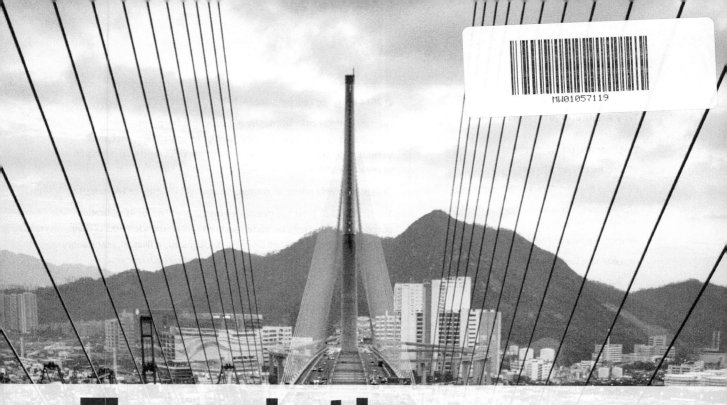

Foundations
of Investments

Troy Adair
Lehigh University

John Nofsinger
University of Alaska Anchorage

✷ Cengage

Australia • Brazil • Canada • Mexico • Singapore • United Kingdom • United States

Foundations of Investments, **1e**
Troy Adair and John Nofsinger

SVP, Product: Erin Joyner

VP, Product: Thais Alencar

Portfolio Product Director: Joe Sabatino

Sr. Portfolio Product Manager:
Aaron Arnsparger

Product Assistant: Flannery Cowan

Sr. Learning Designer: Brandon Foltz

Sr. Subject Matter Expert: Brian Rodriguez

Content Manager: Renee Schnee

Digital Project Manager:
Christopher Comeaux

Product Marketing Manager: Colin Kramer

Content Acquisition Analyst: Ashley Maynard

Production Service: Lumina Datamatics Ltd.

Designer: Chris Doughman

Cover Image Source: Nikada/Getty Images

Library of Congress Control Number: 2022912917

ISBN: 978-0-357-13042-1

LLF ISBN: 978-0-357-13046-9

Cengage
200 Pier 4 Boulevard
Boston, MA 02210
USA

Cengage is a leading provider of customized learning solutions. Our employees reside in nearly 40 different countries and serve digital learners in 165 countries around the world. Find your local representative at **www.cengage.com**.

To learn more about Cengage platforms and services, register or access your online learning solution, or purchase materials for your course, visit **www.cengage.com**.

Notice to the Reader

Publisher does not warrant or guarantee any of the products described herein or perform any independent analysis in connection with any of the product information contained herein. Publisher does not assume, and expressly disclaims, any obligation to obtain and include information other than that provided to it by the manufacturer. The reader is expressly warned to consider and adopt all safety precautions that might be indicated by the activities described herein and to avoid all potential hazards. By following the instructions contained herein, the reader willingly assumes all risks in connection with such instructions. The publisher makes no representations or warranties of any kind, including but not limited to, the warranties of fitness for particular purpose or merchantability, nor are any such representations implied with respect to the material set forth herein, and the publisher takes no responsibility with respect to such material. The publisher shall not be liable for any special, consequential, or exemplary damages resulting, in whole or part, from the readers' use of, or reliance upon, this material.

Printed at CLDPC, USA, 10-22

Brief Contents

Contents

About the Authors

Troy A. Adair, Jr., is a professor (teaching) in the Decision and Technology Analytics Department of the College of Business at Lehigh University, where he also codirects the computer science and business degree program and the fintech minor. Professor Adair received his BS degree in computers/information science from the University of Alabama at Birmingham, his MBA from the University of North Dakota, and his PhD in business from Indiana University. Prior to joining Lehigh University, his previous positions included managing research computing infrastructure and support services for Harvard Business School; acting as a senior business intelligence consultant in the financial services industry to HSBC, JP Morgan Chase, and the United Services Automobile Association (USAA); serving as the banking/risk management professor for the Ross School of Business at the University of Michigan; and overseeing a variety of academic functions as the associate provost/associate vice president for institutional effectiveness at Berkeley College.

Dr. Adair is a vocal advocate for the use of technology to enhance business processes and the author of numerous textbooks leveraging technology in the business decision-making processes, including *Finance: Applications & Theory* (6th edition, McGraw-Hill), *Corporate Finance Demystified* (2nd edition, McGraw-Hill), and *Introduction to R for Business* (2nd edition, dataDicts).

John R. Nofsinger is dean and the William H. Seward Endowed Chair in international finance at the College of Business and Public Policy, University of Alaska Anchorage. He holds a BS from Washington State University, an MBA from Chapman University, and PhD from Washington State University. He has been a finance professor at Marquette University, Washington State University, and University of Alaska Anchorage.

Dr. Nofsinger is one of the world's leading experts in behavioral finance and has recently been working in the biology of finance and socially responsible investing. He is a prolific scholar who has published in multiple disciplines. He has published 74 articles in prestigious scholarly journals and practitioner journals, including the *Journal of Finance, Journal of Financial and Quantitative Analysis, Journal of Business, Journal of Business Ethics, Journal of Corporate Finance, Financial Analysts Journal, Financial Management,* and *Journal of Banking and Finance,* among many others. Professor Nofsinger is an award-winning writer who has authored/coauthored 16 finance trade books, textbooks, and scholarly books that have been translated into 11 languages. Two of his books, *The Psychology of Investing* and *The Biology of Investing,* are popular with investment advisors. As such, John is a frequent speaker on investment topics and has presented over 50 times at practitioner associations, industry conferences, businesses, and individual investor associations.

Why We Wrote This Book

Investing can be a very personal or professional activity. Virtually everyone makes investments. For example, important investment decisions are made when allocating your pension plan (like a 401k or 403b plan at work). Those decisions have a significant impact on your level of wealth in retirement. Other people choose to select specific assets for their portfolio, such as mutual funds, stocks, and bonds. Each of these investments has common characteristics, such as the potential return and the risk you must bear. Some lucky few will even make a career in the investments industry. This book is appropriate for students wanting to direct their own portfolios, be financial advisors, or be institutional money managers.

Theory is important, but practical implementation is critical. All investors should understand the theory that underpins the investing world as well as the language of Wall Street. But the primary focus of the book is to teach the practical skills and tools that lead to making investment decisions. As a book focused on the practice of investing, the illustrations and examples use real securities and real data.

This book is designed for a semester-long or two-quarter course. The primary tool used is the spreadsheet. We wrote this book to be the most spreadsheet-dominate textbook available. The examples are solved using spreadsheets in a manner that illustrates the functions available for direct computations. Students can easily replicate all analysis using their own data and situations.

We believe this approach offers several advantages:

- Students already have access to spreadsheets and have usually taken a course on spreadsheet basics.
- Spreadsheets are the most popular tool of choice in investment jobs.
- Spreadsheets are particularly good for analysis and data visualization.
- Spreadsheet analysis can be easily shared with others and clearly understood by colleagues.

Spreadsheets are implemented in Excel Expert boxes throughout each chapter. The Excel functions used are summarized at the end of the chapters for easy reference. All the end-of-chapter problems are solved using spreadsheets, though some problems do not need the power of a spreadsheet to solve. Lastly, the end-of-chapter cases are also spreadsheet oriented.

Skills-Based Pedagogy and Organization

From Theory to Practice to Implementation. Many investment books are strong on the underlying theory and do well to describe the world of investing. However, most books fall short in giving students the skills to implement investment tasks. For example, theory helps us understand math and visualize portfolio construction. Practice illustrates the regulations and implications of diversification in mutual funds and other portfolios. Yet, many students have not been taught the skills to download the data from 50 stocks and determine their portfolio weights to construct the portfolio desired. An advantage of this text is the ***implementation phase of the investment process***. We teach the implementation ability through spreadsheets. After the theory is presented, every investment process is illustrated and solved through spreadsheets. We demonstrate how to optimize return under the constraints of minimizing risk. We implement functions for different returns, data handling, probability distributions, and regression analysis. We even illustrate powerful graphing tools to demonstrate charting in technical analysis.

Organization. The book is organized into six parts. Part One covers the underlying investments environment, which sets the stage with discussion on the types and attributes of financial instruments, securities markets and transactions, and mutual funds and other investment companies. Part Two introduces portfolio theory, covering return and risk measurement, portfolio diversification, asset allocation and CAPM, asset pricing models and efficient markets, and portfolio performance analytics. Parts Three, Four, and Five cover the major investing activities, from stocks (common and preferred) to debt (corporate bonds and government securities) to derivative securities (futures, contracts, options, and derivative valuation). The closing chapter in this edition covers technical analysis.

Key Features

Foundations of Investments is a book about investment learning and doing. This textbook identifies places on the Internet to obtain information and data. That data is then used in spreadsheets to create investment solutions that lead to good decision making. Investment spreadsheet analysis is shown and thoroughly explained via Excel Expert example boxes and offers hands-on practice with questions, problems, and case studies. This helps students implement their investment strategies, whether in their personal portfolio or in a professional job.

Objective-Based Learning. Clear and concise learning objectives start each chapter and are tied to text, questions, and problems. The eBook in MindTap includes links to subheads with each objective for ease of navigating to specific parts of the chapter for targeted comprehension.

5-1 Measuring Return

5-1a The Components of Return

Return refers to the possible compensation or loss you experience when investing in an asset. Before buying an investment, you expect the return to be positive; however, after the fact, your realized return can be negative. In either case, return usually comes from two basic sources: income and capital appreciation.

Income refers to cash flows that are generated by your investment while you own the asset. If you invest your money in a bank savings account, your income will be the interest that the savings account pays. If you buy stocks, your income may include any cash dividends that are paid. But income can also be negative. If you buy a rental property that requires more in repair expenses than it generates in rent, you will experience negative income.

Key Equations. Key equations within the chapter are screened and numbered to highlight their importance when learning the underlying theory. All equations are summarized at the end of each chapter for use in studying and working the end-of-chapter problems.

$$Total\ Return = Income + (Price_{Received} - Price_{Paid}) \qquad \text{5-1}$$

where

$Income$ = cash flows generated by the asset while the investor owned it
$Price_{Received}$ = the net selling price received by the investor
$Price_{Paid}$ = the net price paid by the investor to purchase the asset (including any brokerage costs and/or commissions)

Excel Expert Boxes. Most examples in the text are shown as **Excel Expert** boxes. Example solutions are presented through spreadsheets so students can shift from theory to practice by implementing suggested functions and formulas within Excel to build important problem-solving skills.

Excel Expert 5-1

The easiest way to calculate *total dollar return* is to write your own function, as shown below in cell C5. The best way to calculate the HPR in Excel is to use the *RATE(nper, pmt, pv, [fv], [type], [guess])* function, setting *nper* = 1, *pmt* = Income, *pv* = $-Price_{Paid}$, *and fv* = $Price_{Received}$, as shown below in cell C6:

Note that we will always set *nper* equal to 1 in this situation, as we are defining the length of time between when we bought the asset and when we sold it as "1 period," regardless of how long or short a time it is. This will change when we "standardize" our holding period (see below), but not when we want to calculate a pure HPR.

	A	B	C
1	Income	$ 0.60	
2	Price$_{Paid}$	$ 10.00	
3	Price$_{Received}$	$ 12.00	
4			
5	Total Return	$ 2.60	=B1+(B3-B2)
6	HPR	26.00%	=RATE(1,B1,-B2,B3)

Real Company Data. To generate interest and provide relevance, real data—from leading companies such as Tesla, AMD, JP Morgan, Apple, Walmart, and many more— is used throughout to describe and demonstrate actual performance.

Figure 17-1: Tesla Stock Prices with Moving Averages and Support and Resistance Lines

Data Source: Yahoo! Finance

World of Investing Applications. Each chapter provides students with "in the news" examples of popular topics in the investing world, such as Bitcoin volatility, socially responsible investing (SRI), GameStop (GME) Short Squeeze, and many more.

The World of Investing

Bitcoin Volatility

Which investment is riskier, Bitcoin or the stock market? This chapter introduces standard deviation of returns as a measure of risk. A higher standard deviation indicates a larger dispersion of returns around the mean, which is a higher risk. But that may not give you a feel for how this volatility impacts you.

Consider the cryptocurrency Bitcoin that was introduced in 2014. Since its introduction, its monthly return and standard deviation through May 2021 has been 8.37%, and 23.33%, respectively. That is a very high return and risk! As a comparison, the stock market average return and risk (as proxied by the S&P 500 Index) was 1.03% and 4.16%. The graph visually illustrates how much more volatile Bitcoin is compared to the stock market. Bitcoin frequently loses 30% in value or gains 30% or more in a single *month*. When the stock market declines 30% over a *quarter*, it is described as a terrible bear market.

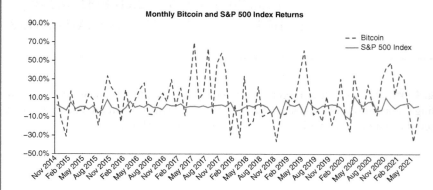

The extreme volatility of Bitcoin and other cryptocurrencies causes significant doubt over their ability to actually be used as a currency for day-to-day purchases. Imagine getting a paycheck in Bitcoin worth $5,000 and then a week later it is only worth $4,000. Until crypto prices stabilize, they are unlikely to be taken seriously as a currency.

Questions and Problems. Questions cover key terminology and conceptual understanding, while problems provide computational practice applying the methods described in the chapter. Many problems include an Excel data file as indicated in the problem.

	A	B	C
1	Income	$ 0.60	
2	Price$_{Paid}$	$ 10.00	
3	Price$_{Received}$	$ 12.00	
4			
5	Total Return	$ 2.60	=B1+(B3-B2)
6	HPR	26.00%	=RATE(1,B1,-B2,B3)

Case Studies. Case studies ask students to use real data from companies such as Pfizer (PFE). In addition to solving for multiple requirements, case studies ask students to justify their conclusions after performing a deeper investment analysis.

Case Study

Download all available historical monthly adjusted prices for Pfizer Inc. (PFE) and use it to answer the following questions:

a. Over what one-year calendar (January to December) holding period was the HPR the highest? The lowest? Research these time periods and provide an intuitive explanation or why.

b. Graph the average and standard deviation in monthly returns for all the one-year holding periods you used

above, then graph all these combination of average and standard deviation in returns on a scatter plot. Over time, has PFE always consistently had higher average returns when the standard deviation was highest? Give examples to support your answer.

c. Is the distribution of PFE monthly returns normally distributed? Provide a histogram to assess the distribution.

Online Learning Platform: MindTap

Cengage MindTap

Today's leading online learning platform, MindTap for Adair/Nofsinger *Foundations of Investments,* 1e, gives you complete control of your course to craft a personalized, engaging learning experience that challenges students, builds confidence, and elevates performance.

MindTap introduces students to core concepts from the beginning of your course using a simplified learning path that progresses from understanding to application and delivers access to eTextbooks, study tools, interactive media, auto-graded assessments, and performance analytics.

Use MindTap for Adair/Nofsinger *Foundations of Investments,* 1e, as is, or personalize it to meet your specific course needs. You can also easily integrate MindTap into your learning management system (LMS).

Active Learning in MindTap

Microsoft Excel Activities

Powered by Microsoft and integrated in MindTap, over 100 unique Excel activities provide students with algorithmic versions of textbook problems so they can learn and apply the techniques and functions presented in the textbook in the live Excel application delivered directly from Office Online servers.

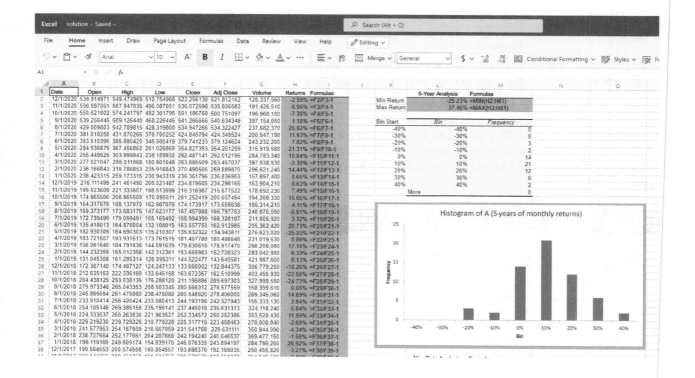

Feedback. Students receive real-time feedback on their answers with function support directly from Office Online, source calculations including Excel dialog box steps for apps such as Solver, and personalized Excel solution files to compare their own Excel solutions against.

Cloud Save. For online versions of activities, Excel work is saved continuously in the cloud along with the assignment so students can always access their Excel file with their homework within MindTap. In addition to these activities being auto-graded, instructors can easily review Excel work for each student for all completed activities in the MindTap gradebook.

Excel Tutorial Videos/Problem Walk-Throughs. Created by Troy Adair and John Nofsinger, each Excel activity in MindTap includes a problem walk-through video that shows students how to solve a similar problem.

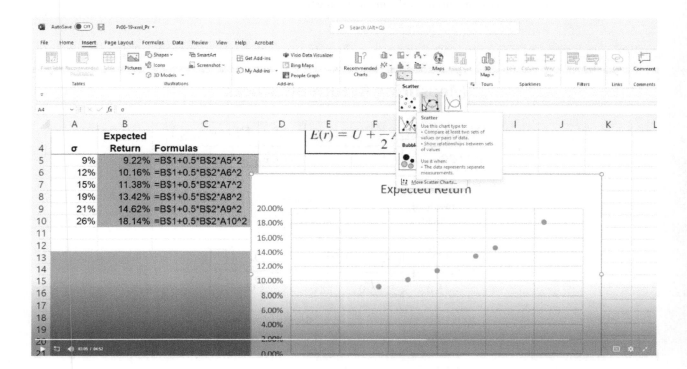

Quizzes and Homework Assignments

Check Your Knowledge reading quizzes, "Learn It" assignments that focus on fundamental concepts, additional algorithmic textbook problems with solutions, and test bank questions are all available in MindTap to form a rich, comprehensive set of questions for any assignment or for assessment needs.

Chapter Overview Videos

Created by Dr. Mark Morpurgo, FCPA, each chapter includes an overview video that prepares students for success by outlining the main topics and themes covered in the reading, homework, and assessments.

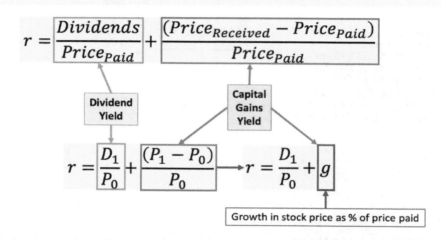

Cengage Finance

Measuring Return on Stocks

Instructor and Student Resources

Additional instructor and student resources for this product are available online. Instructor assets include PowerPoint® slides, a Solutions and Answers Guide, and a test bank powered by Cognero®. Student resources include Excel data files for specific problems and case studies as shown in the textbook. Sign up or sign in at **www.cengage.com** to search for and access this product and its online resources.

Acknowledgments

We would like to acknowledge the work of reviewers who have provided comments and suggestions for improvement of this first edition of this text. Thanks to:

Adam Lei, Midwestern State University

Allan A. Zebedee, Clarkson University

Anne Macy, PhD, West Texas A&M University

Anthony Gu, The State University of New York College

Axel Grossmann, Georgia Southern

Benjamas Jirasakuldech, Slippery Rock University

Cathy Marsh, Assistant Professor, Augustana University

Chunda Chen, Lamar University

Corey Shank Ph.D, Miami University

David A. Lesmond, Tulane University

David J. Charron, Jr., Springfield Technical Community College

Dazhi Zheng, West Chester University

Dr. Diane Rizzuto Suhler, Columbia College

Dr. Gary Kayakachoian, The University of Rhode Island

Dr. James Falter, CFP, CFA, Walsh University

Dr. Rahul Verma, University of Houston-Downtown

Dr. Ronnie Clayton, Glenn Huie Eminent Scholar Chair, Jacksonville State University

Felix Meschke, The University of Kansas

G. Michael Phillips, California State University

Ji Chen, University of Colorado Denver

John Paul Broussard, PhD, CFA, FRM, PRM, University of Oklahoma

John S. Walker, Kutztown University

Karl Leonard Hicks, CFP®, AEP®, MBA

Khaled Abdou, Penn State University Berks

Kwang Soo Cheong, PhD, Johns Hopkins University

Larry Devan, Adjunct Professor of Finance and Accounting, Hood College

Loren M. Rice, Clarke University

Mahfuzul Haque, Indiana State University

Marek Kolar, Trine University

Mark Hassell, Pensacola Christian College

Michael A. Matousek, Portland Community College

Michael Nugent, Stony Brook University

Piman Limpaphayom, PhD, CFA, Portland State University

Professor Michael Dotto, University of Massachusetts Boston

Schuyler Banks, Business Professor, SUNY Erie Community College

Scott D. Below, East Carolina University

Sharon O'Reilly, MBA, CPA, Accounting Instructor, Gateway Technical College

Shengxiong Wu, Texas Wesleyan University

Stevan H. Labush, RFC, Johnson & Wales University

Suzanne K. Hayes, Finance Professor, University of Nebraska-Kearney

Tom Arnold, PhD, CFA, CIPM, University of Richmond

William G. Stough, CPQA, MBA, CGMA, Waynesburg University

Zhenhu Jin, Valparaiso University

We would like to especially thank Ohaness Paskelian, University of Houston-Downtown, for his significant contribution in reviewing the chapter manuscript and developing the solutions manual. We would also like to thank Dr. Olson Pook, Newmarket Editing and Consulting, who provided valuable structural suggestions on earlier drafts of the manuscript.

We are also indebted to the entire team at Cengage who worked on this title: Senior Portfolio Product Manager Aaron Arnsparger; Content Manager Renee Schnee; Senior Learning Designer Brandon Foltz; Product Marketing Manager Colin Kramer; Digital Project Manager Christopher Comeaux; Senior Subject Matter Expert Brian Rodriguez; Designer Chris Doughman; Product Assistant Flannery Cowan; and Senior Project Manager at Lumina Datamatics Limited, Manoj Kumar, for their editorial counsel and support during the preparation of this text.

Troy A. Adair, Jr.
John R. Nofsinger

Part

1

The Investments Environment

Part 1 of this text covers the importance of investors for the flow of cash through the economy (Chapter 1), common investment securities (Chapter 2), the mechanics of buying and selling financial assets and the markets they trade (Chapter 3), and mutual funds and other investment company products.

Chapter

1

Introduction to Investments

Learning Objectives

After completing this chapter, you should be able to:

LO 1-1   Describe the difference between real assets and financial assets.
LO 1-2   Explain the system of cash flows between companies, investors, and the government.
LO 1-3   Understand the factors involved in assessing value.
LO 1-4   Describe the characteristics of an efficient market.
LO 1-5   Recognize how asset-specific risk and asset allocation contribute to portfolio diversification.
LO 1-6   Understand the importance of integrating the macroeconomic environment into the investing process.
LO 1-7   Become acquainted with careers in the investment service sector.

defined contribution plan
An employee-funded retirement program in which the employee makes the funding and investment decisions

investment
The purchase of an asset for the purpose of storing and (possibly) increasing value over time

The world of investing is a thrilling one! It is exciting for many reasons. For example, it is a world in which innovation flourishes. New investment products, ideas, and processes are constantly being created. Also, the investment world is vitally important to an economy because it provides companies with the capital they need to grow. Investing is also extremely important to your financial future. Decades ago, there were pension plans that paid for an employee's retirement years. Those plans are largely gone. They have been replaced with **defined contribution plans**, usually referred to as a 401(k) or an individual retirement account (IRA). These plans require the employee to make the investment decisions that will determine how much money they have when they retire. Then the retiree must invest that money in a manner that will support their spending.

Successful investing involves more than just . . . buy low and sell high. Building wealth requires knowledge, effort, and time. So, let's start with the basics. An **investment** involves allocating resources, usually money, with the expectation of generating some benefit in the future. If you've ever dropped a coin in a piggy bank as a small child, or deposited money in a savings account, then you've made an investment, and you probably already understand this concept at an instinctual level.

Consider your expectations when funding a 401(k) plan, a type of defined contribution plan. Essentially, you are putting aside some of your current wages today and forgoing some current spending with the expectation that you will earn three possible future benefits:

1. interest on any of your own money you've put in;
2. the eventual right to the company's matching contributions and its investment growth; and
3. the potential ability to take money out of the plan in the future and taxed at a (potentially) lower tax rate.

Because of these potential future benefits, putting money into a 401(k) or an IRA therefore qualifies as an *investment*.

In fact, this definition for *investment* is pretty broad, and we find ourselves applying it to a lot of situations that most people would agree are a little different than these instances. For example, paying for a college degree (as many of you are in the process of doing) is often referred to as an "investment in the future." You're investing time and money today in the expectation that it will pay off with a higher salary and/or greater job satisfaction in the future. People are said to make an investment in themselves through diet or exercise.

Even in finance, there's a lot of ambiguity about exactly what the term *investment* means: we are all probably pretty comfortable with using that term to describe the process of individual investors purchasing shares of stock or other financial securities; however, chief financial officers and government regulators habitually use *investment* to describe the process of firms purchasing machinery, plant, and equipment to support their projects.

That latter example is probably not what springs to mind when you've signed up to take a class on *Investments*. So, to cut through all this ambiguity, we're going to use the phrase *investment* in this text as *the purchase of an asset for the purpose of storing and (possibly) increasing value over time.* We'll call all such transactions investments, even if in the end there is only a transfer of ownership from a seller to a buyer. The purchase of stocks, bonds, options, commodity contracts, cryptocurrency, and even antiques, stamps, and real estate are all considered to be investments. If these assets are acting as stores of value, they are investments for that individual.

1-1 The Study of Investments

Now that we've agreed on a common definition of what an investment is, we also need to discuss what the *study of investments* is. To put it bluntly, it's not just about buying investments. It's the study of *which* individual investments to buy, *how much* to invest in each, *when* to buy and sell them, and *how* all the individual investments interact with each other. And underpinning all those decisions is the basic measurement of *what* they're worth, formally referred to as **valuation**.

As we'll see, there are a lot of different varieties of investments out there, each with its own subtleties concerning timing and amount of cash flows to be received. One main goal of this text is to expose you to those different varieties, giving you the tools and knowledge necessary to correctly value all those different types of investments.

Once we understand each investment's characteristics, in a perfect world, it would be a straightforward application of the **time value of money** (TVM) concept you likely learned in an earlier course to compute its value. But we're *not* operating in

valuation
The process of determining the current worth of an asset—the present value of future benefits

time value of money
The concept that the money you have now is worth more than the same amount received in the future due to its potential ability to grow

a perfect world. In the real world, all investments are an "iffy" proposition, carrying uncertainties about when and how much value we're going to get back for our investment. So, the second goal of this text is to teach you how to measure and incorporate those uncertainties into an asset's valuation. Of course, the purpose of valuing an asset is to determine whether the market selling price is a good deal, fair deal, or bad deal to purchase. This relates to how efficiently markets price assets.

correlated
The degree of return co-movement between two assets

diversified portfolio
A portfolio of assets that includes various asset categories, such as stocks, bonds, and cash, for the purpose of reducing risk

We also must consider that the uncertainty or variabilities in the cash flows of investments may be linked to or **correlated** with one another, implying that investing in multiple assets at the same time may result in some of the risks or uncertainties of individual investments "cancelling out" when they are held together in a **diversified portfolio**. So, a third goal of this text is to teach you how to evaluate which risks may cancel each other out and to what extent they may do so.

Finally, investment decisions are not made in a vacuum, they must take into account the economic environment at the time they are being made as well as the needs and preferences of the investor. For example, investment decisions for a person entering the workforce during the COVID-19 pandemic would obviously be very different from the investment decisions of a person approaching retirement a decade earlier. So, our final goal in this text will be to teach you how to use the investment tools in any investor situation.

This text will guide you through acquiring the knowledge and skill set you need to make these kinds of decisions. Part I will introduce you to the types of investments and the investments environment that they are traded in. Part II will introduce coverage of investment companies, describing how they operate and the services they provide as middlemen between investors and the assets in which they invest. Part III will provide you with the necessary tools to measure expected risks of real and financial assets in a diversified portfolio and then show you how to use these tools to develop basic valuation formulas for different types of assets. Part IV will go into detail concerning using these tools to value common and preferred stocks, and Part V will cover using these tools to value debt securities, such as bonds. Part VI will expand our discussion of risk, return, and valuation to cover **derivative securities**, such as options and forward contracts, and Part VII will cover analyzing portfolio performance and using this information to optimize portfolio composition.

derivative security
A financial instrument with value stemming from changes in the value of some other (possibly financial) asset

To kick things off, the remaining sections of this chapter will provide some basic fundamentals about the different types of assets we will consider, the sources of uncertainty concerning the cash flows from those assets, and how investors take that uncertainty into account when valuing those investments. We'll then look at how the uncertainty and risks of individual investments interact to reduce risk when those individual investments are held as part of a diversified portfolio. We then illustrate how investment environment, which frequently changes, impacts investment decisions by discussing two declining market periods and two recovery periods. We end by discussing careers in the investment field.

1-2 Real vs. Financial Assets

real asset
Physical asset that has a value due to its substance and properties, like precious metals, commodities, real estate, land, equipment, and natural resources

For many of you reading this, you'll be using this book in a second (or later) finance class as part of a business curriculum. It usually follows an *Introduction to Finance* course, which tends to focus on what is called corporate finance or financial management. Much of that course focuses on the efficient use of **real assets**, defined as assets that either contribute to production or create income or wealth. Most real assets have a physical existence, with the most common examples being real estate and land, machinery, precious metals, and commodities. However, certain intangible assets like patents, trademarks, and intellectual property can also create income, so they are considered real assets, too.

For example, if you are a farmer who owns land, seeds, and equipment, those real assets can be used together to produce crops that you can either consume yourself or sell to others. But if you are an independent musician and own the copyright to an original song that you wrote and recorded, you can earn income from that song every time it is played, so the song's copyright is considered a real asset.

Real assets do have a part to play in investments, and we'll be discussing their critical role in portfolio diversification later in the text. Most of the assets that we'll be analyzing as investments will be **financial assets**, which are nonphysical assets whose values are derived from either a contractual claim on real assets or on the cash flows produced by those real assets.

The most common types of financial assets are stock and bonds. In a corporate finance course, you dealt with stocks and bonds as *sources* of capital, which the firm *sold* to raise the money to invest in the real assets required for capital budgeting projects. The investments arena considers *buying* those same stocks and bonds from the firm (or from other investors) because owning them gives us a claim on the cash flows of the firm.

In addition to stocks and bonds, other types of financial assets include cash, bank deposits, certificate of deposits (CDs), loans made, corporate receivables, derivative securities, and cryptocurrencies. We'll discuss each of these in more detail in Chapter 2.

Another way to think about the difference between real and financial assets is from an economic point of view. You will realize that this means that real assets are those used to *produce* economic output, while financial assets merely serve to *allocate* how that output is divided up. If you take some of your wages and use them to buy a machine (a real asset) that turns raw materials into finished goods, then by running that machine you are not only adding to the amount of goods available in the economy but reaping the **profits** as well (i.e., the difference between what you sell the finished goods for and what the raw materials and running the machines cost you). On the other hand, if you go to the stock market and buy a share of Apple, Inc.'s common stock (a financial asset) from another investor, you are *not* adding any capital or productive capacity to the company (that only happens when the company first sells that share of stock). Instead, you are merely changing whom the proceeds of that initial investment go to.

There's another aspect of the difference between real and financial assets that we need to recognize. Real assets, being actual physical items, often have some aspect of "uniqueness" that (if used correctly) can convey at least a limited form of **monopoly power** to the owner. For example, if you own a particular corner lot on a busy intersection frequented by commuters, and if the traffic pattern is such that most of the commuters will be taking a right at that corner on their way into work, and if the lot is sized and zoned such that you can build a drive-through coffee shop there with "easy off, easy on" access to the street traffic pattern, you can make a ton of money. The "abnormally large" (i.e., "monopolistic") profits it generates are in part due to its ideal location and the fact you own that particular lot and no one else can ever own it unless you sell it to them. Others will try to compete with you by building on lots close to yours or by offering discounts to coffee drinkers that are willing to put up with the inconvenience of turning left against traffic to save a buck or two. But if your lot has unique features that really make it the best one for this purpose in that area, then you're going to make a lot of money.

Financial assets, on the other hand, don't tend to have quite that same aspect of uniqueness. Every share of a company's common stock has exactly the same rights and

financial asset
An investment instrument issued by corporations, governments, or other organizations that offer legal rights to debt or equity cash flow

profit
Financial gain earned from the difference between the revenue and the expenses from an investment asset or business

monopoly power
A firm's ability to price its product or service substantially above the competitive level and persist in doing so

risks as every other share, and therefore the same value. For example, in mid-2021, there were just over 500 million shares of Amazon common stock outstanding, and every single share of that stock had exactly the same value and rights as every other one of those 500 million shares.

So, unlike real assets, whose uniqueness of their physical attributes tends to give their owners at least a small amount of monopoly power due to that uniqueness, financial assets find themselves in the position of trading in markets that bear a much closer resemblance to the concept of "pure competition" that you may have run into in an Economics class. Because of this pure competition, as discussed in the financial markets in Chapter 3, lots of investors wanting to buy and sell lots of similar financial assets make for a very competitive environment, and it's that competitiveness that will allow us to depend on financial assets being "fairly priced" in those markets. By "fairly priced," we mean that we'll be able to develop valuation formulas for financial assets based on observable prices for other financial prices that are "similar enough."

1-3 Cash Flows and the Sources of Uncertainty

Let's continue exploring the differences between corporate finance and financial investing. Even though many business students and all finance majors take courses in both corporate finance and investing, they often don't have a clear view of exactly how these topics fit together. Put simply, they're just different points of view on the same system of cash flows depicted below in **Figure 1-1**.

In this system, investors band together to fund companies. The investors' money becomes the companies' capital. The companies use that capital to invest in projects. When the projects return cash flows to the firm, any profits are usually subject to taxation by federal, state, and/or local governments. Of the remaining after-tax profits, some are retained in the firm to fund future operations and the rest are paid out to investors (where they are taxed again).

Figure 1-1: System of Financial Cash Flows

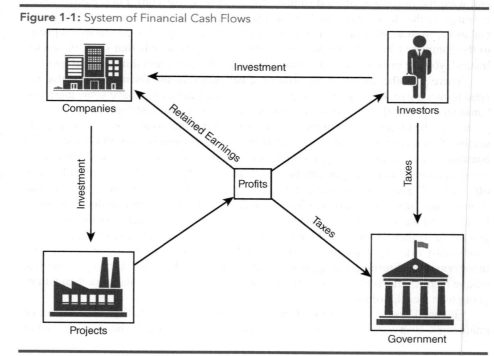

If we look at this system from the viewpoint of the corporation, the focus is on decisions concerning (1) the form and amount of funding received from investors, (2) which projects to put the funds in, (3) how to manage taxes, and (4) how much of the revenues of existing projects to keep versus paying back the firm's investors (shown in **Figure 1-2.**).

If we put ourselves in the shoes of the investors, the focus turns to decisions such as (1) which firms and what types of financial instruments to invest in, (2) what terms and maturities of return cash flows to seek, and (3) how to best manage the timing and amounts of taxes paid. That leads us to the decision-making environment covered here in Investments (depicted in **Figure 1-3**).

Of course, the descriptions of these two primary areas of finance sound a little . . . simplistic. That's because (as with many things in business) the "devil is in the details." For example, this seemingly simple system of cash flows is complicated by the fact that all the depicted cash flows are subject to uncertainty (refer **Figure 1-4**).

A firm's investments in projects are not "sure things," as the demand for the goods and services produced by those projects are subject to change over time in a competitive macroeconomic environment. That change could negatively affect the firm's operations as well as their ability to sell those products and services at their hoped-for prices.

Likewise, due to the uncertainty inherent in projects' cash flows, firms face uncertainty in their total earnings and therefore cannot guarantee the amount and timing of the returns they can give back to investors. Even if firms could perfectly forecast the

Figure 1-2: Corporate Finance Decisions

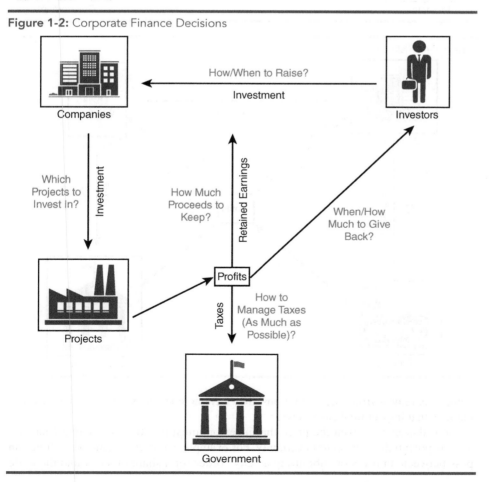

Figure 1-3: Investment Decisions

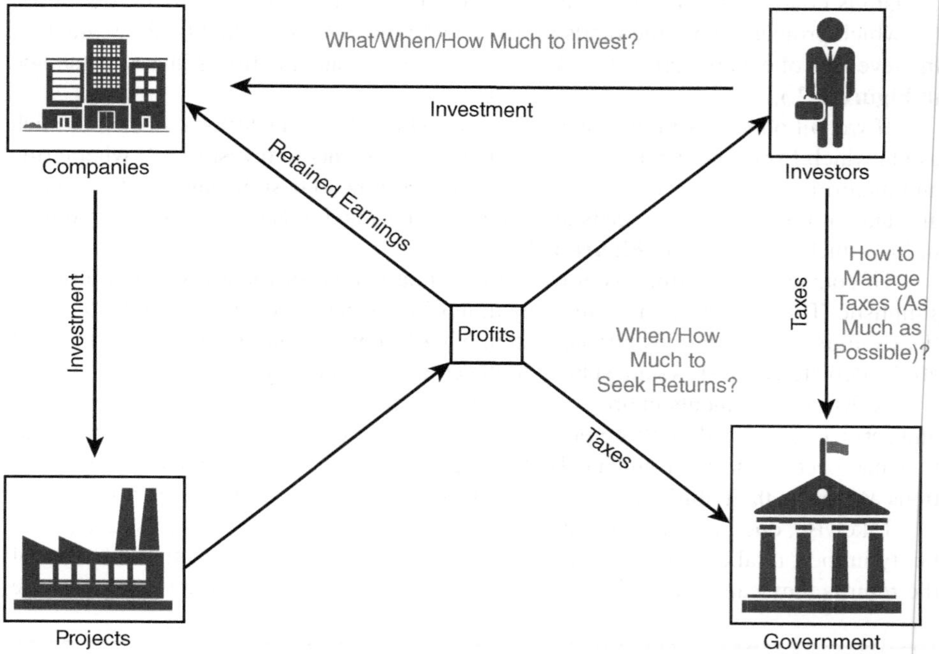

Figure 1-4: Risks in Financial Cash Flows

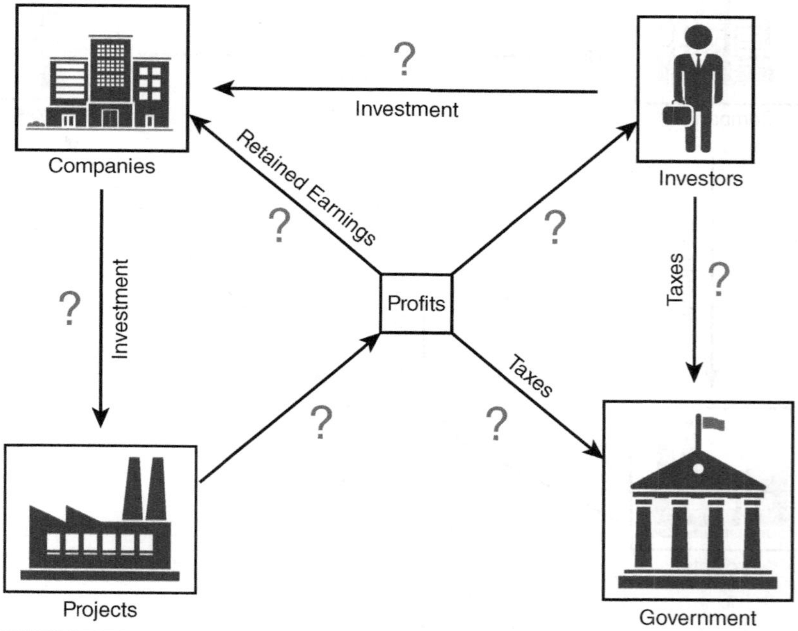

before-tax returns from their operations, they have no control over government tax regulations that impact final cash flows.

For that matter, even the price that investors must pay for a particular financial asset is potentially subject to uncertainty. For example, a nontrivial amount of time can pass between an investor submitting a "buy" order for a share of stock and the trade actually being fulfilled on the stock market. In fact, many stock traders submit their buy orders as an "at-the-market" purchase, meaning they are committing to pay the prevailing price for the stock at the time the trade occurs, not necessarily the price they see when they first place the order.

The second factor making this seemingly simple system of cash flows more complex than it might seem is the fact that new information is constantly arriving about projects' and firms' future prospects. This steady stream of information causes the valuation of financial instruments to be in a constant state of flux. That constant stream of new information is likely to affect each individual security differently, implying that yesterday's optimized portfolio of various securities is going to be "less than optimal" today as its components' expected returns and risks change relative to one another.

And the last complicating factor is the fact that there are just so many (and so many *kinds of*) participants in this system. In the United States alone, there were over 3,500 publicly traded corporations in 2020, with many of them issuing multiple classes of financial securities each. There are also billions of individual investors, as well as innumerable financial intermediaries such as investment banks, stockbrokers, venture capitalists, and so forth. Finding the right mix of investments for so many people when there are so many choices is a daunting task.

1-4 Valuation

Assets have value because of the future benefits they offer. The process of determining what an asset is worth today is called *valuation*. As implied in our discussion of financial cash flows in the previous section, asset valuation is based on both the expected future cash flows for an investment and on the risks concerning the timing and amount of those cash flows.

In cases where the expected future cash flows have relatively little risk, this valuation is relatively easy. For example, the bonds of the U.S. federal government pay a fixed amount of interest each year and mature at a specified date. Thus, the future cash flows are known with a great deal of certainty.

However, the future cash flows of other types of assets are not so readily identified. For example, although you may anticipate receiving future dividends when you purchase a share of Alphabet (GOOGL) common stock, neither their payment nor their amount can be known with certainty. Forecasting future benefits and their volatility is difficult but crucial to the process of valuation. Without forecasts and an evaluation of the asset, you cannot know if the asset should be purchased or sold.

Rational investors are generally **risk averse**. This means that they will only take risk when they feel they will be compensated for the risk with a higher expected return. But that doesn't mean they're all *equally* risk averse. An investor with a long-time horizon and considerable additional savings can afford to take risks that someone with a shorter horizon and less savings would be uncomfortable with.

risk averse
The degree to which a person desires to avoid risk

Because the valuation of some assets is complicated and the future is uncertain, people may have different estimates of the future cash flows. It is therefore easy to understand why two individuals may have completely divergent views on the worth of a particular asset. One person may believe that an asset is overvalued at the current market price and hence seek to sell it, while another may seek to buy it at the same time in the belief that it is undervalued. Since valuation is open to subjectivity, this can lead to one person's buying a particular investment while the other is selling. Note that every stock traded on a stock exchange has a buyer and a seller. But this does not mean that one person is irrational or incompetent—they can just weigh factors differently in the process of valuation. Also, a person's perception or estimate of an asset's value can change.

In fact, even if two investors were to completely agree on the timing and amounts of expected future cash flows for a particular investment, they may have different preferences concerning the timing of the cash flows they expect to receive.[1] For that matter, even the same investor over time can be expected to see their preference for the timing of cash flows change. When you are young and have a longer investment horizon (e.g., you are many years away from retiring), you normally have a preference for longer-term investments. As you get older and closer to retirement, you may change your preferences from a growth to income orientation and will probably find yourself putting a greater portion of your wealth in shorter-term investments.

Regardless of what motivates the purchase of an investment, the buyer does so in anticipation of a **return**. The total return on an investment is what the investor earns. This may be in the form of **income**, such as dividends on shares or interest on bonds, or in the form of **capital gains** (as the result of a rise in the asset's price). Not all assets offer both income and capital appreciation. Some stocks pay no current dividends but may grow or appreciate in value, whereas other assets (like savings accounts) do not appreciate in value but solely return interest income.

Return is frequently expressed in percentages, such as the **rate of return**, which is the annualized return that is earned by the investment relative to its cost. Investors anticipate that the return will be at least as great as that of other assets of similar risk — otherwise they would not make the purchase. Of course, the element of risk means the *realized* return may be quite different from the anticipated rate of return.

Risk in finance is the uncertainty that the anticipated return will be achieved. As we will discuss later in the text, there are many sources of risk, and the investor must be willing to bear these risks to achieve the expected return. Even relatively safe investments involve some risk; there is no completely safe investment. For example, savings accounts that are insured still involve an element of risk. If the rate of inflation exceeds the rate of interest that is earned on these accounts, the investor suffers a loss of purchasing power.

While the term *risk* has a negative connotation, it's helpful to remember that uncertainty works both ways. For example, events may occur that cause the value of an asset to rise more than anticipated. Certainly, the stockholders of Slack Technologies reaped larger-than-anticipated returns when Salesforce.com announced it was acquiring the firm for more than 50% premium over the preannouncement price. The price paid for the stock was considerably higher than the price the security commanded before the announcement of the merger.

A term that is frequently used in conjunction with risk is **speculation**. Many years ago, virtually all investments were called *speculations*. Today, the word implies a high degree of risk; however, risk is not synonymous with speculation. Speculation has the connotation of gambling, in which the odds are against the player. Many securities are risky, but over a period of years, the investor should earn a positive return. The odds are not really against the investor, and such investments are risky but not speculative.

The term *speculation* is rarely used in this text, and when it is, the implication is that the individual runs a good chance of losing the funds invested in the speculative asset. Although a particular speculation may pay off handsomely, the investor should not expect that such gambles will consistently reap large returns. After the investor adjusts for the larger amount of risk that must be borne to own such speculative investments, the anticipated return may not justify the risk involved.

---

return
The sum of income plus capital gains earned on an investment in an asset

income
The flow of money produced by an asset, e.g., dividends and interest

capital gain
An increase in the value of a capital asset, such as a stock

rate of return
The annual percentage return realized on an investment

risk
The possibility of loss; the uncertainty of future returns

speculation
An investment that offers a potentially large return but is also very risky; a high probability that the investment will produce a loss

---

[1]For example, one of the strongest rationales for most investors in using a tax-deferred retirement account such as a 401(k) or an individual retirement account (IRA) is that many of them expect their total income to be less after they retire than it is before they retire. In a nation such as the United States, where personal income is subject to a progressive tax (i.e., one where lower incomes are taxed at lower rates than are higher incomes), moving income through time using one of these tax-deferred retirement accounts therefore allows investors to reduce taxes on income earned today by moving it to a more-favorably-taxed tomorrow.

A Walk Down Wall Street

Are Cryptocurrencies Investments?

Cryptocurrencies were originally created to be like digital cash to be used in purchasing transactions that replace traditional currency like the U.S. dollar or the euro. Since then, its real-world use has evolved. Many retail investors started buying it as a speculative investment, which dramatically increased its price. Institutional investors and the media have noticed. For example, the most popular (and first to be launched, in 2009) crypto is Bitcoin; its price is shown on CNBC along with stock and bond market indicators as well as on the financial menu of popular website Yahoo! Finance.

Bitcoin has the largest market capitalization of all of the cryptos (other popular cryptos are Ether, Tether, Dogecoin, Litecoin, and Bitcoin cash). A crypto is a decentralized form of digital cash that eliminates the need for traditional intermediaries like banks and governments to make financial transactions. The U.S. dollar is backed and regulated by the U.S. government. Bitcoin, on the other hand, is powered through peer-to-peer technology and software-driven cryptography driven by blockchain. This creates a currency backed by code rather than gold or the U.S. central bank.

The U.S. Securities and Exchange Commission does not regulate cryptocurrencies, thus, many institutions are not allowed to own it. However, starting in 2021, many of those institutional investors started considering ways to taking positions in cryptos. Brokerage firms, pension funds, investment advisory firms, and others have announced their intension to gain exposure to cryptocurrencies.

What are the pros and cons of buying some cryptos? Make no mistake, Bitcoin is a very speculative asset that experiences extreme volatility. Over the past five years, the price of Bitcoin averages a change of 2.72% (up and down) per day. It experienced a rise of 25.2% one day and a decline of −37.2% another day. Additionally, because a cryptocurrency is electronic money, keeping it secure from hackers is a risk. Lastly, cryptos are not protected by the Securities Investor Protection Corporation, which insures investors up to $500,000 if a brokerage fails or funds are stolen. On the positive side, there is a big potential for growth in the number of investors buying cryptos, which would increase their prices. Other investors like that the cryptos are not associated with a government's central bank.

The bottom line is that cryptos have become their own asset class for investors.

Besides involving risk and offering an expected return, stores of value have marketability or liquidity. These terms are sometimes used interchangeably, but they may also have different definitions. Marketability implies that the asset can be bought and sold. Many financial assets, such as the stock of Procter & Gamble, are readily marketable.

The ease with which an asset may be converted into money is its **liquidity**. Unfortunately, the word *liquidity* is often used in two contexts. In investments, liquidity usually means ease of fully converting an asset into cash. A savings account with a commercial bank is very liquid because you can get your cash without cost. But shares of IBM would be less liquid, since you could sustain a loss or a trading cost. But writing about trading liquidity usually means the ability to sell an asset without affecting its price. In that context, liquidity refers to the depth of the market for the asset. You may be able to buy or sell 1,000 shares of IBM stock without affecting its price, in which case the stock is liquid. If you try to sell 1,000 shares of a very small firm, your selling pressure might lower the price, in which case the stock is illiquid.

All financial assets that serve as stores of value possess some combination of marketability, liquidity, and the potential to generate future cash flow or appreciate in price. These features, along with the risk associated with each asset, should be considered when including the asset in an individual's portfolio. Since assets differ with regard to their features, you need to know the characteristics of each asset. Much of the balance of this text describes each asset's features as well as its sources of risk and return and how it may be used in a well-diversified portfolio.

liquidity
The ease with which assets can be converted into cash with no or minimal loss or cost

1-5 Efficient and Competitive Markets

Sports analytics provides an enormous amount of statistics for fans and gamblers to contemplate. For example, there are simple statistics about a basketball player's free throw percentage. More complicated statistics are available, like the chance a player will pass versus shoot the ball during the final minute of a close game. New players to the league have few statistics available on them. Why?

You likely know why. If someone only plays one or a few games, we're not so sure that their performance across such a small sample is indicative of their "typical" performance, right? Maybe they had an unusually hot or cold shooting day. Without more information about the player, most of us would be hesitant to judge their abilities or future behavior so soon.

law of large numbers (LLN)
From probability and statistics, a concept that states that as a sample size grows, its sample mean gets closer to the population average

Our tendency to instinctively not want to base a judgment on a small sample is an application of what statisticians call the **law of large numbers (LLN)**. Put simply, the LLN implies that as the size of a sample grows, its mean gets closer to the average of the whole population. In other words, we are more confident about a basketball player's free throw percentage after a thousand attempts than after only ten. Note that small-sized samples are likely to *not* be representative of the population as a whole, and that drives us to instinctively discount abnormally high or low results when they occur in samples of small size.

In many ways, this analogy also applies to investing. Individuals tend to talk about the one-time big returns ("I bought GameStop stock and it doubled within a week") or the lost opportunities ("After GameStop doubled in price, I failed to sell it before the price dropped"). But what matters is the return you earn after making *many* investments over an *extended* period of time. Unless you have special skills or knowledge, that return should tend to be comparable to the return earned by other investors in comparable investments.

Why is this so? The answer lies in the fact that investors participate in efficient and competitive financial markets. Economics teaches us that a market with many participants (i.e., buyers and sellers) who may enter and exit freely will be a competitive market. That certainly describes financial markets, where investors may participate freely in the purchase and sale of stocks and bonds. Virtually anyone, from a child to a grandmother, may own an investment, even if it is just a savings account. Many firms, including banks, insurance companies, and mutual funds, compete for the funds of investors. The financial markets are among the most (and perhaps *the* most) competitive of all markets.

Competitive financial markets also tend to be extremely efficient at making sure that new information is rapidly taken into account by valuations. As is explained throughout this text, asset valuations depend on future cash flows, such as interest or dividend payments. If new information suggests that these flows will be altered, the market rapidly adjusts the asset's price. Thus, an efficient financial market implies that a security's current price embodies all the known information concerning its potential return and risk.

If an asset (such as a stock) were undervalued and offered an excessive return based on the information available at that time, all investors would seek to *buy* it, which would drive the price up and reduce the return that subsequent investors would earn. That is, the buying would move the price up to its true value. Conversely, if the asset were overvalued and offered an inferior return, all investors would seek to *sell* it, which would drive down its price and increase the return to subsequent investors. The fact that there are sufficiently informed investors in the financial markets means that a security's price will reflect the investment community's consensus regarding the asset's true value and also that the expected return will be consistent with the amount of risk the investor must bear to earn the return.

This concept of an efficient financial market has an important and sobering corollary. Efficient markets imply that investors (or at least the vast majority of investors) cannot expect on average to consistently beat the market. Of course, that does not mean an individual will *never* select an asset that does exceedingly well. Individuals can earn large returns on particular assets, as the stockholders of many firms know. Certainly, an investor who owned DocuSign (DOCU) stock on Friday, June 4, 2021, enjoyed the one day 19.8% increase in price when the firm announced a stellar quarterly earnings report. But the concept of efficient markets implies that this investor is just as likely to select a firm that underperforms as one that will earn abnormally large returns.

If efficient markets imply that investors cannot expect to *outperform* the market consistently, they also should not consistently *underperform* the market. (That is, you would not always be the investor who *sold* DocuSign just prior to the large increase in its price.) Of course, some securities may decline in price and inflict large losses on their owners, but efficient markets imply that the individual who constructs a well-diversified portfolio will not always select the stocks and bonds of firms that fail.

While the concept of efficient financial markets permeates investments, the question remains of how efficient markets are. Are some securities markets more efficient than others? Are there times when highly efficient markets become temporarily less efficient? Do exceptions to the efficient market hypothesis exist? Many of the various investment techniques and methods of analysis covered in later chapters are often used in an attempt to identify "mispricings": that is, situations where an asset is not worth what it is selling for, and where profit opportunities can be realized by buying underpriced assets or by selling overpriced ones.

1-6 Diversification and Portfolio Construction

Rational investors are risk averse. That is, they generally avoid risk unless that risk offers additional return as compensation.

Let's look at risk and expected return between stocks. Consider three stocks (A, B, and C) that all have the same risk and are trading in an efficient market as described in the previous section. If stock B offers higher expected returns than stocks A and C (see Before, **Figure 1-5**), but the same risks, then all rational risk-averse investors would want to buy B instead of A and C. Likewise, anyone who already owned A or C would want to sell them (presumably to turn around and buy B). But if everyone wants to buy B and sell A and C, think about what that is going to imply for the prices of A, B, and C. Since demand for B is high, its price will go up, while C's price and possibly A's price will go down.

When prices of financial assets change, expected returns go in the opposite direction. So, if stock B were dominating stocks A and C, market forces would drive its return down (and stock C's expected returns up) until they were all offering the same returns for equivalent amounts of risk (see After, Figure 1-5). We'll see that this holds true for all the valuation formulas we'll use in later chapters—if price goes up (down), expected returns go down (up).

But what about when you have to choose between investments that have different levels of risk? Well, that's when things get a bit more complicated. In general, you have to offer a risk-averse investor higher expected return to get them to invest in assets with more expected risk. However, some of the risk of holding an asset, called the **asset-specific risk**, can be canceled out if the asset is held as part of a *well-diversified portfolio*. In such a situation, if the asset-specific risks

asset-specific risk
The chance that problems with an individual asset will reduce the value of the portfolio

Figure 1-5: Risk and Expected Return

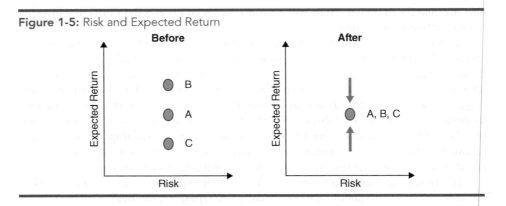

of each asset are truly random and uncorrelated with the asset-specific risks of the other assets, then we can expect "bad" unexpected surprises in returns on one of the assets in our portfolio to be at least partially offset by "good" unexpected surprises in other assets in the portfolio.

As discussed later in the text, to achieve diversification, the returns on each of your individual investments must not be highly correlated with one another. Factors that negatively affect one security must have a positive impact on others. For example, higher oil prices may be good for ExxonMobil but bad for British Airways. By combining a variety of nonperfectly correlated assets in your portfolio, you can achieve diversification and reduce some of your portfolio's risk.

Notice, however, that we said "some" of the risk can be canceled out—not "all." Certain types of **systemic risks** will affect the returns on all assets to some extent and therefore can't be completely cancelled out in diversified portfolios. An example of systemic risk can be seen by examining the economic impact of the 2020 COVID-19 pandemic. When people in an economy must "lock down" in their homes to prevent the spread of the disease, then they spend less money at local businesses and can't work. The resulting decline of consumption and income impacts the entire economy.

Asset allocation refers to the amount of a portfolio allocated to different assets. Risk-adverse investors use their finite resources to acquire diverse types of assets that include stocks, bonds, precious metals, collectibles, and real estate. But even within such a diversified portfolio, the investment amounts allocated to different sectors or geographic regions differ. How well you allocate your portfolio to the different types of assets determines how well (or not) you are diversified. Allocation within asset type is also important. For example, you may tilt your allocation toward energy stocks and away from airlines if you anticipate high oil prices. Your diversification among stocks, bonds, and other assets remains the same, but the allocation between two sectors is altered.

The terms *diversification* and *asset allocation* are going to be used quite often in this text. As we will see, diversification is important because it reduces your risk exposure, while asset allocation is important because it has a major impact on the return your portfolio earns. If diversification is all about reducing asset-specific risk, then we can think about asset allocation as the process of knowingly choosing to put a higher concentration of our wealth in the sector(s) in which we want to place bets that sector-specific risk will come out in our favor.

systemic risk
Return volatility associated with the overall market

asset allocation
The process of diversifying an investment portfolio across various asset categories, such as stocks, bonds, and cash

1-7 The Financial Crises of 2008 and 2020 and Associated Recoveries

One of our goals is to illustrate the importance of integrating the macroeconomic environment into the investing process. The two most recent stock bear markets (defined as a 20% or more decline) occurred in 2008 and 2020. However, their causes were very different and so were the recoveries.

Both of these financial crises, as well as the ones the proceeded them, share one common underlying cause: a sudden and dramatic increase in risk and uncertainty brought upon by an unexpected event that caused a shift in expectations and risk aversion for large portions of the investment community.

The causes of the Great Recession of 2008 have been extensively analyzed and well documented, with the main culprits being identified as excessive risk-taking by banks and the bursting of the U.S. housing bubble, both combining to cause the value of securities tied to U.S. real estate (such as bank stocks) to fall precipitously. The bear market started in October of 2007 and lasted until March of 2009 and registered a decline of over 50%. The most shocking time of the bear market was the five-day crash of October 6–10, 2008, that dropped the market 18%. The extent of the fall in value hit the banking and finance sectors very hard and spawned an international banking crisis.

It took about four years for the stock market to fully recover from the Great Recession. While that seems like a long time, because the stock market had lost half of its value, it needed to *double* its value to return to previous levels. Governments around the world supported their financial institutions, which eventually regained their lost value.

The primary initial causes of the COVID-19 financial crisis are even more easily identifiable, as widespread lockdowns around the globe resulted in massive business closures, many of which will be permanent. Investors' reaction to the pandemic news brought selling pressure that dropped the overall stock markets worldwide by about a third in a shocking six weeks. Due to the lack of customer mobility, investors dumped firms related to the travel sector like those in the cruise, hotel, airline, and restaurant industries.

While investors reacted to the reduction in expected profitability of many firms, like Norwegian Cruises, Royal Caribbean, and Carnival, they also quickly realized the increase in expected profitability of firms that supported remote work, like DocuSign and Zoom. Indeed, after the initial decline in March 2020, investors bought the stock of technology firms, which ended 2020 with great returns. In 2021, as the pandemic slowly subsided, investors started buying back the travel-oriented firms that they had previously dumped in anticipation of pent-up travel demand.

These examples illustrate several important points about the macroeconomic environment. First, the economy and the stock market cycle up and down over time, though both trend higher. Second, it isn't just one stock market—it is a market of stocks. In other words, some companies' stocks or an industry can be thriving at the same time others are struggling. Lastly, investors should be aware of the changing environment and adjust their portfolios accordingly.

1-8 Investment Careers

Those of you who are really interested in making a career in investments have probably watched finance movies like, *Wall Street, The Wolf of Wall Street, The Big Short, Boiler Room*, and others that feature investments prominently in their stories. If you haven't, you should. The protagonists in those movies have been portrayed in a less-than-flattering light. They are just movies, after all. The real investment world is not as glamorous but can be very rewarding in both a personal finance sense and through the pleasure of helping others.

Remember that the characters in all those movies, and the investment professionals whom we read about every day in the financial news, are working in the business of *providing investment advice*. That is, they usually don't make money by trading on their own account, but instead run (or, at least, work for) financial firms that help investors decide what financial assets to invest in. Some investment professionals give that advice directly to their customers, while others implement decisions directly in the portfolios. While no stockbroker or investment analyst can guarantee that a particular investment will "outperform" the market, they *can* help investors determine if their expected returns are justified by the risks and how those risks and returns will fit in the portfolio.

Investment professionals work in many places. Any business that has its own portfolio to manage or has clients with money to manage employ investment professionals. Employment opportunities are most numerous with brokerage firms, investment banks, commercial banks, savings institutions, insurance carriers, investment institutions (like mutual funds, pension funds, and hedge funds), investment financial planning firms, and real estate companies. Even large businesses often employ people with investment skills in their benefits department to administer the pension plan.

The various kinds of roles available include stockbroker, securities analyst, portfolio manager, financial planner, and investment banker. A stockbroker works with individuals and institutions in advising and executing buy and sell orders of selling financial securities. A securities analyst is an expert in specific industries and provides advice about the valuation and prospects of firms in those industries. They often provide recommendations to the portfolio manager, who makes the final decisions on what to buy and sell in the creation or management of the portfolio. A financial planner helps individuals and families navigate the process of saving, investing, and ultimately providing retirement income. Lastly, investment bankers are the intermediaries between the companies and governments seeking new capital and investors with capital to offer. Thus, they work with companies to issue securities and distribute them to investors.

Careers in financial planning, portfolio management, and investments also have professional certifications and license requirements. For example, passing the Series 7 exam given by the Financial Industry Regulatory Authority (www.finra.org) is required for you to become a registered representative (broker) who acts as an account executive for clients. To become an investment advisor and provide research and opinions on securities and the securities market, you must pass the Series 66 (or comparable) exam. (For information on the Series 66 exam, see the North American Securities Administrators Association [NASAA] webpage at www.nasaa.org.)

While professional designations are not required for you to buy and sell securities and to construct a portfolio, you should consider pursuing one if you plan on a career in some aspect of investments. The following list, in alphabetical order, provides several financial professional designations and where you may obtain information concerning them.

- Chartered Alternative Investment Analyst (CAIA), granted by the CAIA Association (www.caia.org)
- Chartered Financial Analyst (CFA), granted by the CFA Institute (www.cfainstitute.org)
- Certified Financial Planner (CFP), granted by the Certified Financial Planner Board of Standards (www.cfp.net)
- Chartered Financial Consultant (ChFC), granted by the American College of Financial Services (www.chfc-clu.com)

securities analyst
A financial professional who analyzes and makes recommendations regarding stocks and other financial assets

portfolio manager
A finance professional in charge of making buy, sell, and hold decisions for a portfolio

financial planner
A person who guides customers through the investment process to meet current and long-term financial goals

investment banker
A finance professional who helps companies and governments acquire capital through the issuance of financial securities

Conclusion

This chapter has introduced many of the important foundational financial concepts that apply to investing. These concepts include the following:

- capital flow
- types of financial assets
- risk and expected return
- asset valuation
- risk aversion
- asset allocation
- diversification
- market efficiency

Each of these themes reappears throughout this text. Even though a chapter may be devoted to a specific topic, such as mutual funds or bonds, these specific assets ultimately must fit into a portfolio. It is important to know the characteristics, like risks and expected return, of a specific security. But ultimately, the characteristics of each individual asset will interact with the other assets in your portfolio. In addition, the success of your portfolio will depend on the macro environment.

Key Terms

asset-specific risk – The chance that problems with an individual asset will reduce the value of the portfolio

asset allocation – The process of diversifying an investment portfolio across various asset categories, such as stocks, bonds, and cash

capital gain – An increase in the value of a capital asset, such as a stock

correlated – The degree of return co-movement between two assets

defined contribution plan – An employee-funded retirement program in which the employee makes the funding and investment decisions

derivative security – A financial instrument with value stemming from changes in the value of some other (possibly financial) asset

diversified portfolio – A portfolio of assets that includes various asset categories, such as stocks, bonds, and cash, for the purpose of reducing risk

financial asset – An investment instrument issued by corporations, governments, or other organizations that offer legal rights to debt or equity cash flow

financial planner – A person who guides customers through the investment process to meet current and long-term financial goals

income – The flow of money produced by an asset, e.g., dividends and interest

investment banker – A finance professional who helps companies and governments acquire capital through the issuance of financial securities

investment – The purchase of an asset for the purpose of storing and (possibly) increasing value over time

law of large numbers (LLN) – From probability and statistics, a concept that states that as a sample size grows, its sample mean gets closer to the population average

liquidity – The ease with which assets can be converted into cash with no or minimal loss or cost

monopoly power – A firm's ability to price its product or service substantially above the competitive level and persist in doing so

portfolio manager – A finance professional in charge of making buy, sell, and hold decisions for a portfolio

profit – Financial gain earned from the difference between the revenue and the expenses from an investment asset or business

rate of return – The annual percentage return realized on an investment

real asset – Physical asset that has a value due to its substance and properties, like precious metals, commodities, real estate, land, equipment, and natural resources

return – The sum of income plus capital gains earned on an investment in an asset

risk averse – The degree to which a person desires to avoid risk

risk – The possibility of loss; the uncertainty of future returns

securities analyst – A financial professional who analyzes and makes recommendations regarding stocks and other financial assets

speculation – An investment that offers a potentially large return but is also very risky; a high probability that the investment will produce a loss

systemic risk – Return volatility associated with the overall market

time value of money – The concept that the money you have now is worth more than the same amount received in the future due to its potential ability to grow

valuation – The process of determining the current worth of an asset—the present value of future benefits

Questions

1. **Real vs. Financial Assets.** Compare and contrast real assets with financial assets. (LO 1-1)
2. **Capital Flow: Corporate vs. Investor View.** Regarding the flow of capital between investors, corporations, and the government, how does the view of the corporation differ from the view of the investor? (LO 1-2)
3. **Capital Flow Factors.** What are the complicating factors that make the flow of capital among corporations and investors uncertain?
4. **Valuation.** What factors are involved in assessing value? (LO 1-3)
5. **Risk Aversion.** What are the ramifications of an investor being risk averse? (LO 1-3)
6. **Market Efficiency.** Why might a market be efficient? (LO 1-4)
7. **Asset Specific Risk.** What is an asset-specific risk and how does it relate to portfolio diversification? (LO 1-5)
8. **Oil Prices and Diversification.** How would an increase in oil prices impact petroleum companies and airline firms? How does this relate to diversification? (LO 1-5)
9. **Financial Crisis Recovery.** How did the recoveries after the financial crises of 2008 and 2020 differ for investor opportunities? (LO 1-6)
10. **Investment Professional Roles.** Discuss four kinds of investment professionals, including their primary roles in the industry. (LO 1-7)

Case Study

Financial Information

To be successful in this course and in your investment life, you will need access to good information. Investment professionals often have access to expensive information sources and analytical tools, like a Bloomberg Terminal. However, there are also many free financial websites that are very useful:

- Bloomberg: bloomberg.com
- CNN/Money: cnn.com/business
- Google: google.com/finance
- MarketWatch: marketwatch.com
- Morningstar: morningstar.com
- MSN Money: msn.com/en-us/money
- Yahoo! Finance: finance.yahoo.com

The purpose of this case is to explore one information source you will use during this course and in your personal financial life. Start by picking a public company to explore and finding its ticker symbol on Yahoo! Finance. Once you have found the company, locate the following information:

A. From the Summary tab, find the closing stock price, PE ratio, earnings per share, dividend, capitalization, beta, and volume of shares traded.

B. From the Financials tab, obtain an annual income statement and a balance sheet. Comment on the firm's financial statements.

C. From the Statistics tab, obtain the valuation measures, profitability, management effectiveness, and share statistics.

D. Historical stock price data can be found in the historical data. This is useful for obtaining a history of daily, weekly, or monthly stock returns. Select years of monthly prices. Next, click the Download link to receive a csv file for your spreadsheet. Note that the data is sorted as oldest month first. Next, compute a monthly return using the Adj Close column (this column adjusts the price for dividends and share splits) for each month starting at the second month. [Example: For spreadsheet row 3, compute the return as $= (F3 - F2)/F2$]. Compute the five-year monthly average return. Comment on the monthly returns and average return.

Example:

	A	B	C	D	E	F	G	H	I	J	K
1	Date	Open	High	Low	Close	Adj Close	Volume	Return			
2	7/1/2016	23.8725	26.1375	23.5925	26.0525	24.33785	2.74E+09				
3	8/1/2016	26.1025	27.5575	26	26.525	24.77926	2.52E+09	1.81%	=(F3-F2)/F2		
4	9/1/2016	26.535	29.045	25.6325	28.2625	26.54543	3.87E+09	7.13%			
5	10/1/2016	28.1775	29.6725	28.07	28.385	26.66048	2.75E+09	0.43%	Average =	3.13%	=AVERAGE(H3:H62)
6	11/1/2016	28.365	28.4425	26.02	27.63	25.95136	2.89E+09	-2.66%			
7	12/1/2016	27.5925	29.505	27.0625	28.955	27.33548	2.44E+09	5.33%			
8	1/1/2017	28.95	30.61	28.60	30.2375	28.64066	2.35E+09	4.77%			

Types and Attributes of Financial Instruments

After completing this chapter, you should be able to:

LO 2-1 Identify the differences between financial instruments and securities.
LO 2-2 Compare and contrast primary market transactions and secondary market transactions.
LO 2-3 Detail the division of capital, risk, return, and control imposed on a firm by a mixture of different types of primary market issues.
LO 2-4 Define the allocation of risk, return, and control created by primary market equity issues.
LO 2-5 Explain the impact of bond maturity on bond interest rates.
LO 2-6 Define the allocation of risk, return, and control created by primary market debt issues.
LO 2-7 Compare and contrast the different types of money market instruments.
LO 2-8 Explain the difference between futures contracts and options.
LO 2-9 Define and explain how foreign exchange instruments are used by investors.

As previously discussed, financial assets are nonphysical assets whose values are derived from either a contractual claim on real assets or on the cash flows produced by those real assets. In some circles, you will hear the terms *financial assets*, *financial instruments*, and *securities* used interchangeably, but this is not quite correct.

A **financial instrument** refers to a contract that generates a financial asset to one of the parties involved and an equity claim or financial liability to the other party. Equity-based financial instruments represent ownership of an asset, while debt-based financial instruments represent a loan made by an investor to the borrower, which could be a company or government.

All financial instruments *can* technically be traded, but those that are created with the *specific intention of being publicly traded* are called securities. Accordingly, most financial instruments fall into one or more of the following

financial instrument
A contract that generates a financial asset

five categories: equity securities, debt securities, money market instruments, derivative instruments, and foreign exchange instruments. We will discuss each type of instrument in detail later in the chapter, with an eye toward identifying which types are best suited for achieving various investment goals. However, first let's focus on why equity and debt are "securities" while the other three are referred to as "instruments."

2-1 Securities vs. Financial Instruments

As its name implies, the Securities and Exchange Commission (SEC) heavily regulates publicly traded securities. Other types of financial instruments are less-heavily regulated.

One need for additional regulation on long-lived, publicly traded securities such as equity securities (i.e., stocks) and long-term bonds sold by corporations is self-evident. Because these types of securities can expect to be traded between multiple pairs of buyers and sellers throughout their lifetime, careful documentation of the ability of the firm to pay back the securities' purchasers and the rights accruing to the owners of the securities (a process usually referred to as **due diligence**) is necessary to ensure that every buyer knows exactly what they're getting into. Likewise, careful tracking of who rightfully owns the securities is necessary to ensure that investors receive payments from the firm and are allowed the right to exercise control of the firm's activities as specified for their type of security.

For private equity and debt placements where the buyer is *not* expected to resell the instrument, there is presumably no need for such careful tracking. In this case, the SEC operates under the rule of *caveat emptor* (Latin for "let the buyer beware"), assuming that someone wealthy enough to participate in a private placement should have the resources to perform their own due diligence.

2-1a Primary Market Transactions

Public corporations raise capital to purchase productive assets and often fund those purchases by taking out a loan or by selling (issuing) stocks or bonds. Two methods exist to facilitate this transfer. The first is the direct investment that occurs when people or financial institutions directly supply capital to firms. The direct sale of an entire issue of bonds or stock to a financial institution, such as a private equity firm or a hedge fund, is called a **private placement**. A direct transfer also occurs when securities are initially sold to investors in the primary market through investment bankers. These securities may be subsequently bought and sold in the secondary markets.

As a result, when a public firm *does* issue new stocks or bonds for sale to the public, it will do so through an **underwriter**, usually an investment bank that is in a position to evaluate the risks of the issue for the public after having been granted access to the firm's proprietary information to do so. Because the issue is supported by the underwriter, who *does* presumably have access to the firm's own proprietary information, the underwriter's reputation helps assure investors that the issue is worth investing in. And, as a result, the firm is able to earn enough capital from the sale of the new issue of financial instruments that it can afford to purchase the productive assets it needs to act on its proprietary plans. Such a sale by an issuing firm is referred to as transacting in the **primary market** to denote that it is the first time the securities have been sold.

Private placements are especially important for small emerging firms. The size of these firms or the risk associated with them often precludes their raising funds from traditional sources, such as commercial banks. Firms that do make private placements of securities issued by emerging firms are called **venture capitalists**. Venture capital is a major source

due diligence
The investigation or exercise of care that a reasonable business or person is normally expected to take before entering into an agreement or contract with another party

private placement
The nonpublic sale of securities

underwriter
A large financial institution that guarantees the performance of a public security issue

primary market
Sale or purchase of securities by the firm that issued them

venture capitalist
A firm specializing in investing in the securities of small, emerging companies

of finance for small firms or firms developing new technologies. The venture capitalists thus fill a void by acquiring securities issued by small firms with exceptional growth potential.

Once the emerging firm grows, the securities purchased by the venture capitalist or private equity firm may be sold to the general public through an **initial public offering** (IPO), which is the traditional process of selling new securities to the general public. Firms use the services of an investment banker to issue new securities and sell them to the general public. Firms sell securities when internally generated funds are insufficient to finance the desired level of investment spending. The firm obtains outside funding from the general public at a time when it benefits it the most. Such outside funding may increase public interest in the firm and its securities.

initial public offering (IPO)
The first sale of common stock to the general public

Underwriting Process

In most instances, corporations seeking additional investment capital hire an investment bank as an underwriter to act in the role of advisor and distributor. Investment banking services include underwriting of debt and equity securities, such as advising on mergers, acquisitions, privatization, and restructuring, and participating in real estate, project finance, and leasing activities. Successful underwriters have a roster of regular customers—such as pension funds, mutual funds, and insurance companies—for new issues. Highly respected investment bankers must be sure to bring only high-quality IPOs to the attention of their regular institutional customers or risk the loss of their source of capital for their issuers. Because of the large fees they charge issuers, investment bankers are always on the prowl for more companies with securities to sell and for more institutional customers.

The investment bank does not usually sell all the securities by itself but instead forms a **syndicate** to market them. The syndicate is a group of brokerage houses that join together to underwrite a specific sale of securities. The members of the syndicate may bring in additional brokerage firms to help distribute the securities. The firm that manages the sale is frequently referred to as the *lead underwriter*. It is the lead underwriter that allocates the specific number of securities that each member of the syndicate is responsible for selling.

syndicate
A selling group assembled to market an issue of securities

The use of a syndicate has several advantages. First, the syndicate may have access to more potential buyers for the securities. Second, its use will reduce the number of securities that each brokerage firm must sell. The uptick in the number of potential customers and the drop in the amount that each broker must sell increases the probability that the entire issue of securities will be sold. Thus, syndication makes possible both the sale of a large offering of securities and a reduction in the risk borne by each member.

In some cases, the firm seeking funds may not choose to negotiate the terms of the securities with an underwriter. Instead, the firm designs the issue and auctions the securities to the investment banker making the highest bid. In preparation for bidding, the investment banker will form a syndicate as well as determine the price it is willing to pay. The underwriter and its syndicate that wins the auction and purchases the securities mark up the price of the securities and sell them to the general public. Obviously, if the investment banker bids too high, it will be unable to sell the securities for a profit. Then the underwriter may sustain a loss when it lowers the securities' price in order to sell them.

Types of Agreements

The agreement between the investment bankers and the firm may be one of two types. The investment bankers may make a **best-efforts agreement** in which they agree to make their best effort to sell the securities but do not guarantee that a specified amount of money will be raised. The risk of selling the securities rests with the firm issuing the securities. If the investment bankers are unable to find buyers, the firm does not receive the desired amount of money.

best-efforts agreement
An agreement with an investment banker who does not guarantee the sale of a security but who agrees to make the best effort to sell it

firm commitment
An agreement with an investment banker who guarantees a sale of securities by agreeing to purchase the entire issue at a specified price

The alternative is a firm commitment, an underwriting in which the investment bankers purchase (i.e., underwrite) the entire issue of securities at a specified price and subsequently sell them to the general public. Most sales of new securities are made through firm commitments, and best-effort sales are generally limited to small securities issues by less-well-known firms. In an underwriting, the investment bankers pay the expenses with the anticipation of recouping these costs through the sale. Because the underwriters have agreed to purchase the entire issue, they must pay the firm for all the securities even if the syndicate is unable to sell them. Thus, the risk of the sale rests with the underwriters.

It is for this reason that the pricing of the underwritten securities is crucial. If the initial offer price is too high, the syndicate will be unable to sell the securities. When this occurs, the investment bankers have two choices: (1) to maintain the offer price and hold the securities in inventory until they are sold or (2) to let the market find a lower price level that will induce investors to purchase the securities. Neither choice benefits the investment bankers. If the underwriters purchase the securities and hold them in inventory, they either must tie up their own funds, which could be earning a return elsewhere or borrow funds to pay for the securities. Like any other firm, the investment bankers pay interest on these borrowed funds. Thus, the decision to support the offer price of the securities requires that the investment bankers invest their own capital or, more likely, borrow substantial amounts of capital. In either case, the profit margins on the underwriting are substantially decreased and the investment bankers may even experience a loss on the underwriting.

Instead of supporting the price, the underwriters may choose to let the price of the securities fall. The inventory of unsold securities can then be sold, and the underwriters will not tie up capital or have to borrow money from their sources of credit. If the underwriters make this choice, they take losses when the securities are sold at less than cost. But they also cause the customers who bought the securities at the initial offer price to sustain a loss. The underwriters certainly do not want to inflict losses on these customers: if they experience losses continually, the underwriters' market for future security issues will vanish. Therefore, the investment banks try not to overprice a new issue of securities, as overpricing will ultimately result in their suffering losses.

There is also an incentive to avoid underpricing new securities. Underpriced issues will be readily sold; the price will then rise as demand has exceeded supply. The buyers of the securities will be satisfied, as this underpricing will have led to an increase in price. The initial purchasers of the securities reap windfall profits; however, these gains are really at the expense of the company whose securities were underpriced. If the underwriters had assigned a higher price to the securities, the company would have raised more capital. Underwriting is a competitive business, and each security issue is negotiated individually. Hence, if one investment banker consistently underprices securities, firms will choose competitors to underwrite their securities.

The Prospectus

preliminary prospectus
Initial document detailing the financial condition of a firm that must be filed with the SEC to register a new issue of securities

registration
Process of filing information with the SEC concerning a proposed sale of securities to the general public

Once the terms of the sale have been agreed upon, the managing house may issue a preliminary prospectus. This is often referred to as a *red herring,* a term connoting that the document should be read with caution, as it is not final nor complete. (The phrase "red herring" is derived from British fugitives' rubbing herring across their trails to confuse pursuing bloodhounds.) The preliminary prospectus informs potential buyers that the securities are being registered with the Securities and Exchange Commission (SEC) and may subsequently be offered for sale. Registration refers to the disclosure of information concerning the firm, the securities being offered for sale, and the use of the proceeds from the sale. While there are exceptions, generally unregistered corporate securities may not be sold to the general public. The debt of governments (e.g., state and municipal bonds), however, is *not* registered with the SEC and may be sold to the general public.

The cost of preparing the red herring is borne by the issuing firm. This preliminary prospectus describes the company and the securities to be issued; it includes the firm's income statement and balance sheets, its current activities (such as a pending merger or labor negotiation), the regulatory bodies to which it is subject, and the nature of its competition. The preliminary prospectus is thus a detailed document concerning the company and is, unfortunately, usually tedious reading.

The preliminary prospectus does not include the price of the securities. That will be determined on the day that the securities are issued. If prices decline or rise, the price of the new securities may be adjusted for the change in market conditions. In fact, if prices decline sufficiently, the firm has the option of postponing or even canceling the underwriting.

An important part of the IPO process is the **road show**, where the investment banker discusses the investment merits of the corporation's securities to institutional investors and the general public. This is a useful means of drumming up interest in the offering and determining investors' appetite for the firm's securities under different pricing scenarios. Throughout this process, the issuing corporation and the investment banker come to agreement on several things, including the amount of capital needed by the corporation, type of security to be issued, price of the security to be issued, and amount of compensation (or commission) paid by the firm to the investment banker.

road show
A series of sales presentations to potential investors by the underwriting firm

After the SEC accepts the registration statement, a final prospectus is published. The SEC does not approve the issue as to its investment worth but rather sees that all information has been provided and that the prospectus is complete in format and content. Except for changes that are required by the SEC, it is virtually identical to the preliminary prospectus. Information regarding the price of the security, the underwriting discount, and the proceeds to the company, along with any more recent financial data, is added. The dating app Bumble conducted its IPO in early 2021. Its founder and CEO Whitney Wolfe Herd became a billionaire and the youngest woman to take a company public. The IPO was priced at $43 per share and sold 50 million shares, which raised $2.15 billion for the firm. The stock closed at $70.31, 64% above its IPO price on its first day of trading.

The cost of the underwriting (also called *flotation costs* or *underwriting discount*) is the difference between the price of the securities to the public investor and the proceeds that go to the firm. If a firm is offering shares at a price of $43, then the underwriters will keep a portion as their fee. For example, a 7% fee is common, which means that the underwriters take $3.01 per share. Thus, the sale of 50 million shares earns over $150 million in fees. Underwriting fees tend to vary with the dollar value of the securities being underwritten and the type of securities being sold. Some of the expenses are fixed (e.g., preparation of the prospectus), so the unit cost for a large underwriting is smaller. Also, because it may be more difficult to sell speculative bonds than high-quality bonds, underwriting fees for speculative issues tend to be higher.

Volatility of IPOs

The new-issue market (especially for common stock) is extremely volatile. There have been times when the investing public seemed willing to purchase virtually any new security that was being sold on the market. At other times, new companies have simply been unable to raise money and large well-known companies were able to do so only under onerous terms.

The market for IPOs is volatile regarding not only the number of securities that are offered but also the price changes of new issues. It is not unusual for prices to dramatically rise and fall. In Bumble's IPO, the shares were sold for $43 per share in the primary market and then started trading at $76 on the stock exchange. The next day, the price hit $84.80 but closed at $75.46. A few months later, the stock was trading in the $30s before rebounding to the $50s.

Lockups

In addition to price volatility caused by speculative buying of an IPO, insiders could possibly use a new public issue of securities as a means to sell their stock. Such sales may also lead to price volatility, although in this case it would be price declines and not increases. (There is an additional ethical question concerning insiders profiting at the expense of the general investing public.) To understand the possible source of the price volatility, consider a privately held company that is considering going public. Before the IPO, managers and other employees are allowed to purchase the stock in a "nonpublic" or "private" transaction (e.g., $1 a share) or granted options to buy the stock at a low price. Because there is no market in the stock, the price cannot be determined, so the sale price to insiders could be artificially low. (Such stock sales and the granting of options prior to the IPO are often viewed as "compensation" for those employees.)

While lockups are not required by the SEC and are negotiated by the issuing firm and the underwriter, the full disclosure agreements laws do require that issuing firms disclose potential sales by insiders. Because large sales may destabilize the market and cause the stock's price to fall, underwriters prefer long lockups. The period can range from 90 to 365 days, but 180 days is the most common. If there were no lockup agreement, insiders could sell shares immediately provided they had met the SEC requirement to disclose the possible sale of previously restricted stock.

Shelf Registrations

The preceding discussion was cast in terms of firms initially selling their stock to the general public (i.e., the "initial public offering" or "going public"). Firms that have previously issued securities and are currently public also raise funds by selling new securities. If the sales are to the general public, the same basic procedure applies. The new securities must be registered with and approved by the SEC before they may be sold to the public, and the firm often uses the services of an investment banker to facilitate the sale.

There are, however, differences between an IPO and the sale of additional securities by a publicly held firm. The first major difference concerns the price of the securities. Because a market already exists for the firm's stock, the problem of an appropriate price for the additional shares is virtually eliminated. This price will approximate the market price on the date of issue. Second, because the firm must periodically publish information (for instance, the annual report) and file documents with the SEC, there is less need for a detailed prospectus. Many publicly held firms construct a prospectus describing a proposed issue of new securities and file it with the SEC. This document is called a *shelf registration*. After the shelf registration has been accepted by the SEC, the firm may sell the securities whenever the need for funds arises. For example, UDR Inc. filed a shelf registration for $1.5 billion in debt securities, preferred stock, and common stock. This shelf registration offers the issuing firm flexibility. The securities do not have to be issued but can be quickly sold if the management deems that the conditions are optimal for the sale. In addition, the firm does not have to sell all the securities.

The management of UDR Inc. may choose to sell the debt but not the stock or to sell only the common stock (up to the limit covered by the registration). The remaining securities may be subsequently issued when conditions warrant their sale.

Direct Listing

Some companies can avoid the negative aspects of the IPO process by using a direct listing, also known as a *direct public offering*. The direct listing process allows a private firm's investors and the company to sell existing shares directly to the public through a secondary exchange without the use of an underwriter. Thus, the firm avoids having to pay underwriters and lockup agreements. This process does not allow for the creation of new shares of stock for sale and thus may limit the amount of capital raised. Direct listings are better suited for well-known companies that don't necessarily need new financing.

direct listing
Existing outstanding shares are sold to the public for the first time on a secondary market with no underwriters involved

Prior to 2020, while a few companies had used a direct listing, there was no official process that had been approved by the SEC. However, on December 22, 2020, the SEC announced its approval of a NYSE proposal to allow companies to raise capital through direct listings. This regulatory consent paves the way for more firms to circumvent the traditional initial public offering process. For the first half of 2021, the largest direct listing was Coinbase. The company's direct listing set a reference price of $250 but hit a high of $429.54 before closing out their first day of trading at $328.28 on April 14. Over the ensuing weeks, the stock slipped below its initial $250 price.

Special Purpose Acquisition Companies (SPACs)

Special purpose acquisition companies (SPACs) are another way to take a private firm public rather than using the traditional IPO. First, the SPAC conducts its own IPO to become a publicly traded stock that is essentially all cash from the raised capital. Its sole purpose is to acquire one or more unspecified private companies within two years after going public. That is, the SPAC raises the capital in its IPO and then goes looking for private companies to purchase. When those private companies are purchased, they become publicly traded firms. The SPAC becomes the public version of the previously private company. For example, the SPAC VectolQ Acquisition purchased Nikola—a rival for electric car company Tesla—in June of 2020. Before the acquisition, the SPAC traded as ticker VTIQ; afterward, the new company began trading with ticker symbol NKLA.

SPAC
Investment vehicle that raises capital in its IPO and then goes looking for a private company to purchase, which causes that firm to become a publicly traded firm

Why would firms prefer to go public through being acquired by a SPAC instead of the traditional IPO process? One reason is that the SPAC IPO is significantly shorter than the traditional IPO. The normal IPO process takes about six months or longer, while the SPAC process can be completed in less than four months. In addition, there are no historical financial data reporting and much less involvement from the SEC. This is likely why SPACs have become popular. In 2019, 59 SPACs conducted their IPOs. In 2020, the number of SPACs raising capital rose to 248.

Regardless of the rise in popularity, investors need to be wary. When you buy the stock of a SPAC, you are essentially gambling on the ability of its sponsor to find good private companies to buy and to get a good deal on that purchase. Thus, the reputation and intent of the SPAC team is what matters. For example, SPAC Soaring Eagle Acquisition Corp. had no trouble raising capital in its IPO because the acquisition team had found previous success taking DraftKings public in 2019 and Skillz in 2020. The recent popularity of taking a firm public via a SPAC merits close observation to see if it will last or is just a fad.

A Walk Down Wall Street

Celebrity SPACs

Celebrity influencers are drawing attention from regulators, who warned recently about the dangers of investing in SPACs simply because of famous backers. Athletes, pop-culture figures, and politicians have become sponsors. The following list includes celebrity SPAC sponsors, the SPAC, and the name of the firm if one has been acquired.

Athletes

- **Shaquille O'Neal**, Forest Road Acquisition Corp. (taking Beachbody public) and Forest Road Acquisition Corp. II
- **Serena Williams**, Jaws Spitfire Acquisition Corp. (one of real estate investor Barry Sternlicht's SPACs)
- **Alex Rodriguez**, Slam Corp.
- **Colin Kaepernick**, Mission Advancement Corp.
- **Stephen Curry**, Dune Acquisition Corp.
- **Patrick Mahomes, Justin Verlander, Naomi Osaka, Saul "Canelo" Álvarez, Robert Lewandowski**, Disruptive Acquisition Corp.
- **Peyton Manning, Andre Agassi, Steffi Graf**, NewHold Investment Corp. (investing in a deal to take crowd-safety company Evolv Technology public)
- **Roger Staubach**, Victory Acquisition Corp.

Singers and other pop-culture figures

- **Ciara**, Bright Lights Acquisition Corp.
- **Jay-Z**, The Parent Co. (formerly Subversive Capital Acquisition Corp.)
- **Sammy Hagar**, Victory Acquisition Corp.
- **Joanna Coles**, Northern Star Acquisition Corp. (taking BarkBox Inc. public), Northern Star Investment Corp. II–IV

Why are celebrities getting involved? The sponsor gets a 20% stake, called a "promote," and there's much less regulatory scrutiny. The celebrity sponsor doesn't have to invest much of their own money but does provide name recognition. Investment professionals handle the acquisition of the private company. Regulators are concerned that investors may be drawn to these SPACs for the wrong reasons and fail to understand the risks involved.

2-1b Corporate Risk, Return, and Control Ramifications of Primary Market Transactions

Let's start with the basic equity ownership structure and build from there. When a firm is financed entirely with equity, the shareholders of the firm provide all the capital, bear all the risk, get all the returns, and have complete control of the actions of the firm as shown in this simple diagram (refer **Figure 2-1**).

Sometimes a firm will sell two different classes of equity: A shares and B shares. If both classes provided the same amount of capital and were co-equal in terms of risk, return, and control, then all four of these aspects would be split evenly between the two classes. However, it wouldn't make much sense to issue two classes of stock that were exactly the same. It would be more efficient to have only one class of shareholders if they were truly equal in every way. Instead, what normally happens is that one of the classes gets less control in return for less risk or more return, as shown in **Figure 2-2**.

Now the details in terms of how much risk and return both classes would bear, as well as how much capital they would provide and how much control over the firm they

Figure 2-1: Capital, Risk, Return, and Control in an All-Equity Firm

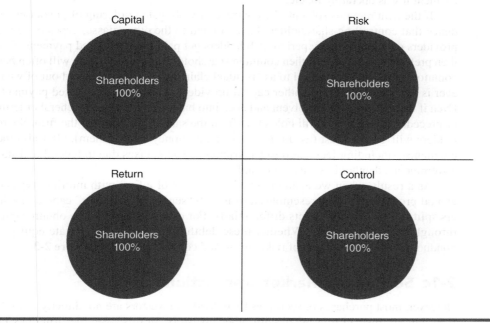

Figure 2-2: Capital, Risk, Return, and Control in a Two-Class All-Equity Firm with Differential Rights

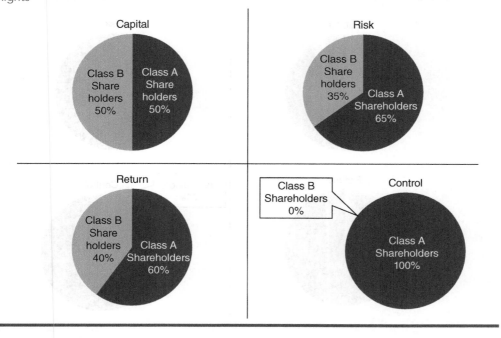

would exercise, would depend upon the business risk of the firm, the economic environment it was operating in, etc.

If the firm remains solvent, the contractually obligated ordering of payout precedence that controlling shareholders have granted to the other classes/types of capital providers dictate that every period, debtholders get paid their promised payments first, then preferred shareholders, then common shareholders. As a result, you will often hear common shareholders referred to as "residual claimants," as they get paid out of whatever is left over after all the other capital providers receive their promised payments. Even if the firm becomes insolvent and goes into bankruptcy, the same general ordering or precedence in payouts still holds true from the sale of the assets of the firm. Shareholders will get paid last (assuming there is any money left for them), after all other claimants—including fees owed to bankruptcy lawyers, taxes due to federal and state governments, debtholders, etc.—are paid.

As a result, when we examine the four aspects of a firm with multiple types of capital providers, it often resembles a firm with "senior" and "junior" capital providers splitting those four aspects differentially. For example, firms often obtain capital through borrowing money. Whether these debtholders are banks, private equity, or bondholders, the distribution of risk, return, and control is shown in **Figure 2-3**.

2-1c Secondary Market Transactions

However, most purchases of securities by individual investors are not directly from the firm, but are instead transacted with other investors. In this case, the firm does not receive any proceeds from the transaction, meaning that there is no net investment in productive assets. Instead, for every investment by the buyer in one of these "later"

Figure 2-3: Capital, Risk, Return, and Control in a Firm with Debt and Equity

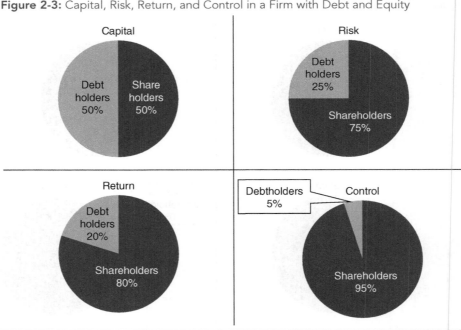

transactions, there is an equal sale by the seller (or multiple sellers). The seller trades the security for cash and the buyer trades cash for the security. These transactions occur in secondhand markets; as such, securities markets are often referred to as **secondary markets**.

Note that since secondary market transactions do not alter the amount or types of capital in the firm or the number and type of claimants, they also will not affect the division of the four aspects of capital, risk, return, and control that we discussed earlier for primary market transactions. Only primary market transaction will do so.

For that reason, in the following discussion of the different major types of financial instruments, we will cover whether each is normally traded in a primary market transaction, in a secondary market transaction, or in both. And for those that are traded in primary market transactions, we will discuss the relative impact on the aspects of the firm's capital, risk, return, and control.

secondary market
A market where securities trade after issuance by the firm

2-2 Equity Securities

A corporation is an artificial legal economic unit established (i.e., chartered) by a state. **Stock** represents ownership, or equity, in a corporation. Under state laws, the firm is issued a certificate of incorporation that indicates the name of the corporation, the location of its principal office, its purpose, and the number of shares of stock that are authorized (i.e., the number of shares that the firm may issue). In addition to a certificate of incorporation, the firm receives a **charter** that specifies the legal relationship between the corporation and the state. At the initial meeting of stockholders, bylaws are established that set the rules by which the firm is governed, including such issues as the voting rights of the stockholders.

Firms may issue both preferred and common stock. When investors normally think of stock, they are thinking of common stock, which has the equity control rights of the firm, as illustrated in Figures 2-1 to 2-3 above. However, there is another type of stock—*preferred stock*—that some firms issue in addition to their common stock. As the name implies, preferred stock holds a position superior to common stock in some respects. Specifically, preferred stock receives dividend payments before common stock and, in the case of liquidation, preferred stockholders are compensated before common stockholders. Preferred stock is legally equity and hence represents ownership. However, its features are more similar to the characteristics of debt than of common stock. For example, preferred stock does not have any control rights and generally pays a fixed dividend. The relationship between the four aspects of common and preferred stock in the same firm would be similar in spirit to that shown in Figure 2-3.

In the eyes of the law, a corporation is a legal entity that is separate from its owners. It may enter into contracts and is legally responsible for its obligations. Creditors may sue the corporation for payment if it defaults on its obligations, but the creditors cannot sue the stockholders. Therefore, an investor knows that if they purchase stock in a publicly held corporation, such as General Electric, the maximum that can be lost is the amount of the investment. If a large corporation (e.g., Christopher & Banks in 2021) does go bankrupt, **limited liability** means its stockholders are safe from the firm's creditors. Stockholders in privately held corporations who pledge their personal assets to secure loans do not have limited liability. In that case, if the corporation defaults, the creditors may seize the assets that the stockholders have pledged. In this event, the liability of the shareholders is not limited to their investment in the firm.

stock
The shares into which ownership of a corporation is divided

charter
The document that establishes the existence of a corporation and specifies its allowed activities

limited liability
A legal status where an investor's financial liability is limited to their investment in a firm

2-2a Allocation of Control to Shareholders

Because stock represents ownership in a corporation, investors have all the rights of ownership. These rights include the ability to vote the shares. The stockholders elect a board of directors that selects the firm's management. Management is then responsible to the board of directors, which in turn is responsible to the firm's stockholders. If the stockholders do not think that the board is doing a competent job, they may elect another board to represent them.

For publicly held corporations, such democracy rarely works seamlessly. Stockholders are usually widely dispersed, while the firm's management and board of directors generally form a cohesive unit. Rarely do the individual investor's votes mean much. There have, however, been exceptions. In May 2021, shareholders voted to unseat at least two board members for Exxon Mobil Corporation in a bid to force the company's leadership to reckon with the risk of failing to adjust its business strategy to match global efforts to combat climate change.

As mentioned above, some corporations have two or more classes of common stock. For example, Alphabet, Inc. (GOOGL), the current incarnation of Google, Inc., has class A, class B, and class C common shares. Having different classes of common stock like this facilitates controlling the corporation by a few stockholders, since voting rights often differ between the classes. In the case of GOOGL, class B shares have 10 votes for every 1 vote available to the owner of a share of the class A stock, while the class C shares get no votes at all.

Even if there are no proxy battles, there is always the possibility that if a company does poorly, another firm may offer to buy the outstanding stock held by the public. Once such purchases are made, the stock's new owners may remove the board of directors and establish new management. To some extent, this encourages a corporation's board of directors and management to pursue the goal of increasing the value of the firm's stock.

2-2b Allocation of Return to Shareholders

Since stockholders are owners, they are entitled to the firm's earnings. These earnings may be distributed in the form of cash dividends or be retained by the corporation. If they are retained, the individual's investment in the firm is increased (i.e., the stockholder's equity increases). However, for every class of stock, the individual investor's relative position is not altered. Some owners of common stock cannot receive cash dividends, whereas others have their earnings reinvested. The distribution or retention of earnings applies equally to all stockholders. (Some firms, however, do offer stockholders the option to use their dividends to purchase shares instead of receiving the cash.)

2-2c Allocation of Risk to Shareholders

Although limited liability is one of the advantages of investing in publicly held corporations, stock ownership does involve risk. As long as the firm prospers, it may be able to pay dividends and grow. However, if earnings fluctuate, dividends and growth may also fluctuate. It is the owners—the stockholders—who bear the business risk associated with these fluctuations. This is one source of the volatility in stock prices. If the firm should default on its debt, it can be taken to court by its creditors to enforce its obligations. If the firm should fail or become bankrupt, the stockholders have the last claim on its assets. Only after all the creditors have been paid will the stockholders receive any funds. In most cases of bankruptcy, what is left over is nothing. Even if the corporation survives bankruptcy proceedings, the amount received by the stockholders is uncertain.

2-3 Fixed-Income Securities

Debt securities are longer-term debt instruments where the issuer is essentially borrowing money from the investor. The investor plays the role of a lender lending money to the issuing entity. Longer-term debt securities often yield higher returns than money market instruments (see below). Debt instruments also represent a claim on the assets of the issuing entity in the event of a failure to pay the debt's interest payments or repay the principal.

You'll often hear debt securities referred to as **fixed-income securities** because the investor or lender often predetermines the terms of the debt instrument. For example, a debt instrument will be issued with a certain maturity, a certain principal amount, and a set coupon rate. This fixes all of the future cash flows. However, as you'll remember from your Introduction to Finance class, fixed-income securities' prices and returns can fluctuate and vary as the going interest rate changes over time. Since the future cash flows are fixed, a change in the discount rate used to value the security causes the price to change.

debt securities
Longer-term debt instruments

fixed-income securities
A category that includes bonds, preferred stocks, and other instruments with fixed-income cash flows

2-3a Fixed-Income Issuers and Their Attributes

Most fixed-income bonds (i.e., long-term debt instruments) are issued by large corporations; federal governments; or state, county, or municipal governments.

As we will discuss in Chapter 13, there are many risk factors that go into determining the price and/or coupon rate on bonds. But both federal governments and state, county, or municipal governments (usually referred to collectively as **munis**) enjoy lower **default risk** than corporate bonds. While corporation can't make customers buy their products, federal governments have the power to print money to use to repay their bond obligations, implying that, for large and stable governments, there is virtually no risk of a federal government defaulting on its bonds. Munis, while not capable of printing money, can (within limits) raise taxes and use the proceeds to pay back their bonds. While this is not quite as much of a "sure thing" as federal governments enjoy, it still makes most muni bonds fairly safe.

Another advantage that both federal and muni bonds enjoy is that the interest paid on their bonds is not taxed the same as corporate bond interest payments in the United States. Federal government bonds are not taxed at the state level, and munis are not taxed at either the federal level or in the state that issued them.

muni
A bond issued by a state, a county, or municipal governments

default risk
Lender risk that the borrower will fail to pay the interest payments and repay the principal

2-3b Interest and Maturity

All bonds (i.e., long-term debt instruments) have similar characteristics. They represent the indebtedness (liability) of their issuers in return for a specified sum, which is called the principal. Virtually all debt has a maturity date, which is the particular date by which it must be paid off. When debt is issued, the length of time to maturity is set: it may range from one day to 20 or 30 years or more. (Disney has an outstanding bond that matures in 2093.) If the maturity date falls within a year of the date of issuance, the debt is referred to as short-term debt. Long-term debt matures more than a year after it has been issued. (Debt that matures in 1 to 10 years is sometimes referred to as intermediate-term debt.) The owners of debt instruments (bondholders) receive the return of the principal and a flow of payments, which is called interest, in return for the use of their money. Interest should not be confused with other forms of income, such as the cash dividends that are paid by common and preferred stock. Dividends are distributions from earnings, whereas interest is an expense of borrowing.

yield
The potential return on a bond

yield to maturity
The estimated annual rate of return for a bond assuming that the investor holds the asset until its maturity date

current yield
A bond's annual interest payments divided by the current price of the bond

yield curve
Yields plotted against different maturities

When a fixed-income debt instrument such as a bond is issued, the rate of interest to be paid by the borrower is established. This rate is frequently referred to as the bond's coupon rate[1] (e.g., the 2.5% for the Apple bond in **Table 2-1**). The amount of interest is usually fixed over the lifetime of the bond. (There are exceptions; for example, see the section on variable interest rate bonds later in this chapter.) The return earned by the investor, however, need not be equal to the specified rate of interest because bond prices change and thus capital gains or losses may occur. They may be purchased at a discount (a price below the face amount or principal) or at a premium (a price above the face amount of the bond). The return actually earned depends on the interest payments received, the purchase price, and what the investor receives upon selling or redeeming the bond.

The potential return offered by a bond is referred to as the **yield**. Yield is frequently expressed in two ways: the **current yield** and the **yield to maturity**. Current yield refers only to the annual flow of interest or income as compared to the bond price. The yield to maturity refers to the yield that the investor will earn if the debt instrument is held from the moment of purchase until it is redeemed at par (face value) at the maturity date. The difference between the current yield and the yield to maturity is discussed in the section on the pricing of bonds in Chapter 13.

Generally, the longer the term to maturity, the higher will be the interest rate. This relationship is illustrated in **Figure 2-4**, which plots the yield to maturity of various U.S. government securities as of June 2020 and June 2021. This figure, which is frequently referred to as a **yield curve**, indicates that bonds with the longest time to maturity have the highest interest rates. This is referred to as a positively sloped yield curve. For example, in June 2020, the short-term securities with three months to maturity had a yield of 0.15%, five-year bonds paid 0.32%, and the bonds that mature in 20 years paid 1.24%. The figure also illustrates that one year later, the yields decreased in the short-term bonds, but increased in long-term bonds. The yields on the 1- through 12-month securities were virtually nonexistent (less than 0.05%). Yields on the 20-year bonds were 2.2%. This combination made the slope of the yield curve steeper.

The positive relationship between yields and the term to maturity makes intuitive sense. The longer the term, the longer the time the investor must tie up their funds. To induce investors to lend their funds for lengthier periods, it is usually necessary to pay them more interest. Also, there is more risk involved in purchasing a bond with a longer term to maturity, since the future financial condition of the issuer is less certain. This means that investors will generally require additional compensation to bear the risk associated with long-term debt.

Table 2-1: Ratings for Selected Bonds Maturing in 2025

Issuer	Coupon Rate of Interest	S&P's Rating	Moody's Rating
Apple	2.500%	AA+	A2
Bank of America	4.000	BBB+	Baa3
FedEx	3.200	BBB	Baa1
General Motors Financing	4.000	BBB	Ba1
Merck	2.750	AA	A2
Waste Management	3.125	A	Baa2

Source: Schwab

[1]The term *coupon* is a historical term stemming from the old days, when a coupon book was issued to the bondholder. The cash payment for interest payments was paid when the coupon was redeemed.

Figure 2-4: Positively Sloped Yield Curves

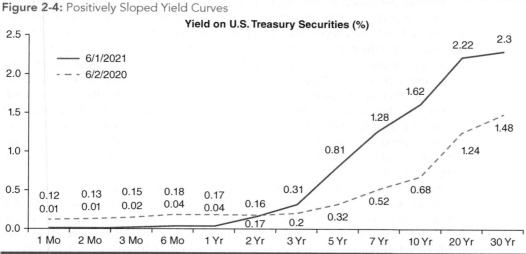

Although the positive slope relationship between time and yield does usually exist, there have been periods when the opposite has occurred (i.e., when short-term interest rates exceeded long-term interest rates). This is referred to as an inverted yield curve. This happened from 1978 to 1979, and then again in 1981, 2000, and 2007. The yields on Treasury securities (securities issued by the Treasury Department) in February 2007 are illustrated in **Figure 2-5**. In this case, the yield curve has a negative slope, which indicates that as the length of time to maturity increased, the interest rates declined. Thus, securities maturing in less than a year had a yield of greater than 5%, while the long-term debt that matured after 10 years yielded lower than 4.75%.

Such a yield curve can be explained by inflation expectations. When the Board of Governors of the Federal Reserve pursues a tight monetary policy in order to fight inflation, short-term interest rates rise. Long-term rates typically do not rise as much as short-term rates in anticipation that the fight against inflation will be won and thus short-term rates will eventually decline. Indeed, the figure also shows the flat yield curve five months earlier. Note that short-term interest rates rose while long-term rates declined. While the negative yield slope has not occurred often, you should be aware that this is a likely consequence the next time inflation is high.

Figure 2-5: Yield Curves (Yields on Federal Government Securities)

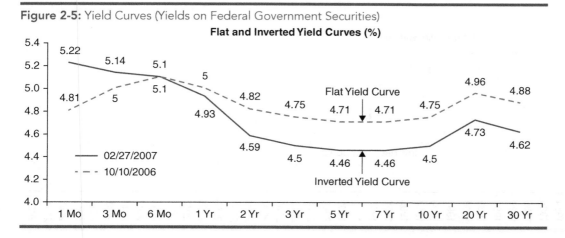

Figures 2-4 and 2-5 also illustrate that interest rates do change. (You should remember that the interest rate is the current rate paid for credit. That rate should not be confused with the coupon rate, which is fixed when the debt is issued.) Although all interest rates fluctuate, short-term rates fluctuate more than long-term rates. These differences in fluctuations are illustrated in **Figure 2-6**, which plots the yields on a three-month Treasury bill and on a 30-year Treasury bond. As may be seen in the figure, the fluctuations for the short-term debt are greater than for the 30-year bond. For example, the yields on the three-month Treasury bill decreased from 7% in late 1990 to below 4% in early 1992 while the yield on the bond declined from 8.5 to 7.9% during the same period. Figure 2-6 also illustrates how quickly rates can change. Short-term rates fell 2% in less than a year in 2020 as central banks around the world loosen monetary policy.

Note that interest yields have steadily declined during the past 30 years. For investors who have seen long-term yields at less than 4% for the past decade, seeing that they were over 10% (and as high as 14%) in the 1980s might seem like a shock. The figure also shows that the difference between the long-term yield and the short-term yield, called the **yield spread**, can vary substantially. When the short-term yield is higher than the long-term yield, the yield curve is inverted, as described above. Currently, investors are in a low-interest rate environment. However, post-COVID price increases have some worried that inflation will rise. You should watch the yield spread to see how central banks and investors are reacting to potential future inflation.

yield spread
The long-term Treasury bond yield less the government short-term Treasury Bill yield

2-3c The Indenture

Each debt agreement has terms that the debtor must meet. These are stated in a legal document called the *indenture*. (For publicly held corporate bond issues, the indenture

Figure 2-6: Yields on Treasury Bills and Treasury Bonds (1980–2021)

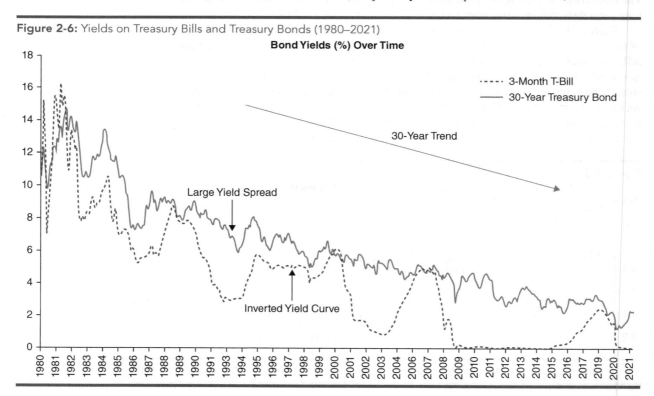

is filed with the Securities and Exchange Commission.) These terms include the coupon rate, the date of maturity, and any other conditions required of the debtor. One common requirement is the pledging of collateral, which is property that the borrower must offer to secure the loan. For example, the collateral for a mortgage loan is the building. Any other assets owned by the borrower, such as securities or inventory, may also be pledged to secure a loan. If the borrower defaults on the debt, the creditor may seize the collateral and sell it to recoup the principal. Default occurs when the borrower fails to meet not only the payment of interest but any of the terms of the indenture. The other conditions of the indenture are just as important as meeting the interest payments on time, and often they may be more difficult for the debtor to satisfy. Examples of common loan restrictions include (1) limits on paying dividends, (2) limits on issuing additional debt, and (3) restrictions on merging or significantly changing the nature of the business without the prior consent of the creditors. In addition, loan agreements usually specify that if the firm defaults on any other outstanding debt issues, this debt issue is also in default, in which case the creditors may seek immediate repayment. Default on one issue, then, usually puts all outstanding debt in default.

These examples do not exhaust all the possible conditions of a given loan. Since each loan is separately negotiated, there is ample opportunity for differences among loan agreements. During periods of scarce credit, the terms of a loan agreement will be stricter, whereas during periods of lower interest rates and more readily available credit, the restrictions will tend to be more lenient. The important point, however, is that if any part of the loan agreement is violated, the creditor may declare that the debt is in default and may seek a court order to enforce the terms of the indenture.

2-3d The Role of the Trustee

Many debt instruments are purchased by individual investors who may be unaware of the terms of the indenture. To protect their interests, a **trustee** is appointed for each publicly held bond issue. It is the trustee's job to see that the terms of the indenture are upheld and to take remedial action if the company defaults on the terms of the loan. For performing these services, the trustee receives compensation from the issuer of the debt.

trustee
An agent appointed to act in the interest of bondholders

Trustees are usually commercial banks that serve both the debtor and the bondholders. They act as transfer agents for the bonds when ownership is changed through sales in the secondary markets. These banks receive from the debtor the funds to pay the interest, and this money is then distributed to the individual bondholders. It is also the job of the trustee to inform the bondholders if the firm is no longer meeting the terms of the indenture. In case of default, the trustee may take the debtor to court to enforce the terms of the contract. If there is a subsequent reorganization or liquidation of the company, the trustee continues to act on behalf of the individual bondholders to protect their principal.

2-3e Forms of Debt

Debt instruments are issued in one of two forms: (1) registered bonds or (2) bearer bonds to which coupons are attached. Registered bonds are similar to stock certificates. These bonds are registered in the owner's name. Delivery of the bonds is made to the registered owner, who also receives the interest payments from the trustee bank. When the bond is sold, it is registered in the name of the new owner by the transfer agent.

While bonds may be registered in the name of the owner, most registered bonds are issued in book form. No actual bonds are printed. Instead, a computer record of owners is maintained by the issuer or the issuer's agent, such as a bank. If a bond is sold only in book form, the investor cannot take delivery, and the bond must be registered in the street name of the investor's brokerage firm or whoever is holding the bond for the investor. Such a system is obviously more efficient than physically issuing the bond.

Bearer bonds are entirely different. Ownership is evidenced by mere possession and is transferred simply by passing the bond from the seller to the buyer. No new certificates are issued. Securities in this form are easy to transfer. They are like currency in that they may not be recoverable if the bonds are stolen since they may not be traceable. For this reason, many brokerage firms will not accept bearer bonds for sale or to put on an account unless the individual has proof of purchase.

Under current federal law, all newly issued corporate and municipal bonds must be registered in the name of the owner or whoever holds the bond for the owner (e.g., a brokerage firm). The primary reason for this ban on issuing bearer bonds with coupons attached is that they are an easy means to evade taxes. When the coupons are cashed, there may be no record of the interest payment, so income taxes may not be paid. Since possession is indication of ownership, the bonds may also be used to evade estate taxes. When the owner dies, the bonds may pass to an heir without being included in the estate. Since the transfer of ownership through the estate is avoided, the value of the bonds may not be reported for purposes of estate taxation. Given the ease with which these bonds facilitate tax evasion, it should hardly be surprising that the federal government outlawed bearer bonds.

2-3f Allocation of Control to Bondholders

Unlike stockholders, bondholders in a firm have limited control of the firm in terms of day-to-day operations. What forms of control they do exercise are normally seen if the firm approaches financial distress or when certain corporate actions are undertaken.

Control shifts to creditors as the firm becomes distressed, particularly when the firm is closer to default or bankruptcy. From a legal perspective, the fiduciary responsibility of the board shifts to creditors as soon as the firm is in the "zone of insolvency." Even if the firm is further from insolvency, cash flow shortfalls such that a firm violates a covenant or misses a scheduled debt payment trigger control rights for debtholders.

Even when firms are not near distress, certain corporate actions—such as changes to financial structure, pledges of collateral, asset sales, or acquisitions—can require the consent of a specified percentage of bondholders. Further, a decline in firm value creates incentive for creditors to exercise their control rights—such as covenant violations giving the creditors the ability to intervene in managerial decisions.

2-3g Allocation of Return to Bondholders

Under normal situations, the only returns that bondholders receive are those that they were promised when the bond was first issued by the company, which are the stated coupon rate paid in periodic interest payments and the bond's maturity value paid at the end of its life.

Some financially strong firms and federal governments may actually set up the repayment schedules on certain bond issues so that all of the interest is paid at the end of the bond's life, along with the maturity value. Such bonds are referred to as zero-coupon bonds (or simply "zeros") due to the fact that they pay zero interest until maturity. Obviously, such firms and governments have to be very strong financially in order to convince potential buyers that there is minimal chance of default on such bonds.

On the other hand, some financially weak firms will often issue what are called **participating bonds**, which are bonds that that pay the holder dividends as well as interest. The bonds are not only the corporation's debt obligation, bearing interest at a stated rate, but also an equity instrument, entitling the bondholder to receive a portion of the corporation's earnings. Participating bonds are frequently issued by financially weak corporations who must offer an extra inducement to attract investors.

participating bond
A bond that pays both interest and a form of dividends

2-3h Allocation of Risk to Bondholders

An important characteristic of all debt is risk. There are several sources of risk:

- risk that the interest will not be paid (i.e., risk of default);
- risk that the principal will not be repaid;
- risk that the price of the debt instrument may decline;
- risk that inflation will reduce the purchasing power of the interest payments and of the principal when it is repaid;
- risk that the bond will be retired (i.e., called) prior to maturity, thereby denying the investor the interest payments for the term of the bond; and
- risk that interest rates will fall, resulting in lower interest income when the proceeds are reinvested.

These risks vary with different types of debt. The general belief is that there is no risk of default on the interest payments and principal repayments of the debt of the federal government. The reason for this absolute safety is that the federal government has the power to tax and to create money. The government can always issue the money that is necessary to pay the interest and repay the principal.

Even though the federal government can refund its debt and hence is free of the risk of default, the prices of the federal government's bonds can and do fluctuate. In addition, the purchasing power of the dollar may decline as a result of inflation, and, therefore, the purchasing power of funds invested in debt also may decline. Thus, investing in federal government securities is not free of risk, since the investor may suffer losses from price fluctuations of the debt or from inflation.

The debt of firms, individuals, and state and local governments involves even greater default risk, for all these debtors may default on their obligations. To aid buyers of debt instruments, several companies have developed credit rating systems. The most important of these services are Moody's, Fitch, and S&P's. Although these firms do not rate all debt instruments, they do rate the degree of risk of a significant number. (The word "credit" is derived from the Latin word *credo*, which means "I believe." The implication is that creditors believe the borrower will pay the interest and repay the principal.)

Note that Table 2-1 gives the risk classifications presented by Moody's and S&P's. The rating systems are quite similar and shown in **Table 2-2**. Each classification of debt involving little risk (high-quality debt) receives a rating of triple A, while debt involving greater risk (poorer-quality debt) receives progressively lower ratings. Bonds rated triple B or better are considered investment grade, while bonds with lower ratings are often referred to as junk bonds or high-yield securities. The growth in this poor-quality debt was one of the phenomena within the financial markets during the 1980s.

Even within a given rating, both Moody's and S&P's fine-tune their rankings. Moody's adds the numbers 1 through 3 to indicate degrees of quality within a ranking, with 1 representing the highest rank and 3 the lowest. Thus, a bond rated A1 has a higher rating than a bond rated A3. Standard & Poor's uses + and − to indicate shades of quality. Thus, a bond rated A+ has a higher rating than an A bond, which, in turn, has a better rating than an A− bond.

Table 2-2: Ratings from Bond Credit Rating Agencies

Moody's	S&P's	Fitch	Rating descriptions	
Aaa	AAA	AAA	Prime	
Aa1	AA+	AA+	High grade	Investment grade
Aa2	AA	AA	High grade	Investment grade
Aa3	AA−	AA−	High grade	Investment grade
A1	A+	A+	Upper medium grade	Investment grade
A2	A	A	Upper medium grade	Investment grade
A3	A−	A−	Upper medium grade	Investment grade
Baa1	BBB+	BBB+	Lower medium grade	Investment grade
Baa2	BBB	BBB	Lower medium grade	Investment grade
Baa3	BBB−	BBB−	Lower medium grade	Investment grade
Ba1	BB+	BB+	Noninvestment grade, speculative	Noninvestment grade (high-yield bonds, junk bonds)
Ba2	BB	BB	Noninvestment grade, speculative	Noninvestment grade (high-yield bonds, junk bonds)
Ba3	BB−	BB−	Noninvestment grade, speculative	Noninvestment grade (high-yield bonds, junk bonds)
B1	B+	B+	Highly speculative	Noninvestment grade (high-yield bonds, junk bonds)
B2	B	B	Highly speculative	Noninvestment grade (high-yield bonds, junk bonds)
B3	B−	B−	Highly speculative	Noninvestment grade (high-yield bonds, junk bonds)
Caa1	CCC+	CCC	Substantial risks	Noninvestment grade (high-yield bonds, junk bonds)
Caa2	CCC	CCC	Extremely speculative	Noninvestment grade (high-yield bonds, junk bonds)
Caa3	CCC−	CCC	Default imminent with little prospect for recovery	Noninvestment grade (high-yield bonds, junk bonds)
Ca	CC	CCC	Default imminent with little prospect for recovery	Noninvestment grade (high-yield bonds, junk bonds)
Ca	C	CCC	Default imminent with little prospect for recovery	Noninvestment grade (high-yield bonds, junk bonds)
C		DDD	In default	Noninvestment grade (high-yield bonds, junk bonds)
/	D	DD	In default	Noninvestment grade (high-yield bonds, junk bonds)
/	D	D	In default	Noninvestment grade (high-yield bonds, junk bonds)

Since the rating services analyze the comparable data, their ratings of specific debt issues should be reasonably consistent. This consistency is illustrated in Table 2-1, which gives the ratings for several different bond issues. Generally, both S&P's and Moody's assigned comparable ratings such as the AA and A2 ratings for the Apple bond. When the ratings differ, the discrepancies are small. Standard & Poor's rated the General Motors Financing bond BBB2, which is marginally lower than the Ba1 rating by Moody's.

These ratings play an important role in the marketing of debt obligations. Since the possibility of default may be substantial for poor-quality debt, some financial institutions and investors will not purchase debt with a low credit rating. Many financial institutions, especially commercial banks, are prohibited by law from purchasing bonds with a rating below Baa (Moody's) or BBB (S&P's and Fitch). Thus, if the rating of a bond issued by a firm or a municipality is low or declines from the original rating, the issuer may have difficulty selling its debt. Corporations and municipal governments try to maintain good credit ratings because high ratings reduce the cost of borrowing and increase the market-ability of the debt.

Besides the risk of default, creditors are also subject to the risk of price fluctuations. Once debt has been issued, the market price of the debt will rise or fall depending on market conditions called **interest rate risk**. If interest rates rise, the price of existing debt must fall so that its fixed interest payments relative to its price become competitive with the higher rates. In the event that interest rates decline, the opposite is true. The existing higher fixed-interest payment bonds make their debt more attractive than comparable newly issued bonds with lower coupons. Buyers will be willing to pay more for the higher coupon existing bonds than the new debt issue. The details of these bond price fluctuations are explained in Chapter 13, which discusses the valuation of debt instruments.

interest rate risk
The potential that a rise in overall interest rates will reduce the value of a bond or other fixed-rate investment

There is, however, one feature of debt that partially compensates for the risk of price fluctuations. The holder knows that the debt ultimately matures. The principal must be repaid. If the price of the bond decreases and the debt instrument sells for a discount (i.e., less than the face value), the value of the debt must appreciate as it approaches maturity, because on the day of maturity, the full amount of the principal must be repaid.

Since interest rates fluctuate, bondholders may also bear reinvestment rate risk. When cash payments are received, the market may be offering lower interest rates than before. The converse would also apply if interest rates were higher.

Bondholders and creditors also endure the risk associated with inflation, called **purchasing power risk**, which reduces the purchasing power of money over time. During periods of inflation, the debtor repays the loan in money that purchases less. Creditors must receive a rate of interest that is at least equal to the rate of inflation to maintain their purchasing power. If lenders anticipate inflation, they will demand a higher rate of interest to help protect their purchasing power. For example, if the rate of inflation is 3%, the creditors may demand 6%. Although inflation still causes the real value of the capital to decline, the higher interest rate partially offsets the effects of inflation. If creditors do not anticipate inflation, the rate of interest may be insufficient to compensate for the loss in purchasing power. Inflation, then, hurts the creditors and helps the debtors, who are repaying the loans with money that purchases less.

> **purchasing power risk**
> The chance that future cash flows won't be worth as much because of inflation

If the investor acquires bonds denominated in a foreign currency, there is the additional risk that the value of the currency will decline relative to the dollar. This is called **foreign exchange rate risk**. Payments received in yen, euros, or pounds have to be converted into dollars before they may be spent in the United States, so fluctuations in the value of the currency affect the number of dollars the investor will receive. Of course, the value of the foreign currency could rise, which means the investor receives more dollars, but the value could also fall.

> **foreign exchange rate risk**
> The risk that business or investment cash flows will be impacted by changes in the exchange rates between currencies

All the sources of risk to bondholders (default, fluctuations in bond prices from fluctuations in interest rates, reinvestment rate risk, loss of purchasing power from inflation, and foreign exchange rate risk) are essentially the same as the sources of risk to investors in stock, with the caveat that such risks are born first by the shareholders, who therefore act to shelter bondholders from the worst of those risks.

While a diversified bond portfolio reduces the risk identified with a specific asset (i.e., the default risk), the risks associated with bond investments in general are not reduced by diversification. Even diversified bond investors must still bear interest rate risk, reinvestment risk, purchasing power risk from inflation, and foreign exchange rate risk.

2-4 Money Market Instruments

Money market instruments are highly marketable short-term debt securities. Due to the shortness of their term as well as the relative strength of firms issuing them, money market instruments are generally low-risk investments and are generally seen as providing investors with an alternative to savings and time deposits offered by banks. Because of this, they tend to offer lower yields than either stocks or debt securities.

> **money market instrument**
> Short-term debt security that trades in liquid markets

Many money market instruments trade in large denominations among institutional investors. However, some money market instruments are available to individual investors via **money market funds**. These are considered to be safe, short-term choices for "parking your money" if you want to take your funds out of the market for a short period.

> **money market fund**
> Mutual fund that invest solely in money market instruments

Money market instruments include treasury bills (T-bills), repurchase agreements (commonly referred to as *repos*), certificates of deposit (CDs), commercial paper issued by corporations, banker's acceptances, and tax anticipation notes. While individual investors may acquire these securities directly, the large denominations of some short-term securities (e.g., the minimum denomination of negotiable CDs and commercial paper is $100,000) encourage most small investors to park their money through money market funds.

2-4a Treasury Bills

T-bill
A short-term U.S. government security

The safest short-term security is the U.S. Treasury bill (commonly referred to as a T-bill), which is issued by the U.S. federal government. T-bills can have maturities of just a few days or up to one year. The most common maturities at issues are 4, 8, 13, 26, and 52 weeks. There is no question that the federal government will redeem the principal on these short-term obligations. (The pricing of and yields earned on T-bills are covered in Chapter 14.) The short-term nature of the bills also implies that if interest rates were to rise, the increase would have minimum impact on the bills price, and the quick maturity means that investors could reinvest the proceeds in the higher-yielding securities.

2-4b Repurchase Agreements

repurchase agreement
A sale of a security in which the seller agrees to buy back (repurchase) the security at a specified price at a specified date

A repurchase agreement (or "repo") is a sale of a security in which the seller agrees to buy back (repurchase) the security at a specified price at a specified date. Repos are usually executed using federal government securities, and the repurchase price is higher than the initial sale price. The difference between the sale price and the repurchase price is the source of the return to the holder of the security. By entering into the repurchase agreement, the investor (the buyer) knows exactly how much will be made on the investment and when the funds will be returned.

2-4c Certificates of Deposit

CDs
Negotiable certificates of deposit issued by commercial banks

Negotiable certificates of deposit (jumbo CDs) are issued by commercial banks. As their name implies, the CDs are "negotiable," which means they may be bought and sold. The ability to buy and sell jumbo CDs differentiates them from the certificate of deposit that most savers acquire at their banks. Savings CDs cannot be bought and sold—you redeem them at the issuing bank and probably pay a penalty for early redemption. Jumbo CDs are also differentiated from savings CDs because they are issued in units of $100,000, which precludes most individual investors from acquiring negotiable CDs.

Large American banks with foreign operations also issue Eurodollar certificates of deposit (Eurodollar CDs). These CDs are similar to domestic negotiable CDs except they are issued either by the branches of domestic banks located abroad or by foreign banks. Eurodollar CDs are denominated in dollars (instead of a foreign currency) and are actively traded, especially in London, which is the center of the Eurodollar CD market. Because they are issued in a foreign country, these CDs are considered riskier than domestic CDs, so Eurodollar CDs offer higher yields to induce investors to purchase them.

2-4d Commercial Paper

commercial paper
A short-term debt issued by a corporation

Commercial paper is a promissory note (i.e., debt) issued by a corporation that matures in 270 days or less. Only firms with excellent credit ratings are able to sell commercial paper. Hence, the risk of default is small, and the repayment of principal is virtually assured. Once again, the term is short, so there is little risk from an investment in commercial paper.

2-4e Banker's Acceptances

Banker's acceptances are short-term promissory notes guaranteed by a bank. These acceptances arise through international trade. Suppose a firm ships goods abroad and receives a draft drawn on a specific bank that promises payment after two months. If the firm does not want to wait for payment, it can take the draft to a commercial bank for acceptance. Once the bank accepts the draft, the draft may be sold. The buyer purchases the draft for a discount, which becomes the source of the return to the holder. Banker's acceptances are considered to be good short-term investments because they are supported by two parties: the firm on which the draft is drawn and the bank that accepts the draft.

banker's acceptance
A short-term debt issued by a corporation but guaranteed by a bank

2-4f Tax Anticipation Notes

Tax anticipation notes are issued by states or municipalities to finance current operations before tax revenues are received. For example, property taxes are typically paid once or twice per year. Yet, municipality expenses occur all during the year. As the taxes are collected, the proceeds are used to retire the debt. Similar notes are issued in anticipation of revenues from future bond issues and other sources, such as revenue sharing from the federal government. These anticipation notes do not offer the safety of Treasury bills, but the interest is exempt from federal income taxation. (The tax exemption of interest paid on state and local municipal debt is discussed in Chapter 14.) Commercial banks and securities dealers maintain secondary markets in them, so the notes may be liquidated should the noteholder need cash.

tax anticipation note
Debt issued by states or municipalities to be repaid from future tax revenues

Money market mutual funds can invest in any of the money market instruments (negotiable CDs, Eurodollar CDs, Treasury bills, commercial paper, repurchase agreements, banker's acceptances, and tax anticipation notes). Some of the funds, however, do specialize, such as the Schwab U.S. Treasury Money Fund, which invests solely in U.S. government securities or securities that are collateralized by obligations of the federal government. Other funds invest in a wider spectrum of short-term debt obligations. For example, as of June 2021, the Fidelity Money Market Fund had almost 36% of its assets in commercial paper, 24% in U.S. Treasury repos, 11% Certificates of Deposit, and the remaining allocation in various other short-term assets.

2-4g Yields on Money Market Instruments

The yields earned on investments in money market funds closely mirror the yields on short-term securities. Since the Schwab U.S. Treasury Money Fund invests solely in government or government-backed securities, the yield it offers investors mirrors the return on these government securities. This relationship must occur because when the short-term debt held by the fund matures, the proceeds can be reinvested only at the going rate of interest paid by short-term government securities. Hence, changes in short-term interest rates paid by these securities are quickly transferred to the individual money market mutual fund.

Prior to 2008, the risk of loss from an investment in a money market mutual fund was considered virtually nonexistent. Money market mutual fund shares were always priced at their $1.00 net asset value (NAV). The short-term debt instruments held by the fund could decline and cause the NAV to fall below the $1.00 (called "breaking the buck"). This had occurred once before when the Mercury Finance Corporation defaulted on its commercial paper, but the Strong family of funds covered the losses sustained by its money market mutual funds and maintained the $1.00 NAV.

This changed in 2008 with the financial crisis. When Lehman Brothers filed for bankruptcy, it defaulted on its commercial paper. The value of several money funds fell below $1.00, which caused investors to rush to withdraw funds. Such withdrawals would have the same effect as the runs on banks during the 1930s. The money funds could not liquidate sufficient assets at their face value and sustain the $1.00 NAV of mutual fund shares. In order to stop the run on money market mutual funds, the U.S. Treasury offered temporary guarantees for most money market funds and the Federal Reserve guaranteed certain commercial paper issuers. These actions by the U.S. federal government stopped massive withdrawals from the money funds.

The guarantees achieved the same objective as that of the Federal Deposit Insurance Corporation (FDIC). FDIC insures bank deposits up to a specified limit. If a bank were to fail, FDIC would reimburse each depositor up to the limit. As most individuals do not have more than the limit on deposit, these investors know that their principal is safe and will not make a massive run on banks to withdraw deposits. (You should realize that deposit insurance is not automatic but must be purchased from FDIC by the bank. A few banks have chosen not to purchase the insurance. If safety of your principal is a major concern, you should deposit funds only in an account insured by FDIC.)

2-5 Financial Derivative Instruments

derivative instrument
An instrument whose value is linked to the value of something else

A financial **derivative instrument** is a contract that derives its value from an underlying asset or factor. In short, the value of a derivative depends on the value of something else. When the value of the underlying factor changes, the value of the derivative instrument also changes.

For example, a popular type of derivative security is a call option, which gives the buyer the right (but not the obligation, as we'll discuss later) to buy a certain number of shares of an underlying stock at a certain price, called the "strike price."

Although you'll hear about derivatives being used to increase the riskiness of an investor's position (by speculating, or for leveraging a position) most buyers of derivative securities are using them to **hedge** a risk in a position they already have.

hedge
To insure a position in financial instruments against risk

Common derivatives include futures and options. Common underlying assets or factors include stocks, bonds, currency exchange rates, commodity prices (like metals, agricultural products, etc.), market indices, and interest rates. However, derivatives can derive their value from almost anything, including weather data and political election outcomes.

2-5a Futures Contracts

commodity
A basic good used in commerce that is interchangeable with other goods of the same type

A **commodity** such as corn may be purchased for current delivery or for future delivery. Investing in futures refers to a contract to buy or to sell (deliver) a commodity in the future. For this reason, these contracts are often referred to as futures. A **futures contract** is a formal agreement between a buyer or seller and a commodity exchange. In the case of a purchase contract, the buyer agrees to accept a specific commodity that meets a specified quality in a specified month. In the case of a sale, the seller agrees to deliver the specified commodity during the designated month.

futures contract
A binding agreement to buy or sell a commodity in the future

Investing in commodity futures is considered to be very speculative. For that reason, investors should participate in this market only after their financial obligations and primary financial goals have been met. There is a large probability that the investor will suffer a loss on any particular purchase or sale of a commodity contract. Individuals who buy and sell commodity contracts without wanting to deal in the actual commodities are generally referred to as speculators, which differentiates them from the growers, processors, warehouses, banks, and other dealers who also buy and sell commodity futures but really wish to buy or sell the actual commodity.

The primary appeal of commodity contracts to speculators is the potential for a large return on the investment resulting from the leverage inherent in commodity trading. This leverage exists because (1) a futures contract controls a substantial amount of the commodity and (2) the investor must make only a small payment to buy or sell a contract (i.e., there is a small margin requirement). These two points are discussed in detail later in this chapter.

Like stocks and bonds, commodity futures are traded in several markets. One of the most important is the Chicago Mercantile Exchange (CME, or "the MERC"), which acquired the Chicago Board of Trade (www.cmegroup.com) and formed the CME Group Inc. CME Group subsequently acquired the New York Mercantile Exchange (NYMEX). The CME Group trades a variety of commodity futures, such as corn and soybeans, and financial futures for currencies, debt, and equity instruments. Other commodities (e.g., coffee and cocoa and energy resources such as oil and natural gas) trade through the Intercontinental Exchange (www.theice.com).

Individuals acquire commodity futures through brokers who act on behalf of the investor by purchasing and selling the contracts through a commodity exchange. The investor opens an account by signing an agreement that requires the contracts to be guaranteed. Since trading commodity contracts is considered to be speculative, brokers will open accounts only after the investor has proved the capacity both to finance the account and to withstand the losses.

Once the account has been opened, the individual may trade commodity contracts. These are bought and sold in much the same way as stocks and bonds. However, the use of the words "buy" and "sell" is misleading. The individual does *not* buy or sell a contract, but *enters a contract to buy or sell*. A buy contract, also called the long side of the contract, specifies that the individual will accept delivery and hence "buy" the commodity. A sell contract, sometimes called the short side of the contract, specifies that the individual will make delivery and hence "sell" the commodity.

A commodity contract specifies whether the contract is a buy or a sell, the type of commodity and the number of units, and the delivery date (i.e., the month in which the contract is to be executed and the commodity is bought or sold). While a futures contract is an agreement to exchange the product for cash in the future, both the buy-side and sell-side of the contract must put up a set amount of cash in advance, called margin, in order to assure that they will be able to uphold their side of the agreement.

Although a futures contract appears to involve a buyer and a seller, the actual contract is made between the individual and the exchange. If an individual buys a contract, the exchange guarantees the delivery (the sale). If an individual sells a contract, the exchange guarantees to take delivery (the purchase). When a contract is created, the exchange simultaneously makes an opposite contract with another investor. While the exchange has offsetting buy and sell contracts, the effect is to guarantee the integrity of the contracts. If one of the parties were to default (e.g., the buyer), the seller's contract is upheld by the exchange.

2-5b Options

option
The (nonbinding) right to buy or sell stock at a specified price for a specified length of time

An **option** is often defined as the right to choose. In the securities markets, an option is the right to buy or sell stock at a specified price within a specified time period. The value of an option is derived from (i.e., depends on) the underlying security for which the option is a right to buy or sell. Hence, options are often referred to as derivative securities. Options take various forms, including calls, puts, and warrants. Some securities, such as the convertible bonds discussed in the previous chapter, have options built into them.

Investors in options do not receive the benefits of owning the underlying stock. These investors purchase the option because they expect the price of the option to rise (and fall) more rapidly (in percentage terms) than the underlying stock. Since options offer this potential leverage, they are also riskier investments; an individual could easily lose the entire amount invested in an option.

The details of futures contracts are discussed in Chapters 15 and 16.

2-6 Foreign Exchange Instruments

foreign exchange instruments
Contracts involving the exchange of one currency for another

Another category of financial instruments is **foreign exchange instruments**. These are contracts involving different currencies. There are many currencies in the world, and there are several different instruments commonly used to trade in currencies.

The value of one currency relative to another depends on the exchange rate between the two currencies, which can either be fixed or floating. Types of foreign exchange instruments purchased and sold by investors typically include spot contracts, futures contracts, and options.

You can trade foreign currencies all over the world 24 hours a day via banks and brokerages. The foreign exchange market is the largest market in the world. Speculating in foreign exchange markets is very risky.

Conclusion

There is a wide variety of financial instruments and securities available to investors, ensuring that just about any reasonable combination of risk, return, and maturity can be obtained through careful selection amongst the choices we've covered.

In the next chapter, we will go into the details of how these securities and instruments are traded on the financial markets. These details, along with the attributes of each type that we've covered in this chapter, will help shape our expectations concerning what types of available investments can be used for obtaining various investment goals and will inform us on what the mechanics of making such investments will involve.

Key Terms

banker's acceptance – A short-term debt issued by a corporation but guaranteed by a bank

best-efforts agreement – An agreement with an investment banker who does not guarantee the sale of a security but who agrees to make the best effort to sell it

CDs – Negotiable certificates of deposit issued by commercial banks

charter – The document that establishes the existence of a corporation and specifies its allowed activities commercial paper – A short-term debt issued by a corporation

commodity – A basic good used in commerce that is interchangeable with other goods of the same type

current yield – A bond's annual interest payments divided by the current price of the bond

debt securities – Longer-term debt instruments

default risk – Lender risk that the borrower will fail to pay the interest payments and repay the principal

derivative instrument – An instrument whose value is linked to the value of something else

direct listing – Existing outstanding shares are sold to the public for the first time on a secondary market with no underwriters involved

due diligence – The investigation or exercise of care that a reasonable business or person is normally expected to take before entering into an agreement or contract with another party

financial instrument – A contract that generates a financial asset

firm commitment – An agreement with an investment banker who guarantees a sale of securities by agreeing to purchase the entire issue at a specified price

fixed-income securities – A category that includes bonds, preferred stocks, and other instruments with fixed-income cash flows

foreign exchange instruments – Contracts involving the exchange of one currency for another

foreign exchange rate risk – The risk that business or investment cash flows will be impacted by changes in the exchange rates between currencies

futures contract – A binding agreement to buy or sell a commodity in the future

hedge – To insure a position in financial instruments against risk

initial public offering (IPO) – The first sale of common stock to the general public

interest rate risk – The potential that a rise in overall interest rates will reduce the value of a bond or other fixed-rate investment

limited liability – A legal status where an investor's financial liability is limited to their investment in a firm

money market fund – Mutual fund that invest solely in money market instruments

money market instrument – Short-term debt security that trades in liquid markets

muni – A bond issued by a state, a county, or municipal governments

option – The (nonbinding) right to buy or sell stock at a specified price for a specified length of time

participating bond – A bond that pays both interest and a form of dividends

preliminary prospectus – Initial document detailing the financial condition of a firm that must be filed with the SEC to register a new issue of securities

primary market – Sale or purchase of securities by the firm that issued them

private placement – The nonpublic sale of securities

purchasing power risk – The chance that future cash flows won't be worth as much because of inflation

registration – Process of filing information with the SEC concerning a proposed sale of securities to the general public

repurchase agreement – A sale of a security in which the seller agrees to buy back (repurchase) the security at a specified price at a specified date

road show – A series of sales presentations to potential investors by the underwriting firm

secondary market – A market where securities trade after issuance by the firm

SPAC – Investment vehicle that raises capital in its IPO and then goes looking for a private company to purchase, which causes that firm to become a publicly traded firm

stock – The shares into which ownership of a corporation is divided

syndicate – A selling group assembled to market an issue of securities

T-bill – A short-term U.S. government security

tax anticipation note – Debt issued by states or municipalities to be repaid from future tax revenues

trustee – An agent appointed to act in the interest of bondholders

underwriter – A large financial institution that guarantees the performance of a public security issue

venture capitalist – A firm specializing in investing in the securities of small, emerging companies

yield curve – Yields plotted against different maturities

yield spread – The long-term Treasury bond yield less the government short-term Treasury Bill yield

yield to maturity – The estimated annual rate of return for a bond assuming that the investor holds the asset until its maturity date

yield – The potential return on a bond

1. **Instruments vs. Securities.** What are the fundamental differences between financial instruments and securities? (LO 2-1)

2. **Primary vs. Secondary Market Transactions.** Why do we differentiate between primary and secondary market transactions? (LO 2-2)

3. **Division of Capital, Risk, Return, and Control.** Explain why bondholders are willing to accept a lower rate of return than stockholders in the same firm. (LO 2-3)

4. **Division of Capital, Risk, Return, and Control.** Explain why equity ownership (stocks) is often much more valuable than debt ownership (bonds) in public corporations. (LO 2-3)

5. **Primary Market Equity Issue.** What effect does a primary market equity issue have on the firm? What is this used for? (LO 2-4)

6. **Bond Rates and Maturity.** If you have two bonds of different maturities issued by the same firm, which would you expect to have a higher coupon rate? Why? (LO 2-5)

7. **Primary Market Debt Retirement.** Under what condition would a firm decide to retire some of its outstanding debt early? (LO 2-6)

8. **Money Market Instruments.** Why are money market instruments called that? (LO 2-7)

9. **Futures vs. Options.** What are the differences between futures contracts and options? (LO 2-8)

10. **Foreign Exchange Instruments.** Explain how a foreign exchange instrument could be used by an investor to hedge currency risk. (LO 2-9)

Case Study

Identify a publicly traded corporation that has at least two different classes of equity and investigate the firm to answer the following questions:

   a. How do the different classes vary in terms of risk, return, and control?

   b. Which class of shares was the "original" type of shares? Why do you think the other classes were issued?

   c. Identify bond issues by the firm. What are the coupon rates, maturity dates, and credit ratings of those bonds?

   d. Are options traded on this stock? What are the characteristics of these options?

Securities Markets and Transactions

After reading this chapter, you should be able to:

LO 3-1 Describe the role of market makers and distinguish between securities exchanges and over-the-counter markets.

LO 3-2 Understand the options for trading foreign stocks.

LO 3-3 Describe the price-weighted and value-weighted stock index designs.

LO 3-4 Describe the major stock indexes and what they measure.

LO 3-5 Contrast the different types of brokerage firms.

LO 3-6 Differentiate between the types of security orders and identify the costs of investing in securities.

LO 3-7 Compute margin debt and returns for long and short positions.

LO 3-8 Understand short positions and explain the source of its profit.

LO 3-9 Describe the purpose of federal securities laws and their role in regulation in securities markets.

LO 3-10 State the purpose of the Securities Investor Protection Corporation (SIPC).

Securities are bought and sold every day by investors who never meet each other. The market transfers stocks and bonds from individuals who are selling to those who are buying. This transfer may occur on an organized exchange, such as the New York Stock Exchange or Nasdaq. Transactions are made in either round lots or odd lots. A **round lot** is the normal unit of trading; for stocks, that is usually 100 shares. Smaller transactions, such as 37 shares, are called **odd lots**. The vast majority of trades are round lots or multiples of round lots. The volume and value of transactions for many stocks are substantial. For example, on July 20, 2021, some 953,300 shares of Google (parent is Alphabet: GOOG) traded. At the closing price of $2,622.03, the total value of those trades was approximately $2.5 billion (= $2,622.03 × 954,200). Note that this is not an unusual daily trading value for Google or many other large popular companies. In fact, a normal day can produce 12 billion trades.

round lot
The general unit of trading in a security, normally 100 shares

odd lot
A trade that is not a multiple of 100 shares

That is a lot of trades and money changing hands! In this chapter, you will learn the mechanics of trading. This includes buying, selling, and selling short. It also discusses the types of orders to be placed to ensure either a timely trade or a precise price. But first the chapter discusses the various stock exchanges and trading systems that handle this enormous amount of trading. Was that trading associated with the market rising or falling? How can we tell? Note that every share bought is also a share sold. Nevertheless, we can measure the general movement of the equity market through stock indexes. There are many stock indexes to measure whatever part of the market you are interested in.

3-1 Major Securities Exchanges

A securities exchange does not participate in the buying and selling of those securities; rather, it provides the space and electronic platform for the buyers and sellers. In some ways it is like a farmer's market. Farmers and producers of products pay the farmer's market to have space to sell their goods. Buyers come to the market because they know they'll have a variety of goods to choose from. Farmers and buyers both benefit from the marketplace. Similarly, companies pay stock exchanges to be listed. Investors buy and sell with each other through the stock exchange marketplace. Stock exchanges are very important to investors because they provide liquidity. Most people would not buy stocks if it were difficult to later sell. The existence of the exchanges provides that assurance that stocks owned can be sold at any time.

3-1a New York Stock Exchange

Located in New York City, on the corner of Wall Street and Broad Street, the New York Stock Exchange (NYSE) is the largest and best-known exchange in the world. The opening bell of the NYSE rings at 9:30 a.m. Eastern Standard Time (EST) and the closing bell rings at 4 p.m. (EST). While the NYSE is known for its trading floor, there are two methods of trading: floor brokers and all electronic. Regardless of the method of exchange, all stock transactions are conducted through an **agency auction**. Trading on the NYSE takes place in the form of bids and offers by exchange members, who are acting as agents for institutions or individual investors. Buy and sell orders meet directly on the trading floor or electronic market, and prices are determined by the interplay of supply and demand.

agency auction
Brokers represent buyers and sellers, and prices are determined by supply and demand

designated market maker (DMM)
The NYSE market maker responsible for maintaining fair and orderly markets for assigned securities

Both the physical and automated auction markets are managed by the **designated market maker** (DMM). Every NYSE stock has a DMM. The DMM supervises trading in a company's stock to ensure that trading (buying and selling) goes smoothly. If trading were to become volatile, the DMM would step in and buy or sell the securities for their own account—in effect, offering to buy securities from sellers and sell securities to buyers. By making a market in individual securities, the DMM makes it possible for the investor to buy and sell stocks.

The NYSE is actually a part of the publicly traded Intercontinental Exchange, Inc. (ticker: ICE). That means you can own stock in the stock exchange! Through consolidation of exchanges in the United States, ICE operates three related stock exchanges: the NYSE, NYSE American, and NYSE Arca. The NYSE trades the mid- and large-cap companies. The American Stock Exchange, which was acquired by the NYSE, now operates as NYSE American and provides a marketplace for small-cap companies. NYSE Arca is a fully electronic market for exchange-traded portfolios (see Chapter 4).

To be listed on the NYSE, both domestic and foreign-based firms are expected to meet certain governance and reporting standards. At a minimum, the company must be a going concern—or be the successor to a going concern. In determining eligibility for listing, particular attention is given to such qualifications as the degree of national interest in the company, its relative position and stability in the industry, and its business prospects. To be listed, a company must meet initial and continuing listing standards. For example, a domestic firm must have a minimum of 400 round lot shareholders, 1.1 million shares publicly held, market capitalization of $100 million, and a share price of $4.00. The annual listing fee for a company is based on firm size and starts at about $70,000. To be listed on NYSE American, a firm needs only a minimum of $50 million market capitalization and $2 share price. The NYSE recognizes that a firm may periodically become unprofitable and lose investors. If that persists, the firm will then fail to meet the continuing listing standards and be delisted from the exchange.

Table 3-1 shows the level of trading on the three NYSE marketplaces. For the NYSE, the trading of over 3,400 issues generated over 4 billion shares traded for July 14, 2021. Nearly 1,400 issues traded higher, called advances, while nearly 1,900

Table 3-1: The Daily Market Digest for NYSE Exchanges, July 14, 2021

NYSE	Latest Close	Previous Close	Week Ago
Issues traded	3,437	3,466	3,448
Advances	1,395	835	1,578
Declines	1,889	2,483	1,703
Unchanged	153	148	167
New highs	114	140	211
New lows	36	19	38
Adv. volume	1,457,253,616	950,746,128	1,389,572,098
Decl. volume	2,539,490,422	2,715,309,837	2,658,085,087
Total volume	4,027,562,997	3,735,388,347	4,070,269,473

NYSE American	Latest Close	Previous Close	Week Ago
Issues traded	285	283	285
Advances	86	89	89
Declines	185	185	186
Unchanged	14	9	10
New highs	3	8	3
New lows	3	2	4
Adv. volume	158,633,399	90,823,653	32,608,033
Decl. volume	194,611,733	179,272,127	254,299,819
Total volume	359,090,343	276,489,154	289,743,463

NYSE Arca	Latest Close	Previous Close	Week Ago
Issues traded	1,511	1,530	1,532
Advances	793	274	922
Declines	685	1,232	576
Unchanged	33	24	34
New highs	96	140	181
New lows	15	14	28
Adv. volume	531,914,336	282,550,769	653,646,874
Decl. volume	475,580,887	726,411,387	417,483,060
Total volume	1,013,802,141	1,035,734,562	1,081,410,100

Source: Wall Street Journal

issues traded lower, called declines. 114 issues reach a new high, while 36 reached a 12-month low. There was far less trading on the NYSE American. Only 285 issued traded, generating 359 million shares traded. NYSE Arca has over 1,500 issues, generating over 1 billion shares traded.

3-1b Nasdaq

The National Association of Securities Dealers Automated Quotations, or simply the *Nasdaq exchange*, was the world's first electronic stock market and began in 1971. Today, Nasdaq, Inc. (ticker: NDAQ) is a premier global electronic marketplace for buying and selling securities. There are about 3,400 companies listed on its trading platforms and trade in derivatives, bonds, and commodities.

What distinguishes Nasdaq is its use of computers and a vast telecommunications network to create an electronic trading system that allows market participants to meet over the computer rather than face-to-face. Since making its debut as the world's first electronic stock market, Nasdaq has been at the forefront of innovation, using technology to bring millions of investors together to trade some of the world's leading companies. While nearly all securities exchanges include electronic trading systems, Nasdaq continues to be the leader.

One of the major differences between the Nasdaq exchange and the NYSE is Nasdaq's structure of competing market makers. On the NYSE, a stock is assigned one DMM as its market maker. On Nasdaq, each market maker, referred to as a **dealer**, competes for customer order flow by displaying buy and sell quotations for a guaranteed number of shares. Once an order is received, the dealer will immediately purchase for or sell from its own inventory. All of this typically occurs in a matter of seconds. Therefore, when you buy a stock on the NYSE, your trade with another investor is facilitated by the DMM. When you buy a stock on Nasdaq, you are buying from a dealer.

Table 3-2 shows the trading on Nasdaq and can be compared with the trading on the NYSE shown in Table 3-1. Nasdaq had over 4,500 issues trading on July 14, 2021. More issues traded higher than lower, and all trading generated 4.4 billion shares changing hands. While this was more shares than traded on the NYSE alone, it was fewer shares than traded on the three combined NYSE exchanges.

dealer
A market maker who buys and sells securities for their own accounts

Table 3-2: The Daily Market Digest for Nasdaq Exchange, July 14, 2021

Nasdaq	Latest Close	Previous Close	Week Ago
Issues traded	4,536	4,542	4,526
Advances	1,387	1,072	1,479
Declines	2,961	3,294	2,839
Unchanged	188	176	208
New highs	95	128	154
New lows	129	75	113
Adv. volume	1,579,672,365	2,108,120,026	1,935,350,335
Decl. volume	2,815,216,312	2,267,791,841	2,623,512,706
Total volume	4,436,756,706	4,532,743,610	4,584,494,466

Source: Wall Street Journal

3-1c Over-the-Counter Markets

Securities of public companies with shares that are not listed on an exchange are traded over-the-counter (OTC). All major unlisted stocks are included in the OTC Bulletin Board (OTCBB) stock market. OTCBB is a regulated interdealer quotation service that displays real-time quotes, last-sale prices, and volume information in OTC equity securities. The Penny Stock Reform Act of 1990 mandated the Securities and Exchange Commission to establish an electronic system that met the requirements of section 17B of the Exchange Act. This system was designed to facilitate the widespread publication of quotation and last-sale information. Investors may access this information for many OTC stocks and bonds by simply entering the security's symbol into the system.

The OTCBB provides investors with access to more than 17,000 securities that trade about 35 billion shares per day. The OTCBB is a quotation medium for subscribing members, not an issue-listing service. It should not be confused with the Nasdaq stock market, which is also an electronic stock market. OTCBB securities are traded by a community of market makers that enter quotes and trade reports through a highly sophisticated computer network. Many of the stocks that trade OTC are priced at less than $1 and referred to as penny stocks.

over-the-counter
The informal market for shares not listed on an exchange

penny stocks
Equities priced below $1

3-1d Internationalization of Markets

Foreign companies, like U.S. companies, issue a variety of securities as a means to acquire funds. These securities subsequently trade on foreign exchanges or foreign OTC markets. For example, there are stock exchanges in London, Paris, Tokyo, Hong Kong, and other foreign financial centers. Investors can buy and sell stocks through these exchanges in much the same way that they purchase U.S. stocks and bonds. Thus, foreign securities may be purchased through the use of U.S. brokers who have access to trading on these exchanges. In addition, some stock exchanges operate in multiple countries. For example, Euronext lists 1,900 companies in regulated markets in Amsterdam, Brussels, Dublin, Lisbon, Oslo, and Paris.

The easiest way for American investors to acquire foreign stocks is to purchase companies such as Alibaba Group or Nokia, whose shares are traded on a U.S. exchange. (Foreign stock exchanges also list U.S. securities.) American securities markets do not actually trade the foreign shares but trade receipts for the stock, called American Depositary Receipts (ADRs), or American Depositary Shares. These ADRs are created by large financial institutions, such as investment banks. The ADRs are sold to the public and continue to trade in the United States.

There are two types of ADRs. *Sponsored* ADRs are created when the firm wants the securities to trade in the United States. The firm employs a bank to perform the paperwork to create the ADRs and to act as transfer agent. In this case, the costs are absorbed by the firm. All ADRs listed on the NYSE are sponsored ADRs. *Unsponsored* ADRs are created when a brokerage firm believes there will be sufficient interest in a stock or bond to make a market in the security. The brokerage firm buys a block of securities and hires a commercial bank to create the ADRs and to act as transfer agent. However, fees for this service and for converting dividend payments from the foreign currency into U.S. dollars will be paid by the stockholders, not the issuing firm.

American depositary receipts (ADRs)
Domestic shares issued to represent ownership in foreign securities held by a trustee

3-1e Electronic Communications Networks (ECNs)

Large institutional investors often prefer to trade with each other directly because sending a large order to the floor of a stock exchange can impact the market price. A large buy order can cause the market price to rise, while large sell orders can cause prices to fall. Sometimes, adverse price effects of large buy or sell orders can be mitigated when large institutional investors deal directly with other large institutions. One way they accomplish this is through electronic communications networks, or ECNs. ECNs are electronic trading systems that automatically match buy and sell orders at specified prices.

Institutional investors, broker–dealers, and market makers who subscribe to ECNs can place trades directly. ECNs post orders on their systems for other subscribers to view. The ECN will then automatically match orders for execution. If a subscriber wants to buy a stock through an ECN, but there are no sell orders to match the buy order, the order can't be executed. If the order is placed through an ECN during regular trading hours, an ECN that cannot find a match may send the order to another ECN or a stock exchange for execution. Some of the different ECNs include Instinet, SelectNet, and NYSE Arca.

3-2 Indices to Measure the Markets

Given the tens of thousands of stocks that trade around the world, the stock market is a big place. So, what does it mean to say the stock market was down today? Table 3-2 illustrates that even on a down day, many stocks rose in price. Some even made a new high. Can it be a down day when more than half of the stock went up? Yes, but it depends on how you measure the stock market. We measure the market through a stock index—and there are many. A subsample of stocks is used to compute most indexes. The subsample that is used is an important factor. The following section will illustrate that stock index design is also an important factor.

3-2a Stock Index Design

Imagine that you have three stocks with which to create a stock index. The three stocks are:

- Goliath: $50 price with 100 million shares outstanding, for a $5,000 million capitalization
- Midriff: $30 price with 20 million shares outstanding, for a $600 million capitalization
- Miniature: $100 price with 1 million shares outstanding, for a $100 million capitalization

How might you create a stock index with these three stocks? Your first inclination might be to average the prices for an index level of 60 (= ($50 + $30 +$100) ÷ 3). Now consider that the prices change to Goliath $49, Midriff $31, and Miniature $103. Thus, the new index level is 61 (= ($49 + $31 + $103) ÷ 3). So, this was an up day. The index rose from 60 to 61, which is a 1.67% increase (= (61−60) ÷ 60).

This index strategy is called a **price-weighted index** and the general formula is

price-weighted index
A stock index computed by components' prices being summed and then divided by a divisor

stock split
The number of shares issued to shareholders increases simultaneously with a price decline so that the value of each holding remains the same

$$Index\ Level_t = \frac{\sum_{i=1}^{n} P_{it}}{divisor}$$ **3-1**

where n is the number of stocks in the index and P is the stock price for the ith index component company at any given point in time t. The divisor in this example is 3. However, that number changes over time due to changes in the number of shares outstanding for a firm and the firms in the index. For example, if Miniature does a two for one **stock split**, the stock price would change from $103 to

$51.50, but every stock would be split into two, so every investor would have double the number shares and the shares outstanding would be 2 million. You would not want the index to plummet because of a stock split. Thus, the divisor would need to change from 3 to 2.1557 in order to keep that index level the same. To determine the new divisor, first compute the level of the index before the stock split. Then adjust the stock price for the split and solve **Equation 3-1** for the divisor. Thus, the new divisor would be 2.1557 (= ($49 + $31 + $51.50) ÷ 61). Another example occurs when the components of the index change. For example, perhaps one of these three companies gets taken over by a fourth company. Again, an adjustment would need to be made to keep the index level stable during the transition.

Now consider a different index strategy. Instead of averaging the prices, add the market capitalizations. This is called a **value-weighted index**. In this example, the added capitalization would be 5,700 million (= $5,000 + $600 + $100). However, we might want to scale this number to start at a more manageable level. So, we divide by the original market value and multiply by the number at which we want to start. If we want to start at 100, the index base value is 100 in the general formula:

value-weighted index
A stock index computed by components' market capitalization being summed and then divided initial index capitalization, then multiplied by a base value

$$Value\text{-}weighted\ index = \frac{total\ current\ market\ value\ of\ all\ firms\ in\ index}{original\ market\ value\ of\ firms\ in\ index} \times index\ base\ value$$

$$= \frac{\Sigma P_t Q_t}{\Sigma P_0 Q_0} \times index\ base\ value \qquad \textbf{3-2}$$

where P is price and Q is number of outstanding shares. For this example, the original index level would be 100 (= {($5,000 + $600 + 100) ÷ ($5,000 + $600 + 100)} × 100). The value-weighted index does not need to be adjusted for stock splits. The market capitalization is not impacted by a stock split. After the prices change, the new index level would be 98.65 (= {($4,900 + $620 + 103) ÷ ($5,000 + $600 + 100)} × 100) for an index decrease of −1.35% (= (98.65−100) ÷ 100).

Notice that our price-weighted index increased and the value-weighted index decreased. What causes this disparity? A price-weighted index is impacted more by the highest priced firms. In this case, the smallest company, Miniature, has the highest price. Note that if Miniature's price increased by 10%, the index would rise by 3.33. However, if the smallest price stock, Midriff, rose by 10%, the index would rise by only 1. Alternatively, the value-weighted index is impacted the most by the largest companies. If the largest company's (Goliath) price rose by 10%, then the value-weighted index would rise by 8.77—compared to an increase of only 0.18 when the smallest company (Miniature) rose by 10%. In short, the high-price stocks drive the level for the price-weighted index, and the largest stocks drive the level for the value-weighted index. Which is better? The largest companies are more important to employment, investors, and the overall economy, so value-weighted indexes are better. Besides, it is odd that a stock split would cause a company to go from being more important in a price-weighted index to less important when nothing about the firm's business operations and prospects change.

3-2b Major Stock Indexes

Dow Jones Industrial Average

In 1882, Charles H. Dow and Edward Davis Jones started Dow Jones & Co. From an unpainted basement office next to the NYSE, they published a tip sheet called the

Customer's Afternoon Letter, a precursor to the *Wall Street Journal.* At that time, people on Wall Street found it difficult to discern whether stocks were generally rising, falling, or treading water. Thus, beginning with 11 stocks, they invented the first stock average in 1884. Most of the stocks were railroads. Given that this far predates computers and calculators, the mechanics of the first stock average were simple. Just add up 11 stock prices and divided by 11. The railroad index eventually was renamed the *Dow Jones Transportation Average.* On May 26, 1896, Dow began tracking a 12-stock industrial average. This became one of today's most popular indexes: the *Dow Jones Industrial Average (DJIA).* In 1916, the industrial average was expanded to 20 stocks; it grew to 30 on October 1, 1928, where it remains today. The *Dow Jones Utility Average* came along in 1929.

These Dow Jones indices are price-weighted indexes but by tradition are commonly referred to as "averages." None of the original components of the DJIA remain in the index today after General Electric was dropped in 2018. The editors of the *Wall Street Journal* determine the companies; the components in today's DJIA are shown in **Table 3-3**. These 30 stocks, often called blue chips, represent about 18% of the total U.S. market capitalization. Note that the highest-priced stocks are UnitedHealth Group and The Home Depot. The lowest priced stocks are Walgreens Boots Alliance and Cisco Systems. Because of more than a hundred years of stock splits and changes in the components of the DJIA, the divisor has gotten very small: it was 0.14748071991788 at the end of June 2018. For every $1 of change in a component's price, the DJIA moves 6.781 points.

blue chips
A large-cap company with a sterling business reputation

Standard & Poor's 500 Index

The Standard & Poor's Corporation introduced a 90-stock average in 1928; however, it was not until 1957 that it offered the expanded index of 500 stocks. Today, the *S&P 500 Index* is the most popular value-weighted market index. It is important to recognize

Table 3-3: The 30 Companies in the Dow Jones Industrial Average, July 16, 2021

Company	Symbol	Weight	Price	Company	Symbol	Weight	Price
3M Company	MMM	3.811849	199.37	Johnson & Johnson	JNJ	3.167979	168.10
American Express Company	AXP	3.252273	170.10	JPMorgan Chase & Co.	JPM	2.92507	151.91
Amgen Inc.	AMGN	4.640487	246.85	McDonald's	MCD	4.457035	234.75
Apple Inc.	AAPL	2.793737	145.92	Merck & Co., Inc.	MRK	1.465734	78.02
Boeing Company	BA	4.191359	217.74	Microsoft Corporation	MSFT	5.287743	280.40
Caterpillar Inc.	CAT	3.977802	207.95	NIKE, Inc. Class B	NKE	3.042291	159.85
Chevron Corporation	CVX	1.906018	98.62	Procter & Gamble Company	PG	2.618376	140.51
Cisco Systems, Inc.	CSCO	1.009456	53.56	Salesforce.com, Inc.	CRM	4.470206	238.43
Coca-Cola Company	KO	1.061951	56.40	Travelers Companies, Inc.	TRV	2.927328	156.39
Dow Inc.	DOW	1.164873	60.01	UnitedHealth Group Inc.	UNH	7.903485	419.70
Goldman Sachs Group Inc.	GS	7.024798	364.80	Verizon Communications Inc.	VZ	1.064021	56.46
The Home Depot, Inc.	HD	6.071976	321.54	Visa Inc. Class A	V	4.676612	247.80
Honeywell International Inc.	HON	4.380455	230.33	Walgreens Boots Alliance, Inc.	WBA	0.870221	46.07
Intel Corporation	INTC	1.050098	55.00	Walmart Inc.	WMT	2.665415	141.56
International Business Machines	IBM	2.642648	138.90	The Walt Disney Company	DIS	3.464889	179.31

that stocks in the S&P 500 Index are not the 500 largest companies in the United States, but rather are the most important companies in each of the 11 sectors of the economy. **Figure 3-1** shows that in mid-2021, information technology was by far the largest U.S. economic sector and thus represented 27.4% of the total equity market capitalization. The utilities, real estate, materials, energy, consumer staples, and industrials sectors combined do not match the size of information technology. In 2021, the 505 companies in the S&P 500 Index covered about 80% of the total U.S. equity market capitalization. Note that Standard & Poor's targets 500 companies for the index, but 5 companies have two classes of shares listed, which brings the total to 505.

The variation in the size of the companies in the index is dramatically skewed. The largest stock in the index, Apple Inc., represents 5.9% of the index market value. The largest 10 stocks (Apple, Microsoft, Amazon, Facebook, Alphabet A, Alphabet C, Berkshire Hathaway, Tesla, Nvidia, and JP Morgan Chase) out of the 505 total represent 27.4% of the index market value.

Although the DJIA is a long-time favorite with media, the S&P 500 Index is preferred as an investment **equity benchmark** in the investment industry. That is, institutional investors, such as mutual funds, pension funds, and even hedge funds, compare their performance to the S&P 500 Index. If you beat the S&P 500 performance after costs over time, you are considered a top fund manager. Many individual investors simply try to match the S&P 500 Index return. Have you ever heard the phrase, "If you can't beat 'em, join 'em"? In the investment industry, investors use investment products based on the S&P 500 Index to "join 'em." Chapter 4 describes the different investment products that simply buy the stocks in the S&P 500 Index to replicate the index return. These products are very popular!

equity benchmark
A performance standard to be evaluated against

Nasdaq Composite Index

The three most popular stock indices are S&P 500, DJIA, and Nasdaq. The *Nasdaq Composite Index* includes over 2,500 companies (almost all stocks) that trade on the Nasdaq Stock Exchange. Note that many foreign companies trade on the Nasdaq and therefore the Index is not focused only on U.S. companies. However, the Nasdaq Composite is a value-weighted index and thus is driven by the largest companies, which are mostly U.S. technology-oriented firms. Indeed, technology stocks represent about 50% of the Nasdaq Composite market capitalization. This high proportion is because many of the largest companies in the world trade on Nasdaq and are technology firms. For example, some of the largest 20 companies trading on Nasdaq are Apple, Microsoft, Amazon, Facebook, Alphabet (Google), PayPal, Intel, etc.

Figure 3-1: Sector Weights (%) Breakdown of the S&P 500 Index, June 2021

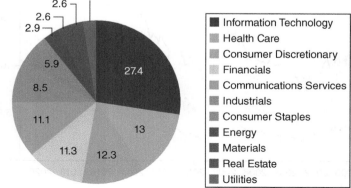

Source: S&P Dow Jones Indices—S&P 500 Fact Sheet, June 2021

How do the DJIA, S&P 500 Index, and Nasdaq Composite compare? **Figure 3-2** shows the three indexes since 1990. Note the spike and subsequent crash in the Nasdaq in 2000. This is known as the *technology bubble*. It took nearly 15 years for the Nasdaq Composite to reclaim a new high. The bubble's impact is well demonstrated by the Nasdaq Composite because it is skewed toward technology companies. Many of the large tech companies in the Nasdaq Composite are also components of the DJIA, which shows a less dramatic increase and decrease in about 2000. All 30 of the DJIA companies are also components of the S&P 500 Index. However, of the three indices, the S&P 500 is the broadest measure of stocks across the economy. The financial crisis of 2008 is also clearly indicated in the figure. Since the DJIA had a larger portion of financial firm components than the other indexes, its decline was greater. Finally, note that the steep but brief pandemic-fueled decline of March 2020 shows up as just a blip in the graph.

3-2c Indexes by Market Capitalization

There are many ways to choose stocks for an index. One popular way to examine stocks is by market capitalization. Note that in a broad value-weighted index of stocks, the large-capitalization stocks dominate the index movements. Thus, the industry likes to isolate the medium and small stocks in their own indices to get a clear picture of their performance. Two index providers are particularly known for their different market-cap indexes, Wilshire and Russell.

Figure 3-2: Performance of the DJIA, S&P 500 Index, and Nasdaq Composite since 1990

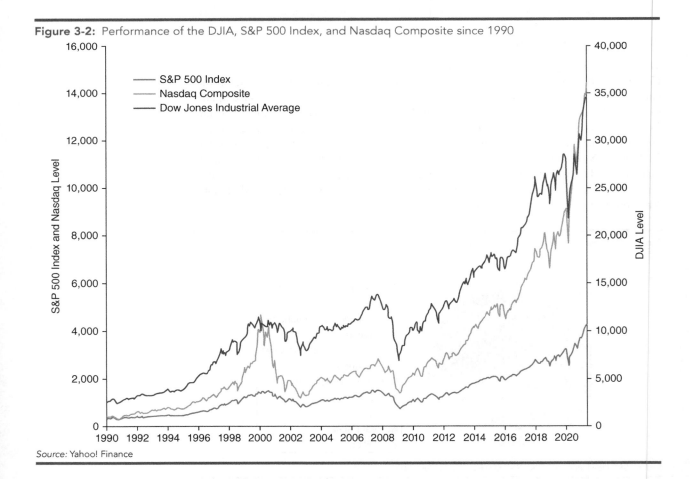

Source: Yahoo! Finance

FT Wilshire Equity Indexes

The FT Wilshire 5000 Index is the most comprehensive measure of the U.S. stock market. This market benchmark is designed to represent the performance of all U.S.-headquartered equity securities with readily available price data. To be included in the index, a security must be the primary equity issue of a U.S. company. Originally called the Wilshire 5000 Total Market Index, the *FT Wilshire 5000 Composite Index* was created in 1974 by the founder of Wilshire Associates and was named for the nearly 5,000 stocks it contained at the time. It now includes a variable number of companies, reflecting changes in the number of U.S. securities. *Financial Times* partnered with the Wilshire Indexes in 2021 and renamed them the FT Wilshire Indexes.

The FT Wilshire Indexes provide three important indexes to measure large-, medium-, and small-sized firms. The *FT Wilshire US Large Cap Index* is a subset of the FT Wilshire 5000 components and includes all stocks ranked above the 85th percentile by market capitalization. In 2021, this large-cap index consisted of 518 firms for which the mean was $71.6 billion in market capitalization. The *FT Wilshire US Mid Cap Index* contains the 309 firms in the range of the 70th to 85th percentile of market capitalization of the FT Wilshire 5000 Index firms. It has a mean market capitalization of $22.2 billion. Lastly, the *FT Wilshire US Small Cap Index* contains 1,202 firms with a mean market capitalization of $4.88 billion.

Figure 3-3 shows these three indices since 1998. Note that the small- and mid-cap indexes move together quite closely. Also, they are more volatile than the large-cap index. That is, they experience larger swings in index levels.

Russell Indexes

Russell produces a family of U.S. equity indexes. All Russell equity indexes are market-cap-weighted and include only common stocks incorporated in the United

Figure 3-3: FT Wilshire Capitalization Based Indexes

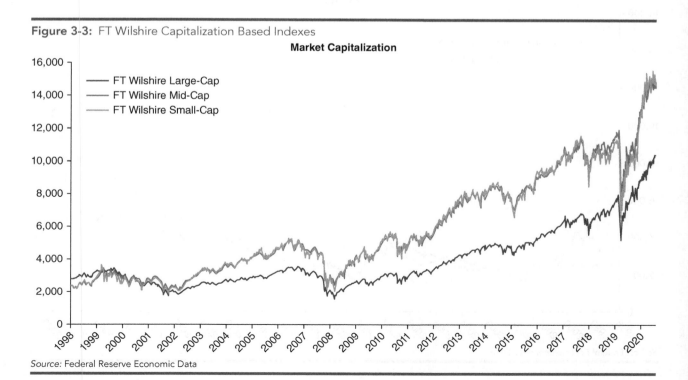

Source: Federal Reserve Economic Data

States and its territories. All these indexes are subsets of the *Russell 3000 Index*, which includes the 3,000 largest U.S. companies and represents approximately 98% of the investable U.S. equity market. However, the most popular of the Russell Indexes is likely the one that measures small-cap stocks, the *Russell 2000 Index*. Its components are the smallest 2,000 stocks of the Russell 3000 Index, which represents only about 10% of the total market capitalization. The Russell 2000 Index is widely reported in the media to gauge the performance of the small-cap stocks.

3-2d Value and Growth Indexes

Some investors look for fast-growing companies. Other investors want a good deal. Thus, the value and growth dimensions are common categories for companies. Growth stocks tend to have faster business growth and greater future potential. However, they often have high prices to reflect that potential. Value stocks are companies that are currently trading below what they are worth. Thus, they are a good deal and could provide a superior return. Wilshire uses statistical analysis to categorize companies as growth or value by using six factors. Growth firms have higher (1) projected price-to-earnings ratio, (2) projected earnings growth, (3) price-to-book ratio, (4) trailing revenue growth, (5) trailing earnings growth, and (6) lower dividend yield.

Wilshire produces value and growth indices that are also stratified by market capitalization. Thus, they provide a U.S. large-cap value index and a U.S. large-cap growth index. They have value and growth indexes for mid-cap and small-cap firms, too. **Figure 3-4** shows the *Wilshire US Large-Cap Value* and growth indexes. Note that the growth index was impacted by the technology bubble in 2000. However, since 2012, growth firms have dramatically outperformed value firms.

Figure 3-4: Wilshire Value and Growth Indexes

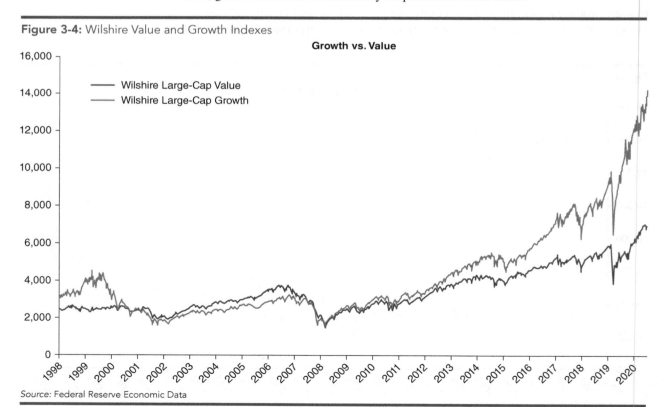

Source: Federal Reserve Economic Data

3-2e Indexes by Sector and Industry

Note that Figure 3-1 above shows the 11 sector breakdowns of the S&P 500 Index. Standard & Poor's also offers an index for each of these sections. For example, there is an *S&P 500 Health Care Index* that contains the 64 companies in the S&P 500 Index that are classified as being in the health care sector. The largest of these companies is Johnson & Johnson and UnitedHealth Group. The *S&P 500 Energy Index* comprises the 22 companies in the S&P 500 that classify as being in the energy sector.

You can drill down to even more focused baskets of stocks. Instead of following the *S&P 500 Financials Index*, you can follow just the banking industry with the *S&P Banks Select Industry Index,* which includes 95 firms in the asset management and custody banks, diversified banks, regional banks, other diversified financial services, thrifts, and mortgage finance subindustries. Other finance industry indexes include the *S&P Insurance Select Index*, *S&P Mortgage Finance Select Index*, and *S&P Regional Banks Select Index.* Whether you are looking to follow precious metals, biotechnology, aerospace, or most anything else, there is an index for you.

Excel Expert 3-1

FAANG stocks

In 2013, the media started to use the term FANG stocks to represent the prominent technology companies: Facebook (FB), Amazon (AMZN), Netflix (NFLX), and Alphabet (GOOG). In 2017, Apple (AAPL) was added, and the term changed to FAANG stocks. Each of the FAANG companies had shown extraordinary growth in both revenues and net profits. Can you create a FAANG Stock Index? Yes, of course! Let's do it.

First, download the prices of the five FAANG stocks from Yahoo! Finance for the past five years. Put them together in a spreadsheet. Let's start at the beginning of 2017 (so delete the older observations). The analysis here goes through July 16, 2021. In addition, get the number of shares outstanding from Yahoo! Finance from each of the company Financials tab. The Balance Sheet reports the Ordinary Share Number for several years. Get the shares number from the 2017 figures.

	A	B	C	D	E	F
1		FB	AMZN	AAPL	NFLX	GOOG
2	Shares =	2.91E+09	4.84E+08	2.05E+10	4.33E+08	6.95E+08
3				**Daily Prices**		
4	Date	FB	AMZN	AAPL	NFLX	GOOG
5	1/3/2017	116.86	753.67	29.0375	127.49	786.14
6	1/4/2017	118.69	757.18	29.005	129.41	786.9
7	1/5/2017	120.67	780.45	29.1525	131.81	794.02

The next step is to compute the initial market capitalization of each stock, the sum total, and the daily capitalizations. Note that we are assuming that the shares outstanding do not change during the period.

I	J	K	L	M	N	O	P	Q
	Index Base Value =	20000						
	Initial Market Cap =	1.90123E+12	=SUM(I5:M5)					
=B5*$B$2		**Daily Market Cap**					=(SUM(I6:M6)/$K$2)*$K$1	
FB	AMZN	AAPL	NFLX	GOOG		Date	FAANG Index	DJIA
3.39595E+11	3.64776E+11	5.95408E+11	55253272703	5.46197E+11		1/3/2017	20000.00	19881.76
3.44913E+11	3.66475E+11	5.94742E+11	56085389864	5.46725E+11		1/4/2017	20081.11	19942.16
3.50667E+11	3.77738E+11	5.97766E+11	57125530463	5.51672E+11		1/5/2017	20354.91	19899.29

(Continued)

Note that we selected a base value of 20,000 to be close the DJIA in 2017. Now, we create the value-weighted FAANG Index each day by summing up that day's market capitalization of the five stocks, dividing by the initial market cap, and multiplying by the base as shown in column P. The DJIA levels are shown for comparison:

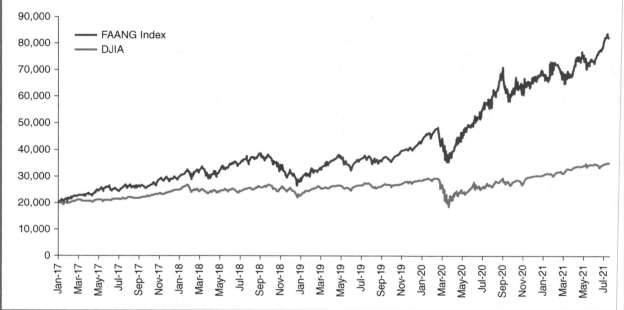

3-2f Global Stock Market Indexes

There are large stock markets in Japan, England, China, and dozens of other countries. There are also stock indexes of these markets to help you assess their performance and trends. Indeed, there are indexes that focus on a region, like Europe. There are also indexes that focus on the development level of the economy, like emerging markets. From the U.S. investor's perspective, do you want those indexes measured in their local currency, like euros or the yen? Or would you prefer the indexes to measure prices in U.S. dollars? Rest assured, there are indexes for regional and global markets in a variety of currencies.

Foreign Stock Indexes

Each country with a stock exchange has at least one stock index that measures the performance of the market in the domestic currency. Some of the most well-known and followed foreign stock indexes are:

- *Nikkei 225 Index* of Japan is a price-weighted average of 225 stocks from the first (most liquid) section of the Tokyo Stock Exchange.
- *FTSE 100* of the United Kingdom (pronounced "footsie") is a value-weighted index of the 100 largest capitalization companies on the London Stock Exchange (LSE).
- *TSE-35* of Canada is a value-weighted index of 35 blue chip Canadian companies that trade on the Toronto Stock Exchange.
- *Hang Seng Index* of Hong Kong includes the most important 30 companies on the Hong Kong Stock Exchange.

- *All Ordinaries* of Australia includes 300 companies listed on the Australia Stock Exchange.
- *DAX Performance Index* of Germany represents 30 of the largest and most liquid German companies that trade on the Frankfurt Exchange.
- *SZSE Composite Index* of China is an index of 500 stocks that are traded at the Shenzhen Stock Exchange.
- *CAC 40* of France includes the 40 most significant stocks among the 100 largest market caps on the Euronext Paris exchange.
- *IBOVESPA* of Brazil in an index of about 70 stocks that account for most of the trading and market capitalization on the Brazilian stock market.
- *MERVAL* of Argentina is a price-weighted index of 22 companies listed on the Buenos Aires Stock Exchange.
- *KOSPI* of South Korea is the Korea Composite Stock Price Index includes over 900 components.

Four of these indexes (Nikkei 225, DAX Performance, Shenzhen Component, and MERVAL) are shown in **Figure 3-5**. Some points of interest are that the Argentina stock market has really exploded upward since 2014. Also, the Chinese market experienced an extreme bubble that deflated during the financial crisis of 2008. The Shenzhen Component Index has yet to regain its peak 13 years later. Lastly, the Japanese market has largely traded sideways until the last few years.

MSCI Global Indexes

MSCI, formerly known as Morgan Stanley Capital International, is an industry leader in providing global equity benchmark indexes for more than 50 years. MSCI

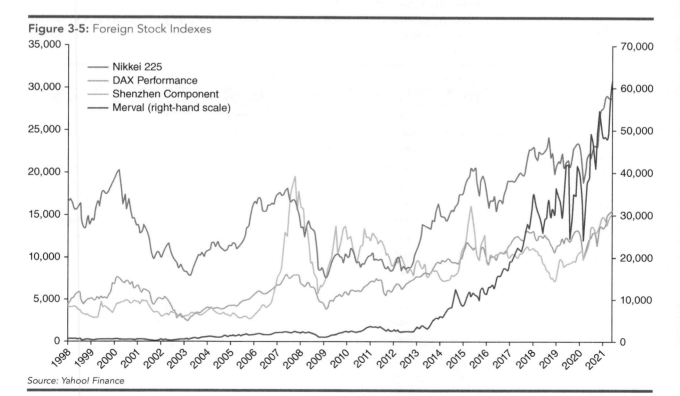

Figure 3-5: Foreign Stock Indexes

Nikkei 225
DAX Performance
Shenzhen Component
Merval (right-hand scale)

Source: Yahoo! Finance

indexes are the most widely used benchmarks for international portfolio managers. MSCI now calculates over 225,000 indices daily. Essentially, MSCI has an index for every country's stock market in both U.S. dollars and in their domestic currency. In additional, MSCI has popular regional and global indices. U.S investors tend to refer to indices covering stock worldwide as "global" indexes when they include the United States and "international" indexes when they omit the United States.

The *Europe, Australasia, Far East (EAFE) Index* is perhaps MSCI's most famous index. The MSCI EAFE stock index is designed to measure the investment returns of developed countries outside North America. The international index now includes over 900 stocks from 21 countries. The most recent addition was Portugal in 1997. For a broader global index, consider the *MSCI All Country World Index (ACWI)*, which contains about 2,900 stocks from 50 countries (23 developed and 27 emerging), which is similar to EAFE but includes stocks from the United States and Canada.

Note how the international indexes differentiate between emerging and developing markets. An equity market develops in a country as economic growth accelerates and companies begin to raise capital in the public markets. These are known as emerging markets. These markets display gross domestic product (GDP) per capita that is substantially below the average for developed economies. The governments of emerging-market countries sometimes limit or ban foreign ownership in their public companies. Lax government regulation, irregular trading hours, and/or less sophisticated back-office operations, including clearing and settlement capabilities, are also common in emerging markets. Some emerging markets also feature restrictions on repatriation of initial capital, dividends, interest, and/or capital gains. You can follow these emerging markets individually or as a group with the *MSCI Emerging Markets Index*, which captures over 1,300 companies in 27 countries. **Table 3-4** shows how MSCI categorizes countries into emerging or developed market status.

Emerging versus developed market status is only one way to classify stocks worldwide. For example, you might be interested in the largest of companies around the

Table 3-4: MSCI Emerging and Developed Markets

Developed Markets			Emerging Markets		
Canada	EMEA	Pacific	Americas	EMEA	Asia
United States	Austria	Australia	Argentina	Czech Republic	China
	Belgium	Hong Kong	Brazil	Egypt	India
	Denmark	Japan	Chile	Greece	Indonesia
	Finland	New Zealand	Colombia	Hungary	Korea
	France	Singapore	Mexico	Kuwait	Malaysia
	Germany		Peru	Poland	Pakistan
	Ireland			Qatar	Philippines
	Israel			Russia	Taiwan
	Italy			Saudi Arabia	Thailand
	Netherlands			South Africa	
	Norway			Turkey	
	Portugal			United Arab Emirates	
	Spain				
	Sweden				
	Switzerland				
	United Kingdom				

world, thus a global large-cap index might suit your needs. Or you may want to follow specific sectors or industries from a global perspective. MSCI has world global sector indexes, too. These indexes follow the major companies within a sector or industry, no matter where the firms operate.

3-2g The Volatility Index (VIX)

One popular index, the *Volatility Index (VIX)*, is a measure of investors' expectations or "sentiment" about near-term stock market volatility. Since the VIX is a gauge of investor expectations, it also measures market psychology and is often referred to as the "fear" index.

The actual calculation of the VIX is based on the S&P 500 Index options and is expressed in percentages. (Options are explained in Chapters 14 and 15). For example, a numerical value of 20 suggests that market participants expect the S&P 500 to swing by 20% over the next 12 months. Low values such as 10 suggest little volatility—market participants are not pessimistic or may even be complacent. As they become more pessimistic and the stock market becomes more volatile and less certain, the value of the index rises. A value of 50 suggests an expectation of large swings in the S&P 500.

During 2005–2006, the value of the VIX fluctuated between 10 and 18 and remained in that range through July 2007. As financial problems started to emerge and people became more aware of them, the VIX rose. By January 2008, the index had risen to over 38 and continued to increase through the year. During October, the VIX rose from 39 to a historic 89 in a matter of days and ended the month at 55. As the financial crises receded, the VIX also declined and by 2012 stood at 23. The market slide of March 2020 during the pandemic shot the VIX up to an intraday high of 85.47 on March 18. However, the VIX was back into the 20s by May as the market recovery looked to continue.

3-3 Buying and Selling Securities

3-3a Brokerage Firms

Individual investors usually purchase stocks and bonds through a broker, who buys and sells securities for their customers' accounts. While a few companies (e.g., ExxonMobil) offer investors the option to purchase shares directly from the corporation, most purchases are made through brokerage firms, such as Merrill Lynch, Charles Schwab, E*TRADE, or Robinhood. Many brokerage firms also act as market makers and may be referred to as *broker–dealers* since different divisions within the firm perform both functions. The firm has individuals who buy and sell for the firm's account (i.e., are securities dealers) and other individuals who buy and sell for customers' accounts (i.e., are brokers).

Brokers must pass the Series 7 exam (known formally as the General Securities Representative Qualification Examination) administered by the Financial Industry Regulatory Authority (FINRA). This competency examination covers an extensive range of financial terms and topics as well as securities regulations. Once the individual has passed the test, they are referred to as a registered representative and can buy and sell securities for customers' accounts.

Although registered representatives have passed this proficiency examination, do not assume that the broker is an expert. There are many aspects of investing, and even

broker
An agent who handles buy and sell orders for an investor.

Series 7 exam
The General Securities Representative Qualification Examination, which assesses the competency of an entry-level registered representative

registered representative
A person who works for a financial firm trading investment products and securities for clients

a person who spends a considerable portion of the working day servicing accounts cannot be an expert on all the aspects of investing. Thus, many recommendations are based on research that is done by analysts employed by the brokerage firm rather than by individual salespersons.

Traditionally, stock brokerage firms were categorized into full-service, discount, and online groups. Full-service brokerage firms provide clients with investment research, financial advice, retirement services, and other services and products. They pay for this service through high commission costs on the buy and sell trades that can amount to hundreds of dollars. Examples of full-service broker–dealers are CitiFinancial, Merrill Lynch Wealth Management, and Morgan Stanley. Discount brokerage firms charge a low commission per trade but don't give their clients advice. Examples of discount broker firms are E-Trade Financial Corp., Fidelity Investments, Charles Schwab Corp., Interactive Brokers, and TD Ameritrade. Online brokers have no human interaction and simply execute your trades. They charge deeply discounted commissions that are less than $5 per trade. Popular examples are Robinhood, Webull, TradeStation, and Coinbase. However, these distinctions are now blurred. All the traditional discount brokerage firms provide their services online. In addition, by 2019, the discount and online brokerage firms all zeroed out their commission fees on popular stocks.

How can broker firms afford to not charge commissions on trades? Broker firms have shifted their revenue model from commissions to **payment for order flow**. In essence, the broker steers the client's order to a particular market maker. That market maker or high-speed trader executes the trade. To get these orders, the market maker pays the brokerage firm a fee (fractions of a penny per share), called *payment for order flow*. The trade execution can be at an improved price for the client. However, the concern is that the payments discourage brokers from obtaining the best trades for their customers.

You should realize that brokers make their living through transactions (i.e., buying and selling for their customers' accounts), regardless of whether that is from commissions or payment for order flow. Thus, the broker's advice on investing may be colored by the desire to secure commissions. Also, online broker trading platforms are designed to encourage trades. You should always weigh the impact of a specific investment decision in terms of fulfilling your financial goals.

3-3b Types of Orders

With a brokerage account, buying and selling a security is easy. Consider that you wish to purchase 50 shares of Bank of America stock. A quick search reveals the bank's stock **ticker symbol** to be BAC. Before entering an order, you should obtain a price quote. While your broker will provide a quote, prices are readily available on the Internet. After typing in the ticker symbol, you will obtain both bid and ask quotes and the price of the last trade. The quoted **bid** is the highest price that a *market maker* is willing to pay to buy a security. Thus, it is the highest currently available price at which you can sell shares of stock to the market maker. The quoted **ask** is the lowest price a market maker is willing to accept to sell a stock. So, this is the quoted offer at which you can presently buy shares of stock. The **bid–ask spread** is the difference between the bid price and the ask price. As an investor, you always pay the higher price (*ask price*) to buy and receive the lower price (*bid price*) to sell. Therefore, the bid–ask spread represents a cost to you and the profit margin earned by the market maker.

The Bank of America stock quote shown in **Figure 3-6** from Yahoo! Finance shows a bid price of $39.97 and an ask price of $39.98 for a $0.01 bid–ask spread per share. The 4000 number shown for the bid price indicates the maximum number of shares the market maker is willing to buy at that price. BAC is a large and liquid stock.

payment for order flow
The compensation a brokerage firm receives for steering client orders to a market maker for trade execution

ticker symbol
The unique stock identifier assigned for trading in a particular market

bid
The highest price at which a dealer is willing to buy shares

ask
The lowest price at which a dealer is willing to sell shares

bid–ask spread
The difference between the bid and the ask prices, which represents a cost to traders

Figure 3-6: Yahoo! Finance Stock Information Page

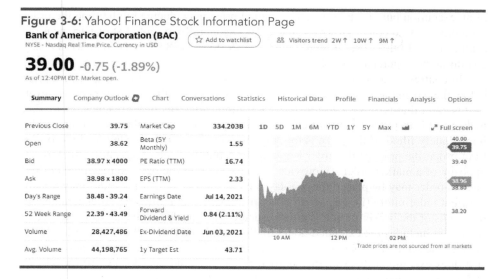

Other common stocks can have bid–ask spreads as high as $0.15. The quote also shows the price of the last trade, its change from yesterday's close, and the price range for the day and the past 52 weeks. This data gives you some context on where the price is now relative to recent trends.

Figure 3-7 illustrates the decision steps for purchasing stock. It shows that you want to buy 50 shares of BAC. You may request that your broker buy the security at the best price currently available, which is the asking price set by the market maker. Such a request is a **market order**. When you enter a market order, you are assured

market order
An order placed with a broker to buy or sell at the current price

Figure 3-7: Stock Trading Demonstration

Ticker	Quantity	Action
BAC	50	Buy ▼
		Buy
		Sell
		Sell Short

Ticker	Quantity	Action	Price
BAC	50	Buy	Market ▼
			Market
			Limit
			MKT on Close
			Stop
			Stop Limit

Ticker	Quantity	Action	Price	Limit	Duration
BAC	50	Buy	Limit	$ 38.75	Fill or Kill ▼
					Fill or Kill
					Day
					GTC
					Day + Ext.

of an execution but not the price. The quoted price may change by the time the order is entered and executed. However, the order is generally executed at or very near the asking price. In this case, it would cost $1,949.00 (= $38.98 × 50 shares) plus any commissions to purchase the shares.

In contrast to a market order, you may consider a limit order to specify a price below the current asking price and wait until the price declines to the specified level. In this case, that is $38.75. For a fill or kill limit order, the order reaches the market maker and if the current market price meets the desired price, then the order will be immediately filled. If the price is too high, the order will be canceled (or killed). For limit order, the price of the order is guaranteed, but the execution is not, which is the opposite of a market order. To provide a longer time for the price to reach the desired one, an order may be placed for one day (i.e., a day order), or the order may remain in effect indefinitely (i.e., a good-till-canceled order). Such an order remains on the books of the broker until it is either executed or canceled. You can also place a day order that includes the extended hours trading using the Day + Ext limit order. If the price of the security does not decline to the specified level, the purchase is never made. If it does execute at the $38.75 specified price, is would cost $1,937.50 (= $38.75 × 50 shares) plus any commissions. While a good-till-canceled order may remain in effect indefinitely, brokerage firms generally have a time limit (e.g., one month or three months) that specifies when the order will be canceled if it has not been executed.

Sell orders work in a similar manner. You can sell with a market order or a limit order. In a limit order, you may be seeking to sell at a higher price than the current bid price and you can use fill or kill, day, or good to canceled orders.

When you own shares of a stock, you can place an order to sell it when its price reaches a certain level. To do so, you place a stop order to sell. The market price reaches that designated level and it triggers a market order to sell. There are two strategies for using stop orders. One uses the stop order to lock in a profit. For example, say that you bought 50 shares of BAC at $38.75 and want to automatically sell if the price climbs 50%. In that case, you would place a stop order at $58.13. If or when the market price reaches that level, the 50 shares are sold. The other strategy is to protect against certain losses. For example, you may believe that if BAC declines 20%, then it is time to get out before you lose any more. This is referred to as a stop loss, and its stop order should be placed at $31.00. Whether the stop order is used for locking in a specific profit or for limiting losses, once the price level is reached, the order executes as a market order. A second option is to place a stop-limit order. In this case, you specify the level when the order executes and also a limit price and duration.

It is easy to confuse limit orders and stop orders because they both specify a price. The limit order specifies a price at which a stock is to be bought or sold. Limit orders are filled in order of receipt. A limit order to buy stock at $10 may not be executed if other investors have previously entered purchase orders at that price. (Because individuals tend to think in terms of simple numbers, such as $10 or $15, it may be a wise strategy to enter the buy order at $10.05 so that the order is executed before all orders placed at $10. The same applies to sell orders.) When the price is reached for a stop order, the order becomes a market order and is executed. Since the stop becomes a market order, the actual price at which it is executed may not necessarily be the specified price, like any market order.

3-3c Cash and Margin Accounts

Investors usually set up their brokerage account as a cash account. That simply means you need to have the cash in the account to cover any purchases you make. It's very

limit order
An order placed with a broker to buy or sell at a specified price

fill or kill
An order to be immediately executed or canceled depending on the trading price

day order
An order placed with a broker that is canceled at the end of the day if it is not executed

good-till-canceled order
An order placed with a broker that remains in effect until it is executed by the broker or canceled by the investor

stop order
A sell order at a specific price designed to limit an investor's loss or to assure a profit

stop loss
A stop order placed to limit a loss in a position

Excel Expert 3-2

Consider the dynamics of buying and selling stock. Your brokerage charges $5 per trade in commission fees. The stock shows a bid price of $46.23 per share and an ask price of $46.28 per share. What would be the cost of purchasing 200 shares? What proceeds would you receive if you sold 200 shares?

	A	B	C
1	Quantity (shares)	200	
2	Bid Price	$ 46.23	
3	Ask Price	$ 46.28	
4	Commission (per trade)	$ 5.00	
5			
6	Cost to Purchase	$9,261.00	=B1*B3+B4
7	Proceeds from Sale	$9,241.00	=B1*B2-B4

Note that buying stock is done at the ask price and there is a $5 commission charge. Selling stock is done at the bid price and you also pay the commission.

---

straightforward: if you want to buy $1,000 of stock, you need to have at least $1,000 in cash in your account. However, in a different type of account, you can borrow money to invest. A **margin account** is a brokerage account that holds securities purchased with a combination of cash and borrowed funds. You pay interest payments on that borrowed money. Brokerages earn a portion of their total profit by making such loans. The loan in the margin account is collateralized by stocks or bonds. In other words, if the value of those securities purchased with borrowed money drops sufficiently, you will be asked to either put up more collateral or sell some of the securities held in the account.

Minimum initial equity (called **initial margin**) for stock purchases in the United States is 50% of the total amount invested. This means that you can buy up to $10,000 worth of stock with only $5,000 of investment capital. The percentage amount of equity of a position is calculated by

$$Percent\ equity = \frac{equity}{stock\ value} = \frac{stock\ value - debt}{stock\ value} \qquad \textbf{3-3}$$

where the percent equity is simply the market value of equities held in the account minus the amount of **margin debt** borrowed, all expressed as a percentage of the market value of equities held in the account. Note that investors who do not borrow money to invest will have an equity percentage of 100%. This means 100% of the value of a stock position is owned free and clear by the investor.

When a stock's value declines, the investor remains obligated to pay back the margin debt. In other words, it is your equity portion of the stock position that loses value with the stock's price. The brokerage firm considers your equity to be their collateral. Thus, they will allow the equity of the position to decline only so far

margin account
An account that holds securities purchased with a combination of cash and borrowed funds

initial margin
The minimum starting equity for an investment position

margin debt
The amount borrowed to buy or maintain a security investment

maintenance margin
The ongoing minimum equity required for a margin account

before demanding that you pay back some of the loan or sell the stock position. The Federal Reserve Board sets a minimum **maintenance margin** for common stocks of 25% equity, but most brokers have 30% minimum equity requirements. Many brokers require higher initial and maintenance margins for highly concentrated accounts that hold fewer than three securities and for accounts that hold especially volatile securities (e.g., tech stocks). Securities that exhibit lower price volatility, such as Treasury bonds, may have lower minimum initial and maintenance margin requirements. Consider a previously purchased stock position of $10,000. The stock was purchased with $5,000 equity and $5,000 margin debt. How far can the stock position decline before the margin reaches 30%?

Solve for stock value in the margin equation:

$$0.30 = \frac{\text{stock value} - \$5,000}{\text{stock value}}$$

margin call
A broker's demand for additional collateral when the equity has declined below the maintenance margin level

Solving results in stock value = $7,143. This shows that when the $10,000 stock position declines 28.6% to $7,143, the brokerage firm's maintenance margin minimum will be triggered. In Wall Street terminology, a **margin call** is a formal notification by one's broker, demanding additional collateral because of adverse price movements. The investor will be asked to increase the account's equity back to the maintenance margin level within three business days or sell at least some of the stock position to pay down a portion of the margin debt.

In this example, how much additional cash is required to bring the position back to a 50% margin? Again, use the percent equity equation:

$$0.50 = \frac{\$7,143 - \text{new debt total}}{\$7,143}$$

Solving results in new debt total = $3,571.50. Since the new margin debt total must be $3,571.50 and the current debt is $5,000, the investor must pay down the loan by $1,428.50 (= $5,000 − $3,571.50).

Although margin accounts are a low-risk proposition for brokerage firms, they entail substantial risks for margin account investors. Buying stocks with borrowed funds, called *buying on margin,* is risky for investors because it magnifies returns. Big gains become bigger gains, but big losses become bigger losses. Thus, the use of margin account debt can greatly amplify the typical risks of stock and bond investors. In addition, the process forces the investor to implicitly agree to sell in the event of a sharp downturn in the value of their portfolios. Temporary market downturns can cause a margin call and force the liquidation of margin account securities at ruinously low prices.

Table 3-5 illustrates how the use of margin debt increases the volatility of returns earned on investment. Notice how the use of 50% initial margin debt increases the volatility of returns earned on the purchase of 1,000 shares of stock at $10. The initial investor equity is $5,000 and initial margin debt is $5,000. The investor's equity will double from $5,000 to $10,000 with a 50% rise in the stock's price from $10 to $15. In other words, the investor gets a 100% return when the stock price increases only 50%. Using margin debt leverages, or magnifies, the return. But that works in both directions for price changes. The equity gets wiped out by a 50% decline in the stock's price from $10 to $5 per share. In this example, the required maintenance margin is 30%. Notice that a margin call is triggered at a price between 7 and 8, specifically

Table 3-5: Leverage Increases Potential Gains and Losses

Investment results with an initial purchase of 1,000 shares at $10 using 50% initial margin, $5,000 of equity.

Stock Price	Investor Equity	Stock Price Change	Equity Return	Required Equity With 30% Maintenance Margin	Excess Equity (Deficit)
$5	$0	−50.0%	−100.0%	$1,500	($1,500)
6	1,000	−40.0%	−80.0%	1,800	(800)
7	2,000	−30.0%	−60.0%	2,100	(100)
8	3,000	−20.0%	−40.0%	2,400	600
9	4,000	−10.0%	−20.0%	2,700	1,300
10	5,000	0.0%	0.0%	3,000	2,000
11	6,000	10.0%	20.0%	3,300	2,700
12	7,000	20.0%	40.0%	3,600	3,400
13	8,000	30.0%	60.0%	3,900	4,100
14	9,000	40.0%	80.0%	4,200	4,800
15	10,000	50.0%	100.0%	4,500	5,500

at $7.14. This means that the investor's broker will demand additional equity if the stock's price falls by more than 28.6%. If the investor is unable or unwilling to quickly provide additional equity, the broker will sell part of the investor's position to get back to the maintenance margin level, and the investor will recognize a significant loss. In that event, the investor is unable to "weather the storm" of even a short-term decline in the stock's price. This makes stock purchases using margin debt risky. In making a margin purchase, the investor becomes open to the possibility of being forced to sell if the stock falls substantially for even a brief period. Also note that the margin debt's interest payments must be considered in the calculation of an investor's true return when buying on margin.

As the previous discussion explains, margin accounts can increase the percentage returns on your investments. By borrowing some of the cost of an investment, you are able to leverage your returns. However, here are some realities that anyone who buys stock on margin should know.

1. The interest on the borrowed funds is a short-term rate that your broker sets, and the rate will increase with a general increase in interest rates.
2. While the Federal Reserve sets the minimum margin requirement, your broker can set a higher minimum rate and can raise that minimum rate without giving you advance written notice.
3. If you receive a margin call, the brokerage firm can determine which assets in your account will be sold to meet the margin call.
4. If you receive a margin call, you are not entitled to an extension of time.
5. It is possible to lose more funds than you deposit with the broker, and you are responsible for that additional loss.

In summary, the use of margin can magnify your return, but as the above points indicate, the use of margin increases your personal risk.

Excel Expert 3-3

You purchase 100 shares of a $75 stock using 50% initial margin. What is the margin debt to be borrowed, and what is your equity? At what price would the stock need to decline in order reach the maintenance margin of 30%? If the stock price climbs to $100, what is your equity and return? If the price drops to $50, what is your equity and return?

	A	B	C
1	Initial stock price	$ 75.00	
2	Number of shares	100	
3			
4	Initial margin	50%	
5	Maintenance margin	30%	
6			
7	Initial stock value	$7,500.00	
8	Amount borrowed	$3,750.00	=B7*0.5
9	Initial equity	$3,750.00	=B8
10			
11	Stock price to reach maintenance	$ 53.57	=(B8/0.7)/100
12			
13	Potential stock price	$ 100.00	
14	Equity at this price	$6,250.00	=B2*B13-B8
15	Investor return at this price	66.67%	=(B14-B9)/B9
16			
17	Potential stock price	$ 50.00	
18	Equity at this price	$1,250.00	=B2*B17-B8
19	Investor return at this price	-66.67%	=(B18-B9)/B9

Note that when the stock climbs to $100 from $75, it is a 33.3% return for the stock. Using a 50% margin, that becomes a 66.7% return for you. However, a 33.3% decline to $50 represents a −66.7% return. Of course, you would have received a margin call when the price reached $53.57.

3-3d The Short Sale

Buy low and sell high. For most people, this implies that the investor first buys the security and then sells it at some later date. Can you reverse the order and sell a security first and then buy it back later at a (hopefully) lower price? The answer is yes. Sometimes, investors identify a company with poor and deteriorating fundamentals. If their assessment is correct, the investor could profit from the expected decline in the company's stock price using a **short sale**. A short sale is the sale of borrowed stock. The borrower hopes to repurchase identical shares to return to the lender to **cover the short** at a lower price, thus making a profit. The brokerage firm is the lender in the short sale. The broker profits from a client short selling through the net interest income derived from security borrowing because it is like margin debt lending; the broker also profits from the brokerage commissions generated from the trades. If you borrow stock to sell short and the company pays a dividend, you owe the dividend to the brokerage. Therefore, there is a holding cost for short positions that can be substantial in the case of stocks that pay a high dividend.

The mechanics of the short sale can be illustrated by a simple example of a normal stock purchase, sometimes referred to as a *long position*. If the current price of the XYZ Inc. is $50 per share, the investor may buy 100 shares at $50 per share for a total

short sale
The sale of borrowed stock used to profit from a falling stock price

cover the short
To return borrowed shares to the broker

cost of $5,000. Such a purchase represents taking a long position in the stock. If the price subsequently rises to $75 per share and the stock is sold, the investor will earn a profit of $2,500 (=$7,500 − $5,000).

Now contrast that with a short position. The investor simultaneously borrows and sells the stock to buy it back at some time in the future. The investor borrows and sells 100 shares of XYZ short at $50 ($5,000). Such a sale is made because the investor believes that the stock is *overpriced* and that the price of the stock will *fall*. Although the investor has sold the securities, the proceeds of the sale are not delivered to the seller but rather held by the broker. These proceeds will be subsequently used to repurchase the shares. In addition, the short seller must deposit with the broker an amount of money equal to the margin requirement for the purchase of the stock. Thus, if the margin requirement is 60%, the short seller must deposit $3,000 (=$5,000 × 0.6) with the broker. This money protects the broker (i.e., it is the short seller's collateral) and is returned to the short seller plus any profits or minus any losses when the investor covers the short position.

If the price of a share declines to $40, the short seller can buy the stock for $4,000. This purchase is no different from any purchase made on an exchange. The stock is then returned to the broker, and the loan of the stock is repaid. The short seller will have made a profit of $1,000 because the shares were purchased for $4,000 and sold for $5,000. The investor's collateral is then returned by the broker plus the $1,000 profit.

If the price of the stock had risen to $60 per share and the short seller had purchased the shares and returned them to the broker, the short position would have resulted in a $1,000 loss. The proceeds from the short sale would have been insufficient to purchase the shares. The short seller would have to use $1,000 of the collateral in addition to the proceeds to buy the stock and cover the short position. The broker would owe the short seller only what was left of the collateral ($2,000) after the transactions had been completed.

Although the purchase of stock on margin is risky, the short sale of stock is an inherently riskier proposition. If a stock is bought, the potential loss is limited to the amount invested. The potential gain from a stock purchase is unlimited. With a short sale, the potential gain is limited to the amount of proceeds obtained when the borrowed stock is sold short. If such a company went bankrupt, and its stock price went to zero, all sale proceeds could be kept by the short seller. Although the potential gain from a short-sale transaction is limited, the potential loss is unlimited. Short sellers lose enormous amounts of money when they are on the wrong side of an overpriced stock that continues to gallop skyward.

Margin Call Risk for Short Sellers

Selling short is even riskier than purchasing a stock on margin because a rise in stock price both cuts the short seller's equity *and* increases the short seller's margin requirement. Consider the case where an investor sells short 1,000 shares of a stock at $10 per share. The sale nets $10,000 in proceeds, which is held by the broker. To enter this position, the investor must put some cash at risk as well. The investor can deposit cash of between 50 and 100% of the $10,000 position. Using a 50% initial margin, the investor would need $5,000 to establish the $10,000 short position. The broker would then hold the $10,000 proceeds of the sale and the $5,000 cash deposit. The equity percentage for a short seller is given by the expression:

$$Percentage\ equity = \frac{equity}{current\ stock\ value} = \frac{stock\ value\ when\ sold\ +\ cash\ -\ current\ stock\ value}{current\ stock\ value} \qquad \textbf{3-4}$$

If the price of the stock declines to $7 per share, then the equity of the position becomes $8,000 (= $10,000 + $5,000 − [$7 × 1,000]), for a profit of $3,000. This decline in the stock price increases the equity percentage to 1.14 (= $8,000/$7,000), or 114%. **Table 3-6** shows the equity in the position for various stock price levels. Note that an increase in price to $15 per share completely wipes out the investor's equity.

Short sales with a 50% initial margin trigger a 30% maintenance margin call following only a 15.4% rise in price. To see that this is the case, remember that margin debt for a short seller consists of two parts: initial margin debt plus any debt incurred from a *rising* stock price. Consider **Equation 3-4**.

$$0.30 = \frac{\$10,000 + \$5,000 - 1,000 \times P}{1,000 \times P}$$

Solving for the price in **Equation 3-4** yields P = $11.54. Note that this represents a 15.4% increase over the original stock price of $10. A stock price increase of only 15.4% triggers a margin call. The investor will have to either add more cash to the margin account or buy back the shares and close the short position at a loss.

Compare the use of margin in buying versus selling short (**Table 3-5** versus **Table 3-6**). In the case of a stock purchase with a 50% margin debt, a typical 30% margin call occurs only when the stock price has fallen by at least 28.6%. In the case of a short sale transaction with 50% margin debt, a similar margin call occurs when the stock price has risen by only 15.4%. Following adverse price moves, a margin calls occur about twice as fast for short sellers as they do for stock buyers. The reason for this difference is simple: when a stock price falls, the margin buyer's equity and required margin both decline. When a stock price rises, the short seller's equity falls while the amount of required margin rises. This "squeezes" the short seller.

Short-Interest Ratio

The short selling of a stock requires that the shares must eventually be repurchased. Such repurchases imply future demand for the stock, which may increase its price.

Table 3-6: Short Sale Potential Gains and Losses

Investment results with an initial short sale of 1,000 shares at $10 using a 50% initial margin.

Stock Price	Investor Equity	Stock Price Change	Equity Return	Required Equity With 30% Maintenance Margin	Excess Equity (Deficiency)
$5	$10,000	−50%	100%	$1,500	$8,500
6	9,000	−40%	80%	1,800	7,200
7	8,000	−30%	60%	2,100	5,900
8	7,000	−20%	40%	2,400	4,600
9	6,000	−10%	20%	2,700	3,300
10	5,000	0%	0%	3,000	2,000
11	4,000	10%	−20%	3,300	700
12	3,000	20%	−40%	3,600	(600)
13	2,000	30%	−60%	3,900	(1,900)
14	1,000	40%	−80%	4,200	(3,200)
15	0	50%	−100%	4,500	(4,500)

Excel Expert 3-4

You *sell short* 100 shares of a $75 stock using a 50% initial margin. What is the amount of cash you must contribute for the trade? At what price would the stock need to increase in order reach the maintenance margin of 30%? If the stock price climbs to $100, what is your equity and return? If the price drops to $50, what is your equity and return?

	A	B	C
1	Initial stock price	$ 75.00	
2	Number of shares	100	
3			
4	Initial margin	50%	
5	Maintenance margin	30%	
6			
7	Initial stock value when sold	$7,500.00	
8	Cash equity from investor	$3,750.00	=B7*0.5
9			
10	Stock price to reach maintenance	$ 86.54	=((B7+B8)/1.3)/100
11			
12	Potential stock price	$ 100.00	
13	Equity at this price	$1,250.00	=B7+B8-B2*B12
14	Investor return at this price	–66.67%	=(B13-B8)/B8
15			
16	Potential stock price	$ 50.00	
17	Equity at this price	$6,250.00	=B7+B8-B2*B16
18	Investor return at this price	66.67%	=(B17-B8)/B8

Note that when the stock climbs to $100 from $75, it is a 33.3% return for the stock. The short position using a 50% margin returns –66.7%. Of course, you would have received a margin call when the price increased to just $86.54. If the stock price falls as anticipated, the 33.3% decline to $50 represents a 66.7% return for you.

Of course, the argument could be expressed in reverse. Increased short selling suggests that those in the know are anticipating lower stock prices. For either reason, some investors track short sales as a means to forecast price changes.

Such tracking requires obtaining data on short sales. The number of shares that have been sold short is referred to as the **short interest**. Because companies have differing amounts of stock outstanding, the absolute number of shares sold short may be meaningless. Instead, the number of shares short is often divided by the number of shares outstanding and expressed as the **short-interest ratio**. The numerical value of the short-interest ratio is easy to interpret. A ratio of 2.11 indicates that it will take 2.11 days of trading to cover (on the average) existing shorts. Note that the short-interest ratio definition varies in the industry. Yahoo! Finance calculates it as the number of short shares divided by the average daily volume on that day. Other information sources calculate the short interest as percentage of float, percentage of all outstanding shares, and percentage of average daily volume. The implication of the ratio, however, is ambiguous. Does a higher ratio suggest that a stock's price will rise or fall? The answer to that question can be argued either way. A high numerical value implies that it will take several days for all the existing short positions to be covered. This future buying of the shares by the short sellers will drive up the price of the stock, so a high short-interest ratio is bullish. There is, however, an exact opposite interpretation. A high short-interest ratio

short interest
The number of shares sold short in a firm

short-interest ratio
Short interest expressed in terms of an average day's trading volume

indicates that knowledgeable investors are shorting the stock in anticipation of a price decline. Thus, the high short-interest ratio is bearish and forecasts a declining stock price.

The number of shares sold short and the short-interest ratio are readily available. Data on the short interest may be found online. **Figure 3-8** shows the Share Statistic for Bank of America (BAC) from the Statistics tab from Yahoo! Finance. BAC's short interest is 83.09 million shares, which is a low amount given the 8.57 billion shares outstanding. Note that the short interest declined from the previous month. The short-interest ratio is 2.11 days.

At times, however, aggressive speculators may try to force short sellers to cover their short position, called a **short squeeze**. If speculators can bid up the stock price, short sellers will lose money and experience a margin call. The short seller can either deposit more money with the brokerage or buy back shares to cover the short. That short covering can bid up the price and force more short sellers to cover. When a volatile stock is pushed sharply higher by momentum players, the effect of frantic short covering can resemble throwing kerosene on a raging fire. If momentum investors jump into an appreciating stock, they will "squeeze" short sellers to cover their short positions at truly wild prices. Making matters worse for short sellers is the fact that widely published short-interest data identify prime short-squeeze candidates. A successful short seller must master both the economics and the psychology of the situation.

short squeeze
The pressure on short sellers through margin calls caused by rapidly appreciating stock prices

Figure 3-8: Bank of America Share Statistics from Yahoo! Finance

Share Statistics

Avg Vol (3 months) [3]	44.29M
Avg Vol (10 days) [3]	40.79M
Shares Outstanding [5]	8.57B
Implied Shares Outstanding [6]	N/A
Float	8.54B
% Held by Insiders [1]	0.12%
% Held by Institutions [1]	72.96%
Shares Short (Jun 15, 2021) [4]	83.09M
Short Ratio (Jun 15, 2021) [4]	2.11
Short % of Float (Jun 15, 2021) [4]	1.10%
Short % of Shares Outstanding (Jun 15, 2021) [4]	0.97%
Shares Short (prior month May 14, 2021) [4]	90.25M

Footnotes

[1] Data provided by Refinitiv.
[2] Data provided by EDGAR Online.
[3] Data derived from multiple sources or calculated by Yahoo Finance.
[4] Data provided by Morningstar, Inc.
[5] Shares outstanding is taken from the most recently filed quarterly or annual report and Market Cap is calculated using shares outstanding.
[6] Implied Shares Outstanding of common equity, assuming the conversion of all convertible subsidiary equity into common.
[7] EBITDA is calculated by S&P Global Market Intelligence using methodology that may differ from that used by a company in its reporting.

A Walk Down Wall Street

GameStop Short Squeeze: Amateurs vs. the Wall Street Giants

In early 2021, shares of game retailer GameStop (GME) surged more than 700% in January following the speculative involvement of amateur investors. GameStop opened January 4 with a price of $19.03 and more than doubled to $43.03 by January 21. However, the real surge occurred during the following five trading days as the share price topped $483 in the morning of Thursday, January 28. Individual investors were coordinating their buying of GME and other assets, such as AMC Entertainment and the DogeCoin cryptocurrency, via social media platform Reddit (specifically on the r/WallStreetBets subreddit, a part of the platform where members can discuss trading strategies). Much of the trading occurred through no-commission online brokerage platforms such as Robinhood.

  GameStop was ripe for a short squeeze. Consider its share statistics from Yahoo! Finance and compare them to those of Bank of America shown earlier. GME had 61.78 million shares sold short out of 69.75 shares outstanding. This represents 88.58% of the shares. Bank of America only had 0.97% of its shares sold short. The investors kept buying shares, which drove up the price. Wall Street investors, such as hedge funds, that were short received margin calls. They had to either add cash to their account or cover the short by buying the stock. But the individual investors were not selling. Shares were hard to find, which drove the price up more. As such, more hedge funds wanted to cover their short position, and so on. The result was the dramatic price increase. The media reported that over a two-day period, short sellers lost $1.9 billion.

Share Statistics

Avg Vol (3 months) [3]	25.58M
Avg Vol (10 days) [3]	115.8M
Shares Outstanding [5]	69.75M
Float	46.89M
% Held by Insiders [1]	27.33%
% Held by Institutions [1]	122.04%
Shares Short (Jan 15, 2021) [4]	61.78M
Short Ratio (Jan 15, 2021) [4]	2.81
Short % of Float (Jan 15, 2021) [4]	226.42%
Short % of Shares Outstanding (Jan 15, 2021) [4]	88.58%
Shares Short (prior month Dec 15, 2020) [4]	68.13M

  The party ended when Robinhood and other brokerages restricted trading in GameStop and AMC. GameStop's stock lost 44% that day. Limited trading was allowed the next day, but the rally had broken. The shares fell back to the $40s in a few weeks. This time, it was the amateur investors who lost their money. However, they didn't give up; for the next six months, the stock bounced between $140 to $300 while the percentage of outstanding shares sold short declined to 13.94%.

3-4 Regulation

Like many industries, the securities industry is subject to a substantial degree of regulation from both the federal and state governments. Since the majority of securities are traded across state lines, most regulation is at the federal level.

The purpose of these laws is to protect the investor by ensuring honest and fair practices. The laws require that the investor be provided with information upon which to base decisions. Hence, these acts are frequently referred to as the *full disclosure laws*, because publicly owned companies must inform the public of certain facts relating to their firms. The regulations also attempt to prevent fraud and the manipulation of stock prices. However, they do not try to protect investors from their own folly and greed. The purpose of legislation governing the securities industry is not to ensure that investors will profit from their investments; instead, the laws try to provide fair market practices while allowing investors to make their own mistakes.

While much of the laws pertaining to the financial markets are federal regulations, there are state laws as well, frequently called *blue sky laws* because fraudulent securities were referred to as pieces of blue sky. Although there are differences among the state laws, they generally require that (1) securities firms and brokers be licensed, (2) financial information concerning issues of new securities be filed with state regulatory bodies, (3) new securities meet specific standards before they are sold, and (4) regulatory bodies be established to enforce the laws.

3-4a Federal Securities Laws

Modern federal legislation governing the securities industry was created in the aftermath of the 1929 stock market crash and the ensuing Great Depression. The Securities Act of 1933 primarily concerns the issuing of new securities. It requires that new securities be "registered" with the Securities and Exchange Commission (SEC). As discussed in Chapter 2, registration consists of supplying the SEC with information concerning the firm, the nature of its business and competition, and its financial position. This information is then summarized in the prospectus, which makes the formal offer to sell the securities to the public. Once the SEC has determined that all material facts that may affect the value of the firm have been disclosed, the securities are released for sale in its initial public offering.

Although the Securities Act of 1933 applies only to new issues, the Securities Exchange Act of 1934 (and subsequent amendments) extends the regulation to existing securities. This act forbids market manipulation, deception and misrepresentation of facts, and fraudulent practices. The SEC was also created by this act to enforce the laws pertaining to the securities industry. A summary of the SEC's objectives is provided in **Table 3-7**.

Under the Securities Exchange Act of 1934, publicly held companies are required to keep current the information on file with the SEC. This is achieved by having the firm file timely reports with the SEC. Perhaps the most important is the **10-K report**, which is the firm's annual report to the SEC. Because it gives detailed statements of the firm's financial position, the 10-K is the basic source of data for the professional financial analyst. The content of the 10-K includes audited financial statements; breakdowns of sales and expenses by product line; information concerning legal proceedings; and management compensation, including deferred compensation and incentive options. Although the 10-K is not automatically sent to stockholders, a company must supply stockholders with this document upon written request, and it is generally available through the company's website and a stockbroker. The **10-Q report** is the firm's

10-K report
A required annual report filed with the SEC by publicly held firms

10-Q report
A required quarterly report filed with the SEC by publicly held firms

Table 3–7: Summary of the SEC objectives

Objectives of the SEC

1. To ensure that individuals have sufficient information to make informed investment decisions.

2. To provide the public with information by the registration of corporate securities prior to their sale to the general public and to require timely and regular disclosure of corporate information and financial statements.

3. To prevent manipulation of security prices by regulating trading in the securities markets, by requiring insiders to register the buying and selling of securities, and by regulating the activities of corporate officers and directors.

4. To regulate investment companies (e.g., mutual funds) and investment advisors.

5. To work in conjunction with the Federal Reserve to limit the use of credit to acquire securities.

6. To supervise the regulation of member firms, brokers, and securities dealers by working with FINRA, which is the self-regulatory association of brokers and dealers.

quarterly report to the SEC. Like the 10-K, it is a detailed report of the firm's financial condition. The quarterly report that the firm sends to its stockholders or places on their website is usually a summary of the 10-Q.

The **8-K report** provides specific information about material changes and must be filed with the SEC within 15 days after an event that may affect the value of the firm's securities. This document often details materials previously announced through a press release. The SEC has the power to suspend trading in a company's securities for up to 10 days if, in its opinion, the public interest and the protection of investors necessitate such a ban on trading. If a firm fails to keep investors informed of material events, the SEC can suspend trading pending the release of the required information. Such a suspension is a drastic act and is seldom used; most companies frequently issue news releases that inform the investing public of significant changes affecting the firm.

Individuals as well as firms may have to file forms with the SEC. Any stockholder who acquires 5% of a publicly held corporation's stock must submit a **13-D report**. This document requires crucial information, such as the intentions of the stockholder acquiring the large stake. Many takeover attempts start with the acquiring stockholder accumulating a substantial stake in the corporation. The required filing of the 13-D means that once the position reaches 5% of the outstanding shares, the buyer's intentions can no longer be hidden.

All the forms that are filed with the SEC are readily available through EDGAR, which is an acronym for electronic data gathering, analysis, and retrieval. All publicly held firms (and mutual funds) are required to file information electronically. Anyone may readily download a firm's 10-K or 10-Q by accessing EDGAR from the SEC's website, www.sec.gov.

The disclosure laws do not require that the company tell everything about its operations. All firms have trade secrets that they do not want to be known by their competitors. The purpose of the full disclosure laws is not to restrict the corporation but to (1) inform the investors so that they can make intelligent decisions and (2) prevent a firm's employees from using privileged information for personal gain.

It should be obvious that employees—ranging from the chief executive officer (CEO) to the mailroom clerk—may have access to information before it reaches the public. Such information (called *inside information*) may significantly enhance the employees' ability to make profits by buying or selling the company's securities before the announcement is made. Such profiteering from inside information is illegal.

8-K report
A document filed with the SEC that describes a change in a firm that may affect the value of its securities

13-D report
A document filed with the SEC by an individual who acquires 5% of a publicly held firm's stock

In addition to employees, there are others who are subject to the inside information laws. A person could have access to inside information through business relationships, family ties, or being informed ("tipped off") by insiders. Use of such privileged information even by nonemployees is also illegal. Officers and directors of the company must report their holdings and any changes in their holdings of the firm's securities to the SEC. Thus, it is possible for the SEC to determine if transactions have been made prior to any public announcement that affected the value of the securities. If insiders do profit illegally from the use of such information, they may be prosecuted under criminal law and their gains may have to be surrendered to the firm.

Sarbanes–Oxley Act of 2002

The large increase in stock prices experienced during 1998 and into 2000 and the subsequent decline in prices may be partially attributed to fraudulent (or at least questionable) accounting practices and securities analysts' touting of stocks. These scandals led to the creation of the Sarbanes–Oxley Act, which was intended to restore public confidence in the securities markets. The main provisions encompass the following:

- The independence of auditors and the creation of the Public Company Accounting Oversight Board
- Corporate responsibility and financial disclosure
- Conflicts of interest and corporate fraud and accountability

Sarbanes–Oxley created the Public Company Accounting Oversight Board, whose purpose is to oversee the auditing of the financial statements of publicly held companies. The board has the power to establish audit reporting rules and standards and to enforce compliance by public accounting firms. Firms and individuals who conduct audits are prohibited from performing non-audit services for clients that they audit.

Corporate responsibility and financial disclosure require that a publicly held firm's CEO and chief financial officer (CFO) certify that the financial statements do not contain untrue statements or material omissions. These officers are also responsible for internal controls to ensure that they receive accurate information upon which to base their certifications of the financial statements. Corporate personnel cannot exert improper influence on auditors to accept misleading financial statements. Directors and executive officers are also banned from trading in the firm's securities during blackout periods when the firm's pensions are not permitted to trade the securities. Personal loans to executives and directors are prohibited, and senior management must disclose purchases and sales of the firm's securities within two business days.

Conflicts of interest revolve around the roles played by securities analysts and by investment bankers. Investment bankers facilitate a firm's raising funds. Analysts determine if securities are under- or overvalued. Both are employed by financial firms such as Goldman Sachs. If a securities analyst determines that a stock is overvalued, this will damage the relationship between the investment bankers and the firm wishing to issue securities. Hence, there is an obvious conflict of interest between the securities analysts and the investment bankers working for the same financial firm. The investment banking division tends to earn more money for the investment bank, so they have the potential to influence analysts. Thus, the analyst and investment bank divisions need to be independent of each other. Sarbanes–Oxley seeks to create or strengthen a firewall between securities analyst and investment banking divisions. Penalties for violating Sarbanes–Oxley and existing corporate fraud laws, which prohibit destroying documents and impeding or obstructing investigations, were increased, with penalties including fines and imprisonment of up to 20 years.

Other Regulations

Although the Securities Act of 1933, the Securities Exchange Act of 1934, and the Sarbanes–Oxley Act of 2002 are the backbone of securities regulation, other laws pertaining to specific areas of investments have been enacted. These include the Public Holding Company Act of 1935, which reorganized the utility industry by requiring better methods of financial accounting and more thorough reporting and by constraining the use of debt financing. The Investment Company Act of 1940 extended the regulations to include mutual funds and other investment companies. The Securities Investor Protection Act of 1970 is designed to protect investors from brokerage firm failures and bankruptcies. The act also created the SIPC, which is discussed in a later section.

In addition to the laws affecting the issuing of securities and their subsequent trading, laws require disclosure by investment advisors (the Investment Advisers Act of 1940). Investment advisory services and individuals who "engage for compensation in the business of advising others about securities shall register" with the SEC. This registration brings investment advisors within the regulation of the SEC. Under this law, investment advisors must disclose their backgrounds, business affiliations, and the compensation charged for their services. Failure to register with the SEC can lead to an injunction against supplying the service or to prosecution for violating securities laws.

Besides the state and federal securities laws, the industry itself regulates its members. The stock exchanges and the trade association, the Financial Industry Regulatory Authority (FINRA), have established codes of behavior for their members. These include relationships between brokers and customers, the auditing of members' accounts, and proficiency tests for brokers. While such rules may not have the force of law, they can have a significant impact on the quality and credibility of the industry and its representatives.

Securities Investor Protection Corporation

Most investors are aware that accounts in virtually all commercial banks are insured by the Federal Deposit Insurance Corporation (FDIC—www.fdic.gov). As of 2021, if an insured commercial bank were to fail, the FDIC would reimburse the depositor for any losses up to $250,000. This insurance has greatly increased the stability of the commercial banking system.

Like commercial banks, brokerage firms are also insured by an agency that was created by the federal government—the Securities Investor Protection Corporation (SIPC). The SIPC (www.sipc.org) is managed by a seven-member board of directors. Five members are appointed by the president of the United States, and their appointments must be confirmed by the Senate. Two of the five represent the public, and three represent the securities industry. The remaining two members are selected by the secretary of the treasury and the Federal Reserve board of governors.

The SIPC performs a role like that of the FDIC. Its objective is to preserve public confidence in the securities markets and industry. Although the SIPC does not protect investors from losses resulting from fluctuations in security prices, it does insure investors against losses arising from the failure of a brokerage firm. The insurance provided by the SIPC protects a customer's cash and securities up to $500,000. (Only $100,000 of the $500,000 insurance applies to cash balances on an account.) If a brokerage firm fails, the SIPC reimburses the firm's customers up to this specified limit. If a customer's claims exceed the $500,000 limit, that customer becomes a general creditor for the remainder of the funds. The cost of this insurance is paid for by the brokerage firms that are members of the SIPC. All brokers and dealers that are registered with the SEC and all members of national securities exchanges must be members of the SIPC.

Conclusion

In this chapter, we discuss the mechanics of stock trading. We start by describing the various types of stock exchanges and how trading is conducted either at a physical trading floor or done electronically. With thousands of stocks, it may be difficult to know if the market was generally up or down in a given day. Stock indexes help us assess those trends. The details and implications of index design are illustrated. There are many indices available for you to track the entire market, large-cap stocks, small-cap stocks, growth stocks, international stocks, and more.

Investors like you trade through a brokerage account. Thus, we discuss the characteristics of full-service brokerage firms versus online no-commission brokerage firms, including the various costs and fees of trading. You can limit your stock purchases to the capital you provide or open a margin account and borrow some of the funds to invest. Normally, investors use their funds to purchase stocks to seek income and capital gains. However, sophisticated investors sometimes sell shares short when they anticipate a decline in a stock price. When placing trades, you can use market orders to guarantee execution or limit orders to guarantee a specific price.

There is a lot of government regulation in financial markets to protect the public from fraud all throughout the system—from corporate behavior to broker behavior. However, as later chapters illustrate, the main risk for investors is that securities prices can decline. Regulation does not protect investors from investment risk.

Chapter Equations

$$Price-weighted\ Index\ Level_t = \frac{\sum_{i=1}^{n} P_{it}}{divisor} \qquad \text{3-1}$$

$$Value\text{-}weighted\ index = \frac{total\ current\ market\ value\ of\ all\ firms\ in\ index}{original\ market\ value\ of\ firms\ in\ index} \times index\ base\ value$$

$$= \frac{\Sigma P_t Q_t}{\Sigma P_0 Q_0} \times index\ base\ value \qquad \text{3-2}$$

$$Percent\ equity = \frac{equity}{stock\ value} = \frac{stock\ value - debt}{stock\ value} \qquad \text{3-3}$$

$$Percentage\ equity = \frac{equity}{current\ stock\ value} = \frac{stock\ value\ when\ sold\ +\ cash\ -\ current\ stock\ value}{current\ stock\ value} \qquad \text{3-4}$$

Excel Functions

SUM(A2:A10)

Key Terms

8-K report – A document filed with the SEC that describes a change in a firm that may affect the value of its securities

10-K report – A required annual report filed with the SEC by publicly held firms

10-Q report – A required quarterly report filed with the SEC by publicly held firms

13-D report – A document filed with the SEC by an individual who acquires 5% of a publicly held firm's stock

agency auction – Brokers represent buyers and sellers, and prices are determined by supply and demand

American depositary receipts (ADRs) – Domestic shares issued to represent ownership in foreign securities held by a trustee

ask – The lowest price at which a dealer is willing to sell shares

bid – The highest price at which a dealer is willing to buy shares

bid–ask spread – The difference between the bid and the ask prices, which represents a cost to traders

blue chips – A large-cap company with a sterling business reputation

broker – An agent who handles buy and sell orders for an investor.

cover the short – To return borrowed shares to the broker

day order – An order placed with a broker that is canceled at the end of the day if it is not executed

dealer – A market maker who buys and sells securities for their own accounts

designated market maker (DMM) – The NYSE market maker responsible for maintaining fair and orderly markets for assigned securities

equity benchmark – A performance standard to be evaluated against

fill or kill – An order to be immediately executed or canceled depending on the trading price

good-till-canceled order – An order placed with a broker that remains in effect until it is executed by the broker or canceled by the investor

initial margin – The minimum starting equity for an investment position

limit order – An order placed with a broker to buy or sell at a specified price

maintenance margin – The ongoing minimum equity required for a margin account

margin account – An account that holds securities purchased with a combination of cash and borrowed funds

margin call – A broker's demand for additional collateral when the equity has declined below the maintenance margin level

margin debt – The amount borrowed to buy or maintain a security investment

market order – An order placed with a broker to buy or sell at the current price

odd lot – A trade that is not a multiple of 100 shares

over-the-counter – The informal market for shares not listed on an exchange

payment for order flow – The compensation a brokerage firm receives for steering client orders to a market maker for trade execution

penny stocks – Equities priced below $1

price-weighted index – A stock index computed by components' prices being summed and then divided by a divisor

registered representative – A person who works for a financial firm trading investment products and securities for clients

round lot – The general unit of trading in a security, normally 100 shares

Series 7 exam – The General Securities Representative Qualification Examination, which assesses the competency of an entry-level registered representative

short interest – The number of shares sold short in a firm

short-interest ratio – Short interest expressed in terms of an average day's trading volume

short sale – The sale of borrowed stock used to profit from a falling stock price

short squeeze – The pressure on short sellers through margin calls caused by rapidly appreciating stock prices

stock split – The number of shares issued to shareholders increases simultaneously with a price decline so that the value of each holding remains the same

stop loss – A stop order placed to limit a loss in a position

stop order – A sell order at a specific price designed to limit an investor's loss or to assure a profit

ticker symbol – The unique stock identifier assigned for trading in a particular market

value-weighted index – A stock index computed by components' market capitalization being summed and then divided initial index capitalization, then multiplied by a base value

Questions

1. **Stock Exchanges.** What is the difference between an agency auction market and an over-the-counter negotiated market? Include in your answer an example of both types of markets. (LO 3-1)

2. **Foreign Securities.** What is an American depository receipt (ADR)? Give examples. (LO 3-2)

3. **Stock Index Design.** What are the differences between a price-weighted index and a value-weighted index? What are the implications of those differences? (LO 3-3)

4. **Major Stock Indexes.** What are the major stock indexes, and what are they trying to measure? (LO 3-4)

5. **Brokerage Firms.** What are the differences in services and costs between a full-service stock brokerage firm and a discount online brokerage firm? (LO 3-5)

6. **Trading Orders.** What is the difference between each pair of items? (LO 3-6)

   a. market order and limit order
   b. fill or kill order and good-until-canceled order
   c. stop order and stop loss order

7. **Brokerage Firms.** Why is it riskier to buy stock on margin? (LO 3-7)

8. **Short Selling.** The following questions concern short selling: (LO 3-8)

   a. When should an investor sell short?
   b. How can investors sell stock they do not own?
   c. How is a short position closed?
   d. How does the investor profit from a short sale?
   e. What is the risk associated with a short position?

9. **Federal Regulations.** What are the main securities laws passed by Congress to regulate the investment industry? What part of the industry does each law regulate? (LO 3-9)

10. **SIPC.** What is the purpose of the Securities Investor Protection Corporation (SIPC)? (LO 3-10)

Problems

1. **Price-Weighted Index.** Suppose a given component of the DJIA is priced at $60 while another is priced at $110. If the divisor is 0.11, how much does the index change when the $60 stock loses 10% and when the $110 stock gains 10%? (LO 3-3)

2. **Price-Weighted Index.** Consider a price-weighted index like the DJIA with only three stocks. If the stock prices are $30, $50, and $70, and the divisor is 0.18, what is the index level? If the stocks change to $25, $53, and $76, what would the new index level be and what is the index return? If the $76 stock conducted a 2-for-1 stock split, what should the new divisor be? (LO 3-3)

3. **Value-Weighted Index.** Consider a market value-weighted index like the S&P 500 Index with only three stocks. The first stock price is $50 and has 300 shares outstanding. The second and third stocks sell for $65 and $90 with shares outstanding of 100 and 200, respectively. Each stock originally had 100 shares each that sold for $30, $75, and $50, respectively. If the base index value is 100, what is the value of the index? (LO 3-3)

4. **Value-Weighted Index.** Suppose that Apple Inc. represents a 5% weighting on a value-weighted index. If the index is at 8,000, and Apple's stock price increases by 10%, how much will this cause the index to increase? (LO 3-3)

5. **Price vs. Value-Weighted Indexes.** Two stock indexes, one price-weighted average and one value-weighted index, are to be created from the following three stocks: Lifestyle Retail (share price = $24.15, shares outstanding = 20.67 million), Frenzy Fast Food (share price = $32.75, shares outstanding = 1,272 million), and Mango Tech, Inc. (share price = $39.83, shares outstanding = 817.17 million). (LO 3-3)

   a. If the divisor for the price-weighted average is 0.9673, what is the index value?
   b. If the beginning value of the value-weighted index is $74,705.06 million and the Index base value is 100, what is the current value of this index?
   c. If the price of the three stocks change to Lifestyle = $30, Frenzy = $35, and Mango = $35, what is the value of the two indexes? Why are they different?

6. **Bid–Ask Spreads.** Giant firm American International Group, Inc. (AIG) has a bid of 35.34 and an ask of 35.39, whereas small company Ambac Financial Group, Inc. (ABK) has a bid of 3.07 and an ask of 3.11. Calculate the bid–ask spread as a percentage of the ask price for each firm. What do these calculations tell you about the cost of trading small-cap versus large-cap stocks? (LO 3-6)

7. **Market Depth.** Verizon Communications (VZ) has a bid of 36.05 and a bid size of 1,000. The ask is 36.07, and the ask size is 800. How much money is represented for you to sell shares? (LO 3-6)

8. **Market Depth.** MBIA, Inc. (MBI) has a bid of 6.99, a bid size of 1,500, an ask of 7.00, and an ask size of 800. How much money is represented for you to buy shares? (LO 3-6)

9. **Market and Limit Orders.** One order is a market order for the purchase of 200 shares. A second order is a fill or kill limit order set at $49.50 for the purchase of 200 shares. When the two orders arrive at the stock exchange, the bid quote is $49.48 and the ask quote is $49.52. What is the value of each trade? (LO 3-6)

10. **Margin for Long Position.** A stock sells for $10 per share. You purchase 100 shares using a 50% margin. A year later, the price has risen to $15.50. What is the initial equity you must have to initiate the trade? What is your percent equity position at the end of the year? (LO 3-7)

11. **Margin for Short Position.** A stock sells for $50 per share. You sell short 100 shares using a 50% margin. A year later, the price has fallen to $43.50. What is the initial equity you must have to initiate the trade? What is your percent equity position at the end of the year? (LO 3-7)

12. **Margin Call.** Assume an investor went long Citigroup, Inc.(C) at a price of $25.55 using a 50% margin. At what price would the investor face a 30% maintenance margin call? (LO 3-7)

13. **Margin Call.** Assume an investor shorted GE at a price of $46.43 using a 50% margin. At what price would the investor face a 30% maintenance margin call? (LO 3-7)

14. **Returns Using Margin.** You purchase 100 shares of stock at $100. The margin requirement is 40%. What are the dollar and percentage returns if: (LO 3-7)
    a. you sell the stock for $112 and bought the stock for cash?
    b. you sell the stock for $90 and bought the stock on margin?
    c. you sell the stock for $60 and bought the stock on margin?

15. **Short Position Margin.** Assume an investor shorted 1,000 shares of Pfizer, Inc. (PFE) at $21.55 using a 50% margin. Following a sharp rise in the stock to $26, the investor has received a maintenance margin call. At this point, the investor is required to wire sufficient funds to bring the account equity back to 50%. How much in additional funds must be added to the account? (LO 3-7)

16. **Cash vs. Margin Investing.** Investor A makes a cash purchase of 100 shares of AB&C common stock for $55 a share. Investor B also buys 100 shares of AB&C but uses a margin. Each holds the stock for one year, during which dividends of $5 a share are distributed. The margin requirement is 60%, and the interest rate is 10% annually on borrowed funds. What is the dollar amount and percentage earned by each investor if they sell the stock after one year? (LO 3-7)
    a. $40
    b. $55
    c. $60
    d. $70

17. **Short Selling and Return.** An investor sells a stock short for $36 a share. A year later, the investor covers the position at $30 a share. If the margin requirement is 60%, what is the percentage return earned on the investment? (LO 3-7)

18. **Short Selling and Return.** A speculator sells a stock short for $50 a share using a 50% margin. The company pays a $2 annual cash dividend. A year later, the seller covers the short position at $42. What is the percentage return on the position (excluding the impact of any interest expense and commissions)? (LO 3-7)

19. **Cash vs. Margin.** Investor A buys 100 shares of SLM Inc. at $35 a share and holds the stock for a year. Investor B buys 100 shares on margin. The margin requirement is 60%, and the interest rate on borrowed funds is 8%. (LO 3-7)

    a. What is the interest cost for investor A?
    b. What is the interest cost for investor B?
    c. If they both sell the stock for $40 after a year, what percentage return does each investor earn? In both cases, the value of the stock has risen the same. Why are the percentage returns different?

20. **Short Position Maintenance Margin.** Assume a speculator sold 3,000 shares of mortgage lender Fannie Mae (FNM) short at $30 with an initial margin of 50% and subsequently received a 30% maintenance margin call. Calculate the dollar amount that must be deposited to bring the account equity back up to 50%. (LO 3-7)

Case Study

Investing an Inheritance

The Kelleher brothers, Victor and Darin, could not be more different. Victor is assertive and enjoys taking risks, while Darin is reserved and exceedingly risk averse. Both have jobs that pay well and provide fringe benefits, including medical insurance and pension plans. You are the executor for their grandfather's estate and know that each brother will soon inherit $85,000. Neither has an immediate need for the cash, which could be invested to meet some long-term financial goal.

Once the funds have been received, you expect Victor to acquire some exceedingly risky investment (if he does not immediately squander the money). You would be surprised, however, if Darin chose to do anything other than place the funds in a low-yielding savings account. Neither alternative makes financial sense to you, so before the distribution of the funds, you decide to offer financial suggestions that would reduce Victor's risk exposure and increase Darin's potential return.

Given the brothers' ages and financial condition, you believe that equity investments are appropriate. Such investments may satisfy Victor's propensity to take risks and increase Darin's potential return without excessively increasing his risk exposure (willingness to assume risk). Currently, the stock of Choice Juicy Fruit is selling for $70 and pays an annual dividend of $1.80 a share. The company's line of low-to-no-sugar juice offers considerable potential. The margin requirement set by the Federal Reserve is 50%, and brokerage firms are charging 5% on funds used to purchase stock on margin. While commissions vary among brokers, you decide that $70 for a 100-share purchase or sale is a reasonable amount to use for illustrative purposes. Currently, commercial banks are paying only 3$ on savings accounts.

To give the presentation focus, you decide to answer the following questions:

1. What is the percentage return earned by Darin if he acquires 100 shares, holds the stock for a year, and sells the stock for $80?
2. What is the percentage return earned by Victor if he acquires 100 shares on margin, holds the stock for a year, and sells the stock for $80? What advantage does buying stock on margin offer Victor?
3. What would the percentage returns be if the sale prices had been $50 or $100?
4. What would the impact be on the brothers' returns if the rate of interest charged by the broker increased to 10%?
5. If the maintenance margin requirement were 30% and the price of the stock declined to $50, what impact would that have on each brother's position? At what price of the stock would they receive a margin call?

Mutual Funds and Other Investment Companies

After reading this chapter, you should be able to:

LO 4-1   Describe the structures, advantages, and disadvantages of buying mutual funds.
LO 4-2   Identify the costs and pricing of investing in mutual funds.
LO 4-3   Distinguish among the types of mutual funds based on their portfolios or investment strategies.
LO 4-4   Assess mutual fund performance.
LO 4-5   Describe the features and advantages associated with exchange-traded funds (ETFs).
LO 4-6   Understand the dynamics of various investment objectives of ETFs.
LO 4-7   Compare and contrast closed-end funds with ETFs and mutual funds.
LO 4-8   Describe shares selling for a discount and shares selling for a premium from their net asset values (NAVs).
LO 4-9   Compare and contrast hedge fund and mutual fund investment objectives and fees.
LO 4-10   Differentiate among the types of real estate investment trusts. (REITs).

Many people find selecting specific securities and managing their own portfolios to be difficult. Instead, they pass the decisions to the managers of investment companies. These portfolio managers invest the funds on behalf of clients. In many cases, the portfolios of investment companies are well-diversified, holding a wide spectrum of stocks, bonds, or a combination of both. Thus, the investor receives both the benefits of professional management and diversification. You may be interested in using investment companies in your portfolio. Or you may be interested in the many investment jobs they create.

We use the term "investment company" to encompass all types of investment portfolios for which an investor can buy. There are several types of investment companies that focus on various investment topics, and they have different structures. As explained in this chapter, these different organizational structures determine who can buy their shares, how they can buy shares, the costs to trading, what the financial firm can own, tax ramifications, and more. By far, the most popular is the mutual fund (see **Figure 4-1**). In addition to mutual funds, we explain the dynamics of exchange-traded funds, closed-end funds, unit trusts, hedge funds, and real estate investment trusts. The Investment Company Institute (ICI—www.ici.org) reports in its 2021 *Investment Company Fact Book* that there were $29.7 trillion in U.S.-registered investment company total net assets. Note that hedge funds are not included in **Figure 4-1**. They are not "registered" investments, which is explained later in the chapter.

Figure 4-1: Net Assets in U.S.-Registered Investment Companies in 2020, by Type

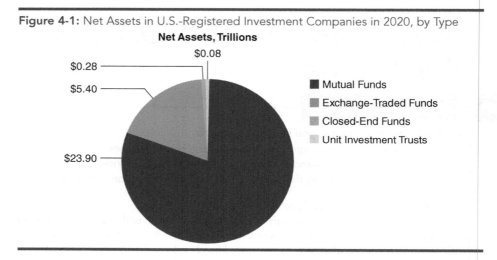

Net Assets, Trillions

$0.08
$0.28
$5.40
$23.90

- Mutual Funds
- Exchange-Traded Funds
- Closed-End Funds
- Unit Investment Trusts

4-1 Mutual Funds

mutual fund
An open-end investment company

A mutual fund manages a portfolio of securities. Investors buy into that portfolio through purchasing shares of the fund. The performance of the securities in the fund's portfolio (including costs and fees) directly determines the investment success of the investors who own shares of the fund. However, mutual fund shares are not traded in the secondary markets like stocks and bonds. Instead, an investor purchases shares directly from the fund. The rationale for mutual funds is simple and appealing. The investment company receives the money from many investors, combines that capital, and uses that money to purchase securities. The individual investors receive (1) the advantage of professional management of their money; (2) the benefit of ownership in a diversified portfolio; (3) the potential savings in commissions, as the investment company buys and sells in large blocks; and (4) custodial services (e.g., the collecting and disbursing of funds).

The advantages and services help explain why mutual funds are so popular, driving dramatic growth in assets. There are over 9,000 mutual funds in the United States that create portfolios of stocks, bonds, and money market securities. As **Figure 4-1** illustrates, mutual fund assets in the United States were $29.3 trillion in 2020. This represents a more than doubling of assets in 10 years since the 2011 value of $12.7 trillion.

There are several interesting characteristics that arise from investors buying and selling fund shares directly from the mutual fund company. The fund creates new shares for each new purchase of the fund. This gives mutual funds an **open-end fund** structure, which means that they can create an unlimited number of shares. They delete shares that are sold back to them by investors. Because the mutual fund keeps all the accounting records, there is no need to only trade in whole shares. Thus, investors tend to buy in round dollar amounts and get fractional shares. For example, if you purchase $5,000 of a mutual fund priced at $23.44 per share, you will receive 213.31058 shares (= $5,000 ÷ $23.44).

open-end fund
A mutual fund that continuously offers to sell and buy shares

This example mentioned buying shares "priced at" $23.44 per share. However, the value of mutual fund shares is precisely measured and known as its **net asset value (NAV)**. The NAV is the value of all the securities in the portfolio less any liabilities, then divided by the total number of shares issued to investors. Thus, the NAV may be obtained as follows:

net asset value (NAV)
A per-share value of a mutual fund's stock, bond, and cash reserve holdings

$$NAV = \frac{Total\ Value\ of\ Securities\ -\ Liabilities}{Number\ of\ Shares} \qquad \textbf{4-1}$$

Therefore, if a mutual fund owned $245.5 million in stocks, $187.3 million in bonds, and $2 million in cash and had $.8 million in liabilities and 18.5153 million shares outstanding, then its NAV would be $23.44 per share (= ($245.5 million + $187.3 million + $2 million − $0.8 million) ÷ 18.5153).

As long as the fund exchanges shares with investors at a price equal to the NAV, then the NAV is not impacted. Thus, the open-end fund has no limit to the number of shares it could issue. Changes in the NAV occur when the value of the securities in the portfolio changes. Thus, changes in the NAV represent the investment performance to the investors.

Note that there is some uncertainty as to the NAV at which you will trade. This is because trades are conducted after the capital markets have closed so that the portfolio value can be accurately computed. When you place an order during the day, it is executed at the *NAV as of the end of the day*. The NAV will change during the day as the stock and bond prices fluctuate. Since there is no secondary market in the shares of mutual funds, you cannot specify limit orders or stop-loss orders for the purchase and sale of mutual funds as you can for stocks.

4-1a Mutual Fund Costs

While there are many advantages of mutual funds for investors, there are also costs. Think of the costs in two areas, *transacting fund shares* and *holding fund shares*.

Excel Expert 4-1

Changes in the NAV

Consider the mutual fund described in the text example and illustrated at Day 0 here. The next day (Day 1), the stock market generally rises, pushing up the value of the stocks in the portfolio by 1%. The bond value of the portfolio declines by 0.5%. Notice that the NAV of the fund increases to $23.53 per share, a 0.35% return for investors.

	A	B	C	D	E	F
1	*In millions*	Day 0	Day 1	Day 2		
2	Stock's value	$ 245.50	$ 247.96	$ 247.46		
3	Bond's value	$ 187.30	$ 186.36	$ 186.18		
4	Cash	$ 2.00	$ 2.00	$ 2.00		
5	Liabilities	$ 0.80	$ 0.80	$ 0.80		
6						
7	Shares outstanding	18.5153	18.5153	18.5153		
8						
9	NAV =	$ 23.44	$ 23.52	$ 23.49	=(D2+D3+D4-D5)/D7	
10	Daily return =		0.35%	-0.16%	=(D9-C9)/C9	

On Day 2, the portfolio's stock value and bond value fall 0.2% and 0.1%, respectively. The resulting NAV falls to $23.49 per share, a –0.16% decline for investors.

Transacting Costs

load fee
A sales commission

front-end load
A commission paid at the time of a fund purchase

low-load fund
A fund that charges sales fees ranging from 1 to 3%

back-end load
Commissions paid when a fund is sold

no-load fund
A mutual fund that does not charge a commission for buying or selling shares

asset-based fee
A fee charged as a percentage of the assets under management

Many mutual fund investors pay one-time sales commissions, or a **load fee**. Sales commissions are often charged at the time of purchase as a simple percentage of the amounts invested. Such **front-end loads** range from 4 to 8.5% (or $400 to $850 per $10,000 invested) on the high end. Funds that charge sales fees ranging from 1 to 3% (or $100 to $300 per $10,000 invested) are called **low-load funds**. Another form of sales charge is the **back-end load**, which is assessed when an investor sells fund shares. Back-end loads may be as high as 6% for redemptions that take place within one year of the original investment. These charges typically decline over time and may disappear by the seventh year after the original purchase of fund shares.

The way investors come to invest in a mutual fund often determines the front-end load they pay. If you do your own research and find a fund you like, going directly to the fund will likely allow you to *pay no load charges*. Alternatively, if someone helps you find the fund, then loads might apply. For example, the load fee ranges from 0 for **no-load funds** that you find yourself, to 1 to 3% for low-load funds that may go to your financial advisor, to 4 to 8.5% for high-load funds for specialty funds or funds sold by mutual fund salespersons. That is, advisors and salespersons are often compensated by recommending specific mutual funds through the load fee. However, over the past few decades, the way that people compensate their financial advisors has significantly changed, moving away from front-end loads toward **asset-based fees**. This transition moves the costs from up-front fees to annual costs, which will be explained shortly.

How prevalent are load fees? As the industry changes from compensating financial professionals using loads to level fees, the prevalence of loads has diminished. ICI's 2021 *Investment Company Fact Book* reports that while the amount of assets in loaded funds has remained mostly the same since 2010, the assets in no-load funds has

Figure 4-2: Net Assets in Load and No-Load Mutual Funds in 2020

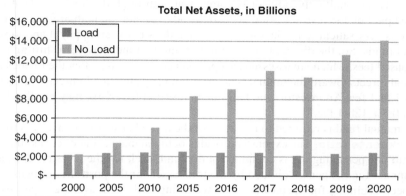

increased by a multiple of seven. In 2020, no-load funds managed $14,150 billion in assets, while loaded funds managed only $2,520 billion (refer **Figure 4-2**).

The manner in which funds implement the load fee is a little tricky. The fee is a percentage of the offer price and not a percentage of the NAV, which makes the fee larger than it would be if it were based on the NAV. **Equation 4-2** shows that the NAV is divided by 1 minus the load fee percentage:

$$Offer\ Price = \frac{NAV}{(1\ -\ Load\ Fee)} \qquad \textbf{4-2}$$

Thus, to purchase shares of a mutual fund with an NAV of $23.44 while paying a 2% load fee, the offer price would be $23.9183673 per share (= $23.44/(1 − 0.02)). A $5,000 purchase would provide 209.0443686 shares (= $5,000/$23.9183763) valued at $4,900.00 (= 209.0443686 × $23.44). Thus, the load fee represents $0.4783673 per share and a total of $100.

Holding Costs

In addition to loading charges, investors in mutual funds have to pay a variety of other expenses. Each mutual fund is required to disclose in its prospectus these various costs. The costs associated with researching specific assets, brokerage fees charged when the fund buys and sells securities, and compensation to management are all mutual fund costs that are charged quarterly to the fund investors. These expenses are the cost of owning the shares and are wrapped together as the **management fee**. These fees are in addition to any sales fees (loading charges) the investor pays when the shares are purchased. The costs of owning the shares are generally expressed as a percentage of the fund's assets. A management fee of 1.6% indicates that the fund's expenses are $1.60 for every $100 of assets per year. It should be obvious that the fund must earn at least $1.60 for each $100 in assets just to cover these costs, so if a fund earns 11.2% on its assets, the investor nets 9.6%.

Some funds also charge investors an additional amount to cover marketing and distribution costs. These marketing charges are formally referred to as **12b-1 fees**, after the 1980 U.S. SEC rule that permits this practice. There is no legal limit to the 12b-1 fees that a fund may charge, but such fees normally run between 0.25 and 1% of the fund's average annual net assets.

management fee
A fee charged against the portfolio to fund the operation of fund

12b-1 fees
Marketing expenses charged to the mutual fund shareholder

As mentioned earlier, many investors buy mutual funds recommended by their advisor. Traditionally, the advisor is compensated through the load fee. That is, the load fee paid by the investor often goes to the advisor, not the mutual fund. However, that fee is very salient to the investor, who often does not want to pay it and looks for no-load funds. So, the distribution structure of mutual funds has been shifting toward asset-based fees, which are assessed as a percentage of the assets that the financial professional directs toward the mutual fund. The fund pays this fee indirectly through the fund's 12b-1 fee. An investor who balks at an up-front fee of 4% may not flinch at an annual 0.5% 12b-1 fee.

expense ratio
Total fees and trading costs expressed as a percentage of fund assets

A mutual fund is required to report all of the annual costs to the investors together as the **expense ratio**. The expense ratio adds both the management fee and the 12b-1 fees into one percentage. It is computed at the fund level, not the investor level, as the total annual fund expenses divided by the total assets of the portfolio. Expense ratios have been declining for the past decade. According to the ICI, average expenses have fallen from 1.46% in 2010 to 1.16% in 2020 for U.S. equity mutual funds. The largest funds tend to charge expenses that are half of small funds expenses.

Excel Expert 4-2 illustrates how fees and loads negatively impact an investor's return. It shows why investors seek no-load and low-expense funds.

Excel Expert 4-2

Impact of Fund Expenses and Loads

You want to invest $5,000 in a mutual fund. Consider four funds that are identical except for their loads and expenses (the impact of the expenses and loads is illustrated in the spreadsheet below). One fund is no load and low expenses. The second fund in no load with high expenses. The third and fourth funds have low load with low expense and high load with high expenses, respectively. What is the value of each portfolio after five years given the returns shown?

	A	B	C	D	E	F	G	H
1	Money to invest	$ 5,000.00						
2	NAV	$ 23.44						
3	Year 1 return	7%						
4	Year 2 return	12%						
5	Year 3 return	-6%						
6	Year 4 return	4%						
7	Year 5 return	10%						
8		No Load	No Load	Low Load	High Load			
9		Low Expense	High Expense	Low Expense	High Expense			
10	Front-End Load	0.0%	0.0%	2.0%	5.0%			
11	Expense Ratio	0.2%	1.8%	0.3%	2.0%			
12								
13	Shares Purchased	213.3105802	213.3105802	209.0443686	202.6450512	=$B$1/($B$2/(1-E10))		
14	Value, End Year 1	$ 5,339.30	$ 5,253.70	$ 5,227.27	$ 4,980.85	=E13*$B$2*(1+$B$3)*(1-E11)		
15	Value, End Year 2	$ 5,968.06	$ 5,778.23	$ 5,836.98	$ 5,466.98	=E14*(1+$B$4)*(1-E11)		
16	Value, End Year 3	$ 5,598.75	$ 5,333.77	$ 5,470.30	$ 5,036.18	=E15*(1+$B$5)*(1-E11)		
17	Value, End Year 4	$ 5,811.06	$ 5,447.27	$ 5,672.05	$ 5,132.88	=E16*(1+$B$6)*(1-E11)		
18	Value, End Year 5	$ 6,379.38	$ 5,884.14	$ 6,220.53	$ 5,533.24	=E17*(1+$B$7)*(1-E11)		

Invest $5,000 in the no-load, low-expense fund, and you end the five years with $6,379.38, for a 27.59% return for the five years. Note that paying higher loads and expenses costs you money! The no-load, high-expense fund results in $495.24 less money. Of course, the high-load and high-expense fund provides a much lower $5,533.24 value, representing only 10.66% return. The interesting comparison is between the no-load, high-expense fund and the low-load, low-expense fund. Which one is better? In this case, it's the low-load, low-expense fund.

A, B, and C Shares

Some funds have adopted different classes of shares, and the fees for each class differ. Class A shares have front-end load fees but tend to have lower 12b-1 fees and lower annual expenses. Class B shares have no front-end loads but have exit fees and higher 12b-1 fees. Class C shares do not have front- or back-end load fees. They do, however, have higher 12b-1 fees and higher annual expenses. If held for many years, class C shares will be more expensive, as the 12b-1 fees offset the benefit associated with no loads. If the investor anticipates holding the shares for many years, class A shares would be better, but the individual cannot know when the investment is made which alternative will prove to be the best. That will be known only after the fact.

4-1b Mutual Fund Portfolios

Mutual fund portfolios may be diversified or specialized. Diversified portfolios might include money market instruments, stocks, and bonds. Specialized portfolios might include only money market instruments, or only stocks from the banking industry. You might classify a fund by **investment type** or **investment style**. *Investment type* refers to the type of securities the fund acquires, such as equities (stocks) or bonds. *Investment style* refers to the fund's investment philosophy or strategy. Investors have different objectives, so various types of mutual funds are needed to help them achieve their goals. As shown in **Table 4-1**, most funds fit into one of four basic types: money market funds, bond funds, stock funds, and blend mutual funds. There can be many styles within each category.

investment type
The kind of securities held by the fund, such as stocks or bonds

investment style
A fund's investment philosophy or strategy

Investors think of **money market mutual funds** as a place to hold cash. As the name implies, they acquire money market instruments (detailed in Chapter 2), which are short-term securities issued by banks, nonbank corporations, and governments. Common short-term securities in these funds are negotiable certificates of deposit (CDs), short-term debt of the federal government (Treasury bills), commercial paper issued by corporations, repurchase agreements (commonly referred to as *repos*), bankers' acceptances, and tax anticipation notes. Since the purpose of money market mutual funds is the stability of principal, and they have no growth and little income potential, they compete directly with banks and other depository institutions for the deposits of savers.

money market mutual fund
A fund that invests in cash reserves, or short-term IOUs

Bond funds invest in fixed-income securities. Bond funds provide little growth potential but do offer moderate-to-high income potential with low-to-moderate stability of principal. Investors primarily own bond funds to provide income through interest payments and also to offset some of the risk of equity holdings. Common categories of bond funds classify funds by whether they own taxable bonds or tax-exempt bonds. The tax status of the interest payments is transferred to the fund investor. Tax-exempt funds tend to specialize in the municipal bonds of a single state because citizens of that state experience tax-exempt status for both federal and state income tax purposes. Taxable bond funds can be further classified by characteristics of the bonds in the portfolio by:

bond fund
a fund that buys debt instruments

- average time to maturity (short, medium, long)
- credit risk (low to high)
- magnitude of the interest payments (low-to-high yields)
- type of issuer (government, corporate, asset-backed, etc.)

These classifications determine the degree of income potential and the level of principal stability.

Table 4-1: Types and Styles of Mutual Funds

Style	Objective	Securities Held	Capital Growth Potential	Income Potential	Stability of Principal
Money Market Funds					
Taxable money market	Current income, stability of principal	Cash investments	None	Low	Very high
Tax-exempt money market	Tax-free income, stability of principal	Municipal cash investments	None	Low	Very high
Bond Funds					
Taxable bond	Current income	Wide range of government and/or corporate bonds	None	Moderate to high	Low to moderate
Tax-exempt bond	Tax-free income	Wide range of municipal bonds	None	Moderate to high	Low to moderate
Stock Funds					
Equity income	Current income, capital growth	High-yield stocks, convertible bonds	Moderate to high	Moderate	Low to moderate
Value funds	Current income, capital growth	Low P/E, P/B stocks	Moderate to high	Low to moderate	Low to moderate
Growth and income	Current income, capital growth	Dividend-paying stocks	Moderate to high	Low to moderate	Low to moderate
Domestic growth	Capital growth	U.S. stocks with high potential for growth	High	Very low	Low
International growth	Capital growth	Stocks of companies outside the U.S.	High	Very low to low	Very low
Aggressive growth	Aggressive growth of capital	Stocks with very high potential for growth	Very high	Very low	Very low
Small cap	Aggressive growth of capital	Stocks of small companies	Very high	Very low	Very low
Specialized	Aggressive growth of capital	Stocks of industry sectors	High to very high	Very low to moderate	Very low to low
Blended Funds					
Balanced	Current income, capital growth	Cash, bonds, and stocks	Moderate	Moderate to high	Low to moderate
Life cycle	Current income, capital growth	Cash, bonds, and stocks	Varies over time	Varies over time	Varies over time

stock fund
A fund that makes equity investments

Investors use **stock funds** to generate growth, income, and diversification. They are generally higher risk than bond funds and money market funds and therefore generally offer higher returns in the long run. Some portfolios are focused on generating income and thereby invest in stocks with higher dividend yields. Portfolios focused on growth tend to own the stock of fast-growing companies. These companies usually do not pay any dividends because they need that capital to reinvest in the company. A "growth" fund portfolio manager identifies firms offering exceptional growth based on the industry's potential and the firm's position within the industry. Many technology stocks illustrate the difference between the growth and value approaches. Amazon (AMZN) may appeal to growth portfolio managers because the company has potential for growth through its dominant sales position on the Internet.

Another delineation between styles of stock funds is the size of the companies in the portfolio. The most common categories are micro-capitalization (micro-cap), small-cap, medium-cap, and large-cap funds. Large-cap funds own large-cap companies, which have market capitalizations of $10 billion or greater. Although these large-cap companies may only represent 5% of the number of firms, they represent about 90% of the total market capitalization. Note that the largest companies have over $1 trillion in market cap. Mid-cap companies range from $2 to $10 billion, and small-cap companies range from $300 million to $2 billion. Micro-cap firms have less than $300 million in market capitalizations. There are thousands of small- and micro-cap stocks; however, together, they represent only a tiny portion of the total overall market capitalization.

Morningstar (morningstar.com) is an information powerhouse in the mutual fund industry. They provide a lot of metrics and ratings to help investors understand the characteristics of mutual fund portfolios. One convenient way to summarize the portfolio strategy of a particular fund is the Morningstar **style box**. The diagram illustrates the location of a fund's portfolio based on the portfolio's average market capitalization and value/growth orientation. A growth strategy is described above. Alternatively, a value manager acquires stocks that are deemed undervalued or "cheap" by fundamental analysis and analytical tools described in a later chapter. Value investors are sometimes called **contrarian** investors because value stocks are often out of favor with many investors and the media. **Figure 4-3** illustrates the style boxes for a small-cap value fund and a fund with a balanced portfolio of large-cap stocks.

There are many other strategies that equity mutual funds may employ to try to earn great returns for investors. A **momentum strategy** buys the companies that other investors are buying and whose stock is rising. Another example is **market timing** strategy. Market timers attempt to move in and out of various groups of stocks to buy low and sell high. This could involve **sector rotation** or simply jumping between the stock market and cash securities. The danger of market timing is that many investors have bad timing.

Blended funds own a mixture of securities that sample the attributes of many types of assets. Instead of investing in a stock fund and a bond fund, investors often simply choose one fund, the balanced mutual fund. In addition to stocks, a balanced fund's portfolio may also include short-term debt securities (e.g., Treasury bills), bonds, and preferred stock. Such a portfolio seeks a balance of income from dividends and interest plus some capital appreciation. The **lifecycle fund** (or target retirement fund) is a special type of blended fund. This mutual fund is designed to replicate the stock/bond mix an investor wants over their lifetime. For example, when younger, you likely want more growth potential and thus have a larger portion of stocks. When retired, you likely want both less risk and more income. Thus, you would own more bonds and dividend paying stocks. The lifecycle fund begins with a larger allocation in stocks and then over the decades shifts to more bonds. You would pick the lifecycle fund that has a target date similar to your planned retirement year.

style box
Morningstar's depiction of a fund's portfolio expressed in market capitalization and value/growth orientation

contrarian
An investor who goes against the consensus concerning investment strategy

momentum strategy
The strategy of buying and holding securities that have been rising

market timing
The attempt to time the purchase and sale of securities to market lows and highs, respectively

sector rotation
A form of market timing in which investors rotate between sectors over time

blended fund
a fund that buys stocks and debt instruments

lifecycle fund
A blended fund that starts with higher equity allocation and slowly changes to higher debt securities allocation as the retirement date nears

Figure 4-3: Example of Morningstar's Style Box

Small-Cap Value Fund

	Value	Blend	Growth
Large			
Mid			
Small	•		

Balanced Large-Cap Fund

	Value	Blend	Growth
Large		•	
Mid			
Small			

fund family
A mutual fund firm that offers many portfolio choices

An advantage of investing in mutual funds is convenience. Most investment companies offer a "family" of mutual funds, or fund family. Fund families like T. Rowe Price, Vanguard, Fidelity, and others offer dozens, even hundreds, of different mutual fund portfolios to choose from. A fund family always offers money market funds and various types of stock, bond, and balanced funds. You can easily move money from one fund to another as your needs or investment priorities change. Most mutual funds also provide extensive record-keeping services. This helps investors keep track of transactions, follow fund performance, and assist in completing tax returns.

4-1c Popular Specialized Mutual Funds

Many funds have been created to offer investors specialized strategies. For example, a mutual fund may limit itself to investments in the securities of a particular:

- sector of the economy (e.g., Fidelity Select Multimedia);
- industry, such as gold (e.g., INVESCO Gold); or
- country, such as Japan (e.g., T. Rowe Price Japan Fund).

The returns of these funds are likely to be more volatile because they are less diversified than typical large-cap or balanced funds. Nevertheless, you may believe that given the current economic environment, a particular industry such as banking may outperform other industries. Using a banking-focused mutual fund is a way to tilt your portfolio toward your investment forecast. Investors do this with sector-, industry-, and country-focused funds.

Index Funds

index fund
A fund whose portfolio mimics a specific index of the market

Most stock mutual funds do not outperform standard stock market indexes over time. This is partially because funds have trading costs and charge management fees. So, if you can't beat 'em, join 'em. In 1975, John Bogle started the first index fund. An index fund duplicates a specific index of the market. The fund's purpose is almost diametrically opposite to the traditional purpose of a mutual fund. Instead of identifying specific securities for purchase, the management of these funds seeks to duplicate the composition of an index of the market. This simple idea powered the company that Bogle created, The Vanguard Group, to become a financial powerhouse. Today, Vanguard manages over $7 trillion in investment assets, and the Vanguard 500 Index Fund is the largest mutual fund in the United States—followed by the Fidelity 500 Index Fund and the Vanguard Total Stock Market Index Fund.

passively managed
An investment style in which securities are not chosen by a manager but instead identified in an index

Why is index investing so popular? Index funds are essentially passively managed investments since the fund duplicates the index. Once the portfolio is constructed, changes are infrequent and occur in response to changes in the composition of the index. Such minimal changes reduce the cost of managing the fund, so they are a cost-effective means to buy the market. Like the Vanguard 500 Index Fund, most index funds are designed to mimic the Standard & Poor's 500 index. Matching the Nasdaq-100 Index is also popular. However, indexing can be used to match the returns of any stock or bond market benchmark, or index. When an index strategy is employed, a computer staff simply attempts to replicate the investment results of the benchmark index by holding the index securities. Index funds make no attempt to use stock selection or traditional active management techniques to try to beat the market. Indexing can be described as a passive investment approach that emphasizes broad diversification and low portfolio-trading activity.

The biggest advantage of index fund investing is the low cost. According to the ICI, in 2020, the average actively managed equity fund had an annual expense ratio of about 0.71% of assets under management. The average index fund expense ratio was only 0.06%. In addition, index funds incur far less trading costs.

In short, indexing is a time-tested investment strategy that offers long-term investors an efficient means for achieving market-matching results that typically beat actively managed mutual funds.

Socially Responsible Funds

One of the most popular investment trends of this decade is socially responsible investing (SRI). SRI has evolved over the past six decades. Public interest in ethical investment vehicles took off in 1971 as a reaction to the Vietnam War. Some investors wondered how corporations used their capital for manufacturing weapons and Agent Orange, a chemical sprayed on Vietnamese jungles. As a response to some public outcry, the Pax Fund launched an SRI portfolio for these socially conscious investors. It focused on avoiding companies profiting from the war. Later, other mutual funds excluded companies making products considered harmful to society and shunned firms profiting from doing business in countries with oppressive governments.

Fast forward to today: SRI investing is frequently called sustainable investing or environmental, social, and governance (ESG) investing. The basis of sustainable investing is personal values. Your values can differ from others in both focus and veracity. Values derive from strong beliefs stemming from social, political, and religious beliefs. These funds can target topics like social values, civil rights, and climate change. Since values differ among people, hundreds of investment opportunities are available through mutual funds to serve different social investing goals. The key is to understand your values and the strength of your convictions. You may need to reflect on your values to align your investing goals.

To form SRI portfolios, sustainable mutual funds can use negative and positive screens. A negative screen simply avoids companies that have problematic products, typically alcohol, gambling, polluters, tobacco, and weapons. Instead of simply avoiding companies doing bad things, today's socially responsible investors often take a positive approach and seek to find companies doing good things. As such, funds may use a positive screen technique to identify the firms with socially desirable values, such as having women on the board of directors or supporting specific social justice issues.

To assist investors in locating and assessing sustainable mutual funds, Morningstar (Morningstar.com) has an ESG rating system. The rating evaluates how effectively each mutual fund invests in a sustainable portfolio and reports using the Morningstar Sustainability Score.

Sustainalytics computes company-level ESG Risk Ratings, which measures the degree to which a company's economic value may be at risk due to ESG factors. **Table 4-2** shows the issues that factor into the ESG Risk Ratings. Notice that they cover a range of ethics, human rights, climate change, etc.

A higher portfolio sustainability risk score represents a worse ESG risk profile. Conversely, a lower sustainability risk score indicates that the mutual fund has a more ESG friendly portfolio. Notice that only 3 of the 20 material ESG issues in **Table 4-2** relate directly to climate change and greenhouse gas measurements. Thus, a company could score poorly in carbon emissions but well on the other 17 material issues, resulting in a moderate sustainability risk category.

actively managed
An investment strategy in which the portfolio manager chooses securities to outperform an index

socially responsible investing (SRI)
An investment strategy in which companies are selected that have positive social impacts

sustainable investing
An investment strategy that considers environmental, social, and corporate governance (ESG) criteria to generate financial returns and positive societal impact

environmental, social, and governance (ESG) investing
an investment strategy in which securities must meet ESG standards

negative screen
A way to select securities by filtering out companies that fail certain criteria

positive screen
A way to select securities by identifying companies that excel in certain criteria

ESG Risk Ratings
A measure of the degree to which a company's economic value may be at risk due to ESG factors

Table 4-2: Twenty Material Issues of Sustainalytics' ESG Risk Ratings

ESG Issue Categories	
Product environmental and social impact	Human rights
Business ethics	Human rights–supply chain
Data privacy and security	Human capital
Bribery and corruption	Access to basic services
Community relations	Resource use
Land use and biodiversity	Resource use–supply chain
Land use and biodiversity–supply chain	Carbon–products and services
Occupational health and safety	Carbon–own operations
Product governance	Emissions, effluents, and waste
Resilience	ESG Integration–financials

You can find these scores for individual companies at the Sustainalytics' website (www.sustainalytics.com/esg-ratings/). For example, the ESG Risk Rating in mid-2021 of several well-known companies are as follows: Apple Inc., 16.7 (Low Risk), Tesla Inc., 31.3 (High Risk), General Electric, 42.6 (Severe Risk), Bank of America, 26.3 (Medium Risk), Facebook Inc., 31.6 (High Risk), and Amazon.com, 27.4 (Medium Risk). Are some of these scores surprising? Tesla might be high because of its car production and the landfill impact of the batteries.

Morningstar uses the Sustainalytics company–level measure to compute an asset-weighted average ESG risk score for each mutual fund portfolio. In addition to the ESG Ratings, Morningstar began reporting fund-level carbon risk in May 2018 to focus more directly on climate change. Morningstar uses the Sustainalytics company–level **Carbon Risk Ratings**. A company's Carbon Risk shows how consistent the firm's activities and products are related to the transition to a low-carbon economy. The score assesses two dimensions: exposure and management. *Exposure* measures the material carbon risks across a firm's entire value chain. *Management* measures a firm's ability to manage reducing emissions and related carbon risks. Morningstar's mutual fund Carbon Risk Score is the asset-weighted sum of the Sustainalytics carbon risk scores of the fund's portfolio holdings. Higher carbon risk scores denote higher carbon risks in the fund's portfolio.

Carbon Risk Ratings
A measure of how consistent a firm's activities and products are related to the transition to a low-carbon economy

Table 4-3: Morningstar Social Responsibility Ratings for Popular U.S. Mutual Funds, August 2021

Mutual Fund	Sustainability				Carbon Risk
	Total	E	S	G	
Fidelity 500 Index Fund	21.48	3.72	10.07	7.65	6.29
American Funds Growth Fund of America Fund	22.79	3.44	10.41	7.76	5.82
T. Rowe Price Value Fund	22.93	4.85	10.11	7.97	9.27
Dodge & Cox International Stock Fund	24.26	4.31	10.56	9.00	10.93
Vanguard FTSE Social Index Fund	20.39	2.71	9.93	7.63	4.25
Calvert US Large-Cap Responsible Index Fund	21.22	3.22	9.89	7.45	5.22
Green Century Balanced Fund	18.05	2.54	8.28	6.81	4.80
Parnassus Mid-Cap Fund	20.83	4.02	9.09	5.92	7.34

You can check Morningstar's sustainability scores and Carbon Risk Score to evaluate how well a mutual fund performs on the ESG and Carbon Risk dimensions. Simply click the *Portfolio* link on the fund's Morningstar page. **Table 4-3** shows scores for four popular mutual funds and four socially responsible– focused funds.

The Fidelity 500 Index Fund replicates the S&P 500 index. Thus, it represents a proxy for the sustainability and carbon risk of the overall U.S. stock market. In August 2021, this index fund had a Sustainability Rating of 21.48 and a Carbon Risk Score of 6.29. Now compare the other three popular funds with the Fidelity 500 Index Fund. For example, the American Funds Growth Fund of America has a higher Sustainability Score than the market overall. This comes from a higher S (social) rating and higher G (governance) rating. Interestingly, it has a lower E (environment) rating. Confirmation of the lower environmental rating comes from the Carbon Risk Score, which is lower than the overall market. The Dodge & Cox International Stock fund has the highest Sustainability Score and Carbon Risk Score of these funds. This may not be surprising because it focuses on owning non-U.S. companies, and many countries have less stringent sustainability laws and enforcement.

Now examine the four popular socially responsible funds. All of them have lower Sustainability Scores than the overall market. Indeed, with one exception, their E, S, and G scores are lower, too. The exception is the Parnassus Mid-Cap Fund's E score. This is confirmed from its higher Carbon Risk score.

Information on socially responsible funds may be obtained from US SIF, the Forum for Sustainable and Responsible Investment (www.ussif.org), a nonprofit organization that promotes the practice of social investing. The US SIF website shows 180 sustainable mutual funds.

4-1d Mutual Fund Returns

Mutual fund performance is best measured by the fund's *total return*, consisting of dividend and interest income and both realized and unrealized appreciation. A fund's total return is reflected by the change in the value of an investment in the fund over time. Mutual funds produce current income for shareholders from investments in interest-bearing securities, such as short-term and long-term bonds, and from dividends paid on common stocks owned by the fund. After expenses, all mutual fund income is paid out to fund shareholders in the form of income distributions. Depending on the type of fund, income distributions may be paid monthly for money market funds and short-term bond funds or on a quarterly, semiannual, or annual basis for stock and long-term bond funds. Fund shareholders can choose to receive income distributions in cash or to have their dividends reinvested in additional shares of the fund. You designate the method of dividend payment when you open an account and can change your selection at any time.

income distribution
Payment of interest and dividends

When securities in the fund portfolio have risen in value, the fund generates unrealized capital gains. Unrealized capital gains raise the net asset value (NAV) of a fund. If a fund sells securities at a profit, a taxable capital gain is realized. Realized capital gains are typically allocated to mutual fund shareholders in December in the form of a capital gains distribution. When a fund pays out realized capital gains, the fund's NAV is reduced by the amount of the distribution. As in the case of income dividends, capital gains distributions may be received by a shareholder in cash or reinvested for further appreciation. Of course, stocks and bonds can also fall in value, and funds periodically incur capital losses that reduce the NAV. Likewise, you can suffer losses on your mutual fund investments by selling shares at a lower price lower than you paid.

unrealized capital gains
An increase in fund value caused by a rise in the value of fund investments

capital gains distribution
Payment of realized capital gains

Excel Expert 4-3

End-of-Year Distributions

A mutual fund in which you own 276.3245 shares begins the last quarter of the year with an NAV of $34.597 per share. At the end of the quarter, the fund declares an income distribution of $0.511 per share and a capital gains distribution of $1.245 per share. Before the distribution, the NAV of the fund is $38.109. If you want your distributions reinvested in more shares, how many shares will you have after the distribution?

	A	B	C	D	E	F
1	Shares owned	276.3245		Combined distribtuion	$ 1.756	=B3+B4
2	NAV start	$ 34.597		Value of distribution	$ 485.226	=E1*B1
3	Income distribution	$ 0.511		NAV after distribution	$ 36.353	=B5-E1
4	Capital gains distribution	$ 1.245				
5	NAV before distribution	$ 38.109		New shares	13.3476	=E2/E3
6				Total shares	289.6721	=B1+E5

If you choose to take the distributions as cash, you get $485.23. If you take additional shares, you get 13.3476 more shares. Investors wanting to build their wealth usually choose to take more shares.

Historical Returns

The return performance of a mutual fund is impacted by its (a) costs, (b) asset allocation, and (c) security selection. As for *costs*, management fees and trading costs have been discussed. The higher the annual costs, the lower the net return of the fund to the investor. For stock funds, *asset allocation* is the type of stocks in the portfolio classified by size and style. This determines its Morningstar category. **Figure 4-3** shows the annual 5-, 10-, and 15-year returns for each category. Note that these returns include the expense ratio costs but not any loads. Paying a load to purchase the fund would reduce the returns. For the previous 15 years (ending June 30, 2021), large blend stocks earned an average 9.82% per year. This beat mid-cap blend (9.31%) and small blend (9.19%). However, index funds beat all three categories and averaged 11.19% per year. Several observations are clear:

- Large-cap funds outperformed mid-cap and small-cap funds
- Growth funds outperformed value funds
- Index funds outperformed large blend funds

Security selection is stock picking. A portfolio full of winners does very well. When a fund picks the wrong stocks, it underperforms is category. Morningstar ranks all the funds within a category and reports each fund's percentile rank. For example, BNY Mellon Appreciation Investor Fund is in the large blend category. In 2018, it selected the wrong stocks for its portfolio and ranked in the 59th percentile. It did much better in 2019 and 2020, ranking in the 4th and 7th percentiles, respectively. Indeed, it is very difficult for a fund to outperform its peers every year.

The easiest way to evaluate a fund's performance is to compare its return to the performance of its category competitors. Morningstar classifies stock funds into the categories shown in **Figure 4-4**, large blend, large growth, etc. **Exhibit 4-1** shows how Morningstar presents a fund's performance. The performance of BlackRock Capital Appreciation, a large growth fund, can be found by using the Performance link on the fund's Morningstar page. Note that in 2020, the fund earned a 40.59% return. Comparing this return to the 1,289 funds in the large growth category shows that its return was

Figure 4-4: Mutual Category Returns over 5, 10, and 15 Years, Ending June 30, 2021

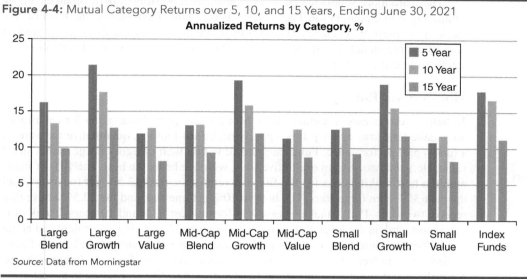

Source: Data from Morningstar

Exhibit 4-1: Morningstar Portfolio Comparison for BlackRock Capital Appreciation K Fund, August 16, 2021

Total Return %	2011	2012	2013	2014	2015	2016	2017	2018	2019	2020	YTD
Investment	-8.78	14.29	34.29	8.72	7.29	0.03	33.19	2.11	32.33	40.59	18.33
+/- Category	-6.32	-1.05	0.37	-1.28	3.69	-3.20	5.52	4.20	0.44	4.73	2.23
+/- Index	-11.42	-0.96	0.81	-4.33	1.63	-7.05	2.98	3.62	-4.06	2.10	0.29
Quartile Rank	☰	☰	☰	☰	☰	☰	☰	☰	☰	☰	☰
Percentile Rank	91	59	44	67	20	79	17	13	48	28	30
# of Investment in Cat.	1,683	1,681	1,712	1,710	1,681	1,463	1,363	1,405	1,360	1,289	1,259

YTD Investment as of Aug 13, 2021 | Category: Large Growth as of Aug 13, 2021 | Index: Russell 1000 Growth TR USD as of Aug 13, 2021

Trailing Returns ⬭ Day End   Month End   Quarter End

	-Day	1-Week	1-Month	3-Month	YTD	1-Year	3-Year	5-Year	10-Year	15-Year
Total Return %	0.31	-0.16	1.83	15.90	18.33	35.57	24.14	24.00	18.37	13.55
+/- Category	0.19	-0.10	0.11	2.34	2.23	2.02	1.61	2.57	0.76	0.91
+/- Index	0.06	-0.33	-0.19	0.76	0.29	0.98	-0.90	0.56	-1.15	-0.54
Quartile Rank	☰	☰	☰	☰	☰	☰	☰	☰	☰	☰
Percentile Rank	20	61	50	23	30	27	32	19	36	30
# of Investments in Cat.	,285	1,285	1,284	1,274	1,259	1,236	1,133	1,019	763	555

USD | Investment return as of Aug 13, 2021 | Category: Large Growth as of Aug 13, 2021 | Index: Russell 1000 Growth TR USD as of Aug 13, 2021 | Inception date Dec 31, 1997 | Time periods greater than 1 year are annualized

higher than the average large growth fund by 4.73%. This stellar performance ranked it in the top 28 percentile. This good performance persisted into the first half of 2021. Note that this BlackRock fund did not beat its competitors every year. It underperformed the large growth average fund in 2011, 2012, 2014, and 2016. Trailing returns shows that the fund earned an annual 24.0% for the past five years, which beat the average category return by 2.57% per year.

There are more sophisticated ways to evaluate a portfolio's performance then by comparing it to a competitor. These methods take into consideration the level of risk taken by the portfolio manager. The rewards for taking risk are discussed in the context of asset pricing models in Chapters 7 and 8. These models lead to formal portfolio evaluation as described in Chapter 9.

Morningstar Ratings

star rating
Morningstar's backward-looking rating for a fund's past performance

To help investors assess mutual funds, Morningstar provides a rating for each fund, often called the star rating. It is a purely backward-looking, quantitative measure of a fund's past performance. Funds are ranked within their category (large blend, small value, etc.) and issued from one to five stars, with five being the best. The 10% of funds with the best rankings receive the five-star rating, the next 22.5% get four stars, and the next 35% earn three stars. The bottom 10% get one star, and the 22.5% above that receive two stars. Performance is assessed for the past 3, 5, and 10 years. Think of it as a report card on the level of the fund's past success. Star ratings are calculated at the end of every month. Note that past performance may not be strongly related to future performance. Indeed, there is much turnover each year in the five-star designed funds. Nevertheless, the mutual funds strongly advertise their five-star rating to attract more investors.

Morningstar Analyst Rating
An analyst grade on expected fund performance

Because the Morningstar star ratings are exclusively backward looking, they also offer the Morningstar Analyst Rating. The analyst rating provides a forward-looking assessment of a fund's ability to outperform its peer group over a full market cycle. Funds are assigned a rating of gold, silver, bronze, neutral, or negative that reflects analysts' conviction in a fund's prospects. Analysts evaluate funds based on five key pillars—people, parent, process, performance, and price. Each analyst evaluation comes from face-to-face interviews with the fund management team, along with analysis of proprietary Morningstar data and fund documents. **Exhibit 4-2** shows examples of Morningstar Star Ratings along with Morningstar Analyst Ratings. Note that the past performance rating, the stars, does not necessarily predict the analyst forward-looking rating. A five-star rating can accompany a bronze or worse analyst rating.

Exhibit 4-2: Examples of Morningstar Star and Analyst Ratings

4-1e Tax Efficiency

While fees affect the fund's return, taxes affect the return the investor retains. Mutual fund returns are before tax are reported before the investor pays the taxes, but income and capital gains taxes affect the final return the investor. **Table 4-4** illustrates how taxable distributions impact the profit of mutual fund investors. Consider three funds that have the same NAV and portfolio return. However, Fund A manages the portfolio in such a manner that no end-of-year distributions are needed, Fund B has an income distribution, and Fund C has a capital gains distribution.

The NAV of each is $20, and each earns a return of 10%. The investor buys one share for $20. Fund A consists solely of stocks that are never sold, so at the end of the second year, the fund's NAV is $22 ($20 × 1.1), and the investor has stock worth $22.

Fund B collects interest of 10% on its debt securities. Thus, during the first year, the fund earns $2 and distributes $2. The fund's earnings initially increase its NAV to $22, but after the $2 income distribution, the NAV returns to $20. The individual reinvests the $2 into 0.1 share and has 1.1 shares worth $22.

Fund C invests in stock that appreciates 10%, then sells it and distributes the gain. The fund's NAV initially increases to $22, but after the $2 capital gain distribution, the NAV returns to $20. The individual reinvests the $2 into 0.1 share and has 1.1 share worth $22.

All three cases end with the investor having a value worth $22. However, there is a tax difference. Fund A had no security sales, and the investor has no tax obligations. Fund B's $2 distribution is subject to income taxes (24% in this example), and Fund C's $2 distribution is subject to capital gains taxation (15% in this example). There is an obvious difference in the investor's tax obligations generated by each fund. After taxes, Fund A provided a higher value (via higher profit), followed by Fund C and then Fund B.

The ability of the fund to generate returns without generating large amounts of tax obligations is the fund's *tax efficiency*. Obviously, if the fund never realizes any capital gains and does not receive any income, there will be no distributions and the investor has no tax obligations. This is unlikely for most holding periods. At the other extreme are the funds that frequently turn over their portfolios. Each security sale is a taxable event. Such frequent turnover implies the fund will not generate long-term capital gains, but rather short-term gains. The capital gains and the distributions will be short term, which are taxed at a higher rate than are long-term gains.

Table 4-4: Demonstration of How Taxable Distributions Impact Investors

	Fund A	Fund B	Fund C
Beginning NAV	$20.00	$20.00	$20.00
Shares owned	1	1	1
Return	10%	10%	10%
Pre-distribution NAV	$22.00	$22.00	$22.00
Distribution	$0.00	$2.00 income	$2.00 capital gains
Post-distribution NAV	$22.00	$20.00	$20.00
Shares owned	1	1.1	1.1
Pre-tax value	$22.00	$22.00	$22.00
Tax (24% income, 15% capital gain)	$0	$0.48	$0.30
After-tax value	$22.00	$21.52	$21.70

If the fund turns over its portfolio less frequently, the capital gains it realizes and the subsequent distributions may be long term. Since long-term capital gains are taxed at favorable (lower) rates, the fund's ability to generate long-term instead of short-term capital gains is more favorable to the investor from a tax perspective.

4-2 Exchange-Traded Funds (ETFs)

The inability of most mutual funds to consistently outperform the market (or outperform an appropriate benchmark) led to increased interest in index mutual funds, which mirror a specific index, as described in the previous section.

Financial markets are not static. New products are developed all the time. Since index mutual funds became very popular, why not a version that can be traded on the equity markets like stocks? Thus, the creation of the index mutual fund led to the development of the exchange-traded fund (ETF). Index mutual funds permit investors to take a position in the market as a whole without having to select individual securities. Purchases and redemptions, however, occur only at the end of the day when the fund's NAV is determined. The first ETF, Standard & Poor's Depositary Receipts, or SPDRs (pronounced "spiders"), tracked the S&P 500 index (ticker: SPY) and overcame this limitation. The shares are bought and sold on an exchange *during operating hours.*

exchange-traded fund (ETF)
A tradeable fund share that mimics an index or basket of stocks

The first SPDR, the SPY, was launched in 1993 and comprised all the stocks in the S&P 500 stock index. The second SPDR was based on the S&P MidCap 400 stock index (ticker MDY) and was followed by nine "Select Sector SPDRs" based on the Standard & Poor's sectors. These sectors include basic industry, consumer products, utilities, health care, financial, technology, and energy stocks. If you believe that large-cap energy companies will do well, you do not have to select specific companies. You can buy the energy SPDRs ETF. Since each sector SPDR includes *virtually all* the stocks in the appropriate subsection, there is no selection process for the ETF. Operating expenses for most ETFs are minimal, and the performance of the SPDR should mirror the return earned by the subsection (e.g., energy).

ETFs have become very popular. There are over 1,000 ETFs sponsored by financial firms like Blackrock, State Street Global Advisors, iShares, Invesco, Vanguard, and others. **Table 4-5** shows the 10 largest ETFs by assets under management (AUM). Note that the top four are tracking the largest part of the U.S. stock market by indexing to

Table 4-5: Ten Largest ETFs by Assets Under Management (AUM), 2021

ETF	Index Tracked	AUM (billion)	Avg. Daily Share Volume (million)
SPDR S&P 500 (SPY)	S&P 500 Index	$388	62.1
iShares Core S&P 500 (IVV)	S&P 500 Index	$296	4.1
Vanguard Stock Market (VTI)	CRSP US Total Market Index	$263	3.3
Vanguard S&P 500 (VOO)	S&P 500 Index	$247	3.6
Invesco QQQ (QQQ)	NASDAQ-100 Index	$182	35.8
Vanguard FTSE Developed Markets (VEA)	FTSE Developed ex-US Index	$104	7.1
iShares Core MSCI EAFE (IEFA)	MSCI EAFE Investable Index	$100	6.9
iShares Core U.S. Aggregate Bond (AGG)	Bloomberg Barclays US Aggregate	$89	5.6
Vanguard Value (VTV)	CRSP US Large Cap Value Index	$84	2.4
Vanguard Growth (VUG)	CRSP US Large Cap Growth Index	$82	0.7

the S&P 500 index or the CRSP U.S. Total Market Index. The fifth largest ETF tracks the Nasdaq-100 Index, which is heavily weighted toward technology stocks. Notice that there are ETFs that track international markets, the bond market, and value and growth styles. The trading value for ETFs is large. Some of the most popular stocks, like Apple, Microsoft, and Alibaba, have an average daily volume that is between 15 million and 80 million shares. Two highly traded ETFs, SPY and QQQ, average 62.1 million and 35.8 million shares daily, respectively.

Their appeal is obvious. The advantages include: (1) portfolio diversification; (2) a passive portfolio with minimal turnover, resulting in lower operating expenses; (3) lower taxes, as the index fund has few realized capital gains; and (4) intraday buying and selling. Consider the SPDRs S&P 500 ETF as an example. Its portfolio represents ownership in the 500 companies in the S&P 500 index and its expense ratio is only 0.095%. Another advantage for sophisticated investors is the opportunity to sell an index short (see Chapter 3). If you believe the stock market, or a sector, is overpriced, you may sell the ETF short. Such short sales are not possible with mutual funds and would require substantial commissions to short all of the individual stocks in the index.

4-2a ETF Pricing and Performance

Because ETFs trade in the secondary markets like stocks, they have a trading price. Selling for less than the NAV is referred to as a **discount**, while selling greater than the NAV is a **premium**. Can the ETF shares have a price that differs from its NAV? The answer is a qualified yes, but any discount or premium should be small.

discount
The difference between the traded price and the NAV when shares are selling for less than the NAV

premium
The difference between the traded price and the NAV when shares are selling for more than the NAV

The reason for the small discount or premium is that ETF shares may be created (and redeemed) by authorized participants. When demand for an ETF rises, a financial institution creates more shares, usually a minimum of 50,000. The financial institution then buys the securities that compose the ETF's portfolio and exchanges them for shares in the ETF. The net effect is the creation of new shares, which satisfies the increased demand for the ETF. The reverse occurs when the supply rises relative to the demand for the ETF. Unlike mutual funds, whose shares are created and redeemed at their NAV at the end of the day, this process for the creation and redemption of ETFs is continuous throughout the day.

Because the ETFs permit large financial institutions to exchange shares in the companies that compose an ETF's portfolio, any difference between the ETF's price and its NAV will be eradicated through the process of creation or redemption of the ETF's shares. Suppose that as a result of increased demand, the ETF sold for a premium. Financial institutions would buy the underlying shares that compose the ETF's portfolio (buy low) and create new ETF shares to sell into the market (sell high). They would make a small profit, which serves as their incentive. The buying of the underlying securities might push those prices slightly up, while the selling of the ETF shares might push those prices slightly down. The net effect is to reduce or eliminate the premium.

The simultaneous buying and selling of ETF shares and the underlying securities is an illustration of **arbitrage**. Arbitrage is the simultaneous selling and buying of the same security or commodity to take advantage of the differences in prices. If the price of the ETF's NAV (which is a measure of the combined prices of the stocks in the ETF portfolio) differs from the trading price of the ETF on the stock exchange, *arbitrage assures that the price differences are erased*. Arbitrage is an important concept in finance and economics because it causes prices to be fair.

arbitrage
The simultaneous buying and selling of securities in different markets to take advantage of price differences

Although the potential for arbitrage assures that an ETF will sell for approximately its NAV, the NAV may not track the index well. Consider an ETF designed to track an index of foreign stocks, such as the EAFE. (The EAFE is an index of major stocks traded in Europe, Australasia, and the Far East.) Suppose the index rises by 10%. The ETF NAV should also increase by 10%. It might not. One reason why the return may be less is the expenses associated with the ETF. The return might be 9.8% after operating expenses are subtracted. Of course, all investment companies have operating expenses, so this discrepancy between the investor's return and the change in the benchmark index should be expected.

There is, however, an important reason why the change in the ETF's value may not be equal to the change in its benchmark. Suppose an ETF mimicked an index that encompassed 100 stocks. To achieve the same percentage change as the benchmark, the ETF would have to *own all 100 stocks in the same proportion as the index.* ETFs rarely do this. Instead, they own a set of stocks that are highly correlated with the index. For example, iShares US Medical Devices (IHI) tracks the Dow Jones U.S. Medical Equipment index. The fund usually invests 90% of its assets in the stocks in the index. The fund, however, does not invest in all the stocks in the index, and over 50% of its assets are in just 10 stocks. The fund may also invest in other assets that management believes will track the index. For this reason, the change in an ETF's price can deviate from the change in the index. The difference is referred to as the **tracking error**. Tracking error is the standard deviation of the difference between the returns of the portfolio and the returns of the benchmark as shown in **Equation 4-3**. If you acquire an ETF with a large tracking error, you may not earn the return generated by the underlying index.t

tracking error
The standard deviation of the difference between the returns of the portfolio and the returns of the benchmark

$$Tracking\ Error = \sqrt{\sum_{t=1}^{n}\left(\frac{[NAV\ Return - Benchmark\ Return]^2}{n-1}\right)} \qquad \textbf{4-3}$$

Excel Expert 4-4

Tracking Error

The annual returns for the Vanguard S&P 500 ETF (SPY) are shown below using the fund's price and the NAV. The index that it tracks is the S&P 500 Index. The index returns are also shown. What is the ETF's tracking error?

	A	B	C	D	E	F
1						
2		Return by NAV	Return by Price	Index Return	Difference	
3	2020	18.35%	18.40%	18.40%	-0.05%	=B3-D3
4	2019	31.46%	31.47%	31.49%	-0.03%	
5	2018	-4.42%	-4.47%	-4.38%	-0.04%	
6	2017	21.78%	21.74%	21.83%	-0.05%	
7	2016	11.93%	12.04%	11.96%	-0.03%	
8	2015	1.35%	1.32%	1.38%	-0.03%	
9	2014	13.63%	13.64%	13.69%	-0.06%	
10	2013	32.33%	32.31%	32.39%	-0.06%	
11	2012	15.98%	16.01%	16.00%	-0.02%	
12	2011	2.09%	2.04%	2.11%	-0.02%	
13						
14				Tracking Error =	0.015%	=STDEV.S(E3:E12)

Source: Vanguard.com

First, note that the return via the NAV is very close to the return via the ETF price. These numbers indicate that there is very little price discount or premium. Now compare the NAV return to the index return. Again, they are very close. The Difference column shows this. The standard deviation of the Difference column is the Tracking Error column, shown to be 0.015%. This is a very small tracking error.

An ETF's expenses and tracking error impact its performance. To assess performance, just like for mutual funds, Morningstar provides its star ratings and analyst ratings for ETFs. Remember, Morningstar compares performance of a fund to its category competitors. However, it does not categorize ETFs separately. Instead, it combines ETFs and mutual funds. An ETF that tracks the S&P 500 index or Total Market Index would be categorized as a large blend fund. Thus, its star ratings derive from its performance relative to all large blend ETFs and mutual funds.

4-2b Investment Objectives of ETFs

While there were only 30 ETFs at the beginning of 2000, the number has subsequently exploded. According to the Investment Company Institute (ICI), the number of ETFs grew to 2,207 by the end of 2020. Total assets under management grew from $6 billion in 2000 to over $5.4 trillion in 2020. Initial ETFs mimicked broad stock indexes, but some new ETFs grew to track other securities, like bonds, while others became increasingly specialized and covered increasingly smaller and more narrowly defined segments of the financial market. **Figure 4-5** shows the AUM for each category of ETF investment objective. Domestic equity that tracks broad stock measures encompass nearly half of the ETF assets, with $2.66 trillion. Domestic sector ETFs hold $521,455 million. Bond ETFs and global equity ETFs are the second and third largest objectives. Examples of bond ETFs are iShares Core U.S. Aggregate Bond ETF and Vanguard Total Bond Market ETF. Examples of global ETFs are iShares Global 100 ETF and SPDR MSCI ACWI ex-US ETF. A much smaller amount of money is being managed in ETFs with a commodity or hybrid investment objective. Examples of commodity ETFs are iShares Gold Trust and Invesco DB Agriculture Fund ETF.

In a sense, ETFs let passive investors actively manage their positions. Instead of having to select individual securities (as active portfolio management requires), you may move between sectors and types of securities. Even if you want to acquire individual assets in a specific sector, ETFs offer flexibility.

Figure 4-5: ETF Assets Under Management by Investment Objective, 2020

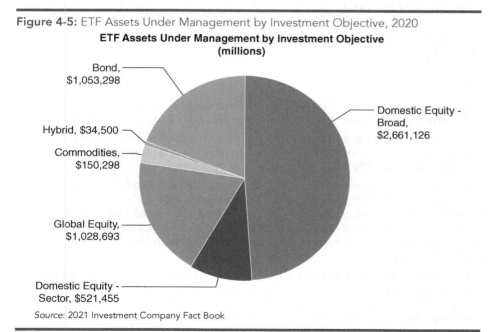

ETF Assets Under Management by Investment Objective (millions)

- Bond, $1,053,298
- Hybrid, $34,500
- Commodities, $150,298
- Global Equity, $1,028,693
- Domestic Equity - Sector, $521,455
- Domestic Equity - Broad, $2,661,126

Source: 2021 Investment Company Fact Book

4-2c Leveraged and Short ETFs

leveraged ETF
An ETF that uses debt and derivative securities to magnify an index's return

One type of ETF that has gained in popularity is the leveraged ETF, which seeks to duplicate a multiple of the daily change in an index. For example, ProShares Ultra Dow30 (DDM) generates a return that is twice the daily performance of the Dow Jones Industrial Average, as measured from its NAV. If the average rises 3%, DDM should generate a return of 6%. Suppose the Dow is 35,000 and the ETF is $75. If the Dow rises by 3% to 36,050 (= 35,000 * 1.03), the ETF should increase by 6% to $70.50 (=$75 * 1.06). Of course, leverage works both ways, so if the average were to decline by 2%, the ProShares Ultra Dow would decline by 4%. Thus, leverage ETFs entail a lot of risk.

Note that if a portfolio owns the 30 companies in the DJIA in the right proportions, it should earn the same return as the DJIA. How do leveraged ETFs obtain two times the return of the DJIA? In other words, how do leveraged ETFs obtain their leverage? They have three ways of gaining leverage and may use all of them simultaneously:

- Overweight the companies that drive the DJIA the most, which are the higher priced stocks (see Chapter 2)
- Borrow money to invest in more stocks of the 30 DJIA, which is called "using margin" (see Chapter 3)
- Use derivative securities, like options and futures, that have leverage as a part of their structure (see Chapters 15 and 16)

How well has ProShares Ultra Dow30 performed? As of the end of the second quarter of 2021, its five-year annualized NAV return was 26.87% when the DJIA earned 16.65%. The 10-year annualized return was 22.12% when the DJIA earned 13.48%. Both historical returns represent about 1.6 times the DJIA return. While it hasn't earned two times the DJIA in the long run, it certainly has demonstrated that its leverage multiplies the index return.

short ETF
An ETF that tries to replicate the opposite direction of an index's daily change

The short ETF seeks a return that is in the opposite direction of its index. When the index is up (down) for the day, the short ETF should be down (up) that day. For example, the ProShares Short Dow30 (DOG) seeks a return that is −1 times the DJIA return for the day. Its 5-year and 10-year annualized returns are −16.40% and

A Walk Down Wall Street

Mutual Funds Are Converting to ETFs

Exchange-traded funds are experiencing enormous growth in popularity and assets under management. The first ETF was introduced in 1993. In less than 30 years, ETF AUM have increase from $0 to over $5.1 trillion.

That growth is expected to continue as investors and financial advisors favor ETFs over mutual funds for their relative lower cost and tax efficiency. Instead of offering new ETFs from scratch, some fund providers are converting some of their existing mutual funds to ETFs.

For example, Guinness Atkinson was the first to convert two of its mutual funds into ETFs and plans to do more. It is converting these funds into its SmartETF structure, which are *actively managed* ETFs. Dimensional Fund Advisors, a global asset manager, introduced its own ETFs in 2020 and then converted four of its U.S. mutual funds to ETFs in 2021. These are to be actively managed ETFs. This made Dimensional one of the largest global active ETF issuers in the industry. JPMorgan announced it plans to convert four mutual funds to actively managed ETFs worth $5 billion in 2022.

This conversion to ETFs also accompanies a new trend in introducing actively managed ETFs. ETFs were built on the foundation of passively tracking indexes. These new actively managed ETFs have a manager or team making decisions on the underlying portfolio allocation instead of following a passive investment strategy. Because these active ETFs have hired managers, they have higher costs then traditional ETFs.

−14.20%, respectively, when the DJIA earned 16.65% and 13.48%. However, investors typically don't hold a short ETF over long periods of time. They hold it over short periods of time when they have concerns about the market and want to hedge their long positions. For example, if you owned the ProShares Short Dow30 during the month-long market decline reaction to COVID-19 (February 12 to March 23, 2020), you would have earned a 48% return when the DJIA declined −37%. To accomplish their objective, the short ETF can short stocks (see Chapter 3) and use derivative securities (see Chapters 14 and 15).

4-3 Closed-End Investment Companies

A security that has some similarity with exchange-traded funds is the **closed-end fund** (CEF). For example, closed-end mutual funds are bought and sold through the securities markets, like ETFs. The shares are originally sold to the public through an initial public offering (IPO) and subsequently traded on an exchange. However, unlike ETFs, no new shares are created after the listing. The number of shares and the dollar amount of debt that the company may issue are pre-specified.

closed-end fund
A mutual fund that trades as a security on an exchange

4-3a Discounts and Premiums

Since the number of shares can't expand and contract to meet changes in demand, CEF shares prices may often deviate from the fund's net asset value (NAV). Thus, while ETF prices are very close to their NAV, a CEF can experience large discounts or premiums to NAV. **Equation 4-4** illustrates the calculation of the CEF discount or premium:

$$Discount\ or\ Premium = \frac{Price - NAV}{NAV} \qquad \textbf{4-4}$$

These differences between the investment company's NAV per share and the stock price are illustrated in **Table 4-6**, which gives the NAV, the price, and the discount or the premium for several closed-end funds.

CLM has a high premium of 20.7%. However, the difference between the fund price and the NAV has varied a lot over time. For example, on March 18, 2020, CLM had a discount of −28.5%. One year later, it had a premium of 37.3%. Note that the discount/premium is not necessarily related to an investment strategy. Both CLM and RVT have a value strategy and yet one has a premium and the other a discount.

Table 4-6: Examples of Closed-End Funds with Large Discounts and Premiums, August 20, 2021

Closed-End Fund	Ticker	NAV	Price	Discount or Premium
Cornerstone Strategic Value	CLM	$10.29	$12.42	20.7%
John Hancock Financial Opportunities	BTO	$36.81	$41.15	11.8%
Gabelli Multimedia	GGT	$8.83	$9.54	8.0%
Royce Value Trust	RVT	$20.11	$18.25	−9.3%
MQ Global Infrastructure	MGU	$27.36	$23.73	−13.3%
Eagle Capital Growth	GRF	$11.44	$9.29	−19.0%

The cause of this price to NAV difference is not really known. But it likely includes several factors. First, the number of shares can't adjust to demand changes like an ETF. Second, the portfolio is actively managed so the contents of the portfolio may only be transparent once per quarter when the fund must report to the SEC. There may also be a potential capital gains taxation impact if some funds are expected to have a capital gains distribution.

Investors in closed-end funds earn returns in a variety of ways. First, if the CEF collects dividends and interest on its portfolio, this income is distributed to the stockholders. Second, if the value of the firm's assets increases, the company may sell the assets and realize the gains. These profits are then distributed as capital gains. Such distributions usually occur in a single payment near the end of the calendar year and, for most individuals, the tax year. Third, the NAV of the portfolio may increase, which will cause the market price of the company's stock to rise. In this case, the investor may sell the shares in the secondary market and realize a capital gain. Fourth, the market price of the shares may rise relative to the NAV (i.e., the premium may increase, or the discount may decrease).

Some investors view the status of a discount or premium as an indicator to buy and sell CEFs. If the shares are selling for a sufficient discount, they are considered for purchase. If the shares are selling for a small discount or at a premium, they are sold. However, this strategy often frustrates investors because discounts sometimes get larger. Consider that you buy a CEF with a price of $18 and NAV of $20. This CEF is trading at a −10% discount (= [$18 − $20]/$20). You hope the discount closes to zero or even becomes a premium to capture a nice return. But a change in the discount can occur through either a change in the price, NAV, or both. The NAV can rise to $21, but the price could stay the same, increasing the discount. The NAV could remain the same and the price could fall, which also increases the discount and gives you a loss. The best scenario is when the NAV rises and the price rises more, closing the discount. In that case, you would earn a return higher than the NAV return. Regardless, CEF investing includes an additional investment risk that mutual funds and ETFs do not suffer— price to NAV discount/premium risk.

Closed-end funds are not nearly as popular as mutual funds or ETFs. The ICI reports that total assets managed within the CEF structure at the end of 2020 was $279 billion, which is only about 5.5% of the assets in ETFs. While the investment objective for CEFs varies from equities to bonds, they have found a niche in the fixed income arena. **Figure 4-6** shows that 62% of CEF portfolios are targeted to fixed income, whether they focus on global bonds, domestic municipal bonds, or domestic taxable bonds.

4-3b Unit Trusts

unit trust
Privately held type of closed-end fund

A variation on the closed-end fund is the fixed-unit investment trust, commonly referred to as a **unit trust** or unit investment trust (UIT). These trusts, which are formed by brokerage firms and sold to investors, hold a fixed portfolio of securities. The portfolio is designed to meet a specified investment objective, such as the generation of interest income, in which case the portfolio would include federal government or corporate bonds, municipal bonds, or mortgage loans.

A unit trust is a passive investment, as its assets are not traded but frozen. No new securities are purchased, and securities originally purchased are rarely sold. The trust collects income (e.g., interest on its portfolio) and, eventually, the repayment of principal. The trust is self-liquidating because as the funds are received, they are not reinvested but distributed to stockholders. Such trusts are primarily attractive to retirees who seek a steady, periodic flow of payments. If the investor needs the funds earlier,

Figure 4-6: CEF Investment Objectives Composition, 2020

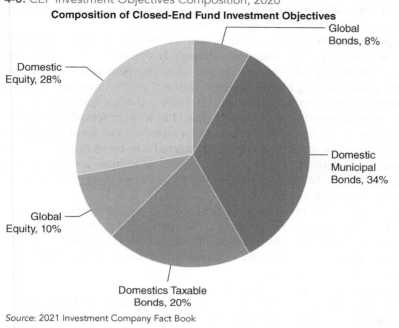

Composition of Closed-End Fund Investment Objectives

Source: 2021 Investment Company Fact Book

the shares may be sold back to the trust at their current NAV, which may be lower than the initial cost.

Unit trusts are also of interest to investors whose financial goals are matched by the objectives of the trust. Such individuals acquire shares in a diversified portfolio of assets that are sold in affordable units. Unlike other investment companies, the fixed portfolio means that operating expenses, which would reduce the current flow of income to the owners of the trust, are minimal.

As with any investment, however, unit trusts do have disadvantages. The investor pays an initial up-front fee of 3–5% when the trust is formed, and even though there are minimal management fees, the trustees do have custodial expenses that are paid from the earnings of the trust. Although a trust may acquire high-quality debt instruments, there is no certainty that the bonds will not default. There is always the risk that the realized return may be less than anticipated.

The ICI reports that unit trusts managed only $73 billion of assets at the end of 2020, which is only 1.5% of the assets managed through ETFs.

4-4 Hedge Funds

The word *hedge* generally implies a course of action designed to reduce risk, and the phrase "hedge fund" might imply a type of mutual fund that pursues low-risk strategies. However, neither inference is correct. Hedge funds (and private equity firms) are pools of money that are used to acquire a variety of assets with the intent to earn high returns or produce return streams other than traditional stock and bond portfolios. Investments with return streams that are different from stocks and bonds increase an investor's ability to diversify. The strategies employed often require taking substantial

hedge fund
A limited partnership of investors in a portfolio using high-risk methods seeking high returns

risks and may not be allowed within a mutual fund. A simple example is that a hedge fund portfolio could consist entirely of one company stock, like Tesla. Mutual funds have diversification rules that would prevent this strategy.

In order to use investment strategies that are not available to mutual funds, hedge funds must raise capital in nonpublic offerings. Hedge funds are generally organized as limited partnerships: the fund's managers serve as general partners, while the investors are limited partners. Hedge funds are "private" organizations that generally limit the number of investors to fewer than 100. Each individual (or financial institution, such as an endowment fund or pension plan) has to meet specified criteria in order to participate. Accredited investors need a minimum net worth of $1,000,000 and minimum annual income of $200,000. The required investment is also substantial, with minimums of $1,000,000 being common. Because hedge funds are private, they are not subject to many of the disclosure requirements and other regulations associated with public investment companies.

Hedge fund portfolio managers are exceedingly well compensated through salary and performance bonuses. The hedge fund fee structure for many decades was typically referred to as a 2 and 20. This represents a management fee that is 2% of the value of the assets under management and an incentive fee that is 20% of the fund's performance. This is a very large cost to investors. Hedge funds would have to really perform well to overcome such high costs to investors.

If the fund does not generate a positive return in a given year, the investors still pay the management fee. If the fund loses 10%, the managers continue to collect the 2% of the NAV, but there is no incentive fee that year. (A $1 billion portfolio generates a fee of $20,000,000!) In many cases, the performance bonus may not be restored until the fund recoups the lost 10%, which is referred to as the high-water mark. But fund managers may get around this inconvenience by closing and liquidating the fund and starting a new hedge fund. This process wipes out the poor performance and ends the need to recoup the losses before performance bonuses are resumed.

Since a hedge fund is private, no secondary market exists for its shares. Once the individual invests in a hedge fund, that person cannot sell the shares. The fund generally has a withdrawal policy to define when and how an investor may liquidate a position. There are, however, significant limitations on the withdrawals. For example, the hedge fund may refuse to repurchase shares until a period of time has elapsed. A one-year lockup is not unusual, and longer periods are common. One reason that a hedge fund uses a lengthy lockup is because their strategy may involve long-term investments. For example, a hedge fund could fund a movie production. The fund may also limit repurchases to some percentage of the outstanding shares. These exit policies should be clearly detailed in the fund's general offering statement, and a potential investor should obviously read that statement carefully prior to acquiring the shares.

Traditional mutual funds are precluded from using risky strategies—such as selling short or buying stocks and bonds of firms in bankruptcy—but hedge funds may follow such strategies. A common hedge fund practice is to buy a particular stock and simultaneously short another. If the fund's analysts thought that Home Depot was undervalued relative to Lowe's, the fund would buy Home Depot and short Lowe's. The proceeds of the short sale would be used to cover the cost of the long position. Of course, identical movements in the two stocks would offset each other. A $1 increase in Home Depot would be offset by a $1 increase in Lowe's if the same number of shares were bought and sold short. But that is not the point. The expectation is that Home Depot will increase relative to Lowe's or that Lowe's will decline relative to Home Depot. If the analysis is correct and Home Depot proves to be undervalued relative to Lowe's, the gains more than offset the losses. The price of Home Depot rises more than the price of

accredited investor
A sophisticated investor requiring a minimum $1 million in net worth and $200,000 in annual income

high-water mark
The highest end-of-year value of a portfolio

lockup
The amount of time an investor is prevented from redeeming shares

Excel Expert 4-5

Hedge Fund Fees Scenarios

Consider a hedge fund that charges the traditional 2 and 20 fees. That is a 2% management fee on assets and a 20% incentive fee on profits over a threshold of 8%. Also, losses need to be made up before incentive fees are paid. Assume you invest $1 million in the fund, and it earns the five years of pre-fee returns shown in column B. Hedge funds take the management fee quarterly, but we will assume end-of-year (EOY) management fee and incentive fee payments here. Given the portfolio returns, what are the fee payments and your return each year?

	A	B	C	D	E	F	G	H	I	J	K
1			Management Fee	2%							
2			Incentive Fee	20%							
3			Threshold Level	8%							
4			Initial Investment	$ 1,000,000		=D7*$D$1		=IF((F8-I7)-I7*(C8)>0,$D$2*((F8-I7)-I7*(C8)),0)			
5											
6	Year	Fund Return	Threshold Level	Value Pre-Fees	Mgt Fee	Post Mgt Fee Value	Incentive	Total Fees	EOY Value	Investor Return	
7	1	18.0%	8.0%	$ 1,180,000	$ 23,600	$ 1,156,400	$ 15,280	$ 38,880	$ 1,141,120	14.11%	
8	2	-10.0%	8.0%	$ 1,027,008	$ 20,540	$ 1,006,468	$ -	$ 20,540	$ 1,006,468	-11.80%	=(I8-I7)/I7
9	3	15.0%	18.0%	$ 1,157,438	$ 23,149	$ 1,134,289	$ -	$ 23,149	$ 1,134,289	12.70%	
10	4	11.0%	8.6%	$ 1,259,061	$ 25,181	$ 1,233,880	$ 403	$ 25,585	$ 1,233,477	8.74%	
11	5	25.0%	8.0%	$ 1,541,846	$ 30,837	$ 1,511,009	$ 35,771	$ 66,608	$ 1,475,238	19.60%	
12											
13		=(I7-I9)/I9+D3			Sum =	$ 123,307		$ 51,454	$ 174,761		
14			=I10*(1+B11)								

For the first year, the 18% return builds the value of the investment to $1,180,000. After the 2% management fee of $23,600, the value drops to $1,156,400. The incentive fee is paid as 20% of all profits above an 8% return. Note that 8% of the $1,000,000 beginning-of-year value is $80,000. Thus, the incentive fee is paid on $76,400 (=$156,400 − $80,000) of the profit for a fee of $15,280 (=0.20 * $76,400). While the hedge fund portfolio earned 18%, after fees, you only earned 14.11%. Note from the spreadsheet that no incentive fee is paid in year 2 because the fund lost money. No incentive fee is paid in year 3 because the fund had not reached the high-water mark of the loss plus 8% threshold. Because it did not reach the high-water mark in year 3, there is still some makeup needed in year 4. Thus, the profit needs to be 8.6% in year 4 to reach the high-water market.

Lowe's, and the two positions generate a net profit. Note that this strategy is independent of the overall move in the stock market. In other words, this strategy could earn a profit in an up market and a down market.

While such a combination of a long and a short may appear to be a hedge position, it is not. The strategy may produce large losses and is certainly not comparable to true hedge positions, which are neutral. The above positions using Home Depot do not lock in a price but are designed to take advantage of an anticipated price change in one stock relative to the other. If the anticipated price changes were to occur, the strategy would generate a profit. If, however, the price of Lowe's rises relative to Home Depot, the loss on the short in Lowe's would exceed the gain on the long position in Home Depot, and there would be a net loss on the strategy.

Table 4-7 shows the difference between mutual funds and hedge funds in four key areas: investors, fees, investment practices, and pricing. Mutual funds are available to the public, while hedge funds are only available to accredited investors. Thus, you may see many mutual funds advertisements, but you will not see hedge fund ads. Mutual fund costs are generally much lower than hedge funds costs. Can a hedge fund earn a high enough return pre-fees to overcome these high costs? Sure, but they may not do so consistently. A major difference between the two types of funds is how they invest.

Table 4-7: Comparison of Mutual Funds and Hedge Funds

	Mutual Funds	Hedge Funds
Who invests	100 million Americans own mutual fund shares. The only qualification for investing is having the minimum investment to open an account with a fund company—often $1,000 or less.	Only accredited investors are eligible to invest. The typical investor is a wealthy individual or an institution such as a pension fund. A minimum investment of $1 million or more is often required.
Fees	Mutual fund shareholders pay, on average, an annual expense ratio of roughly 1.2% of assets. Index funds expense ratios are much less. Sales charges and other distribution fees are subject to specific regulatory limits.	Hedge fund investors often pay a portfolio management fee of 1 to 2% of net assets, plus a performance-based fee that can run as high as 20% of profits per year. Fees are not subject to specific regulatory limits.
Investment practices	Securities laws restrict a mutual fund's ability to leverage, or borrow against, the value of securities in its portfolio. Investment policies must be fully disclosed to investors in the prospectus.	High leverage strategies are common. Investment policies do not have to be disclosed, even to investors in the fund.
Pricing and liquidity	Mutual funds must value their portfolio securities and compute their NAV daily. They generally must also allow shareholders to redeem shares on at least a daily basis.	There are no specific rules on valuation or pricing. As a result, hedge fund investors may be unable to determine the value of their investment at any given time. In addition, lockups often apply to new investors.

Source: Investment Company Institute

Hedge funds often borrow substantial amounts of money to leverage their portfolios, a practice very limited for mutual funds. Hedge funds also use derivative securities to execute investment strategies that are not available to mutual funds. Lastly, there is a lot of transparency in what mutual funds portfolio hold and their values. However, hedge fund portfolio compositions are purposely kept secret so competitors can't steal their investment ideas.

Hedge fund portfolio managers have nearly complete discretion as to how to run the fund. In addition, they often create highly leveraged portfolios. By doing this, small changes in the prices of the assets they hold can create large returns—positive and negative. Thus, their strategies have led to some large hedge fund losses:

- In 2006, Amaranth lost $6 billion in a matter of days. The fund took large positions in natural gas that were heavily leveraged (i.e., financed with debt). When natural gas prices declined, the value of Amaranth's assets declined from over $9 billion to $3.5 billion. For example, the London-based hedge fund White Square Capital had to close its doors.
- Melvin Capital Management was one of the best-performing hedge funds until it took large positions against retail investors in meme-stocks such as GameStop, AMC, and others in January 2021. Melvin lost more than $6 billion, or 54.5%, in just a few weeks. Melvin wasn't the only hedge fund to lose billions of dollars during this short-squeeze event.
- Madoff Investment Securities, LLC, was a well-respected hedge fund for decades. It turned out to be a Ponzi scheme that scammed investors out of about $65 billion. Bernard L. Madoff pleaded guilty to multiple federal crimes of fraud, money laundering, perjury, and theft and was sentenced to 150 years in prison.
- Perhaps the most important hedge fund failure occurred in 1998. Long-Term Capital Management (LTCM) had an equity base of $4.5 billion but was able to borrow more than $200 billion. While this huge amount of leverage initially produced spectacular results for the investors, the collapse of the Russian financial system led to widespread selling of poorer-quality debt. LTCM was unable to liquidate its positions and sustained large losses. In the end, the Federal Reserve stepped in and essentially forced large banks to put in additional funds. Note that other hedge funds took positions against LTCM's portfolio and profited from the debacle.

Despite these disastrous outcomes, the hedge fund industry is still large. Five of the largest funds are Bridgewater Associates, Renaissance Technologies, Man Group, Millennium Management, and Elliott Management. Barclay Hedge reports that in mid-2021, hedge funds had over $4 trillion in assets under management.

Private equity firms are also large pools of cash but are different from hedge funds. While hedge funds use a variety of strategies to increase returns, the primary objective of private equity firms is to make large, focused investments. For example, an equity firm may use its cash to acquire a company and take it private. The intent is to make the acquired firm exceedingly profitable (often through aggressively cutting costs) and then sell the firm to another company or to resell the firm to public stockholders through an IPO. If the acquired firm does prosper and the company is sold, the private equity firm may reap a large return on its investment. In a variation on this strategy, a firm with a minority of public stockholders may be taken private. The majority stockholders (often a family or the firm's management) use the help of a private equity firm. After the minority stockholders are bought out, the company becomes private. Once the firm is private, SEC and Sarbanes–Oxley disclosure requirements no longer apply. Management may then direct the firm without the oversight and regulations imposed on publicly held firms.

private equity firm
A private investment firm that purchases, operates, and resells companies

Hedge funds and private equity firms are obviously not appropriate for and not available to the vast majority of investors. They do, however, appeal to a select group of investors, and the dollar amount invested in hedge and private equity firms has grown dramatically. Their alleged advantages include higher returns and the potential for diversification of a traditional portfolio. The word *alleged* applies because returns cannot be verified. Hedge funds self-report their returns. While funds with high returns have an incentive to announce superior results, funds with inferior returns need not report their performance. All mutual funds must report returns, so an average fund return encompasses the best and the worst performers. An average of hedge fund returns, however, will have an upward bias if inferior-performing funds are excluded from the calculation.

Their potential for diversifying a traditional stock and bond portfolio is also difficult to verify. To do so, you need to know the hedge fund's monthly returns to compare them to traditional portfolios. Failure to report returns or the selective reporting of returns increases the difficulty of estimating meaningful comparisons.

One means to overcome or at least reduce these disadvantages is to acquire shares in a fund that invests in different hedge funds. This fund of funds offers the potential for diversification since it owns positions in several hedge funds. Presumably, the management of a fund of funds has better access to information and may be able to make more informed investment decisions. However, from the individual's perspective, these funds are expensive, since the investor *pays two sets of management fees,* one to the managers of the fund of funds and a second to the managers of the hedge funds acquired by the fund of funds.

fund of funds
A mutual fund that owns the shares of other mutual funds

4-5 Real Estate Investment Trusts (REITs)

Buying, building, and managing real estate properties take an enormous amount of time, expertise, and capital. One of the easiest and most promising ways for investors with limited time and expertise to effectively invest in real estate is through publicly traded real estate investment trusts (REITs). There are over 225 publicly traded REITs, most trading on the NYSE. Real estate investment trusts are a special form of closed-end fund that focuses on real estate investments rather than stock or bond

real estate investment trust (REIT)
A publicly traded company that manages property and/or mortgage loans

portfolios. For REITs, the investment portfolio comprises a pool of real estate assets that may include real estate property or loans on real estate property. To qualify as an REIT, the trust must distribute at least 90% of its taxable income to shareholders annually in the form of dividends. Thus, REITs are popular for investors seeking income. An example is Camden Property Trust, a real estate company engaged in the ownership, development, acquisition, management, and disposition of multifamily apartment communities. It trades on the New York Stock Exchange under the ticker symbol CPT. As of July 2021, it owned interests in or operated 169 multifamily properties containing 57,611 apartment units located across the United States. A big advantage that REITs have over direct real estate ownership is liquidity. They can be easily and quickly bought and sold with minimal transaction costs, just like stocks. For example, on August 20, 2021, there were 546,670 shares of Camden Property Trust that traded at over $146 per share.

The price performance of REITs over time also gives a good benchmark to judge the performance of real estate investing. The National Association of Real Estate Investment Trusts (Nareit) is the REIT industry's association (see www.reit.com). Members are REITs and other businesses that own, operate, and finance income-producing real estate. The association develops and follows REIT indexes. According to the Nareit, the FTSE All REITs index represents a market capitalization of $1.58 trillion as of July 2021. **Figure 4-7** shows how a $1,000 investment would grow if it were invested at the end of 1999 in the stock market and in three REIT indexes. Note that the FTSE Nareit All REITs index ends 2020 with over $8,038, which is more than double the S&P 500 index investment, which ends at only $3,765. This includes the real estate crisis of 2007/2008.

REITs own and operate everything from golf courses and casinos to self-storage units and hospital buildings. REITs are commonly categorized by the type of real estate assets owned and by their focus on equity or debt instruments. Equity REITs own real properties, and their value is determined by the value of their real estate holdings and the cash flow generated. Over 90% of publicly traded REITs are equity REITs. The market capitalization of the All Equity REITs Index was $1.06 trillion in July 2021. Mortgage REITs lend money to owners and developers of real estate and purchase existing mortgages or mortgage-backed securities. The price of mortgage REITs is determined by the net interest generated and the credit quality of their loan portfolios. Hybrid REITs

equity REIT
An REIT with an ownership position in real estate

mortgage REIT
An REIT that invests in real estate–oriented debt

hybrid REIT
An REIT that generates income from real estate debt and equity

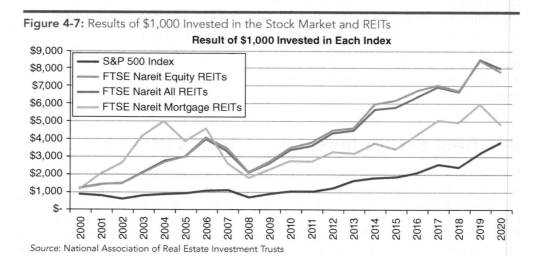

Figure 4-7: Results of $1,000 Invested in the Stock Market and REITs

Source: National Association of Real Estate Investment Trusts

Table 4-8: Annual Return Statistics for Stocks and REITs, 1975 to 2020

	S&P 500 Index	FTSE Nareit All REITs	FTSE Nareit Equity REITs	FTSE Nareit Mortgage REITs
Average Return	13.46%	13.43%	14.22%	10.91%
Median Return	15.90	15.16	16.66	16.26
Min. Return	−35.49	−37.34	−37.73	−42.35
Max. Return	37.40	48.97	47.59	77.34
Std Dev.	16.10	17.99	17.07	26.85
Correlation with Stocks		0.47	0.46	0.25

combine the investment strategies of equity REITs and mortgage REITs by investing in both properties and mortgages. **Figure 4-7** also shows the performance of the FTSE Nareit Equity and Mortgage REITs Indexes. Since 90% of REITs are equity REITs, the All REITs Index and the Equity REITs Index have similar performance.

While **Figure 4-7** shows that REITs experienced better performance since 2000, **Table 4-8** shows that the average annual return on REITs since 1975 has been much closer to the S&P 500 index return. The average return for stocks is 13.46%, which is similar to the All REITs Index average of 13.43%. The Equity REITs Index return is a little higher, but the Mortgage REITs Index average is much lower, at 10.91%. The REITs indexes are very volatile. That can be seen from their larger range (minimum to maximum returns) and high standard deviation of returns. The Mortgage REITs Index is especially volatile. The concept of correlation is introduced in Chapter 6. However, knowledgeable investors know that the relatively low level of correlation of 0.47 between stocks and REITs means that some risk reduction can be achieved in a portfolio that combines REITs and stocks. The opportunity for risk reduction is even greater with stocks and mortgage REITs.

Equity REITs and mortgage REITs have very different return characteristics. Equity REITs have earned an average 14.22% annual return during the period of 1975 to 2020, while mortgage REITs have returned only 10.91%, on average. Mortgage REITs have earned lower returns with a much higher volatility. This may explain why equity REITs have dominated mortgage REITs over the last 45 years in popularity.

4-5a Real Estate Stocks and Mutual Funds

Investors also get some real estate exposure in their portfolios through common stock ownership. The companies that own, manage, and develop hotels, resorts, and time-share properties have values that are closely tied to the real estate industry. Examples include Hyatt Hotels Corporation (ticker: H) and Marriott International, Inc. (ticker: MAR). Both can be thought of as real estate companies.

While Marriott is similar to an equity REIT, the government-sponsored enterprise known as Fannie Mae (ticker: FNMA) is similar to mortgage REITs. Fannie provides loans for the acquisition or refinancing of homes and multifamily apartment buildings. The company focuses on increasing the supply of funds that mortgage lenders can make available to homebuyers and multifamily investors. It primarily buys mortgages from lenders, creates pools of such mortgages, and then sells these mortgage-backed securities to investors. In addition, Fannie holds a $160 billion mortgage portfolio of its own.

In addition to investing in REITs and real estate–oriented companies, investors can also invest in mutual funds that have a real estate emphasis. There are hundreds of real estate mutual funds available. These funds invest in a portfolio of REITs and real estate–oriented companies. While an investor can easily and quickly obtain a diversified real estate portfolio through mutual funds, the investor pays a cost in the form of management fees and loads.

Investors can also get a diversified exposure to real estate investment opportunities using ETFs with a real estate focus. The iShares Cohen & Steers REIT ETF (ticker: ICF) tracks the Cohen & Steers Realty Majors Index, which is broadly diversified by both geographic region and property type through 30 REITS. The iShares U.S. Real Estate Index Fund (IYR) tracks the Dow Jones REIT Composite Index. The performance characteristics of these two exchange-traded funds are similar.

Conclusion

Instead of directly investing in securities, individuals may buy shares in investment companies. These firms, in turn, invest the funds in various assets, such as stocks and bonds. This chapter reviews these financial firms, particularly mutual funds, ETFs, closed-end funds, unit trusts, hedge funds, and REITs.

Mutual funds offer professional management, diversification, and custodial services. Dividends and the interest earned on the firm's assets are distributed to stockholders in either cash or additional shares. In addition, if the value of the fund's assets rises, the shareholders profit as capital gains are realized and distributed. Mutual funds may be classified by the types of assets they own. Some stress income-producing assets—such as bonds, preferred stock, and common stock of firms—that distribute a large proportion of their income. Other mutual funds stress growth in their NAVs through investments in firms with the potential to grow and generate capital gains. A disadvantage to owning mutual funds is the expenses and load fees.

ETF shares trade through the secondary securities markets, so they may be readily bought and sold by investors. As the result of an arbitrage process, the price of an ETF tends to equal its NAV. The first ETFs tracked an aggregate market index such as the S&P 500 stock index. Subsequently, ETFs were created to track sectors of the S&P 500 and to track other indexes or to replicate investment strategies.

Closed-end funds are like ETFs in that they trade in the secondary securities markets. Their structure is different, however, which leads to the shares often selling for a premium above, or a discount from, the NAV. Returns from an investment in a closed-end fund are earned from distributions, increases in the fund's market price, and changes in the discount or premium relative to the fund's NAV.

Hedge funds and private equity firms offer a small number of investors an alternative to traditional assets. Hedge funds frequently employ risky strategies to increase returns. Participation in a hedge fund is limited to individuals and institutions such as endowment funds or pension plans with substantial cash to invest. Hedge funds and private equity firms are not publicly traded. These alternative investments are appropriate only for investors who understand and can accept the risk associated with these funds.

REITs are investment companies that specialize in real estate and trade on secondary exchange markets. REITs make loans to develop properties, originate and acquire mortgage loans, or manage properties such as apartments and shopping malls and lease the buildings to tenants such as Wal-Mart stores. REITs offer individuals a means to invest in real estate without owning and operating the properties.

Chapter Equations

$$NAV = \frac{Total\ Value\ of\ Securities\ -\ liabilities}{Number\ of\ Shares}$$

4-1

$$Offer\ Price = \frac{NAV}{(1\ -\ Load\ Fee)}$$

4-2

$$Tracking\ Error = \sqrt{\sum_{t=1}^{n}\left(\frac{[NAV\ Return\ -\ Benchmark\ Return]^2}{n-1}\right)}$$

4-3

$$Discount\ or\ Premium = \frac{Price\ -\ NAV}{NAV}$$

4-4

Excel Functions

STDEV.S(number1,[number2],…)   IF(logical_test,[value_if_true],[value_if_false])

Key Terms

12b-1 fees – Marketing expenses charged to the mutual fund shareholder

accredited investor – A sophisticated investor requiring a minimum $1 million in net worth and $200,000 in annual income

actively managed – An investment strategy in which the portfolio manager chooses securities to outperform an index

arbitrage – The simultaneous buying and selling of securities in different markets to take advantage of price differences

asset-based fee – A fee charged as a percentage of the assets under management

back-end load – Commissions paid when a fund is sold

blended fund – A fund that buys stocks and debt instruments

bond fund – A fund that buys debt instruments

capital gains distribution – Payment of realized capital gains

Carbon Risk Ratings – A measure of how consistent a firm's activities and products are related to the transition to a low-carbon economy

closed-end fund – A mutual fund that trades as a security on an exchange

contrarian – An investor who goes against the consensus concerning investment strategy

discount – The difference between the traded price and the NAV when shares are selling for less than the NAV

environmental, social, and governance (ESG) investing – an investment strategy in which securities must meet ESG standards

equity REIT – An REIT with an ownership position in real estate

ESG Risk Ratings – A measure of the degree to which a company's economic value may be at risk due to ESG factors

exchange-traded fund (ETF) – A tradeable fund share that mimics an index or basket of stocks

expense ratio – Total fees and trading costs expressed as a percentage of fund assets

front-end load – A commission paid at the time of a fund purchase

fund family – A mutual fund firm that offers many portfolio choices

fund of funds – A mutual fund that owns the shares of other mutual funds

hedge fund – A limited partnership of investors in a portfolio using high-risk methods seeking high returns

high-water mark – The highest end-of-year value of a portfolio

hybrid REIT – An REIT that generates income from real estate debt and equity

income distribution – Payment of interest and dividends

index fund – A fund whose portfolio mimics a specific index of the market

investment style – A fund's investment philosophy or strategy

investment type – The kind of securities held by the fund, such as stocks or bonds

lifecycle fund – A blended fund that starts with higher equity allocation and slowly changes to higher debt securities allocation as the retirement date nears

leveraged ETF – An ETF that uses debt and derivative securities to magnify an index's return

lockup – The amount of time an investor is prevented from redeeming shares

load fee – A sales commission

low-load fund – A fund that charges sales fees ranging from 1 to 3%

management fee – A fee charged against the portfolio to fund the operation of fund

market timing – The attempt to time the purchase and sale of securities to market lows and highs, respectively

momentum strategy – The strategy of buying and holding securities that have been rising

money market mutual fund – A fund that invests in cash reserves, or short-term IOUs

Morningstar Analyst Rating – An analyst grade on expected fund performance

mortgage REIT – An REIT that invests in real estate–oriented debt

mutual fund – An open-end investment company

negative screen – A way to select securities by filtering out companies that fail certain criteria

net asset value (NAV) – A per-share value of a mutual fund's stock, bond, and cash reserve holdings

no-load fund – A mutual fund that does not charge a commission for buying or selling shares

open-end fund – A mutual fund that continuously offers to sell and buy shares

passively managed – An investment style in which securities are not chosen by a manager but instead identified in an index

positive screen – A way to select securities by identifying companies that excel in certain criteria

premium – The difference between the traded price and the NAV when shares are selling for more than the NAV

private equity firm – A private investment firm that purchases, operates, and resells companies

real estate investment trust (REIT) – A publicly traded company that manages property and/or mortgage loans

sector rotation – A form of market timing in which investors rotate between sectors over time

short ETF – An ETF that tries to replicate the opposite direction of an index's daily change

socially responsible investing (SRI) – An investment strategy in which companies are selected that have positive social impacts

star rating – Morningstar's backward-looking rating for a fund's past performance

stock fund – A fund that makes equity investments

style box – Morningstar's depiction of a fund's portfolio expressed in market capitalization and value/growth orientation

sustainable investing – An investment strategy that considers environmental, social, and corporate governance (ESG) criteria to generate financial returns and positive societal impact

tracking error – The standard deviation of the difference between the returns of the portfolio and the returns of the benchmark

unit trust – Privately held type of closed-end fund

unrealized capital gains – An increase in fund value caused by a rise in the value of fund investments

Questions

1. **Mutual Fund Advantages and Disadvantages.** What are the advantages and disadvantages of owning mutual funds? (LO 4-1)

2. **Mutual Fund Costs.** Describe the different costs of buying, owning, and selling mutual funds. (LO 4-2)

3. **Mutual Fund Objectives.** What are the various investment objectives and Morningstar categories for mutual funds? (LO 4-3)

4. **Mutual Fund Performance.** How can you assess a mutual fund's performance over time? (LO 4-4)

5. **ETF Advantages.** What advantages do ETFs have over mutual funds? (LO 4-5)

6. **ETF Investment Objectives.** What are the various investment objectives of ETFs? (LO 4-6)

7. **ETF vs. Closed-End Funds.** Compare and contrast closed-end funds with ETFs. (LO 4-7)

8. **Premiums and Discounts.** What are fund premiums and discounts and how do they complicate fund performance? (LO 4-8)

9. **Hedge Fund Objectives.** Describe a hedge fund structure. What are the primary differences between hedge funds and mutual funds, from the investor's perspective? (LO 4-9)

10. **REIT Objectives.** What are real estate investment trusts? Describe the various REIT investment objectives. (LO 4-10)

Problems

1. **NAV Calculation.** Suppose a mutual fund owned $322.2 million in stocks, owned $417.8 million in bonds, had $50.2 million in cash, had $1.3 million in liabilities, and had 25.6681 million shares outstanding. (LO 4-2)

   a. What is the fund's NAV?
   b. The next day, the stock portion of the portfolio increases by 0.7% and the bond portion declines by 0.2%. The cash, liabilities, and shares outstanding remain unchanged. What is the new NAV?
   c. What is the return for investors that day?

2. **Open-End Fund.** An open-end fund closes the day with an NAV of $56.684, total assets of $344,883,045, and shares outstanding of 6,084,310.299. You buy $8,000 worth of shares. How many shares do you buy? What is the new NAV, total assets of the fund, and shares outstanding? (LO 4-2)

3. **Mutual Fund Returns.** You own shares of three mutual funds, as shown below. What is the value of the three positions and your total portfolio yesterday and today? What was your dollar value change? (LO 4-2)

	Shares	NAV Yesterday	NAV Today
Growth Stock Fund	214.658	$ 57.441	$ 56.982
International Stock Fund	130.554	$ 36.119	$ 38.052
High Grade Bond Fund	75.7664	$ 44.512	$ 45.488

4. **Offer Price with Load.** Consider the three mutual funds below with different front-end loads. You wish to purchase $5,000 of one fund. In each case, (LO 4-2)

   a. what would be the offer price?
   b. how many shares could you purchase?
   c. what would be the load fee?

	Load	NAV
High-Load Fund	5%	$ 25.00
Low-Load Fund	2%	$ 25.00
No-Load Fund	0%	$ 25.00

5. **Mutual Fund Costs.** Mutual funds charge their management fees and 12b-1 fees quarterly. Specifically, they charge one-quarter of the advertised annual fees four times per year. Consider the three mutual funds below with different expense ratios. The NAV at the end of each quarter is shown. For each fund, what are the fees paid at each quarter and the sum for the year? The data are in the file, **ch4_pr05.xlsx**.(LO 4-2)

	Expense Ratio	Shares	NAV Qtr 1	NAV Qtr 2	NAV Qtr 3	NAV Qtr 4
High Expense	2.0%	200	$ 25.6250	$ 26.1375	$ 26.6603	$ 27.1935
Medium Expense	1.1%	200	$ 25.6250	$ 26.1952	$ 26.7780	$ 27.3738
Low Expense	0.3%	200	$ 25.6250	$ 26.2464	$ 26.8829	$ 27.5348

6. **Front-End vs. Back-end Loads.** Calculate the future value of $10,000 invested for five years in a fund earning 12% per year and featuring a front-end load of 5%. Perform the same calculation assuming a deferred back-end load of 5% instead. In terms of investment impact, what's the difference between front-end and back-end loads? (LO 4-4)

7. **Imapcts of Costs on Returns.** A mutual fund has a 1.6% expense ratio and begins with a $124.655 NAV. It experiences the annual returns shown below. What are the end-of-year NAVs after fees for each year? What are the after-fee returns each year? (LO 4-4)

Money to Invest	$ 10,000.00
NAV	$ 124.655
Expense ratio	1.6%
Year 1 return	5%
Year 2 return	−12%
Year 3 return	18%
Year 4 return	4%
Year 5 return	23%

8. **Share Classes.** A fund you are reviewing sells Class A shares with a front-end load of 5% and Class B shares with 12b-1 fees of 0.5% annually. Assume the portfolio rate of return net of operating expenses is 10% annually. Both have an NAV of $50, and you plan to invest $10,000. If you plan to sell the fund after four years, are Class A or Class B shares the better choice for you? (LO 4-4)

9. **Fund Distributions.** A mutual fund in which you own 165.2595 shares begins the last quarter of the year with an NAV of $152.756 per share. At the end of the quarter, the fund declares an income distribution of $1.532 per share and a capital gains distribution of $2.095 per share. Before the distribution, the NAV of the fund is $168.908. If you want your distributions reinvested in more shares, how many shares will you have after the distribution? (LO 4-4)

10. **Tax Implications of Distributions.** Assess the tax consequences of three mutual fund distributions. Fund A manages the portfolio in such a manner that no end-of-year capital gains distribution is needed. Fund B has a large income distribution and moderate capital gains distribution. Fund C has a moderate income distribution and large capital gains distribution. The NAV of each is $55 before the distribution. Conduct the analysis as if you owned $5,000 of each fund. Given the information below, what are the distributions and taxes owed for each fund if the tax rates are 24% for interest income and 15% capital gains? The data are in the file, **ch4_pr10.xlsx**. (LO 4-4)

	Fund A	Fund B	Fund C
Pre-distribution NAV	$55.00	$55.00	$55.00
Value owned	$5,000	$5,000	$5,000
Income gains distribution	$1.00	$2.50	$1.00
Capital gains distribution	$0.00	$1.00	$2.50

11. **Buying ETFs.** An ETF trades for $34.56 in the stock market. It costs you $10 commission to place a trade. How much does it cost to purchase 100 shares of the ETF? (LO 4-5)

12. **Tracking Error.** Monthly returns for an ETF's NAV and for the index it tracks are in the data file, **ch4_pr12.xlsx**. What is the ETF's tracking error? (LO 4-5)

13. **Leveraged ETF Performance.** The SPDR Dow Jones Industrial Average ETF (ticker: DIA) aims to mimic the Dow Jones Industrial Average (DJIA) return. However, the ProShares Ultra Dow30 (ticker: DDM) and the ProShares UltraPro (ticker: UDOW) aim to double and triple the DJIA return, respectively. Consider that the NAVs of DIA, DDM, and UDOW all start at $350, and the DJIA earns −15% in the first year and −15% in the second year. If the three ETFs are successful in their objectives, what is the NAV of each ETF at the end of the second year? (LO 4-6)

14. **Short ETF Performance.** The SPDR Dow Jones Industrial Average ETF (ticker: DIA) aims to mimic the Dow Jones Industrial Average (DJIA) return. However, the ProShares Short Dow30 (ticker: DOG) aims to short the DJIA and earn −1x the DJIA return. The ProShares Ultra-Short Dow30 (ticker: DXD) and ProShares UltraPro Short Dow30 (ticker: SDOW) aim to earn −2x and −3x the DJIA return, respectively. Consider that the NAVs of DIA, DOG, DXD, and SDOW all start at $400, and the DJIA earns 12% in the first year and −12% in the second year. If the three ETFs are successful in their objectives, what is the NAV of each ETF at the end of the second year? (LO 4-6)

15. **Closed-End Fund Returns.** A closed-end investment company is currently selling for $10, and its NAV is $10.63. You decide to purchase 100 shares. During the year, the company distributes $0.75 in dividends. At end of the year, you sell the shares for $12.03. At the time of the sale, NAV is $13.52. What percentage return do you earn on the investment? What role does the NAV play in determining the percentage return? (LO 4-8)

16. **Premium Dynamics.** Consider a closed-end fund that has an NAV of $10.50 and a price of $12.30. What is the closed-end fund's premium in dollars and percentage? If the NAV were to increase 10% to $11.55 and the price rose to $13.16, what would be the return to the investor and the new premium? (LO 4-8)

17. **Discount Dynamics.** Consider a closed-end fund that has an NAV of $27.60 and a price of $23.20. What is the closed-end fund's discount in dollars and percentage? If the NAV were to increase 10% to $30.36 and the price rose to $26.68, what would be the return to the investor and the new premium? (LO 4-8)

18. **Hedge Fund Fees.** Consider two investments. At the end of the year, before fees, you have a $1 million investment in a hedge fund that charges 1.5% in management fees and 15% in incentive fees over a threshold of 8%. Also at the end of the year is the second investment of $1 million in a mutual fund that has an expense ratio of 1.5%. *Compute the fees* for each investment if the hedge fund had earned 15% and the mutual fund had earned 12%. (LO 4-9)

19 **Hedge Fund Returns.** Consider two investments. At the end of the year, before fees, you have a $1 million investment in a hedge fund that charges 1.5% in management fees and 15% in incentive fees over a threshold of 8%. Also at the end of the year is the second investment of $1 million in a mutual fund that has an expense ratio of 1.5%. *Compute the after fee return* for each investment if the hedge fund had earned 15% and the mutual fund had earned 12%. (LO 4-9)

20. **Buying REITs.** You wish to buy an equity REIT and a mortgage REIT in equal proportions. You have a total of $10,000 to invest in REITs. If the equity REIT is trading at $163.22 per share and the mortgage REIT is trading at $45.90 per share, how many share of each REIT should you buy? (LO 4-10)

Case Study

Is Berkshire Hathaway a Fund?

Warren Buffett started an investment partnership with $100 in 1956 and has gone on to accumulate a personal net worth more than $100 billion. Today, Buffett, nicked named the Oracle of Omaha, runs Berkshire Hathaway (BRK) like a combination of a private equity firm and a closed-end mutual fund. He combines a stable of wonderful operating businesses, such as Geico Insurance, with a handful of core investment holdings, such as stock in the Coca-Cola Company.

Buffett looks for companies that enjoy strong franchises, pricing flexibility, high return on equity (ROE), high cash flow, owner-oriented management, and predictable earnings growth. He also looks for companies that are not natural targets of regulation. Berkshire operates businesses in insurance (like GEICO), railroads (like BNSF Railway), energy, manufacturing (like Fruit of the Loom), service, and retailing. In addition, it takes large positions in other public firms. His largest investment positions are in Apple, Bank of America, The Coca-Cola Company, and American Express Company.

Each year, the investors and the media anticipate the Berkshire's annual meeting. In preparation, Buffett writes his annual letter to shareholders. Over the years, his letters have provided many investment advice nuggets, such as these:

- We simply attempt to be fearful when others are greedy and to be greedy only when others are fearful.

- It's far better to buy a wonderful company at a fair price than a fair company at a wonderful price.
- Price is what you pay. Value is what you get.
- Whether we're talking about socks or stocks, I like buying quality merchandise when it is marked down.
- Risk comes from not knowing what you're doing.
- Beware of geeks bearing formulas.
- Success in investing doesn't correlate with IQ ... what you need is the temperament to control the urges that get other people into trouble in investing.
- Our favorite holding period is forever.

If you think of Berkshire Hathaway as a fund, then its performance would be compared to the S&P 500 index. Below is the annual returns of Berkshire Hathaway since 1965. Also shown is the annual return of the S&P 500 index with dividends.

Given the data in the file, **ch4_case_study.xlsx**, compute and interpret the following:

1. What is the average annual return for BRK and for the S&P 500 index:
   a. over the entire period?
   a. by decade?

2. Which one experiences more volatility over time?

3. Compute the tracking error as if BRK was indexing to the S&P 500 Index.

Part

2

Portfolio Theory

Part 2 of this text covers the calculation of investment returns and risks (Chapter 5), the theory and application of diversification and portfolio construction (Chapter 6), the theory and application of the Capital Asset Pricing Model (Chapter 7), the application of other asset pricing models and the role of efficient markets in investing (Chapter 8), and portfolio performance measures (Chapter 9).

Measuring Return and Risk

As we've previously discussed, when you make an investment, you do so with the expectation of that investment generating some benefit in the future, which usually takes the form of a monetary return. That monetary return includes the return of your investment and then some income and/ or capital gain.

Why do investors ask for that additional monetary return over and above what they put in? Humans tend to exhibit what we call a "propensity for current consumption"—they want to spend right now rather than waiting. Investing is about foregoing current consumption for larger consumption in the future. Thus, the most basic component of return is compensation for waiting. However, with investments, your "expectation" of receiving a return is *not* the same thing as its "certainty" of receiving the expected return. Even U.S. government Treasury bills, commonly perceived to be one of the safest investments around, carry a slight uncertainty about what their guaranteed return in dollars will be worth in terms of spending power. And potential returns from investments made in other entities (such as companies, municipal governments, etc.) that *don't* have the ability to print their own currency can be even riskier.

In this chapter, we're going to take our first tentative steps toward figuring out how much more an investor wants/needs/requires to invest their money in an uncertain investment. For most investments, there is at least some risk of not receiving any profits and possibly not getting back some or all of the original investment. We start with a discussion of what return is and how to measure it. We then present a similar discussion on how to measure risk using historic returns and how to use that measurement as a proxy for the uncertain future investment risk. Once we have those ideas under our belt, we'll make an initial attempt at determining if there is a "price" for risk; that is, if the amount of return expected/required from investing in an asset can be tied to the amount of uncertainty there is in the future returns to that asset.

Treasury bills
A short-term U.S. government debt obligation backed by the Treasury Department with a maturity of one year or less

5-1 Measuring Return

5-1a The Components of Return

Return refers to the possible compensation or loss you experience when investing in an asset. Before buying an investment, you expect the return to be positive; however, after the fact, your realized return can be negative. In either case, return usually comes from two basic sources: income and capital appreciation.

Income refers to cash flows that are generated by your investment while you own the asset. If you invest your money in a bank savings account, your income will be the interest that the savings account pays. If you buy stocks, your income may include any cash dividends that are paid. But income can also be negative. If you buy a rental property that requires more in repair expenses than it generates in rent, you will experience negative income.

Capital appreciation refers to the change in value of the asset between the time you buy it and when you sell it. If you invest in a stock, your capital appreciation will be the difference between the net amount you pay for the stock at the beginning of your investment and the net amount you receive for selling the stock when you end your investment. But, just as with income, capital appreciation can be negative, too. If you buy a bond trading at a premium (i.e., selling for more than face value) and hold it until maturity, the price will decline to match the face value of the bond at maturity and give you a capital loss.

Assuming that you get a return from both sources, you can calculate your total dollar return as:

return
Compensation for investing in an asset

income
Cash in-flows from an investment, like dividends, interest payments, or rent

capital appreciation
The increase in value of an investment

$$Total\ Return = Income + (Price_{Received} - Price_{Paid}) \qquad \textbf{5-1}$$

where

$Income$ = cash flows generated by the asset while the investor owned it
$Price_{Received}$ = the net selling price received by the investor
$Price_{Paid}$ = the net price paid by the investor to purchase the asset (including any brokerage costs and/or commissions)

Of course, it is much more typical to quote returns as a proportion, measuring "money I got back over how much I put in." This proportion is calculated by taking the total return divided by the amount invested:

$$r = \frac{Income + (Price_{Received} - Price_{Paid})}{Price_{Paid}} \qquad \text{5-2}$$

In practice, this proportion is often stated as a percentage rate and is calculated by multiplying by 100%. For example, if you pay $100 for an asset that gives you a total return of $4, you will earn $\frac{\$4}{\$100} = 0.04$, which could also be expressed as $0.04 \times 100\% = 4\%$. In practice, you'll often find that return and rate are used interchangeably and jointly referred to as a "percentage rate."

holding period
The amount of time that an investment is held by an investor

This percentage rate r can be calculated over an actual **holding period**, defined as the time between buying and subsequently selling an asset—or any other potential time period if we are willing to substitute the prevailing market prices we *could have* paid for or sold the asset. To differentiate between these two situations, we normally refer to the return earned over a holding period in which the asset was actually bought and sold as the **holding period return (HPR)**, while using the more generic "return" to refer to any situation involving potential returns that could have, hypothetically, been earned. This is often based on the calendar, as in a daily return or a monthly return.

holding period return (HPR)
The investment return over a specified period

For example, if an investor buys a share of stock for $10, earns $0.60 in dividends while they own it, and then sells the stock for $12, the total dollar return would be [$0.60 + ($12−$10)] = $2.60, while the HPR would be calculated as:

$$r = \frac{\$0.60 + (\$12 - \$10)}{\$10} = 0.26 \text{ or } 26\%$$

Excel Expert 5-1

The easiest way to calculate *total dollar return* is to write your own function, as shown below in cell C5. The best way to calculate the HPR in Excel is to use the *RATE(nper, pmt, pv, [fv], [type], [guess])* function, setting *nper* = 1, *pmt* = Income, *pv* = −Price$_{Paid}$, *and fv* = Price$_{Received}$, as shown below in cell C6:

Note that we will always set *nper* equal to 1 in this situation, as we are defining the length of time between when we bought the asset and when we sold it as "1 period," regardless of how long or short a time it is. This will change when we "standardize" our holding period (see below), but not when we want to calculate a pure HPR.

	A	B	C
1	Income	$ 0.60	
2	Price$_{Paid}$	$ 10.00	
3	Price$_{Received}$	$ 12.00	
4			
5	Total Return	$ 2.60	=B1+(B3-B2)
6	HPR	26.00%	=RATE(1,B1,-B2,B3)

When we calculate returns in this manner—using the actual prices and intervening cash flows that occurred over a particular historic time frame—we are computing what is called a **realized return**. Particularly for financial assets, there is a tendency to group the components of **Equation 5-2** into subparts based on "differing mechanisms of revenue accrual." Sounds impressive, doesn't it? Well, all it really means is that if the different parts of the return come from different places, then it just makes sense to organize the total return so that we can update the different subcomponents individually and quickly.

realized return
The amount or percentage of money gained or lost over a holding period

For example, stock prices arise from the buying/selling activities occurring on the stock markets on which the stocks trade, while stock dividends are announced and paid by the firm itself, so we often see the total return to a stock broken into two parts:

$$r = \frac{Income + (Price_{Received} - Price_{Paid})}{Price_{Paid}}$$

$$r = \frac{Income}{Price_{Paid}} + \frac{(Price_{Received} - Price_{Paid})}{Price_{Paid}}$$

Given that we're talking about stocks, this can be more specifically written as:

$$r = \frac{Dividends}{Price_{Paid}} + \frac{(Price_{Received} - Price_{Paid})}{Price_{Paid}}$$

Substituting in commonly used variables in stock pricing, this is usually written as:

$$r = \frac{D_1}{P_0} + \frac{P_1 - P_0}{P_0} \qquad \textbf{5-3}$$

where
D_1 = Dividends received during the holding period
P_1 = Price received at end of holding period
P_0 = Price paid at beginning of holding period

Finally, and as you may remember from your corporate finance class, this is often written as

$$r = \frac{D_1}{P_0} + g \qquad \textbf{5-4}$$

where g = growth in stock price as a percentage of price paid. To differentiate the two parts of r here, you'll often hear $\dfrac{D_1}{P_0}$ referred to as the **dividend yield** and g referred to as the **capital gains yield**.

dividend yield
A measure of annual return from the dividend income only

For example, Exxon Mobil Corporation (ticker: XOM) started 2020 priced at $69.78 per share and ended the year at $41.22. During the year, it paid a total of $3.48 per share in dividends. Thus, its one-year return includes a dividend yield of $3.48/$69.78 = 4.99% and a capital gains yield (a loss) of ($41.22 − $69.78)/$69.78 = −40.93%. Thus, the total return was 4.99% + −40.93 = −35.94%.

capital gains yield
A measure of an investment's return based solely on the capital appreciation

Similarly, it is also common for the total return to a bond to be broken down as:

$$r = \frac{Income + (Price_{Received} - Price_{Paid})}{Price_{Paid}}$$

$$= \frac{Income}{Price_{Paid}} + \frac{(Price_{Received} - Price_{Paid})}{Price_{Paid}}$$

$$= \frac{Coupon\ Payments}{Price_{Paid}} + \frac{(Price_{Received} - Price_{Paid})}{Price_{Paid}}$$

$$= \frac{C}{P_0} + \frac{(P_1 - P_0)}{P_0}$$

$$= \frac{C}{P_0} + g \qquad \text{5-5}$$

where $\frac{C}{P_0}$ is referred to as the **current yield** and g is again referred to as the capital gains yield. Consider a 10-year Treasury bond that begins the year priced at $934.52 per bond and pays $11.25 in total interest payments during the year. The bond's price increases to $1,012.81 by the end of the year. The bond's current yield was $11.25/$934.53 = 1.20% and the capital gain yield was ($1,012.81−$934.52)/$934.52 = 8.38% for a total return of 9.58%.

So, if you're calculating the realized return on a stock or bond, you typically take the dividend yield or current yield from one data source and the capital gains yield from another. However, in some cases, financial intermediaries such as stock exchanges or banks actually go out of their way to gather all the components necessary for you to compute total return in one place. A case in point is Yahoo! Finance's calculation of adjusted close prices, discussed below.

5-1b Realized vs. Expected vs. Required Returns

Before we get into the use of adjusted prices, however, we need to clarify a couple of other "types" of return that you will hear discussed. While realized returns are calculated based on what *has* happened, you will also hear mention of *expected returns* and *required returns*.

Expected returns are similar to realized returns but are calculated using our best guesses about what income and selling price we will actually receive. As a result, the expected returns themselves are just guesses, too, and often turn out to be wrong. Nevertheless, you can only make buy decisions on expected return (unless you know the future). As we will discuss in more detail later in this chapter, that uncertainty leads to risk, for which investors must be compensated for.

As guesses, formulas for expected returns are usually written using the **expectations operator**, $E()$, to indicate which parts we're guessing about. For example, expected return on a share of stock would be calculated as:

$$E(r) = \frac{E(D_1)}{P_0} + \frac{E(P_1) - P_0}{P_0}$$

$$= \frac{E(D_1)}{P_0} + E(g) \qquad \text{5-6}$$

Notice that we're not guessing about everything here. We can usually safely assume that you can know the price you are paying for an asset with a great degree of certainty, while the anticipated future cash inflows are *educated* guesses.

Although **Equation 5-6** is very close to **Equation 5-4**, and is often used interchangeably with it, they are not exactly equal to one another because of the uncertainty in expected returns. Because of this, if we wanted to equate realized return to expected return for a particular asset class, we would normally write an equation something like this:

$$r = E(r) + U \qquad\qquad \textbf{5-7}$$

where U stands for the "surprise"; that is, the difference between what we expected to get and what we actually received. This leads us to the topic of the required return, which, before you buy an asset, is the minimum amount of expected return to compensate you for the risk of holding the asset.

required return
The minimum amount of expected return to compensate for the risk of holding an asset

If U were completely random, and if investors were completely risk-neutral, then they wouldn't ask for any "extra" return to compensate them for the anticipated distribution of U, as they could use the techniques we'll discuss in Chapter 6 to form portfolios where the U portions of the individual assets' expected returns could be expected to cancel each other out. But, as previously discussed, people tend to be risk averse, and it often isn't possible to *completely* cancel out all the Us, so the more uncertainty about the returns on an asset, the more compensation in the form of $E(r)$ that investors will require to get them to invest in the asset in the first place.

5-1c HPR Using Adjusted Closing Prices

Financial assets trade frequently on an exchange and in great volume. There are financial information providers that track such information. We can access the historical information needed to calculate our returns through those third parties rather than keeping track of it ourselves. This also comes in handy when we want to take a look at the historic returns and risks for assets that we haven't held in the past but which we are now considering.

For example, many small investors turn to the Yahoo! Finance website (finance. yahoo.com) when they want to research a stock. If you go to the site and enter a company's name or ticker symbol in the search box, you will be presented with a very impressive set of information on the company's "summary" page. For example, here is the summary page for Walmart Inc. (WMT) as shown in **Figure 5-1**.

The statistics reported here are very valuable, and we'll discuss how to compute them and other similar indicators ourselves throughout the text. For now, let's take a look at the "Historical Data" page in **Figure 5-2**.

As shown in the dropdown selected in **Figure 5-2**, we can select historic prices for a variety of time periods. In most cases, we can even select "max" to get all the historic data for a company's stock price back to when it first went public.

Yahoo! doesn't provide all the intraday prices for each stock, but instead the daily open, high, low, closing and adjusted closing prices. Of these prices, the most useful to someone researching a stock to calculate either actual or hypothetical "what-if" holding period returns is the adjusted close price. *Adjusted close* is the closing price after adjustments have been made for all subsequent stock splits and dividend distributions.[1] The easiest way to understand the net effect of these adjustments is that they

adjusted close
An end-of-day stock price that is adjusted for subsequent dividends and stock splits

[1] Yahoo! Finance uses the same standards for computing split and dividend adjustments as does the *Center for Research in Security Prices (CRSP)*, which is affiliated with the University of Chicago Booth School of Business, and which has long been accepted as the standard for such adjustments for academic studies.

Figure 5-1: Yahoo! Finance Stock Information Page

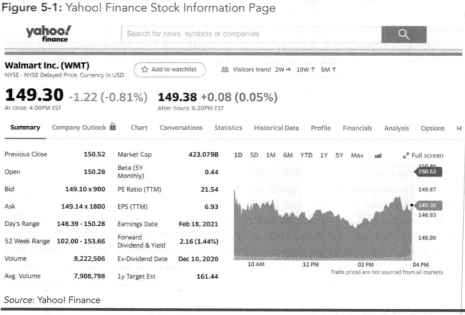

Source: Yahoo! Finance

Figure 5-2: Yahoo! Finance Historical Data Page

Time Period: Dec 03, 2019 - Dec 03, 2020 ⌄   Show: Historical Prices ⌄   Frequency: Daily ⌄   **Apply**

Date	Open	High	Low	Close*	Adj Close**	Volume
Dec 03, 2020			148.39	149.30	149.30	8,222,506
Dec 02, 2020			149.53	150.52	150.52	7,842,600
Dec 01, 2020			151.66	152.64	152.64	7,645,100
Nov 30, 2020			150.10	152.79	152.79	10,887,600
Nov 27, 2020			151.10	151.60	151.60	3,666,500
Nov 25, 2020	151.25	152.39	151.21	151.83	151.83	4,611,100
Nov 24, 2020	151.74	151.98	150.27	151.36	151.36	5,718,400
Nov 23, 2020	150.37	151.40	149.37	150.93	150.93	6,185,700
Nov 20, 2020	151.17	152.76	149.81	150.24	150.24	7,312,400
Nov 19, 2020	149.46	152.45	149.32	152.12	152.12	6,196,900

Source: Yahoo! Finance

retroactively adjust previous prices to be on the same basis as the latest stock price. If the stock were split, for example, two-for-one sometime in the past, then each current share is only half as "big" (i.e., only has half as large a claim on ownership) as shares before the split. So, the prices from before the split are each divided by two so that the amount of ownership/earning "power" is the same for before and after the split. Likewise, if a stock that used to sell for $10 pays out a $1 dividend, prices from before the ex-dividend date have $1 subtracted from them, sort of along the intuitive lines of "Yeah, you paid $10 for the share, but you got $1 of it back, so your effective net cost was $10 − $1 = $9."

This means that Yahoo! Finance's adjusted close at the beginning of any holding period we choose has been adjusted for subsequent effects, such as dividends or stock splits. So, we can calculate HPR using adjusted close simply by taking the change in adjusted close as a percentage of the starting adjusted close since income is already factored in. Mathematically, this is simply an algebraic rearrangement of the parts of **Equation 5-2**:

$$
\begin{aligned}
HPR &= \frac{Income + (Price_{Received} - Price_{Paid})}{Price_{Paid}} \\
&= \frac{Price_{Received} - (Price_{Paid} - Income)}{Price_{Paid}} \\
&\approx \frac{Adjusted\ Price_{Received} - Adjusted\ Price_{Paid}}{Adjusted\ Price_{Paid}} \\
&\approx \frac{Adjusted\ Price_{Received}}{Adjusted\ Price_{Paid}} - 1 \qquad\qquad \textbf{5-8}
\end{aligned}
$$

As the "$\approx$" symbol in **Equation 5-8** implies, we are taking a little liberty here in that we go from having $Price_{Paid}$ in the denominator to replacing it with *Adjusted Price$_{Paid}$*. As long as the two aren't very different from one another, this is an acceptable approximation.

Also notice that we developed **Equation 5-4** for *any* price on a given day, though it is a common convention to use closing prices as "the" price for a day for a couple of different reasons. First, if you aren't actually buying or selling a stock on a given day, the closing price, which theoretically holds true from the close of the markets on one day to the opening of the markets on the next trading day, is arguably the "usual" price for that day. Investors, traders, financial institutions, regulators, and other stakeholders typically use it as a reference point for determining performance over a specific time, such as one year, a week, and shorter time frames such as one minute or less. Secondly, many "redemptions" of assets that are invested in stocks, such as the redemption of fund shares to a mutual fund, actually *do* happen at the closing price.

Circling back to our WMT data from Yahoo! Finance, note that the adjusted close on November 27, 2019, was $116.7135, while the adjusted close on November 27, 2020, was $151.60, which would allow us to calculate the one-year HPR for Walmart over that period as:

$$
\frac{\$151.60}{\$116.7135} - 1 = 0.2989 \text{ or } 29.89\%
$$

5-1d Standardizing HPR

As its name implies, the HPR is very useful for calculating the rate of return during the period that you own an asset, but using the HPR to compare the performance of multiple assets won't be very informative if the holding periods for each of the assets are different. For example, suppose someone who had bought Walmart Inc. (WMT) stock on November 27, 2019, and sold it on November 27, 2020, would have had the one-year HPR of 29.89% that we computed above, while someone who bought Intel Corporation

Excel Expert 5-2

When you download historical prices from Yahoo! Finance, the data file you receive is already arranged in a format conducive to calculating returns, with the rows corresponding to dates and the different columns corresponding to different types of prices. To use adjusted close values for a particular holding period, we just have to identify the appropriate rows and column from the table to reference:

	A	B	C	D	E	F	G	H	I
1	Date	Open	High	Low	Close	Adj Close	Volume	Return	
11914	11/19/2019	120.11	120.36	119.71	119.89	117.8241	3715400		
11915	11/20/2019	120.21	120.48	118.4	119.13	117.0771	5075900		
11916	11/21/2019	118.83	120	118.67	119.86	117.7946	4302400		
11917	11/22/2019	120.15	120.3	119.27	119.36	117.3032	3843100		
11918	11/25/2019	120	120.02	117.9	118.92	116.8708	5881500		
11919	11/26/2019	118.96	119.3	118.45	119.19	117.1361	6292500		
11920	11/27/2019	119.39	119.8	118.73	118.76	116.7135	3434100	29.89%	=(F12172/F11920)-1
12172	11/27/2020	152.15	152.72	151.1	151.6	151.6	3666500		

Note that here we have hidden the intervening rows corresponding to the dates between the start and end of our holding period so as to make it easier to see where we are getting the numbers from.

(INTC) stock on September 27, 2015, and sold it on the same November 27, 2020, date would have had a five-year HPR of 57.51%. Obviously, 57.51% is *bigger* than 29.89%, but is it *better*? Well, we can't really say, as the difference in holding periods means that we're "comparing apples to oranges." We know that earning the 57.51% HPR for INTC would have meant tying up our money for five years, but we don't know what else we could have done with our money between 2015 and 2019 if we had invested it in WMT.

In order to be able to make "fair" comparisons between different assets, we really have to standardize the lengths of the holding periods to a common size. The most popular choice for such a common size is a year, due to several logical reasons. First, many rates, particularly those for borrowing, are already quoted on annual terms, so expressing an asset's return as an annual rate allows us to easily discuss assets in a "what rate it costs versus what rate it earns" context. Secondly, the regulatory and tax environment that investment decisions are made in often shifts on an annual basis, including changes in tax rates and brackets, changes in the tax basis of income versus capital appreciation, and so forth, so it makes sense that we have to reevaluate our investment decisions on an annual basis, as well. Finally, as we will discuss in later chapters, differential changes in the individual assets in a portfolio often require investment portfolios to be "rebalanced" on an annual basis, meaning that the HPR for at least some of your assets actually *will* be on an annual basis.

The most appropriate way to measure annual returns on an asset is, if possible, to measure the net price paid for the asset at the beginning of the year, the net selling price of the asset at the end of the year, and any income that occurs during that year, and then to apply **Equation 5-2** above (or, if using adjusted prices, to apply **Equation 5-8**).

For example, since we have data available for INTC for the same holding period that we do for WMT, it is fairly simple to calculate its one-year HPR ending on November 27, 2020, using adjusted close prices, as well:

$$\frac{\$47.45}{\$57.09043} - 1$$

or -16.89%

Excel Expert 5-3

The calculations for the one-year HPR for INTC are the same as those we used for WMT, it's just that the pricing data is different:

	A	B	C	D	E	F	G	H	I
1	Date	Open	High	Low	Close	Adj Close	Volume	Return	
10005	11/14/2019	57.61	58.04	57.57	57.81	56.40741	12119000		
10006	11/15/2019	58.17	58.7	57.62	57.96	56.55377	16112100		
10007	11/18/2019	57.7	58.48	57.57	58.25	56.83674	16097500		
10008	11/19/2019	58.48	58.65	57.75	58.35	56.93431	17061900		
10009	11/20/2019	58.26	58.36	57.37	57.9	56.49523	18542300		
10010	11/21/2019	57.49	58.3	57.41	58.22	56.80747	16139000		
10011	11/22/2019	58.34	58.65	57.49	57.61	56.21227	15690200		
10012	11/25/2019	58	58.84	58	58.81	57.38316	15011700		
10013	11/26/2019	58.95	59.13	58.45	58.9	57.47097	22338700		
10014	11/27/2019	58.53	58.59	57.91	58.51	57.09043	18184200	-16.89%	=(F10266/F10014)-1
10266	11/27/2020	47.36	48.1	47.36	47.45	47.45	15921400		

Note that we have once again hidden the intervening rows corresponding to the dates between the start and end of our holding period so as to make it easier to see where we are getting the numbers from.

You'll be immediately struck by the fact that INTC lost money (a return of −16.89%) while WMT made money (a return of 29.89%) over the same period. Does this mean that people who invested in INTC at the start of that holding period expected to lose money, or that people investing in INTC at the end of the holding period expected to lose money going forward? No, and no, but for different reasons. First, anyone who invested in INTC on November 27, 2019, and expected to hold the stock for the next year certainly did not expect to lose money. As we said before, realized returns should be equal to expected returns *on average*—on average across investments and across different holding periods.

During this one-year period, INTC experienced continuing delays in the technological advancement for their flagship product line of Central Processing Units (CPUs), while AMD, their primary rival, continued to make technological breakthroughs allowing AMD to expand their market shares in both the desktop and laptop CPU markets. To the extent that investors without inside knowledge of the two firms could not have anticipated the effects of these events on INTC share prices, those effects were unanticipated and would fall under the category of idiosyncratic or nonsystematic risk, which we will discuss in more depth below; those effects could have been mitigated by holding INTC in a well-diversified portfolio, which we will discuss in Chapter 6.

What returns should we expect from INTC and WMT in the future? If we were standing there on November 27, 2020, thinking about investing in INTC for the *next* year, should the fact that it had just earned –16.89% return influence our expectations of the future returns?

Using the past to predict what is going to happen in the future, called forecasting, is not usually handled by simply using the latest single past return to predict the next expected return. We will cover some of the more advanced forecasting techniques in Chapters 7 and 8, so we'll defer our discussion of those advanced techniques until then. For now, there is a forecasting technique we *can* use that, while simple, will greatly improve the accuracy of our forecasts: we can use an average of multiple past (or "historic") returns to predict future return.

idiosyncratic risk
Risk that is unique to a particular asset, also called nonsystematic risk

nonsystematic risk
Risk that is unique to a particular asset, also called idiosyncratic risk

forecasting
Predicting future values of a variable

5-1e Arithmetic vs. Geometric Averages

arithmetic average
The sum of a set of numbers divided by the number of observations

There are actually two different types of average returns we can use to measure the "typical" return across multiple periods. The first, the **arithmetic average**, is just the sum of a selection of the historic returns divided by the number of returns. By "selection," we mean that you can choose any range of historic returns on which you feel comfortable basing an estimate of future returns. However, the usual convention that investors use is to take the past five years' worth of returns.[2]

$$Arithmetic\ Average = \frac{\sum_{t=1}^{n} r_t}{n}$$ 5-9

For example, the past five years' worth of returns on INTC were 6.45%, 28.84%, 10.77%, 24.75%, and −16.89%, respectively. The calculation of those yearly returns is included below in **Excel Expert 5-4**. The arithmetic average return over those five years would be:

$$\frac{6.45\% + 28.84\% + 10.77\% + 24.75\% - 16.89\%}{5} = 0.1078\ or\ 10.78\%$$

Note that the arithmetic average gives us a measure of the average one-year return during that five-year period if we had purchased INTC for a single one-year period with a constant amount of money in each successive one-year period. Say, for example, if we invested $1,000 at the beginning of each year, then sold and cashed out at the end of each year. Thus, we would not be reinvesting the proceeds from one year to the next.

Excel Expert 5-4

Excel uses the *AVERAGE(number1,[number2],…)* function for calculating the arithmetic average:

	A	B	C	D	E	F	G	H	I	J
1	Date	Open	High	Low	Close	Adj Close	Volume		Return	
9005	11/24/2015	34.33	34.44	33.9	34.36	30.0381	21413500			
9006	11/25/2015	34.26	34.74	34.14	34.45	30.11677	17939400			
9007	11/27/2015	34.54	34.68	34.4	34.46	30.12552	6620900		6.45%	=(F9259/F9007)-1
9259	11/28/2016	35.43	35.66	35.21	35.51	32.06759	13549000		28.84%	=(F9510/F9259)-1
9510	11/27/2017	44.42	44.61	44.27	44.49	41.31431	18202100		10.77%	=(F9762/F9510)-1
9762	11/27/2018	46.94	48.22	46.59	48.07	45.76206	27621000		24.75%	=(F10014/F9762)-1
10014	11/27/2019	58.53	58.59	57.91	58.51	57.09043	18184200		-16.89%	=(F10266/F10014)-1
10266	11/27/2020	47.36	48.1	47.36	47.45	47.45	15921400			
10267							Arithmetic Average		10.78%	=AVERAGE(I9007,I9259,I9510,I9762,I10014)

Note that we used the same approach for calculating the previous four years' worth of returns as we did for calculating the latest year's return in **Excel Expert 5-3**, but that we had to adjust the start and end dates when November 27 of a particular year was not a trading date for the stock markets. In each such case, we used the closest trading day to calculate as close to an annual return as possible.

---

[2]To be simplistic, the normal convention is to take five years of monthly returns, not annual ones, but we'll clarify and expand on that in Chapter 7.

The **geometric average** return, on the other hand, will give us the average one-year return if we had kept the money invested in INTC for the entire five-year period. In effect, geometric averages assume **compound interest**, while arithmetic averages assume **simple interest**. To calculate a geometric average, we solve for the "nth" root of a "long" HPR computed using each of the n individual "short" rates:

$$Geometric\ Average = \left(\sqrt[n]{\prod_{t=1}^{n}(1 + r_t)} \right) - 1 \qquad \textbf{5-10}$$

For example, for every dollar invested in INTC during the five-year period we are considering, it would have grown to $(1+0.0645) \times (1+0.2884) \times (1+0.1077) \times (1+0.2475) \times (1-0.1689) = 1.5751$ dollars at the end of the five-year period. Taking the 5th root of that and subtracting 1 would give us a geometric average return of 0.0951, or 9.51%.

If you will remember back to your discussions of rate and time value of money (TVM) in earlier finance classes, you shouldn't be too surprised to see that the geometric average return (the rate necessary to get the same FV *with* compounding) is less than the arithmetic average return (the rate necessary *without* compounding).

Which return—arithmetic average return or geometric average return—should we use? It depends on your expected holding period. If you are planning to keep an asset for the same length of time as the "short" holding period in our description above, then you should probably use the arithmetic average. If you plan on holding it for an indefinite period, then the geometric average return is probably the best measure.

5-1f Arithmetic Average as a Special Case of Probabilistic Expected Return

In our discussion of arithmetic average return, we were implicitly putting equal weight on each of the past historic returns in our calculation of an estimated average return to

geometric average
The average compounded growth of an investment

compound interest
Interest earned on both principal and earlier interest

simple interest
Interest earned on principal alone

Excel Expert 5-5

While there is a *GEOMEAN()* function in Excel, its use is restricted to instances where the individual values are all positive, which we don't have here due to the past year's return being negative. Luckily, there are a variety of ways to handle the same problem in Excel: we can solve for the geometric average return using much the same approach that we did manually above but making use of the *FVSCHEDULE(principal, schedule)* function, which uses a schedule of interest rates to compute the future value (FV) at the end:

	A	B	C	D	E	F	G	H	I	J
1	Date	Open	High	Low	Close	Adj Close	Volume		Return	
9005	11/24/2015	34.33	34.44	33.9	34.36	30.0381	21413500			
9006	11/25/2015	34.26	34.74	34.14	34.45	30.11677	17939400			
9007	11/27/2015	34.54	34.68	34.4	34.46	30.12552	6620900		6.45%	=(F9259/F9007)-1
9259	11/28/2016	35.43	35.66	35.21	35.51	32.06759	13549000		28.84%	=(F9510/F9259)-1
9510	11/27/2017	44.42	44.61	44.27	44.49	41.31431	18202100		10.77%	=(F9762/F9510)-1
9762	11/27/2018	46.94	48.22	46.59	48.07	45.76206	27621000		24.75%	=(F10014/F9762)-1
10014	11/27/2019	58.53	58.59	57.91	58.51	57.09043	18184200		-16.89%	=(F10266/F10014)-1
10266	11/27/2020	47.36	48.1	47.36	47.45	47.45	15921400			
10267								Arithmetic		
								Average	10.78%	=AVERAGE(I9007,I9259,I9510,I9762,I10014)
10268										
								Geometric		
10269								Average	9.51%	=(FVSCHEDULE(1,I9007:I10014))^(1/5)-1

Note that the FVSCHEDULE() function only gives us the FV of the $1 principal; we still have to take its 5th root (raising something to the 1/5 power is the same as taking a 5th root) and subtract 1 to get the geometric average rate of return.

be used as our best guess for the return for a "short" holding period. It's easy to see this if we rewrite **Equation 5-9** slightly:

$$Arithmetic\ Average = \frac{\sum_{t=1}^{n} r_r}{n}$$

$$= \sum_{t=1}^{n}\left(\frac{1}{n} \times r_t\right) \qquad \textbf{5-11}$$

Looking closely at **Equation 5-11**, we can see that the arithmetic average can be interpreted as putting an equal "weight" of $1/n$ on each of the n historic returns we are using to predict future returns. Note that in our example, n = 5, each annual return is multiplied by 1/5, or 0.20. If the actual relation between past realized returns and future expected returns differed only by random uncertainty U values, as discussed previously, then giving each historic observation equal weight like this would probably be the best approach for estimating future expected return. But, in fact, we can do a little better than that if common sense tells that some of the previous historic returns represent situations that are "more likely" to happen in the future, while others represent "less likely" situations.

For example, let's turn back to our calculation of the arithmetic average return for INTC that we covered in **Excel Expert 5-4**. Suppose we thought that each of the four positive returns (6.45%, 28.84%, 10.77%, and 24.75%) was slightly more likely to represent what we could expect in the future, and that the negative return (-16.89%) was slightly less likely to represent the future. To be precise, suppose we gave the four positive returns each a probability of 0.22 of happening, and the negative return a probability of $1 - (4 \times 0.22) = 0.12$ of happening. Then we could calculate a "probability adjusted" weighted average return as a proxy for our expectation of the future return:

$$Probabilistic\ Expected\ Return = E\ (r) = \sum_{t=1}^{n}(p_t \times r_t) \qquad \textbf{5-12}$$

In this case, this would give us an adjusted expected return of $(0.22 \times 6.45\%) + (0.22 \times 28.84\%) + (0.22 \times 10.77\%) + (0.22 \times 24.75\%) + (0.12 \times -16.89\%) = 13.55\%$

If you're feeling a little uneasy about somewhat arbitrarily putting more weight on some of the past historic returns and less weight on others, let me point out that this is where the "art" of forecasting comes into play. If we really think that last year's negative return was an anomaly, then we obviously *should* assign a lesser weight to it; the question of how much less is the one that requires experience and insight to answer correctly.

If the idea of giving *any* historic returns less weight than others still strikes you as questionable, realize that we already did that when we first started talking about the arithmetic average: taking an average of the past five years' returns implicitly involves assigning weights of 0 (zero) to any returns that are more than five years old.

5-1g The Relationship Between Geometric Average Return, Effective Rates, and Nominal Rates

In our discussion of the geometric average return, we referred to "long" and "short" rates of return. Both of these rates are effective rates, in that they represent rates of return that could actually be earned in an investment, but for different lengths of time.

Excel Expert 5-6

Excel has a handy function for multiplying two (or more) *vectors* together called *SUMPRODUCT(array1, [array2],[array3]…)*. In the example below, we have put our returns in one column (i.e., vector) and our probabilities in another, so all we need to do to compute the probabilistic weighted average return is to apply the *SUMPRODUCT()* function.

	A	B	C	D	E	F	G	H	I	J	K
1	Date	Open	High	Low	Close	Adj Close	Volume		Return	Probability	
9002	11/19/2015	33.22	34.73	33.13	34.30	29.99	45381600				
9003	11/20/2015	34.48	35.29	34.48	34.66	30.30	41137700				
9004	11/23/2015	34.66	34.85	34.41	34.48	30.14	20152900				
9005	11/24/2015	34.33	34.44	33.90	34.36	30.04	21413500				
9006	11/25/2015	34.26	34.74	34.14	34.45	30.12	17939400				
9007	11/27/2015	34.54	34.68	34.40	34.46	30.13	6620900		6.45%	0.22	
9259	11/28/2016	35.43	35.66	35.21	35.51	32.07	13549000		28.84%	0.22	
9510	11/27/2017	44.42	44.61	44.27	44.49	41.31	18202100		10.77%	0.22	
9762	11/27/2018	46.94	48.22	46.59	48.07	45.76	27621000		24.75%	0.22	
10014	11/27/2019	58.53	58.59	57.91	58.51	57.09	18184200		-16.89%	0.12	
10266	11/27/2020	47.36	48.10	47.36	47.45	47.45	15921400				
10267									Probablistic Weighted Avg	13.55%	=SUMPRODUCT(I9007:I10014,J9007:J10014)

Note that, as we have done here, it often helps to keep track of returns versus probabilities if we keep returns in a percentage format and probabilities in a decimal format.

Equation 5-10 can be generalized to give us an equation for converting between any two effective rates for the same asset but for different holding periods.

For example, you may remember reading a discussion of effective annual rate (EAR) computation in the context of a credit card with monthly payments from your Introduction to Finance course. Most credit cards charge interest on the basis of your outstanding monthly balance: if you have, say, a balance of $500, then they will charge you a monthly rate of interest on that balance. Let's suppose your credit card has a 1.5% monthly interest rate (they don't quote it that way, but we'll go over that in a moment). Then, if you kept the $500 balance unpaid, and made interest-only payments each month, you would pay them $500 × 0.015 = $7.50 in interest per month.

The point is, that monthly rate of 1.5% is an effective rate, as it represents the cash flows *from* you (and *to* the company that lent you money), but it's a *monthly* effective rate. If you wanted to convert it to an effective annual rate, you would just need to realize that there are 12 months in a year, and then use a version of **Equation 5-10** to compute:

$$r_{Annual} = (1 + r_{Monthly})^{12} - 1$$

$$= 1.015^{12} - 1$$

$$= 0.1956 \text{ or } 19.56\% \qquad \textbf{5-13}$$

This winds up being much simpler than **Equation 5-10** because we're not trying to convert different monthly rates into an average monthly rate, but rather into an annual rate, so we can get rid of the 12th root calculation. Also, all the 12 monthly rates are the same, so the product function Π gets converted into a simple exponent.

Why bother with this? Didn't we say before that we could simply choose prices at the beginning and end of our holding period as well as income during the holding period to compute returns? Well, it turns out that while you can find that information on financial assets trading frequently in liquid markets, you can't do that with all assets. In

Excel Expert 5-7 〉〉

Excel has an *EFFECT(nominal_rate,npery)* function, ostensibly just for converting between nominal annual rates and effective annual rates, but, in fact, it can convert between nominal and effective rates for the same length of time, no matter what the time in question is. For the problem as stated, converting 1.50% per month to an effective annual rate consists of first converting the 1.50% effective monthly rate into a "lie" (see below for more details) for the length of time you want to know the "truth" (i.e., effective rate) for, and then passing that lie and the number of real ("short") periods inside the lie to the *EFFECT()* function:

	A	B	C
1	Rate$_{Short}$	1.50%	
2	Short Periods per Long	12	
3			
4	Rate$_{Long}$	19.56%	=EFFECT(B1*B2,B2)

Note, though, that we could convert that 1.50% effective monthly rate to an effective quarterly rate simply by changing cell B2 to 3 (i.e., there are three months in a quarter), or to any other effective rate we wished by choosing the appropriate number of "short times in the long time" in cell B2. That is why we referred to the rates as Rate$_{Short}$ and Rate$_{Long}$. They are both actual, effective rates. We just have to go through a nominal "lie" inside the *EFFECT()* function to get from one to the other.

particular, it can be close to impossible to find that kind of information on real assets that trade infrequently on nonpublic marketplaces. In many cases, the best you can do is to keep track of what you paid for the asset when you bought it, what you got for it when you sold it, and what the intervening income flows were. Those numbers will give you an HPR for the length of time you owned the asset, which you can then convert to an equivalent HPR for a standard length of time (e.g., that often-used annual time frame we talked about earlier) using yet another version of **Equation 5-10**:

$$r_{Short} = \sqrt[t]{(1 + r_{Long})} - 1 \qquad \text{5-14}$$

where t = number of short periods in a long period

For example, suppose that you owned a 1999 first edition Shadowless holographic Charizard #4 Pokémon card that you bought on eBay back in 1999 for $100, and which you sold in 2020 for $36,000.[3] Your HPR would be $\frac{\$36,000-\$100}{\$100}$ = 35,900%. Impressive, right? But your equivalent annual rate of return over those 21 years would be:

$$\sqrt[21]{(1 + 359)} - 1 = 32.35\%$$

Still impressive, but much more comparable to the return of other investments.

---

[3]This is a real price.

Excel Expert 5-8

Excel also has a *NOMINAL(effect_rate,npery)* function that converts from a "long" effective rate to a "long" nominal rate. We can then convert that "long" nominal rate into a "short" rate by simply dividing it by the number of "short" periods in the "long" period. This is fairly easy to implement:

▲	A	B	C
1	Rate$_{Long}$	35900.00%	
2	Short Periods per Long	21	
3			
4	Rate$_{Short}$	32.35%	=NOMINAL(B1,B2)/B2

Note that in all of this conversation about effective rates, we have completely disregarded **nominal rates**, of which the **annual percentage rate (APR)** is the most popular. There's a reason for this popularity. In the 1800s, Mark Twain popularized the saying, "There are three kinds of lies: lies, damned lies, and statistics." If he were alive today, I think he would be tempted to add "… and APRs."

APRs and other nominal rates are lies, both in the sense that they can't be used in mathematical formulas without messing them up, and (in the particular case of the APR) in the sense that they were imposed on the American public so as to provide a "fairer" way to judge the rates being charged on consumer loans because they were easier to compute without a calculator. In fact, they did just the opposite, causing people to systematically understate the rates they were being charged on consumer loans.

Turning back to our example of a credit card charging 1.50% interest per month that we discussed earlier, that monthly rate was equivalent to an annual effective rate of 19.56%. However, the rules for calculating the APR, laid out in the Truth in Lending Act of 1968, would simply take that 1.50% monthly rate and multiple it by the number of payments per year: $1.50\% \times 12 = 18\%$. As you should probably already be able to guess (due to the APR formula not involving exponentiation), the APR for the credit card is lower than the EAR because it ignores compound interest.

In the end, about the only useful thing about APRs and other nominal rates is that it *is* easy to get an effective rate out of them (though it's not usually the effective rate for the holding period you want or need). For example, dividing an APR of 18% based on monthly payments gets us quickly back to our 1.5% effective monthly rate, which we can then convert to an effective rate for the holding period we're interested in by using **Equation 5-13**.

nominal rates
Annualized interest rates based on simple interest only

annual percentage rate (APR)
A nominal rate consisting of the periodic effective rate multiplied by the number of payments per year

5-2 Measuring Risk

Risk refers to the uncertainty that the actual return the investor realizes from an asset will equal the expected return, which we already touched upon when we developed **Equation 5-7**:

$$r = E(r) + U$$

As we will discuss in Chapter 6, some of this risk is asset- or firm-specific; it can be cancelled out by holding multiple assets together in a diversified portfolio so that

risk
A measure of the dispersion of actual returns around the expected return

the firm-specific portions of the risks of each asset offset each other. However, some of the sources of risk are common to all assets, and no amount of diversification in your investment portfolio will allow you to eliminate it. This implies that we will eventually need to rewrite **Equation 5-7** in a slightly more advanced form:

$$r = E(r) + U_{Diversifiable} + U_{Non\text{-}divesifiable} \qquad \textbf{5-15}$$

However, as a first step toward dealing with both diversifiable and non-diversifiable risk, we are going to start with single-asset portfolios. By holding a single asset like this, we won't be making any attempt at measuring or mitigating the diversifiable risk, which allows us to treat (for now) all the risk as non-diversifiable. Once we've got a handle on measuring this **total risk** and have developed a formula for how expected return has to compensate investors for risk in this chapter, we'll move on to how that total risk of an investment changes in a diversified portfolio in Chapter 6.

5-2a The Law of Large Numbers (LLN) and the Benefit of Recency

In statistics and probability theory, the **law of large numbers (LLN)** is a theorem that describes the result of performing the same experiment many times. According to the LLN, the average of the results obtained from a large number of trials should be close to the expected value and will tend to become closer to the expected value as more trials are performed.

In the context of Investments, those "multiple experiments" of the LLN are analogous to the repeated holding period returns that we earn from investing in an asset for period after period. *Everything else held constant*, if past realized returns to an asset can be used to forecast the future expected returns of that asset, then the LLN tell us that we are better off using as many historic returns as possible to predict expected future returns. But, in the real world, *"everything else"* is *not "held constant."* That is, common sense tells us that, over time, the technological, competitive, regulatory, etc., environments facing individual businesses and/or investments in assets changes. If we take historic returns of a firm or asset from far back in the past, we run the risk of those returns having been made in a far different environment than we expect going forward. In effect, we have to worry about older historic returns being "stale" and not representatives of the potential future returns we are trying to forecast.

To some extent, we've already subtly alluded to such concerns in previous examples. When we chose to calculate INTC's average one-year HPRs, we only went back five years instead of all the way back to when the firm first went public. And, even though the choice of a five-year period may have seemed a little arbitrary at the time, we actually chose it rather carefully, as most investment professionals agree that using historic returns that are more than five years old runs the risk of using stale data.

However, going back to the concept of the LLN, using a sample of only five annual historic returns to predict the future expected return doesn't really seem to fit the definition of a "large number." Indeed, it is not, but no one ever said that we have to use *annual* returns. The way that most investment professionals get around this issue it to use the past 60 *monthly* returns[4] as their historic sample and use those to predict the future expected monthly return. Doing so involves an additional step of converting

total risk
Diversifiable plus non-diversifiable risk of an asset

law of large numbers
A theorem stating that the average of the results obtained from a large number of trials will tend to become closer to the expected value as more trials are performed

---

[4]In fact, some investment professionals feel that even going back five years can run the risk of dipping into stale data, particularly if the firm has acquired another business. Accordingly, you will also find some investors using the latest 52 weekly returns, or some other similar combination of more but shorter holding periods, to forecast expected returns.

the expected monthly returns to an annual return. This estimation procedure gracefully sidesteps the issue of returns more than five years old being stale, while giving us enough historic observations to reduce our forecast error in line with the LLN.

Implementing such a procedure in the real world is actually fairly simple. Going back to Yahoo! Finance, but this time using AMD as an example, we can select "Monthly" frequency on the Historical Data page as shown in **Figure 5-3**.

This, in turn, will give us monthly price data, which we can download to compute monthly returns after selecting an appropriate historic range of observations as shown in **Figure 5-4**.

Figure 5-3: AMD Historical Data on Yahoo! Finance

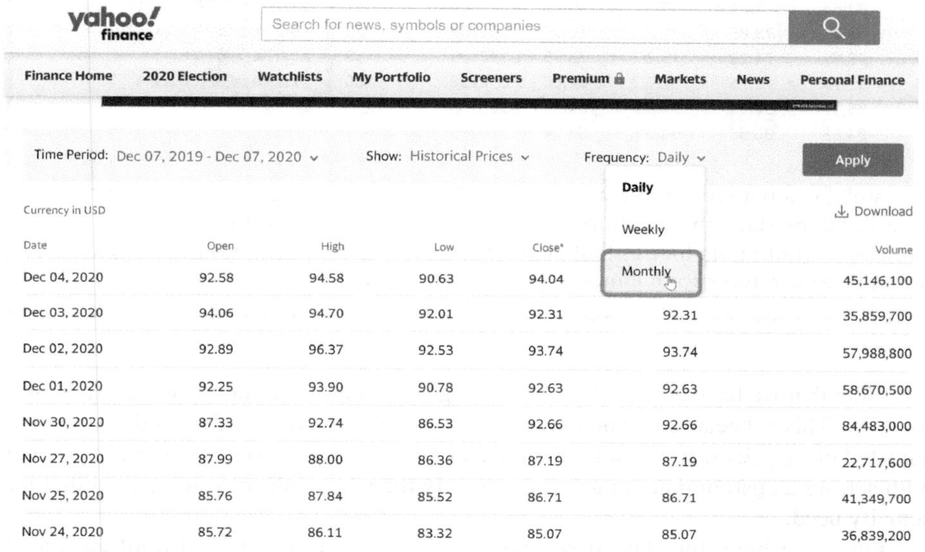

Date	Open	High	Low	Close*		Volume
Dec 04, 2020	92.58	94.58	90.63	94.04		45,146,100
Dec 03, 2020	94.06	94.70	92.01	92.31	92.31	35,859,700
Dec 02, 2020	92.89	96.37	92.53	93.74	93.74	57,988,800
Dec 01, 2020	92.25	93.90	90.78	92.63	92.63	58,670,500
Nov 30, 2020	87.33	92.74	86.53	92.66	92.66	84,483,000
Nov 27, 2020	87.99	88.00	86.36	87.19	87.19	22,717,600
Nov 25, 2020	85.76	87.84	85.52	86.71	86.71	41,349,700
Nov 24, 2020	85.72	86.11	83.32	85.07	85.07	36,839,200

Source: Yahoo! Finance

Figure 5-4: Selection of Historical Range for Monthly Price Data on Yahoo! Finance

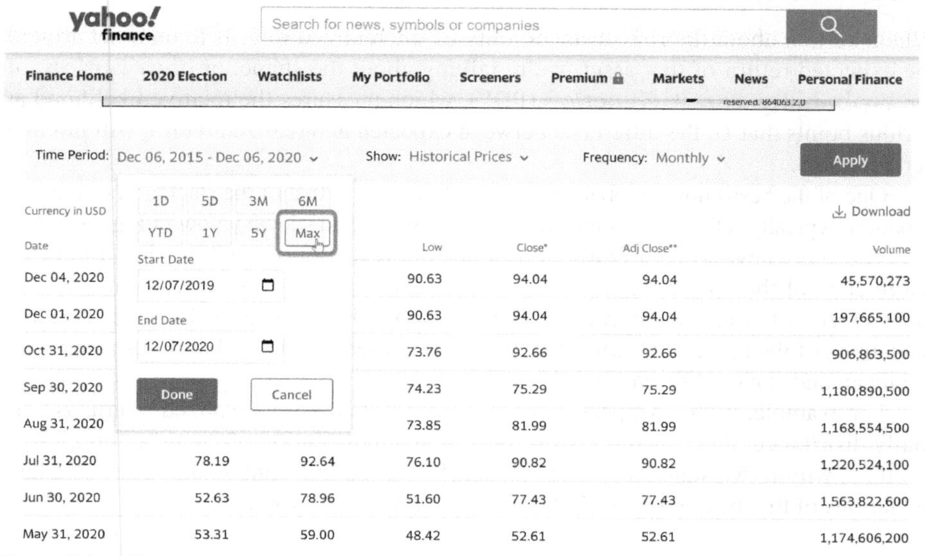

Date	Open	High	Low	Close*	Adj Close**	Volume
Dec 04, 2020			90.63	94.04	94.04	45,570,273
Dec 01, 2020			90.63	94.04	94.04	197,665,100
Oct 31, 2020			73.76	92.66	92.66	906,863,500
Sep 30, 2020			74.23	75.29	75.29	1,180,890,500
Aug 31, 2020			73.85	81.99	81.99	1,168,554,500
Jul 31, 2020	78.19	92.64	76.10	90.82	90.82	1,220,524,100
Jun 30, 2020	52.63	78.96	51.60	77.43	77.43	1,563,822,600
May 31, 2020	53.31	59.00	48.42	52.61	52.61	1,174,606,200

Source: Yahoo! Finance

The trickiest part in converting the downloaded monthly adjusted close prices to monthly returns lies in ensuring that you choose the correct rows to get the latest 60 monthly returns. First, our choice of the "Max" history to download implies that there will be a large number of older data that we can get rid of. You may find it helpful to sort the data on Date in descending order, and then delete the rows for the older Dates at the bottom as a first step.

	A	B	C	D	E	F	G	H	I	J
1	Date	Open	High	Low	Close	Adj Close	Volume	Observation	Monthly Return	
58	8/1/2020	78.19	92.64	76.1	90.82	90.82	1.22E+09	57	-9.72%	=F59/F58-1
59	9/1/2020	91.92	94.28	73.85	81.99	81.99	1.17E+09	58	-8.17%	=F60/F59-1
60	10/1/2020	83.06	88.72	74.23	75.29	75.29	1.18E+09	59	23.07%	=F61/F60-1
61	11/1/2020	75.85	92.74	73.76	92.66	92.66	9.07E+08	60	1.49%	=F62/F61-1
62	12/1/2020	92.25	96.37	90.63	94.04	94.04	1.98E+08			
63	12/4/2020	92.58	94.58	90.63	94.04	94.04	45570273			

Note that you also have to be careful when it comes to the *latest* downloaded observation. Depending on what day of the month you download the data, this latest row may represent prices from other than the end-of-the-month/beginning-of-next-month time frames that all the other rows do, so you may have to leave it out (in the spirit of only including historic returns for full-month periods), as we do here.

Note that we have chosen the "Max" range of prices, even though there is a choice for "5Y." This is because to calculate 60 monthly returns, we actually need 61 monthly adjusted close prices. It is just more convenient to choose "Max" rather than to bother with setting a custom date range to get exactly the 61 months of pricing data that we actually need.

Once we have the data downloaded, it is a straightforward application of **Equation 5-8** to calculate the 60 monthly returns.

5-2b The Distribution of Monthly Returns

distribution
The mathematical function that gives the probabilities of occurrence of different possible outcomes for an experiment

probability density function
A function measuring the relative likelihood at various points that a given number will fall in a certain range

When we talk about the risk or uncertainty of the realized returns to an asset around the expected return of that asset, we're talking about the shape, or **distribution**, of the **probability density function** (PDF), which measures the relative likelihood at various points that U, the difference between expected and realized return, will fall in a certain range.

One of the best-known probability density functions is that of the standard normal distribution, typically referred to as the "bell-shaped curve" and shown below in **Figure 5-5**.

There are several nice features of a normal distribution such as this. First, the parameters of the normal distribution are well known, and, if we can assume that an asset's series of returns are normally distributed, this allows us to easily "map" possible deviations of the realized returns from the expected return into probabilities using only the mean and standard deviation.

For example, if the unexpected component, U, of an asset's realized returns is normally distributed, then it will lie within one standard deviation of the mean 68.27% of the time, within two standard deviations 95.45% of the time, and within three standard deviations of the mean 99.73% of the time, as shown in **Figure 5-6**.

Figure 5-5: Probability Density of Standard Normal Distribution

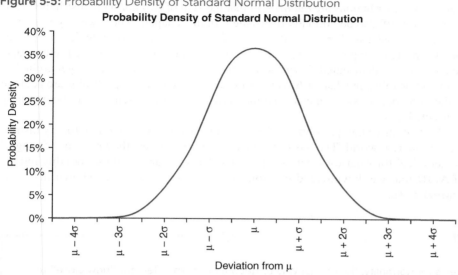

Figure 5-6: Mapping of Normal PDF into Probabilities

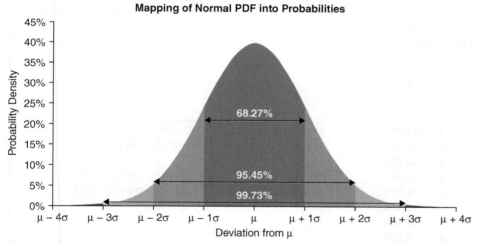

Being able to put "caps" like these on the chances that U will be outside these ranges is extremely helpful to risk-averse investors.

Even more important, for other types of distributions, we typically have to measure and keep track of up to four **moments** of the distribution to map deviation from the mean into probabilities like this. In addition to worrying about the mean and variance (i.e., squared standard deviation) of the distribution, we'd also have to keep track of the distribution's **skewness** (a measure of symmetry, or whether the graph looks the same to the left and right of the center point) and **kurtosis** (a measure of how "fat" the far-left and far-right tails of the distribution are). For the normal distribution, we only need the mean and standard deviation to map deviations from the mean into probabilities, which helps to greatly simplify our calculations.

moments
Attributes of a statistical distribution used to describe its shape

skewness
A measure of distribution symmetry

kurtosis
A measure of how "fat" the tails of a distribution are

Another big advantage of dealing with variables that are normally distributed is that normal distributions are *additive*, in that the sum of two normally distributed variables will itself also be normally distributed. In this chapter, where we're going to be dealing with one asset's returns at a time, this assumption of normality on the part of the unexpected component of realized return translates into total realized returns also being normally distributed. It will also come in really handy when we get around to forming portfolios in Chapter 6, as we will see that the fact that portfolios are additive in their component assets means that the portfolio's realized returns will be normally distributed, too.

So that raises the question of whether realized stock returns *are* normally distributed in the real world. The answer is that, for our purposes, they're "close enough." To get a feel for what we mean by that, let's start by graphing those monthly returns of AMD that we downloaded previously using a **histogram** as shown in **Excel Expert 5-10**.

histogram
A bar graph used to indicate frequencies of occurrence in various ranges

Excel Expert 5-10

Though there are statistical tests for normality, the easiest way to get a fundamental feel for "how close" to normal a distribution is to graph it as a histogram, which is a bar chart measuring the frequencies of different ranges, or "bins," of the variable in question, and then to compare the resulting distribution to what the normal distribution would look like.

Excel has a bundled add-in called the "Analysis ToolPak" that provides drop-down guided access to a basic set of data analysis tools. Though this add-in gets installed with Excel, it is not enabled by default, and so the first thing you need to do in using those analysis tools (of which creating a histogram is one) is to enable the add-in.

Once that is ready, the easiest way to set things up to graph a histogram for our purposes is to first calculate the sets of values shown below:

	A	H	I	J	K	L	M
1	Date	Observation	Monthly Return				
2	12/1/2015	1	-23.34%		Max Return	47.18%	=MAX(I2:I61)
3	1/1/2016	2	-2.73%		Min Return	-41.05%	=MIN(I2:I61)
4	2/1/2016	3	33.18%				
5	3/1/2016	4	24.56%		Mean	7.39%	=AVERAGE(I2:I61)
6	4/1/2016	5	28.73%		Standard Deviation	17.24%	=STDEV.S(I2:I61)
7	5/1/2016	6	12.47%				
8	6/1/2016	7	33.46%		Bin Start		
9	7/1/2016	8	7.87%			-50%	
10	8/1/2016	9	-6.62%			-40%	
11	9/1/2016	10	4.63%			-30%	
12	10/1/2016	11	23.24%			-20%	
13	11/1/2016	12	27.27%			-10%	
14	12/1/2016	13	-8.55%			0%	
15	1/1/2017	14	39.44%			10%	
16	2/1/2017	15	0.62%			20%	
17	3/1/2017	16	-8.59%			30%	
18	4/1/2017	17	-15.86%			40%	
19	5/1/2017	18	11.53%			50%	

As you can see, we first start by using four statistical functions: *MAX()* and *MIN()*, to get an idea of the range of our observations, and *AVERAGE()* and *STDEV.S()*, to get an idea of where the center (i.e., mean or

(Continued)

arithmetic average) and of what the sample standard deviation of our data is. Seeing that our return data seems to be in the range from −50% to 50%, we then (somewhat arbitrarily) choose to make our histogram bins as shown in cells K9:K19. After setting up our bin range, we then run the Data Analysis tool on the Data ribbon bar, setting up our inputs as shown:

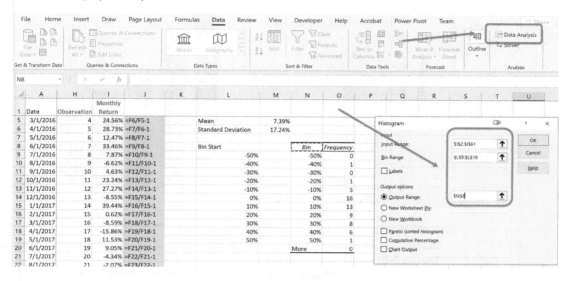

The trickiest part in converting the downloaded monthly adjusted close prices to monthly returns lies in ensuring that you choose the correct rows to get the latest 60 monthly returns. First, our choice of the "Max" history to download implies that there will be older data that we can get rid of. (You may find it helpful to sort the data on Date in descending order and then delete the rows for the older Dates at the bottom as a first step.)

	A	B	C	D	E	F	G	H	I	J
1	Date	Open	High	Low	Close	Adj Close	Volume	Observation	Monthly Return	
58	8/1/2020	78.19	92.64	76.1	90.82	90.82	1.22E+09	57	-9.72%	=F59/F58-1
59	9/1/2020	91.92	94.28	73.85	81.99	81.99	1.17E+09	58	-8.17%	=F60/F59-1
60	10/1/2020	83.06	88.72	74.23	75.29	75.29	1.18E+09	59	23.07%	=F61/F60-1
61	11/1/2020	75.85	92.74	73.76	92.66	92.66	9.07E+08	60	1.49%	=F62/F61-1
62	12/1/2020	92.25	96.37	90.63	94.04	94.04	1.98E+08			
63	12/4/2020	92.58	94.58	90.63	94.04	94.04	45570273			

Note that you also have to be careful when it comes to the latest downloaded observation. Depending on what day of the month you download the data, this latest row may represent prices from other than the end-of-the-month/beginning-of-next-month time frames that all the other rows do, so you may have to leave it out (in the spirit of only including historic returns for full-month periods), as we do here.

If we then create a column chart of the resulting frequencies for each bin, it shows us a rough distribution of our sample of returns for AMD, as shown in **Figure 5-7**.

Though this looks only vaguely bell-shaped, we can lay an actual graph of a normal distribution with the same mean and standard deviation as the AMD returns on top of it for comparison, as shown in **Figure 5-8**. You can do this by using the NORM. DIST(x,mean,standard_dev,cumulative) Excel function. Use the Bin column for the *x* variables and the mean and standard deviation of the sample. Cumulative should be set to 0.

Figure 5-7: Histogram of AMD Returns

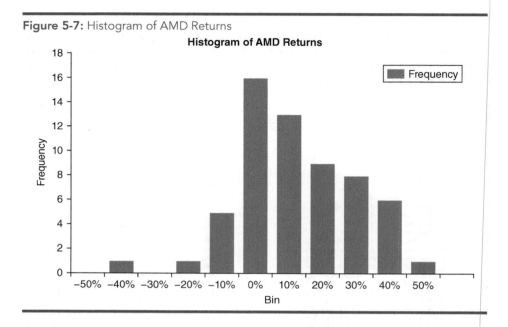

Figure 5-8: Histogram of AMD Returns vs. Normal Distribution

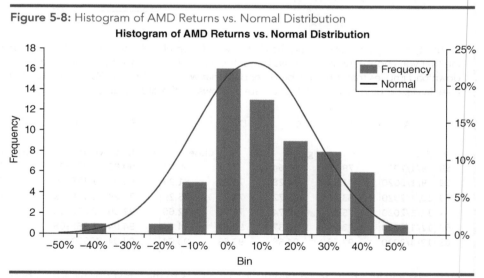

To the layman's eye, AMD's return distribution doesn't appear to be very close to a normal distribution. But in practice, it's not that far off. In fact, some aberration from a theoretically "perfect" normal distribution is to be expected, as a sample size of 60 returns, though large enough to make us feel comfortable about using them to forecast expected future returns, is still a fairly small sample size in the statistical world. In such situations, we'll sometimes go back and use all available returns for the histogram (though our reasoning for not using stale data for forecasting still holds), which, in AMD's case, would yield the histogram shown in **Figure 5-9**.

Doing so makes AMD's histogram of monthly returns look much more similar what we would expect from a normal distribution, implying that part of the "weirdness" of the histogram we saw in **Figure 5-8** was due to random sampling error.

Figure 5-9: Histogram of All Available Monthly Returns for AMD from March 1980 through November 2020

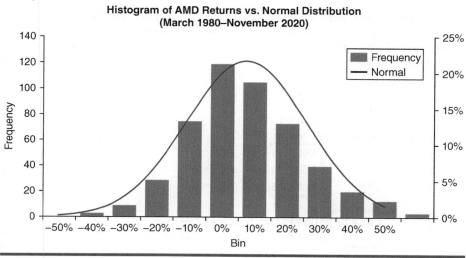

Over the years, many researchers have run similar and more precise comparisons between stock return distributions and equivalent normal distributions. Their consensus is the same as what we just determined: for most analyses, particularly those we're going to be doing in this text, returns seem to be closely distributed to a normal distribution for our purposes.

5-2c Calculating Standard Deviation of Returns

We've already discussed the mean, or arithmetic average, in **Equation 5-9** as a special case of the probabilistic expected return, which is shown in **Equation 5-12**.

In either case, to calculate the standard deviation, we first find the appropriate expected return using either **Equation 5-9** or **Equation 5-12** and then use it to find the sum of the "weighted" squared deviations of the actual returns around that expected return, taking the square root so that the standard deviation is expressed in the same basis as the returns and their mean.

For example, if we were in a situation where we were explicitly estimating the expected return using probabilities as per **Equation 5-12**, and we thought that there was a 0.30 probability of earning a 10% return, a 0.30 probability of earning a 12% return, and a 0.40 probability of earning a 17% return, we would calculate the expected return using **Equation 5-12** as:

$$E(r) = (0.30 \times 10\%) + (0.30 \times 12\%) + (0.40 \times 17\%) = 13.40\%$$

And then we would calculate the standard deviation as:

$$\sigma = \sqrt{\sum_{t=1}^{n} (p_t \times [r_t - E(r)]^2)}$$

$$= \sqrt{0.30 \times [10\% - 13.40\%]^2 + 0.30 \times [12\% - 13.40\%]^2 + 0.40 \times [17\% - 13.40\%]^2}$$

$$= 3.04\% \hspace{6cm} \textbf{5-16}$$

Excel Expert 5-11

As previously demonstrated, the easiest way to compute the expected return is using the *SUMPRODUCT()* function, shown below in cell C6. Calculating the standard deviation also involves the same function, but inside a *SQRT()* function and with *SUMPRODUCT()* being applied to the probabilities in column A with the squared deviations from the expected return, calculated in column C.

	A	B	C	D	E
1	Probability	Return	Squared Deviations		
2	0.3	10%	0.001156	=(B2-$B$6)^2	
3	0.3	12%	0.000196	=(B3-$B$6)^2	
4	0.4	17%	0.001296	=(B4-$B$6)^2	
5					
6	E(r)	13.40%	=SUMPRODUCT(A2:A4,B2:B4)		
7	σ	3.04%	=SQRT(SUMPRODUCT(A2:A4,C2:C4))		

If, on the other hand, we were using the historic returns shown below (and carefully selected to allow us to compare with the probabilistic example) to calculate the arithmetic average and historic standard deviation to use as estimates of expected future return and volatility, then our calculations would be as shown:

$E(r) = Arithmetic\ Average$

$$= \frac{10\% + 10\% + 10\% + 12\% + 12\% + 12\% + 17\% + 17\% + 17\% + 17\%}{10}$$

$$= 13.40\%$$

$$\sigma = \sqrt{\sum_{t=1}^{n}\left(\frac{[r_t - E(r)]^2}{n}\right)} \qquad \text{5-17}$$

$$= \sqrt{\frac{\left(\begin{array}{l}[10\% - 13.40\%]^2 + [10\% - 13.40\%]^2 + [10\% - 13.40\%]^2 + \\ [12\% - 13.40\%]^2 + [12\% - 13.40\%]^2 + [12\% - 13.40\%]^2 + \\ [17\% - 13.40\%]^2 + [17\% - 13.40\%]^2 + [17\% - 13.40\%]^2 + [17\% - 13.40\%]^2\end{array}\right)}{10}}$$

$$= 3.04\%$$

As we can see, if the forward-looking probabilities of the various returns are set equal to their relative frequencies of occurrence observed when using historic data, we get the same expected return and standard deviation using either approach.

However, there is one fundamental difference between using the forward-looking, probabilistic approach to calculating expected returns and the approach based on using the historic distribution of returns as a proxy for the distribution of expected returns. In the former, if we're guessing about the future, we might as well guess about the *entire* future population of possible returns. That is, we should include every expected return that could possibly happen. And we have been, which is why the probabilities under that approach have summed up to 1.0.

> ## Excel Expert 5-12
>
> Calculating the average and standard deviation of historical returns like these in Excel involves only the use of the *AVERAGE()* and *STDEV.P()* ("P" for Population: see below) functions:
>
> | | A | B | C | D |
> |---|---|---|---|---|
> | 1 | Time Period | Return | | |
> | 2 | 1 | 10% | | |
> | 3 | 2 | 10% | | |
> | 4 | 3 | 10% | | |
> | 5 | 4 | 12% | | |
> | 6 | 5 | 12% | | |
> | 7 | 6 | 12% | | |
> | 8 | 7 | 17% | | |
> | 9 | 8 | 17% | | |
> | 10 | 9 | 17% | | |
> | 11 | 10 | 17% | | |
> | 12 | | | | |
> | 13 | E(r) | 13.40% | =AVERAGE(B2:B11) | |
> | 14 | σ | 3.04% | =STDEV.P(B2:B11) | |

But when we're using the distribution of historic returns as a proxy for future expected returns, it's important that we realize that the historic record for that asset *cannot* possibly constitute the population of all eventual realized returns. (Obviously not, if we're using the past returns to predict future returns that haven't happened yet.) So, therefore, we're working with only a sample of the returns for that asset.

When you are calculating statistics on a sample instead of on an entire population, the mean is an unbiased estimator of the expected return, so we're still good to use **Equation 5-9** when calculating the expected future return based on historic realized rates. However, the convention for the calculation of standard deviation when using only a sample from a population is that we normally "correct" it by using **Equation 5-18** instead of **Equation 5-17**:

$$\sigma = \sqrt{\sum_{t=1}^{n}\left(\frac{[r_t - E(r)]^2}{n-1}\right)} \qquad \text{5-18}$$

Notice that the only difference between the two equations is that while we divided each term by n in **Equation 5-17**, we divide by $n\text{-}1$ in **Equation 5-18**. Dividing by a consistently smaller number like that, we get a slightly larger sample standard deviation than we would an equivalent population standard deviation.

$$= \sqrt{\frac{\begin{pmatrix}[10\% - 13.40\%]^2 + [10\% - 13.40\%]^2 + [10\% - 13.40\%]^2 + \\ [12\% - 13.40\%]^2 + [12\% - 13.40\%]^2 + [12\% - 13.40\%]^2 + \\ [17\% - 13.40\%]^2 + [17\% - 13.40\%]^2 + [17\% - 13.40\%]^2 + [17\% - 13.40\%]^2\end{pmatrix}}{9}}$$

$$= 3.20\%$$

The only difference in calculating a sample standard deviation rather than a population standard deviation is that we use the *STDEV.S()* function instead of the *STDEV.P()* function:

	A	B	C	D
1	Time Period	Return		
2	1	10%		
3	2	10%		
4	3	10%		
5	4	12%		
6	5	12%		
7	6	12%		
8	7	17%		
9	8	17%		
10	9	17%		
11	10	17%		
12				
13	E(r)	13.40%	=AVERAGE(B2:B11)	
14	σ	3.20%	=STDEV.S(B2:B11)	

5-3 Return vs. Risk: The Historical Record

OK, so now we know how to measure both return and risk. Also, we've been sort of implicitly assuming that because investors are risk averse, they will demand/expect to *get* more return for investing in assets with more risk. Does that actually happen?

5-3a Is Risk "Priced" into Returns?

Formally phrased, our question about the relationship between expected return and risk becomes one of whether risk is included in the price that investors pay for assets, and, in turn, whether that risk is compensated for by a lower purchase price, causing the investor to realize a higher return.

By and large, the answer is yes. For example, if we were to calculate the average and standard deviations of the past five years' worth of monthly returns for the three stocks we have been using in our previous examples (AMD, INTC, and WMT), we would see the relationship as shown in **Figure 5-10**.

Admittedly, this is a rather small sample (we'll deal with that in a moment), but, overall, the stock with the highest standard deviation in returns also has the highest average return. In general, this would seem to support the idea that risk is "priced" in the market, with expected/realized return being higher for assets with more risk in order to compensate investors for that higher risk. The one troubling thing about this graph is the relationship between the risk/return for INTC and that for WMT. Over the five-year period, WMT has earned a higher average return but has also had lower volatility, which seems to counter the idea of the market pricing risk.

The World of Investing

Bitcoin Volatility

Which investment is riskier, Bitcoin or the stock market? This chapter introduces standard deviation of returns as a measure of risk. A higher standard deviation indicates a larger dispersion of returns around the mean, which is a higher risk. But that may not give you a feel for how this volatility impacts you.

Consider the cryptocurrency Bitcoin that was introduced in 2014. Since its introduction, its monthly return and standard deviation through May 2021 has been 8.37%, and 23.33%, respectively. That is a very high return and risk! As a comparison, the stock market average return and risk (as proxied by the S&P 500 Index) was 1.03% and 4.16%. The graph visually illustrates how much more volatile Bitcoin is compared to the stock market. Bitcoin frequently loses 30% in value or gains 30% or more in a single *month*. When the stock market declines 30% over a *quarter*, it is described as a terrible bear market.

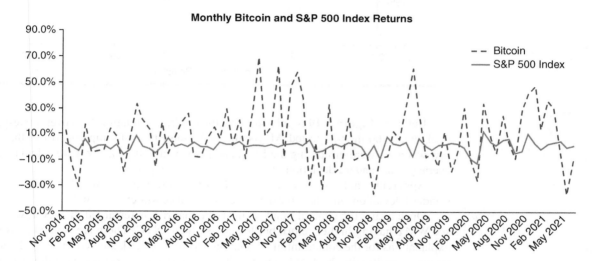

The extreme volatility of Bitcoin and other cryptocurrencies causes significant doubt over their ability to actually be used as a currency for day-to-day purchases. Imagine getting a paycheck in Bitcoin worth $5,000 and then a week later it is only worth $4,000. Until crypto prices stabilize, they are unlikely to be taken seriously as a currency.

Figure 5-10: Standard Deviation vs. Average Return for Selected Stocks

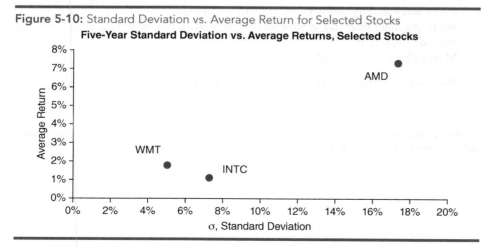

Figure 5-11: Standard Deviation vs. Average Return for Selected Stocks from 3/1980 to 11/2020

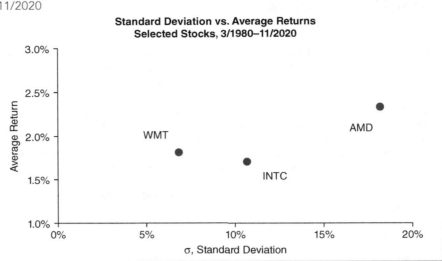

But wait! **Figure 5-10** is only showing the risk/return relationships over a five-year (technically, 60-month) period. Maybe this is the same type of sampling artifact that we saw when we were discussing the LLN, and perhaps it will go away if we calculate the average and standard deviation of returns over a longer period.

Apparently not, as shown below in **Figure 5-11**, which shows the averages and standard deviations in return for the three stocks since March of 1980.[5]

Once again, the general trend seems to be that risk is rewarded; however, we still see WMT having higher return but lower risk than INTC. There are several possible explanations for the counterintuitive relationship between risk and return being demonstrated, specifically, by INTC and WMT here. These explanations boil down to the following:

1. Imperfections of the relationship between risk and return are being driven by the fact that we're looking at a sample, not the population of all returns that will ever happen.
2. There might be a systematic difference between what we *expect* to get in terms of return and volatility and what we actually experience.
3. We're graphing total risk against returns. Should all risk be priced, even if we can mitigate some of it?
4. Maybe different classes of assets have different "prices" for risk.

We'll address these one-by-one in the next subsections.

---

[5]All three companies were actually formed significantly earlier than 1980, but historical stock market data for both AMD and INTC was only available through Yahoo! Finance back to March of 1980.

5-3b The Effect of Sampling on Compensation for Risk

Even though we have extended the calculation of historic average and standard deviations as far back in time as we can, it is still possible that what we're seeing is an artifact of sampling that might go away if we could take a large enough sample.

Possible, but we would deem it "not likely." Even in much broader samples, we still see a nonperfect relationship between risk and return. For example, we see the same general trend toward pricing risk but with inconsistencies even when we graph a broader sample, such as the S&P 500 shown in **Figure 5-12**.

5-3c Our Inability to Perfectly See Investors' Expectations

It is possible that there is some small "disconnect" between the risk/return relationship seen in historical returns and the risk/return relationship expected in future returns. That is, even though strict pricing of risk hasn't held in the past, investors might still expect it to hold more strictly in the future.

Such a disconnect between the realized compensation for risk and the expected future compensation for risk is simply impossible to either prove or disprove. We will never be able to perfectly discern investors' future expectations of the price for risk and use historical returns as a method of calculating a proxy for such, but it will always be an *inexact* proxy. We'll touch upon this subject again once we've had a chance to examine the pricing of risk in portfolios in Chapter 6 and when we develop a formula for pricing non-diversifiable risk in Chapter 7.

Figure 5-12: Risk vs. Return for All Components of the S&P 500 Index

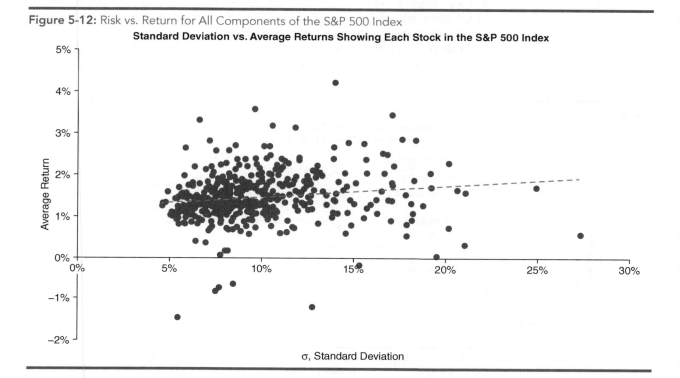

5-3d Should All Uncertainty Be Priced?

We are graphing "stand-alone" standard deviation, which represents the total uncertainty reflected in **Equation 5-7**. As we previously discussed, some of that uncertainty is diversifiable in the sense that it would be offset if the asset were held in a well-diversified portfolio. The point here being that maybe it's not all the standard deviation that matters and should be priced, but rather only the portion of the standard deviation that we can't get rid of. (This will be the primary topic of Chapter 6.)

5-3e Is There Only One "Price" for Risk?

As we've already noticed, returns aren't quite perfectly normally distributed. It's also possible that, in practice, the *distributions* of different classes of assets are of different types, as well. In particular, notice that the three stocks we've been using in our examples could be grouped into two classes. WMT is a retailer that sells a rather broad selection of **staple goods**, while AMD and INTC are "tech stocks." The demand for staple goods is relatively stable in even bad times, but there's also an upper limit on how many staple goods most consumers can use, which presumably would impose an upper ceiling on just how much profit (and return) WMT could earn. Tech stocks, on the other hand, operate in a very fluid, dynamic marketplace, that not only has more volatility, but also the potential to "knock it out of the park."

So far, we've been looking at the risk/return relationship using only the returns to shares of common stock as examples. But even if we expand our examination to include the more common classes of assets we see in the financial markets, as shown in **Figure 5-13**, we still see that while there's definitely a general trend toward more risk being compensated with more return, there are some cases where the risk/return relationship is a little inconsistent.

In short, it's likely that the "return for risk" relationship is different for those two classes of assets, which is what we'll explore in Chapter 8.

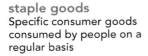

staple goods
Specific consumer goods consumed by people on a regular basis

Figure 5-13: Major Asset Classes Standard Deviation vs. Returns

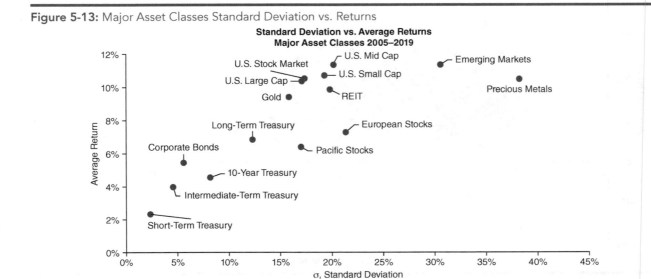

Conclusion

Mellody Hobson, the president and co-CEO of Ariel Investments (and former chairwoman of DreamWorks Animation, who negotiated the acquisition of DreamWorks by NBCUniversal in August 2016), once said, "The biggest risk of all is not taking one."[6]

In this chapter, we've started laying the groundwork for proving that there is a direct trade-off between risk and returns. As we will see in later chapters, investing toward any reasonable financial goal will require that investors invest their money in assets that are riskier than such low-risk assets as money market funds and bonds. To successfully do so, we will need to be able to measure how much risk we're being asked to take on; calculate what additional level of compensation above and beyond the risk-free rate we will require for taking on that risk; and, after we've made the investment, determine whether the actual realized risks and returns match our expectations.

We've taken a first good step toward realizing those goals, having seen that we can use both arithmetic and geometric averages of historic returns as proxies for expected future returns. We've also seen that the dispersion of returns around those average returns, measured by the standard deviation, can serve as a good measure of uncertainty about those average returns.

We will continue to build on these ideas in the next chapter, modeling and measuring how average and standard deviation in returns is affected by keeping an asset as part of a well-diversified portfolio. We will also use that analysis to develop more usable models for pricing risk in the asset markets.

Chapter Equations

$$Total\ Return = Income + (Price_{Received} - Price_{Paid}) \qquad \text{5-1}$$

$$r = \frac{Income + (Price_{Received} - Price_{Paid})}{Price_{Paid}} \qquad \text{5-2}$$

$$r = \frac{D_1}{P_0} + \frac{P_1 - P_0}{P_0} \qquad \text{5-3}$$

$$r = \frac{D_1}{P_0} = g \qquad \text{5-4}$$

$$r = \frac{C}{P_0} + g \qquad \text{5-5}$$

$$E(r) = \frac{E(D_1)}{P_0} + E(g) \qquad \text{5-6}$$

$$r = E(r) + U \qquad \text{5-7}$$

$$HPR \approx \frac{Adjusted\ Price_{Received}}{Adjusted\ Price_{Paid}} - 1 \qquad \text{5-8}$$

---

[6]Johnson, K. (2015). 14 quotes to get inspired for business growth and leadership. *Black Enterprise*. Retrieved December 1, 2020, www.blackenterprise.com/15-quotes-inspire-business-growth-leadership/

$$\text{Arithmetic Average} = \frac{\sum_{t=1}^{n} r_t}{n} \tag{5-9}$$

$$\text{Geometric Average} = \left(\sqrt[n]{\prod_{t=1}^{n} (1 + r_t)} \right) - 1 \tag{5-10}$$

$$\text{Arithmetic Average} = \sum_{t=1}^{n} \left(\frac{1}{n} \times r_t \right) \tag{5-11}$$

$$\text{Probabilistic Expected Return} = E(r) = \sum_{t=1}^{n} (p_t \times r_t) \tag{5-12}$$

$$r_{Annual} = (1 + r_{Monthly})^{12} - 1 \tag{5-13}$$

$$r_{Short} = \sqrt{(1 + r_{Long})} - 1 \tag{5-14}$$

$$r = E(r) + U^t_{Diversifiable} + U_{Non\text{-}divesifiable} \tag{5-15}$$

$$\sigma = \sqrt{\sum_{t=1}^{n} (p_t \times [r_t - E(r)]^2)} \tag{5-16}$$

$$\sigma = \sqrt{\sum_{t=1}^{n} \left(\frac{[r_t - E(r)]^2}{n} \right)} \tag{5-17}$$

$$\sigma = \sqrt{\sum_{t=1}^{n} \left(\frac{[r_t - E(r)]^2}{n - 1} \right)} \tag{5-18}$$

Excel Functions

RATE(nper, pmt, pv, [fv], [type], [guess])
AVERAGE(number1,[number2],...)
FVSCHEDULE(principal, schedule)
SUMPRODUCT(array1,[array2],[array3]...)
EFFECT(nominal_rate,npery)
NOMINAL(effect_rate,npery)
MAX()

MIN()
AVERAGE()
STDEV.S()
SQRT()
STDEV.P()
NORM.DIST(x,mean,standard_dev,cumulative)

Key Terms

adjusted close – **An end-of-day stock price that is adjusted for subsequent dividends and stock splits**

annual percentage rate (APR) – **A nominal rate consisting of the periodic effective rate multiplied by the number of payments per year**

arithmetic average – **The sum of a set of numbers divided by the number of observations**

capital appreciation – **The increase in value of an investment**

capital gains yield – **A measure of an investment's return based solely on the capital appreciation**

compound interest – **Interest earned on both principal and earlier interest**

current yield – **A measure of income return computed as income over investment value**

distribution – The mathematical function that gives the probabilities of occurrence of different possible outcomes for an experiment

dividend yield – A measure of annual return from the dividend income only

expectations operator – The use of $E()$ to denote that a value is an expectation

expected returns – The amount of profit or loss that an investor anticipates receiving on an investment

forecasting – Predicting future values of a variable

geometric average – The average compounded growth of an investment

histogram – A bar graph used to indicate frequencies of occurrence in various ranges

holding period – The amount of time that an investment is held by an investor

holding period return (HPR) – The investment return over a specified period

income – Cash in-flows from an investment, like dividends, interest payments, or rent

idiosyncratic risk – Risk that is unique to a particular asset, also called nonsystematic risk

kurtosis – A measure of how "fat" the tails of a distribution are

law of large numbers – A theorem stating that the average of the results obtained from a large number of trials will tend to become closer to the expected value as more trials are performed

moments – Attributes of a statistical distribution used to describe its shape

nominal rates – Annualized interest rates based on simple interest only

nonsystematic risk – Risk that is unique to a particular asset, also called idiosyncratic risk

probability density function – A function measuring the relative likelihood at various points that a given number will fall in a certain range

realized return – The amount or percentage of money gained or lost over a holding period

required return – The minimum amount of expected return to compensate for the risk of holding an asset

return – Compensation for investing in an asset

risk – A measure of the dispersion of actual returns around the expected return

simple interest – Interest earned on principal alone

skewness – A measure of distribution symmetry

staple goods – Specific consumer goods consumed by people on a regular basis

total risk – Diversifiable plus non-diversifiable risk of an asset

Treasury bills – A short-term U.S. government debt obligation backed by the Treasury Department with a maturity of one year or less

Questions

1. **Return Components.** What are the primary components of return? (LO 5-1)

2. **Holding Period Returns.** What factors go into calculating a holding period return? (LO 5-2)

3. **Different Returns.** What are the differences between the expected return, the required return, and the realized return? (LO 5-3)

4. **Arithmetic and Geometric. Averages** What is the basic difference between arithmetic and geometric average returns? Which will always be higher? (LO 5-4)

5. **Adjusted Close Prices.** How many adjusted close prices would you need to calculate the past 40 quarterly returns? Why? (LO 5-5)

6. **Data Staleness.** How do the law of large numbers and data "staleness" fit together? (LO 5-6)

7. **Effective Interest Rates.** If you wanted an effective quarterly interest based on daily interest rates, how would you go about constructing it? (LO 5-7)

8. **Standard Deviation.** Why do we use the population standard deviation for probabilistic situations but the sample standard deviation when calculating standard deviation on historic data? (LO 5-8)

9. **Distribution Normality.** What are the advantages of a stock's returns being normally distributed? (LO 5-9)

10. **Historical Relationship of Risk and Return.** Historically, does higher risk always offer higher return? Why or why not? (LO 5-10)

Problems

1. **Return Components.** If you buy a share of stock for $12, earn total dividends $0.75 while owning it, and then sell it for $10, what is your dollar return? Your total rate of return? (LO 5-1)

2. **Return Components.** If you buy a bond for $1,059.05, earn interest payments totaling $34.00 during the year, and then sell it for $1,096.26, what is your income yield? Your capital gains yield? (LO 5-1)

3. **Holding Period Returns.** The year-end closing prices of stock XYZ are shown below for the past five years. Ending in Year 5, what were the one-, two-, three-, four-, and five-year HPRs? (LO 5-1)

XYZ Stock	Year 0	Year 1	Year 2	Year 3	Year 4	Year 5
Price at End of Year	$23	$28	$34	$32	$34	$33
Dividends During Year	$3	$3	$3	$3	$3	$3

4. **Holding Period Returns.** The year-end prices for one ounce of gold is shown below. What is the five-year HPR for the periods 2011 to 2015 and 2016 to 2020? What is the 10-year HPR over that span? The data are in the file, **ch5_pr04.xlsx**. (LO 5-2)

2010	2011	2012	2013	2014	2015	2016	2017	2018	2019	2020
$1405.50	$1531.00	$1657.50	$1205.50	$1206.00	$1060.00	$1145.90	$1291.00	$1279.00	$1514.75	$1887.60

5. **Different Returns.** An investment that cost $10 was expected to have a price of $12 at the end of the year but actually had a year-end price of $13. What were the expected and realized returns for the year? (LO 5-3)

6. **Different Returns.** An investment that cost $20 was expected to have a price of $24 at the end of the year but actually had a year-end price of $18. What were the expected and realized returns for the year? (LO 5-3)

7. **Arithmetic and Geometric Averages.** Calculate the arithmetic and geometric average rates of return for the five-year period shown below. (LO 5-4)

	Year 1	Year 2	Year 3	Year 4	Year 5
Return	6%	12%	4%	15%	8%

8. **Arithmetic and Geometric Averages.** Calculate the arithmetic and geometric average rates of return for the 10-year period shown below. **ch5_pr08.xlsx**. (LO 5-4)

	Year 1	Year 2	Year 3	Year 4	Year 5	Year 6	Year 7	Year 8	Year 9	Year 10
Return	6%	12%	4%	15%	8%	3%	21%	6%	5%	18%

9. **Adjusted Close Prices.** Historical data for Kohl's Corporate (KSS) are provided in the data file, **ch5_pr09.xlsx**. What were the monthly returns for the past 12 full months? (Data from Yahoo! Finance) (LO 5-5)

10. **Adjusted Close Prices.** Historical data for NIKE, Inc. (NKE) are provided in the data file, **ch5_pr10.xlsx**. What was the total annual return for 2020? (Data from Yahoo! Finance) (LO 5-5)

11. **Data Staleness.** Download all available monthly returns for Pfizer, Inc. (PFE) from Yahoo! Finance and calculate the average and standard deviation of monthly returns using the latest one-year, three-year, five-year, and seven-year periods, all ending at the end of 2020. If you were asked to use one of these sets of statistics as a proxy for your future expectations for PFE returns, which would you choose? Why? (LO 5-6)

12. **Data Staleness.** Download all available monthly returns for Tesla, Inc. (TSLA) from Yahoo! Finance and calculate the average and standard deviation of monthly returns using the latest one-year, three-year, five-year, and seven-year periods, all ending at the end of 2020. If you

were asked to use one of these sets of statistics as a proxy for your future expectations for TSLA returns, which would you choose? Why? (LO 5-6)

13. **Effective Interest Rates.** You are offered a credit card with an APR of 21.4%, based on monthly compounding. What is the annual effective rate? If you took a cash advance of $100 against that card and made no payments for an entire year, how much would you owe at the end of that year? (LO 5-7)

14. **Nominal Interest Rates.** A load has an annual effective rate of 9.38%. For monthly compounding, what is the annual percentage rate? What is the monthly rate charged? (LO 5-7)

15. **Standard Deviation.** You expect the economy to go through a boom, bust, or remain steady with probabilities of 0.3, 0.3, and 0.4. You are considering investing in a stock that you think will yield an HPR of 20% in a boom, −33% in a bust, and 6% in a steady state. What are your expected return and standard deviation in returns for that stock? (LO 5-8)

16. **Probabilistic Expected Return.** You know the past five annual returns of a stock to be 18%, −5%, 11%, −23%, and 8%. However, you believe that the −23% return is less likely to occur in the future than the rest. Thus, you place a probability of 0.08 on that return and 0.23 on each of the other four returns. What is the probabilistic expected return? (LO 5-4)

17. **Distribution Normality.** Download all available monthly returns for NVIDIA Corporation (NVDA) from the Yahoo! Finance site. Create histograms for NVDA's monthly returns for the past five years and for all available monthly returns ending in 2020. Which histogram seems to show NVDA as being closer to a normal distribution? (LO 5-9)

18. **Distribution Normality.** Download all available monthly returns for Citigroup Inc. (C) from the Yahoo! Finance site. Create histograms for C's monthly returns for the past five years and for the past 10 years ending in 2020. Which histogram seems to show C as being closer to a normal distribution? (LO 5-9)

19. **Relationship Between Risk and Return.** Download data from the Yahoo! Finance site to compute five years of monthly returns ending at the end of 2020 for the following four stocks: Citigroup (C), NVIDIA (NVDA), Tesla (TSLA), and Pfizer (PFE). Compute the average and standard deviation of returns for each stock, graphing that average and standard deviation for each of the four stocks on a scatter plot. Does there seem to be a positive relationship between risk and return over those five years? Why or why not? (LO 5-10)

20. **Risk and Return Relationship.** Graph risk versus return for the following 10 stocks on the same scatter plot. Do they show a positive relationship between risk and return? Which stocks stick out? Why? The data are in the file, **ch05_pr20.xlsx**. (LO 5-10)

	Stock 1	Stock 2	Stock 3	Stock 4	Stock 5	Stock 6	Stock 7	Stock 8	Stock 9	Stock 10
Return	6%	12%	4%	16%	8%	3%	21%	6%	5%	17%
Std Dev.	12%	17%	7%	21%	8%	4%	32%	10%	8%	29%

Case Study

Download all available historical monthly adjusted prices for Pfizer Inc. (PFE) and use it to answer the following questions:

a. Over what one-year calendar (January to December) holding period was the HPR the highest? The lowest? Research these time periods and provide an intuitive explanation or why.
b. Graph the average and standard deviation in monthly returns for all the one-year holding periods you used

above, then graph all these combination of average and standard deviation in returns on a scatter plot. Over time, has PFE always consistently had higher average returns when the standard deviation was highest? Give examples to support your answer.
c. Is the distribution of PFE monthly returns normally distributed? Provide a histogram to assess the distribution.

Portfolios and Diversification

The previous chapter laid the groundwork for the fundamental finance concept that there is a direct trade-off between risk and expected return. In short, higher expected return comes with higher risk. Thus, to attain any reasonable financial goal, you must invest money in assets that have some risk. We've seen that we can use both arithmetic and geometric averages of historic returns as proxies for expected future returns. We've also seen that the dispersion of returns around those average returns, measured by the standard deviation, can serve as a good measure of risk about those average returns.

While risk and expected return are positively related, not all forms of risk should be expected to produce high expected returns. Indeed, betting on the toss of a coin entails risk. However, the continued betting on coin flips would net you an expected return of zero. The important concept for this chapter is that risks that can be diversified away should not be rewarded with high expected returns. Therefore, the ability to form a well-diversified **portfolio** to eliminate those risks is of paramount importance to investors. This chapter presents the theory, tools, and practice of forming portfolios of risky assets.

portfolio
A combination of investment assets

After we determine which portfolios are the best we can create with the risky assets available, then we determine which one is the best for you. Each investor chooses the portfolio that gives them the highest welfare, or satisfaction. Since everyone has a different capacity to take on risk, each investor chooses a different portfolio.

6-1 Risky Assets and Return Comovement

6-1a Two Risky Assets

Whether holding two stocks improves diversification and reduces risk compared to holding one stock depends on the comovement of returns between them. If the monthly stock returns of the two stocks are always the same, then there is no opportunity for diversification. If the monthly stock returns often differ, then these two stocks might be combined in a portfolio to reduce risk.

Figure 6-1 illustrates this point using the daily stock price of two companies over one year. Stock A (top line in red) is very volatile, that is, has much risk. However, it does earn a profit for the year. Stock B (bottom line in blue) is also volatile and also earns a profit. Note that sometimes the stock price movements appear to move in the same direction. At other times, the prices move in the opposite direction. Because of this difference, there may be an opportunity to combine the two stocks in a portfolio to reduce risk. The portfolio of the two stocks shown (middle line in gray) is created by investing half your money in stock A and half in stock B. Note that the portfolio has a profit for the year. In addition, its volatility appears to be lower than stock A or B. Combining these two stocks allowed you to earn a profit with less risk than owning either of the two stocks individually.

diversification
The reduction of risk through owning a variety of different types of assets

Figure 6-1: Combining Two Stocks Can Reduce Volatility

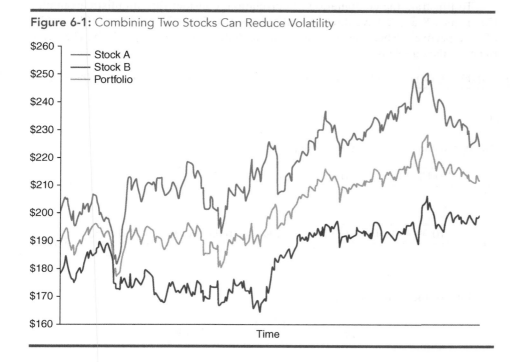

The figure is only a visual illustration of portfolio risk reduction. Investment professionals formally conduct portfolio analysis using statistical analysis of returns instead of prices. Return comovement between two assets is measured using the statistical tools of covariance and correlation. The first step is to compute the **covariance** of a sample, which is an absolute measure of comovement:

covariance
An absolute measure of comovement that varies between plus and minus infinity

$$Covariance_{ij} = \frac{\sum_{t=1}^{N}\{(r_{it} - average\ return_i) \times (r_{jt} - average\ return_j)\}}{N-1} \qquad \textbf{6-1}$$

where i and j are different individual securities or indexes and there are N time periods. Other than covariance being positive or negative, it can be difficult to interpret. Therefore, covariance is often used to compute the **correlation**. Correlation is often denoted as ρ and is a relative measure of comovement that varies between -1 and $+1$:

correlation
A measure of comovement that varies between -1 and $+1$

$$Correlation_{ij} = \rho_{ij} = \frac{covariance_{ij}}{\sigma_i \times \sigma_j} \qquad \textbf{6-2}$$

Again, i and j are different individual securities or indexes.

Correlation has a straightforward interpretation. A value of -1 means that returns from two assets are perfectly inversely correlated. In that case, a positive return of 10% in one asset would correspond with a negative return of -10% in the other asset. A correlation value of $+1$ means that returns from two different assets are perfectly in sync. They move in lockstep fashion up and down together. Asset returns are uncorrelated when they have a correlation of zero. This means that the two asset returns are not related. If one return is positive, the other could be positive or negative. The best opportunity for diversification and risk reduction occurs with assets that have negative correlation.

To illustrate the computation of correlation, consider this simplistic example. Companies X and Y have three annual returns of (15%, 8%, -5%) and (9%, -2%, 5%), respectively. Thus, the average returns are 6.0% and 4.0%, respectively. The covariance of the sample is:

$$Cov_{X,Y} = \frac{(0.15 - 0.06) \times (0.09 - 0.04) + (0.08 - 0.06) \times (-0.02 - 0.04) + (-0.05 - 0.06) \times (0.05 - 0.04)}{3-1}$$

$$= \frac{0.0022}{2} = 0.0011$$

The two standard deviations of a sample are:

$$\sigma_X = \sqrt{\frac{(0.15 - 0.06)^2 + (0.08 - 0.06)^2 + (-0.05 - 0.06)^2}{3-1}} = \sqrt{\frac{0.0206}{2}} = 10.15\%$$

$$\sigma_Y = \sqrt{\frac{(0.09 - 0.04)^2 + (-0.02 - 0.04)^2 + (0.05 - 0.04)^2}{3-1}} = \sqrt{\frac{0.0062}{2}} = 5.57\%$$

Finally, the correlation is:

$$\rho_{X,Y} = \frac{0.0011}{0.1015 \times 0.0557} = 0.1946$$

This correlation of 0.19 is low for two companies and provides some diversification opportunities. However, computing covariances, standard deviations, and correlations with only three observations is not very useful. Instead, it is typical to use samples of five years of monthly returns. Thus, using Excel or statistical programs is common. **Excel Expert 6-1** illustrates this.

To get a flavor of the correlations commonly seen within the stock market, **Table 6-1** shows the correlations of 10 popular stocks using 60 months of returns. Correlation table often appear like this, with just half of the table shown. Note that the correlation of JPM (JP Morgan) and GS (Goldman Sachs) is the same as the correlation of GS and JPM, thus the upper half of the table is redundant and not shown. The table shows that the correlation between JPM and GS is 0.831, which is high. These two stocks tend to move together. This is not surprising as they are both financial companies. There is low correlation between JPM and Apple (AAPL) and Walmart (WMT). Thus, if you owned JPM, there are good opportunities to reduce risk by buying AAPL or WMT. Interestingly, Walmart is a good candidate for diversification will all of the companies in the table.

Excel Expert 6-1

Computing Correlation

Returns for three companies over 60 months are shown below. Stock A and Stock B are in the same industry. Stock C is a company in a different sector. Covariances and correlations are computed between Stock A and B and Stock A and C.

	A	B	C	D
1	Month	Stock A	Stock B	Stock C
2	1	4.002%	10.526%	-2.919%
3	2	16.594%	23.031%	0.586%
4	3	7.634%	9.532%	-1.860%
5	4	-1.924%	-4.231%	-2.752%
6	5	7.670%	8.172%	6.278%
7	6	-3.068%	-7.151%	1.621%
8	7	-0.956%	-2.577%	5.068%
9	8	-5.032%	-5.603%	4.549%
10	9	11.260%	5.390%	-3.071%
11	10	0.438%	1.546%	5.695%
12	11	-0.447%	-0.706%	-2.400%
13	12	5.083%	6.373%	0.719%
14	13	5.340%	2.230%	11.735%
15	14	4.494%	2.128%	11.362%
16	15	2.315%	3.198%	1.563%
17	16	8.163%	5.154%	8.518%
18	17	0.373%	-1.852%	-15.563%

	A	B	C	D	E	F
51	50	21.352%	21.974%	10.119%		
52	51	7.796%	14.368%	-5.655%		
53	52	1.259%	3.389%	-2.183%		
54	53	15.202%	17.815%	-7.524%		
55	54	3.438%	2.354%	4.549%		
56	55	1.038%	6.978%	3.434%		
57	56	7.410%	6.764%	1.515%		
58	57	-5.297%	2.363%	-0.321%		
59	58	-2.417%	-1.225%	1.085%		
60	59	5.990%	10.305%	3.893%		
61	60	-1.619%	-1.951%	-1.130%		
62		1.93%	2.07%	1.48%	= Average	
63		7.16%	8.84%	5.08%	= St. Dev.	
64	Covariance (A,B) =		0.0052	=COVARIANCE.S(B2:B61,C2:C61)		
65	Covariance (A,C) =		0.0008	=COVARIANCE.S(B2:B61,D2:D61)		
66	Correlation (A,B) =		0.829	=CORREL(B2:B61,C2:C61)		
67	Correlation (A,C) =		0.206	=CORREL(B2:B61,D2:D61)		

The computed covariances are hard to interpret because their magnitude can vary depending on the standard deviation of the stocks over the sample period. However, the correlations computed are easier to interpret. The correlation of 0.829 between Stocks A and B is quite high. Note that the maximum correlation is 1. This is expected because these two companies are in the same industry. The correlation between Stocks A and C of 0.206 is low for two stocks. Thus, there is an opportunity to diversity using companies A and C.

Table 6-1: Correlation Between 10 Popular Stocks: Five Years of Monthly Returns

	JPM	GS	AAPL	BA	HD	DIS	MMM	CVX	WMT	IBM
JPM	1									
GS	0.831	1								
AAPL	0.259	0.406	1							
BA	0.580	0.516	0.196	1						
HD	0.380	0.414	0.331	0.355	1					
DIS	0.690	0.624	0.337	0.455	0.329	1				
MMM	0.540	0.471	0.356	0.421	0.516	0.296	1			
CVX	0.639	0.619	0.151	0.551	0.533	0.521	0.525	1		
WMT	0.212	0.222	0.285	0.182	0.377	0.245	0.367	0.198	1	
IBM	0.529	0.576	0.319	0.444	0.643	0.378	0.642	0.544	0.196	1

Data Source: Yahoo! Finance

6-1b Asset Classes

As the correlations in Table 6-1 suggest, most stocks move together to some degree. There are not many stocks that have a negative correlation. That suggests that diversification might be found by combining stocks with other asset classes. **Table 6-2** uses monthly returns since 2000, to compute the correlation between various segments of

Table 6-2: Correlation Between Major Asset Classes: Monthly Returns Since 2000

Panel A Average and Standard Deviation of Monthly Returns

	S&P 500 Index	Nasdaq Composite	Russell 2000	Long-Term Treasury Bond	3-Month T-Bill	Nikkei 225	DAX Performance	Shenzhen Component
Average	0.511%	0.695%	0.764%	0.475%	0.128%	0.317%	0.493%	0.933%
St. Dev.	4.311%	6.291%	5.837%	3.262%	0.146%	5.510%	5.967%	8.362%

Panel B Correlations

	S&P 500 Index	Nasdaq Composite	Russell 2000	Long-Term Treasury Bond	3-Month T-Bill	Nikkei 225	DAX Performance	Shenzhen Component
S&P 500 Index	1							
Nasdaq Composite	0.853	1						
Russell 2000	0.705	0.733	1					
Long-Term Treasury Bond	−0.380	−0.298	−0.334	1				
3-Month T-Bill	−0.103	−0.157	−0.080	0.072	1			
Nikkei 225	0.523	0.526	0.651	−0.310	−0.125	1		
DAX Performance	0.683	0.656	0.755	−0.320	−0.051	0.612	1	
Shenzhen Component	0.149	0.160	0.284	−0.093	0.144	0.272	0.282	1

Source: Yahoo! Finance; the long-term Treasury Bond market is proxied by the Vanguard Long-Term Treasury Fund Investor Shares (VUSTX)

the stock market, bond market, cash, and foreign stock markets. Panel A shows that the highest returns during this period were in China (as measured by the Shenzhen Component), with an average 0.933% per month return. The next two highest markets were the Russell 2000 and the Nasdaq Composite. The largest standard deviations were in the Chinese, Nasdaq, and German (as measured by the DAX Performance) markets. The lowest return and risk were recorded with the 3-month Treasury Bill.

Panel B of the table shows the correlations between these markets. The highest correlation is between the S&P 500 Index and the Nasdaq Composite. This is not surprising, as these indexes are dominated by large companies, and some of those companies are in both indexes. More interesting is the high correlation between the S&P 500 Index and the Russell 2000, which is a small company index. The German stock market appears to be fairly highly correlated with the U.S. stock market.

Note that the largest negative correlation in the table is the one between the S&P 500 Index and the long-term Treasury Bonds. This suggests that your portfolio should consist of both stocks and bonds to reduce risk no matter whether you are primarily a stock investor or bond investor. In addition, the Chinese stock market appears to have a low (but positive) correlation with the U.S. stock market, as well as with the Japanese and German markets.

This section argues that using a low correlation between assets allows you to reduce risk, the kind of risk for which you do not get compensated for. The next section mathematically shows how this works.

6-2 Portfolio Theory

6-2a Portfolio Risk and Return

Probably the most important task for any investor is the proper formation of the investment portfolio. A well-designed portfolio combines stocks, bonds, and other assets in such a way as to achieve an efficient trade-off between risk and expected return. There are two difficult tasks: security selection and asset allocation.

As an illustration, consider forming a two-stock portfolio from the following three stocks:

security selection
The process of selecting the assets for a portfolio

asset allocation
The way a portfolio is divided between different investments

Stock	Return
A	8.3%
B	10.6%
C	12.3%

Portfolio 1 consists of 50% Stock A and 50% Stock B. Portfolio 2 consists of 50% Stock A and 50% Stock C. Finally, Portfolio 3 consists of 70% Stock A and 30% Stock C. The return of each portfolio would therefore be:

	1st Return		Weight		2nd Return		Weight		Return
Portfolio 1	8.3%	×	0.5	+	10.6%	×	0.5	=	9.45%
Portfolio 2	8.3%	×	0.5	+	12.3%	×	0.5	=	10.3%
Portfolio 3	8.3%	×	0.7	+	12.3%	×	0.3	=	9.50%

The difference between Portfolio 1 and Portfolio 2 is security selection. They both allocate 50% to each stock, choose Stock A, but choose a different second stock. That security selection difference drives the difference in portfolio returns, 9.45% versus 10.3%. The difference between Portfolio 2 and Portfolio 3 is asset allocation. They both hold the same stocks but allocate different amounts of the portfolio to each. That asset allocation differences drives the portfolio return differences, 10.3% versus 9.50%. Thus, both security selection and asset allocation are important for your investment success.

Of course, this simple illustration only uses return. Building a successful portfolio is about achieving an efficient trade-off between expected return and risk. Thus, the next step is to detail the tools for computing portfolio return and portfolio risk.

The expected return for a portfolio can be expressed as the weighted average of the asset returns in the portfolio. The weights are the portfolio portions of each asset.

$$E(r_P) = \sum_{i=1}^{N} w_i \times E(r_i) \qquad \text{6-3}$$

In this expression, w_i is the portfolio weight, or percentage, devoted to a given security i, and $E(r_i)$ is the expected rate of return on security i. This equation works for the realized return of a portfolio too. Portfolio 3 in the example above shows that the portfolio return uses this formula for the result of 9.50% (= 0.7×8.3% + 0.3×12.3%).

The standard deviation of a portfolio is much more complicated and is calculated using the expression:

$$\sigma_{Port} = \sqrt{\sum_{i=1}^{N} w_i^2 \times \sigma_i^2 + \sum_{i=1}^{N} \sum_{\substack{j=1 \\ j \neq i}}^{N} 2 \times w_i \times w_j \times \rho_{i,j} \times \sigma_i \times \sigma_j} \qquad \text{6-4}$$

In this expression, σ_{Port} is the portfolio standard deviation, where; w_i and w_j are the portfolio weights in security i and j, respectively; σ_i^2 is the variance of returns for individual securities and σ_i is the standard deviation of returns; $\rho_{i,j}$ is the correlation of returns for securities i and j.

Now that you see the equation for portfolio risk, how does diversification reduce risk? The most direct answer is the correlation shown as the third-to-last variable. Note that in the equation, weights, variances, and standard deviations have positive values. However, correlation can be zero or even negative. A negative value would cause a subtraction in the summation procedure and reduce the portfolio standard deviation of returns.

From the simple example above, stock return standard deviations and correlations are:

Stock	St. Dev.	Correlation	A	B	C
A	15.2%		1		
B	21.7%		0.45	1	
C	29.3%		0.26	0.78	1

The Portfolio 1 standard deviation of owning 50% of Stock A and 50% of Stock B would be

$$\sigma_{Port\ 1} = \sqrt{0.5^2 \times 0.152^2 + 0.5^2 \times 0.217^2 + 2 \times 0.5 \times 0.5 \times 0.45 \times 0.152 \times 0.217}$$

$$= \sqrt{0.02497} = 15.8\%$$

The Portfolio 2 standard deviation of owning 50% of Stock A and 50% of Stock C, and Portfolio 3 standard deviation of owning 70% Stock A and 30% Stock C would be:

$$\sigma_{Port\ 2} = \sqrt{0.5^2 \times 0.152^2 + 0.5^2 \times 0.293^2 + 2 \times 0.5 \times 0.5 \times 0.26 \times 0.152 \times 0.293}$$

$$= \sqrt{0.03303} = 18.2\%$$

$$\sigma_{Port\ 3} = \sqrt{0.7^2 \times 0.152^2 + 0.3^2 \times 0.293^2 + 2 \times 0.7 \times 0.3 \times 0.26 \times 0.152 \times 0.293}$$

$$= \sqrt{0.02391} = 15.5\%$$

Of these three portfolios, which might you want to hold? Compare the expected returns and risks of each portfolio. Portfolio 2 has the highest expected return, but it also has the highest risk. Portfolio 3 has the second highest expected return and lowest risk. No one should want Portfolio 1 because it has the lowest expected return but not the lowest risk. Portfolio 3 is a **dominating portfolio** compared to Portfolio 1 because it offers higher return and less risk. Some people may want Portfolio 2 and others may want Portfolio 3.

dominating portfolio
A portfolio that is superior to others based on better risk and/or return

Equation 6-4 becomes very large, very quickly. The first summation will have the same number of terms as the number of assets in the portfolio. However, the double summation sign means that there will be a term for how each stock in the portfolio comoves with each other stock. For two stocks, that is only one term. For four stocks, there are six terms. However, with 10 stocks, there will be 45 terms in that portion of the equation. Most mutual fund portfolios have dozens, if not hundreds of stocks. Thus, it is often easier to use a spreadsheet to compute the realized risk of a portfolio.

Figure 6-2 illustrates the power of diversification in reducing risk. Five years of monthly returns were obtained from Dow Jones Industrial Average stocks to create the figure. It is assumed that each addition of a stock results in a portfolio that is equally

Figure 6-2: Standard Deviation (Risk) of a Portfolio as Stocks Are Added

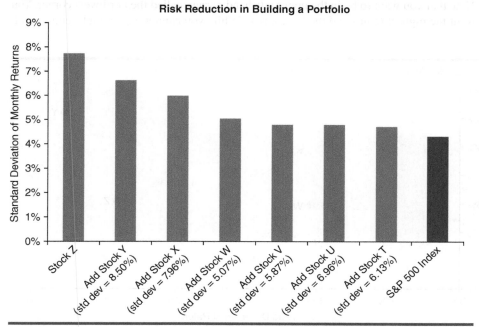

Risk Reduction in Building a Portfolio

weighted among the stocks. That is, a four-stock portfolio contains one-quarter of each stock. We start with Stock Z, which has a standard deviation of monthly returns of 7.76%. Now we add Stock Y and see how the magic of diversification works. Note that Stock Y has a standard deviation of returns of 8.50%, which is higher than that of Stock Z. Yet, the resulting portfolio of two stocks has a risk level of 6.64%. Do you see the magic? You start with one stock, add a stock with higher risk, and yet the total risk of the portfolio declines! The reason is that the two stocks have a correlation of 0.34. Adding stocks with low correlation reduces risk. Now let's add Stock X, which has a risk level of 7.96%: higher than the existing two-stock portfolio standard deviation of return. Yet, the new portfolio has an even lower risk of 6.0%.

As we add stocks to the portfolio, the risk level declines. However, note that the magnitude in the change in risk declines too. That means there is a limit to how much risk can be reduced through diversification in the stock market. If you owned the S&P 500 Index, you would own over 80% of the stock market and still have a portfolio risk measured at a 4.33% standard deviation of monthly returns over this five-year period. We call this base level of risk **systematic risk** (or sometimes **undiversifiable risk**). Systematic risk is the minimum amount of risk you must take to invest in the stock market. This is the risk you get rewarded for taking over time. The difference in the level of risk in the portfolios and the systematic level of risk is called **unsystematic risk** (or **diversifiable risk**). You are not rewarded for taking unsystematic risk and should therefore diversify it away.

6-2b Portfolio Creation

The benefits of diversifying away the unsystematic risk becomes visually clear in the next few figures. **Figure 6-3** shows the seven stocks labeled T through Z on a graph of average monthly return (*y*-axis) and standard deviation of return, that is, risk (*x*-axis). Note that you want to be in the upper left-hand corner, called the northwest corner. You want the highest return and the lowest risk. While you cannot expect high returns with

systematic risk
The risk inherent to the overall investment market

undiversifiable risk
The risk inherent to the overall investment market

unsystematic risk
The portion of risk in an investment asset or portfolio that can be eliminated through diversification

diversifiable risk
The portion of risk in an investment asset or portfolio that can be eliminated through diversification

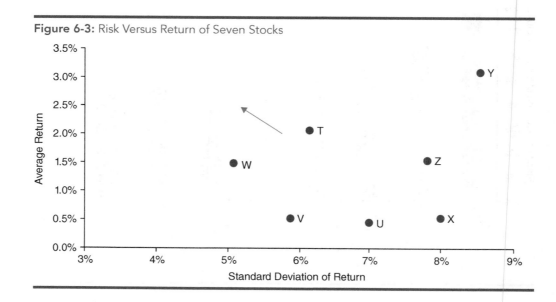

Figure 6-3: Risk Versus Return of Seven Stocks

Figure 6-4: Risk Versus Return of Equally Weighted Portfolios from Seven Stocks

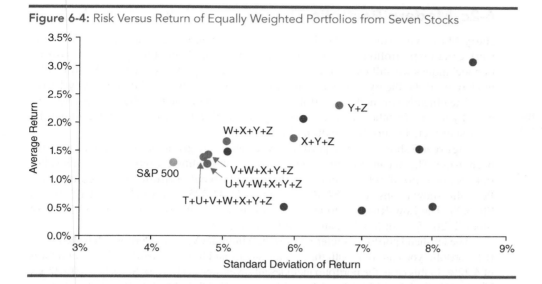

minimal risk, you can move in that direction by removing the diversifiable risk from your portfolio.

If you could only buy one stock, which of these would it be? Note that W, T, and Y dominate all other stocks based on risk and return. In other words, you would never want to own only stock V when you could own W and get higher return for lower risk. Since W, T, and Y dominate, which of those would you want? The answer depends on your personal level of risk aversion and your needs. People who want low risk will own stock W. People who can handle a middle amount of risk might pick stock T, and people with higher risk tolerance might pick stock Y.

Now let's start combining these stocks into equally weighted portfolios, as shown in **Figure 6-4**. Combining stocks Y and Z provides a portfolio with good return and much less risk than either Y or Z alone. That is, the portfolio Y+Z moves from Y and Z independently toward the northwest corner because some of the unsystematic risk is removed. As you add more stocks to the portfolio, the risk gets smaller but begins to converge toward a **minimum variance portfolio**.

Which of these portfolios might you want? The only portfolio that is dominated by others is Portfolio U to Z. Portfolio T to Z has both higher return and lower risk. Thus, you won't want Portfolio U to Z. All of the other portfolios are acceptable and their ownership depends on the investor's risk and return preferences.

However, Figure 6-4 does not show the best portfolios you can create with these seven stocks. It merely shows portfolios with equally weighted portions in each stock. For example, you don't have to form a portfolio of 50% Y and 50% Z. It might be better to have 60% Y and 40% Z. Or any other combination. Note that the beginning of this section (6-2 Portfolio Theory) mentions that portfolio decisions include both security selection and asset allocation. Choosing Stocks Y and Z is the security selection. Deciding on how much of the portfolio should be invested in Y and invested in Z is the asset allocation.

The practice of portfolio theory is all about selecting the securities and determining the allocation among them that deliver the highest expected return for any level of risk desired. Note that this is the same as determining the lowest risk possible for the level of expected return desired. Creating these portfolios is illustrated in the next section.

minimum variance portfolio
The portfolio of risky assets with the lowest risk possible as measured by variance (standard deviation) of return

6-2c Modern Portfolio Theory

Harry Markowitz won the 1990 Nobel Memorial Prize in Economic Sciences for his work creating portfolio theory. He developed the theory behind the portfolio construction techniques we still use today. He called it "modern portfolio theory." We still call it modern portfolio theory, which is interesting because he developed it in the early 1950s.

efficient portfolios
The highest return portfolios for a given level of risk

The objective of modern portfolio theory is to determine the **efficient portfolios** of risky assets. In other words, how can you combine the stocks available to get the highest expected return for the desired level of risk?

Figure 6-5 shows the best portfolios you can create given the seven stocks we have been using. This means that these portfolios reflect the highest return for each level of risk. A portfolio of 100% Stock Y is the far right-hand portfolio. The Medium-Risk Portfolio shown consists of 57.065% of Stock Y, 41.325% of Stock T, and 1.610% of Stock W. The Low-Risk Portfolio shown consists of 35.908% of Stock W, 32.547% of Stock T, 26.455% of Stock Y, and 5.090% of Stock Z.

The left-hand portfolio is referred to as the Minimum Variance Portfolio. It is the lowest risk portfolio you can form with these seven stocks and has a standard deviation of returns of 4.22%. In this case, the portfolio includes all seven stocks (12.07% Stock T, 7.40% Stock U, 16.11% Stock V, 48.64% Stock W, 1.14% Stock X, 4.24% Stock Y, 10.39% Stock Z).

Technically, there are an infinite number of portfolios along the curve. The next section discusses which one of these portfolios you might prefer.

How do you find these efficient portfolios? Markowitz shows us that it is an optimization problem. You vary the weights in the return and standard deviation equations such that the result is the highest return for the risk specified. **Equations 6-2** and **6-3** are rewritten below for a three-stock portfolio with stocks Blue, Red, and Brown.

$$E(r_P) = w_{Blue} \times E(r_{Blue}) + w_{Red} \times E(r_{Red}) + w_{Brown} \times E(r_{Brown})$$

$$\sigma_{Port} = \sqrt{ \begin{array}{c} w_{Blue}^2 \times \sigma_{Blue}^2 + w_{Red}^2 \times \sigma_{Red}^2 + w_{Brown}^2 \times \sigma_{Brown}^2 + 2 \times w_{Blue} \times w_{Red} \\ \times \rho_{Blue, Red} \times \sigma_{Blue} \times \sigma_{Red} + 2 \times w_{Blue} \times w_{Brown} \times \rho_{Blue, Brown} \times \sigma_{Blue} \\ \times \sigma_{Brown} + 2 \times w_{Brown} \times w_{Red} \times \rho_{Brown, Red} \times \sigma_{Brown} \times \sigma_{Red} \end{array} }$$

Figure 6-5: The Efficient Portfolios from Seven Stocks

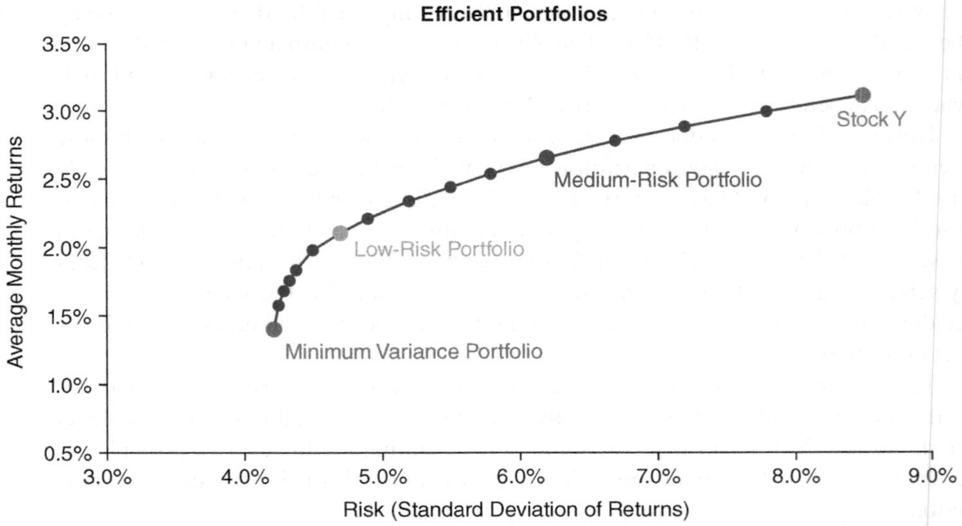

Efficient Portfolios

The optimization problem is formally written as:

Maximize $E(r_p)$ subject to

ρ_{Port} = desired risk level

$0 \leq w_{Blue} \leq 1$

$0 \leq w_{Red} \leq 1$

$0 \leq w_{Brown} \leq 1$

$w_{Blue} + w_{Red} + w_{Brown} = 1$

There are many programs that can provide the answer to this optimization problem, and Excel is one of them. **Excel Expert 6-2** illustrates the Solver function in Excel to find the efficient portfolios given the risky assets to choose from. If you haven't added the Solver add-in to your Excel, you will need to do so to solve portfolio optimization problems.

Excel Expert 6-2

Computing Efficient Portfolios

Find the efficient set of portfolios using three stocks: Blue, Red, and Brown. First, obtain the returns of the stocks. In this case, five years of monthly returns (60 observations) are found for the three stocks.

Second, create a Portfolio column of returns that uses weights of the three stocks (as shown in column I) and the returns of the stocks (shown in columns A, B, and C). The value in cell E2 is shown next to it in green. Note that the values in the Portfolio cells are the sum of the multiplication of the weights in column I with the returns. Once the formula in cell E2 is created, it can be copied and pasted to all of the Portfolio rows. Note that the weights of the stocks must add to 1 (or 100%) as shown in cell I5.

Third, compute the average monthly return and the portfolio standard deviation, as done in cells G4 and G5, and shown in cells G8 and G9. Note that the spreadsheet image shows a portfolio that is equally weighted with the three stocks to start the process.

	A	B	C	D	E	F	G	H	I
1	Blue	Red	Brown		Portfolio				**Weights**
2	6.06%	0.59%	6.94%		4.527%	=$I$2*A2+$I$3*B2+$I$4*C2		Blue =	33.33%
3	4.17%	-1.86%	5.15%		2.484%			Red =	33.33%
4	2.61%	-2.75%	6.99%		2.282%	Port Ave =	1.708%	Brown =	33.33%
5	5.33%	6.28%	-0.51%		3.700%	Port Std Dev =	4.685%	Sum =	100%
6	1.32%	1.62%	3.00%		1.981%				
7	6.96%	5.07%	1.95%		4.659%				
8	-1.66%	4.55%	-6.63%		-1.245%	Port Ave =	=AVERAGE(E2:E61)		
9	0.51%	-3.07%	-1.57%		-1.377%	Port Std Dev =	=STDEV.S(E2:E61)		
10	-2.48%	5.70%	3.46%		2.227%				

The next phase of the process is to set up the Solver tool in Excel. From the Data menu, select Solver. A Solver Parameters screen will pop up. The optimization problem constraints need to be set up. The screenshot below shows that the weights for each of the three stocks must be less than or equal to 1 and the sum of the three weights must equal 1. Note that the weights must also be non-negative, which is handled by checking the Make Unconstrained Variables Non-Negative box.

(Continued)

For the first optimization, choose to find the minimum variance portfolio as shown here in the Set Objective section.

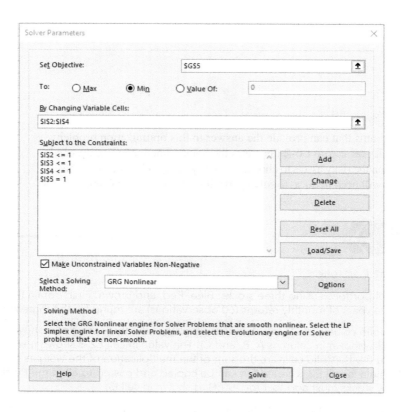

To create a constraint, click the Add box on the right-hand side and identify the cell reference, the mathematical indicator, and the constraint as shown here.

After all of the constraints are entered, this optimization problem is solved by clicking the Solve button on the bottom. The solution for the minimum variable portfolio is shown. The standard deviation of this portfolio is 4.399%, and it averaged a monthly return of 1.663%. The minimum variance portfolio is made up of 27.07% Blue, 56.90% Red, and 16.03% Brown.

	F	G	H	I
				Weights
	=$I$2*A2+$I$3*B2+$I$4*C2		Blue =	27.07%
			Red =	56.90%
	Port Ave =	1.663%	Brown =	16.03%
	Port Std Dev =	4.399%	Sum =	100%
	Port Ave =	=AVERAGE(E2:E61)		
	Port Std Dev =	=STDEV.S(E2:E61)		

Now we know the minimum variance portfolio. We start finding the efficient portfolios by changing the Solver Parameters to Max the return (Cell G4) for a specific level of risk. Start with a standard deviation a little higher than the minimum variance portfolio and begin solving the optimization problem. Keep increasing the risk and solving until there is no solution. Start with a standard deviation of 4.5% by adding this constraint.

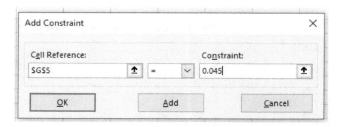

After changing to a Max optimization problem and adding the additional constraint, the Solver Parameters should look like this.

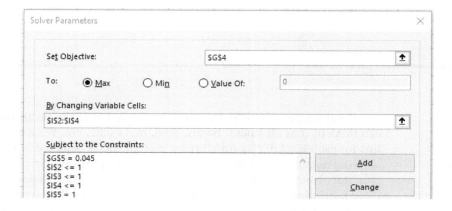

The solution finds the asset allocation that produces the highest return (1.754% per month) for the level of risk identified (standard deviation of 4.5%). Continue to solve for higher risk levels and record the risk and return for each solution. To change the risk constraint, click on it and then click that Change button on the right-hand side.

(Continued)

The Excel image below shows the solutions for six optimization problems. These are then graphed using the Scatter Plot to illustrate the efficient portfolios. Of course, if you want to know the allocation for an efficient portfolio between the dots, just quickly use Solver to compute the desired solution.

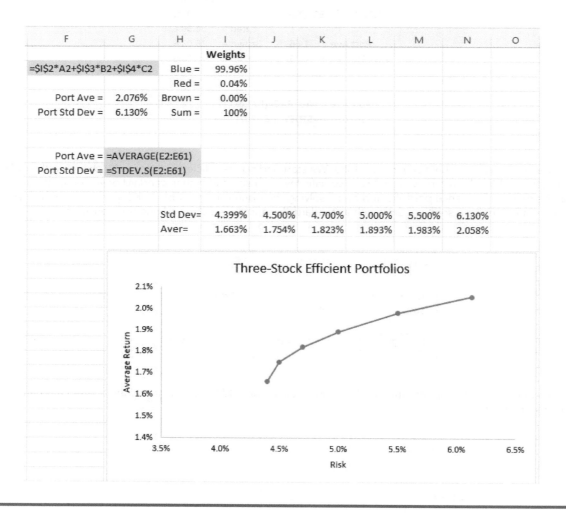

What happens if <u>all</u> risky assets are included in the portfolio analysis? You can think of it as all stocks, bonds, gold, real estate, etc. What are the best portfolios for each level of risk for all risky assets? This is depicted in **Figure 6-6**. When all risky assets are included, the set of efficient portfolios is called the **efficient frontier**. Note that all investors want a portfolio on the efficient frontier because these portfolios dominate all others. That is, they have the highest expected return for any given level of risk. This means that all the unsystematic risk has been diversified away. Any portfolio on the efficient frontier should be rewarded for the level of risk taken. That is why the slope of the efficient frontier is upward sloping.

efficient frontier
All of the efficient portfolios

Figure 6-6: The Efficient Frontier

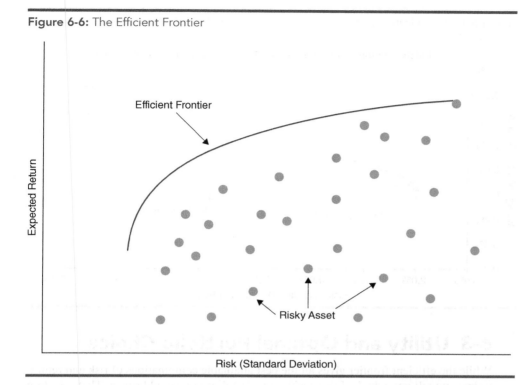

6-2d Portfolios with International Diversification

Consider international diversification from a U.S. investor's point of view. The investor can diversify domestically with stocks and bonds. Since 2000, the monthly average return and standard deviation for the S&P 500 Index and for long-term Treasury Bonds are shown in **Figure 6-7**. The opportunities for diversification are much expanded if foreign market stocks are introduced. The figure shows the risk and return for two developed markets, Germany (DAX Performance) and Japan (Nikkei 225), and an emerging market, China (Shenzhen Component).

Note that the efficient frontier for these investments is a substantial improvement for the U.S. investor compared to the domestic choices. Even if the main objective of a U.S. investor is to obtain the minimum risk with these risky assets, then that investor would allocate a portion of the portfolio internationally. The minimum variance portfolio, in this case, is made up of 57.1% Treasury Bonds, 29.8% U.S. stocks, 9.5% Japanese stocks, and 3.6% Chinese stocks. This is another example illustrating that lowering risk in a portfolio often means including some high-risk assets.

For the investor who wants a high-risk (and expected return) portfolio, the main portion of the portfolio would be allocated to Chinese stocks. The best way to lower some of that risk is to include U.S. Treasury Bonds. The portfolio represented by the third dot from the right on the efficient frontier is made up of 85.2% Chinese stocks, 14.0% U.S. Treasuries, and 0.8% U.S. stocks.

Which of these portfolios on the efficient frontier might you want? We explore which portfolio on the efficient frontier is right for you.

Figure 6-7: Diversification with U.S. Stocks, Treasury Bonds, and International Stocks Since 2000

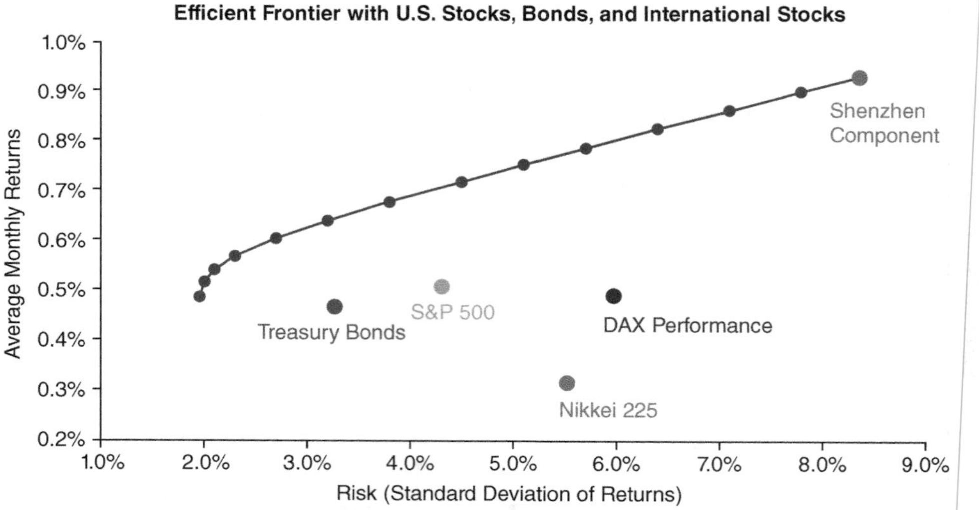

Efficient Frontier with U.S. Stocks, Bonds, and International Stocks

6-3 Utility and Optimal Portfolio Choice

While the efficient frontier gives all the best attainable combinations of risk and return, it does not tell you *which* of these efficient portfolios you should select. That selection depends on your willingness to bear risk. The combining of the efficient frontier and your willingness to bear risk determines your **optimal portfolio**.

optimal portfolio
The best portfolio for an investor based on risk, return, and utility

6-3a Utility Theory

In the previous section, we mentioned that investors want to be in the northwest corner of the risk/return graph. Investors want high return with low risk. In the real world, expected return and risk are positively correlated, which means that high return comes with high risk and low return comes with low risk. Investors will take risk if they are adequately compensated for that risk through sufficient expected return. Some people can handle higher risk levels better than others. These ideas are formalized in the economic utility theory. **Utility** is a measure of a person's welfare. It is a score to assess how much better or worse off a person is between portfolio choices with different risk and expected return characteristics. A popular utility equation is:

utility
A measure of satisfaction or welfare obtained by a portfolio

$$U = E(r) - \frac{1}{2} A\sigma^2 \qquad \textbf{6-5}$$

risk aversion
The magnitude of preferring lower uncertainty (risk)

The variable A is a measure of a person's level of **risk aversion**. The higher the value, the more a person doesn't want to take risk as measured by the variance of returns, σ^2. The equation shows that your utility is higher with higher expected return, but lower with a higher risk. More risk-averse investors (as denoted with larger A) demand a higher expected return in order to invest in higher-risk portfolios.

Note that our efficient portfolios are characterized on the risk/return graph by expected return versus risk. Thus, we rearrange **Equation 6-5**:

$$E(r) = U + \frac{1}{2}A\sigma^2 \qquad \textbf{6-6}$$

What combinations of portfolio characteristics provide the same utility? We use indifference curves to illustrate this. An investor has the same utility level for each point on an indifference curve. That means the investor does not care which portfolio is chosen on the indifference curve. Consider the indifference curves shown in **Figure 6-8**. First note that the curves are upward sloping. This represents the risk-return trade-off. Investors only accept more risk when they receive higher expected return. Investor A is more risk averse than Investor B, with the risk aversion coefficients being 5 and 3, respectively. In Equation 6-5, the utility level, U, is set for 0.1% for both Investors A and B. Investor A gains the same utility (or welfare) from any of the portfolios on the blue curve. To illustrate this, three specific portfolios are denoted on the graph. Investor A is indifferent to which portfolio is owned because they all provide the same utility level.

The yellow curve is the indifference curve for Investor A when the utility level is set to 0.3% and shown as Investor A*. This simply shifts the curve upward. Both indifference curves represent a level of satisfaction, with the higher curve indicating a higher level of satisfaction. Thus, investors prefer the indifference curve with the highest utility level, which are the curves highest on the graph. Also note that the curve for Investor A is steeper than for Investor B (gray line), which means Investor A demands a higher return to compensate for higher risk than does Investor B.

indifference curves
A line showing all the portfolios for which an investor would be indifferent to owning

Figure 6-8: Indifference Curves of Investor A (High Risk Aversion) and Investor B (Low Risk Aversion)

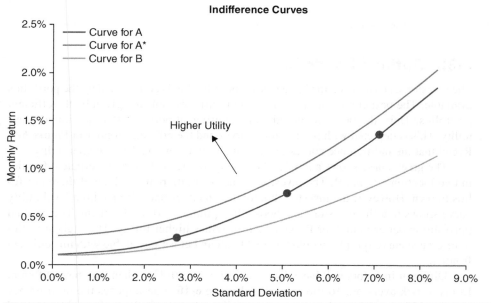

The World of Investing

Dangers of Under-Diversified Portfolios

Portfolios that have a lot of governance supervision are typically very well diversified. For example, mutual funds are regulated by the Securities and Exchange Commission. They have very strict rules that force them to be well diversified. The pension plan portfolios managed for public state and local employees, as well as corporate employees, are regulated and well diversified.

Who may not be well diversified? Interestingly, those considered both the most unsophisticated and the most sophisticated of investors are sometimes dangerously under-diversified. Specially, individual novice investors and hedge funds.

Many hedge funds take big bets on undiversified positions. When they pay off, they pay off big. When they fail, so does the hedge fund. For example, Amaranth Advisors, with $9 billion in assets under management (AUM), lost $6 billion in one year on natural gas bets. Hedge fund Marin Capital failed when sophisticated credit bets collapsed when General Motors' stocks fell. Two Nobel Prize of Economics winners founded the hedge fund Long-Term Capital Management (with others). Its credit arbitrage was successful for four years until it made a big bet that the Russian debt default situation would be short. It wasn't, and LTCM collapsed. These are examples of mega-sized hedge funds. There are dozens of examples of under-diversified small hedge fund collapse.

Many individual investors also struggle with not diversifying their investments. Over the years, research has shown that:

- Corporate employees invest too much in their company's stock within their 401k plan. When that company fails, the employees lose much of their retirement money and their job!
- Defined contribution retirement plans are often 100% invested in the stock market OR 100% invested in fixed income (bonds and cash).
- Individual investor portfolios tend to be dominated by their home country companies with very little international diversification.
- Stock brokerage account analysis shows that investors tend to own fewer than five stocks and those stocks are in similar industries.
- Many Robinhood investors mainly own meme stocks that are highly correlated.

Under-diversified portfolios contain much unsystematic risk. That might yield some temporary high returns, but usually end in disaster.

6-3b Optimal Portfolios

The investor seeks to reach the highest level of utility but is constrained by the portfolios available. The best combinations of risk and return available are given by the efficient portfolios. Thus, the investor should pick the efficient portfolio that maximizes their utility. This is depicted with indifference curves and the efficient frontier in **Figure 6-9**. Recall that the indifference curves that are higher in the graph depict higher utility.

The green curve shows a low level of utility. It intersects with the efficient frontier in two locations, A and B. The investor would be indifferent in which of these portfolios to own. However, the investor shouldn't own either one. The medium level utility curve shows that the investor can choose the optimal portfolio for them. The optimal portfolio is better than A or B because it provides higher utility. The highest utility indifference curve (purple) would be great to attain but isn't available with this efficient frontier.

Different investors will have different optimal portfolios when they have different levels of risk aversion. To illustrate this, **Figure 6-10** superimposes the indifference curves of Figure 6-8 on the efficient portfolios from the U.S. stocks and bonds and international stocks shown in Figure 6-7. The figure shows the optimal portfolios for Investor A and Investor B in the global portfolio opportunity sets.

Figure 6-9: Portfolio Allocations to Seven Stocks and Investor Utility

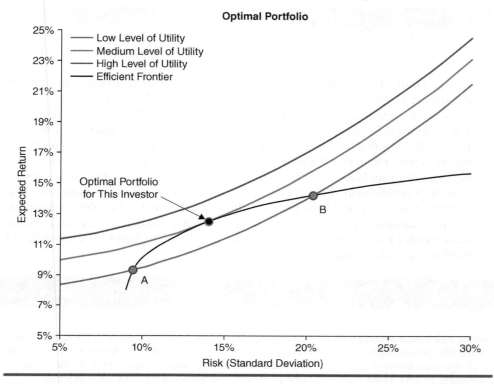

Figure 6-10: Optimal Portfolios for High Risk-Aversion Investor A and Low Risk-Aversion Investor B Using Global Opportunity Set

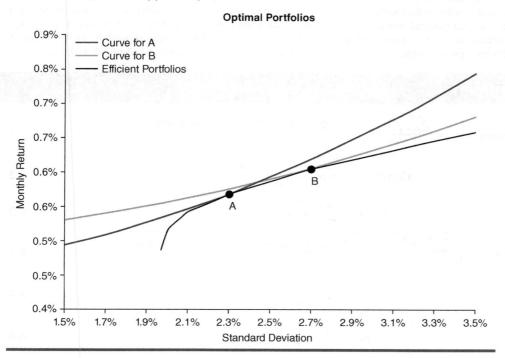

Table 6-3: Optimal Global Portfolios for High Risk-Aversion Investor A and Low Risk-Aversion Investor B

	Utility (A)	S&P 500	LT Treasuries	Nikkei 225	DAX Perf	Shenzhen
Investor A	0.437%	31.1%	50.8%	0.0%	0.0%	18.1%
Investor B	0.497%	27.5%	46.3%	0.0%	0.0%	26.2%

Recall that Investor A is more risk averse than Investor B, which is shown with the steeper indifference curve in blue. The optimal portfolio for Investor A is the indifference curve that is the highest and intersects with the efficient frontier only once. This is shown as Portfolio A. Similarly, Portfolio B is shown as the optimal portfolio for Investor B. Note that Investor B gets higher utility from a portfolio that has more risk but offers more return than Portfolio A. In fact, for this solution, Investor B has a slightly higher utility than Investor A. **Table 6-3** shows the allocations of the two portfolios. Note that to obtain more risk, yet have an efficient portfolio, Investor B owns less of the S&P 500 Index and Long-Term Treasuries, but much more of the Shenzhen Component.

Each investor will pick the efficient portfolio that maximizes their utility. Since each investor has a different level of risk aversion, they will pick different efficient portfolios as their optimal portfolio.

Conclusion

Risk emanates from several sources, which include fluctuations in market prices, fluctuations in interest rates, changes in reinvestment rates, fluctuations in exchange rates, loss of purchasing power through inflation, and government defaults. These sources of risk are often referred to as systematic risk because the returns on assets tend to move together (that is, there is a systematic relationship between security returns and market returns). Systematic risk is also referred to as nondiversifiable risk because it is not reduced by the construction of a diversified portfolio.

Portfolio theory is built around risk and return. Portfolios that offer the highest return for a given amount of risk are referred to as *efficient* because unsystematic risk has been diversified away. Portfolios that do not offer the highest return for a given level of risk are *inefficient*. Together, these efficient portfolios form the *efficient frontier*, which are the set of the best portfolios available using the risky assets offered.

Investors choose the portfolio on the efficient frontier that maximizes their *utility*, which is a measure of satisfaction or welfare. Your utility is also influenced by your level of *risk aversion*. People with high risk aversion demand a high return compensation to take risk. People with low risk aversion are much more comfortable investing in higher-risk portfolios. Thus, each investor desires a different *optimal portfolio* on the efficient frontier because of their different levels of risk aversion.

Chapter Equations

$$Covariance_{ij} = \frac{\sum_{t=1}^{N}\{(r_{it} - average\ return_i) \times (r_{jt} - average\ return_j)\}}{N-1}$$
6-1

$$Correlation_{ij} = \rho_{ij} = \frac{covariance_{ij}}{\sigma_i \times \sigma_j}$$
6-2

$$E(r_P) = \sum_{i=1}^{N} w_i \times E(r_i)$$
6-3

$$\sigma_{Port} = \sqrt{\sum_{i=1}^{N} w_i^2 \times \sigma_i^2 + \sum_{i=1}^{N}\sum_{\substack{j=1\\j\neq i}}^{N} 2 \times w_i \times w_j \times \rho_{ij} \times \sigma_i \times \sigma_j}$$
6-4

$$U = E(r) - \frac{1}{2}A\sigma^2$$
6-5

$$E(r) = U + \frac{1}{2}A\sigma^2$$
6-6

Excel Functions

AVERAGE(number1, [number2], …)
CORREL(array1, array2)
COVARIANCE.S(array1, array2)

Solver
STDEV.S(number1, [number2], …)

Key Terms

asset allocation – **The way a portfolio is divided between different investments**

correlation – **A measure of comovement that varies between −1 and +1**

covariance – **An absolute measure of comovement that varies between plus and minus infinity**

diversifiable risk – **The portion of risk in an investment asset or portfolio that can be eliminated through diversification**

diversification – **The reduction of risk through owning a variety of different types of assets**

dominating portfolio – **A portfolio that is superior to others based on better risk and/or return**

efficient frontier – **All of the efficient portfolios**

efficient portfolios – **The highest return portfolios for a given level of risk**

indifference curves – **A line showing all the portfolios for which an investor would be indifferent to owning**

minimum variance portfolio – **The portfolio of risky assets with the lowest risk possible as measured by variance (standard deviation) of return**

optimal portfolio – **The best portfolio for an investor based on risk, return, and utility**

portfolio – **A combination of investment assets**

risk aversion – **The magnitude of preferring lower uncertainty (risk)**

security selection – **The process of selecting the assets for a portfolio**

systematic risk – **The risk inherent to the overall investment market**

undiversifiable risk – **The risk inherent to the overall investment market**

unsystematic risk – **The portion of risk in an investment asset or portfolio that can be eliminated through diversification**

utility – **A measure of satisfaction or welfare obtained by a portfolio**

Questions

1. **Relationship Between Risky Assets.** Why can two risky assets be combined into a portfolio that has less risk? (LO 6-1)

2. **Comovement of Risky Assets.** Describe the relationship between correlation of asset returns and diversification potential. (LO 6-2)

3. **Asset Classes and Diversification.** Which asset class has the best potential for combining into a portfolio for greater diversification? Why? (LO 6-3)

4. **Portfolio Risk.** Portfolio return is the weighted average of the asset returns in the portfolio. Explain why portfolio standard deviation of returns is not the weighted average of the asset risks. (LO 6-4)

5. **Dominating Portfolios.** How do some portfolios dominate others? What does that mean? (LO 6-5)

6. **Diversifiable and Undiversifiable Risk.** What kinds of risk can be diversified away through portfolio construction? What kinds of risks are not diversified away? (LO 6-6)

7. **Minimum Variance Portfolio.** What is the minimum variance portfolio and why is it important? (LO 6-7)

8. **Efficient Portfolios.** What makes a portfolio efficient? (LO 6-8)

9. **Utility Theory.** What does utility measure in the context of selecting a portfolio? (LO 6-9)

10. **Optimal Portfolio.** What is the optimal portfolio for an investor? Do other investors desire that portfolio? Why? (LO 6-10)

Problems

1. **Covariance.** Compute the covariance between each of the three pairs of stocks A, B, and C. The data are in the file **ch6_pr01.xlsx**. (LO 6-2)

Return A	Return B	Return C
12.0%	5.2%	−1.5%
−5.0%	−7.5%	6.0%
3.0%	8.4%	11.3%
17.0%	10.6%	3.0%
8.5%	9.4%	18.6%
−5.7%	2.1%	5.6%
8.6%	3.7%	−6.8%
10.4%	12.5%	8.9%

2. **Correlation.** Compute the correlation between each of the three pairs of stocks A, B, and C. The data are in the file **ch6_pr02.xlsx**. (LO 6-2)

Return A	Return B	Return C
12.0%	5.2%	−1.5%
−5.0%	−7.5%	6.0%
3.0%	8.4%	11.3%
17.0%	10.6%	3.0%
8.5%	9.4%	18.6%
−5.7%	2.1%	5.6%
8.6%	3.7%	−6.8%
10.4%	12.5%	8.9%

3. **Correlation of Asset Classes.** Compute the correlation between each of the three pairs of asset class returns shown. Which pairs of asset classes are the best to combine to reduce risk? The data are in the file **ch6_pr03.xlsx**. (LO 6-3)

4. **Portfolio Return.** Stock X had a return of 8.5% last year. Stocks Y and Z earned −2.3% and 11.8%, respectively. What is the portfolio return under the following scenarios? (LO 6-4)

   a. The portfolio is equally weighted with the stocks.
   b. The portfolio holds stocks X, Y, and Z with weights 0.5, 0.3, and 0.2, respectively.
   c. The portfolio holds stocks X, Y, and Z with weights 0.25, 0.4, and 0.35, respectively.

5. **Portfolio Return.** What is the average portfolio return of a portfolio with weights of 0.4 in the Russell 2000, 0.4 in Treasuries, and 0.2 in French Stocks? The data are in the file **ch6_pr05.xlsx**. (LO 6-4)

6. **Portfolio Risk.** Stock X has a standard deviation of 3.5% last year. Stocks Y and Z have risk levels of 6.3% and 4.8%, respectively. The correlation between the stocks is $P(X,Y) = 0.2$, $P(X,Z) = 0.7$, $P(Y,Z) = -0.2$. What is the portfolio standard deviation under the following scenarios? (LO 6-4)

   a. The portfolio is equally weighted with the stocks.
   b. The portfolio holds stocks X, Y, and Z with weights 0.50, 0.3, and 0.2, respectively.
   c. The portfolio holds stocks X, Y, and Z with weights 0.25, 0.4, and 0.35, respectively.

7. **Portfolio Risk.** What is the standard deviation of return of a portfolio with weights of 0.4 in the Russell 2000, 0.4 in Treasuries, and 0.2 in French Stocks? The data are in the file **ch6_pr07.xlsx**. (LO 6-4)

8. **Portfolio Return and Risk.** You own a portfolio with an expected return of 9.5% and standard deviation of 14.8%. You are considering reallocating 20% of the portfolio to a different asset class that has an expected return of 11% and standard deviation of 17%. The correlation between your portfolio and the other asset class is 0.7. What would be your new return and risk and how much did they change? (LO 6-4)

9. **Dominating Portfolios.** Consider Stock Blue and Stock Red. Given the scenarios below, does one stock dominate the other? (LO 6-5)

   a. Stock Blue has a return and risk of 6% and 8%, while Stock Red has a return and risk of 5% and 7%.

   b. Stock Blue has a return and risk of 6% and 8%, while Stock Red has a return and risk of 6% and 7%.

   c. Stock Blue has a return and risk of 6% and 8%, while Stock Red has a return and risk of 5% and 9%.

10. **Minimum Variance Portfolio.** Find the minimum variance portfolio. What is the standard deviation? What is the allocation to the three asset classes? The data are in the file **ch6_pr10.xlsx**. (LO 6-7)

11. **Minimum Variance Portfolio.** Find the minimum variance portfolio. What is the standard deviation? What is the allocation to the three asset classes? The data are in the file **ch6_pr11.xlsx**. (LO 6-7)

12. **Efficient Portfolio.** Given the three assets and returns, find the highest return portfolio that has a standard deviation of 17%. What is the average return? What is the allocation to the three asset classes? The data are in the file **ch6_pr12.xlsx**. (LO 6-8)

13. **Efficient Portfolio.** Given the three assets and returns, find the highest return portfolio that has a standard deviation of 20.5%. What is the average return? What is the allocation to the three asset classes? The data are in the file **ch6_pr13.xlsx**. (LO 6-8)

14. **Efficient Portfolio.** Given the three assets and returns, find the lowest risk portfolio that has a return of 10.2%. What is the standard deviation of return? What is the allocation to the three asset classes? The data are in the file **ch6_pr14.xlsx**. (LO 6-8)

15. **Efficient Portfolio.** Given the three assets and returns, find the lowest risk portfolio that has a return of 9.3%. What is the standard deviation of return? What is the allocation to the three asset classes? The data are in the file **ch6_pr15.xlsx**. (LO 6-8)

16. **Efficient Portfolios.** Given the four asset classes and returns, find the portfolio indicated. What is the standard deviation of return and the allocation to the four asset classes? The data are in the file **ch6_pr16.xlsx**. (LO 6-8)

   a. Minimum variance portfolio.

   b. Portfolio with the lowest risk and a return of 9%.

   c. Portfolio with the lowest risk and a return of 10%.

17. **Utility.** An investor with risk aversion of A = 3 reviews the four investments shown below. What utility does the investor get with each investment? Which should the investor choose? (LO 6-9)

Investment	Expected Return	Standard Deviation
A	15%	19%
B	10%	17%
C	20%	25%
D	8%	12%

18. **Utility.** Consider an investor with risk aversion of A = 4. The investor owns a portfolio with expected return of 10% and standard deviation of 15%. (LO 6-9)

   a. If an alternative portfolio had an expected return of 12%, what standard deviation would it need for the investor to be indifferent?

   b. Should the investor switch to a portfolio with expected return of 8% and standard deviation of 11%? Why or why not?

19. **Indifference Curves.** Consider an investor with risk aversion of A = 3 and utility of 0.08. (LO 6-9)

   a. Compute the expected returns for which this investor would be indifferent for standard deviations of 7%, 10%, 13%, 16%, 20%, and 25%.

   b. Graph this indifference curve.

20. **Optimal Portfolio.** Consider an investor with risk aversion of A = 3 is examining the portfolios along the efficient frontier. (LO 6-10)

   a. Compute the investor's utility for each portfolio.

   b. Which of these would be the optimal portfolio?

Return	8.0%	9.0%	9.9%	10.5%	11.5%	12.5%	13.4%	14.4%
St. Dev.	9.0%	9.2%	9.8%	10.4%	11.9%	14.0%	17.0%	21.0%

Case Study

Portfolios with Standard & Poor's Sectors

The famous S&P 500 Index represents Standard & Poor's 11 sectors of the economy. You can invest in the market as a whole through several available S&P 500 Index exchange-traded funds (ETFs). You can also focus a portfolio on one or more sectors through Standard & Poor's SPDR ETFs.

All 11 sectors have an associated SPDR ETF. However, only nine of them have been available for at least 10 years. The file, **ch6_case_study.xlsx**, shows 10 years of monthly returns for the nine sector ETFs with available data (prices obtained from Yahoo! Finance). The sectors are Consumer Discretionary, Consumer Staples, Energy, Financials, Health Care, Industrials, Materials, Technology, and Utilities. The two missing sectors are Communications Services and Real Estate.

This case explores the risk/return relationships between the sectors and the various portfolios that can be formed with them.

   a. Compute the average monthly returns and standard deviation of returns for each of the nine sectors. What do you notice about the risk and return of these sectors?

   b. Compute the correlation between each of the nine sectors. What sector(s) appears to be less correlated with the others?

   c. Compute the minimum variance portfolio. What is the standard deviation and sector allocation for this portfolio? What do you observe about the portfolio allocation?

   d. Compute eight points on the efficient frontier and show the efficient frontier on a graph.

Risk-Free and Risky Asset Allocation and the CAPM

A traditional tenet of investment theory is that expected returns are positively related to the amount of risk taken. If you want to avoid risk, you can simply buy money market securities, such as T-bills, and earn the **risk-free rate**. Investors who want a return higher than the risk-free rate must be willing to take on some investment risk. What, exactly, is this risk/return relationship? In other words, how much risk should you take to obtain the expected return you desire? Stated another way, how much extra expected return is earned for each unit of risk taken? The answer to these questions lies at the heart of **asset pricing theory**. Asset pricing models can be used to predict the return that should be earned on various investments.

    In the prior chapter, modern portfolio theory explained the construction of a diversified portfolio constructed in the framework of all risky

risk-free rate
The certain future return from the risk-free asset

asset pricing theory
Models of expected return expressed as risk-free rates, risks, and risk premiums

risk-free asset
A security with a certain future return

capital asset pricing model
Method for predicting how investment expected returns are determined in an efficient capital market

assets and utility maximization. The next step in the evolution of portfolio theory is to recognize the existence of a **risk-free asset** that provides the risk-free rate. The addition of a risk-free rate changes the investor's opportunity set and allows for even more efficient portfolios than those on the efficient frontier. This concept subsequently led to the development of the **capital asset pricing model** (CAPM) by William F. Sharpe, John Lintner, and Jan Mossin. The CAPM is among the most important *theoretical concepts* in finance as it advances the relationship between risk and expected return and is easier to implement than modern portfolio theory. Further, the CAPM extends the concept of optimal diversified portfolios to the market in general and to the valuation of individual securities. That is, the concept is applied in both a *macro* context that specifies the relationship between risk and expected return overall, and a *micro* context that specifies the relationship between risk and return on a specific asset.

7-1 Capital Market Line

7-1a Capital Allocation Line

Consider an asset that has no risk. That is, its cash flow payoff is completely known and is assured to occur during a short period of time. In practice, the U.S. Treasury bill is considered a risk-free asset. Thus, the T-bill yield is considered to be the risk-free rate. An important theoretical assumption is that investors can lend or borrow at the risk-free rate. For example, you are lending at the risk-free rate when you own T-bills. Borrowing at the risk-free rate is a bit of a theoretical stretch. Not many entities are as safe as the U.S. government. Nevertheless, in the investment context, borrowing at the risk-free rate is done when using margin. As discussed in Chapter 3, you can borrow money from your stockbroker to buy more investment assets. Since the broker holds your investment assets as collateral, the broker loan rate is low and is seldom much above the three-month Treasury bill rate.

Figure 7-1 shows the efficient frontier as developed from modern portfolio theory in the previous chapter. Near the bottom left corner is the risk-free asset. Note that by definition, it is located on the *y*-axis, where risk is zero. Its location on the *y*-axis depicts the risk-free rate. From the risk-free asset, a line is drawn that is tangent to the efficient frontier. The tangent line is the one that intersects with the efficient frontier in only one place. The intersection is depicted as portfolio P. This line is called the **capital allocation line** (CAL).

capital allocation line
Most efficient portfolios for some risky assets and the risk-free asset

If you could locate your investment portfolio on the CAL, note that it dominates the efficient frontier in every place except for portfolio P, which is the same. In other words, you can achieve higher expected return for the same level of risk on the CAL as compared to the efficient frontier.

Figure 7-2 shows that finding the right portfolio on the CAL improves the investor's utility as compared to the efficient frontier. The figure shows the efficient frontier and the CAL. The indifference curve in orange represents the best this investor can achieve locating on the efficient frontier as determined by the level of risk aversion. However, the green indifference curve shows the best portfolio choice on the CAL. Since the green indifference curve is higher than the orange curve, it indicates higher utility. By locating on the CAL, the investor discovers a new and better optimal portfolio than can be obtained on the efficient frontier.

How do you locate your portfolio on the CAL? This is where the lending and borrowing at the risk-free rate comes in. Consider the CAL shown in **Figure 7-3**. You can

Figure 7-1: Capital Allocation Line

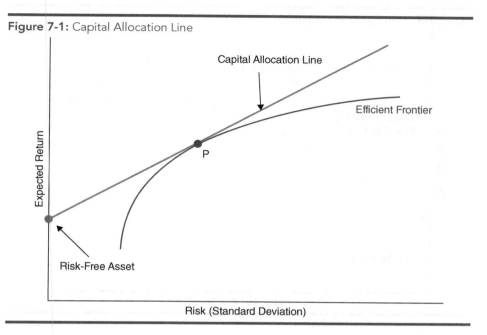

Figure 7-2: New Optimal Portfolio on the Capital Allocation Line

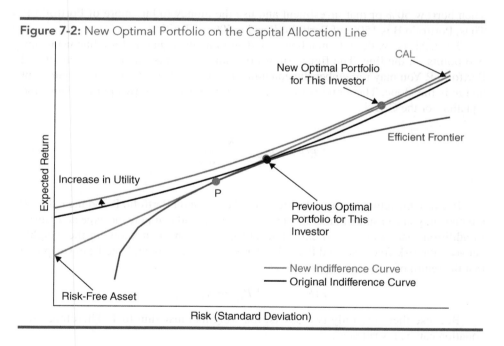

locate your portfolio anywhere on the CAL through owning Portfolio P and either borrowing or lending at the risk-free rate. If you want to be to the left of Portfolio P, like
Portfolio A, then you own Portfolio P and own T-bills, which is lending at the risk-free
rate. Portfolio A represents a portfolio that is constructed with 75% of Portfolio P and
25% of T-bills. Note that Portfolio A dominates the portfolio on the efficient frontier
that has the same level of risk.

Portfolios on the CAL and to the right of P must use margin and borrow at the
risk-free rate. Portfolio B is constructed with first investing all money in Portfolio P.

Figure 7-3 Locating on the Capital Allocation Line

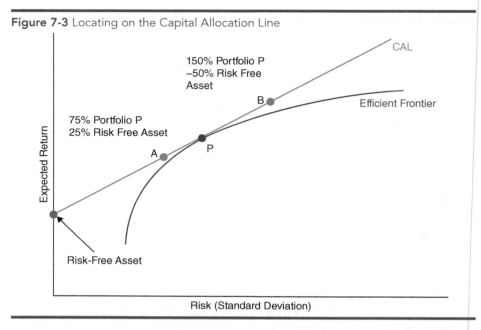

Then borrow 50% of that investment and use the money to buy more of Portfolio P. Thus, Portfolio B is 150% of Portfolio P and −50% of T-bills.

The CAL is, by definition, a line. You determine the equation for a line using any two points on the line. The figure shows two known points, the risk-free asset and Portfolio P. You may remember the equation, $Y = b + mX$, where b is the Y-intercept and m is the slope. The slope is the rise over run between the two points. Thus, the equation for the CAL is:

$$E(R) = R_{free} + \frac{R_P - R_{free}}{\sigma_P}\, \sigma \qquad \qquad 7\text{-}1$$

Because the return on the risk-free asset, the return on Portfolio P, and the risk of P are known, you can simply enter the desired risk level and compute the expected return. In addition, once the desired expected return is known, then knowing the weights between the risk-free asset and Portfolio P are easy to determine. Note from Chapter 6 that the return of a two-asset portfolio is:

$$E(R) = w_{free} * R_{free} + w_P * R_P$$

Because there are only two assets, the weights must sum to 1. Therefore, this equation can be rewritten as:

$$E(R) = (1 - w_P) * R_{free} + w_P * R_P$$

Solving for the weight of Portfolio P results in:

$$E(R) = R_{free} + w_P * (R_P - R_{free}) \qquad \qquad 7\text{-}2$$

Excel Expert 7-1

Allocation to the CAL

Consider that the T-bill yield is 1.5%. Given the risky assets available to you, you have assessed the efficient frontier and determined that your capital allocation line includes T-bills and a portfolio (Portfolio P) with expected return of 9% and a standard deviation of 14%.

If you desire a portfolio with a standard deviation of 11%, what expected return should you be expecting? Also, what allocation to T-bills and to the risky portfolio P should you construct for this optimal portfolio?

Or, if you desire a portfolio with a standard deviation of 17%, what expected return should you be expecting and what allocation should you construct for this optimal portfolio?

The spreadsheet below shows that for the first scenario, you should allocate 21% of your money to T-bills and 79% to the risk portfolio. This provides the desired risk (standard deviation) level of 11% and expected return of 7.39%. For the second scenario, invest all of the money in the risky portfolio and then borrow an additional 21% and invest it in the risky portfolio.

	A	B	C	D	E	F	G	H
1	CAL				Optimal Portfolio 1	Optimal Portfolio 2		
2	Risk-Free Rate =	1.5%		St. Dev. =	11.0%	17.0%		
3	Risky Portfolio Returns =	9.0%						
4	Risky Portfolio St. Dev. =	14.0%						
5				E(R) =	7.39%	10.61%	=B2+((B3-B2)/B4)*F2	
6				Allocation to				
7				T-Bills =	0.21	-0.21	=1-F8	
8				Port P =	0.79	1.21	=(F5-B2)/(B3-B2)	

7-1b The Capital Market Line

The next innovation in the theory is to recognize that all investors have the same opportunity set of risky assets and the risk-free asset. In other words, every investor can invest in Treasury securities and can invest in stocks and bonds from all over the world. Given this assumption, the efficient frontier described earlier would represent the most efficient portfolios of risky assets available for everyone. While this may seem like a subtle change, the ramifications are enormous. As will be demonstrated, this innovation allows for the overall pricing of risk. That is, it leads to asset pricing models that specify the return reward for taking risk.

Figure 7-4 repeats the graph from **Figure 7-1** to illustrate the capital market line. Note that it is essentially the CAL, only using the assumption that it describes all investors' opportunity set. The intersection of the line coming from the risk-free asset that is tangent to the efficient frontier is referenced as M, the market portfolio.

The market portfolio plays a central role in asset pricing models. Consider the demonstration of Portfolio P in the CAL. The investor facing the CAL is best off by investing in Portfolio P and the risk-free asset. Thus, if all investors face the same efficient frontier, then each and all investors would own the market portfolio and some combination of lending or borrowing at the risk-free rate. If you want more risk, you will buy the market portfolio and borrow more money to buy more of the market portfolio. If you want less risk, you will split your portfolio between the market portfolio and T-bills.

capital market line
Most efficient portfolios with *all* risky assets and the risk-free asset

market portfolio
The portfolio with all risky securities in proportion to their value

Figure 7-4: Capital Market Line

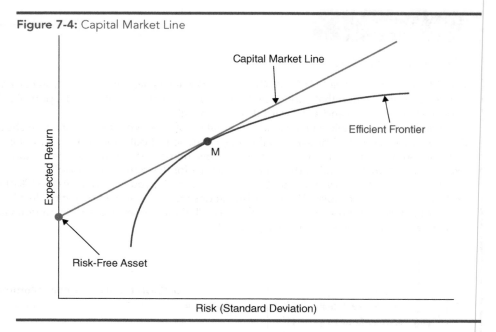

That deserves a restatement: *All investors should own the market portfolio.* That is an important aspect of the theory because it allows for the pricing of risk. The market portfolio is the ultimate diversified portfolio that has eliminated ALL diversifiable risk.

Theory also demonstrates that in equilibrium, this portfolio is the size-weighted portfolio of all risky assets. If one stock is left out of the market portfolio, then its demand would be zero and its price would fall. This would cause its expected return to be abnormally high given its risk, so investors would want to buy it. They would continue buying it until it no longer offered an abnormally high expected return. However, it would then be held by investors and be a part of the market portfolio. For practical purposes, the application of this theory uses a pervasive stock index, like the S&P 500 Index, as a proxy for the market portfolio.

Using the same procedure for the equation of the CAL, the equation for the CML is

$$E(R) = R_{free} + \frac{R_M - R_{free}}{\sigma_M} \sigma \qquad \textbf{7-3}$$

The slope of the line indicates the additional return associated with each additional unit of risk. Rearranging the variables shows that the expected return for any point on the CML (call it portfolio Z) can be represented as

$$E(R_Z) = R_{free} + \frac{\sigma_Z}{\sigma_M} (R_M - R_{free}) \qquad \textbf{7-4}$$

Expected Return = Risk Free Rate + Portion of Market Risk × (Market Risk Premium)

> ### Excel Expert 7-2 ⟫
>
> #### Market Risk Premium
>
> Say that historically, the market portfolio has earned an average of 11% per year with a standard deviation of 16%. T-bills currently yield 2%. Consider two scenarios: (A) you want a portfolio with a risk level of 14% standard deviation, and (B) you want a portfolio with an expected return of 13%. Using the CML, what are the characteristics of the portfolios in these two cases?
>
> First, note that the market risk premium computes to be 9%.
>
> For scenario (A), use **Equation 7-4** to determine the expected return of a portfolio with the desired standard deviation. The spreadsheet computation shows a return of 9.88%. Next, use **Equation 7-2** to determine the allocation to the market portfolio and to T-bills. The spreadsheet shows that 87.5% of the desired portfolio is invested in the market portfolio and 12.5% in T-bills.
>
> | | A | B | C | D | E | F | G | H | I | J | K |
> |---|---|---|---|---|---|---|---|---|---|---|---|
> | 1 | | | | If want portfolio with | | | | If want portfolio with | | | |
> | 2 | Average Market Return = | 11% | | St. Dev. = | 14% | | | Expected Return = | 13% | | |
> | 3 | Market St. Dev. = | 16% | | | | | | | | | |
> | 4 | T-Bill Yield = | 2% | | Then | | | | Then | | | |
> | 5 | | | | Expected Return = | 9.88% | =B4+(E2/B3)*(B6) | | St. Dev. = | 19.56% | =(I2-B4)*B3/B6 | |
> | 6 | Market Risk Premium = | 9% | =B2-B4 | Allocation to M = | 87.5% | =(E5-B4)/B6 | | Allocation to M = | 122.22% | =(I2-B4)/B6 | |
> | 7 | | | | Allocation to T-Bill = | 12.5% | =1-E6 | | Allocation to T-Bill = | -22.22% | =1-I6 | |
>
> For scenario (B), use **Equation 7-4** to determine the standard deviation of a portfolio with the desired expected return. The spreadsheet computation shows a standard deviation of 19.56%. Next, use **Equation 7-2** to determine the allocation to the market portfolio and to T-bills. The spreadsheet shows that 122.22% of the desired portfolio is invested in the market portfolio. To do that, you need to borrow 22.22% of the portfolio from the broker using a margin account.

This shows you that the reward for taking risk is the **market risk premium** (defined as $R_M - R_{free}$). In addition, the risk taken is measured as a proportion of the risk of the market portfolio (denoted as σ_Z/σ_M). Any investor can only buy T-bills and earn the risk-free rate. If you want more expected return than that, **Equation 7-4** and the CML show you how much risk to take to earn the appropriate market risk premium to obtain the desired return.

market risk premium
Risk-reward for taking market risk, defined as the return on the market less the risk-free rate

7-2 Capital Asset Pricing Model in Theory

7-2a Pricing Individual Securities

In the introduction to this chapter, we wrote that asset pricing theory is applied in both a *macro* context that specifies the relationship between risk and the return overall, and a *micro* context that specifies the relationship between risk and the return on a specific asset. The CML is that macro application. To extend to the micro context and determine the risk premium for individual assets, we need two insights:

(1) only the systematic risk of a security should be rewarded with a risk premium, and
(2) in equilibrium, all investments should offer the same reward to risk ratio.

The previous chapter demonstrated that the variance (or standard deviation) of an investment measured its total risk, which is composed of systematic plus unsystematic risk. In this chapter, it was demonstrated that the risk premium for the market is determined by the risk of the market portfolio. This completely diversified portfolio has no unsystematic risk. Thus, the systematic risk of a security is its association with the market risk. That is formally defined as the covariance of the security and the market portfolio. Consider the company Coca-Cola, Inc. (ticker: KO). Coke's systematic risk is now measured as $Cov(R_{KO} - R_{free}, R_M - R_{free})$.

All securities should offer the same reward-to-risk ratio. The theory developed the market portfolio, whose reward-to-risk ratio is characterized as

$$Market\ reward\ to\ risk\ ratio = \frac{E(R_M) - R_{free}}{\sigma_M^2} \qquad \textbf{7-5}$$

Since the reward-to-risk ratio for Coke must be the same as the market portfolio, then

$$\frac{E(R_{KO}) - R_{free}}{Cov(R_{KO} - R_{free}, R_M - R_{free})} = \frac{E(R_M) - R_{free}}{\sigma_M^2}$$

Solving for the expected return for Coke produces

$$E(R_{KO}) = R_{free} + \frac{Cov(R_{KO} - R_{free}, R_M - R_{free})}{\sigma_M^2} \times (E(R_M) - R_{free}) \qquad \textbf{7-6}$$

This is the CAPM that prices individual securities, in this case, the stock of Coke. From the equation, note that Coke investors start with the risk-free rate. Then the appropriate risk premium starts with Coke's systematic risk that is standardized by the market risk. This standardized systematic risk is then multiplied by the market risk premium to determine the risk premium for Coke.

beta
Measure of the market risk of an asset or portfolio

It is customary to reflect the standardized security systematic risk as **beta** and denoted with the Greek letter β. Thus, Coke's beta is

$$\beta_{KO} \frac{Cov(R_{KO} - R_{free}, R_M - R_{free})}{\sigma_M^2} \qquad \textbf{7-7}$$

The general and most familiar form of the CAPM is, therefore,

$$E(R) = R_{free} + \beta \times (E(R_M) - R_{free}) \qquad \textbf{7-8}$$

Figure 7-5 breaks down the CAPM equation. The expected return for a security is the risk-free rate plus the company risk premium. That company risk premium is the company risk measured by beta times the market risk premium.

Figure 7-5: Characteristics of the CAPM

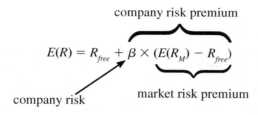

$$E(R) = R_{free} + \beta \times (E(R_M) - R_{free})$$

company risk premium

company risk

market risk premium

In the CAPM framework, a beta is easy to interpret

- The risk-free asset has a beta of 0,
- The market portfolio has a beta of 1,
- Beta measures systematic risk in units of market risk, and
- Higher beta means higher risk.

Excel Expert 7-3

CAPM Exercises

Consider that the market return is 9.5% and the risk-free rate is 2.2%. Stocks A, B, and C have betas of 0.5, 1, and 1.5, respectively. What is the market risk premium? For each stock, what is its expected return and company risk premium?

	A	B	C	D	E	F	G	H
1	Market Return =	9.5%		Stock A	Stock B	Stock C		
2	Risk-free Rate =	2.2%	Beta =	0.5	1	1.5		
3								
4	Market Risk Premium =	7.3%		Stock A	Stock B	Stock C		
5		=B1-B2	Expected Return =	5.85%	9.50%	13.15%	=$B$2+F2*$B$4	
6			Stock Risk Premium =	3.65%	7.30%	10.95%	=F2*$B$4	

As the spreadsheet shows, the market risk premium is 7.3%.

Using the CAPM of **Equation 7-8**, Stock A has an expected return of 5.85%. That comes from a 2.2% risk-free rate and 3.65% stock risk premium. The return is low because Stock A has low risk. The beta of 0.5 indicates that Stock A has only half of the systematic risk of the market.

Stock B has a beta of 1, which is the same as the market portfolio. Therefore, its expected return and risk premium is the same as the market, 9.5% and 7.3%. Stock C has more systematic risk than the market. Its expected return is therefore higher. Stock C has an expected return of 13.15% and stock risk premium of 10.95%.

The World of Investing

Are T-Bills Really Risk-free?

The risk-free asset is a theoretical concept. As a practical application, the U.S. Treasury Bill is generally considered the best proxy for the risk-free asset. The T-bill yield is therefore taken to be the risk-free rate that is very important to the CAPM. The T-bill is considered to be a good risk-free proxy: it is considered to be free of default risk because it is fully backed by the U.S. federal government.

Is the T-bill really free of default risk? Arguments in favor include that the U.S. government has never defaulted on its debt obligations. This is true through severe economic crises and world wars. T-bills are very short-term instruments that mature in three months, six months, or one year, when issued. Also, T-bills are very liquid. That is, hundreds of billions of dollars of T-bills trade every day. So, if you need to buy or sell, there is an incredibly active market available to do so.

The arguments for caution include the knowledge that many countries have defaulted on their debt. Here is an abbreviated list of countries that have defaulted since 1990. Some might surprise you: Argentina, Brazil, Greece, Iceland, Mexico, Morocco, Nigeria, Russia, South Africa, Thailand, Venezuela, Zimbabwe, and many more. In addition, the U.S. government has an enormous amount of debt. At the end of 2021, the total national debt was $29 trillion, which is over $86,000 for every citizen. If you add to this debt all the unfunded liability, like Social Security, Medicare, Veteran benefits, etc., the total becomes $158 trillion, or nearly $475,000 per citizen. See the U.S. Debt Clock for a running total (usdebtclock.org).

Lastly, the U.S. government has a debt ceiling limit. That debt limit is routinely increased to make room for new borrowing. However, periodically, politicians use the debt limit to play political chicken. They refuse to vote for the debt increase until they get their bill passed. This caused recent debt ceiling crises in 2011, 2013, and 2021. When U.S. debt reaches the limit, there is no cash available to pay maturing bills and bonds. Thus, there would be a default on those securities. It has not come to that yet, but are the U.S. T-bills really a risk-free asset, or are they simply the best proxy we have?

7-2b Security Market Line

security market line
Linear risk-return trade-off for individual stocks

The CAPM equation is the specification of the relationship between risk and return for the *individual* asset. At the micro level, this relationship is referred to as the **security market line** (SML). This relationship is very similar to the capital market line and is depicted in **Figure 7-6**.

The similarities of the capital market line and the SML are immediate. The *y*-axis is the same, and the relationship between risk and expected return is represented as a straight line. The difference is the measure of risk on the *x*-axis. The CML uses the portfolio's standard deviation, while the SML uses the individual security's beta.

The difference between the two concepts, however, is more than the distinction between the two measures of risk. Both the CML and the SML are part of the CAPM, which seeks to explain security returns. The capital market line, or the macro component, suggests that the return on a well-diversified portfolio depends on the yield of a risk-free security and the portfolio's response to an aggregate measure of risk—the portfolio's standard deviation. The SML, or the micro component, suggests that the return on an individual asset depends on the risk-free rate and the security's response to changes in the market, with that response being measured by an index of the security's market risk—beta.

Figure 7-6 shows the market portfolio, M, has a beta of one and an expected return of R_M. When beta is zero, the return is the risk-free rate. The figure also depicts a stock A that has a beta of 1.2. The SML relationship shows the expected return of stock A is R_A, which represents the return of the risk-free rate plus the stock A risk premium.

Consider that through other analysis, you think the return of stock A will be higher, as shown as A*. In this case, you would be claiming that the stock is *underpriced*.

Figure 7-6: Security Market Line

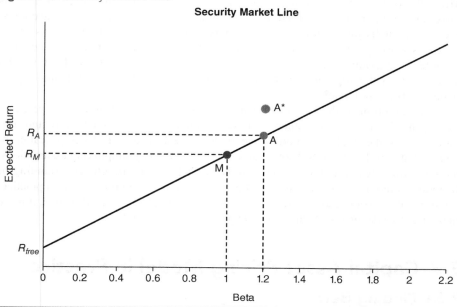

Given stock A's risk (beta of 1.2), the stock should only be expected to earn its CAPM predicted expected return. To earn more than that, the stock needs to be underpriced. If so, the stock would earn its expected return given its risk and potentially the return from its repricing back to an efficient price.

In addition to being a theory of the determination of security returns, the CAPM plays an important role in the valuation of securities and the analysis of portfolio performance. For example, in Chapter 11, the SML component of the CAPM is used to determine the required return for an investment in common stock. This return is then used in the dividend-growth model to determine the value of a common stock. The model is also used in portfolio evaluation in Chapter 9, in which the realized return is compared to the required return specified by using the CAPM. Thus, the CAPM not only is an integral part of the theory of portfolio construction and the determination of security returns but also establishes a criterion for assessing portfolio performance.

7-2c CAPM Basic Assumptions

The CAPM is a comprehensive theory to provide a complete description of how investment returns are determined. It is a method for predicting how investment returns are generated in a capital market. However, the CAPM theory entails a few important underlying assumptions. These basic assumptions are:

- Securities are efficiently priced.
- Investors hold efficient portfolios.
- It is possible to borrow and lend as much as desired at the risk-free rate.
- Investors have the same expectations about investment risk and returns.
- The model has a one-period time horizon.
- Investments are infinitely divisible.
- There are no market frictions, like no taxes or transaction costs.
- Investors fully anticipate inflation.
- Capital markets are in equilibrium.

Some criticize the CAPM for such a restrictive set of underlying assumptions. After all, taxes and transaction costs exist in the real world. Although, transactions costs have dramatically decreased over time and taxes are avoided in some accounts, like institutionally managed pensions and individual defined contribution plans. However, it is worth pointing out that a model can be a useful predictive device even if its underlying assumptions fail to be met. If a model such as the CAPM can predict stock returns with a high degree of accuracy, then the restrictiveness of its underlying assumptions is a moot point.

The attraction of the CAPM is that it offers powerful and intuitively pleasing predictions about risk measurement and the relation between expected return and risk. Unfortunately, the empirical record of the model is weak. The CAPM's empirical problems probably reflect both its theoretical failings, due to many simplifying assumptions, and the difficulties in its implementation. Nevertheless, a thorough understanding of the model is important for two reasons. First, the CAPM is commonly used in practice. Therefore, it is advantageous to know its strengths and weaknesses. And second, it is the theoretical foundation on which other asset pricing theory is built.

7-3 Capital Asset Pricing Model in Practice

7-3a Finding Beta

Beta is a very useful measure of risk. Many investors want to know a stock's beta, but can't compute it themselves. Thus, they look to financial information sources. For institutional investors, Bloomberg is the most popular. Individual investors use information provided by their stock brokerage firm or use free online websites, like Yahoo! Finance, MarketWatch, and Morningstar. To locate a firm's beta, go to yahoofinance.com and enter the stock's ticker symbol. On the stock's Summary page, you will find its beta, as shown in **Exhibit 7-1**. The 3M Company has a beta of 0.98, which is very close the market risk of 1.

Similarly, you can find betas on the MarketWatch and Morningstar websites. **Table 7-1** shows the beta estimates for the 30 Dow Jones Industrial Average stocks. First, review the betas from Yahoo! Finance.

A beta of 1 is the same risk as the market portfolio. Thus, it makes sense that firms whose business fluctuates with the economy have a beta near 1. Examples are 3M, Caterpillar, and Home Depot. It seems odd to have two competitors, like American Express and Visa, with very different betas: 1.23 and 0.97, respectively. On the other hand, Walgreens and Walmart have identical betas of 0.50. These are low-risk firms because people often shop more in their stores when economic times are poor. The companies with the highest market risk are Dow, Boeing, and Goldman Sachs, with betas of 1.71, 1.57, and 1.50, respectively.

Now review the MarketWatch beta column. In some cases, the beta estimate is very similar to the one from Yahoo! Finance, like Apple's beta estimates of 1.23 and 1.20. In other cases, like Johnson & Johnson, the beta estimates are somewhat similar: 0.72 and 0.64. But in many cases, the estimates are very different. Why are these beta estimates so different? It likely comes down to how they were computed. The beta generated by Yahoo! Finance uses five years of monthly returns and the S&P 500 Index as the proxy for the market portfolio. Other sites use only three years of monthly returns.

Morningstar also provides beta estimates for stocks and for mutual funds. The beta estimates from Morningstar are very close to those of Yahoo! Finance. Morningstar computes beta the same way as Yahoo! Finance. The likely reason there are small differences stem from how often the beta is estimated and the website data is updated.

Morningstar also provides beta estimates for ETFs and mutual funds as shown in **Exhibit 7-2**. You can use the Risk link in the menu of the Morningstar page for the

Exhibit 7-1: 3M Company's Beta on Yahoo! Finance, October 20, 2021

3M Company (MMM)
NYSE - NYSE Delayed Price. Currency in USD

☆ Add to watchlist   ⧉ Visitors trend 2W ↓ 10W ↑ 9M ↑

182.42 +0.11 (+0.06%)   **182.42** 0.00 (0.00%)
At close: 4:03PM EDT   After hours: 06:46PM EDT

Summary   Company Outlook ✅   Chart   Conversations   Statistics   Historical Data   Profile   Financials   Analysis   Options

Previous Close	182.31	Market Cap	105.555B	1D 5D 1M 6M YTD 1Y 5Y Max ⎍ ⤢ Full screen
Open	182.59	Beta (5Y Monthly)	0.98	183.40
Bid	181.64 x 900	PE Ratio (TTM)	18.04	182.87
Ask	182.54 x 1400	EPS (TTM)	10.11	
Day's Range	182.04 - 183.18	Earnings Date	Oct 26, 2021	182.42
52 Week Range	156.13 - 208.95	Forward Dividend & Yield	5.92 (3.25%)	181.80
Volume	1,693,340	Ex-Dividend Date	Aug 20, 2021	10 AM 12 PM 02 PM 04 PM
Avg. Volume	2,400,032	1y Target Est	193.46	Trade prices are not sourced from all markets

Source: Yahoo! Finance

SPDR S&P 500 Index Trust ETF (ticker: SPY) as shown. Note that the ETF has a beta of 1.00 as measured over the previous five years. This should not be a surprise because this ETF is trying to replicate the S&P 500 Index, which is also the proxy for the market portfolio.

Morningstar varies its proxy for the market portfolio depending on the category of fund. For example, Morningstar uses the S&P 500 Index for U.S. stock portfolios as shown in **Table 7-2**. The American Funds Growth Fund of America is a large company stock fund with a risk level very similar to the S&P 500 Index. The S&P 500 Index ETF has the exact same risk as the S&P 500 Index (also shown above). Even the iShares Core S&P Small-Cap ETF, which shares no stocks in common with the S&P 500 Index, and the technology-laden Nasdaq Index ETF (QQQ) use the S&P 500 Index as the market portfolio proxy. Morningstar uses the MSCI ACWI Ex USA as the market proxy for international stock funds. The Bloomberg US Agg Bond TR is used for bond funds, and the Morningstar Mod Tgt Risk TR is used for blended funds with both stocks and bonds. Note that this means you can't directly compare the Morningstar beta of the Fidelity Balanced fund (1.22) with the beta of Invesco QQQ (1.03) because their computation uses different market portfolio proxies.

Note that to implement the CAPM equation to compute the expected return of one of these funds, you would need the beta shown, a risk-free rate, and the expected return for the market proxy shown in column 3 of the table.

7-3b Estimating Beta

While the CAPM is framed in terms of computing expected returns so that you know what to expect in the future, all the variables in the model must be computed using past data. In addition, the model itself does not direct us on the important details of estimating beta. For example, what is the best proxy for the market portfolio? The discussion above shows that some financial information providers, like Morningstar,

Table 7-1: Betas for the 30 Companies in the Dow Jones Industrial Average, October 20, 2021

Company	Yahoo! Finance Beta	Market Watch Beta	Morning-star Beta	Company	Yahoo! Finance Beta	Market Watch Beta	Morning-star Beta
3M Company	0.98	0.86	0.98	Johnson & Johnson	0.72	0.64	0.73
American Express Company	1.23	1.30	1.25	JPMorgan Chase & Co.	1.14	1.19	1.17
Amgen Inc.	0.68	0.81	0.69	McDonald's Corporation	0.60	0.80	0.62
Apple Inc.	1.22	1.20	1.23	Merck & Co. Inc.	0.42	0.65	0.40
Boeing Company	1.57	1.61	1.58	Microsoft Corporation	0.80	1.19	0.80
Caterpillar Inc.	0.93	1.11	0.94	NIKE Inc. Class B	0.90	0.97	0.90
Chevron Corporation	1.24	1.20	1.27	Procter & Gamble Company	0.42	0.61	0.44
Cisco Systems Inc.	0.92	1.04	0.92	Salesforce.com inc.	1.04	1.15	1.04
Coca-Cola Company	0.64	0.68	0.64	Travelers Compa-nies Inc.	0.77	0.99	0.76
Dow Inc.	1.71	1.38	1.71	UnitedHealth Group Inc	0.79	1.04	0.79
Goldman Sachs Group Inc.	1.50	1.24	1.51	Verizon Commu-nications Inc.	0.45	0.48	0.47
Home Depot Inc.	0.99	1.06	1.00	Visa Inc. Class A	0.97	1.13	0.98
Honeywell Inter-national Inc.	1.19	1.03	1.18	Walgreens Boots Alliance Inc	0.50	0.81	0.51
Intel Corporation	0.59	1.23	0.60	Walmart Inc.	0.50	0.53	0.49
International Busi-ness Machines	1.18	0.95	1.20	Walt Disney Company	1.20	0.97	1.20

Source: Yahoo! Finance, MarketWatch.com, Morningstar.com

use different market portfolio proxies that depend on the category of the fund being analyzed. Also, should the risk measurements (variances, co-variances, etc.) be computed using monthly returns, annual returns, daily returns? How long should the time period be? Lastly, what is the proxy for the risk-free rate? Even if you think it should the T-bill yield, there are T-bills with different durations (i.e., three months, six months, one year).

To estimate beta, you need a time-series set of returns for your company (or portfolio), the risk-free rate, and a market portfolio proxy. The most common choices are to use the 3-month T-bill yield and the S&P 500 Index and to use monthly returns over a five-year period. One caution is that the 3-month T-bill yield is quoted as an annual rate. Thus, yield for the month is the quoted yield divided by 12. Step 1 is to obtain this data.

excess return
A security or portfolio return less the risk-free rate.

Step 2 is to convert the company and market portfolio returns to **excess returns**. To do that, simply subtract the risk-free rate from the company and index returns, like $R_{KO} - R_{free}$.

For Step 3, you have several options using a spreadsheet. You can use **Equation 7-7** and compute the covariance of KO excess returns and Index excess returns, divided by the variance of the Index excess returns. The most common procedure is to recognize

Exhibit 7-2: The SPDR S&P 500 ETF Page on Morningstar, October 20, 2021

SPDR® S&P 500 ETF Trust SPY ★★★★ 🛡 Silver

Analyst rating as of Mar 15, 2021

Quote   Fund Analysis   Performance   Risk   Price   Portfolio   Parent   Crowd Sense

Risk (3-Yr   5-Yr   10-Yr)

Morningstar Risk & Return ⓘ

Risk vs. Category

Average

Low — Average — High

Return vs. Category

Above Average

Low — Average — High

Category: Large Blend as of Sep 30, 2021 | Rankings are out of 1,102 funds.

Risk & Volatility Measures ⓘ

Trailing	Fund	Category	Index
Alpha	-0.09	-1.37	-0.15
Beta	1.00	1.00	1.03
R²	100.00	94.98	99.76
Sharpe Ratio	1.03	0.92	1.02
Standard Deviation	15.17	15.66	15.60

USD | Fund as of Sep 30, 2021 | Category: Large Blend as of Sep 30, 2021 | Index: Russell 1000 TR USD as of Sep 30, 2021 | Calculation Benchmark: S&P 500 TR USD

Source: Morningstar.com

Table 7-2: The Betas of Large Mutual Funds and ETFs from Morningstar

Mutual Fund or ETF	Fund Beta	Market Portfolio Proxy
American Funds Growth Fund of America	1.01	S&P 500 TR
Fidelity Balanced	1.22	Morningstar Mod Tgt Risk TR
Dodge & Cox International Stock Fund	1.26	MSCI ACWI Ex USA NR
Vanguard Core Bond Investor	1.09	Bloomberg US Agg Bond TR
SPDR S&P 500 ETF	1.00	S&P 500 TR
iShares Core S&P Small-Cap ETF	1.24	S&P 500 TR
Invesco QQQ ETF	1.03	S&P 500 TR

Source: Morningstar.com

that empirically, the relationship between the firm's excess returns and the market excess returns involves error. Thus, a linear regression is computed as,

$$R_{KO} - R_{free} = \hat{\alpha}_{KO} + \hat{\beta}_{KO} \times (R_M - R_{free}) + \varepsilon \qquad \textbf{7-9}$$

where R_{KO} is the rate of return on an individual security (Coca-Cola in the example), R_{free} is the return on the risk-free asset, the intercept term is described by the Greek letter α (**alpha**), the slope coefficient is beta, and the random disturbance or error term is depicted by the Greek letter ε (epsilon).

The intercept term α shows the anticipated rate of return when either $\beta = 0$ or $R_M = R_{free}$. Theoretically, alpha should be zero over time. A non-zero alpha is referred to as an **abnormal return**. When $\alpha > 0$, investors enjoyed higher returns than should be expected given the firm's level of market risk (beta).

alpha
Portion of return that can't be explained as compensation for risk

abnormal return
Same as alpha

Excel Expert 7-4

Estimating Beta

There are (at least) three methods for computing beta in a spreadsheet. This illustration uses five years of monthly returns for Coca-Cola (KO), the 3-month T-bill yield, and the S&P 500 Index. As the spreadsheet below shows, first subtract the monthly T-bill yield from the month's return of KO and the S&P 500 Index. The first estimate shows the three functions of INTERCEPT, SLOPE, and RSQ. The INTERCEPT is the alpha of **Equation 7-9**. SLOPE computes the slope of the line between KO and the index, which is beta. Lastly, RSQ computes the R^2 for the regression to determine the quality of fit in the beta estimation.

During these five years, KO has a beta of 0.62. Yahoo! Finance reports a beta of 0.64. The difference is likely a difference in the exact months used in the analysis. KO's return underperformed that level of market risk by –0.15% per month. The fit was moderately good with an R^2 of 0.314. For the second method of computing beta, note that **Equation 7-8** shows that it is computed as the covariance of KO and the market, then divided by the variance of the market. Row 6 of the spreadsheet shows that equation provides the same estimate of beta as the SLOPE function.

	I	J	K	L	M	N	O	P	Q
1	KO		KO - T-Bill	S&P - T-Bill		Market Proxy = S&P 500 Index			
2	-3.01%		-3.04%	3.54%		alpha =	-0.15%	=INTERCEPT(K2:K61,L2:L61)	
3	-0.46%		-0.48%	-0.15%		beta =	0.62	=SLOPE(K2:K61,L2:L61)	
4	-2.56%		-2.58%	-0.15%		R^2 =	0.314	=RSQ(K2:K61,L2:L61)	
5	1.01%		0.98%	-1.97%					
6	-4.83%		-4.87%	3.38%		beta =	0.62	=COVARIANCE.S(K2:K61,L2:L61)/VAR.S(L2:L61)	
7	3.62%		3.58%	1.78%					

A third method is to estimate the linear regression. To do that, under the Data menu, select Data Analysis. Scroll down to Regression and select it. The Regression data input window will appear. Select the company excess return range as the Y Range and the market excess return range for X. Enter the cell for your output data and click OK.

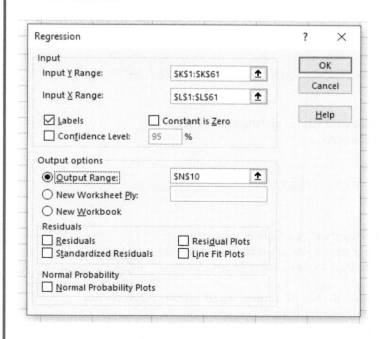

(Continued)

The regression analysis produces the following SUMMARY OUTPUT. The results are the same as found using the SLOPE, etc., functions. However, there is additional information that might be valuable to you. For example, the t Stat shown indicates that the underperformance (alpha) is not statistically significant.

SUMMARY OUTPUT

Regression Statistics	
Multiple R	0.560491702
R Square	0.314150948
Adjusted R Squa	0.302325964
Standard Error	0.039998861
Observations	60

ANOVA

	df	SS	MS	F	gnificance F
Regression	1	0.042504321	0.042504321	26.56671	3.2E-06
Residual	58	0.092794716	0.001599909		
Total	59	0.135299037			

	Coefficients	Standard Error	t Stat	P-value	Lower 95%	Upper 95%	ower 95.0%	Jpper 95.0%
Intercept	-0.0014751	0.005361841	-0.275110635	0.784209	-0.01221	0.009258	-0.01221	0.0092578
S&P - T-Bill	0.618708943	0.120037649	5.15429074	3.2E-06	0.378427	0.85899	0.378427	0.8589904

In summary, if you have returns from your firm or portfolio, the risk-free rate, and the market portfolio proxy, you can estimate beta.

7-3c Model Specification Problems

In the analysis above, what would KO's beta estimate be if different model specification choices were made? What if a different market portfolio proxy was used? Or a different time period? **Table 7-3** shows the beta estimate and model fit via R^2 for each model specification. Specification 1 repeats the estimation shown in **Excel Expert 7-4**. The S&P 500 Index is selected as the market portfolio proxy and the estimation is conducted using monthly returns for the most recent five years. The KO beta estimate is 0.62 for Specification 1. The R^2 is 0.314. Specification 2 replaces the S&P 500 Index with the NASDAQ Composite as the market portfolio proxy. Notice that the KO beta estimate falls to 0.39. In addition, the lower R^2 of 0.160 shows that this model is a worse fit than Specification 1. Thus, the S&P 500 Index appears to be a better choice.

Table 7-3: Cola-Cola Betas Estimates Using Different Model Specifications

Specification	Market Proxy	Return Interval	Time Length	Beta Estimate	R^2
1	S&P 500 Index	Monthly	5 years	0.62	0.314
2	NASDAQ	Monthly	5 years	0.39	0.160
3	S&P 500 Index	Monthly	Prior 5 years	0.55	0.233
4	S&P 500 Index	Monthly	1 years	0.91	0.454
5	S&P 500 Index	Weekly	5 years	0.85	0.519

Thus, the relative market risk borne by Coca-Cola shareholders is very different depending on the market index used. Although there is a high degree of correlation between the S&P 500 Index and the NASDAQ Composite returns, slight differences have meaningful effects on the beta estimates. Market index bias is the distortion to beta estimates caused by the fact that market indexes are only imperfect proxies for the market portfolio. The differences in beta computations would lead to differences in expected return. The presence of market index bias makes it imperative that beta comparisons among individual companies reflect identical and appropriate market benchmarks.

market index bias
Distortion of beta estimates caused by imperfect proxies for the market portfolio

An ideal measure of stock market risk would be constant from one period to another. The usefulness of a stock's market risk diminishes if it fails to provide accurate and consistent measures of risk exposure over time. In fact, an important limitation of risk estimators derived from the CAPM is that they vary from one period to another in unpredictable ways. Specification 3 shows the beta estimation is conducted during the five years prior to the original estimation period (year -10 to -5 rather than year -5 to year 0). Comparing to Speculation 1, the beta falls from 0.62 to 0.55 and the model fit weakens. This leads to an interesting question. Did Coca-Cola's level of market risk increase over the 10 years, or is the difference a model estimation issue?

A company's risk level can change. Companies acquire other business to add to their product mix. In addition, a firm expands to international markets. Companies add or reduce their financial level (i.e., debt level). Risk can also change when the power of their competitors changes.

nonstationary beta problem
Implementation difficulty due to betas' inherent instability over time

However, there are model estimation issues too. The beta you estimate today likely differs from the one you will estimate next year. This is the nonstationary beta problem.

If betas can change over time, then maybe using a beta estimate over a short, recent period might be better? Specification 4 shows the result of a one-year estimation period. The beta estimate is quite high compared to the other estimates at 0.91. Actually, short time horizon estimates are the most volatile, i.e., exhibit the least stationarity.

time interval bias
Beta estimation problem derived from dependence on the return interval used

Finally, a time interval bias exists because beta estimates are sensitive to the length of time over which stock return data are measured. This is illustrated in Specification 5, which uses weekly returns instead of monthly returns over the five-year period. Compared to Specification 1, the weekly beta estimate shows a higher beta of 0.85. This is a lot higher than the 0.62 beta estimated over the same time period but using different return time intervals. Which is better? The coefficient of determination, R^2 is higher for the weekly estimation specification, which suggests that in this case, Specification 5 is better.

Clearly, there are difficulties with estimating beta. Many obtain beta estimates from financial websites or other data services. Be cautious about using these betas. First, you may not know how those betas are computed. For example, what market portfolio is used (model specification bias)? What time length and time intervals are used? Lastly, how long ago was the beta computed (nonstationary beta problem)? At least when you compute your own beta estimate, you know the underlying assumptions used.

7-3d Portfolio Betas

How does adding a stock to an existing portfolio change the risk of that portfolio? Answering this question using modern portfolio theory requires substantial computational effort. Portfolio theory describes the risk of a portfolio as the standard deviation of the portfolio. The standard deviation is determined by how each security's return in the portfolio covaries with each of the other assets' returns. Adding a new stock to the portfolio requires computing all the standard deviations of each security and the covariance between all the securities. However, the CAPM provides an easier frame-work for assessing how a new stock will change the risk of an existing portfolio. When two assets are being combined, the risk of the new portfolio is simply the weighted average of the betas of the two assets. More generally, the beta of a portfolio is

$$\beta_P = \sum_{i=1}^{n} w_i \times \beta_i \qquad \qquad 7\text{-}10$$

where w_i is the proportional weight of asset i in the portfolio. An application is illustrated in **Excel Expert 7-5**.

Unlike the beta coefficient for individual securities, the beta for a diversified portfolio is fairly stable over time. Changes in the individual company betas tend to average out. While one stock's beta is increasing, the beta of another stock declines. A portfolio's historical beta, then, is much better suited to forecast its future beta, and thus the portfolio's expected return.

As mentioned earlier, Morningstar provides beta estimates for the mutual funds in its database. **Table 7-4** shows the betas of popular actively managed mutual funds reported by Morningstar. The estimation of these betas is done of the most recent 3-, 5-, and 10-year periods. Note that for each fund, the beta estimation is fairly stationary across time. For example, the behemoth American Funds Growth Fund of America mutual fund has a beta of about 1, no matter how long a time period is used to estimate it. The high-risk fund, DFA U.S. Small Cap Value Portfolio, shows beta estimates between 1.30 and 1.39. The low-risk specialty fund, T. Rowe Price Health Sciences Fund, shows beta estimates between 0.85 and 0.89. So, whether the mutual fund is high risk, low risk, or about the same risk as the market portfolio, its beta estimation is consistent across time.

Excel Expert 7-5

Portfolio Beta

You own a portfolio that represents 40% of Stock A, 35% of Stock B, and 25% of Stock C. The betas of the three stocks are 1.2, 0.9, and 0.8, respectively. What is the portfolio beta? In addition, you are considering adding Stock D that has a beta of 1.3. What would be the portfolio beta if 10% of the portfolio was invested in Stock D?

	A	B	C	D	E	F	G	H	I
1		Beta	Weight			Beta			
2	Stock A	1.20	0.40		Original Portfolio Beta =	0.995	=SUMPRODUCT(B2:B4,C2:C4)		
3	Stock B	0.90	0.35						
4	Stock C	0.80	0.25		Portfolio Considered Beta =	1.0255	=B5*C5+F2*(1-C5)		
5	Stock D	1.30	0.10						

As the spreadsheet shows, your portfolio has a beta of 0.995, which is very close to the same risk as the market in general. Adding 10% of Stock D, which has a beta of 1.3, to that portfolio slightly increases the portfolio beta to 1.0255, which is slightly more than the market risk level.

Table 7-4: The Betas of Popular Mutual Funds Estimated over Different Periods

Mutual Fund or ETF	Beta		
	3- Years	5- Years	10- Years
American Funds Growth Fund of America	1.01	1.00	1.00
Fidelity Magellan	0.96	0.97	1.03
T. Rowe Price Growth Stock	1.03	1.02	1.05
Columbia Dividend Income	0.85	0.86	0.86
Principal MidCap Institutional	1.10	1.08	1.06
DFA U.S. Small Cap Value Portfolio	1.39	1.35	1.30
T. Rowe Price Health Sciences Fund	0.87	0.89	0.85

Source: Morningstar.com

The CAPM characterization of risk has estimation issues for individual stocks. But for diversified portfolios, the framework works very well.

Conclusion

This chapter expands modern portfolio theory to asset pricing by adding a risk-free asset and developing the capital asset pricing model (CAPM). Through the CAPM, the risk–return relationship is defined. Investors who don't want to take risk will earn the risk-free rate. To earn a higher expected return than that, you need to take some market risk. In other words, you need to take some risk to earn some of the market risk premium. How much risk should you take? The CAPM tells you that the risk of the stock or portfolio you choose is measured through the risk of the market portfolio. The level of risk associated with the market risk is called *beta*. A beta of 1 adds the market risk premium to the risk-free rate for the expected return. Lower (beta<1) or higher (beta>1) levels of risk predict commensurate lower or higher expected returns, respectively.

The most common application of the CAPM in industry is to estimate stock or portfolio betas using five years of monthly returns (60 observations). The S&P 500 Index is the most common proxy for the market portfolio and the T-bill yield for the risk-free rate. Other specifications usually result in different beta estimates. Unfortunately, beta estimates for individual stocks are not stationary over time. These issues reduce the practical use of the CAPM as a predictive model of returns. Because of this, other asset pricing models have been developed. They are explored in the next chapter.

Chapter Equations

$$E(R) = R_{free} + \frac{R_P - R_{free}}{\sigma_P} \sigma \qquad \text{7-1}$$

$$E(R) = R_{free} + w_P*(R_P - R_{free}) \qquad \text{7-2}$$

$$E(R) = R_{free} + \frac{R_M - R_{free}}{\sigma_M} \sigma \qquad \text{7-3}$$

$$E(R_Z) = R_{free} + \frac{\sigma_Z}{\sigma_M}(R_M - R_{free}) \qquad \text{7-4}$$

$$Market\ reward\ to\ risk\ ratio = \frac{E(R_M) - R_{free}}{\sigma_M^2} \qquad \text{7-5}$$

$$E(R_{KO}) = R_{free} + \frac{Cov(R_{KO} - R_{free}, R_M - R_{free})}{\sigma_M^2} \times (E(R_M) - R_{free}) \qquad \text{7-6}$$

$$\beta_{KO} \frac{Cov(R_{KO} - R_{free}, R_M - R_{free})}{\sigma_M^2} \qquad \text{7-7}$$

$$E(R) = R_{free} + \beta \times (E(R_M) - R_{free}) \qquad \text{7-8}$$

$$R_{KO} - R_{free} = \hat{\alpha}_{KO} + \hat{\beta}_{KO} \times (R_M - R_{free}) + \varepsilon \qquad \text{7-9}$$

$$\beta_P = \sum_{i=1}^{n} w_i \times \beta_i \qquad \text{7-10}$$

Excel Functions

COVARIANCE.S(array1, array2)
INTERCEPT(known_ys, known,xs)
Regression
RSQ(known_ys, known,xs)

SLOPE(known_ys, known,xs)
SUMPRODUCT(array1,[array2],[array3]...)
VAR.S(array1, array2)

Key Terms

abnormal return – **Same as alpha**

alpha – **Portion of return that can't be explained as compensation for risk**

asset pricing theory – **Models of expected return expressed as risk-free rates, risks, and risk premiums**

beta – **Measure of the market risk of an asset or portfolio**

capital allocation line – **Most efficient portfolios for some risky assets and the risk-free asset**

capital asset pricing model – **Method for predicting how investment expected returns are determined in an efficient capital market**

capital market line – **Most efficient portfolios with *all* risky assets and the risk-free asset**

excess return – **A security or portfolio return less the risk-free rate**

market index bias – **Distortion of beta estimates caused by imperfect proxies for the market portfolio**

market portfolio – **The portfolio with all risky securities in proportion to their value**

market risk premium – **Risk-reward for taking market risk, defined as the return on the market less the risk-free rate**

nonstationary beta problem – **Implementation difficulty due to betas' inherent instability over time**

risk-free asset – **A security with a certain future return**

risk-free rate – **The certain future return from the risk-free asset**

security market line – **Linear risk-return trade-off for individual stocks**

time interval bias – **Beta estimation problem derived from dependence on the return interval used**

Questions

1. **Capital Allocation Line.** How does adding a risk-free asset allow investors to obtain better opportunities than the efficient frontier? (LO 7-1)

2. **Optimal Portfolio.** What are the dynamics involved in assessing your optimal portfolio on the capital allocation line? (LO 7-2)

3. **Market Portfolio.** What is the market portfolio? What role does it play in the CAPM? (LO 7-3)

4. **Expected Return.** What data do you need to obtain to estimate beta of a stock and its expected return? (LO 7-4)

5. **Security Market Line.** What are the differences between the security market line (SML) and the capital market line? What does the SML tell you? (LO 7-5)

6. **CAPM Assumptions.** What are the basic assumptions in the CAPM theory? Which ones seem unrealistic to you? (LO 7-6)

7. **Finding Company Betas.** Betas can be found at various financial websites. Why are the betas found for a company often different? (LO 7-7)

8. **Estimating Beta.** What data would you use to estimate a company's beta? How do you assess whether the proxy for the market portfolio is a good fit? (LO 7-8)

9. **Issues with Estimating Beta.** What are the empirical criticisms of estimating beta? (LO 7-9)

10. **Portfolio Beta.** Given individual securities in a portfolio, explain why estimating portfolio risk is much easier through portfolio beta than through portfolio standard deviation of returns. (LO 7-10)

Problems

1. **Portfolios on CAL.** Consider a CAL in which the risk-free rate is 2%, the risky portfolio P return is 10%, and the portfolio P risk is a standard deviation of 16%. What are the expected returns and risk levels of these 3 portfolios? (LO 7-2)

   a. 25% risk-fee asset and 75% portfolio P
   b. 50% risk-free asset and 50% portfolio P
   c. Borrow 20% at risk-free rate, 120% portfolio P

2. **Portfolios on CAL.** Consider a CAL in which the risk-free rate is 3%, the risky portfolio P return is 11%, and the portfolio P risk is a standard deviation of 17%. What are the allocations to the risk-free asset and portfolio P needed to obtain the following expected returns? (LO 7-2)

   a. 5% expected return
   b. 10% expected return
   c. 13% expected return

3. **Portfolios on CML.** The market portfolio has earned an average of 12% per year with a standard deviation of 18%. T-bills currently yield 1.5%. What are the expected return and asset allocation characteristics of portfolios with the following risk? (LO 7-3)

   a. 5% standard deviation
   b. 18% standard deviation
   c. 21% standard deviation

4. **Portfolios on CML.** The market portfolio has earned an average of 10.5% per year with a standard deviation of 15.5%. T-bills currently yield 1.8%. What are the standard deviation and asset allocation characteristics of portfolios with the following expected return? (LO 7-3)

   a. 3% expected return
   b. 10.5% expected return
   c. 11.5% expected return

5. **Beta.** The market portfolio has a variance of excess returns of 0.0324. Given the covariances with the market excess returns of the following stock's excess returns, what are those stock's betas? (LO 7-4)

   a. 0.0162 covariance
   b. 0.0389 covariance

6. **Expected Return from CAPM.** The market portfolio has an expected return of 11.4% and the T-bill yield is 2.1%. Given the following betas, what are their expected returns? (LO 7-4)

   a. Beta = 0.6
   b. Beta = 1.0
   c. Beta = 1.5

7. **Returns and Premiums.** A company's expected return is 13.5% and it has a beta of 1.1. The market portfolio return is 12% and the risk-free rate is 2.3%. What is the company's excess return and company risk premium? (LO 7-4)

8. **Returns and Premiums.** At the beginning of the year, you bought three stocks with betas shown below. The risk-free rate is 2.6%. Unfortunately, the market portfolio had a negative return of − 8.7% during the year. What is the likely return for each company during the year? (LO 7-4)

   a. Beta = 0.6
   b. Beta = 1.0
   c. Beta = 1.5

9. **Under- or Over-Valued.** A security market line can be characterized by a risk-free rate of 2.3% and a market portfolio return of 11.2%. Determine whether each of the following stocks are over- or under-valued. (LO 7-5)

   a. Expected Return of 12.4% with beta = 1.0
   b. Expected Return of 14% with beta = 1.2
   c. Expected Return of 7.5% with beta = 0.8

10. **Under- or Over-Valued.** A security market line can be characterized by a risk-free rate of 3.1% and a market portfolio return of 13.1%. Analysts report the expected return they believe for each of the following three stocks. If these stocks are properly valued, what should their beta be? (LO 7-5)

    a. Expected Return of 12.0%
    b. Expected Return of 14.8%
    c. Expected Return of 8.5%

11. **Alpha.** During the year, the market portfolio earned a 9.4% return while the risk-free rate was 1.3%. The actual returns of three stocks and their betas are shown below. What is these stock's alpha for the year? (LO 7-8)

    a. Actual Return of 10.4% with beta = 1.0
    b. Actual Return of 10.5% with beta = 1.2
    c. Actual Return of 8.5% with beta = 0.8

12. **Estimating Beta.** In the data file, **ch7_pr12.xlsx**, two years of monthly excess returns for the S&P 500 Index and Stock W, use regression analysis or spreadsheet functions to estimate CAPM parameters of **Equation 7-9**. What is Stock W's alpha, beta, and the R^2 fit of the estimation? What does the alpha estimate mean? (LO 7-8)

13. **Estimating Beta.** In the data file, **ch7_pr13.xlsx**, two years of monthly excess returns for the S&P 500 Index and Stock X, use regression analysis or spreadsheet functions to estimate CAPM parameters of **Equation 7-9**. What is Stock X's alpha, beta, and the R^2 fit of the estimation? What does the alpha estimate mean? (LO 7-8)

14. **Estimating Beta.** In the data file, **ch7_pr14.xlsx**. two years of monthly returns for the S&P 500 Index and Stock Y, and the annual yield for T-bills shown below. Use regression analysis or spreadsheet functions to estimate CAPM parameters of **Equation 7-9**. What is Stock Y's alpha, beta, and the R^2 fit of the estimation? What does the alpha estimate mean? (LO 7-8)

15. **Different Beta Estimates.** You searched three different financial information websites looking for the beta of a company. The betas found are 1.08, 1.23, and 1.12. Given the return on the market portfolio of 12% and risk-free rate of 2.5%, what is the range (min and max) of company risk premiums suggested by these betas? (LO 7-9)

16. **Different Beta Estimates.** You searched three different financial information websites looking for the beta of a company. The betas found are 0.95, 0.84, and 1.02. Given the return on the market portfolio of 11.5% and risk-free rate of 1.5%, what is the range (min and max) of the company's expected return suggested by these betas? (LO 7-9)

17. **Portfolio Beta.** Your portfolio is composed of 1,000 shares of LED stock (beta = 1.3) at a price of $32.45 per share, 500 shares of EPC (beta = 1.2) at $55.88 per share, 2,000 shares of FRED (beta = 0.7) at $22.57 per share, and 700 shares of GILL (beta = 0.9) at $48.90 per share. Calculate the beta of this four-stock portfolio. (LO 7-10)

18. **Portfolio Beta.** Your existing portfolio has a beta of 1.1 and a value of $100,000. Examining each of the following cases separately, what would be the final portfolio beta? (LO 7-10)

    a. Sell $10,000 of the existing portfolio to buy a stock with a beta of 1.4
    b. Convert 20% of the existing portfolio to a low-risk portfolio that has a beta of 0.5
    c. You have an additional $15,000 in cash and buy a stock with a beta of 0.9 to add to the existing portfolio

19. **Portfolio Beta.** Your existing portfolio has a beta of 0.9. There is a risker portfolio available that you could add to your existing portfolio. The riskier portfolio has a beta of 1.4. What portion of the existing portfolio and what portion of the riskier portfolio do you need to have a new portfolio with a beta of 1.1? (LO 7-10)

20. **Portfolio Beta.** You are creating a portfolio with the following stocks. Note each of their beta and their portfolio weight are given. What is the portfolio beta? (LO 7-10)

	Beta	Weight
Stock L	1.5	0.20
Stock M	1.1	0.15
Stock N	0.6	0.22
Stock O	0.8	0.20
Stock P	1.2	0.23

Case Study

Estimating Disney's Beta

The Walt Disney Company, a worldwide entertainment company, was founded in 1923 and is based in Burbank, California. The company's Media Networks include Disney, ESPN, Freeform, FX, and National Geographic and television broadcast network ABC. Its theme parks and resorts include Walt Disney World Resort in Florida, Disneyland Resort in California, Disneyland Paris, Hong Kong Disneyland Resort, and Shanghai Disney Resort. There is also the Disney Cruise Line; Disney Vacation Club; National Geographic Expeditions; and Adventures by Disney and Aulani, a Disney resort and spa in Hawaii. The company's Studio Entertainment segment produces and distributes motion pictures under the Walt Disney Pictures, Twentieth Century Studios, Marvel, Lucasfilm, Pixar, Searchlight Pictures, and Blue Sky Studios banners. Its direct-to-consumer videos streaming services consist of Disney+/Disney+Hotstar, ESPN+, and Hulu.

This case involves downloading data and estimating the beta for The Walt Disney Company for several different indexes as the market proxy and for several different time periods. The data are in the file, **ch7_case_study.xlsx**. There are other broad-based stock indexes that can be used to proxy for the market portfolio other than the S&P500 Index. Whereas the S&P500 Index has about 500 of the largest stocks, the

Russell 1000 Index contains the largest 1,000 companies and the Russell 3000 Index has the largest 3,000 firms. The Wilshire 5000 Index is an attempt to include all companies trading on the U.S. exchanges.

Estimate the alpha, beta, and R^2 fit of Disney for using these market proxies and five years of monthly returns. Are you expecting a beta that is smaller or larger than one?

Step 1:
Using the Yahoo! Finance website, or similar data source, download the monthly prices for the maximum time period possible for the following indexes:

Russell 1000 (ticker ^RUI)
Russell 3000 (ticker ^RUA)
Wilshire 5000 (ticker ^W5000)

Also, download the prices for Disney and the yields on the 13-week T-bills:

The Walt Disney Company (ticker DIS)
13-week T-bills (ticker ^IRX)

Step 2:
Using the index and stock prices, compute the monthly returns for the five-year period ending June 2021. Note that

you need 61 prices to compute 60 returns. Also, compute the monthly T-bill yield in percent from the annualized T-bill yield obtained.

Step 3:
Compute the excess monthly returns for the three indexes and for Disney.

Step 4:
Compute Disney's alpha, beta, and the R^2 fit for the following scenarios:

a. Market Proxy is Wilshire 5000, period is five years.
b. Market Proxy is Russell 3000, period is five years.
c. Market Proxy is Russell 1000, period is five years.
d. Market Proxy is Wilshire 5000, period most recent three years.
e. Market Proxy is Russell 3000, period most recent three years.
f. Market Proxy is Russell 1000, period most recent three years.

What do you observe about the estimates?

Chapter

8

Asset Pricing Models and Efficient Markets

Learning Objectives

After reading this chapter, you should be able to:

LO 8-1 Know the arbitrage pricing theory (APT) asset pricing model.
LO 8-2 Use the Fama–French 3-Factor model.
LO 8-3 Use the 4-Factor asset pricing model.
LO 8-4 Apply the Fama–French 5-Factor model.
LO 8-5 Understand the concept of market efficiency and its ramification for price adjustments.
LO 8-6 Know the forms of information efficiency in the efficient market hypothesis (EMH).
LO 8-7 Assess efficient market anomalies.
LO 8-8 Describe the data-snooping problem.
LO 8-9 Characterize financial asset bubbles.
LO 8-10 Understand the investment implications of the forms of the EMH.

The previous chapter discussed beta coefficients and their use in the capital asset pricing model (CAPM). While the CAPM is a major component in financial theory, it has been criticized as being too limited. The model reduces the explanation of a stock's return to two variables: (1) the market return and (2) the volatility of the stock in response to movements in the market (i.e., the beta). Of course, in a well-diversified portfolio, systematic risk is *the* important source of risk. However, unsystematic risk may be important in the determination of an individual stock's return if the stock's price is responsive to changes in some other variable. For example, an increase in the rate of inflation or a decrease in the euro relative to the dollar could have an important impact on an individual stock's return. Thus, other factors could play an important role in the explanation of security returns. This chapter considers other factors in asset pricing models.

Whether we are talking about modern portfolio theory, the CAPM, or other asset pricing models, they all rely on prices being unbiased reflections of value. That is, if investors can systematically determine stocks that are under-valued, then those stocks' risk and expected return characteristics are not correct. Thus, the model predictions would be systematically inaccurate. The last section of this chapter is devoted to the idea of market price efficiency. Efficiency suggests that investors cannot expect to consistently outperform the market on a risk-adjusted basis.

8-1 Arbitrage Pricing Theory

8-1a Arbitrage Pricing

Arbitrage pricing theory (APT) seeks to understand security returns from a different perspective than CAPM. It is a multivariable model in which security returns are dependent on several variables. APT derives its name from the economic premise that prices cannot differ in two markets. **Arbitrage** is the act of buying a good or security and simultaneously selling it in another market at a higher price. Individuals who participate in these transactions are called *arbitrageurs*. If IBM stock is selling for $150 in New York and $160 in London, an opportunity for a riskless profit exists. Arbitrageurs would buy the stock at the low price in New York and simultaneously sell it in London at the higher price, thus earning the $10 profit without bearing any risk. Of course, the act of buying in New York will drive up the stock's price and the act of selling in London will drive down the price until the prices in the two markets are equal and the opportunity for arbitrage is erased.

arbitrage
Simultaneous buying and selling of the same asset at different markets to capture a mispricing

Arbitrage also implies that portfolios with the same risk generate the same returns. If portfolio A has the same risk as portfolio B, the two are substitutes for each other. Just as the stock of IBM must trade for the same price in New York and London, the returns on portfolios A and B must be the same or an opportunity for arbitrage would exist. Once again, the role of arbitrage is to erase differentials. Differences in returns then must be related to differences in how the portfolios respond to the *changes* in the sources of risk that the investor faces. These changes in risk may be a major determinant of the return the investor earns.

In arbitrage, the security's price movement and return are *not* explained by a relationship between risk and return. The CAPM is built on an assumption concerning investors' willingness to bear risk (i.e., investors must expect to earn a higher return to be induced to bear more risk). While this assumption may be reasonable, APT explains movements in securities prices without making an assumption concerning risk preferences. Security returns are the result of arbitrage as investors seek to take advantage of perceived differences in prices of risk exposure. Thus, it is the difference from expectations that drives the APT models.

Whereas CAPM posits that excess returns on a portfolio are systematically affected by a single market risk factor β, APT suggests that the difference between the expected excess return on a portfolio is explained by the portfolio's return sensitivity to a variety of N risk factors, and therefore:

$$R - R_{free} = E(R - R_{free}) + b_1 F_1 + b_2 F_2 + \cdots + b_N F_N + \varepsilon \qquad \textbf{8-1}$$

The realized return is explained by the expected excess return, $E(R - R_{free})$, adjusted by any deviations in the factors, F_N. The individual parameters (i.e., the estimated coefficients $b_1 \ldots b_N$) measure the responsiveness or sensitivity of the return on the stock (or portfolio) to changes in the respective factors. They are often referred to as **factor loadings** or **factor betas**. The ε represents an error term. If the model captures the important factors, the errors tend to cancel out (i.e., a positive error is canceled by a negative error), and the numerical value of the error term should be zero ($\varepsilon = 0$). If there is a consistent error, the error term will not be equal to zero and the model is miss-specified—that is, at least one important factor has been excluded.

Note that the expected value of each factor is zero. APT factors are unanticipated movements. Thus, their expectation is zero and the realized value is as likely to be negative as it is to be positive. APT allows for an unspecified number of important factors. One of these factors could be the unexpected portion of the CAPM's excess market return, but it does not necessarily need to be. This is because the CAPM and APT are two independent theories.

Intuitively, APT is appealing because it is less limiting than the CAPM. The CAPM makes assumptions concerning risk preferences and explains returns solely in terms of movements in the market. In the CAPM, the impact of asset-specific variables is erased through the construction of a diversified portfolio, so the volatility of the stock relative to the volatility of the market is the prime variable that explains an asset's risk and return. APT, however, suggests that differences in returns are driven by an arbitrage process and that two securities or portfolios with the same risk must generate the same return. APT permits the inclusion of more explanatory variables. The inclusion of these other factors, especially economic variables, such as unexpected changes in industrial production, makes APT an appealing alternative explanation of an asset's return.

8-1b   APT Modeling

To use an APT model, the factor sensitivities must be estimated. This is done in a similar manner to estimating beta in the CAPM. For example, five years of monthly excess returns for a company or portfolio can be regressed on the factors. For example, if three factors are identified, then **Equation 8-1** becomes the regression model:

$$R - R_{free} = \hat{\alpha} + \hat{b}_1 F_1 + \hat{b}_2 F_2 + \hat{b}_3 F_3 + \varepsilon \qquad \text{8-2}$$

The alpha and b variables show "hat" accents, which denotes they are estimated. The $\hat{b}_1$ regression coefficient is the stock's first factor loading and the other b estimates are sensitivities to their factors. This stock is expected to earn a monthly excess return of $\hat{\alpha}$ plus any adjustments due to the realization of the factors and their associated factor betas.

Two problems exist with the implementation of an APT model:

- The theory fails to specify the source of the factors. What are the factors?
- The theory does not state the number of factors. How many factors are there?

These limitations cause each user of the APT framework to specify their own unique model. Which factors might you consider?

The potential factors are numerous. APT generally classifies these variables into *sector* influences and *systematic* influences. An example of a sector variable is a firm's industry. What affects a bank stock may not affect a retailer or an airline. A systematic influence may be unanticipated inflation or the level of currency exchange rates. For example, high-dividend-paying stocks may more readily respond to inflation, which impacts interest rates, while exporting companies may more readily respond to changes in the level of the value of the dollar.

While there could be many possible variables, empirical studies suggest that only a few seem to have a lasting or continuous impact on security returns. For example, a change in inflation may have an important impact on security returns. However, it is unanticipated (rather than anticipated) inflation that has the impact. In competitive financial markets, expected inflation is already incorporated into a security's price. If inflation is expected to rise from 4% to 8%, securities prices would have previously adjusted downward, and yields would be higher. It is the unexpected change that APT is seeking to build into the asset pricing model. The expected return plus the responsiveness to the unexpected change in inflation (and to other factors) determine the realized return.

Since the factors represent unanticipated influences, the outcome of the factors is expected to be zero. If nothing unexpected occurs, the stock should earn $\hat{\alpha}$ because the factors would be zero.

Unexpected events will always occur, so realized returns usually deviate from expected returns. What the investor doesn't know is which unexpected events will occur and how the individual stock will respond to the change. In addition, not all securities or portfolios will respond in the same direction or by the same amount. Two portfolios may respond differently to a change in a particular factor. Hence, the returns on two (or more) portfolios may also differ.

Consider this estimated three-variable multifactor model for stock A and stocks B:

$$R_A - R_{free} = 0.09 + 0.02F_1 - 0.01F_2 + 0.01F_3$$
$$R_B - R_{free} = 0.09 + 0.05F_1 + 0.01F_2 + 0.02F_3$$

The expected excess return on a stock will be 9% plus the impact of three risk factors. However, the estimated parameters for two stocks differ. The stocks have different sensitivities to changes in the factors, so the returns on each stock must differ. For example, the estimated coefficients for the second factor have different signs (minus versus plus), indicating this factor has an opposite impact on the returns of the two stocks.

Suppose the risk-free rate is 0.02 (which is 2%) and the numerical values of the factors are 0, 1, and 2, respectively. The returns on the stocks will be

$$R_A = 0.02 + 0.09 + 0.02 \times 0 - 0.01 \times 1 + 0.01 \times 2 = 0.12$$
$$R_B = 0.02 + 0.09 + 0.05 \times 0 + 0.01 \times 1 + 0.02 \times 2 = 0.16$$

Since the numerical value of factor 1 is 0 during the period, the expected value for this factor and the actual value were the same (i.e., $F_1 = 0$), so this factor had no impact on the returns. The actual values of factors 2 and 3 differed from the expected values. Thus, these two variables affected each security's return. Factor 2 had a negative impact on stock A and a positive impact on stock B, while factor 3 had a positive influence on both stocks, with a slightly larger effect (0.02 versus 0.01) on stock B.

Again, since expected changes are already incorporated into the expected return, APT stresses the importance of unanticipated change. If the actual values and expected values are equal, the factor washes out.

While there may be many possible factors, research suggests these five should be considered:

- unexpected inflation,
- unexpected changes in the level of industrial production,
- unanticipated shifts in the market risk premiums,
- unanticipated corporate bond spread, and
- unanticipated changes in the structure of yields measured by the slope of the curve illustrating term structure of interest rates.

One of the largest problems facing those who seek to apply APT is the measurement of unanticipated changes in the factors. How do you compute the unexpected portion of a variable? Typically, investors use the change from the previous period. For example, if annual inflation is 3.4% at the beginning of the month and 3.6% at the end of the month, then the investor might use a positive 0.2% as the unexpected inflation for the period. A similar process can be used for the level of industrial production, a common economic indicator. The risk premium is typically measured as in CAPM: the return on the market less the risk-free rate. However, APT uses the change in the market risk premium as a proxy for the unanticipated shift in the risk premium. Another type of risk premium is the yield spread between high-risk corporate bonds and low risk corporate bonds. Again, the APT uses the change in the corporate bond yield spread. The last factor mentioned above is the change in the slope of the yield curve. The slope of the yield curve is typically measured as the yield on 10-year Treasury Bonds less the yield on Treasury Bills.

Implementing an APT model is very data intensive, as the investor must choose the factors, compute a time series of the factors, and then estimate the factor sensitivities. There are other multivariable models discussed in the next section for which databases exist and are free to access.

8-2 Multifactor Models

8-2a 3-Factor Model

Fama–French 3-factor model
Common multifactor asset pricing model that incorporates market portfolio, size, and book-to-market based risk factors

firm size
A company's market capitalization (shares outstanding × price)

book-to-market ratio
Accounting book value per share divided by the stock price

The APT model above uses unanticipated systematic influences as factors. However, empirical studies show that average returns on common stocks are also related to firm characteristics such as firm size, price-to-earnings ratio, cash flow-to-price ratio, book-to-market ratio, past sales growth, long-term past return (long-term momentum), and short-term past return (short-term momentum). These patterns in average returns are not explained by the traditional one-factor CAPM. Thus, most multifactor models start with the CAPM market portfolio return factor and then add additional risk factors. Note that this is a risk factor approach (like CAPM), and not an arbitrage approach (like APT). The most common multifactor models try to capture risk premiums for systematic risks.

One of the most common multifactor models is referred to as the Fama–French 3-factor model. The first factor is the CAPM excess market portfolio return. The other two risk factors attempt to capture the empirical findings that firm size and book-to-market ratio explain much of a stock's variation in returns over time. How does the model capture firm level variables, like firm size, into a systematic risk factor?

Consider how the CAPM factor is designed. It is the return on the most important risky portfolio, the market portfolio, less the no-risk portfolio called the risk-free asset. The other two factors are created in a similar manner. For firm size, all NYSE stocks are ranked by their market capitalization so that the midpoint is determined. Then all stocks trading in the NYSE, NASDAQ, and AMEX exchanges that are larger than that midpoint are combined to form a value-weighted portfolio called *big*. The firms from the three exchanges that are smaller than the midpoint form a value-weighted portfolio called *small*. The factor SMB (small minus big) is the return on the small portfolio minus the return on the big portfolio. The portfolios are reshuffled once per year. This factor is often referred to as the *size premium*.

The third factor is constructed by sorting all NYSE firms into three groups by their book-to-market (B/M) ratio to find the 70th and 30th percentiles. The *book* is the accounting book value of their equity, while the *market* is their market capitalization. The firms from all three exchanges with B/M ratios higher than the 70th percentile breakpoint are designated for the *value* portfolio while the firms with B/M ratios smaller than the 30th percentile breakpoint form the *growth* portfolio. The HML (high minus low) factor is the return on the value portfolio minus the return on the growth portfolio. This factor is often referred to as the *value premium*.

The Fama–French 3-Factor model is:

$$R - R_{free} = \alpha + b_1(R_m - R_{free}) + b_2(\text{SMB}) + b_3(\text{HML}) + \varepsilon \qquad \textbf{8-3}$$

It shows that the firm or portfolio excess return is related to an abnormal return (α), three risk factors, and their associated factor loadings. Note that the b_1 coefficient is interpreted like the CAPM beta. A positive b_2 indicates the stock or portfolio loads with small company returns. A negative value indicates it is sensitive to large company returns. A positive b_3 indicates the firm's return is sensitive to value stock returns, while a negative b_3 means the firm returns moves with growth stocks.

Consider the estimated 3-Factor model for a stock:

$$R - R_{free} = 0 + 1.1(R_m - R_{free}) - 0.5(\text{SMB}) + 0.6(\text{HML})$$

Note that this company is a little riskier than the market portfolio and is sensitive to large firm returns and value stock returns. If the next month's market results in a market return of 0.9%, an SMB factor of –0.1%, and an HML factor of 0.4%. If the risk-free rate for the month was 0.1% for the month, what is the expected return on the stock for the month?

$$R = 0.1 + 1.1(0.9 - 0.1) - 0.5(-0.1) + 0.6(0.4) = 1.27\%$$

This stock should earn 1.27% next month. Note that the CAPM alone would predict 0.98%, but the SMB factor exposure contributed 0.05% and the HML factor contributed 0.24%.

Data for these factors is readily available in monthly, weekly, and daily time increments. Visit the Data Library maintained at Professor Kenneth French's website at Dartmouth University (http://mba.tuck.dartmouth.edu/pages/faculty/ken.french/index.html). **Exhibit 8-1** shows an image of the Data Library. The library is structured so

Exhibit 8-1: Data Library Hosted by Kenneth French and Dartmouth University

HOME
BIOGRAPHY
CURRICULUM VITAE
WORKING PAPERS
DATA LIBRARY
• U.S. RESEARCH RETURNS
• U.S. RESEARCH BREAKPOINTS
• U.S. BOOK EQUITY DATA
• INTERNATIONAL RESEARCH RETURNS
• DEVELOPED MARKET FACTORS AND RETURNS
CONSULTING RELATIONSHIPS
FAMA / FRENCH FORUM
CONTACT INFORMATION

Current Research Returns

In September 2021, we transitioned from using our proprietary links between CRSP and Compustat data to those provided by CRSP after examining their consistency. We also updated the eligible universe through time to apply time-sensitive evaluation of stocks on criteria such as whether they are investment funds.

	September 2021	Last 3 Months	Last 12 Months
Fama/French 3 Research Factors			
Rm-Rf	-4.37	-0.34	31.50
SMB	0.80	-3.55	22.78
HML	5.09	3.25	36.17
Fama/French 5 Research Factors (2x3)			
Rm-Rf	-4.37	-0.34	31.50
SMB	1.25	-3.99	27.92
HML	5.09	3.25	36.17
RMW	-1.93	3.09	7.77
CMA	2.08	-0.11	9.40
Fama/French Research Portfolios			
Size and Book-to-Market Portfolios			
Small Value	0.64	-0.45	87.63
Small Neutral	-3.47	-3.83	53.80
Small Growth	-4.34	-7.50	48.94
Big Value	-0.25	0.41	60.78
Big Neutral	-3.86	-2.51	34.12
Big Growth	-5.45	0.96	27.13

Source: http://mba.tuck.dartmouth.edu/pages/faculty/ken.french/data_library.html#Research

that the most recent factor values are shown in a table. Click on the U.S. Research Returns link on the menu to access the location to download historical factor values. The first factor, the excess return on the market, is computed using the value-weighted return of all firms incorporated in the United States and listed on the NYSE, AMEX, or NASDAQ as a proxy for the market portfolio. The risk-free asset is proxied by the one-month Treasury Bill.

Exhibit 8-2 shows and image of the links for accessing the data. The annual, monthly, weekly, and daily data access links are shown for the excess market return, SMB, and HML factors. The annual returns are included in the monthly return file. In addition, you can download the returns for the size and B/M portfolios used to construct the factors.

The estimation of **Equation 8-3** is done like CAPM and APT. Typically, five years of monthly excess returns on a stock or portfolio are regressed against the data for the three factors. The alpha and factor beta coefficients are estimated and an R^2 informs you about the fit of the model to explain the returns. For back testing investment ideas, the annual factors are available starting in 1927 and the first daily, weekly, and monthly factors start in July of 1926.

Exhibit 8-2: Access to Fama–French Factor Data

U.S. Research Returns Data (Downloadable Files)

<u>Changes in CRSP Data</u>

Fama/French 3 Factors TXT CSV Details
Fama/French 3 Factors [Weekly] TXT CSV Details
Fama/French 3 Factors [Daily] TXT CSV Details

Fama/French 5 Factors (2x3) TXT CSV Details
Fama/French 5 Factors (2x3) [Daily] TXT CSV Details

Univariate sorts on Size, B/M, OP, and Inv

Portfolios Formed on Size TXT CSV Details
Portfolios Formed on Size [ex.Dividends] TXT CSV Details
Portfolios Formed on Size [Daily] TXT CSV Details

Portfolios Formed on Book-to-Market TXT CSV Details
Portfolios Formed on Book-to-Market [ex. Dividends] TXT CSV Details
Portfolios Formed on Book-to-Market [Daily] TXT CSV Details

Portfolios Formed on Operating Profitability TXT CSV Details
Portfolios Formed on Operating Profitability [ex. Dividends] TXT CSV Details
Portfolios Formed on Operating Profitability [Daily] TXT CSV Details

Portfolios Formed on Investment TXT CSV Details
Portfolios Formed on Investment [ex. Dividends] TXT CSV Details
Portfolios Formed on Investment [Daily] TXT CSV Details

Source: http://mba.tuck.dartmouth.edu/pages/faculty/ken.french/data_library.html#Research

An example of 3-Factor model estimation is shown in **Excel Expert 8-1**.

Excel Expert 8-1

3-Factor Model Estimation

In Excel Expert 7-4 of the previous chapter, the Coca-Cola's CAPM beta was estimated using five years of monthly returns. The estimated results were $\alpha = -0.15\%$, $\beta = 0.62$, and $R^2 = 0.314$.

For the exact same period, the Fama–French 3 Factors were obtained and are shown below. The Excel Regression capability from the Data Analysis menu was used to estimate the 3-Factor model coefficients.

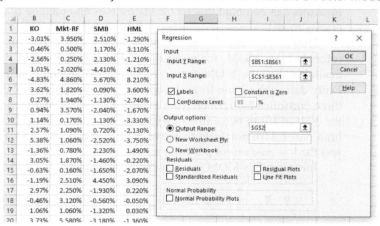

(Continued)

The results show that the market factor beta is 0.68, which is very close to the CAPM estimation. Note that the market portfolio proxy is different between the two analyses. The SMB factor beta is −0.89. The negative SMB beta makes sense because Coke is a large company. The HML factor beta is 0.28. This suggests that Coke is more sensitive to value stock (rather than growth stock) movements. Lastly, the alpha is essentially zero and the R^2 is 0.510.

SUMMARY OUTPUT

Regression Statistics	
Multiple R	0.71443876
R Square	0.51042274
Adjusted R Square	0.48419538
Standard Error	0.03442334
Observations	60

ANOVA

	df	SS	MS	F	Significance F
Regression	3	0.069183535	0.023061	19.46147	9.07313E-09
Residual	56	0.066358106	0.001185		
Total	59	0.135541641			

	Coefficients	Standard Error	t Stat	P-value	Lower 95%	Upper 95%	Lower 95.0%	Upper 95.0%
Intercept	0.00062169	0.004768377	0.130379	0.896734	-0.008930513	0.0101739	-0.00893051	0.010173901
Mkt-RF	0.67802572	0.106416803	6.371416	3.76E-08	0.464847251	0.8912042	0.464847251	0.891204198
SMB	-0.8949285	0.175330617	-5.10423	4.12E-06	-1.246157897	-0.543699	-1.2461579	-0.54369903
HML	0.27848996	0.121730623	2.287756	0.02595	0.034634217	0.5223457	0.034634217	0.522345699

8-2b 4-Factor Model

momentum
Stocks with higher (lower) prior returns will continue to achieve high (low) returns in the future

It is popular to add a **momentum** factor to the Fama–French 3-Factor model. Momentum in stock returns occurs when stocks that performed well in the past, like 3 or 12 months, continue to perform well into the future. Past poor performing stocks tend to continue to perform poorly. Professor Mark Carhart proposed to add a momentum factor to the standard 3-Factor model.

The momentum factor was originally included as UMD, which is the 12 months' return of the equal weighted average of the 50% highest performing stocks minus the 12 months' return of the lowest performing stocks, lagged one month. Scholars and investors can compute this factor themselves and include it as a factor in their asset pricing model.

However, French's Data Library mentioned above includes a similar factor, referred to as MOM, for momentum. **Exhibit 8-3** shows the momentum datasets available. For the MOM factor, monthly and annual data is available from 1927. Daily data is available from the end of 1926. To compute the monthly MOM factor, three portfolios are formed from the prior 2 to 12-month period. The breakpoints are the 30th and 70th percentile of past returns for NYSE stocks. The MOM factor is the high past return portfolio from the NYSE, NASDAQ, and AMEX exchange stocks less the low past return portfolio return.

Including this MOM factor expands the model to the 4-Factor model:

$$R - R_{free} = \alpha + b_1(R_m - R_{free}) + b_2(\text{SMB}) + b_3(\text{HML}) + b_4(\text{MOM}) + \varepsilon \qquad \textbf{8-4}$$

Exhibit 8-3: Momentum Factor Data

```
Sorts involving Prior Returns
```

Momentum Factor (Mom) TXT CSV Details
Momentum Factor (Mom) [Daily] TXT CSV Details

6 Portfolios Formed on Size and Momentum (2 x 3) TXT CSV Details
6 Portfolios Formed on Size and Momentum (2 x 3) [Daily] TXT CSV Details

25 Portfolios Formed on Size and Momentum (5 x 5) TXT CSV Details
25 Portfolios Formed on Size and Momentum (5 x 5) [Daily] TXT CSV Details

10 Portfolios Formed on Momentum TXT CSV Details
10 Portfolios Formed on Momentum [Daily] TXT CSV Details

Short-Term Reversal Factor (ST Rev) TXT CSV Details
Short-Term Reversal Factor (ST Rev) [Daily] TXT CSV Details

6 Portfolios Formed on Size and Short-Term Reversal (2 x 3) TXT CSV Details
6 Portfolios Formed on Size and Short-Term Reversal (2 x 3) [Daily] TXT CSV Details

25 Portfolios Formed on Size and Short-Term Reversal (5 x 5) TXT CSV Details
25 Portfolios Formed on Size and Short-Term Reversal (5 x 5) [Daily] TXT CSV Details

10 Portfolios Formed on Short-Term Reversal TXT CSV Details
10 Portfolios Formed on Short-Term Reversal [Daily] TXT CSV Details

Long-Term Reversal Factor (LT Rev) TXT CSV Details
Long-Term Reversal Factor (LT Rev) [Daily] TXT CSV Details

6 Portfolios Formed on Size and Long-Term Reversal (2 x 3) TXT CSV Details
6 Portfolios Formed on Size and Long-Term Reversal (2 x 3) [Daily] TXT CSV Details

25 Portfolios Formed on Size and Long-Term Reversal (5 x 5) TXT CSV Details
25 Portfolios Formed on Size and Long-Term Reversal (5 x 5) [Daily] TXT CSV Details

10 Portfolios Formed on Long-Term Reversal TXT CSV Details
10 Portfolios Formed on Long-Term Reversal [Daily] TXT CSV Details

Source: http://mba.tuck.dartmouth.edu/pages/faculty/ken.french/data_library.html#Research

What do these four factors look like over time? **Table 8-1** shows the average monthly factors by decade. Note the market risk premium ($R_m - R_{free}$) varies by decade. In some decades, the monthly excess market portfolio exceeds 1%. Yet, it was negative in the 2000s. While early research suggested that small stocks outperformed large stocks, the size premium (SMB) is often negative, suggesting that large stocks outperform small stocks in some decades. The value premium (HML) shows positive values through the 1980s. This created a "value beats growth" perception. However, in the 1990s, 2010s, and so far in the 2020s, growth has outperformed value. The momentum factor shows that recent past winners continue to perform well in all decades. The exception is the 2020s, for which the table has less than two years of data.

Table 8-1: Average Monthly Factors by Decade, %

	$R_m - R_{free}$	SMB	HML	MOM
1920s*	1.163	−1.030	0.205	2.004
1930s	0.462	0.828	0.290	0.019
1940s	0.828	0.384	0.799	0.548
1950s	1.309	−0.054	0.297	0.895
1960s	0.412	0.404	0.284	0.926
1970s	0.098	0.292	0.655	0.823
1980s	0.709	0.010	0.492	0.766
1990s	1.064	−0.115	-0.009	1.135
2000s	−0.147	0.433	0.638	0.089
2010s	1.092	−0.012	−0.198	0.275
2020s^	1.830	0.690	−0.721	−0.097

Source: http://mba.tuck.dartmouth.edu/pages/faculty/ken.french/data_library.html#Research
* July 1926 to December 1929
^ Through September 2021

Excel Expert 8-2

4-Factor Model Estimation

In the previous Excel Expert 8-1, Coca-Cola's 3-Factor model estimates were shown. The momentum factor, MOM, is added to the 4-Factor model. The Excel Regression was redone with the additional variable. The output is shown below.

SUMMARY OUTPUT

Regression Statistics	
Multiple R	0.71534045
R Square	0.51171196
Adjusted R Square	0.4762001
Standard Error	0.0346891
Observations	60

ANOVA

	df	SS	MS	F	Significance F
Regression	4	0.069358279	0.01734	14.40961	4.13776E-08
Residual	55	0.066183362	0.001203		
Total	59	0.135541641			

	Coefficients	Standard Error	t Stat	P-value	Lower 95%	Upper 95%	Lower 95.0%	Upper 95.0%
Intercept	0.00070657	0.00481035	0.146884	0.88376	-0.00893359	0.01034672	-0.00893359	0.010346722
Mkt-RF	0.66133307	0.115839975	5.709023	4.73E-07	0.429184571	0.89348156	0.42918457	0.893481564
SMB	-0.90947572	0.18076122	-5.03137	5.54E-06	-1.2717293	-0.5472221	-1.2717293	-0.547222136
HML	0.24996909	0.143699742	1.739524	0.087537	-0.03801163	0.5379498	-0.03801163	0.537949804
MOM	-0.0594672	0.156052195	-0.38107	0.704618	-0.37220279	0.25326839	-0.37220279	0.253268387

The estimates for the original three factors are very similar to the previous analysis. The new MOM coefficient estimate is −0.06. The negative sign suggests that Coke is not a momentum stock. Also, the low *t*-statistic means that this momentum variable is not important in explaining Coke returns.

8-2c 5-Factor Model and More

In 2015, Professors Fama and French proposed a five-factor model. The 5-Factor model includes the original three factors and then attempts to capture the ability of profitability and corporate investment to predict average stock returns. RMW (robust minus weak) is the return spread between profitable firms and unprofitable firms. Operating profit is computed as annual revenues minus cost of goods sold, interest expense, and selling, general, and administrative expenses divided by book equity. A positive factor beta for RMW indicates the stock or portfolio is sensitive to the movement of profitable firms. CMA (conservative minus aggressive) is the return spread between companies that invest conservatively and those that invest aggressively. Investment is the change in total assets divided by total assets. A positive factor beta for CMA indicates the stock or portfolio is sensitive to the returns of firms with lower capital investment.

The Fama–French 5-Factor model is:

$$R - R_{free} = \alpha + b_1(R_m - R_{free}) + b_2(\text{SMB}) + b_3(\text{HML}) + b_4(\text{RMW}) + b_5(\text{CMA}) + \varepsilon \qquad \textbf{8-5}$$

Exhibit 8-2 shows the links to download the data for the five factors. It is interesting to note that this model ignores momentum. However, if you want, you can download the data for MOM and add it to the 5-Factor Model to create a 6-Factor model!

Excel Expert 8-3

5-Factor Model Estimation

The previous Excel Expert 8-1 showed Coca-Cola's 3-Factor Model estimates. For the 5-Factor model, the two additional factors of RMW and CMA were added. The Excel Regression was redone with the additional variables. The output is shown below.

SUMMARY OUTPUT

Regression Statistics	
Multiple R	0.715203215
R Square	0.511515639
Adjusted R Square	0.466285606
Standard Error	0.035015862
Observations	60

ANOVA

	df	SS	MS	F	Significance F
Regression	5	0.069331669	0.013866	11.3092	1.7263E-07
Residual	54	0.066209972	0.001226		
Total	59	0.135541641			

	Coefficients	Standard Error	t Stat	P-value	Lower 95%	Upper 95%	Lower 95.0%	Upper 95.0%
Intercept	0.000723096	0.004865308	0.148623	0.882405	-0.00903126	0.010477452	-0.00903126	0.010477452
Mkt-RF	0.670352157	0.123566013	5.425053	1.4E-06	0.422617217	0.918087097	0.422617217	0.918087097
SMB	-0.90284896	0.222672166	-4.05461	0.000162	-1.349279768	-0.45641814	-1.349279768	-0.456418142
HML	0.309490818	0.154516675	2.002961	0.050212	-0.000296464	0.619278101	-0.000296464	0.619278101
RMW	-0.03483796	0.343998578	-0.10127	0.919708	-0.724513581	0.654837666	-0.724513581	0.654837666
CMA	-0.10243073	0.303472576	-0.33753	0.737027	-0.710856608	0.505995158	-0.710856608	0.505995158

The 5-Factor beta estimates are very similar to the previous analysis. The new RMW shows a factor loading of −0.03, while the CMA factor beta is −0.10. The statistics shown indicates that these two additional factors are too small to be important in describing Coke's returns.

Active investors are always looking for an edge. Having a better understanding of what moves stock prices might provide an advantage. Therefore, there are always people looking for new and better factors. Here are some examples:

- Liquidity factor: trading frequency of the stock as share turnover.
- QMJ (quality minus junk) factor: high-quality stock returns less low-quality stock returns.
- Volatility factor: captures long-term versus short-term dimensions of relative return variability.

There are likely more factors being used, but those investors don't make them public in order to keep their edge!

8-3 Efficient Markets

8-3a Competitive Markets

Millions of stock market investors—and tens of thousands of professional money managers and security analysts—around the globe seek stock market bargains in a 24-hour trading day. Knowledgeable professional and individual investors comb through reams of widely available financial information looking for clues about which securities may be undervalued or trending. Machine learning and artificial intelligence are doing the same. The daily level of activity is feverish. Any edge, ever so slight, can lead to enormous profits when sufficient leverage is used.

In a world filled with millions of investors hungry for stock market profits, can undervalued stocks really be found? Financial markets are competitive! You need to be aware that an important implication of this competitiveness is that financial markets are very **efficient**. In an efficient stock market, the price for any given stock effectively represents its value. Its value can be viewed as the expected net present value of all future profits. In this calculation, profits are discounted by using a fair or risk-adjusted rate of return. If the stock market is to be perfectly efficient, there must be:

efficient
The condition that a stock price that is an unbiased representation of its value

1. a large number of buyers and sellers of essentially identical securities,
2. information must be free and readily available, and
3. entry and exit by market players must be uninhibited.

Overall, these basic criteria for an efficient market seem easily met in the stock market. In the United States, there are literally thousands of actively traded securities that promise investors a wide array of capital gain and dividend producing opportunities. For any given stock, tens of millions of identical shares of stock trade every day. Moreover, financial and nonfinancial stock market information is widely disseminated to individual investors on the Internet, television, radio, and in the financial press. Hard-to-find information that was sought and prized by professional investors only a decade ago is now instantly published and available to all on the Internet. And finally, not only are millions of eager investors available to bid up the prices of attractive securities, but the supply of available securities quickly adjusts to meet investor demand. When investor demand is high, new supply is created in the form of initial public offerings and seasoned-equity offerings.

At any point in time, prices in an efficient market reflect the interplay of demand and supply. Investors seeking bargains bid up the price of attractive securities. Companies with quickly deteriorating economic fundamentals see their stock prices collapse as demand withers. The price for any stock or bond reflects the collective wisdom of market buyers and sellers regarding the company's future economic prospects.

As such, the market price for a stock is the best available estimate of the company's future economic prospects given all that is presently known in the market. This makes it tough for professionals and amateurs alike to *beat the market.*

The distinction between "beating the market" and "beating the market on a risk-adjusted basis" is important. The popular press often compares a stock or mutual fund return to the return on the market, proxied by the S&P 500 Index. Beat the index and the press anoints your success. However, comparisons should not be made on an absolute basis but instead on a risk-adjusted basis. Of course, if you pursue a risky strategy, you should earn a higher return (i.e., beat the market on an absolute basis). Conversely, if you manage a conservative, low-risk portfolio, you should earn a lower return. Failure to consider risk is, in effect, omitting one of the most important considerations in investing and portfolio construction. To beat the market, the portfolio manager or individual investor must do better than the return that would be expected given the amount of risk taken. This implies that you could earn a lower return than the market but still outperform the market after adjusting for risk. Portfolio performance is the topic of Chapter 9.

8-3b The Efficient Market Hypothesis

Since securities markets are highly competitive, information is readily available, and transactions may be executed with minimal transaction costs, the **efficient market hypothesis** (EMH) argues that a security's price adjusts rapidly to new information and must reflect all known information concerning the firm. Since securities prices fully incorporate known information and prices change rapidly, day-to-day price changes will follow in a random walk over time. A **random walk** essentially means that *price changes are unpredictable and patterns formed are accidental.* Note that in an efficient market, prices change when new information is revealed. If you can't predict whether the next news release will be good or bad, you can't predict whether the price will go up or down as a result of announcement. If prices do follow a random walk, trading rules are useless, and various techniques, such as charting moving averages, cannot lead to superior security selection.

This suggests that investors cannot expect to outperform the market consistently on a risk-adjusted basis. Notice that the hypothesis does not say you can't outperform the market, since obviously some investors may do exceptionally well for a short period. It does imply that you can't beat the market over a long period. Being an occasional winner happens a lot—so does being an occasional loser. Short-term winners and losers cancel out.

It is worth remembering that every transaction involves both buyers and sellers. Through their market activity, each buyer and seller are behaving in such a way as to imply that they know more than the person on the other side of the transaction. If stock and bond markets are perfectly efficient and current prices fully reflect all available information, then neither buyers nor sellers have an informational advantage. In an efficient market, both buyers and sellers have the same information.

Within this context, important characteristics of a perfectly competitive securities market include the following:

- New information arrives at the marketplace in an independent and random fashion.
- Current stock prices reflect all relevant risk and return information.
- Investors rapidly adjust stock prices to reflect unexpected new information.

efficient market hypothesis
Theory stating that security prices fully reflect all available information

random walk
A concept that stock price changes do not follow any patterns or trends

The conventional choice of the term *random walk* to describe the pattern of changes in securities prices is perhaps unfortunate for two reasons. First, it is reasonable to expect that over a period, stock prices will rise. Unless the return is entirely the result of dividends, stock prices must rise to generate a positive return. In addition, stock prices will tend to rise over time as firms and the economy grow. Thus, the term **random walk with drift** is often used.

Second, the phrase *random walk* is often misinterpreted as meaning that securities prices are randomly determined, an interpretation that is completely backward. It is *changes* in securities prices that are random. Securities prices themselves are rationally and efficiently determined by such fundamental considerations as earnings, interest rates, dividend policy, and the economic environment. Changes in these variables are quickly reflected in a security's price. All known information is embodied in the current price, and only new information will alter that price. New information must be unpredictable. If it were predictable, the information would be known, and stock prices would have already adjusted for that information. Hence, new information *must be random*, and a security's price should change randomly in response to that information. If changes in securities prices were not random and could be predicted, then some investors could consistently outperform the market (i.e., earn a return in excess of the expected return given the amount of risk) and securities markets would not be efficient.

Like any theory, the EMH is useful to the extent that it can describe or predict real-world behavior. To the extent that the EMH accurately explains securities prices, it can be useful in helping investors understand the price formation process.

The Speed of Price Adjustments

Note that market efficiency relies on the relationship between information and prices. One implication is that prices must adjust quickly. In highly efficient markets, prices adjust rapidly and accurately as new information is disseminated. In a world of advanced communication, information is swiftly dispersed in the investment community. The market then adjusts a security's price in accordance with the impact of the news on the firm's future earnings and dividends. By the time that you have learned the information, the stock's price probably will have already changed and stabilized. Thus, the investor will not be able to profit from acting on the information.

This adjustment process is illustrated in **Figure 8-1**. Consider that a company makes a positive earnings announcement. Actually, the positive news is unanticipated. This is important because if information is expected, then that expectation is already included in the stock price. Unexpected information is a surprise and gets included into the price very quickly. In this example, the news is released at announcement time 0. The time before the announcement mostly shows the stock price randomly fluctuating around $45 per share. However, in the few minutes before the announcement, the price appears to drift upward a little. This suggests that there is some information leakage. That is, some people (like the accountants) know what is about to be announced. If they trade on this knowledge or have someone else trade on it before the announcement, the price may start to rise. If this story were true, it demonstrate illegal trading from insider information. Nevertheless, prices adjust rapidly to the new information. The price quickly settles into the new price of $48. By the time you learn of this great news, it is too late to react.

Figure 8-1: Price Change from an Unanticipatedly Position Announcement

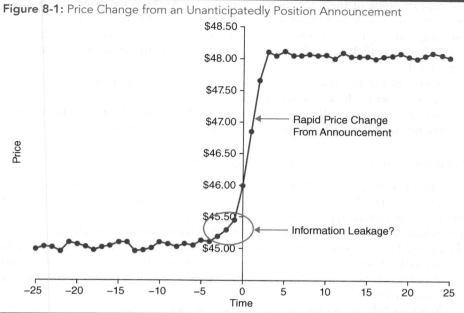

If the market were not efficient and prices did not adjust rapidly or accurately, you would be able to make buy or sell trades to take advantage of the changing price. Consider the gray line in **Figure 8-2**, which shows a **price underreaction**. If you knew that good surprises always took time to be fully integrated into the price, then you could use a trading strategy of buying as soon as possible after the announcement

price underreaction
The tendency for a price to change too slowly in response to an announcement

Figure 8-2: Different Reactions to an Unanticipatedly Position Announcement

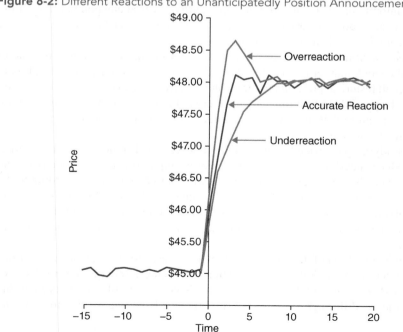

and capture some of the price increase. This only works if the price consistently underreacted . The orange shows a price overreaction. The price increases rapidly, but not accurately. It overshoots the mark. If prices consistently overreacted, then you could short the stock when the price overshoots to capture the decline back to the target level.

A market can be efficient even though stock prices sometimes overreact and underreact to news. The key is that in an efficient market, you can't predict what type of reaction is occurring. Thus, you don't know whether to buy or short unexpected positive news. As long as these reactions are unpredictable, the market is efficient.

price overreaction
The tendency for a price to change too much in response to an announcement

Forms of the Efficient Market Hypothesis

Although you may believe that financial markets are efficient, you may not know *how* efficient. The degree of efficiency is important because it determines the value you place on various types of analysis to select securities. If financial markets are inefficient, then many techniques may aid in selecting securities, and these techniques could lead to superior results. However, as markets become more efficient and various tools of analysis become well known, their usefulness for security selection is reduced, since they will no longer produce superior results (i.e., beat the market on a risk-adjusted basis).

You may believe that the financial markets are weakly, semistrongly, or strongly efficient. These alternative forms of the EMH can be described as:

weak form
Premise that current prices reflect all stock market trading information

semistrong form
Premise that stock prices reflect all public information

strong form
Premise that stock prices reflect all public information and nonpublic information

- **Weak form**: Current prices reflect all stock market information. Trading rules based on past stock market returns and trading volume are futile.
- **Semistrong form**: Current prices reflect all public information. All trading rules based on public information are ineffective.
- **Strong form**: Current prices reflect all public information and nonpublic information. All trading rules are pointless.

Notice how each form of the EMH involves slightly different assumptions regarding the level of information that is incorporated in security prices at any point in time. If the empirical evidence supports none of the various forms of the EMH, then the market must be judged as *not being efficient*, or inefficient.

The *weak form* involves the easiest or lowest hurdle that must be met for one to argue that the stock market is efficient. According to the weak form, stock and bond prices reflect all historical price and trading volume activity. In an efficient stock market, it would not be possible to beat the market on a risk-adjusted basis by buying or selling stocks on the premise that they should continue to rise or fall on price momentum or other price related notions.

Thus, studying past price behavior and other technical indicators of the market will not produce superior investment results. For example, if a stock's price rises, the next change can't be forecasted by studying previous price behavior. According to the weak form of the efficient market hypothesis, technical indicators do not allow you to beat the market. As you might imagine the subset of the investment industry that rely on technical analysis do not agree with the EMH. Technical analysis is described in Chapter 17.

The *semistrong form* of the efficient market hypothesis asserts that the current price of a stock reflects the public's known information concerning the company. Knowledge of the public information includes both the firm's price and volume history and the information learned through studying a firm's financial statements, its industry, and

public information
Information available to the public

the general economic environment. According to the semistrong form, analysis of this material can't be expected to produce market beating results.

The semistrong form description should not be surprising to anyone who thinks about the investment process. Many investors and analysts study the same information. Their thought processes and training are similar, and they are in competition with one another. Certainly, if you perceive a fundamental change in a particular firm, this information will be readily available to other investors, and the price of the security will change. The competition among the potential buyers and the potential sellers will result in the security's price reflecting the firm's intrinsic worth.

Again, as you may expect, the investment community that employs fundamental analysis with public information (see Chapter 11) to select securities doesn't believe the semistrong form of the EMH to be true. Since public information includes historical price and volume data, this form of the EMH negates technical analysis too. Of course, if you can perceive fundamental changes before other investors do, you could outperform the market as a whole. However, few, if any, people should be likely to consistently perceive such changes. Thus, there is little reason to expect investors to achieve *consistently* superior investment results.

There is one major exception to this general conclusion of the semistrong form of the EMH. If you have access to **private information**, you may consistently achieve superior results. In effect, when you have information that is not known by the general investing public, you can incorporate the information into your fundamental analysis to make superior decisions. Examples of such privileged information include inside knowledge of upcoming dividend cuts or increases, new product introductions, potential takeovers, and many more activities that have a significant impact on the value of the firm. If you have advance knowledge of such events and the time to act, you should be able to achieve superior investment returns.

Of course, most investors don't have access to inside information or at least don't have access to information concerning many firms. One person may have access to privileged information concerning a firm for which they work. But the use of such information for personal gain is *illegal*. To continuously beat the market, you would have to have a continuous supply of inside information and use it illegally. Probably few, if any, investors have this continuous supply, which may explain why both fundamental and technical analysts watch sales and purchases by insiders as a means to glean a clue as to the true future potential of the firm as seen by its management.

The strong form of the EMH asserts that the current price of a stock reflects all known (i.e., public) information and all private or inside information concerning the firm. Thus, even access to inside information cannot be expected to result in superior investment performance. Once again, this does not mean that an individual who acts on inside information can't achieve superior results. It means that these results can't be expected and that success in one case will tend to be offset by failure in other cases. Over time, this investor will not achieve superior results.

This conclusion rests on a very important assumption. Inside information can't be kept inside! Too many people know about the activities of a firm. This information is discerned by a sufficient number of investors, and the prices of the firm's securities adjust for the informational content of this inside knowledge. Notice that the conclusion that the price of the stock still reflects its intrinsic value and doesn't require that all investors know this additional information. All that is necessary is for a sufficient number of investors to know. Furthermore, this knowledge need not be acquired illegally. It is virtually impossible to keep some information secret, and there is a continual flow of rumors concerning a firm's activities.

private information
Information that has not been formally released to the public

Note that the price reaction in Figure 8-1 caused by the unexpected positive earnings announcement would not occur if the market were strong form efficient. The news announced would have already been slowly incorporated into the price in the preceding days as the information was informally disseminated through the trades of people in the know.

Is the stock market efficient? If so, to what level? Let's look at the evidence.

Empirical Evidence for the Efficient Market Hypothesis: The Anomalies

While it is generally believed that securities markets are efficient, it is still a hotly debated question as to how efficient they are. This raises a second question: If the financial markets are not completely efficient, what are the exceptions? This question has led to the identification of exceptions to market efficiency, referred to as anomalies. A market anomaly is a situation or strategy that cannot be explained away but would not be expected to happen if the EMH were true. For example, if buying shares in companies that announced a dividend increase led to abnormal returns, such a strategy would imply that securities markets are not completely efficient.

Most empirical testing of various types of technical indicators supports the weak form of the efficient market hypothesis. The evidence suggests that successive price changes are random and that the correlation between stock price changes from one period to the next period is virtually nil. Thus, past price behavior provides little useful information for predicting future stock prices.

At the other extreme, the strong form of the efficient market hypothesis asserts that even access to inside information will not lead to extra returns. Initial empirical evidence does not support the strong form and suggests that insiders may be able to trade profitably in their own stocks. Such evidence suggests that financial markets are not completely efficient. Indeed, that is why we have insider trading laws.

By far, the most research and interest lie with the semistrong form of the efficient market hypothesis. Many studies examine strategies that use publicly available information, such as the data found in a firm's financial statements. These studies generally concluded that the announcement of this information does not produce predictably superior results. Prices change very rapidly once information becomes public, and thus the security's price embodies all known information (see Figures 8-1 and 8-2). If you could anticipate the new information and act before the information became public, you might be able to outperform the market, but once the information becomes public, it rarely can be used to generate superior investment results.

However, many studies found that some accounting information did produce productive strategies. Two of the most important anomalies are the P/E effect and the small-firm effect. The P/E effect suggests that portfolios consisting of stocks with low price/earnings (P/E) ratios have a higher average return than portfolios with higher P/E ratios. Further research showed that the book-to-market (B/M) ratio performed better than the P/E ratio. High B/M firms are known as value stocks and low B/M firms are growth stocks. During the 1990s, the research using decades of data showed that value stocks outperformed growth stocks. Recent decades have shown the opposite. The small-firm effect (or *small cap* for small capitalization) suggests that returns diminish as the size of the firm rises. Size is generally measured by the market value of its stock. If all common stocks on the New York Stock Exchange are divided into five groups, the smallest quintile (the smallest 20% of the total firms) has tended to earn a return that exceeds the return on investments in the stocks that compose the largest quintile, even after adjusting for risk.

---

anomalies
Security prices that deviate from the efficient market hypothesis

P/E effect
The tendency for companies with a low stock price to earnings per share ratio (value stocks) outperform high P/E ratio companies (growth companies)

small-firm effect
The tendency for small capitalization companies to outperform large capitalization companies

value stocks
Securities considered to be temporarily undervalued or unpopular

growth stocks
Companies expected to have above average rates of growth in sales and earnings

Subsequent studies have found that the small-firm effect occurs primarily in January, especially the first five trading days. This anomaly is referred to as the **January effect**. The January effect is often explained by the fact that investors buy stocks in January after selling for tax reasons in December. And there is some evidence that, within a size class, those stocks whose prices declined the most in the preceding year tend to rebound the most during January.

The **neglected-firm effect** suggests that small firms that are neglected by large financial institutions (e.g., mutual funds, insurance companies, trust departments, and pension plans) tend to generate higher returns than those firms covered by financial institutions. By dividing firms into the categories of highly researched stocks, moderately researched stocks, and neglected stocks (based on the number of institutions holding the stock), researchers have found that the last group outperformed the more well-researched firms. This anomaly is probably another variation of the small-firm effect, and both the neglected-firm effect and the small-firm effect suggest that the market gets less efficient as firms get smaller. Because large financial institutions may exclude these firms from consideration, their lack of participation reduces the market's efficiency.

Over the years, scholars have determined that the B/M ratio effect (value versus growth) is actually a proxy for a systematic risk factor. The same is true for the size effect. These risk factors are now included as HML and SMB in the Fama–French 3-Factor model. This illustrates an important aspect to using asset pricing models and studying market efficiency: When is an anomaly proof of market inefficiency or alternatively a systematic risk factor not included in existing models? Indeed, as more anomalies were discovered, more asset pricing factors were created.

January effect
Phenomenon of unusually large positive rates of return for stocks during the first few trading days of the year

neglected-firm effect
The tendency for lesser-known companies to outperform better-known companies

---

The World of Investing

Should I Buy or Sell Company Breakups?

The splitting up of a company is always big news. Corporate breakups seem rarer than company mergers but are just as interesting. The typical way firms split is that one business segment is spun off by assigning it its own stock. For example, company A spins off business B. For every share of A you own, you will end up with that share plus a share of the new company, B. However, the original company A will be fundamentally different, A*. Thus, you start with A and end with A* and B. (Note that this simple example uses a 1 for 1 ratio. Spinoffs can use whatever ratio they want.)

The fall of 2021 brought announcements of some major breakups.

Johnson & Johnson announced it would break up into two companies. One company would be the consumer-oriented business that sells the products like Band-Aids, Tylenol, and baby powder. The other company would be the prescription drug and medical device business. Rivals Pfizer and Merck are also splitting off their consumer product businesses.

General Electric is one of the most storied companies in finance. It was one of the original stocks in the Dow Jones index. But GE had been struggling for years, as indicated by the fact it was booted from the DJIA in the summer of 2018. In the fall of 2021, GE announced it was splitting into three companies. GE Healthcare, which makes MRIs and other hospital equipment, will become its own company. Also, its power unit and renewable energy business will split off into its own company. Other manufacturing, like jet engines, stays in the existing GE Company. GE shares rose 2.65% at the breakup announcement.

If the announcement is unexpected good news, the price of the firm (A) will quickly rise. If you are an investor in the firm, after the spinoff, should you keep A*, B, or both? Research suggests both A* and B beat the market over the next 24 months.

This suggests that the market is not semistrong form efficient. Specifically, you can hear about this breakup, buy shares, and experience returns greater than expected given the risk taken.

Data-Snooping Problem

data-snooping problem
Reliance on chance observations in historical data as a guide to investment decision making

back testing
Backward-looking analysis

Patterns have a tendency to emerge in historical stock return data. But are they real? Can they make you money? This illustrates the **data-snooping problem**. Given sufficient computer time, anyone can find some mechanical trading rule that would have provided superior historical returns. However, such **back testing**, or backward-looking analysis, is an unfair test of the EMH or the usefulness of any investment strategy. An investment strategy is useful only to the extent that it can be used to generate positive abnormal returns in the *future*. While it is important to back test a trading strategy, most strategies were "found" by examining the same historical data. Thus, real back testing needs to test trading strategies in different data sets than they were first identified.

For example, it is a well-known curiosity is that the stock market has tended to perform well during years in which the winner of the NFL Super Bowl comes from the old National Football League as opposed to the old American Football League. The reason for this statistical anomaly is simple. On average, the stock market tends to go up. Because there are more old NFL teams than old AFL teams, the probability of having a Super Bowl winner from the old NFL is higher than that of having a winner from the old AFL. Given the fact that most Super Bowl winners tend to come from the old NFL, and the fact that the stock market tends to rise, there will be a spurious historical correlation in observing an old NFL winner of the Super Bowl and a rising stock market. Obviously, the winner of the Super Bowl has no impact on the performance of the stock market that year, yet that spurious correlation should give you pause when hearing about other correlations.

Dogs of the Dow
Investment strategy that selects the 10 highest dividend yield stocks of the DJIA

Foolish Four
An investment strategy advocated by The Motley Fool that buys four DJIA stocks based on dividend yield and price

Consider the convoluted example of **Dogs of the Dow** morphing into the **Foolish Four**. An investment strategy was proposed in 1988 in the *Wall Street Journal* that was later dubbed the Dogs of the Dow. It was very simple: At the beginning of the year, rank order all 30 Dow Jones Industrial Average stocks by their dividend yield, buy the 10 top yielding stocks, and hold for the year. The strategy purported to outperform the DJIA by over 7.5% per year. Note that the dividend yield is the dividend divided by the price. The top 10 yielders tended to be the firms where the price fell in the previous year, thus they had a high dividend yield and were the previous year's "dogs." This is a simple version of a buy value stocks strategy. Due to its simplicity, this strategy became very popular. However, over the subsequent years, the effectiveness of the strategy diminished.

That is when The Motley Fool claimed to improve upon the strategy. The Motley Fool provides insight and analysis about stocks to retail investors. The strategy combines the dividend yield and price. Essentially, after finding the 10 Dogs, sort them by price. Buy the four stocks with the second-, third-, fourth-, and fifth-lowest price. Buy these Foolish Four stocks to beat the DJIA for the year by even more! This is truly odd. While dividend yield has a basis in value stock strategies, the low or high price of a large company like a DJIA stock is meaningless because they can change their price with a stock split. Besides, if price was important, why skip the lowest one? With only four stocks in the strategy, professional traders quickly determined in late December which stocks the Fool followers would buy in early January. They bought them first in December. When the Fool followers bought in early January, they bid up the price for the traders to sell into. Traders made money . . . Foolish Four followers didn't. This is a great example of how inefficiencies in the market are quickly traded away, thus making the market efficient.

Therefore, before you rush out to take advantage of an alleged anomaly or inefficiency, you should remember several sobering considerations:

1. The spurious empirical results are only *consistent* with inefficiencies, they don't prove their existence.

2. For you to take advantage of an inefficiency, it must be ongoing. Once an inefficiency is discovered and investors seek to take advantage of it, the inefficiency may disappear.

3. Transaction costs are important, and you must pay the transaction costs associated with the strategy. If a substantial amount of trading is required, any excess return may be consumed by transaction costs.

4. You still must select individual issues. Even if small firms outperform the market in the first week of January, you cannot purchase all of them. There is no assurance that the selected stocks will be those that outperform the market in that particular year.

Bubbles

According to the EMH, a stock price accurately reflects all information known about the firm and its business environment. If each stock is priced correctly, then the overall stock market is also priced correctly. A common criticism of the EMH is that the overall market sometimes seems too high or too low relative to fundamental value.

Market bubbles and subsequent crashes are good examples of market inefficiency. Market bubbles are identified after a tremendous inflation in prices and then followed by a dramatic decline. History contains many colorful examples of stock, bond, and commodity markets in which rampant speculation caused a rapid boom in prices followed by a collapse. Noteworthy bubbles have also occurred in major stock markets. Remarkable examples include the Japanese stock market of the 1980s and the tech-stock bubble in the United States that culminated in March 2000.

Panel A of **Figure 8-3** shows the bubble in the Japanese stock market, as measured by the Nikkei 225 Index. The index climbed from 13,757 on March 3, 1986, to 38,915 on December 29, 1989, for a 182% increase in 3.75 years, or nearly 32% annually.

market bubble
A significant overvaluation of economic fundamentals in the stock market

Figure 8-3: Examples of Market Bubbles
Panel A Japan's Nikkei 225 Stock Market

Panel B United States' NASDAQ Composite Stock Market Index

Panel C Cryptocurrency Bitcoin

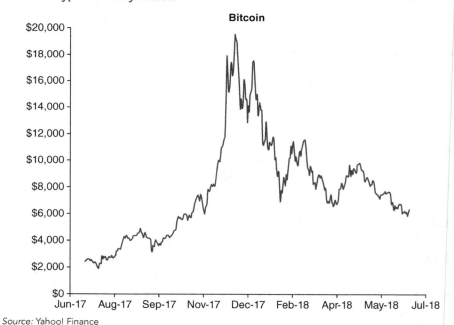

Source: Yahoo! Finance

Then, the index fell to a low of 14,309 on August 18, 1992, for a decline of −63%, or −45% annually. From an efficient market framework, how can the stock market value of a large developed market be "right," nearly triple in a short time to be "right," and then plummet so quickly and be "right" again? It doesn't seem like the value was "right" at the peak. If some of these prices are "wrong," then the market is inefficient.

Panel B of Figure 8-3 shows the dotcom bubble. The dotcom bubble actually impacted most technology firms. Thus, Panel B shows the NASDAQ Composite, an index that is dominated by the tech sector. The parallel between the rise and fall of the Japanese Nikkei and the performance of the Nasdaq tech stocks is striking. Starting at 1419 on October 8, 1998, the NASDAQ climbed to 5048 on March 10, 2000. This is a 255.7% return in just 17 months, or 145% annual return. Then, the dotcom bubble burst, and the NASDAQ declined to 1638 on April 4, 2001, at decline of −67% in just 13 months. Again, this price behavior isn't consistent with an efficient market.

Lastly, the early days of Bitcoin experienced a bubble. Panel C of Figure 8-3 shows the very dramatic cryptocurrency prices. Bitcoin was at $3,155 on September 14, 2017, and skyrocketed 518% to $19,497 in just three months! Bitcoin then plummeted −67% to $6,955 in only one and a half months.

Are these asset price bubbles consistent with an efficient market? The answer to this question is debated in the context of whether bubbles represent rational or irrational behavior. **Rational bubbles** are defined as an inflation and subsequent decline in prices that can be reasonably explained by commensurate changes in the fundamental economics of the situation. That is, prices are efficient in a bubble if they reflect all available information. **Irrational bubbles** are defined as a stark deviation of prices from fundamental values. Irrational bubble theory suggests that assets may go through periods of undervaluation and overvaluation due to episodes of widespread euphoric speculation and pervasive pessimistic panic. In stock markets, irrational bubbles can occur if investors are sometimes overly optimistic in evaluating the potential for future profits. Momentum investors may also display a tendency to buy stocks on the premise that rising prices will become a self-fulfilling prophecy, even when companies do not enjoy favorable business prospects. Stock market bubbles can be difficult to explain as rational and consistent with the market efficiency concept, especially when they occur in large, liquid markets such as Nasdaq in the late 1990s.

rational bubbles
Extreme change in financial asset values that tied to changes in economic fundamentals

irrational bubbles
Extreme change in financial asset values that can't be tied to changes in economic fundamentals

Implications of the Efficient Market Hypothesis

Ultimately, you must decide for yourself the market's degree of efficiency and whether the anomalies are grounds for particular strategies. Any investor who has an inclination toward active investment management may see the anomalies as an opportunity. Those investors who prefer more passive investment management may see them as nothing more than interesting curiosities.

Whether you follow a passive strategy or one that is designed to take advantage of an anomaly, you need to understand the EMH. An efficient market implies that investors and financial analysts are using known information to value correctly what a security is worth. You may not be able to use public information to achieve superior investment results because the investment community is already using and acting on that information, which would make the market semistrong form or strong form efficient. If the investment community did not use this information and properly apply it to security valuation, you could achieve superior investment results, which would mean the market is weak form efficient or inefficient. It is the very fact that investors as a whole are competent and are trying to beat each other that helps produce efficient financial markets.

Table 8-2 demonstrates the implications of each level of market efficiency. First, the market may not be efficient. If this is the case, then all kinds of investment analysis may work to provide returns higher than expected given the level of risk taken. If

Table 8-2: Implications of Market Efficiency Levels

Form of Efficiency	Description	Activities Not Useful	Useful Investment Activities
Inefficient	Prices may be predictably inaccurate.		All investment activities might be productive.
Weak Form	Historical price and volume data are incorporated into the current price.	Charting, technical analysis	Fundamental analysis; asset allocation and portfolio construction
Semistrong Form	All public information is incorporated into the current price.	Charting, technical analysis; fundamental analysis with public information	Fundamental analysis if private information is used; asset allocation and portfolio construction
Strong Form	All public and private information is incorporated into the current price.	Charting, technical analysis; fundamental analysis with public or private information	Asset allocation and portfolio construction

the market is only weak form efficient, then prices already reflect the historical price and volume record. Thus, activities like charting and technical analysis (described in Chapter 17) would not provide superior results. However, conducting fundamental analysis (described in Chapter 11) could produce higher returns. If the market is semistrong form efficient, then price reflect all public information. That include historical prices and volume as well as accounting and economic information. In this case, not only would technical analysis not be useful, but neither would fundamental analysis using public information. You could use fundamental analysis with private information, if you had any. Lastly, if the market is strong form efficient, the prices reflect all public and private information. Thus, no fundamental or technical analysis would produce superior returns. All investments would earn their required risk adjusted return. No matter how efficient the market is, it is wise to use asset allocation and portfolio construction tools to optimize your level of expected return and risk.

Conclusion

This chapter considers multifactor asset pricing models. There are many potential models, but they all fall into two categories. The first uses the concept of arbitrage. In APT models, the excess return on a stock or portfolio is the expected return (or average return) with deviations due to factor loadings on economic arbitrage portfolio factors. These factors have an expected value of zero. But realized values can deviate from zero. Those deviations influence the stocks return. The second category extends the ideas of the CAPM in that excess returns are due to factor loadings on the risk premium factors. These "risk-factor" multifactor models include risk factors based on the market portfolio, firm size, book-to-market ratio, momentum, and others. The true test of a model it whether is explains stocks returns.

These models need market prices to be right so that changes in price are due to exposure to the risk factors. Whether prices are accurate representations of value is a discussion about efficient markets. An efficient market is one in which a security's price adjusts rapidly to new information and must reflect all known information concerning the firm. The efficient market hypothesis organizes the efficient market information framework into weak, semistrong, and strong forms of efficiency. Each requires increasing demands on integrating information into prices. Thinking about market efficiency helps guide investors into what types of investment activities might be worthwhile.

Chapter Equations

$$R - R_{free} = E(R - R_{free}) + b_1F_1 + b_2F_2 + \cdots + b_NF_N + \varepsilon$$ 8-1

$$R - R_{free} = \hat{\alpha} + \hat{b}_1F_1 + \hat{b}_2F_2 + \hat{b}_3F_3 + \varepsilon$$ 8-2

$$R - R_{free} = \alpha + b_1(R_M - R_{free}) + b_2(SMB) + b_3(HML) + \varepsilon \qquad \textbf{8-3}$$

$$R - R_{free} = \alpha + b_1(R_m - R_{free}) + b_2(SMB) + b_3(HML) + b_4(MOM) + \varepsilon \qquad \textbf{8-4}$$

$$R - R_{free} = \alpha + b_1(R_m - R_{free}) + b_2(SMB) + b_3(HML) + b_4(RMW) + b_5(CMA) + \varepsilon \qquad \textbf{8-5}$$

Excel Functions

Regression

Key Terms

anomalies – Security prices that deviate from the efficient market hypothesis

arbitrage – Simultaneous buying and selling of the same asset at different markets to capture a mispricing

back testing – Backward-looking analysis

book-to-market ratio – Accounting book value per share divided by the stock price

data-snooping problem – Reliance on chance observations in historical data as a guide to investment decision making

Dogs of the Dow – Investment strategy that selects the 10 highest dividend yield stocks of the DJIA

efficient – The condition that a stock price that is an unbiased representation of its value

efficient market hypothesis – Theory stating that security prices fully reflect all available information

factor betas – Stock or portfolio sensitivity to a factor in a multifactor asset pricing model

factor loadings – See *factor betas*

Fama–French 3-factor model – Common multifactor asset pricing model that incorporates market portfolio, size, and book-to-market based risk factors

firm size – A company's market capitalization (shares outstanding × price)

Foolish Four – An investment strategy advocated by The Motley Fool that buys four DJIA stocks based on dividend yield and price

growth stocks – Companies expected to have above average rates of growth in sales and earnings

irrational bubbles – Extreme change in financial asset values that can't be tied to changes in economic fundamentals

January effect – Phenomenon of unusually large positive rates of return for stocks during the first few trading days of the year

market bubble – A significant overvaluation of economic fundamentals in the stock market

momentum – Stocks with higher (lower) prior returns will continue to achieve high (low) returns in the future

neglected-firm effect – The tendency for lesser-known companies to outperform better-known companies

P/E effect – The tendency for companies with a low stock price to earnings per share ratio (value stocks) outperform high P/E ratio companies (growth companies)

price overreaction – The tendency for a price to change too much in response to an announcement

price underreaction – The tendency for a price to change too slowly in response to an announcement

private information – Information that has not been formally released to the public

public information – Information available to the public

random walk – A concept that stock price changes do not follow any patterns or trends

random walk with drift – Slight upward bias to inherently unpredictable daily stock prices

rational bubbles – Extreme change in financial asset values that tied to changes in economic fundamentals

semistrong form – Premise that stock prices reflect all public information

small-firm effect – The tendency for small capitalization companies to outperform large capitalization companies

strong form – Premise that stock prices reflect all public information and nonpublic information

value stocks – Securities considered to be temporarily undervalued or unpopular

weak form – Premise that current prices reflect all stock market trading information

Questions

1. **Arbitrage Pricing Theory.** What are the problems with implementing the APT as an asset pricing model? (LO 8-1)
2. **Fama–French 3-Factor Model.** Describe the Fama-French 3-Factor model and what anomalies it was created to resolve. (LO 8-2)
3. **4-Factor Model.** Describe the risk factors in the 4-Factor model and how they are constructed. (LO 8-3)
4. **Fama–French 5-Factor Model.** Describe the risk factors in the Fama–French 5-Factor model and how they are constructed. (LO 8-4)
5. **Competitive Markets.** What are the three important characteristics of a perfectly competitive securities market? (LO 8-5)
6. **Efficient Market Hypothesis.** Explain how the EMH forms relate potential stock price mispricing. (LO 8-6)
7. **Anomalies.** What are investment anomalies, and how do they relate to the EMH and investment strategies? (LO 8-7)
8. **Data-Snooping.** What is the data-snooping problem in investment research, and how does it relate to the back testing of strategies? (LO 8-8)
9. **Financial Bubbles.** What are financial asset bubbles, and what do they imply about efficient markets? (LO 8-9)
10. **EMH Investment Implications.** Explain how the forms of the efficient market hypothesis frame the types of investment activities that might be worthwhile to investors. (LO 8-10)

Problems

1. **APT Return.** The realized APT model factors in a 3-factor model are $F_1 = 0.5$, $F_2 = 0.8$, and $F_3 = -0.9$. If the risk-free rate for the month is 0.03, what will the returns of these three portfolios with associated APT factor betas be? (LO 8-1)

   a. alpha = 0.10, $b_1 = 0.9$, $b_2 = 0.5$, $b_3 = 0.2$
   b. alpha = 0.11, $b_1 = 1.1$, $b_2 = -0.5$, $b_3 = -0.9$
   c. alpha = 0.09, $b_1 = -1.4$, $b_2 = 0.7$, $b_3 = 0.3$

2. **APT Return.** The estimated parameters of a 4-factor APT model are: (LO 8-1)

$$R - R_{free} = 0.7 - 0.4F_1 + 0.2F_2 + 0.5F_3 + 0.1F_4$$

   If the risk-free rate is 0.025, what will the return of this stock be when the realized factors are the following?

   a. $F_1 = 0.2$, $F_2 = -0.3$, $F_3 = 0.0$, $F_4 = 0.2$
   b. $F_1 = 0.1$, $F_2 = 0.5$, $F_3 = -0.3$, $F_4 = 0.3$
   c. $F_1 = -0.3$, $F_2 = 0.2$, $F_3 = -0.1$, $F_4 = 0.4$

3. **Deviations from APT Model.** The estimated parameters of a 3-factor APT model are: (LO 8-1)

$$R - R_{free} = 0.08 + 0.03F_1 + 0.03F_2 - 0.04F_3$$

   The risk-free rate is 0.01 and the realized factors are $F_1 = 0.2$, $F_2 = -0.3$, $F_3 = 0.0$. What are the stock's deviations from expected APT return if the realized return is the following?

   a. $R = 0.09$
   b. $R = 0.075$
   c. $R = 0.08$

4. **FF 3-Factor Model Return.** The realized Fama–French 3-Factor model factors are $R_m - R_{free}$ = −4.37, SMB = 0.80, and HML = 5.09. If the risk-free rate for the month is 0.00 and the alpha is 0, what will the returns be of these three portfolios with associated factor betas? (LO 8-2)

   a. $\beta = 1.1$, $b_{SMB} = 0.5$, $b_{HML} = -0.3$
   b. $\beta = 0.9$, $b_{SMB} = 1.5$, $b_{HML} = 0.4$
   c. $\beta = 1.2$, $b_{SMB} = -0.3$, $b_{HML} = 0.8$

5. **FF 3-Factor Model Return.** The estimated parameters of the monthly Fama–French 3-Factor model are: (LO 8-2)

$$R - R_{free} = 0.05 + 0.75(R_m - R_{free}) + 0.8(SMB) - 0.5(HML)$$

   If the risk-free rate for the month is 0.20%, what will the return of this stock be when the realized factors are the following?

   a. $R_m - R_{free}$ = −9.55%, SMB = −2.42%, HML = −1.90%
   b. $R_m - R_{free}$ = 8.41%, SMB = 2.90%, HML = −0.44%
   c. $R_m - R_{free}$ = 3.40%, SMB = 2.04%, HML = −2.68%

6. **Deviations FF 3-Factor Model Return.** The estimated parameters of the monthly Fama–French 3-Factor model are: (LO 8-2)

$$R - R_{free} = 0 + 0.7(R_m - R_{free}) + 1.2(SMB) + 1.1(HML)$$

   The risk-free rate is 0.21% and the realized factors are $R_m - R_{free}$ = 3.96%, SMB = −1.74%, HML = 2.17%. What are the stock's deviations from the expected Fama–French 3-Factor model return if the realized return is the following?

   a. $R = 3\%$
   b. $R = 2.5\%$
   c. $R = 3.5\%$

7. **Estimate FF 3-Factor Model Coefficients.** Annual returns and risk premiums are in the data file, **ch8_pr07.xlsx**. Estimate the Fama–French 3-Factor model alpha and factor betas. (LO 8-2)

8. **Estimate FF 3-Factor Model Coefficients.** Annual returns for the stock that make up the health care industry and risk premiums are in the data file **ch8_pr08.xlsx**. Estimate the Fama-French 3-Factor model alpha and factor betas. What do the factor betas indicate about health care stocks? (LO 8-2)

9. **4-Factor Model Return.** The realized 4-Factor model factors are $R_m - R_{free}$ = 2.37, SMB = 1.80, HML = −3.09, and MOM = 0.22. If the risk-free rate for the month is 0.02 and the alpha is 0, what will the returns be of these three portfolios with associated factor betas? (LO 8-3)

   a. $\beta = 1.2$, $b_{SMB} = 0.5$, $b_{HML} = 0.3$, $b_{MOM} = -0.2$
   b. $\beta = 0.8$, $b_{SMB} = 1.2$, $b_{HML} = 0.4$, $b_{MOM} = 0.3$
   c. $\beta = 1.0$, $b_{SMB} = -0.3$, $b_{HML} = -0.8$, $b_{MOM} = 0.7$

10. **4-Factor Model Return.** The estimated parameters of the monthly 4-Factor model are: (LO 8-3)

$$R - R_{free} = 0.05 + 0.75(R_m - R_{free}) + 0.9(SMB) - 0.3(HML) + 0.5(MOM)$$

   If the risk-free rate for the month is 0.20%, what will the return of this stock be when the realized factors are the following?

   a. $R_m - R_{free}$ = −2.50%, SMB = 2.42%, HML = 4.90%, MOM = 0.93%
   b. $R_m - R_{free}$ = 3.43%, SMB = 1.90%, HML = −0.44%, MOM = 2.45%
   c. $R_m - R_{free}$ = 5.40%, SMB = −2.04%, HML = −1.68%, MOM = −0.88%

11. **Deviations 4-Factor Model Return.** The estimated parameters of the monthly 4-Factor model are: (LO 8-3)

$$R - R_{free} = 0 + 1.2(R_m - R_{free}) - 0.3(SMB) + 1.3(HML) + 0.9(MOM)$$

The risk-free rate is 0.32% and the realized factors are $R_m - R_{free} = 2.55\%$, SMB = 2.07%, HML = -1.22%, and MOM = 0.82%. What are the stock's deviations from the expected 4-Factor model return if the realized return is the following?

a. $R = 2\%$
b. $R = 2.8\%$
c. $R = 1.8\%$

12. **Estimate 4-Factor Model Coefficients.** Annual returns and risk premiums are in the data file **ch8_pr12.xlsx**. Estimate the 4-Factor model alpha and factor betas. (LO 8-3)

13. **Estimate 4-Factor Model Coefficients.** Annual returns for the technology industry and risk premiums are in the data file **ch8_pr13.xlsx**. Estimate the 4-Factor model alpha and factor betas. What do the factor betas indicate about technology stocks? (LO 8-3)

14. **FF 5-Factor Model Return.** The realized Fama–French 5-Factor model factors are $R_m - R_{free} = 3.37$, SMB = 0.50, HML = 4.20, RMW = 3.26, and CMA = -0.68. If the risk-free rate for the month is 0.05% and the alpha is 0, what will the returns be of these three portfolios with associated factor betas? (LO 8-4)

a. $\beta = 1.0, b_{SMB} = 0.5, b_{HML} = -0.3, b_{RMW} = 0.4, b_{CMA} = 0.8$
b. $\beta = 0.85, b_{SMB} = 1.2, b_{HML} = 0.5, b_{RMW} = -0.3, b_{CMA} = -0.7$
c. $\beta = 1.2, b_{SMB} = -0.3, b_{HML} = 1.4, b_{RMW} = 0.6, b_{CMA} = 0.3$

15. **FF 5-Factor Model Return.** The estimated parameters of the monthly Fama–French 5-Factor model are: (LO 8-4)

$$R - R_{free} = 0.04 + 1.2(R_m - R_{free}) + 0.6(\text{SMB}) + 0.5(\text{HML}) - 0.6(\text{RMW}) + 1.1(\text{CMA})$$

If the risk-free rate for the month is 0.20%, what will be the return of this stock when the realized factors are the following?

a. $R_m - R_{free} = -1.58\%$, SMB = -3.42%, HML = -0.55%, RMW = -0.65%, CMA = 1.22%
b. $R_m - R_{free} = 4.63\%$, SMB = 2.75%, HML = -0.44%, RMW = 1.64%, CMA = 1.00%
c. $R_m - R_{free} = 3.25\%$, SMB = 3.27%, HML = -3.08%, RMW = 0.25%, CMA = -0.69%

16. **Deviations FF 5-Factor Model Return.** The estimated parameters of the monthly Fama–French 5-Factor model are: (LO 8-4)

$$R - R_{free} = 0 + 1.3(R_m - R_{free}) + 1.1(\text{SMB}) + 0.4(\text{HML}) + 1.8(\text{RMW}) - 0.4(\text{CMA})$$

The risk-free rate is 0.15% and the realized factors are $R_m - R_{free} = 1.55\%$, SMB = 2.76%, HML = -0.94%, RMW = 0.54%, CMA = 2.24%. What are the stock's deviations from the expected Fama–French 5-Factor model return if the realized return is the following?

a. $R = 4\%$
b. $R = 4.5\%$
c. $R = 5\%$

17. **Estimate FF 5-Factor Model Coefficients.** Annual returns and risk premiums are in the data file **ch8_pr17.xlsx**. Estimate the Fama–French 5-Factor model alpha and factor betas. (LO 8-4)

18. **Estimate FF 5-Factor Model Coefficients.** Annual returns for the manufacturing industry and risk premiums are in the data file **ch8_pr18.xlsx**. Estimate the Fama–French 5-Factor model alpha and factor betas. What do the factor betas indicate about manufacturing stocks? (LO 8-4)

19. **Estimate 4-Factor Model Coefficients.** 60 monthly returns for the energy industry and risk premiums are provided in the data file **ch8_pr19.xlsx**. Estimate the 4-Factor model alpha and factor betas. What do the factor betas indicate about energy stocks? (LO 8-3)

20. **Estimate a 6-Factor Model.** 60 monthly returns for the utility industry and risk premiums are provided in the data file, **ch8_pr20.xlsx**. Estimate a 6-Factor model alpha and factor betas by adding the momentum factor to the Fama–French 5-Factor model. What do the factor betas indicate about utility stocks? (LO 8-3, 4)

Case Study

International Asset Pricing

The models described in this chapter are focused on asset pricing in the United States. Each factor is constructed using the returns of the stocks trading on the NYSE, NASDAQ, and AMEX. If you are examining stocks from other countries, should you use these U.S. centric factors?

The answer is likely . . . no.

Ken French's Data Library also includes factor data for asset pricing in developed and emerging markets. Note that for developed markets, the Fama–French 3-Factor and 5-Factor data is available for all developed markets combined, Europe, Japan, and the Asia Pacific. The momentum factor is also available for these markets.

```
Developed Markets Factors and Returns  Details
```

Fama/French Factors

Fama/French Developed 3 Factors TXT CSV Details
Fama/French Developed 3 Factors [Daily] TXT CSV Details
Fama/French Developed ex US 3 Factors TXT CSV Details
Fama/French Developed ex US 3 Factors [Daily] TXT CSV Details
Fama/French European 3 Factors TXT CSV Details
Fama/French European 3 Factors [Daily] TXT CSV Details
Fama/French Japanese 3 Factors TXT CSV Details
Fama/French Japanese 3 Factors [Daily] TXT CSV Details
Fama/French Asia Pacific ex Japan 3 Factors TXT CSV Details
Fama/French Asia Pacific ex Japan 3 Factors [Daily] TXT CSV Details
Fama/French North American 3 Factors TXT CSV Details
Fama/French North American 3 Factors [Daily] TXT CSV Details

Fama/French Developed 5 Factors TXT CSV Details
Fama/French Developed 5 Factors [Daily] TXT CSV Details
Fama/French Developed ex US 5 Factors TXT CSV Details
Fama/French Developed ex US 5 Factors [Daily] TXT CSV Details
Fama/French European 5 Factors TXT CSV Details
Fama/French European 5 Factors [Daily] TXT CSV Details
Fama/French Japanese 5 Factors TXT CSV Details
Fama/French Japanese 5 Factors [Daily] TXT CSV Details
Fama/French Asia Pacific ex Japan 5 Factors TXT CSV Details
Fama/French Asia Pacific ex Japan 5 Factors [Daily] TXT CSV Details
Fama/French North American 5 Factors TXT CSV Details
Fama/French North American 5 Factors [Daily] TXT CSV Details

Developed Momentum Factor (Mom) TXT CSV Details
Developed Momentum Factor (Mom) [Daily] TXT CSV Details
Developed ex US Momentum Factor (Mom) TXT CSV Details
Developed ex US Momentum Factor (Mom) [Daily] TXT CSV Details
European Momentum Factor (Mom) TXT CSV Details
European Momentum Factor (Mom) [Daily] TXT CSV Details
Japanese Momentum Factor (Mom) TXT CSV Details
Japanese Momentum Factor (Mom) [Daily] TXT CSV Details
Asia Pacific ex Japan Momentum Factor (Mom) TXT CSV Details
Asia Pacific ex Japan Momentum Factor (Mom) [Daily] TXT CSV Details
North American Momentum Factor (Mom) TXT CSV Details
North American Momentum Factor (Mom) [Daily] TXT CSV Details

There is also data available for the Fama–French Factors and momentum for emerging markets. The data for emerging markets is less pervasive than for developed markets due to a lack of reliable data.

Emerging Markets Factors and Returns

Fama/French Factors

Fama/French Emerging 5 Factors TXT CSV Details
Emerging Momentum Factor (Mom) TXT CSV Details

Consider the monthly returns for a portfolio of international (non-U.S.) stocks The data are in the file, **ch8_case_study. xlsx**.

a. Download the monthly factor data from the French Data Library for both the 5-Factor model and the momentum factor for all developed markets.

b. Download the monthly factor data from the French Data Library for both the 5-Factor model and the momentum factor for emerging markets.

c. Estimate a 6-Factor model with the Fama–French 5-Factors and momentum for this international portfolio using the developed market data.

d. Estimate a 6-Factor model with the Fama–French 5-Factors and momentum for this international portfolio using the emerging market data.

e. Which model seems to fit better?

Portfolio Performance Analytics

Learning Objectives

After reading this chapter, you should be able to:

LO 9-1 Know how to select a similar fund category and compare a portfolio's performance with its category.

LO 9-2 Use Jensen's alpha and other alpha measures to assess performance.

LO 9-3 Utilize the Treynor Index to compare portfolio performance.

LO 9-4 Use the Sharpe ratio to compare portfolio performance.

LO 9-5 Understand performance attribution.

LO 9-6 Assess the impact of security selection.

LO 9-7 Assess the impact of asset allocation decisions.

LO 9-8 Know the impact of market timing.

LO 9-9 Understand the purpose of active investment management.

The investment industry is obsessed with evaluating portfolio performance. Did you beat the market this quarter? Which mutual fund is the best? How did that hedge fund do last year? As it turns out, the answer is a bit complicated. The reason is that every portfolio has a different level of risk. As the past three chapters indicate, portfolios with different levels of risk should have different returns. Therefore, to compare the performance of two mutual funds, you must account for the risk they took. This chapter is about risk-adjusted performance measures.

The previous chapters describe portfolio theory and asset pricing models that suggest you will earn a **required return** that depends on the level of risk you took. So, how can you earn a return different from the required return? There are several important ways in which to do this. For example, the market may not be entirely efficient. Therefore, you might pick stocks that perform better than expected, which is the purpose of security selection. Or you might put more of your portfolio in the investment classes that did better over the period, which is an aspect of asset allocation. Finally, you might jump into and out of the stock market to buy low and sell high at opportune times, which is called *market timing*.

required return
Return needed to compensate for risk as described by an asset pricing model

9-1 Risk-Adjusted Returns

It should be obvious that returns from funds with different objectives are not comparable. Returns on bond funds are obviously not comparable to returns on growth stock funds. Even returns on funds with the same objective, such as capital appreciation, may not be comparable if they are not equally risky. From the investor's perspective, a return of 15% achieved by a low-risk portfolio is preferred to 15% earned on a high-risk portfolio. If you compare absolute returns, you are implicitly assuming that both funds are equally risky. To compare returns, the investor needs to standardize them for differences in risk to determine if the fund's management outperformed other funds or the market.

There are four common techniques for the measurement of portfolio performance that incorporate both risk and return. These measures are (1) category comparisons, (2) the Jensen alpha, (3) the Treynor index, and (4) the Sharpe index.

9-1a Category Comparisons

The first performance technique, category comparisons, was touched on in Chapter 4 in a discussion of mutual fund performance. In essence, you compare the performance of your portfolio to other portfolios with similar objectives and style.

To conduct a comparison, first identify the after-cost return of your fund. This is the return to the shareholder after accounting for expenses, fees, and trading costs. Second, identify the Morningstar fund category that matches the portfolio's objective.

Table 9-1 shows the Morningstar categories for different types of portfolios. For equity portfolios, there are categories for broad-based U.S. stock portfolios, sector-focused portfolios, and international equity portfolios. The table shows the familiar (from Chapter 4) categories for U.S. equity portfolios that depend on the size of the firms in the portfolios and their value or growth orientation. Alternatively, a portfolio might be concentrated in a specific industry or sector, like energy or health. International equity categories tend to focus on the region of the world, the size of the firms, and the value/growth orientation.

Table 9-1: Morningstar Categories for Stock, Bond, Mixed, and Alternative Mutual Funds

Broad U.S. Stock Portfolios	Sector Focused	International Equity Focus
Large Blend	Communications	China Region
Large Growth	Consumer Cyclical	Diversified Emerging Markets
Large Value	Consumer Defensive	Diversified Pacific/Asia
Leveraged Net Long	Energy Limited Partnership	Europe Stock
Mid-Cap Blend	Equity Energy	Foreign Large Blend
Mid-Cap Growth	Equity Precious Metals	Foreign Large Growth
Mid-Cap Value	Financials	Foreign Large Value
Small Blend	Global Real Estate	Foreign Small/Mid Blend
Small Growth	Health	Foreign Small/Mid Growth
Small Value	Industrials	Foreign Small/Mid Value
	Infrastructure	India Equity
	Miscellaneous Sector	Japan Stock
	Natural Resources	Miscellaneous Region
	Real Estate	Latin America Stock
	Technology	Pacific/Asia ex-Japan Stock
	Utilities	World Small/Mid Stock
		World Large-Stock Growth
		World Large-Stock Value
		World Large-Stock Blend

(Continued)

Taxable Bond	Municipal Bond	Money Market
Bank Loan	High Yield Muni	Money Market—Tax-Free
Emerging Markets Bond	Muni California Intermediate	Money Market—Taxable
Emerging-Markets Local-Currency Bond	Muni California Long	Prime Monday Market
High Yield Bond	Muni Massachusetts	
Inflation-Protected Bond	Muni Minnesota	
Intermediate Government	Muni California Intermediate	
Intermediate Core Bond	Muni National Intermediate	
Intermediate Core-Plus Bond	Muni National Long	
Long Government	Muni National Short	
Long-Term Bond	Muni New Jersey	
Multisector Bond	Muni New York Intermediate	
Nontraditional Bond	Muni New York Long	
Short Government	Muni Ohio	
Short-Term Bond	Muni Pennsylvania	
Stable Value	Muni Single State Interim	
Target Maturity	Muni Single State Long	
Ultrashort Bond	Muni Single State Short	
Preferred Stock	Muni Target Maturity	
Corporate Bond		
World Bond		
World Bond-USD Hedged		

Allocation	Alternative	Commodities
Allocation—15% to 30% Equity	Long-Short Equity	Commodities Focused
Allocation—30% to 50% Equity	Systematic Trend	Commodities Broad Basket
Allocation—50% to 70% Equity	Single Currency	
Allocation—70% to 85% Equity	Trading—Inverse Commodities	
Allocation—85% + Equity	Trading—Inverse Debt	
Convertibles	Trading—Inverse Equity	
Static Allocation—15% to 30% Equity	Trading—Inverse Misc	
Static Allocation—85% + Equity	Macro Trading	
Target Date Retirement	Event Driven	
Target Date 2000–2010	Relative Value Arbitrage	
Target Date 2015	Options Trading	
Target Date 2020	Multistrategy	
Target Date 2025	Equity Market Neutral	
Target Date 2030		
Target Date 2035		
Target Date 2040		
Target Date 2045		
Target Date 2050		
Target Date 2055		
Target Date 2060		
Tactical Allocation		
World Allocation		
Target–Date 2065+		

Source: Information from Morningstar

The fixed income categories are grouped by taxable bonds, municipal bonds, and money market funds. The taxable bond categories involve delineating U.S. corporate bonds, government bonds, and international bonds. In addition, division by the bond maturity length target of the portfolio is common. The muni bond categories tend to be grouped by the state in which the bonds were issued. Also, many portfolios combine stocks and bonds. They can be categorized by the proportion of stocks in the portfolio or by popular target dates used for retirement plan investing.

Once you have the return and the category, two comparisons are common: rank and average. *Comparison by rank* refers to how the portfolio return ranks with all the mutual funds in that category. The *average method* compares the portfolio return to the average of the returns of the funds in the category.

Consider the example from Chapter 4 regarding the performance of BlackRock Capital Appreciation, a large growth fund. **Exhibit 9-1** shows how Morningstar makes the performance comparison. Note that in 2020, the fund earned a 40.59% return. Comparing this return to the 1,289 funds in the Large Growth category shows that its return was higher than the average large growth fund by 4.73%. This stellar performance ranked it in the top 28 percentile. Good performance persisted into the first half of 2021. Note that this BlackRock fund did not beat its competitors every year. It underperformed the large growth average fund in 2011, 2012, 2014, and 2016. Trailing returns shows that the fund earned an annual 24.0% for the past five years, which beat the average category return by 2.57% per year.

Exhibit 9-1: Morningstar Portfolio Comparison for BlackRock Capital Appreciation K Fund, August 16, 2021

Total Return (%)	2011	2012	2013	2014	2015	2016	2017	2018	2019	2020	YTD
Investment	−8.78	14.29	34.29	8.72	7.29	0.03	33.19	2.11	32.33	40.59	18.33
+/− Category	−6.32	−1.05	0.37	−1.28	3.69	−3.20	5.52	4.20	0.44	4.73	2.23
+/− Index	−11.42	−0.96	0.81	−4.33	1.63	−7.05	2.98	3.62	−4.06	2.10	0.29
Percentile Rank	91	59	44	67	20	79	17	13	48	28	30
Quartile Rank	☰	☰	☰	☰	☰	☰	☰	☰	☰	☰	☰
# of Investment in Cat.	1,683	1,681	1,712	1,710	1,681	1,463	1,363	1,405	1,360	1,289	1,259

YTD Investment as of Aug 13, 2021 | Category: Large Growth as of Aug 13, 2021 | Index: Russell 1000 Growth TR USD as of Aug 13, 2021

Trailing Returns | Day End | Month End | Quarter End |

	Day	1 Week	1 Month	3 Month	YTD	1 Year	3 Year	5 Year	10 Year	15 Year
Total Return %	0.31	−0.16	1.83	15.90	18.33	35.57	24.14	24.00	18.37	13.55
+/− Category	0.19	−0.10	0.11	2.34	2.23	2.02	1.61	2.57	0.76	0.91
+/− Index	0.06	−0.33	−0.19	0.76	0.29	0.98	−0.90	0.56	−1.15	−0.54
Percentile Rank	20	61	50	23	30	27	32	19	36	30
Quartile Rank	☰	☰	☰	☰	☰	☰	☰	☰	☰	☰
# of Investment in Cat.	285	1,285	1,284	1,274	1,259	1,236	1,133	1,019	763	555

USD | Investment return as of Aug 13, 2021 | Category: Large Growth as of Aug 13, 2021 | Index: Russell 1000 Growth TR USD as of Aug 13, 2021 | Inception date Dec 31, 1997 | Time periods greater than 1 year are annualized

The category comparison method adjusts for risk by comparing the portfolio performance to its category. It is assumed that all portfolios in the same category have the same level of risk. While not all the category funds will have the same risk, the range of risk levels within the category is likely to be small. All the funds in the Large Blend category are likely to have more similar levels of risk than comparing funds from the Large Blend and Small Growth categories. That is, the difference between risk levels is likely to be far greater between categories than within categories.

Nevertheless, the performance measures that follow are designed to adjust for risk in a more thorough manner using statistical tools.

9-1b Jensen's Alpha

We know that the capital asset pricing model (CAPM) (see Chapter 7) is used to determine the return a fund should earn given its level of risk. Professor Michael Jensen proposed a measure to determine how much the realized return of a mutual fund differs from this required return from the CAPM. The CAPM equation is:

$$E(R) = R_{free} + \beta \times (E(R_M) - R_{free})$$

Note that the equation is cast in terms of expected return. Evaluating performance is about realized returns. You know the realized return, R, of the portfolio as well as the realized return on the market portfolio, R_M. The difference between the realized return of the portfolio and what the return should have been given the realized market return and its beta is referred to as Jensen's alpha and is denoted using the Greek letter α.

The general equation for Jensen's alpha is:

$$R - R_{free} = \alpha + \beta \times (R_M - R_{free}) \qquad \textbf{9-1}$$

Jensen's alpha
Abnormal return measured from the capital asset pricing model (CAPM)

The return on the market is typically proxied by the return on the S&P 500 Index.

In this form, the equation indicates that the realized risk premium earned on the portfolio equals the market risk premium times the beta plus alpha. This form appeals to people who want to estimate alpha and beta using historical data. The equation fits nicely into a linear regression, as demonstrated in **Excel Expert 9-1**. The numerical value of α indicates superior or inferior performance.

When $\alpha_P > 0$, portfolio performance is better than the required return derived from the CAPM. Superior portfolio performance can be due to security selection, which is the selection of stocks with exceptionally good risk-reward characteristics. This is the hallmark of a good stock picker. Few portfolio managers have demonstrated good stock-picking ability that has stood the test of time. Outstanding portfolio performance can also be due to astute risk management through careful market timing. Over the years, few have demonstrated superior stock market timing. Assessing security selection and market timing is explored further later in this chapter.

When $\alpha_P < 0$, portfolio performance is worse than the theoretical expectation. In the case of inferior performance, bad stock picking or bad market timing is sometimes to blame. Most often, inferior portfolio performance is due to excessive operating expenses tied with high portfolio manager compensation or high portfolio turnover.

Note that Jensen's alpha can be used independently of comparisons with other portfolios. Positive alphas are considered good, while negative alphas are bad. The larger the positive alpha, the better. However, you can also compare a portfolio manager's performance relative to another. The portfolio with the higher alpha has the best

security selection
Attempt to pick stocks that outperform the overall stock market

market timing
Investment style that attempts to buy into the stock market before a bull market move and sell before a bear market move

Excel Expert 9-1

Estimating Alpha

ClearBridge Mid Cap Fund Class C (SBMLX) is a Midcap Blend mutual fund. Its monthly prices were downloaded from Yahoo! Finance to compute monthly returns. The spreadsheet below shows the excess monthly returns for the fund and for the S&P 500 Index. Data for five years of monthly return are used. Equation 9-1 was estimated as a linear regression to estimate the beta and the monthly alpha of the fund. Two methods are shown, the first uses the INTERCEPT and SLOPE functions and the other uses the Regression tool.

F	G	H	I	J	K	L	M	N	O	P	Q	R
SBMLX – Tbill	S&P 500 – Tbill											
4.389%	3.536%		alpha =	−0.23%	=INTERCEPT(F2:F61,G2:G61)							
0.874%	−0.147%		beta =	1.17	=SLOPE(F2:F61,G2:G61)							
−0.308%	−0.148%											
−2.180%	−1.970%		SUMMARY OUTPUT									
7.601%	3.380%											
−0.081%	1.778%			Regression Statistics								
4.016%	1.746%		Multiple R	0.827991243								
2.473%	3.676%		R Square	0.685569499								
−1.307%	−0.101%		Adjusted R Square	0.680148283								
0.045%	0.842%		Standard Error	0.034620732								
0.222%	1.083%		Observations	60								
1.211%	0.400%											
0.874%	1.846%		ANOVA									
−1.602%	−0.030%			df	SS	MS	F	Significance F				
2.923%	1.844%		Regression	1	0.151574908	0.151575	126.4605	3.35184E−16				
−0.054%	2.130%		Residual	58	0.069518516	0.001199						
2.248%	2.706%		Total	59	0.221093425							
−6.930%	0.873%											
10.087%	5.500%				Coefficients	Standard Error	t Stat	P-value	Lower 95%	Upper 95%	Lower 95.0%	Upper 95.0%
−3.945%	−4.026%		Alpha =	Intercept	−0.002271756	0.004640904	−0.489507	0.626329	−0.011561534	0.007018023	−0.011561534	0.007018023
−1.095%	−2.830%		Beta =	S&P 500 – Tbill	1.168378375	0.103897741	11.24546	3.35E−16	0.960404451	1.376352299	0.960404451	1.376352299

Both methods show the same results. The fund's beta is 1.17, which means it is riskier than the market portfolio. The alpha for the fund is −0.23% per month. The regression results also show a t Stat of −0.48951, which is not statistically significant. Thus, you might say that the fund's risk-adjusted performance was marginally negative.

performance. Note that because alpha is a risk-adjusted return, you can compare funds from different categories. For example, you can compare a mutual fund in the Large Value stock category to one in the Midcap Growth category. The mutual fund, Invesco Dividend Income R5, is in the Large Value category. Measured from late November 2021, its five-year annual return was 8.08%. Evaluating performance over five years results in an $\alpha = -5.0$ and $\beta = 0.73$. ProFunds Mid Cap Growth is a mutual fund in the Midcap Growth category. Its five-year average return was 11.91% and its $\alpha = -6.1$ and $\beta = 1.09$. Note that the ProFunds mutual fund had higher realized return than the Invesco fund. However, it was also a much riskier portfolio, as measured by beta. Because of that, it has a lower alpha, which means that the Invesco fund performed better on a risk-adjusted basis.

Equation 9-1 is often rearranged to solve for alpha:

$$\alpha = R - R_{free} - \beta \times (R_M - R_{free}) \qquad \textbf{9-2}$$

This form is useful when returns and beta are provided. It illustrates the difference between the realized return and the required return from the CAPM. **Excel Expert 9-2** demonstrates the calculation of alpha.

Excel Expert 9-2

Calculating Alpha

Consider the realized return and beta for four portfolios shown below. The S&P 500 Index return, and the three-month Treasury Bill yield is shown. What is the alpha for each of the four funds?

	A	B	C	D	E	F	G
1	**Portfolio**	**Return**	**Beta**		**CAPM**	**Alpha**	
2	A	7.5%	0.8		7.9%	−0.4%	=B2−E2
3	B	11.0%	1.2		10.7%	0.3%	
4	C	7.0%	0.5		5.9%	1.1%	
5	D	13.0%	1.4		12.0%	1.0%	
6	S&P 500	9.3%	1				
7	3M T−Bill	2.5%	0			=$B$7+C5*($B$6−$B$7)	

Column E shows the return expected from the CAPM for each fund. Column F shows the alpha calculation. Note that the highest risk-adjust return is from the Portfolio C, which had the lowest realized return, but also has the lowest level of risk.

Alpha statistics are readily available online. For example, in November 2021, Yahoo! Finance reported that the five-year alpha for the Fidelity Blue Chip Growth Fund (FBGRX) was 8.69 and its beta was 1.1. Since the alpha is positive, that indicates this fund outperformed the market on a risk-adjusted basis. At the same time, Morningstar reported the alpha to be 7.99 and a beta of 1.1. The difference is likely due to differences in the exact start and end date of the five-year period and the proxy used for the market return.

Jensen's alpha uses the CAPM as the asset pricing model that determines the required return a portfolio should have earned given its level of market risk. However, you can use other asset pricing models for this purpose. For example, you can subtract the realized return of a portfolio from its 3-Factor model return to determine a risk-adjusted return. Over time, many adaptations of the original Jensen's alpha have occurred. Thus, the industry mostly referred to this risk-adjusted performance simply as alpha. When you see an alpha, you should always ask what asset pricing model was used. In addition, the word *alpha* is popular in the investment industry. Investment companies include the term in their names, investment strategies, and more.

alpha
Abnormal return measured from an asset pricing model

9-1c Treynor Index

Professor Jack Treynor developed an alternative measure for risk-adjusted performance that is also based on the CAPM. The Treynor Index is a reward-to-volatility measure that is used to rank portfolios by risk premium per unit of *systematic risk*. A larger Treynor Index is preferred by all investors, regardless of risk preferences. The Treynor Index is

$$Treynor \ index = \frac{R - R_{Free}}{\beta} \qquad \text{9-3}$$

Treynor Index
Risk premium earned relative to systematic risk

reward-to-volatility measure
Excess return earned for each unit of systematic risk taken

Excel Expert 9-3

Estimating the Treynor Index

The ClearBridge Mid Cap Fund Class C (SBMLX) data from Excel Expert 9-1 is used to estimate the Treynor Index for the fund and for the S&P 500 Index. Note that the beta for the S&P 500 Index is 1.

F	G	H	I	J	K	L	M	N
SBMLX – Tbill	**S&P 500 – Tbill**							
4.389%	3.536%		alpha =	−0.23%	=INTERCEPT(F2:F61,G2:G61)			
0.874%	−0.147%		beta =	1.17	=SLOPE(F2:F61,G2:G61)			
−0.308%	−0.148%							
−2.180%	−1.970%			Treynor Index (SBMLX) =	1.01%	=AVERAGE(F2:F61)/J3		
7.601%	3.380%			Treynor Index (SP 500 Index) =	1.20%	=AVERAGE(G2:G61)/1		

The Treynor Index for the S&P 500 Index (1.20%) is higher than for the ClearBridge fund (1.01%), so the S&P 500 Index performed better. This is not surprising because mutual funds experience costs for trading and charge fees. Stock indexes do not include similar costs. So, it is difficult to outperform the market, especially on a risk-adjusted basis.

It is common to use the average monthly returns over a period for the portfolio return, R, and the associated average risk-free rate. β is the beta from the CAPM and is thus a measure of systematic risk for the investment portfolio. The Treynor Index can vary a lot over time because the realized market portfolio return can vary. Thus, to assess portfolio performance, the Treynor Index of a portfolio should be compared to other portfolios' Treynor Indexes. The larger Treynor Index is considered the one with the better performance.

The Treynor index can be computed with returns over a period, like an annual return, instead of averages. **Excel Expert 9-4** illustrates this using the **Excel Expert 9-2** example.

Excel Expert 9-4

Calculating the Treynor Index

Consider the realized return and beta for four portfolios from Excel Expert 9-2. The three-month Treasury Bill yield is also shown. What is the Treynor Index for each of the four funds?

	A	B	C	D	E	F	G	H	I
1	**Portfolio**	**Return**	**Beta**		**CAPM**	**Alpha**		**Treynor Index**	
2	A	7.5%	0.8		7.9%	−0.4%		6.25%	=(B2−$B$7)/C2
3	B	11.0%	1.2		10.7%	0.3%		7.08%	
4	C	7.0%	0.5		5.9%	1.1%		9.00%	
5	D	13.0%	1.4		12.0%	1.0%		7.50%	
6	S&P 500	9.3%	1						
7	3M T–Bill	2.5%	0						

Column H shows the Treynor Index for each fund. Note that ranking the funds by risk-adjusted performance results in the same order, C, D, B, A (best to worst), no matter whether you use alpha or the Treynor Index.

As **Excel Expert 9-4** shows, Jensen's alpha and the Treynor Index are both based on the CAPM and thus provide the same rankings among portfolios. The ordinal rankings they provide are the same, but the information each measure provides is different. Alpha is the abnormal return and can be evaluated itself without comparing to other portfolios. The Treynor Index is a measure of reward to risk and needs to be compared with other portfolios to be useful.

9-1d Sharpe Ratio

Nobel laureate William Sharpe developed a measure of risk-adjusted performance for portfolios that the industry now calls the Sharpe ratio. This **reward-to-variability measure** can be used to provide a ranking of portfolios by the risk premium earned per unit of total risk (systematic and unsystematic). The Sharpe ratio is:

$$Sharpe \ ratio = \frac{R - R_{Free}}{\sigma} = \frac{excess \ return \ on \ portfolio}{total \ risk \ for \ portfolio} \qquad 9\text{-}4$$

Sharpe ratio
Risk premium earned relative to total risk

reward-to-variability measure
Excess return earned for each unit of total risk taken

The portfolio return, R, is the average rate of return during the period. The standard deviation of returns over the period is σ. Poor relative performance exists if the Sharpe ratio < 0 or positive but small. Larger Sharpe ratios are better. Notice that the ratio uses percentages in both the numerator and denominator so that the result is simply a number without the percentage. However, that number represents the amount of excess return earned for each 1% of standard deviation risk. **Excel Expert 9-5** illustrates the calculation of the Sharpe ratio.

Excel Expert 9-5

Estimating the Sharpe Ratio

The ClearBridge Mid Cap Fund Class C (SBMLX) data from Excel Experts 9-1 and 9-3 is used to estimate the Sharpe ratio for the fund and for the S&P 500 Index.

	C	D	E	F	G	H	I	J	K	L	M	N	O
1	SBMLX	S&P 500 Index		SBMLX - Tbill	S&P 500 - Tbill		alpha =	-0.23%					
2	4.414%	3.561%		4.389%	3.536%		beta =	1.17					
3	0.899%	-0.122%		0.874%	-0.147%								
4	-0.284%	-0.123%		-0.308%	-0.148%		Treynor Index (SBMLX) =		1.01%				
5	-2.153%	-1.943%		-2.180%	-1.970%		Treynor Index (SP 500 Index) =		1.20%				
6	7.638%	3.417%		7.601%	3.380%								
7	-0.039%	1.820%		-0.081%	1.778%		Sharpe Ratio (SBMLX) =		0.193	=AVERAGE(F2:F61)/STDEV.S(C2:C61)			
8	4.058%	1.788%		4.016%	1.746%		Sharpe Ratio (SP 500 Index) =		0.278	=AVERAGE(G2:G61)/STDEV.S(D2:D61)			

The Sharpe ratio for the S&P 500 Index (0.278) is higher than for the ClearBridge fund (0.193), so the S&P 500 Index performed better. Again, this is not surprising because mutual funds experience costs for trading and charge fees. Stock indexes do not include similar costs. In addition, the standard deviation for the fund is higher because it is less well diversified than the Index. The higher risk level in the denominator of the ratio causes the ratio to be lower, all else equal.

Jensen's alpha and the Treynor Index will provide the same ranking of a group of portfolios. However, the Sharpe ratio may be different. The reason for the potential difference in the rankings is the measure of risk. The Sharpe ratio uses the standard deviation of the returns as the measure of risk. Using the standard deviation to measure risk does not assume the portfolio is well diversified. In effect, the ratio standardizes the excess return by the variability of the return. The Treynor Index uses the portfolio's beta and does assume the portfolio is well diversified. In effect, it standardizes the excess return by the volatility of the return. If portfolios are not fully diversified, the Sharpe ratio provides a better comparison.

It is important to realize that variability and volatility do not mean the same thing. (This is so at least in an academic usage; words may be interchanged in the popular press.) *Variability* compares one period's return with the portfolio's average return. That is, how much did the return vary from period to period? A variable return implies that over time there will be large differences in the annual returns. *Volatility* compares the return relative to something else. That is, how volatile was the stock's return compared to the market return? A volatile return implies that the return on the portfolio fluctuates more than some base (i.e., the return on the portfolio is more volatile than the return on the market). A portfolio could have a low beta, thus its return relative to the market would not be volatile (i.e., the return on the market would fluctuate more). However, from year to year there could be a large variation in the portfolio's return, so the returns are variable even though the portfolio is less volatile than the market.

Because the measures of risk used in the Sharpe ratio and Treynor Index differ, it is possible for the two measures to rank performance differently. Suppose the average return on a utility fund is 8% with a standard deviation of 9%. If the returns are normally distributed, this indicates that during 68% of the time, the return ranges from −1 to 17% Returns ranging from −1 to 17% may indicate large variability in the return for that type of fund and indicate considerable risk unique to that fund (i.e., a large amount of diversifiable risk). The fund, however, may have a beta of only 0.6, indicating that its returns are less volatile than the market returns. The fund has only a modest amount of nondiversifiable, systematic risk. The large standard deviation may generate an inferior risk-adjusted performance using the Sharpe ratio because the fund has excessive diversifiable risk. The low beta may generate a superior risk-adjusted return when the Treynor Index is used because that index considers only the fund's nondiversifiable risk.

As with the Treynor Index, the Sharpe ratio doesn't indicate whether the portfolio manager outperformed the market or any other portfolio. You must compare the portfolio's Sharpe ratio with the Sharpe ratio of the market or other portfolios to discern whether it was managed well or not.

Risk-adjusted performance measures are available online. For example, Morningstar provides the performance measures shown in **Exhibit 9-2** for Columbia Select Large Cap Value mutual fund in the *Risk* tab. For the preceding five-year period, the fund has an alpha of −5.73%. That is slightly worse than the Large Value category, which has an alpha of −5.43%.

The fund shows a Sharpe ratio of 0.75, which is slightly better than its Large Value category, and not as good as Morningstar's own US Large-Mid Cap Broad Value index. While the Treynor Index is not shown here, we can compute it from the information provided. The excess return on the fund can be inferred by multiplying the Sharpe ratio by the standard deviation (14.08% = 0.75 × 18.78%). The Treynor Index is the excess return divided by the fund's beta, which is 12.35% (= 14.08 ÷ 1.14). Similar calculations for the fund category and Morningstar index produce 12.18% and 13.19%, respectively. Thus, this fund has a better Sharpe ratio than its category, but a worse Treynor Index than the index.

Exhibit 9-2: Morningstar Risk-Adjusted Performance Measures for the Columbia Select Large Cap Value Inst3 (CSRYX) Mutual Fund, November 2021

Risk and Volatility Measures

Trailing	Index	Category	Investment
Alpha	—	−5.43	−5.73
Beta	—	1.01	1.14
R^2	—	86.71	86.55
Sharpe Ratio	0.83	0.74	0.75
Standard Deviation	15.89	16.63	18.78

USD I Investment as of Oct 31, 2021 I Category: Large Value as of Oct 31, 2021 I
Index: Morningstar US Large Mid Brd Val TR USD as of Oct 31, 2021 I Calculation
Benchmark: S&P 500 TR USD

Negative Sharpe Ratios

The Sharpe ratio compares portfolio performance by standardizing the excess return by the portfolio's standard deviation. Higher values come from either higher returns or smaller standard deviations (lower risk) and imply better performance. For example, consider the following investments:

Investment	Return	Standard Deviation	Sharpe Ratio
A	10%	5%	2.0
B	5%	5%	1.0

Both have the same risk, but A earned a higher return and thus has a larger Sharpe ratio, indicating better performance.

Although the ratio correctly ranks risk-adjusted returns during rising markets, the converse isn't necessarily true during declining markets when the numerical value of the ratio is negative. Consider the following three illustrations:

Case 1: The returns differ but the risk is the same.

Investment	Return	Standard Deviation	Sharpe Ratio
A	−10%	5%	−2.0
B	−5%	5%	−1.0

Both investments have the same risk, but Investment A has the larger loss. Its Sharpe ratio is a larger, negative number. Since −1.0 is a smaller negative number than −2.0, the Sharpe ratio indicates that B is superior to A. A smaller negative number is the larger of the two numbers. This result is intuitively correct since a greater loss for the same amount of risk would indicate inferior performance.

Case 2: The returns are equal, but the risk differs.

Investment	Return	Standard Deviation	Sharpe Ratio
A	−10%	5%	−2.0
B	−10%	10%	−1.0

Both investments have the same return, but Investment A has less risk. Once again, the numerical value of its Sharpe ratio is a larger, negative number. Since −1.0 is a smaller negative number than −2.0, the Sharpe ratio again indicates that B was superior to A. Both investments generated the same return, but since B should have lost more but didn't, its performance was better than A. From an investor's perspective, this result makes no sense. Since investors do not want to sustain a loss, lower risk would be preferred to more risk for an equal loss. Perhaps Case 2 is only a mathematical anomaly.

Case 3: Both the returns and risk differ.

Investment	Return	Standard Deviation	Sharpe Ratio
A	−8%	2%	−4.0
B	−10%	10%	−1.0

Investment A loses less and has less risk than Investment B. However, its Sharpe ratio is a larger, negative number. Once again, the Sharpe ratios indicate that B's risk-adjusted performance is superior to A's. This conclusion must be incorrect. A has less risk and a smaller loss. Its performance must be superior, but the Sharpe ratio for A is the larger, negative number and indicates inferior performance. The reason for the larger, negative number is that as risk decreases, the denominator decreases. The lower denominator increases the ratio.

For rising markets and positive returns, the Sharpe ratio accurately ranks performance. However, in declining markets, negative Sharpe ratios need to be interpreted carefully since they may imply that lower risk and smaller losses indicate inferior performance.

9-2 Performance Attribution

Why did a portfolio earn a positive or negative alpha? If markets are efficient (see Chapter 8), then the long-term alpha of a diversified portfolio should be zero. If markets are not completely efficient, then you could earn positive alphas through (1) superior security selection, or (2) overweight (and underweight) asset classes or market sectors. Distinguishing between these reasons for performance is called attribution analysis.

attribution analysis
Evaluation of how active management decisions explain a portfolio's performance against a benchmark

benchmark
Diversified portfolio of similar risk or investment style used as a comparison

bogey
Industry slang for the benchmark

To illustrate attribution analysis, consider this simplified example. A fund has a benchmark of allocating 60% of its investment to stocks and 40% to bonds. The return of an allocation target like this is often called a bogey. The fund is allowed to deviate from this allocation by 10%. To measure performance, the stock portion of the portfolio will be judged against the S&P 500 Index while the bond portion will be compared to the Bloomberg US Aggregate Total Return Index.

Table 9-2 shows that during the year, the fund had a more conservative allocation of 55% stocks and 45% bonds than the target. The return for the fund was 9.405% (= 0.55 × 13.5% + 0.45 × 4.4%), which comes from a 13.5% return from the stock portion of the portfolio and 4.4% from the bond portion. The benchmark portfolio earned 9.00% (= 0.60 × 12.0% + 0.40 × 4.5%). The fund outperformed the benchmark by 0.405%. Where did the outperformance come from?

The fund manager was good in the security selection for stocks. You can observe that by noticing the fund's stock portion of the portfolio earned 13.5%, while the S&P 500 Index earned only 12.0%. That is due to picking better performing stocks for the portfolio than those that make up the index. However, the manager made a poor asset

Table 9-2: Selection and Allocation Attribution Analysis

Asset Class	Allocation Target	Allocation Actual	Benchmark Return	Fund Return
Stocks	0.60	0.55	12.0%	13.5%
Bonds	0.40	0.45	4.5%	4.4%

allocation choice. The fund allocated less of the portfolio (55%) to stocks than the target (60%) and stocks performed better than bonds. So, the analysis indicates that the fund manager executed good security selection, but those performance results were partially offset by the poor allocation decision.

Security selection ability is assessed by comparing the portfolio return in an asset class to the benchmark return for the class. You can combine the selection ability across asset classes by using a weighted average where the weights are the portfolio allocations. For example,

Stock selection ability: $0.55 \times (13.5\% - 12.0\%) = 0.825\%$

Bond selection ability: $0.45 \times (4.4\% - 4.5\%) = -0.045\%$

The sum is 0.78% (= 0.825 + −0.045). Since this is a positive number, the manager demonstrates some security selection ability. The general equation for security selection is:

$$Selection\ Effect = \sum_i [\omega_{pi} \times (R_{pi} - R_{Bi})] \qquad \textbf{9-5}$$

where i represents each of the asset classes or sectors, P designates the fund or portfolio being analyzed, and B identifies the benchmark for that asset class.

Asset **allocation effects** are measured by comparing the difference in allocation from the target and how each asset class's return compared to the total return of the benchmark (or bogey).

allocation effects
Returns generated by how the portfolio weights allocate capital to sectors or asset classes

Stock allocation effect: $(0.55 - 0.60) \times (12.0\% - 9.0\%) = -0.150\%$

Bond allocation effect: $(0.45 - 0.40) \times (4.5\% - 9.0\%) = -0.225\%$

The sum is −0.375% (= −0.150% + −0.225%). Since this is a negative number, the manager demonstrates poor allocation ability. The general equation for the allocation effect is:

$$Allocation\ Effect = \sum_i [(\omega_{pi} - \omega_{Bi}) \times (R_{Bi} - R_B)] \qquad \textbf{9-6}$$

where i represents each of the asset classes or sectors, P designates the fund or portfolio being analyzed, and B identifies the benchmark for that asset class.

Note that the selection effect plus the allocation effect is the amount of return the fund deviated from the target. As previously noted, the fund outperformed by 0.405%, which is explained by the selection effect of 0.780% plus the allocation effect of −0.375%.

Excel Expert 9-6 illustrates a more sophisticated example.

Excel Expert 9-6

Attribution Analysis

A portfolio manager actively tried to beat the S&P 500 Index by overweighting and underweighting various sectors and then picking stocks within each sector. The Excel page below shows the 11 sectors and the allocation of the portfolio to each in column B. Column C shows the return of each sector portion of the portfolio. The benchmark, or bogey, is the S&P 500 Index. Columns D and E show the sector weights and returns of the index. Column G illustrates the deviations of the portfolio allocation from the index allocation. Column I shows the difference in the portfolio return and the bogey return for each sector. Finally, Column K shows the bogey sector return less the bogey total return to illustrate which sectors did better and which did worse.

	A	B	C	D	E	F	G	H	I	J	K	L	M	N	O	P
1		Portfolio		Benchmark			Diff Weights		Sector Return		Sector					
2	Sectors	Weight	Return	Weight	Return				– Sector Bogey		Contribution					
3	Information Technology	28.5%	41.55%	27.6%	43.62%		0.9%		−2.1%		21.95%		Portfolio Return - Bogey Return			
4	Health Care	13.4%	13.40%	13.5%	13.34%		−0.1%		0.1%		−8.33%		0.28%	=C15−E15		
5	Consumer Discretionary	13.2%	28.86%	12.7%	29.63%		0.5%		−0.8%		7.96%					
6	Communication Services	11.4%	26.11%	10.8%	26.91%		0.6%		−0.8%		5.24%		Selection Effect			
7	Financials	10.1%	−1.87%	10.4%	−1.68%		−0.3%		−0.2%		−23.35%		−0.83%	=SUMPRODUCT(B3:B13,I3:I13)		
8	Industrials	8.6%	11.00%	8.4%	10.96%		0.2%		0.0%		−10.71%					
9	Consumer Staples	6.4%	9.85%	6.5%	10.15%		−0.1%		−0.3%		−11.52%		Allocation Effect			
10	Utilities	2.4%	0.56%	2.8%	0.57%		−0.4%		0.0%		−21.10%		1.12%	=SUMPRODUCT(G3:G13,K3:K13)		
11	Materials	2.7%	20.12%	2.6%	20.52%		0.1%		−0.4%		−1.15%					
12	Real Estate	2.2%	−2.25%	2.4%	−2.11%		−0.2%		−0.1%		−23.78%					
13	Energy	1.1%	−33.46%	2.3%	−32.51%		−1.2%		−1.0%		−54.18%	=E13−$E$15				
14		100.0%		100.0%												
15	Return =		21.95%		21.67%	=SUMPRODUCT(D3:D13,E3:E13)				=C13−E13					

The portfolio beat the benchmark by 0.28%. This comes from poor security selection ability and good asset allocation decisions. Specifically, the security selection decisions cost the portfolio −0.83%, while the allocation decisions benefited the portfolio by 1.12%.

9-3 Market Timing

The previous section assesses a portfolio manager's ability to pick stocks and other securities (security selection) and to distribute the portfolio between different asset classes or sectors (allocation effect). One common asset allocation strategy is to rotate between the asset class or sectors depending on the economic environment. In other words, the portfolio might be overweighted to technology and underweighted to utilities at one point. When the economy changes, the manager may rotate the allocation so that utilities are overweighted. This has to do with timing and is called a **sector rotation strategy**.

There is a common strategy, called **market timing** that attempts to jump between stocks and cash to experience the broad market rallies and avoid the bear market declines. Consider a simple strategy in which a portfolio manager owns the S&P 500 Index or cash. At times, the investor's portfolio will have a beta of one and earn the market return. At other times, the portfolio will have a beta of 0 and earn the risk-free rate.

Consider the three graphs in **Figure 9-1**. Panel A shows a portfolio that does not attempt to time the market. It simply holds a portfolio similar to the S&P 500 Index all of the time. Notice that the line that best approximates the relationship between the excess portfolio return and the excess market return is a straight line. Indeed, this line has a slope (beta) of one.

sector rotation strategy
Rotating over time which sectors are over- or under-weighted in a portfolio

market timing
Investment style that attempts to buy into the stock market before a bull market move and sell before a bear market move

Figure 9-1: Demonstration of Various Market Timing Impact

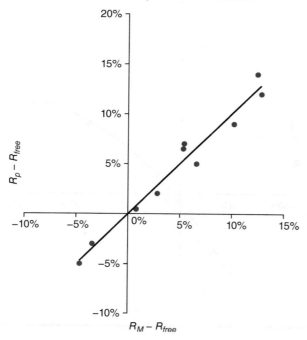

Panel A No Attempt to Time the Market

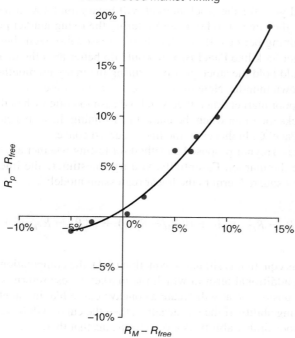

Panel B Good Market Timing

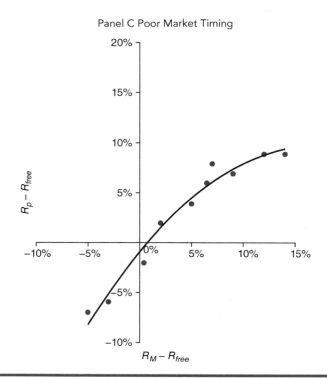

Panel C Poor Market Timing

Even a good year for the stock market will have months with negative returns. Market timing is the attempt to hold stocks during the rising market periods and hold cash during declining periods. If you can do that reasonably well (but not perfectly), your returns might look like Panel B. You would do better than the market in up years because you would hold the stock portfolio during the many up months and hold cash during the few down months. Note the concave curvature of the line.

If you are a poor market timer, then you hold cash too often when the market is rising and hold stocks too often when the market is declining. In such a case, your returns might look like Panel C. In this case, the line is curved convex.

Professor Jack Treynor proposed a method for testing whether a portfolio manager is trying to time the market. Essentially, you try to estimate the lines shown in the figure by adding a squared term to the linear regression model:

$$R_P - R_{Free} = \alpha + \beta(R_M - R_{Free}) + c\,(R_M - R_{Free})^2 + \varepsilon \qquad \textbf{9-7}$$

Note that this equation is similar to equation (9-1), the computation of alpha. However, there is an additional term in which the market excess return is squared. If the coefficient, c, is positive, that will create a concave curve like in Panel B and indicate good market timing ability. If the c is negative, then the curve will be convex like Panel C and indicate poor timing ability. A c of zero means that there is no market timing in the portfolio.

An example is illustrated in **Excel Expert 9-7**.

Excel Expert 9-7

Market Timing

The ClearBridge Mid Cap Fund Class C (SBMLX) data from Excel Experts 9-1, 9-3 and 9-5 is used to test for market timing. First, add a column for the squared market excess return (Column H). Then use the Excel regression to obtain the output below.

	F	G	H	I	J	K	L	M	N	O	P	Q	R	S
1	SBMLX - Tbill	S&P 500 - Tbill	Squared (S&P 500 - Tbill)											
2	4.389%	3.536%	0.00125											
3	0.874%	−0.147%	0.00000			SUMMARY OUTPUT								
4	−0.308%	−0.148%	0.00000											
5	−2.180%	−1.970%	0.00039			*Regression Statistics*								
6	7.601%	3.380%	0.00114			Multiple R	0.831661							
7	−0.081%	1.778%	0.00032			R Square	0.69166							
8	4.016%	1.746%	0.00030			Adjusted R Square	0.680841							
9	2.473%	3.676%	0.00135			Standard Error	0.034583							
10	−1.307%	−0.101%	0.00000			Observations	60							
11	0.045%	0.842%	0.00007											
12	0.222%	1.083%	0.00012			ANOVA								
13	1.211%	0.400%	0.00002				*df*	*SS*	*MS*	*F*	*gnificance F*			
14	0.874%	1.846%	0.00034			Regression	2	0.152922	0.076461	63.93056	2.74E-15			
15	−1.602%	−0.030%	0.00000			Residual	57	0.068172	0.001196					
16	2.923%	1.844%	0.00034			Total	59	0.221093						
17	−0.054%	2.130%	0.00045											
18	2.248%	2.706%	0.00073				*Coefficients*	*andard Err*	*t Stat*	*P-value*	*Lower 95%*	*Upper 95%*	*ower 95.0%*	*pper 95.0%*
19	−6.930%	0.873%	0.00008	alpha =	Intercept	0.000505	0.005324	0.094952	0.924686	−0.01015	0.011166	−0.01015	0.011166
20	10.087%	5.500%	0.00303	beta =	S&P 500 - Tbill	1.165865	0.103812	11.23053	4.51E-16	0.957985	1.373745	0.957985	1.373745
21	−3.945%	−4.026%	0.00162	c =	Squared (S&P 500 - Tbill)	−1.37679	1.297493	−1.06112	0.293112	−3.97498	1.221391	−3.97498	1.221391

The results show that the beta estimate is nearly identical to the one from Excel Experts 9-1, 1.166 versus 1.168. The prior alpha estimate was an insignificant negative number while this estimate shows an insignificant positive number. The estimate for c is negative, but not statistically significant. This means that there may not be any market timing occurring for the fund, but if so, it is poorly done.

These results were estimated using the regression capability of Excel. Specifically, the inputs identify the fund excess return (Column F) as the Y Range and both the market excess return and squared excess returns as two X Range variables (Columns G and H).

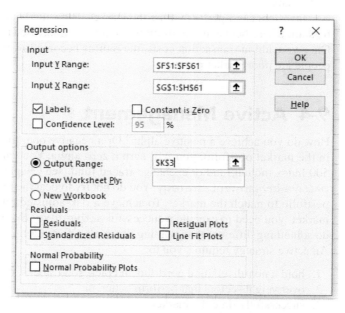

Table 9-3: Benefits and Danger of Market Timing in a Bear Market (Year 1) and Bull Market (Year 2)

Year 1	3-M T-Bill Yield	S&P 500 Index	Year 2	3-M T-Bill Yield	S&P 500 Index
Jan	0.118%	5.618%	Jan	0.198%	7.868%
Feb	0.131%	−3.895%	Feb	0.199%	2.973%
Mar	0.142%	−2.688%	Mar	0.200%	1.792%
Apr	0.147%	0.272%	Apr	0.198%	3.931%
May	0.155%	2.161%	May	0.196%	−6.578%
Jun	0.158%	0.484%	Jun	0.181%	6.893%
Jul	0.163%	3.602%	Jul	0.175%	1.313%
Aug	0.169%	3.026%	Aug	0.163%	−1.809%
Sep	0.178%	0.429%	Sep	0.158%	1.718%
Oct	0.188%	−6.940%	Oct	0.138%	2.043%
Nov	0.194%	1.786%	Nov	0.128%	3.405%
Dec	0.198%	−9.178%	Dec	0.128%	2.859%
	Total Index Return =	−6.24%		Total Index Return =	28.88%
	Perfect Market Timing =	18.69%		Perfect Market Timing =	40.54%
	Terrible Market Timing =	−20.87%		Terrible Market Timing =	−8.14%

Both the benefits and the danger of market timing are illustrated in **Table 9-3**. Note that if you buy and hold the Index, your return would be −6.24% in the first year and 28.88% in Year 2. The first year was a bear market and the second year was a bull market. If you executed a perfect market timing strategy and earned the S&P 500 Index in all up months and earned the T-Bill yield in all stock down months, then you would earn 18.69% and 40.54%, respectively. Great performance! Of course, a perfectly terrible market timing would cause returns of −20.87% and −8.14%, respectively. Awful performance!

Investors can't perfectly time the market. Thus, market timing returns are likely to be somewhere between the minimum and maximum shown in each of the two years. Once you add in transaction costs, the returns become lower. History shows that most people are poor market timers.

9-4 Active Management

passive investment strategy
Investors hold a diversified mix of assets over long periods to match their benchmark return

active investment strategy
Actively buying and selling assets to try to outperform a benchmark or index

How do you achieve a positive alpha? Or a negative one, for that matter? If you invest in the market portfolio, you will earn a zero alpha. You can do this through an S&P 500 Index mutual fund or exchange-traded fund (see Chapter 4). This is one form of a **passive investment strategy**. You do not try to beat the market; you simply set your portfolio to match the market. To achieve a risk-adjusted return that is better than the market, you need to execute a successful **active investment strategy**. You need to do something different than holding the market portfolio.

An active strategy requires you to:

1. hold a non-diversified portfolio and pick good stocks, or
2. overweight sectors that perform better, or
3. successfully time the market.

You can even try all of them at once. To pick good stocks, you need to use various analytical tools, like *fundamental analysis,* which applies discounted cash flow models, analysis of financial statements, and the use of ratios to compare possible investments (see Chapter 11). Fundamental analysis can apply to both a "growth" strategy and a "value" strategy. A growth strategy emphasizes stocks that offer superior potential to generate capital gains. A value strategy emphasizes stocks that are undervalued (under-priced). A similar analysis of sectors might lead you to allocate your portfolio in a way that deviates from the market portfolio allocation.

An alternative method for executing an active investment strategy is to base decisions on price movements and the associated trading volume. This *technical analysis* applies measures of price movements such as moving averages and charts of price patterns. The analyst seeks to perceive changes in the supply and demand for a security and to use that information to determine when to buy and sell the security. This is a form of market timing both into and out of the stock market, as well as into and out of individual securities.

A passive investment approach can be perceptibly different from an active one. One illustration is the buy-and-hold strategy, in which assets are purchased and held for an extended period. Buy and hold, however, does not mean that the investor retains the securities forever. A stock may be sold when the funds are needed. A stock may be sold when the company no longer meets the investor's objectives (e.g., dividends are reduced) or when the fundamentals of the company have changed. While buy and hold may be a passive strategy, some active management remains.

buy-and-hold strategy
A strategy that minimizes transactions by holding investments for long periods of time

The typical investor, however, should take the concept of efficient financial markets seriously (see Chapter 8). Instead of trying to outperform the market, most people should devote their time to developing financial objectives and constructing well-diversified portfolios that meet those objectives. Indeed, professional investors have trouble consistently beating the market on a risk-adjusted basis. For example, studies of mutual fund performance show that on average, mutual funds have a negative alpha.

The World of Investing

Portfolio Manager Performance: Skilled or Lucky?

There are literally millions of speculators and stock pickers trying to beat the market every day. The mutual funds that outperform for the year advertise the accomplishment to gain more investors. If markets are reasonably efficient, then an investor would not be able outperform the market on a risk-adjusted basis over a long time. However, active investors are very likely to either earn a positive or negative alpha in the short term. This is because prices typically move because of information, and it is random whether the next announcement is good or bad news. Being on the right side of the price movement is like calling the right outcome of a coin flip.

What if beating the market for the year is a 50/50 proposition? Consider 4,000 active investment managers trying to beat the market on a risk-adjusted basis. Based on the laws of probability, half of the active investors (2,000) will be successful in outperforming the market the first year. Of these 2,000 investors, 1,000 will win in year two and 500 will have won three years in a row. Four investment managers are likely to beat the market 10 years in a row. But here's the relevant question: Are these investment managers skilled or lucky?

It is not a 50/50 proposition to outperform the market. Most mutual funds don't, primarily due to fees and trading costs. Thus, a 10-year winner is likely to be skilled and not just lucky. However, skilled managers often become victims of their own success. Each year that they outperform, more and more investors invest in the fund and the portfolio grows. A skilled portfolio manager may find good investments to buy with a $100 million portfolio. But when that portfolio grows to $1 billion, performance tends to revert to being average. Indeed, very large portfolios tend to look a lot like the S&P 500 Index!

Conclusion

How did that mutual fund perform? This chapter illustrates that to answer this question, you must take the portfolio's risk under consideration. Risk-adjusted returns, like Jensen's alpha, allow you to assess whether a portfolio manager did better or worse than what would be expected given the risk taken. Return-to-risk measures, like the Treynor Index and Sharpe's ratio, help you compare performance between funds. The larger the measures, the better the performance.

Why did a fund perform better or worse than other funds or the market? Deviations from the required return given the level of risk taken can be due to security selection activities, allocation decisions, and market timing. In other words, to perform differently from the market portfolio, your portfolio needs to look different than the market portfolio. Using these strategies to try to outperform is called *active investment management*. To measure their success, performance attribution techniques can assess a portfolio manager's stock picking, asset allocation, or market timing abilities.

Chapter Equations

$$R - R_{free} = \alpha + \beta \times (R_M - R_{free}) \qquad \text{9-1}$$

$$\alpha = R - R_{free} - \beta \times (R_M - R_{free}) \qquad \text{9-2}$$

$$Treynor\, index = \frac{R - R_{Free}}{\beta} \qquad \text{9-3}$$

$$Sharpe\; ratio = \frac{R - R_{Free}}{\sigma} = \frac{excess\; return\; on\; portfolio}{total\; risk\; for\; portfolio} \qquad \text{9-4}$$

$$Selection\; Effect = \sum_i [\omega_{pi} \times (R_{pi} - R_{Bi})] \qquad \text{9-5}$$

$$Allocation\; Effect = \sum_i [(\omega_{pi} - \omega_{Bi}) \times (R_{Bi} - R_B)] \qquad \text{9-6}$$

$$R_P - R_{Free} = \alpha + \beta(R_M - R_{Free}) + c\,(R_M - R_{Free})^2 + \varepsilon \qquad \text{9-7}$$

Excel Functions

AVERAGE(number1, [number2], ...)
INTERCEPT(known_ys, known,xs)
Regression
SLOPE(known_ys, known,xs)

STDEV.S(number1, [number2], ...)
SUMPRODUCT(array1,[array2],[array3]...)

Key Terms

active investment strategy – Actively buying and selling assets to try to outperform a benchmark or index

allocation effects – Returns generated by how the portfolio weights allocate capital to sectors or asset classes

alpha – Abnormal return measured from an asset pricing model

attribution analysis – Evaluation of how active management decisions explain a portfolio's performance against a benchmark

benchmark – Diversified portfolio of similar risk or investment style used as a comparison

bogey – Industry slang for the benchmark

buy-and-hold strategy – A strategy that minimizes transactions by holding investments for long periods of time

Jensen's alpha – Abnormal return measured from the capital asset pricing model (CAPM)

market timing – Investment style that attempts to buy into the stock market before a bull market move and sell before a bear market move

passive investment strategy – Investors hold a diversified mix of assets over long periods to match their benchmark return

required return – Return needed to compensate for risk as described by an asset pricing model

reward-to-variability measure – Excess return earned for each unit of total risk taken

reward-to-volatility measure – Excess return earned for each unit of systematic risk taken

security selection – Attempt to pick stocks that outperform the overall stock market

sector rotation strategy – Rotating over time which sectors are over- or underweighted in a portfolio

Sharpe ratio – Risk premium earned relative to total risk

Treynor Index – Risk premium earned relative to systematic risk

Questions

1. **Category Comparison.** Harford MidCap Y is a mutual fund with a midcap growth focus. What indexes and fund categories might be used to assess its performance? What data do you use to compare performance? (LO 9-1)

2. **Alpha.** Discuss the importance of selecting the asset pricing model when computing an alpha. (LO 9-2)

3. **Alpha.** Describe how a portfolio manager's performance can be assessed with just its alpha. (LO 9-2)

4. **Treynor Index.** How can you compute the Treynor Index? Discuss the data and procedures you would use. (LO 9-3)

5. **Sharpe Ratio.** What is the difference between the Sharpe ratio and Treynor Index? When would you use one versus the other in evaluating a portfolio? (LO 9-4)

6. **Performance Attribution.** What types of decisions might a portfolio manager make in order to achieve a return that deviates (hopefully greater) from the return expected? (LO 9-5)

7. **Security Selection.** What are stock pickers trying to achieve? How likely is it that they can achieve it? (LO 9-6)

8. **Allocation Effect.** How important is the asset allocation decision to the total portfolio realized return? (LO 9-7)

9. **Market Timing.** Describe the tremendous potential and hazard of market timing. (LO 9-8)

10. **Active Investment Management.** Describe the advantages and disadvantages of active management versus passive management. (LO 9-9)

Problems

1. **Category Comparison.** A portfolio exclusively invests in energy companies (50%) and utilities (50%). The portfolio earned 11% last year. Create a benchmark portfolio from the Morningstar categories. By how much did the portfolio beat its benchmark? (LO 9-1)

Morningstar Category	Return
Financials	–3.5%
Consumer Cyclical	14%
Equity Energy	10.5%
Industrials	5%
Utilities	10%
Technology	13%
Large Blend	11%

2. **Jensen's Alpha.** The market return was 12.5% and the risk-free rate was 3.2%. What is the Jensen's alpha for these three portfolios? (LO 9-2)

    a. Return = 11%, beta = 0.75
    b. Return = 14%, beta = 1.25
    c. Return = 12.5%, beta = 1.05

3. **Alpha.** The realized Fama–French 3-Factor model factors are R_m-R_{free} = 4.37, SMB = 0.70, and HML = 5.09. The risk-free rate for the month was 0.00. The portfolio realized returns and associated factor betas are shown below. What is each portfolio's alpha? (LO 9-2)

    a. R_P = 4%, β = 1.1, b_{SMB} = 0.5, b_{HML} = −0.3
    b. R_P = 6.5%, β = 0.9, b_{SMB} = 1.5, b_{HML} = 0.4
    c. R_P = 10%, β = 1.2, b_{SMB} = −0.3, b_{HML} = 0.8

4. **Treynor Index.** If the return on the S&P 500 Index was 9.3% and the risk-free rate was 2.4%, what is the Treynor Index for the following? (LO 9-3)

    a. S&P 500 Index
    b. Portfolio with Return = 12%, beta = 1.25: is this better or worse than the index?
    c. Portfolio with Return = 10.5%, beta = 1.05: is this better or worse than the portfolio in B?

5. **Sharpe Ratio.** The risk-free rate was 2.7%. What is the Sharpe ratio for each of these three portfolios? (LO 9-4)

    a. S&P 500 Index with Return = 11.4% and standard deviation = 15.7%
    b. Portfolio with Return = 11.8% and standard deviation = 17.3%: is this better or worse than the index?
    c. Portfolio with Return = 10.9% and standard deviation = 16.2%: is this better or worse than the portfolio in B?

Use the data file, **ch9_pr06_09.xlsx** *for problems 6 through 9.*

6. **Jensen's Alpha.** Estimate the Jensen alpha of the portfolio. Is it good or bad? (LO 9-2)
7. **Alpha.** Estimate the 4-Factor model alpha of the portfolio. Is it good or bad? (LO 9-2)
8. **Treynor Index.** Estimate the Treynor Index of the portfolio and of the market portfolio. Which is better? (LO 9-3)
9. **Sharpe Ratio.** Estimate the Sharpe ratio of the portfolio and of the market portfolio. Which is better? (LO 9-4)

10. **Performance Rankings.** Calculate the Treynor Index and Sharpe ratio of each of these portfolios and rank order the portfolios from best to worst using each measure. (LO 9-3, 4)

Portfolio	Excess Return	St.	Beta
Blue	9	20	0.95
Green	11	22	1.2
Red	8	19	0.8
S&P 500	9.5	18.5	1

11. **Security Selection.** Estimate the security selection ability for stocks, bonds, and total for the following portfolio. (LO 9-6)

Asset Class	Allocation Target	Allocation Actual	Benchmark Return	Fund Return
Stocks	0.7	0.65	11.0%	12.5%
Bonds	0.3	0.35	3.5%	3.6%

12. **Security Selection.** Estimate the security selection ability for the sectors and for the total portfolio. The data are in the file, **ch9_pr12.xlsx**. (LO 9-6)

13. **Allocation Effect.** Estimate the asset allocation ability for stocks, bonds, and total for the following portfolio. (LO 9-7)

Asset Class	Allocation Target	Allocation Actual	Benchmark Return	Fund Return
Stocks	0.5	0.55	9.5%	10.0%
Bonds	0.5	0.45	2.5%	2.3%

14. **Allocation Effect.** Estimate the asset allocation ability for the sectors and for the total portfolio. The data are in the file, **ch9_pr14.xlsx**. (LO 9-7)

15. **Performance Attribution.** Estimate the security selection and asset allocation effects for the following portfolio. (LO 9-5)

Asset Class	Allocation Target	Allocation Actual	Benchmark Return	Fund Return
Stocks	0.4	0.35	10.2%	9.8%
Bonds	0.6	0.65	5.7%	6.5%

16. **Performance Attribution.** Estimate the security selection and asset allocation effects for the following global portfolio. The data is in the file, **ch9_pr16.xlsx**. (LO 9-5)

Asset Class	Allocation Target	Allocation Actual	Benchmark Return	Fund Return
Japan	0.1	0.15	7.2%	8.6%
Europe	0.2	0.25	6.7%	6.3%
Emerging Market	0.3	0.27	15.3%	15.5%
North America	0.4	0.33	9.4%	9.5%

17. **Performance Attribution.** Estimate the security selection and asset allocation effects for the following portfolio. The data are in the file, **ch9_pr17.xlsx**. (LO 9-5)

18. **Market Timing.** What are the best and worst annual returns possible by market timing using the risk-free yield (annual return) and the S&P 500 Index monthly returns in file, **ch9_pr18.xlsx**? (LO 9-8)

19. **Sector Rotation.** Consider a strategy of a portfolio being completely invested in one sector and then rotating it to possibly a different sector the next year. The goal is to always own the best sector. See the five sectors and their annual returns shown in file **ch9_pr19.xlsx**. What would your annual return be if you succeeded in always owning the best sector? What annual return would you have if you always owned the worst sector? (LO 9-8)

20. **Market Timing.** Estimate the market parameter in **Equation 9-7** for the portfolio in file **ch9_pr20.xlsx**. Is there evidence of market timing ability? (LO 9-8)

Case Study

Performance Evaluation

Download the following data files from the Kenneth French Data Library (https://mba.tuck.dartmouth.edu/pages/faculty/ken.french/data_library.html):

- 17 Industry Portfolios file (CSV format)
- Fama–French 3-Factors (CSV format)

Use five years of monthly data ending in December 2021. Compute the following for the (1) retail and (2) steel industries:

a. Jensen's alpha
b. FF 3-Factor alpha
c. Treynor Index
d. Sharpe ratio
e. Market timing ability
f. Compare the results for the two industries

Part

3

Investing in Stock

Part 3 of this text covers the macroeconomic environment that investment decisions are made in (Chapter 10) and the mechanics of valuing both common (Chapter 11) and preferred (Chapter 12) stocks.

Chapter 10

The Macroeconomic Environment for Investment Decisions

Learning Objectives

After reading this chapter, you should be able to:

LO 10-1   Define gross domestic product and specify its components.
LO 10-2   Identify the factors that affect a specific rate of interest.
LO 10-3   Differentiate the discount rate, the federal funds rate, and the target federal funds rate.
LO 10-4   Describe the tools of monetary policy and the mechanics of open market operations.
LO 10-5   Contrast the different measures of the money supply.
LO 10-6   Explain how monetary and fiscal policy and a federal government deficit may affect securities prices.
LO 10-7   Determine which investments may be desirable in an inflationary environment.

Investment decisions aren't made in a vacuum, but rather in the context of what's going on in the surrounding environment. Throughout the history of economic markets, there has been an ebb and flow of naturally occurring economic expansions and contractions, and a typical discussion of that history stresses the dual points that (a) the markets have always recovered from any downward "dips" and (b) over the long run, economies around the world have enjoyed steady growth, meaning that a long-term, diversified investment strategy will almost always pay off for the typical investor.

The story that we're going to tell in this chapter will take that approach, but with one important difference: at the time of this writing, economies are still recovering from the effects of the shortages and slowdowns caused by the COVID-19 pandemic. As indicated by the percentage changes in **gross domestic product (GDP)** (a definition is provided later in this chapter) shown in **Figure 10-1**, we *are* in the midst of recovering from the pandemic; however, there is a definite feeling that many of its economic effects were so pervasive and widespread that we are not returning to where we were before the pandemic, but to a "new normal."

gross domestic product (GDP)
the monetary value of all finished goods and services made within a country; usually calculated for years or quarters

Figure 10-1: Percentage Change in GDP

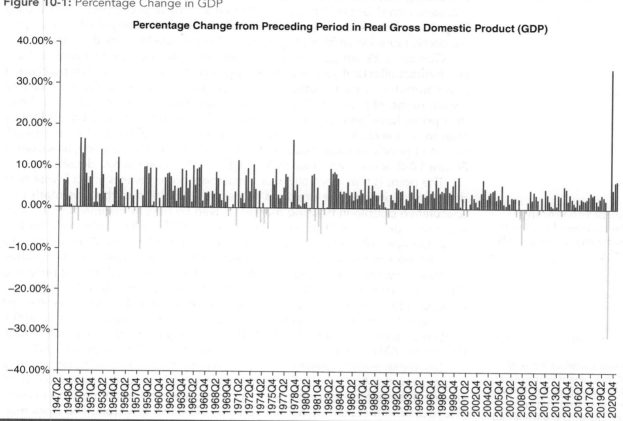

Percentage Change from Preceding Period in Real Gross Domestic Product (GDP)

As Figure 10-1 shows, quarterly GDP shrank by more than 30% at the height of the pandemic, driven largely by the idling of businesses. GDP has rebounded since then, but, unlike in previous **recessions**, that subsequent growth has been spread very unevenly across sectors of the economy, with some sectors extremely well while others languish.

For example, consider the current state of the housing market at the time of the writing of this text: millions of renters—idled from their jobs due either directly to pandemic shutdowns or indirectly to the shuttering or slowing of business operations because of ongoing supply chain problems—have fallen behind on their rent, fearing eviction while accumulating debts they cannot pay. The payments they have missed are, in turn, putting pressure on their landlords and lenders and adding to the fragility of the affordable-housing market. At the same time, prices for owner-occupied housing have soared, while the inventory of for-sale homes has plummeted. This is happening at the same time that we are seeing accelerated existing migration out of big cities into lower-density communities across the United States and boosted demand for larger homes and increased residential mobility across neighborhoods because of the pandemic. These disparate outcomes in housing market segments mirror the pandemic's uneven impact on labor markets, with college-educated professionals working from home while low-wage service workers experience the highest rates of job loss.

And it's not just such direct effects of the pandemic that are causing uncertainty and shifts in the economy: the very same changes in the housing market we just discussed would normally result in significant increases in home building and renovation, but those activities are being stymied by dramatic increases

recession
a period of temporary economic decline during which trade and industrial activity both go down; by common consensus, recessions are generally agreed to occur if GDP falls in two successive quarters

in building material costs: the price of lumber rocketed from about $400 per thousand board feet in February 2020 to an all-time high of over $1,600 in early May. Prices have since fallen to the $800 range—still nearly double their pre-pandemic rates—in what could potentially be the new level for the near term.

Obviously, it's not just the housing market experiencing such sizeable direct and indirect effects: if you've been shopping for a car, or looking to purchase a new computer, or even clothes or other consumer goods, you've noticed that a wide range of products are in short supply. Even when you can find them, their prices have gone up, as evidenced by the fact that inflation, proxied for by changes in the consumer price index (CPI) (a measure of the cost of a "typical" basket of goods and also explained more fully later in this chapter), as shown in **Figure 10-2**, is currently close to the highest it has been in two decades.

subprime lending
the practice of lending to borrowers with low credit ratings

The point is that, normally, many macroeconomic events affect investment decisions. Consider the previous recession, occurring in the aftermath of a speculative bubble in housing markets driven by risky **subprime lending** that saw prices peaking in 2006, dropping sharply 2008, and reaching new lows in 2012. On April 18, 2001, the Federal Reserve System (the "Fed") unexpectedly lowered interest rates and the Dow Jones Industrial Average rose 372 points. Subsequently, on May 15 and July 26, the Fed again lowered interest rates and the stock market yawned; the market did not react. During 2007, the economy continued to grow, but its rate of growth declined. Whether the economy had entered a recession was a big point of debate during the first part of 2008. That debate occurred after the fact! The economy entered into a recession in December 2007, ending a period of economic growth that began in 2001.

Dow Jones Industrial Average (DJIA)
a stock market index of 30 prominent companies listed on stock exchanges in the United States; its components are weighted by their market prices

Do these events matter from the investor's perspective? The positive response to the April 18 decline in interest rates affected investors who owned stocks. But the May 15 decrease in interest rates had no immediate impact. The recession that started in 2007 certainly did affect investors. The stock market, represented by the **Dow Jones Industrial Average (DJIA)** and shown in

Figure 10-2: Changes in Consumer Price Index (CPI)

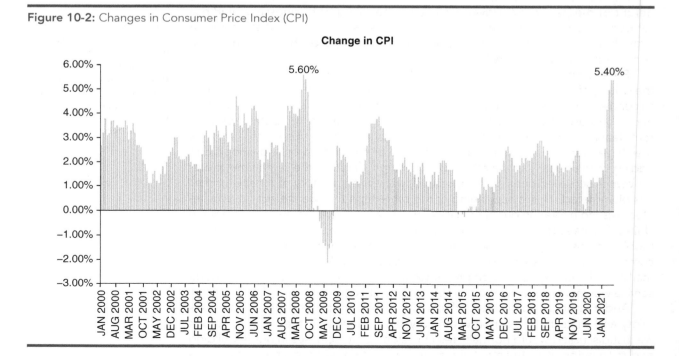

Figure 10-3: DJIA Values in Previous Two Recessions

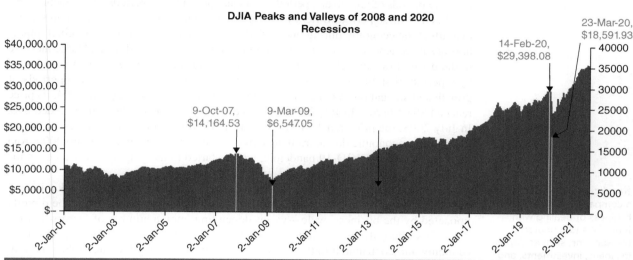

Figure 10-3, fell from $14,164,53 on October 9, 2007, to $6,547.05 on March 9, 2009, a decrease of almost 54%. Recovery was slow, with the market recovery experienced in 2009–2011 only partially recouping the losses generated during 2008, but by 2015 the DJIA and other broad market indices were reaching new highs and then continuing their upward trends into 2020.

As you can see, the recession in 2020 due to the COVID-19 pandemic was not as extreme, with the DJIA falling from $29,398.08 on February 14, 2020, to $18,591.93 on March 23, 2020, a decrease of slightly less than 37%.

So, if we accept the DJIA as a proxy for "the market," the recession of 2020 doesn't seem as extreme as that associated with the housing bubble. However, we should keep in mind that the DJIA is a price-weighted average of 30 blue-chip stocks that are generally the leaders in their industry: such large firms tended to weather the pandemic well, and many emerged stronger than before. Smaller firms, especially mom-and-pop retail businesses, did not do so well during the pandemic, and many are still struggling to recover.

This chapter deals with such topics by briefly introducing the aggregate economic environment in which investment decisions are made. It begins with measures of economic activity, such as gross domestic product, consumer confidence, and consumer prices. Emphasis is then placed on the Fed's monetary policy and its impact on the money supply and interest rates. Since the risk-free rate of interest is part of the **capital asset pricing model** (covered in Chapter 7), anything that affects interest rates should also affect securities prices. The chapter ends with the federal government's fiscal policy and the economic environment that followed the two most recent financial crises.

capital asset pricing model
a pricing model used often to describe the relationship between systematic risk and expected return for stocks

10-1 The Economic Environment

All investment decisions are made within the economic environment. This environment varies as the economy goes through stages of economic prosperity and growth. This process used to be called the *business cycle*; this was an unfortunate choice of words because *cycle* implies a regularly repeated sequence of events, such as the seasons of the year. As we saw earlier, the economy does not follow a regularly repeated sequence of events. Instead, there are periods of growth and periods of stagnation, and even periods of contraction.

Each of these periods differs with regard to length and severity, and circumstances that affect the economy during one period may cease to exist or have marginal impact during subsequent periods. The oil embargo and the resulting sudden and large increase in the price of oil severely affected the economy during the 1970s. This was followed by a period of stable oil prices, but the economy continued to go through periods of growth and stagnation. As of January 1999, oil was $19 a barrel; by late 2004, its price reached $53 a barrel. In July 2006, the price rose to $77; a year later, it exceeded $90. In July 2008, the price reached $147 a barrel. That large increase was a contributing factor to the economic downturn that started in late 2007 and continued into 2009. And the effects of the COVID-19 pandemic, which started to have significant effects on the economy, are continuing to linger as we write this text in 2021.

Even the effect on **financial institutions**, such as commercial banks, investment banks, and insurance companies—all of which one would expect to be directly impacted by the business cycle—varies depending upon a number of factors. During the 1930s, the failures of many commercial banks had an enormous impact on the economy and contributed to the **Great Depression**. During the late 1980s, the failure of many savings and loan associations and commercial banks created a financial crisis; however, unlike those of the 1930s, the financial crisis had little impact on the aggregate economy. Such was not the case with the credit and banking crisis of 2008, which—like the large increase in the price of oil—contributed to the severe decline in the economy. However, the pandemic-driven recession of 2020 seems to have been weathered handily by our financial institutions, presumably because of the vast amount of support pumped into the economy by the federal government.

In many cases, there is a strong relationship between stock prices and the aggregate economy. This was certainly illustrated during 2007–2009, when the aggregate economy experienced a sharp decline, and the decline in stock prices was one of the most severe in history. However, the large plunge in stock prices in October 1987 appears in retrospect to have been a nonevent. At that time, there were predictions that the large decline was forecasting another depression. Such a depression did not occur. Instead, the economy continued to prosper and the stock market rebounded to new highs. Of course, some investors did sustain major losses in October 1987, but other individuals who purchased stocks after the decline did well. Such transfers among investors, however, do not have the same impact on the country that is associated with a decline in the general level of economic activity.

Each of these events is important. The collapse of segments of the banking and financial system and the severe decline in stock prices did inflict losses on investors from 2007 through 2009. It is, however, possible that none of these events will be repeated or repeated simultaneously; the next economic crisis may be perceptibly different from prior crises. If such repetitions were to occur, individuals would soon recognize the patterns and adjust accordingly. Such adjustments, of course, would ensure that the future would not be a replay of the past.

financial institution
a company engaged in the business of dealing with financial and monetary transactions, such as deposits, loans, investments, and currency exchange; types of financial institutions include banks, brokerage firms, insurance companies, trust companies, and investment dealers trading either on their own behalf or on the behalf of clients

Great Depression
a severe worldwide economic depression that took place mostly during the 1930s and was prompted by the U.S. stock market crash of October 1929

10-2 Measures of Economic Activity

Economic activity is measured by aggregate indicators, such as the level of production and national output. Perhaps the most commonly quoted measure is gross domestic product (GDP), which is the total dollar value of all *final* goods and services newly produced within the country's boundaries with *domestic* factors of production. Cars made in the United States by Toyota are included in GDP, while Dell computers produced in Europe or Asia are not. GDP has replaced **gross national product (GNP)** as the primary measure of a nation's aggregate national output. (GNP is the total value of all final goods and services newly produced by an economy and includes income generated abroad—that is, income earned abroad by U.S. firms is added and income earned in the United States by foreign firms is subtracted.) The change from GNP to GDP emphasizes the country's output of goods and services within its geographical boundaries. Alternative measures of economic activity stress prices and employment. Emphasis is often placed on unemployment, especially the rate of unemployment, which measures output lost.

GDP may be computed by adding the expenditures of the sectors of an economy or by adding all sources of income. From the individual investor's perspective, the former is more useful since corporate earnings are related to expenditures by the various sectors of the economy. These expenditures are personal consumption (C), gross private domestic investment (I), government spending (G), and net exports (i.e., exports minus imports, denoted as E). The sum, GDP, is often indicated by the following equation:

$$GDP = C + I + G + E \qquad \textbf{10-1}$$

Equation 10-1 points out the importance to economic activity of personal spending; investment in plant, equipment, and inventory by firms; government spending; and the exporting of goods.

Government taxation, of course, reduces the ability of individuals and firms to spend, but the tax revenues are spent—they contribute to the nation's GDP. Correspondingly, the importing of goods increases the GDP of other nations, while foreign spending here increases GDP. (In a sense, the mercantilists of the fifteenth through seventeenth centuries had it right: export goods and receive gold. However, perhaps they placed the emphasis incorrectly on the accumulation of wealth and national power. They should have said, "Export goods and increase the domestic economy by increasing output and employment.")

Since the GDP is the sum of spending by each sector, if one sector of the economy were to decline, then GDP would also decline if another sector did not increase. For example, a reduction in federal government spending puts pressure on business to expand jobs and invest in plant and equipment. Without such expansion in the business

gross national product (GNP)
GNP for a country is equal to GDP plus residents' investment income from overseas investments minus foreign residents' investment income earned within that country

---

Excel Expert 10-1

In 2020, U.S. personal consumption was $14,147,400 million, government spending was $3,830,200 million, gross private domestic investment was $3,600,400 million, and net exports were −$645,200 million. What was GDP?

	A	B	C
1	Personal consumption	$ 14,147,400	
2	Government spending	$ 3,830,200	
3	Gross private domestic investment	$ 3,600,400	
4	Net exports	-$645,200	
5	GDP	$ 20,932,800	=SUM(B1:B4)

So, 2020 GDP was $20,932,800 million.

sector to offset the decline in government spending, consumer income and spending may not rise and the economy may stagnate.

Equation 10-1 also points out the importance of fiscal and monetary policies on the nation's economy. Excluding the direct impact of government spending, the thrust of a specific policy is its effect on the firms' and consumers' ability to, or incentive to, spend. For example, lower interest rates encourage additional spending by firms on plant, equipment, and inventory and by individuals on durable goods, such as cars and homes. Higher interest rates have the opposite effect. These changes in business and consumer spending have an immediate impact on the aggregate level of output; that is, they affect the level of GDP.

Over time, GDP grows but the rate of growth varies. As the economy expands, employment also tends to increase. There are, however, periods when the economy contracts and unemployment increases. If the contraction lasts for more than two quarters, it is referred to as a *recession*. From 1964 through 2021, the economy experienced six periods of recession as determined by the National Bureau of Economic Research (NBER): December 1969–November 1970, November 1973–March 1975, January 1980–July 1980, July 1981–November 1982, December 2007–June 2009, and February 2020–April 2020. The length of these recessions varied from a few months in 2020 to almost a year and a half from 2007 to 2009. The periods of economic growth also varied from a short period of growth in late 1980 to mid-1981 to the long period of growth that started at the end of 1982 and lasted to July 1990. The following recession ended in March 1991, and economic growth continued for 10 years to the spring of 2001.

The recession of 2001 ended in November; it was very short and mild, and economic growth resumed. During the 2000s, housing prices, fueled by excessive and easy credit, rose dramatically. The situation completely changed in late 2007. Housing prices, which in the aggregate had never declined after World War II, started to fall. Many homeowners failed to make payments on their mortgages and lenders foreclosed on the properties. Bank failures in the United States and worldwide led to the reduction and availability of credit, which precipitated a liquidity and solvency crisis. Major firms were forced into bankruptcy and others received funds from the government in order to survive. The price of a barrel of oil spiked to new highs and unemployment rose dramatically.

During this period, stock prices experienced one of the sharpest declines in history. From a high exceeding 14,200 in 2007, the Dow Jones Industrial Average sank to below 6,500 in 2009, a decline in excess of 50% in less than two years. Since there is a relationship between stock prices and economic activity, securities analysts and portfolio managers follow various indicators of economic activity to help formulate possible investment strategies. These individuals need to know the direction of economic change before it occurs. Hence, the emphasis is placed on leading indicators of economic activity. The NBER (www.nber.org) tabulates a series of economic indicators. Eleven are leading indicators, four are coincident indicators, and seven are lagging indicators. The data are reported individually for each series, and the NBER groups these indicators into three composite indexes.

The Conference Board also publishes composite economic indicators. As with the NBER indicators, some are leading, while others are coincident and lagging indicators. The 10 leading indicators include the following:

1. Average weekly hours of manufacturing production workers
2. Average weekly initial claims for unemployment insurance
3. Manufacturers' new orders (consumer goods and materials)
4. Time for deliveries

5. Manufacturers' new orders of nondefense capital goods
6. Building permits, new private housing units
7. Stock prices (S&P 500 stock index)
8. Money supply (M-2)
9. Interest rate spread (difference between 10-year Treasury bond yields and short-term rates)
10. Index of consumer expectations

Information concerning these indicators may be found at the Conference Board's home page, www.conference-board.org. However, there are two important caveats to consider. First, the time lapse between the initial decline in the index and the subsequent start of the recession differs. The 1973 recession started nine months after the decrease in the index, but the index declined for over a year and a half before the 1990 recession. Second, the index may give false signals. The index decreased in both 1984 and 1987 without a similar decline in the economy.

10-2a Measures of Consumer Confidence

One leading economic indicator that receives special attention is a measure of consumer sentiment or confidence. Consumer confidence affects spending, which has an impact on corporate profits and levels of employment. Two such measures include the **consumer confidence index (CCI)** and the **consumer sentiment index (CSI)**. The CCI is published monthly by the Consumer Research Center of the Conference Board (www.conference-board.org) in the *Consumer Confidence Survey* and in the *Statistical Bulletin*; the CSI is published monthly by the Survey Research Center of the University of Michigan (www.sca.isr.umich.edu). The CSI is used by the Department of Commerce as one of its leading indicators. Both the CCI and the CSI provide indicators of consumer attitudes by focusing on (1) consumer perceptions of business conditions, (2) consumer perceptions of their financial condition, and (3) consumer willingness to purchase durables, such as automobiles, homes, and other large dollar-cost items. An increase in confidence forecasts that consumers will increase spending, which leads to economic growth.

The absolute level of either index is not as important as changes in the index. That is, changes in the indexes suggest changes in consumer optimism or pessimism. A decline in consumer confidence forecasts a reduction in the level of economic activity. Individuals who are worried about losing their jobs or who anticipate a decline in income will demand fewer goods and services and will not borrow to finance durable purchases. An increase in the indexes has, of course, the opposite implication. To some extent, a reduction in consumer confidence and a resulting decline in the demand for goods and services may be a self-fulfilling prophecy. If consumers do cut back and purchase fewer goods and services, firms will have to contract, laying off workers and cutting payrolls.

From an investor's perspective, the change in the economy resulting from a change in consumer confidence could lead to a shift in the individual's portfolio. A reduction in confidence that leads to economic contraction argues for movement out of growth companies into defensive stocks, such as utilities or large firms (IBM or Merck) and debt instruments. The reduction in the level of economic activity should hurt firms' earnings and reduce their capacity to pay dividends or reinvest funds. However, the lower level of economic activity may induce the Fed to pursue a stimulatory monetary policy. At least initially, an easy-money policy will reduce interest rates, as the Fed puts money into the economy. Investors with long-term debt instruments in their portfolios should experience capital gains as bond prices rise in response to lower interest rates.

consumer confidence index (CCI)
an indicator providing an indication of expected future developments of households' consumption and saving, based upon answers to a survey regarding their expected financial situation, their sentiment about the general economic situation, unemployment, and capability of savings

consumer sentiment index (CSI)
an economic indicator produced by the University of Michigan that measures the degree of optimism that consumers feel about the overall state of the economy and their personal financial situation

While investors may follow leading indicators to help formulate investment strategies, the usefulness of the index of leading indicators for trading in stocks is limited, because stock prices are one of the leading indicators. By the time the index of indicators has given a signal, stock prices have (probably) already changed. It is still possible, however, that one of the specific leading indicators leads the stock market. For example, if changes in the stock market precede changes in economic activity by four months, and changes in the money supply precede the change in economic activity by seven months, then changes in the money supply might predict changes in the stock market three months before the event. Unfortunately, there is variation in the individual components of the leading indicators. While a specific indicator may lead one recession by three months, it may lead another recession by nine months. One indicator by itself is not an accurate forecaster. (If it were, there would be no need for an index of leading indicators.)

In addition, it is virtually impossible to tell when an indicator has changed. Peaks and valleys (i.e., changes in the indicators) are generally determined after the fact. It is impossible to tell when a recession has started (or ended) until the change has occurred; the same principle would apply to a specific indicator's forecasting changes in stock prices.

This inability to forecast changes in stock prices is consistent with the efficient market hypothesis. If one variable or an index of several variables could be used to forecast the direction of stock prices, individuals using the technique would consistently outperform the market. Such performance is unlikely using publicly known information, so the inability to use economic data to forecast stock prices is further support for the semi-strong form of the efficient market hypothesis.

10-3 The Consumer Price Index

consumer price index (CPI)
a measure of the average change over time in the prices paid by urban consumers for a typical market basket of consumer goods and services

producer price index (PPI)
a measure of the average selling prices received by domestic producers for their output

personal consumption expenditure (PCE)
a measure of imputed household expenditures defined for a period of time

In addition to aggregate measures of economic activity and leading indicators, measures of inflation can have an important impact on investor behavior. Inflation is a general rise in prices and was previously discussed as an important source of risk. While prices are expressed in units of a currency (e.g., dollars), inflation is generally measured by an index. Two commonly used indexes are the **consumer price index (CPI)** and the **producer price index (PPI)**. The CPI is calculated by the Bureau of Labor Statistics and measures the cost of a basket of goods and services over time. The PPI is calculated by the U.S. Department of Labor and measures the wholesale cost of goods over a period of time. Since goods are manufactured prior to their sale to consumers, changes in the PPI often forecast changes in the CPI. Information concerning federal government statistics such as the CPI may be found through the Bureau of Labor Statistics (stats.bls.gov).

An alternative measure of inflation to the CPI is the index of **personal consumption expenditure (PCE)** computed by the Bureau of Economic Analysis (BEA) (www.bea.gov). Notice the difference in wording. The CPI measures inflation by the change in the prices of a basket of goods and services. The PCE index measures consumer spending. The PCE seeks to take into consideration consumers' response to changes in price. By measuring the response, the PCE measures expenditures and the impact of changes in prices on consumer behavior.

While aggregate prices are measured by an index, the rate of inflation is measured by changes in the index. If the CPI rises from 100 to 105.6 during the year, the annual rate of inflation is 5.6%. Over time, there has been considerable variation in the rate of inflation. During 1930, the inflation rate was −6.0% (i.e., prices in the aggregate fell). During 1980, the rate was 12.4%. For the 1955–2008 period, there were no years in which consumer prices fell.

Excel Expert 10-2

Between June and July 2021, the CPI rose from 242.459 to 243.516. What was the percentage change in the CPI on an annualized basis?

	A	B	C
1	June CPI	242.459	
2	July CPI	243.516	
3	Pct Change	0.4359%	=(B2-B1)/B1
4	Annualized Basis	5.36%	=EFFECT(B3*12,12)

As you can see, the monthly rate of change is simply the ending value minus the beginning value, over the beginning value. To annualize this, we would treat this as a monthly rate. If we take that monthly rate and multiple it by 12, the number of months in a year, we can treat it as a nominal annual rate, which may be converted to an effective annual rate using the EFFECT() function as shown.

The impact of inflation on individuals varies with their consumption of goods and services. Since inflation is a general rise in prices and the CPI measures the price of a basket of goods and services, the impact on individuals depends on the extent to which they consume the particular goods whose prices are inflating. For example, lower housing costs do not affect individuals equally. Individuals seeking to buy may benefit from the lower prices at the expense of those seeking to sell housing. Prices also do not change evenly over geographic areas. Heating costs may rise more in the north than in the south, and correspondingly the cost of air-conditioning may rise more in the South than the North. These differences and other problems—such as how the index is calculated and the inability to adjust the index for technological change in the goods consumed—have led some analysts to argue that the CPI overstates the true rate of inflation. (The Bureau of Labor surveys buying patterns about every 10 years and reconstructs the basket of goods and services consumed by the average household.)

During **deflation**, which is a general decline in prices, the real purchasing power of assets and income rises as the prices of goods and services decline. Since World War II, inflation has been a common occurrence, but deflation is rare. While prices of specific goods and services may decline in response to lower demand or to lower costs of production, prices in general tend to be "sticky"—they do not decline. This stickiness is apparent in the labor market, in which an aggregate reduction in the demand for labor may not result in lower wages. Instead, workers are laid off and individuals looking for jobs are unable to find them, so the level of unemployment rises.

Even though deflation had not happened since the 1950s, the possibility of its occurring during 2008–2009 was a frequent concern facing policymakers and participants in financial markets. The CPI rose approximately 4% during 2007 but was virtually unchanged during the financial crisis in 2008. In addition, there were 12-month periods during which the CPI actually declined. For example, from July 2008 through July 2009, the index declined 2%. The reality, however, was that consumer prices in general were very stable but had the potential to decline. That possibility of deflation raised the fear that economic activity and employment would decline.

deflation
a general decline in the price level of goods and services

10-4 The Fed

In addition to forecasts of aggregate economic activity, investors are concerned with the monetary policy of the **Fed**. The Fed is the country's central bank (www.federalreserve.gov). Although in many countries the central bank is part of the federal government, in the United States it is separate. However, both the federal government and the Fed share the same general goals of full employment, stable prices, and economic growth.

The Fed pursues these economic goals through its impact on the supply of money and the cost of credit. Monetary policy refers to changes in the supply of money and credit. When the Fed wants to increase the supply of money and credit to help expand the level of income and employment, it follows an easy monetary policy. When it desires to contract the supply of money and credit to help fight inflation, it pursues a tight monetary policy.

10-4a Determination of Interest Rates

The impact of the Fed's monetary policy is felt through its effect on the rate of interest—that is, the impact on the cost of borrowing funds. The rate of interest is determined by the demand for and supply of loanable funds. As interest rates decline, the quantity demanded of loanable funds increases. Lower rates increase the profitability of investments in assets such as plant, equipment, and inventory; reduce the cost of carrying a home mortgage; and increase the quantity demanded of borrowed funds. As interest rates rise, the converse applies. Higher returns encourage firms and individuals to spend less and save more.

The actual rate an individual borrower pays (and the investor earns) depends on several variables, such as the term of the loan or the riskiness of the borrower. The types and features of bonds and the impact of fluctuations in interest rates on bond prices is covered in Part IV of this text. A specific interest rate may be expressed as a simple equation:

$$i = i_r + p_i + p_d + p_l + p_{t^*} \qquad \textbf{10-2}$$

The current **nominal interest rate** (i) is the sum of the **real risk-free rate** (i_r) plus a series of premiums: the premium for expected inflation (p_i), the premium for default risk (p_d), the premium for liquidity (p_l), and the premium for the term to maturity (p_t). Thus, the observed current rate of interest is the result of the interplay of several complex variables, each of which is simultaneously affecting the rate.

The real risk-free rate is the return investors earn without bearing any risk in a non-inflationary environment. While no exact measure of the real risk-free rate exists, analysts often use the rate on short-term Treasury bills. The real risk-free rate varies with the general level of economic activity, rising during periods of economic expansion and contracting during periods of economic stagnation.

The **inflation premium** depends on expectations of future inflation. A greater anticipated rate argues for a higher rate of interest. Since inflation may vary from year to year, the expectation also varies. If the expected inflationary rate is 4% for one year and 6% for the second year, the premiums will differ. In this case, the one-year rate of interest would be less than the two-year rate. The investor would have to earn only 4% for a one-year loan to cover the expected rate of inflation but would require a higher interest rate on a two-year loan to be compensated for the higher anticipated rate of inflation in the second year. This relationship would be reversed if the expected rate of inflation were 6% for the next year and 4% for the second year. In that case, the rate on a two-year debt instrument could be lower than the rate on a one-year security. (The inflation premium on the one-year security would have to be 6% to compensate for that year's rate of inflation, while the premium on the two-year security could be 5% annually to compensate the investor for the expected 10% inflation over the two-year time period.)

The **default premium** depends on investors' expectations or the probability that the lender will not pay the interest and retire the principal. The higher the probability of default, the greater will be the interest required to induce investors to purchase the securities. Rating systems give some indication of default risk, and the difference in yields and prices between bonds with different ratings is illustrated in Section IV of the text.

The **liquidity/marketability premium** is related to the ease with which the asset may be converted into cash near its original cost. Although there is an active secondary market in debt securities, there are differences in the depth of these markets. The bonds of a well-known company such as AT&T may be readily sold, but the secondary market for the bonds of a small company may be inactive. The size of an issue of bonds also affects its marketability. A $1 billion bond issue will have an active secondary market. A small issue, however, may not have an active secondary market.

The **term premium** is associated with the time (or term to maturity) when the bond will be redeemed. Investors prefer short-term to long-term bonds. As is explained in Chapter 13, when interest rates rise, bond prices fall, and the amount of the price decline is greater the longer the term of the bond. To compensate for the possibility of higher interest rates inflicting capital losses on bondholders, investors demand a higher interest rate as the term of the bond increases.

As this discussion indicates, the interest rate is affected by many factors. The actual observed current nominal rate of interest is the result of the simultaneous interplay of all these factors. Thus, anomalies in bond yields are possible. For example, the interest rate on a poor-quality bond that matures in one year may be less than the rate on a high-quality bond that matures in 10 years, if the premium for the longer term exceeds the default premium. Another possible explanation for the difference in the yields could be that the poor-quality bond is actively traded, while the higher-quality bond is a small issue with an inactive secondary market. Or investors could anticipate an increase in the rate of inflation. This expectation would lead to higher rates for the 10-year bond but have little impact on the rate paid by the bond that matures within a year.

default premium an additional amount of interest rate necessary to induce an investor to invest their money in a risky security instead of an otherwise equivalent risk-free security

liquidity/marketability premium an interest rate adjustment necessary to get an investor to invest their money in a security that might take time or require a discount to sell

term premium an interest rate adjustment necessary to get an investor to invest their money in a security that will take longer to earn a return

Excel Expert 10-3

If the quoted nominal annual rate on a bond is 8%, but the real risk-free rate is 2%, the premium for expected inflation is 1.5%, the liquidity premium is 0.75%, and the maturity premium is 3%, what is the default premium for the bond?

	A	B	C
1	Nominal annual rate	8.00%	
2	Real risk-free rate	2.00%	
3	Inflation premium	1.50%	
4	Liquidity premium	0.75%	
5	Maturity premium	3.00%	
6	Default premium	0.75%	=B1-SUM(B2:B5)

The default premium will be 0.75%.

10-4b The Impact of the Federal Reserve on Interest Rates

The determination of interest rates is complicated by the actions of the Fed. The Fed seeks to affect the level of economic activity by changing interest rates. Through its impact on the cost of credit, the Fed seeks to control inflation or to stimulate employment and economic growth. The Fed affects interest rates through its power to change the money supply by using the tools of monetary policy: the reserve requirements of banks, the discount rate, and open market operations.

The Fed influences the money supply and interest rates through the lending capacity of the fractional reserve banking system. **Depository institutions** (commercial banks and savings institutions, such as savings and loan associations) must hold reserves against their deposit liabilities. These reserves are divided into required reserves and excess reserves. This division depends on the **reserve requirement**, which is the percentage set by the Fed that depository institutions must hold against deposit liabilities. (Deposit liabilities are primarily checking and savings accounts, but the Fed may set reserve requirements against other accounts, such as time deposits.) If the reserve requirement is 10% and $100 cash is deposited, $10 must be held against the deposit (the required reserve) and $90 is available for lending (the excess reserves). Only a fraction of the new cash (10%) must be held against the deposit liability.

When the commercial banking system lends the excess reserves, the supply of money and credit is expanded. The converse occurs when the reserve requirement is increased and banks are forced to contract their lending. The supply of money and credit declines as excess reserves are removed from the system. By altering the reserve requirement, the Fed affects the capacity of banks to lend and thus affects the supply and cost of credit.

The **discount rate** is the interest rate the Fed charges depository institutions for borrowing reserves. When banks borrow from the Fed, they receive excess reserves. When these reserves are loaned, they expand the supply of money and credit. Depository institutions may also borrow from the Fed when they determine that they have insufficient reserves to meet their reserve requirements. In that case, borrowing the required reserves would not expand the supply of money and credit, because the expansion had already occurred at the time the loans were made. By borrowing the necessary reserves, banks will not have to liquidate assets in order to obtain the funds to meet their reserve requirements. Such liquidations would cause the system to contract, so in this case, borrowing the reserves from the Fed maintains the supply of money and credit.

Although the Fed does change the discount rate, such changes may be more symbolic than substantive. There are other, more effective (and subtler) means to alter the supply of money and credit. Instead of relying on the discount rate and the reserve requirement, the Fed uses the **federal funds rate** (or Fed funds rate) and open market operations. While the term *federal funds rate* includes "federal" and "rate," this rate should not be confused with the discount rate or the rate on federal government debt. The federal funds rate is the interest charged by banks when they lend reserves to each other. Banks with excess reserves can put those funds to work by lending them to other banks in the federal funds market, and the bank in need of reserves acquires them without having to borrow from the Fed.

Unlike the discount rate, the federal funds rate is not set by the Fed. Instead, it is established by the interaction of the demand and supply of funds available in the federal funds market. The Fed, however, can affect the supply of funds and thereby affect the federal funds rate. During the 2000s, the Fed set a target federal funds rate and changed that target as a primary indicator of monetary policy.

Fluctuations in the federal funds rate are illustrated in **Figure 10-4**, which presents the target rate from 2000 through 2021. While the federal funds rate reached 6.5%

depository institution
a financial institution in the United States (such as a savings bank, commercial bank, savings and loan association, or credit union) that is legally allowed to accept monetary deposits from consumers

reserve requirement
the amount of cash that banks must have on hand, in their vaults or in their account at the closest Federal Reserve bank, to return deposits when customers demand them

discount rate
the interest rate charged to commercial banks and other financial institutions for short-term loans they take from the Federal Reserve Bank

federal funds rate
the overnight interest rate that banks charge each other to borrow or lend excess reserves

Figure 10-4: Target Federal Funds Rate, 2000–2021

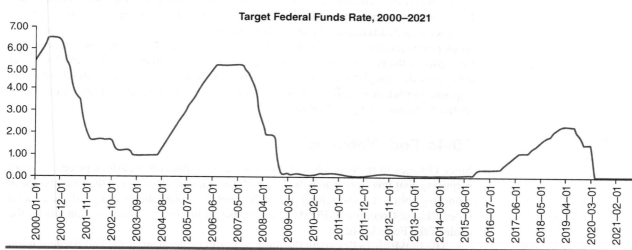

during January 2000, the Fed responded to subsequent sluggish economic behavior by lowering the rate. After economic growth increased during 2003, the Fed began to raise the target rate in 0.25% increments so that by mid-2006, the rate reached 5.25%. The pattern was reversed in 2007, and the target rate was rapidly reduced during 2007–2008 so that by year's end, it was virtually 0% (0.00 to 0.25%). That rate remained in effect until the end of 2015, when the Fed started a series of increases in the federal funds rate. This policy suffered a dramatic reversal with the onset of the COVID-19 pandemic, with the Fed rapidly dropping the target rate down to close to zero, where it has remained since then.

The Fed achieves the desired effect on the federal funds rate through its most important tool of monetary policy, **open market operations**. Open market operations are the buying and selling of securities (primarily short-term Treasury bills) by the Fed. The Fed may buy or sell these securities in any quantity at any time. When the Fed follows an expansionary policy, it purchases securities. When the Fed pays for the securities, the funds are deposited into commercial banks, putting reserves into the banking system. Because only a percentage of the reserves will be required against the deposit liabilities, the remainder become excess reserves. When these newly created excess reserves are loaned by the banking system, the supply of money and credit is increased.

A **contractionary monetary policy** is designed to drain reserves from the banking system. The Fed sells securities, which are then purchased by the general public or banks. When the securities are paid for, funds flow from deposits to the Fed. The effect is to reduce the reserves of depository institutions. The reduction in reserves decreases the banks' capacity to lend and contracts the supply of money and credit.

Open market operations have a direct and immediate impact on interest rates. Purchasing securities increases prices and simultaneously drives down yields. The opposite occurs when the Fed sells securities, which reduces their price and increases yields. The change in yields is transferred to other interest rates. As was explained earlier, interest rates are the result of several factors, including the risk-free rate, the default premium, the liquidity/marketability premium, and the term premium. Since short-term U.S. Treasury bills are the safest of all debt instruments, their yield is often used as the risk-free rate. Changes in that risk-free rate must have an impact on interest rates in general.

open market operations
an instance of a central bank buying or selling short-term Treasuries and other securities in the open market in order to influence the money supply, thus influencing short-term interest rates

contractionary monetary policy
a type of monetary policy that is intended to cut back on the rate of monetary expansion to fight inflation

Changes in monetary policy should also affect stock prices. This impact may be the result of a change in the required return used to discount future cash flows. For example, in the capital asset pricing model, a higher risk-free rate would lead to a higher required return and lower stock valuations. Monetary policy may also affect stock prices through its effect on a firm's earning capacity. An easy monetary policy that reduces the cost of credit may increase earnings, resulting in higher dividends and more growth through the retention of earnings. A tight monetary policy should have the opposite impact. Higher interest rates should reduce earnings, which reduces the firm's ability to expand and pay dividends.

10-4c Fed Watching

Since changes in interest rates can have a major impact on securities prices, it is not surprising that investors watch the Fed with the hope of anticipating the next change in monetary policy. This watching primarily revolves around the meetings of the Federal Open Market Committee (FOMC) and the Board of Governors and statements by the chair of the Fed's board.

The FOMC is individually the most powerful component of the Fed because it has control over open market operations. The committee consists of 12 members, 7 of whom are the members of the board of governors. The remaining 5 members are presidents of some of the 12 Fed district banks. Membership in the Open Market Committee rotates among 11 district bank presidents. The president of the New York district is a permanent member.

The most important individual member of the Fed is the chair of the board of governors, currently Jerome H. Powell. As chair, Powell is the chief spokesperson for the Fed. His frequent testimony to Congress (and the announcements and minutes of board meetings) are scrutinized for clues to future Fed actions. The market may react to the chair's statements, as it did when then chair Alan Greenspan remarked that recent increases in stock prices exhibited "irrational exuberance." The market immediately reacted by declining. The reaction, however, was short-lived. The Dow rose more than 1,000 points within six months after the "irrational exuberance" statement.

10-4d The Money Supply

M1
the portion of the money supply that is composed of currency, demand deposits, and other liquid deposits.

M2
includes M1 plus savings and time deposits, certificates of deposits, and money market funds, all of which are less liquid than the components of M1.

In addition to "Fed watching," analysts track changes in the money supply in an effort to perceive changes in monetary policy. Monetary statistics are released weekly and include data on the money supply. The Fed uses two definitions. The simplest definition of the supply of money (commonly referred to as **M1**) is the sum of currency, coins, and checking accounts (including interest-bearing checking accounts) in the hands of the public. A broader definition (**M2**) adds savings accounts to this definition. Thus, if individuals shift funds from savings accounts to checking accounts, the money supply is increased under the narrow definition (M1) but unaffected under the broader definition (M2).

An alternative measure to determine the direction of change in monetary policy is the "monetary base" or "high-powered money." The monetary base is the sum of coins, paper money (currency), and bank reserves kept within a bank or at the Fed. Since banks' capacity to lend is ultimately related to banks' reserves, changes in the monetary base should mirror current monetary policy.

The measures of the money supply may present conflicting signals, but the consensus is that the Fed systematically expands the money supply over time to maintain economic growth. From the individual investor's perspective, the growth in the money supply is related to economic growth and economic growth is related to stock prices. If the money supply rises too slowly, economic growth will be constrained, which should reduce stock prices. If the money supply rises too rapidly, inflation may result, which is associated with higher rates of interest and lower stock prices. The goal is to determine what rate of growth in the money supply will over time sustain economic growth without creating stagnation or inflation.

Although the monetary policy of the Fed can have an important impact on bond and stock investments, developing a successful investment strategy based on monetary policy is exceedingly difficult, if not impossible. In addition, the stock market is a leading indicator of economic activity. The market anticipates change in monetary policy and often does not react to the policy change unless the change is unanticipated. Hence, to use changes in monetary policy as a guide for an investment strategy, it is necessary to differentiate between expected changes—the effects of which are already embodied in stocks' prices—and unanticipated changes, which can have an impact on stock prices. This means that the investor must correctly anticipate and act before the unexpected change. In efficient financial markets, the investor must have superior insight or luck to use changes in monetary policy to consistently generate superior stock market returns.

10-5 Fiscal Policy

In addition to the monetary policy of the Fed, the fiscal policy of the federal government can have an important impact on the securities markets. Fiscal policy is taxation, expenditures, and debt management by the federal government. The Council of Economic Advisers annually publishes the Economic Report of the President (available at www.gpo.gov), which details the fiscal policy (i.e., taxation and expenditures) of the federal government. Like monetary policy, fiscal policy may be used to pursue the economic goals of price stability, full employment, and economic growth.

fiscal policy
the use of government spending and taxation to influence the economy

Obviously, taxation can have an impact on stock prices. Corporate income taxes reduce earnings and hence reduce firms' capacity to pay dividends and to retain earnings for growth. Personal income taxes reduce disposable income. This reduces demand for goods and services as well as savings that would be invested in some asset. Federal taxes also affect the demand for specific securities, such as tax-exempt bonds discussed in Chapter 14. Thus, the tax policies may affect not only the level of securities prices but also relative prices, as certain types of assets receive favorable tax treatment.

The potential impact of the federal government's fiscal policy is not limited to taxation. Expenditures can also affect securities prices. This should be obvious with regard to the specific products bought by the government. Such purchases may increase a particular firm's earnings and enhance its stock's price. However, expenditures in general, especially deficit spending, in which expenditures exceed revenues, can affect the financial markets and securities prices.

deficit spending
government spending, in excess of revenue raised from taxes, of funds raised by borrowing

When the federal government's expenditures exceed revenues, the federal government may obtain funds to finance this deficit from three sources: (1) the general public, (2) banks, and (3) the Fed. When the federal government sells securities to the general public to finance the deficit, these securities compete directly with all other securities for the funds of savers. This increased supply of federal government securities will tend to decrease securities prices and increase their yields.

A similar conclusion applies to sales of Treasury securities to banks. If the banks lend money to the federal government, they cannot lend these funds to individuals and businesses. The effect will be to raise the cost of loans as the banks ration their supply of loanable funds. Higher borrowing costs should tend to reduce securities prices for several reasons. First, higher costs should reduce corporate earnings, which will have an impact on dividends and growth rates. Second, higher borrowing costs should reduce the attractiveness of buying securities on credit (i.e., margin) and thus reduce the demand for securities. Third, the higher costs of borrowing will encourage banks to raise the rates they pay depositors. Since all short-term rates are highly correlated, increases in one rate will be transferred to other rates. Once again, the higher interest rates in general produce lower securities prices.

If the Fed were to finance the federal government's deficit, the impact would be the same as if the Fed had purchased securities through open market operations. In either case, the money supply would be increased. In effect, when the Fed buys the securities issued to finance the federal government's deficit, the Fed is monetizing the debt because new money is created. This is essentially what occurred during the period of the Fed's quantitative easing, which followed the financial crisis. The federal government ran a sizable deficit that had to be financed. Federal government securities were sold in the financial markets virtually every week and were also sold to the Fed. The Fed's buying of the securities increased the supply of money and created liquidity, which reduced interest rates. The net effect was to maintain interest at historically low levels for an extended period of time, as was illustrated previously in Figure 10-4.

surplus
an amount of an item in an economy that is more than people demand

The opposite of deficit spending is a **surplus**, in which government revenues (receipts) exceed government expenditures (disbursements). Prior to the late 1990s, the federal government had not had a budgetary surplus since the Nixon administration. The period of federal government surpluses, however, did not last long and the federal government was once again operating with expenditures exceeding revenues.

10-6 The 2008–2011 and 2020–2021 Economic Environments

10-6a 2008–2011

Fiscal policy and deficit spending took on a whole new meaning in reaction to the events surrounding the housing bubble of 2007–2008. The financial crisis, the decline in home values, and the large increase in unemployment resulted in the federal government taking unprecedented steps designed to stimulate economic activity. The "stimulus" package proposed by newly elected President Obama and subsequently passed in 2009 by Congress created a federal deficit in excess of a trillion dollars ($1,000,000,000,000).

Simultaneously, the Fed pursued a highly expansionary monetary policy by driving interest rates to historic lows. As of 2009, the discount rate was 0.5% and the federal funds rate was virtually 0%. Previously, open market operations had focused on the buying and selling of Treasury securities; now, however, the Fed extended its purchases to include a variety of debt instruments. Such purchases had the effect of increasing the money supply. **Figure 10-5** plots the one-month percentage changes in M1 and M2 for the period around and including the financial crisis of 2008. The large increases in M1 and M2 are readily apparent. From January 2000 through 2007, M1 rose 22.9%, or 2.9% annually. From January 2008 through December 2011, M1 rose 58.5%, or approximately 1% per month.

The large increase in the money supply led some investors and financial advisors to expect a significant increase in the rate of inflation. During the previous 20 years, the annual rate of inflation ranged between 2 and 4%. These individuals, however,

Figure 10-5: Monthly Percentage Changes in M1 and M2, 2007–2009

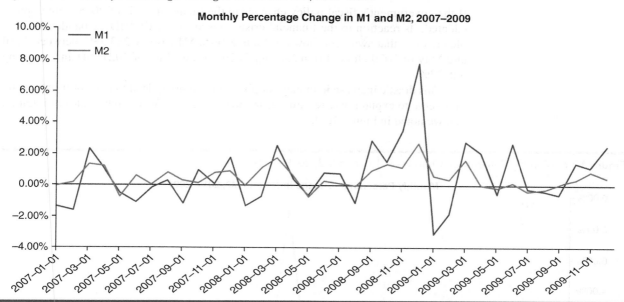

anticipated that inflation would exceed the rate experienced during 1978–1981, when the CPI rose in excess of 13% annually.

This expectation of inflation often changes investor psychology and strategies. Emphasis shifts away from financial assets to physical assets. While the most frequently recommended metal is gold, the concept applies to other metals, such as silver and copper. The same would apply to commodities such as oil and natural gas. The expectation of inflation also encourages individuals to acquire currencies that would appreciate relative to the dollar and debt instruments tied to the rate of inflation. Interest payments and the principal repayment increase with higher interest rates that result from increases in the CPI.

While investors are not precluded from buying assets such as gold or companies that mine gold, they may readily establish positions in precious metals by acquiring shares in exchange-traded funds (ETFs), such as SPDR Gold Shares (GLD). To invest in currencies or variable rate bonds, they may select CurrencyShares Euro Trust (FXE), the Canadian dollar (FXC), or iShares Barclays TIPS bond (TIPS). In fact, an almost unlimited number of possible investments exist that could be used to execute positions designed to take advantage of the expectation of an increase in the rate of inflation.

The rate of inflation, however, did not increase after the financial crisis and the large increases in the money supply. The CPI rose from 210.2 in December 2007 to 233.9 at the end of 2014 for an increase of only 11.3% (less than 2% annually). The price of gold was $833 an ounce at the end of 2007 and did rise dramatically during 2010–2012 to a high of $1,862 in September 2011. Unfortunately, individuals who acquired gold during 2010 through 2012 and maintained their positions subsequently sustained losses as the price closed in 2014 at $1,181. During the same period, however, the S&P 500 rose from 1,115 at the beginning of 2010 to 2,059 at the end of 2014. That value was a historic high for the index.

10-6b 2020–2021

If the government's fiscal policy changes to the financial crisis of 2008 were unprecedented, its reaction to the financial crisis caused by the COVID-19 pandemic completely blew that away. As shown in **Figure 10-6**, M1 rose by 233.38% between April and May of 2020 alone. From January 2020 through July of 2021, M1 increased by 388.27%.

This drastic increase in money supply would naturally lead to fears of inflation and may serve to explain why we are starting to see the significant higher rates of inflation that we noted in Figure 10-2.

Figure 10-6: Monthly Percentage Changes in M1 and M2, 2019–2021

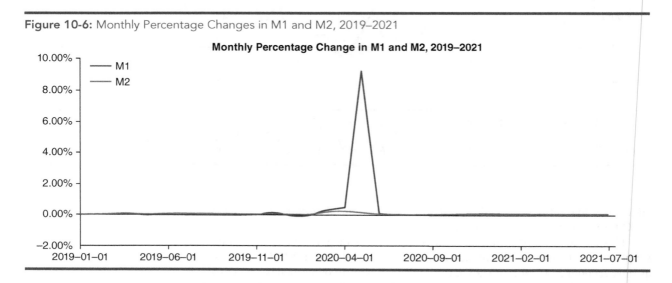

Conclusion

Since portfolio planning, securities analysis, and investment decisions are made in an economic environment, the starting point of any analysis should be the macroeconomy. It affects an individual's employment, income, and wealth and affects a firm's cost of funds and earnings. Measures of economic output and national income include the gross domestic product (GDP). Other economic measures include the consumer confidence index (CCI), the consumer sentiment index (CSI), and the consumer price index (CPI).

The Federal Reserve System (the "Fed") is the nation's central bank. Its goals are full employment, economic growth, and stable prices. The Fed seeks to achieve these economic goals through its impact on the rate of interest or the supply of money. The specific interest rate that a borrower pays depends on the risk-free rate plus a series of premiums related to the expectation of inflation, the borrower's risk of default, and the liquidity of the debt. As the Fed

affects interest rates, it affects the supply of credit and the cost of funds.

The Fed executes monetary policy through its impact on the reserves of the banking system and the supply of money. The discount rate is the rate the Fed charges banks when they borrow reserves. Although the discount rate is one tool of monetary policy, the Fed emphasizes the federal funds rate, which is the rate banks charge each other for borrowing reserves. The Fed affects the federal funds rate through open market operations—the buying and selling of securities by the Fed. Buying securities puts liquidity (money) into the economy, while selling securities has the opposite impact, as it takes liquidity out of the economy.

Fiscal policy is federal government spending, taxation, and debt management. When the federal government spends more than it receives in revenues, it runs a deficit. When the federal government spends less than its revenues, it runs a surplus. Deficit spending by the federal government may be used to stimulate the economy and is often financed by selling securities to the Fed. The Fed's financing of the federal government's deficit will increase the money supply, which may increase the fear of future inflation. To protect themselves from the anticipated inflation, investors often acquire assets such as commodities and precious metals (gold) whose prices tend to rise in an inflationary environment.

Chapter Equations

$$GDP = C + I + G + E \qquad \textbf{10-1}$$

$$i = i_r + p_i + p_d + p_l + p_{t*} \qquad \textbf{10-2}$$

Excel Functions

EFFECT(nominal_rate, npery)
SUM(number 1, [number2], ...)

Key Terms

M1 – the portion of the money supply that is composed of currency, demand deposits, and other liquid deposits.

M2 – includes M1 plus savings and time deposits, certificates of deposits, and money market funds, all of which are less liquid than the components of M1.

capital asset pricing model – a pricing model used often to describe the relationship between systematic risk and expected return for stocks

consumer confidence index (CCI) – an indicator providing an indication of expected future developments of households' consumption and saving, based upon answers to a survey regarding their expected financial situation, their sentiment about the general economic situation, unemployment, and capability of savings

consumer price index (CPI) – a measure of the average change over time in the prices paid by urban consumers for a typical market basket of consumer goods and services

consumer sentiment index (CSI) – an economic indicator produced by the University of Michigan that measures the degree of optimism that consumers feel about the overall state of the economy and their personal financial situation

contractionary monetary policy – a type of monetary policy that is intended to cut back on the rate of monetary expansion to fight inflation

default premium – an additional amount of interest rate necessary to induce an investor to invest their money in a risky security instead of an otherwise equivalent risk-free security

deficit spending – government spending, in excess of revenue raised from taxes, of funds raised by borrowing

deflation – a general decline in the price level of goods and services

depository institution – a financial institution in the United States (such as a savings bank, commercial bank, savings and loan association, or credit union) that is legally allowed to accept monetary deposits from consumers

discount rate – the interest rate charged to commercial banks and other financial institutions for short-term loans they take from the Federal Reserve Bank

Dow Jones Industrial Average (DJIA) – a stock market index of 30 prominent companies listed on stock exchanges in the United States; its components are weighted by their market prices

Fed – a name for the Federal Reserve System, which is the central bank of the United States and is charged with maximizing employment, stabilizing prices, moderating long-term interest rates, supervising and regulating banks, maintaining the stability of the financial system, and providing financial services to depository institutions, the U.S. government, and foreign official institutions

federal funds rate – the overnight interest rate that banks charge each other to borrow or lend excess reserves

financial institution – a company engaged in the business of dealing with financial and monetary transactions, such as deposits, loans, investments, and currency exchange; types of financial institutions include banks, brokerage firms, insurance companies, trust companies, and investment dealers trading either on their own behalf or on the behalf of clients

fiscal policy – the use of government spending and taxation to influence the economy

Great Depression – a severe worldwide economic depression that took place mostly during the 1930s and was prompted by the U.S. stock market crash of October 1929

gross domestic product (GDP) – the monetary value of all finished goods and services made within a country; usually calculated for years or quarters

gross national product (GNP) – GNP for a country is equal to GDP plus residents' investment income from overseas investments minus foreign residents' investment income earned within that country

inflation premium – an interest rate adjustment necessary to compensate an investor for expected inflation

liquidity/marketability premium – an interest rate adjustment necessary to get an investor to invest their money in a security that might take time or require a discount to sell

nominal interest rate – the quoted rate on an investment

open market operations – an instance of a central bank buying or selling short-term Treasuries and other securities in the open market in order to influence the money supply, thus influencing short-term interest rates

personal consumption expenditure (PCE) – a measure of imputed household expenditures defined for a period of time

producer price index (PPI) – a measure of the average selling prices received by domestic producers for their output

real risk-free rate – the theoretical interest rate of an investment that carries zero risk; because even Treasury securities carry the risk of unexpected inflation, the risk-free rate is unobtainable in reality

recession – a period of temporary economic decline during which trade and industrial activity both go down; by common consensus, recessions are generally agreed to occur if GDP falls in two successive quarters

reserve requirement – the amount of cash that banks must have on hand, in their vaults or in their account at the closest Federal Reserve bank, to return deposits when customers demand them

subprime lending – the practice of lending to borrowers with low credit ratings

surplus – an amount of an item in an economy that is more than people demand

term premium – an interest rate adjustment necessary to get an investor to invest their money in a security that will take longer to earn a return

Questions

1. **GDP.** What is the impact on GDP if consumer spending increases? Would the answer be different if the consumer spending were directed toward foreign goods? (LO 10-1)

2. **Inflation.** What differentiates inflation and deflation? If both GDP and unemployment were simultaneously rising, would this period be classified as a recession? (LO 10-2)

3. **Interest Rates.** What factors, besides the expected rate of inflation, may affect the rate of interest a borrower pays? (LO 10-2)

4. **Federal Reserve.** What is the Fed? What are its economic goals? (LO 10-3)

5. **Monetary Policy.** How does the Fed pursue its economic goals? How may the tools of monetary policy affect securities prices? (LO 10-4)

6. **Discount Rate.** What is the difference between the discount rate and the target federal funds rate? (LO 10-3)

7. **Monetary Supply.** What are M1 and M2? How does the Fed alter M1 and M2? (LO 10-5)

8. **Monetary Supply.** Do the fundamental economic goals of fiscal policy differ from those of monetary policy? If the Fed finances the federal government's deficit, what will happen to the supply of money? (LO 10-6)

9. **Recessions.** What are the primary differences between the recession stemming from the housing bubble in 2007–2008 and that arising from the COVID-19 pandemic? (LO 10-7)

10. **Inflation.** How does expanding the monetary supply encourage inflation? (LO 10-7)

Problems

1. **GDP.** If U.S. personal consumption were $12,147,400 million, government spending were $2,805,200 million, gross private domestic investment were $5,345,400 million, and net exports were $1,645,200 million, what would GDP be? (LO 10-1)

2. **Net Exports.** If GDP were $17,147,400 million, government spending were $2,805,200 million, personal consumption were $15,312,000 million, and gross private domestic investment were $5,345,400 million, what would net exports be? (LO 10-1)

3. **Government spending.** If GDP were $18,204,700 million, net exports were −$2,805,200 million, personal consumption were $15,312,000 million, and gross private domestic investment were $5,345,400 million, what would government spending be? (LO 10-1)

4. **Change in CPI.** If the CPI rose from 242.459 to 244.205, what would be the percentage change in the CPI on an annualized effective basis? (LO 10-2)

5. **Change in CPI.** If the CPI rose from 242.459 to 244.205, what would be the percentage change in the CPI on an annualized nominal basis? (LO 10-2)

6. **Change in CPI.** If the CPI fell from 257.314 to 254.205, what would be the percentage change in the CPI on an annualized effective basis? (LO 10-2)

7. **Change in CPI.** If the CPI fell from 257.314 to 254.205, what would be the percentage change in the CPI on an annualized nominal basis? (LO 10-2)

8. **Default premium.** If the quoted nominal annual rate on a bond is 9%, but the real risk-free rate is 1.5%, the premium for expected inflation is 1.75%, the liquidity premium is 1.25%, and the maturity premium is 2%, what is the default premium for the bond? (LO 10-2)

9. **Liquidity premium.** If the quoted nominal annual rate on a bond is 11.5%, but the real risk-free rate is 1.5%, the premium for expected inflation is 1.75%, the default premium is 1.25%, and the maturity premium is 2%, what is the liquidity premium for the bond? (LO 10-2)

10. **Quoted annual rate.** If the default premium on a bond is 3%, but the real risk-free rate is 1.5%, the premium for expected inflation is 1.75%, the liquidity premium is 1.25%, and the maturity premium is 2%, what should be the quoted nominal annual rate for the bond? (LO 10-2)

Case Study

Dealing with Inflation

Suppose that the current trend in the U.S. economy toward increased inflation continues.

a. What actions could you expect the U.S. government to take to try and head off this inflation?

b. Assuming you expected the government to be unsuccessful at staving off inflation, how would that affect your investment strategies? Why?

c. How would your answers to a. and b. change if you expected variants of COVID-19 to continue to have an effect on health, and hence economic stability, in the United States?

Chapter 11

Valuing Common Stock

For many people, the word *investing* is synonymous with buying and selling common stock. Common stocks are a primary instrument of investing, perhaps because of the considerable exposure people have to them. You likely see stock market and company news on social media and news programs and in newspapers. Brokerage firms like Robinhood advertise the attractiveness of such investments throughout the Internet.

When people think of stocks, they usually think about capital appreciation. However, common stocks may pay a dividend, and that constant cash flow is an important part of their total return over time. As the economy prospers and corporate earnings rise, the dividends and the value of common stocks may also increase. For this reason, common stocks are a good investment for people who have less need for current income but desire capital appreciation.

You can easily find information about a stock on the Internet. Does this information help you decide whether you should buy the stock? Information itself does you little good. You need information and the applicable knowledge for financial wisdom. Wisdom is needed because you are facing one of the most elusive and perplexing questions facing every investor. What is the stock worth? Without some estimate of the current value, the decision to buy will be based on hunches, intuition, or tips. Conceptually, the valuation of a stock is the same as the valuation of a bond or any asset. In each case, future cash flows are discounted back to their present value. For debt instruments, this process is relatively easy because debt instruments pay a fixed amount of interest and mature at a specified date. Common stock, however, does not pay a fixed dividend, nor does it mature. These two facts considerably increase the difficulty of valuing common stock.

Three approaches are often used to assess how attractive the business operations are to an investor in valuing a stock: analysis of financial statements, discounted cash flow, and price ratios. Analysis of financial statements employs a variety of accounting measures such as the return on equity (ROE). These measures may be compared to past values from the firm, industry averages, or to a predetermined critical value to determine if the stock should be bought or sold. Discounted cash flow models require estimating future sales, expenses, earnings, and dividends and expressing these values in the present (i.e., discounting future cash flows). This present value is compared to the current price of the stock to make a buy or sell decision. Lastly, price ratios, like the price-to-earnings (PE) ratio, provide a good relative value measure.

This chapter discusses investing in common stocks. Various techniques are used to analyze a firm and its financial statements with the purpose of identifying the stocks that have the greatest potential or are the most undervalued.

11-1 Corporate Form of Business

A corporation is an artificial legal economic entity established (i.e., chartered) by a state. Stock, both common and preferred, represents ownership, or equity, in a corporation. Under state laws, the firm is issued a certificate of incorporation that indicates the name of the corporation, the location of its principal office, its purpose, and the number of shares of stock that are authorized (i.e., the number of shares that the firm may issue). In addition to a certificate of incorporation, the firm receives a **charter** that specifies the relationship between the corporation and the state. At the initial meeting of stockholders, **bylaws** are established that set the rules by which the firm is governed, including such issues as the **voting rights** of the stockholders.

Firms must issue **common stock** and may issue preferred stock. Preferred stock is a much different security than common stocks and is thoroughly discussed in Chapter 12. When investors think of buying a company's stock, they are referring to its common stock.

In the eyes of the law, a corporation is a legal entity that is separate from its owners. It may enter into contracts and is legally responsible for its obligations. Creditors may sue the corporation for payment if it defaults on its obligations, but the creditors cannot sue the stockholders. Therefore, you know that if you purchase stock in a publicly held corporation, such as Apple Inc., the maximum that can be lost is the amount of the investment. If a large corporation (e.g., Pacific Gas and Electric, General Motors, and American Airlines) does go bankrupt, limited liability means its stockholders are safe from the firm's creditors.

charter
A document specifying the relationship between a firm and the state in which it is incorporated

bylaw
A document specifying the relationship between a corporation and its stockholders

voting rights
The rights of stockholders to vote their shares

common stock
A security representing ownership in a corporation with voting rights

11-1a Ownership

Because stock represents ownership in a corporation, investors have all the rights of ownership. These rights include the option to vote the shares. The stockholders elect a board of **directors** that selects the firm's management. Management is then responsible to the board of directors, which in turn is responsible to the firm's stockholders. If the stockholders do not think that the board is doing a competent job, they may elect another board to represent them.

director
A person who is elected by stockholders to determine the firm's goals and policies

For publicly held corporations, such democracy doesn't always work well. Stockholders are usually widely dispersed, while the firm's management and board of directors generally form a cohesive unit. Rarely does the individual investors' votes mean much. There have, however, been exceptions. Shareholders voted to maintain Elon Musk's role as chairman of Tesla's board during the company's 2018 annual shareholder meeting despite a controversial proposal to strip him of that position. (Of course, Musk subsequently stepped down as chairman of Tesla less than four months later as part of a deal to settle fraud charges brought against him by the U.S. Securities and Exchange Commission [SEC], but that's another story.)

proxy battle
A group of shareholders trying to gather enough shareholder proxy votes to win a company vote

Even if there are no **proxy battles**, there is always the possibility that if a company does poorly, another firm may offer to buy the outstanding stock held by the public. Once such purchases are made, the stock's new owners may remove the board of directors and establish new management. To some extent, this encourages a corporation's board of directors and management to pursue the goal of increasing the value of the firm's stock.

Some corporations have two or more classes of common stock. For example, Berkshire Hathaway (BRK) has class A and class B common shares. Having different classes of common stock facilitates control over the corporation by a few stockholders, since voting rights often differ between the classes. In the case of BRK, class A shares have 10,000 votes for every 1 vote available to the owner of a share of the class B stock. The A share rights make them more valuable. At the end of 2021, BRK-A were over $450,000 each, while BRK-B traded for about $300 each.

A stockholder generally has one vote for each share owned, but there are two ways to distribute this vote. With the traditional method of voting, each share gives the stockholder the right to vote for one individual for *each* seat on the board of directors. Under this system, if a majority group voted as a bloc, a minority group could never elect a representative. The alternative system, **cumulative voting**, gives minority stockholders a means to obtain representation on the firm's board.

cumulative voting
A system that permits each stockholder to cast all their votes for one candidate

How cumulative voting works is best explained by a brief example. Suppose a firm has a board of directors composed of five members. With traditional voting, a stockholder with 100 shares may vote 100 votes for a candidate for each seat. The total 500 votes are split among the seats. Under cumulative voting, the individual may cast the entire 500 votes for a candidate for one seat. Of course, then the stockholder cannot vote for anyone running for the remaining four seats. By banding together and casting all their votes for a specific candidate, the minority may be able to win a seat. This technique can't be used to win a majority.

Since stockholders are owners, they are entitled to the firm's earnings. These earnings may be distributed in the form of cash dividends or may be retained by the corporation. If they are retained, your investment in the firm is increased (i.e., the stockholder's equity increases). However, for every class of stock, your relative position is not altered. Some owners of common stock cannot receive cash dividends, whereas others have their earnings reinvested. The distribution or retention of earnings applies equally to all stockholders.

Although limited liability is one of the advantages of investing in publicly held corporations, stock ownership does involve risk. If the firm prospers, it may be able to pay dividends and grow. However, if earnings fluctuate, dividends and growth may also fluctuate. It is the owners—the stockholders—who bear the business risk associated with these fluctuations. If the firm should default on its debt, it can be taken to court by its creditors to enforce its obligations. If the firm should fail or become bankrupt, the stockholders have the last claim on its assets. Only after all the creditors have been paid will the stockholders receive any funds. In most cases of bankruptcy, this amounts to nothing because there is more owed to creditors than the value of the company. If the corporation survives bankruptcy proceedings, the existing shareholders usually receive nothing and some of the creditors become the new owners (stockholders) of the firm.

Preemptive Rights

Some stockholders have **preemptive rights**, which is their prerogative to maintain their proportionate ownership in the firm. If the firm wants to sell additional shares to the general public, these new shares must be offered initially to the existing stockholders in a sale, called a **rights offering**. If the stockholders wish to maintain their proportionate ownership in the firm, they can exercise their rights by purchasing the new shares. However, if they do not want to take advantage of this offering, they may sell their privilege to whoever wants to purchase the new shares.

Preemptive rights may be illustrated by a simple example. If a firm has 1,000 shares outstanding and you have 100 shares, you own 10% of the firm's stock. If the firm wants to sell 400 new shares and the stockholders have preemptive rights, these new shares must be offered to the existing stockholders before they are sold to the public. You would have the right to purchase 40 shares, or 10%, of the new shares. If you buy these shares, then your relative position is maintained, and you continue to own 10% of the firm after the sale of the new stock.

Although preemptive rights are required in some states for incorporation, their importance has diminished, and the number of rights offerings has declined. Some firms have changed their bylaws to eliminate preemptive rights. Investors in companies without preemptive rights can purchase shares in new issues through the open market issue process.

preemptive right
The right of current stockholders to maintain their proportionate ownership in the firm

rights offering
Sale of new securities to existing stockholders

11-1b Cash Dividends

Corporations may pay their stockholders dividends, which can be in the form of cash or additional shares. A **dividend** is a distribution from earnings. Companies that pay cash dividends often have a dividend policy that is known to the investment community. Even if the policy is not explicitly stated by management, the continuation of such practices as paying quarterly dividends implies a specific policy.

While most American companies that distribute cash dividends pay a **regular dividend** on a quarterly basis, there are other types of dividend policies. For example, some companies pay a quarterly dividend plus an additional or **extra dividend**. In 2020, Costco Wholesale (COST), the third-largest retailer in the world, was paying a 70-cent quarterly dividend per share. It then paid a huge $10 per share special dividend in December. Such a policy is appropriate for a firm with fluctuating cash flows. Management may not want to increase the dividend and then have difficulty maintaining the higher dividend. By having a set cash payment that is supplemented with extras in good years, management can maintain a fixed payment that is relatively assured and supplement the cash dividend when the extra is warranted by earnings and cash flow.

dividend
A payment to stockholders that is usually in cash but may be in stock

regular dividend
Steady dividend payments that are distributed at regular intervals

extra dividend
Cash paid in addition to the firm's regular dividend

irregular dividend
Dividend payments that
either don't occur in the
regular intervals or vary in
amount

Other firms pay **irregular dividends**: there is no set dividend payment. For example, real estate investment trusts (frequently referred to as REITs and discussed in Chapter 4) are required by law to distribute their earnings to maintain their favorable tax status. Since the earnings of such trusts can fluctuate, the cash dividends may also fluctuate. The special tax laws pertaining to REITs cause them to have irregular dividend payments. For example, mall operator Simon Property Group (SPG) paid $5.85 per share in 2021, $6.00 in 2020, $8.30 in 2019, $7.90 in 2018, and $7.15 in 2017. The pandemic had a severe impact on shopping malls, which significantly reduced Simon Property's earnings and subsequently, dividends.

Many firms have made dividend payments for years. AT&T, ExxonMobil, and Eli Lilly have paid dividends since the 1880s. Coca-Cola not only has paid cash dividends for over 100 years but also has increased the dividend payment every year for 60 years. While these illustrations may be exceptional, they do suggest that firms may give considerable importance to the paying of cash dividends.

Dividends are paid from earnings. The payment reduces the firm's cash and retained earnings. These funds could be used to acquire more assets or to retire debt. If the new assets generated additional earnings, the firm would grow and be able to pay additional dividends in the future. Cash dividends and the retention of earnings are mutually exclusive. If the firm retains the earnings, its capacity to grow increases. If the firm distributes the earnings, it will have to obtain funds elsewhere to grow.

payout ratio
The ratio of dividends to
earnings

retention ratio
The ratio of earnings not
distributed to total earnings

Management may view dividend policy as the distribution of a certain proportion of the firm's earnings. This policy may be expressed in terms of a **payout ratio**, which is the proportion of the earnings that the firm distributes. Conversely, the **retention ratio** is the proportion of the earnings that are not paid out and are retained. The payout ratio and retention ratio are usually considered in annual terms even though dividends are often paid quarterly to avoid uneven seasonality dividend payments.

$$Payout\ Ratio = \frac{Dividends}{Earnings}\qquad\textbf{11-1}$$

$$Retention\ Ratio = 1 - Payout\ Ratio = \frac{Earnings - Dividends}{Earnings}\qquad\textbf{11-2}$$

For some firms, the payout ratio has remained relatively stable over time. Such consistency suggests that management views the dividend policy in terms of distributing a certain proportion of the firm's earnings to stockholders.

Note that when a firm reduces its dividend amount, the stock price gets hammered. Investors consider dividend reductions as a signal of poor financial health of the firm. Therefore, management is careful about when to increase the cash dividend even if earnings increase. The managers want to be certain that the higher level of earnings will be maintained to pay for a higher dividend. A decrease in earnings may not imply that the firm's capacity to pay the dividend has diminished. For example, an increase in noncash expenses, such as depreciation, reduces earnings but not cash, and the same applies to a write-down of the book value of an asset. In both cases, the firm's capacity to pay the dividend is not affected, because the expense does not affect cash flow. The firm then maintains the dividend payment to signal that the firm's financial condition has not deteriorated.

Excel Expert 11-1

Payout Ratio

Below are the annual earnings and dividends per share for Coca-Cola (KO). Notice that the earnings fluctuate from year to year. If dividends were set by a constant payout ratio, then they would fluctuate, too. However, the dividends appear quite stable in that they increase a few cents per share every year.

	A	B	C	D	E	F	G	H
1		Earnings	Dividends		Payout	Retention		
2		per share	per share		Ratio	Ratio		
3	2021	$ 2.04	$ 1.68		82%	18%	=C3/B3	=1-E3
4	2020	$ 1.80	$ 1.64		91%	9%		
5	2019	$ 2.09	$ 1.60		77%	23%		
6	2018	$ 1.51	$ 1.56		103%	-3%		
7	2017	$ 0.29	$ 1.48		510%	-410%		

Thus, it is no surprise that the payout ratio in column E fluctuates dramatically from year to year. In fact, to keep the dividend stable, Coca-Cola was willing to pay a higher dividend in 2017 and 2018 than they earned those years. Thus, their retention ratio was negative in those years.

This pattern is illustrated in **Excel Expert 11-1**. Coca-Cola maintained (and even increased) its dividend through a temporary decline in earnings. Such action is consistent with management's reluctance to reduce dividends.

While U.S. firms tend to follow a policy of quarterly dividend distributions, firms in other countries may not. Many foreign firms often make only two payments. The first payment may be called a "preliminary" dividend, and the second (made at the end of the firm's fiscal year) may be called a "final" dividend. For example, every year since 2013, AstraZeneca PLC, a British pharmaceuticals firm, has paid a $0.95 per share dividend in February and then distributed $0.45 per share in August.

Many foreign firms pay a cash dividend in their own currency, so the dollar amount tends to vary as the exchange rate varies. For example, if the value of the dollar falls relative to the euro, any dividends that are distributed in euros translate into more dollars when the euros are converted. The converse is also true. If the dollar value of the euro should fall, the dividend buys fewer dollars when the currency is converted.

Distribution of Dividends

The process by which dividends are distributed occurs over time. First, the firm's directors meet. When they declare a dividend, two important dates are established. The first date determines who is to receive the dividend. On the **date of record**, everyone who owns stock in the company at the end of that day receives the dividend.

If you purchase the stock after the date of record, you don't receive the dividend. The stock is traded **ex-dividend**, for the price of the stock does not include the dividend payment. This **ex-dividend date** is two trading days prior to the date of record, because the settlement date for a stock purchase is three working days after the transaction. This process is illustrated by the timeline in **Figure 11-1**.

date of record
The day on which an investor must own shares to receive the dividend payment

ex-dividend
Stock that trades exclusive of any dividend payment

ex-dividend date
The day on which a stock trades exclusive of any dividends

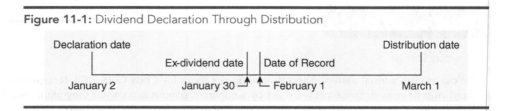

Figure 11-1: Dividend Declaration Through Distribution

In this example, the board of directors declares a dividend on January 2 to be paid March 1 to all stockholders of record on February 1. To receive the dividend, you must own the stock at the close of trading on February 1. To own the stock on February 1, the stock must have been purchased on or before January 29. If the stock is bought January 29, settlement will occur after three days on February 1 (assuming three workdays), so you own the stock on February 1. If you buy the stock on January 30, you don't own the stock on February 1 (the seller owns the stock) and can't be the owner of record on February 1. On January 30, the stock trades exclusive of the dividend (ex-dividend or "ex-div"), and the buyer does not receive the dividend.

The investor should realize that buying or selling stock on the ex-dividend date may not result in a windfall gain or a substantial loss. If a stock that pays a $1.00 dividend is worth $100 on the day before it goes ex-dividend, it cannot be worth $100 on the ex-dividend date. If it were worth $100 on both days, investors would purchase the stock for $100 the day before the ex-dividend date, sell it for $100 on the ex-dividend date, and collect the $1 dividend. Those predictable and easy quick profits simply don't exist in the stock market. If you could do this, the price would bid up and exceed $100 on the day preceding the ex-dividend date and would be less than $100 on the ex-dividend date as a result of the sales. Instead, what happens is that the stock price declines by the dividend amount on the ex-dividend day. Thus, the ex-dividend stock price would be $99 (= $100 − $1). Of course, because of general market fluctuation, the ex-dividend stock price change is not likely to exactly offset the dividend amount.

The second important date established when a dividend is declared is the day on which the dividend is paid, or the **distribution date**. The distribution date may be several weeks after the date of record, as the company must determine who the owners were as of the date of record and process the dividend checks. The company may not perform this task itself, but instead use the services of its commercial bank. The day that the dividend is received by the stockholder is thus likely to be many weeks after the board of directors announces the dividend payment. Many firms try to maintain consistency in their dividend payment dates for their shareholders.

distribution date
The date on which a dividend is paid to stockholders

Dividend Reinvestment Plans

Would you rather have additional shares of stock as the dividend instead of cash? Many corporations that pay cash dividends also have **dividend reinvestment plans** (DRIPs), in which the cash dividends are used to purchase additional shares of stock.

dividend reinvestment plan (DRIP)
A program that permits stockholders to have cash dividends reinvested in stock shares

There are two general types of corporate dividend reinvestment programs. In most plans, a bank acts on behalf of the corporation and its stockholders. The bank collects the cash dividends for the stockholders and in some plans offers the stockholders the option of making additional cash contributions. The bank pools all the funds and purchases the stock on the open market (i.e., in the secondary market). The bank does charge a fee for its service, but this fee is usually modest, and in some cases is paid by the firm. For example, if the commission is $10 per transaction and the amount of the dividend is $100, the commission as a percentage of the amount invested is 10%. If you get $500 in dividends, then the $10 fee only represents a 2% cost.

Excel Expert 11-2

DRIP Purchase

Consider that you own 200 shares of a company that offers a company-sponsored DRIP. The firm is paying a $0.60 dividend per share this quarter. The current price of the stock is $55 per share. How many shares do you purchase, and how much cash remains to be paid?

	A	B	C	D	E	F
1	Stock Price =	$ 55.00				
2	Dividend =	$ 0.60		Total Cash =	$ 120.00	=B3*B2
3	Number of Shares =	200		Shares Purchased =	2	=INT(E2/B1)
4				Remaining Cash =	$ 10.00	=E2-E3*B1

Note that a total of $120 in cash dividends is available. That buys two shares, with $10 left over. After this dividend and reinvestment, 202 shares are owned.

In the second type of reinvestment plan, the company issues new shares of stock for the cash dividend, and the money is directly rechanneled to the company. You may also have the option of making additional cash contributions. This type of plan offers you an additional advantage in that the brokerage fees are completely circumvented. The entire amount of the cash dividend is used to purchase shares, with the cost of issuing the new shares being paid by the company.

The Internal Revenue Service considers dividends that are reinvested to be no different from cash dividends that are received. Such dividends are subject to federal income taxation. The exclusion from federal income taxation of dividend income that is reinvested has been considered as one possible change in the tax code; however, as of 2021, reinvested dividends continued to be subject to federal income tax.

11-1c Stock Dividends

Some firms pay stock dividends in addition to or in lieu of cash dividends. Stock dividends are a form of recapitalization and do *not* affect the assets or liabilities of the firm. Since the assets and their management produce income for the firm, a stock dividend does not by itself increase the potential earning power of the company.

Since a stock dividend is only a recapitalization, the assets and the liabilities are not affected by the declaration and payment of the stock dividend. However, the entries in the equity section of the balance sheet are affected. The stock dividend transfers amounts from retained earnings to common stock and additional paid-in capital. The amount transferred depends on (1) the number of new shares issued through the stock dividend and (2) the market price of the stock.

Note that no funds (i.e., money) have been transferred. While there has been an increase in the number of shares outstanding, there has been no increase in cash and no increase in assets that may be used to earn profits. Thus, there is no change in the book value or market value of the firm. But now there are more shares outstanding representing those values.

For example, say that you owned 100 shares of a $20 stock, worth $2,000. The stock issues 10 dividend shares for each 100 shares owned. After the stock dividend

stock dividend
A dividend paid as stock instead of cash

recapitalization
A modification in a firm's sources of financing, such as the substitution of long-term debt for equity

dilution
A reduction in earnings per share due to the issuing of new securities

is distributed, you own 110 shares that are still worth $2,000. Thus, the price of the stock must fall from $20 to $18.18 (= $2,000 ÷ 110). The price of the stock declines because there are 10% more shares outstanding, but there has been no increase in the firm's assets and earning power. The old shares have been diluted, and hence the price of the stock must decline to indicate this **dilution**.

11-1d Stock Splits

stock split
Company proportionally changes the number of shares outstanding, which affects their par value, earnings per share, and price

After the price of a stock has risen substantially, management may decide to split the stock. The rationale for the **stock split** is that it lowers the price of the stock and makes it more accessible to investors. For example, Apple Inc. split its stock 2-for-1 on February 28, 2005. It split again 7-for-1 on June 9, 2014, and 4-for-1 on August 31, 2020. If the stock price were $150 per share, a 2-for-1 split would double everyone's shares and the price would be cut in half to $75. Firms sometimes believe that a lower price may bring the price per share into a range that should generate increased interest from current and new shareholders. Implicit in this reasoning are the beliefs that investors prefer lower-priced shares and that reducing the price of the stock benefits the current stockholders by widening the market for their stock.

Like the stock dividend, the stock split is a recapitalization. It does not affect the assets or liabilities of the firm, nor does it increase its earning power. The wealth of the stockholder is not immediately increased.

An easy way to find the price of the stock after the split is to multiply the stock's price before the split by the reciprocal of the terms of the split. For example, if a stock is selling for $54 per share and is split 3-for-2, then the price of the stock after the split will be $54 × $\frac{2}{3}$ = $36. Such price adjustments must occur because the old shares are diluted, and the earning capacity of the firm is not increased.

The most common split is 2-for-1, but splits such as 3-for-2 or 3-for-1 are not unusual. There is no obvious explanation for a particular set of terms other than that management wanted to reduce the stock's price to a particular level and selected the terms that would achieve the desired price.

There are also reverse splits, such as the 1-for-10 split executed by First Wave BioPharma Inc. in September of 2021. A reverse split reduces the number of shares and raises the price of the stock. The purpose of such a split is to add respectability to the stock (i.e., to raise the price above the penny stock level). Since many financial institutions, pension plans, and endowments cannot invest in stocks with low prices, the reverse split raises the price sufficiently to be considered for purchase by these potential buyers. A cynic might also suggest that the reverse split is designed to hide poor performance. First Wave's 1-for-10 split raised its $0.545 price to $5.45 per share. Unfortunately for the company and shareholders, its price continued to decline to less than $1.50 by the end of the year.

From the investor's point of view, there is little difference between a stock split and a stock dividend. In both cases, the stockholders receive additional shares, but their proportionate ownership in the firm is unaltered. In addition, the price of the stock adjusts for the dilution of per-share earnings caused by the new shares.

Regular stock splits were very common in the 1990s and 2000s. However, they may be becoming less common. Two trends influence stock splits. First, a couple of decades ago, you had to trade in round lots (units of 100 shares) in order to pay a lower commission rate. Now, however, you can trade single shares with no commissions. Thus, having a price in the range of $30 to $150 is not as important for attracting individual investors. The second trend is that it appears that a high share price may bring prestige to the firm. Near the end of 2021, Alphabet (Google) traded for just over $2,900 per share, Amazon for nearly $3,400 per share, and Berkshire Hathaway A shares for a whopping $450,000 per share.

The federal government taxes cash dividends. Does it also tax shares received in stock dividends and stock splits? There is no taxation of stock dividends and stock splits unless you sell the shares.

11-1e Stock Repurchases and Liquidations

A corporation with excess cash may choose to **repurchase** some of its outstanding stock. Such repurchases are often perceived as an alternative to paying cash dividends. Instead of distributing the money as cash dividends, the company offers to repurchase shares from its stockholders. If you don't want to sell the shares and pay any applicable capital gains taxes, you may retain your shares. If you prefer the money, you may sell the shares. The decision to sell rests with the stockholder, while the decision to distribute cash dividends is made by the firm's management.

repurchase
A company purchasing its own shares of stock

One argument that is often made for repurchasing in preference to distributing cash dividends is the decrease in the number of shares outstanding. The decrease in the number of shares increases earnings per share because the earnings are spread over fewer shares. The higher per-share earnings could, in turn, result in a higher stock price, especially if the PE ratio remains the same. Does a repurchase produce a higher stock price? That is hard to determine because repurchases often take months, if not years, to complete. During that time, the stock price is impacted by many market and firm specific factors.

While the cost of the repurchased shares reduces the firm's equity, the shares aren't retired but held by the company in the firm's "treasury" for future use. If the shares were retired and management subsequently wanted to issue the stock to employees or the public, the shares would have to be reregistered with the SEC in order to be publicly traded again.

Issuing shares to employees or selling the shares back to the public offsets the impact on earnings from the repurchases. Many companies use the repurchases to obtain shares to issue when employees exercise stock options. In this case, current stockholders may be worse off, since the proceeds the company receives when the options are exercised are less than what the company paid to repurchase the shares.

There are some dubious reasons for management to buy back shares:

- Management can repurchase shares to prop up the price of the stock. Such actions often result in the company paying an artificially higher price for the stock and depleting its cash position.
- Management can repurchase shares to reduce the chance of an unwanted takeover. If the firm has a large amount of cash, it may become the prey of another firm. The firm executing the takeover borrows the required cash from another source (such as a group of commercial banks), acquires the firm, and then uses the cash obtained through the takeover to retire the loan. If management believes it is threatened with a hostile takeover, then repurchasing the shares serves two purposes. The reduction in the cash reduces the possibility of the takeover, and the reduction in the number of outstanding shares increases management's proportionate ownership and strengthens its voting control over the firm.

Either of these reasons favors management at the stockholders' expense and may explain why the share buyback did not produce a higher stock price even though earnings per share increased.

liquidated
A company sells all its assets, pays creditors, and ceases operations

Occasionally a firm is **liquidated**. The final distribution of the firm's assets is sometimes called a *liquidating dividend.* This is a bit misleading because the distribution is not really a dividend. It is treated for tax purposes as a distribution of capital and is taxed at the appropriate capital gains tax rate. Thus, liquidating dividends are treated in the same manner as realized sales for federal income tax purposes.

A simple example illustrates how such a liquidating dividend works. A firm decides to liquidate and sells all its assets for cash. The stockholders then receive the cash. If the sales raise $25 per share, a stockholder receives $25 in cash for each share. The capital gain is then determined by subtracting the stockholder's cost basis of the share from the $25. If the stockholder paid $10 for the share, the capital gain would be $15. The stockholder then pays the appropriate capital gains tax. If the cost basis were $40, the investor would suffer a capital loss of $15, which may be used for tax purposes to offset other capital gains or income. In either case, this is no different than if the stockholder had sold the shares for $25. When a firm liquidates, the stockholder cannot postpone the capital gains tax.

11-2 Analysis of Financial Statements

ratio analysis
A method of gaining insight into a company's operation through examining its financial statements

Ratios may be the most frequently used tool to analyze a company. They are readily understood and can be computed with ease. In addition, the information used in **ratio analysis** is easy to obtain because financial ratios employ data available in a firm's annual and quarterly reports. Ratios are used not only by investors and financial analysts but also by a firm's management and its creditors. Management may use ratio analysis to plan, control, and identify weaknesses within the firm. Creditors use the analysis to establish the ability of the borrower to pay interest and retire debt. Stockholders are primarily concerned with performance and employ ratio analysis to measure profitability.

Although a variety of people use ratio analysis, they should select those ratios that are best suited to their specific purposes. A creditor is concerned primarily with the firm's ability to pay interest and repay principal and is less concerned with the rate at which the firm's equipment is used. While the rate at which fixed assets turn over may affect the ability of the company to pay the interest and principal, the typical creditor is more concerned with the firm's capacity to generate cash.

time-series analysis
An analysis of a firm over a period of time

cross-sectional analysis
An analysis of several firms in the same industry at one point in time

Ratios may be computed and interpreted from two perspectives. They may be compiled for a number of years to perceive trends, which is called **time-series analysis**, or may be compared at a given time to several main competing firms or the industry average, known as **cross-sectional analysis**. Time-series and cross-sectional analyses may be used together, as the analyst compares the firm to its industry over a period of years.

One ratio by itself means little, but several ratios together may give a clear picture of a firm's strengths and weaknesses. When they are taken as a group, the ratios often give an indication of the direction in which the firm is moving and its financial position in comparison to other firms in its industry.

The subsequent subsections cover a variety of financial ratios. The illustrations employ data from the balance sheets and income statements of Chloe's Coats (CCS). The balance sheet and income statements for 20X0 and 20X1 are given in **Tables 11-1** and **11-2**.

Table 11-1: CCS Balance Sheet (Thousands)

	20X1	20X0
ASSETS		
Current assets		
Cash and cash equivalents	$998.20	$1,081.60
Accounts receivable	399.50	390.00
Inventories	648.90	533.60
Total current assets	2,046.60	2,005.20
Property, plant, and equipment	1,559.70	1,437.70
Other assets	805.90	829.80
Total assets	$4,412.20	$4,272.70
LIABILITIES AND STOCKHOLDERS' EQUITY		
Current liabilities		
Accounts payable	$420.00	$410.70
Accrued liabilities	612.20	593.30
Short-term debt	141.60	294.80
Total current liabilities	1,173.80	1,298.80
Long-term debt	1,748.60	1,541.80
Other long-term liabilities	617.30	494.50
Total liabilities	$3,539.50	$3,335.10
Stockholders' equity		
Common stock	359.90	359.90
Additional paid-in capital	490.80	434.80
Retained earnings	4,699.60	4,374.70
Treasury stock repurchased at cost	(4,677.70)	(4,231.90)
Total stockholders' equity	872.60	937.60
Total liabilities and stockholders' equity	$4,412.20	$4,272.70

Before proceeding, you need to be forewarned that several ratios have more than one definition. The definition used by one analyst may differ from that used by others. These differences can arise from averaging the data. (See, for instance, the two approaches to inventory turnover discussed next.) Another source of differences can be what is included or excluded. (See, for instance, the various definitions of the debt ratios.)

11-2a Liquidity Ratios

Liquidity is the ease with which assets may be quickly converted into cash without the firm's incurring a loss. If a firm has a high degree of liquidity, it will be able to meet its debt obligations as they become due. Therefore, liquidity ratios are a useful tool for the firm's creditors, who are concerned with being paid.

Table 11-2: CCS Abbreviated Income Statement (Thousands Except Per-Share Data)

	20X1	20X0
Net sales	$6,080.80	$5,671.60
Costs and expenses		
Cost of goods sold	3,548.90	3,255.80
Selling, marketing, administrative	1,476.90	1,510.50
Earnings before interest and taxes (EBIT)	1,055.00	905.30
Interest expense	92.20	96.40
Income taxes	333.90	299.10
Net income	$628.90	$509.80
Net income per share	$2.85	$2.29

current ratio
A measure of liquidity:
current assets divided by
current liabilities

The Current Ratio

The **current ratio** is the ratio of current assets to current liabilities.

$$Current\ Ratio = \frac{Current\ assets}{Current\ liabilities} \qquad \text{11-3}$$

It indicates the extent to which the current liabilities, which must be paid within a year, are "covered" by current assets.

For most industries, it is desirable to have more current assets than current liabilities. It is sometimes asserted that a firm should have at least $2 in current assets for every $1 in current liabilities, or a current ratio of at least 2. If the current ratio is 2, then the firm's current assets could deteriorate in value by 50% and the firm would still be able to meet its short-term liabilities.

Although such rules of thumb are convenient, they need not apply to all industries. For example, electric utilities usually have current liabilities that exceed their current assets (i.e., a current ratio of less than 1). Does this worry short-term creditors? No, because the short-term assets are primarily accounts receivable from electricity users and are of high quality. Should a customer fail to pay an electricity bill, the company threatens to cut off service, and this threat is usually sufficient to induce payment. The higher the quality of the current assets (i.e., the greater the probability that these assets can be converted to cash at their stated value), the less vital it is for the current ratio to exceed 1. The reason for selecting a rule of thumb such as a current ratio of at least 2 is for the protection of the creditors, who are aware that not all current assets will be converted into cash.

Both creditors and equity investors want to know if the firm has sufficient liquid assets to meet its bills. Obviously, a low current ratio is undesirable because it indicates financial weakness, but a high current ratio may also be undesirable. A high current ratio may imply that the firm is not using its funds to best advantage. For example, the company may have issued long-term debt and used it to finance an excessive amount of inventory or accounts receivable. The high current ratio may also indicate that the firm is not taking advantage of available short-term financing or is mismanaging its current assets, which reduces its profitability. A high or low numerical value for the current ratio may be a signal to creditors and stockholders that the management of short-term assets and liabilities should be revised.

The Quick Ratio

The current ratio gives an indication of the company's ability to meet its current liabilities as they become due, but it has a major weakness. It is an aggregate measure of liquidity that does not differentiate between the degrees of liquidity of the various types of current assets, which may be in the form of cash, accounts receivable, or inventory. Cash is a liquid asset, but it may take many months before inventory is sold and turned into cash. This failure of the current ratio to distinguish between the degrees of liquidity has led to the development of the quick ratio, which omits inventory from the calculation. The **quick ratio (acid test)** (both names are used) is determined as either:

quick ratio (acid test)
A measure of liquidity:
current assets excluding
inventory divided by
current liabilities

$$Quick\ Ratio = \frac{Current\ assets\ -\ Inventory}{Current\ liabilities}$$

$$= \frac{Cash\ +\ Cash\ equivalents\ +\ Accounts\ Receivable}{Current\ liabilities} \qquad \text{11-4}$$

It might appear the two definitions are the same, but they are not if the firm has current assets other than cash, cash equivalents, accounts receivable, and inventory. This second definition excludes other current assets such as prepaid expenses, while the first definition doesn't.

A low quick ratio implies that the firm may have difficulty meeting its current liabilities as they become due if it must rely on converting inventory into cash. However, a low quick ratio doesn't indicate that the firm will fail to pay its bills. The ability to meet liabilities is influenced by such factors as:

- the rate at which cash flows into the firm,
- the time at which bills become due,
- the relationship between the company and its creditors and their willingness to roll over debt, and
- the firm's ability to raise additional capital.

The acid test merely indicates how well the current liabilities are covered by cash and by highly liquid assets that may be converted into cash relatively quickly. Because this ratio accounts for less liquid assets, it is a more precise measure of liquidity than is the current ratio.

11-2b Activity Ratios

Activity ratios indicate at what rate the firm is turning its inventory and accounts receivable into cash. The more rapidly the firm turns over its inventory and receivables, the

Excel Expert 11-3

Liquidity Ratios

Compute the liquidity ratios for Chloe's Coats (CCS).

	A	B	C	D	E	F	G	H
1		20X1		20X0	20X1		20X0	
2	ASSETS							
3	Current assets				Current Ratio			
4	Cash and cash equivalents	$998.20		$1,081.60	1.744		1.544	=D7/D13
5	Accounts receivable	399.50		390.00				
6	Inventories	648.90		533.60	Quick Ratio			
7	Total current assets	2,046.60		2,005.20	1.191		1.133	=(D7-D6)/D13
8	LIABILITIES AND STOCKHOLDERS' EQUITY				or			
9	Current liabilities				1.191		1.133	=(D4+D5)/D13
10	Accounts payable	$420.00		$410.70				
11	Accrued liabilities	612.20		593.30				
12	Short-term debt	141.60		294.80				
13	Total current liabilities	1,173.80		1,298.80				

Note the current ratio of 1.74 is below the desired 2. However, it did improve from the previous year. The quick ratio is greater than 1, so the firm has enough liquid assets to pay its liabilities.

more quickly it acquires cash. High turnover indicates that the firm is rapidly receiving cash and is in a better position to pay its liabilities as they become due. Such high turnover need not imply that the firm is maximizing profits. For example, high inventory turnover may indicate that the firm is selling items for too low a price to induce quicker sales but obtain a lower profit. A high receivables turnover may be an indication that the firm is offering large discounts for rapid payment, which could result in lower profits.

Inventory Turnover

inventory turnover
The speed with which inventory is sold

Inventory turnover is defined as annual sales divided by average inventory:

$$Inventory\ Turnover = \frac{Sales}{Average\ inventory}$$

$$or = \frac{Cost\ of\ goods\ sold}{Average\ inventory}$$ **11-5**

Inventory turnover may be defined as either the turnover of sales or the cost of goods sold. This second definition places more emphasis on recouping the cost of the goods. However, creditors may prefer to use sales, since sales produce the funds to service the debt.

This ratio uses average inventory throughout the year. Such an average reduces the impact of fluctuations in the level of inventory. If only year-end inventory was used and was abnormally high at the end of the fiscal year, the turnover would appear to be slower. Conversely, if inventory was lower than normal at the year's end, the turnover would appear faster than in fact it was. Averaging the inventory reduces the impact of these fluctuations. Management may use any number of observations (e.g., monthly or weekly) to determine the average inventory. The information available to investors may be limited to the level of inventory given in the firm's quarterly and annual reports.

average collection period
The number of days required to collect accounts receivable

days sales outstanding
The number of days required to collect accounts receivable

Days Sales Outstanding (Average Collection Period)

The **average collection period**, which is referred to as **days sales outstanding**, measures how long it takes a firm to collect its accounts receivable. The faster the company collects its receivables, the more rapidly it receives cash and can thus pay its obligations, such as its interest expense. The average collection period (ACP) is determined as follows:

$$Average\ Collection\ Period\ (ACP) = \frac{Receivables}{Sales\ per\ day}$$ **11-6**

Sales per day can be computed as the annual sales divided by 360. Note that 365 is also frequently used.

receivables turnover
The speed with which a firm collects its accounts receivable

Receivables turnover, which is another way of viewing the ACP, may be defined as annual credit sales divided by receivables. Some analysts may prefer to average the accounts receivable in the same way that inventory was averaged for the inventory turnover ratio:

$$Receivables\ Turnover = \frac{Annual\ credit\ sales}{Accounts\ receivables}$$ **11-7**

An alternative definition of receivables turnover substitutes annual sales for annual credit sales. Either definition is acceptable as long as it is applied consistently. Although management has access to the information used in both formulas, investors may be limited to the data provided by the firm. If annual credit sales aren't reported by the firm, the investor will have no choice but to use annual sales. The larger the ratio, the more rapidly the firm turns its credit sales into cash.

While days sales outstanding and receivables turnover may on the surface appear to have little interest for stockholders, that conclusion is incorrect. An increase in days sales outstanding (reduction in turnover) indicates that receivables are increasing relative to sales. The firm may be offering more generous credit terms to generate sales or being lax in collection policies. Even though these credit sales may be profitable, they don't generate cash until the receivables are collected. Thus, an increase in days sales outstanding may be a subtle flag that stockholders (and creditors) may interpret as problems that lie ahead!

Fixed-Asset Turnover

Inventory and accounts receivable turnover stress the speed with which current assets flow up the balance sheet. Rapid inventory turnover means inventory is quickly sold and converted into either cash or an account receivable. The ACP tells how long it takes the firm to collect the account (i.e., how long it takes to receive cash from a credit sale).

fixed-asset turnover
Ratio of sales to fixed assets, which tells how many fixed assets are needed to generate sales

Turnover ratios may also be constructed for long-term assets. Such a ratio is the **fixed-asset turnover**.

$$Fixed\text{-}Asset\ Turnover = \frac{Annual\ sales}{Fixed\ assets} \qquad \textbf{11-8}$$

Fixed assets are the firm's plant and equipment, and this ratio indicates the amount of plant and equipment that were used to generate the firm's sales.

Many firms, such as utilities, must have substantial investment in plant and equipment to produce the output they sell. Other firms, especially those providing services, need only modest amounts of fixed assets. Thus, the ratio is obviously sensitive to the firm's industry. Fixed-asset turnover is also hard to interpret. It is a measure of management's ability to efficiently use long-term assets, but a low numerical value isn't necessarily bad, and, conversely, a high value isn't necessarily good. With the passage of time, plant and equipment are depreciated. Their book value diminishes, which would increase the numerical value of the ratio. New investments in plant and equipment would decrease fixed-asset turnover. A low fixed-asset turnover may be indicative of increased investment in plant and equipment and not necessarily inefficient use of fixed assets. Thus, the analyst should consider changes in fixed-asset turnover over time and not the absolute value of the ratio.

Total Asset Turnover

Total asset turnover considers the firm's sales relative to all the assets:

total asset turnover
Ratio of sales to total assets, which tells the amount of sales generated by total assets

$$Total\ Asset\ Turnover = \frac{Annual\ sales}{Total\ assets} \qquad \textbf{11-9}$$

Like the other turnover ratios, total asset turnover (often referred to as the TAT ratio) tells the analyst the amount of sales generated from $1 of assets. However, since it aggregates the firm's total assets, it doesn't differentiate between current and long-term assets. Since it aggregates the assets, it can't indicate the source of any problem that may be identified by receivables, inventory, or fixed-asset turnover.

All the turnover ratios need to be interpreted with caution. These ratios are static, for they use information derived at a given time (i.e., the year-end figures on the balance sheet). The ratios, however, are dealing with dynamic events; they are concerned with the length of time it takes for an event to occur. Because of this problem with time, these turnover ratios, which are based on year-end figures, may be misleading if the firm has (1) seasonal sales, (2) sporadic sales during the fiscal year, or (3) any growth in inventory and sales during the fiscal year. Creditors and bondholders need to be aware of these potential problems since they can lead to incorrect conclusions concerning the firm's capacity to service its debt.

11-2c Profitability Ratios

The amount that a firm earns is particularly important to investors. Earnings accrue to stockholders and either are distributed to them as dividends or are retained. Retained earnings represent an additional investment in the corporation by stockholders. Obviously, a firm's performance is a crucial element in fundamental analysis.

Excel Expert 11-4

Activity Ratios

Compute the activity ratios for Chloe's Coats (CCS).

	A	B	C	D	E	F	G	H
1	**Income Statement**	**20X1**		**20X0**	**20X1**		**20X0**	
2	Net sales	$6,080.80		$5,671.60	Inventory turnover			
3	Cost of good sold	3,548.90		3,255.80	10.28			=B2/((B6+D6)/2)
4	**Balance Sheet**				6.00			=B3/((B6+D6)/2)
5	Accounts receivable	399.50		390.00	Average Collection Period			
6	Inventories	648.90		533.60	23.65		24.75	=D5/(D2/360)
7	Total current assets	2,046.60		2,005.20	Receivables Turnover			
8	Property, plant, and ec	1,559.70		1,437.70	15.22		14.54	=D2/D5
9	Other assets	805.90		829.80	Fixed Asset Turnover			
10	Total assets	$4,412.20		$4,272.70	3.90		3.94	=D2/D8
11					Total Asset Turnover			
12					1.38		1.33	=D2/D10

For inventory turnover, the inventory of the two years is averaged. Annual sales are about 10 times the level of inventory. Thus, inventory turns over 10.3 times a year or about every 35 days (five weeks). Note that the firm takes 24 days to convert its receivables into money. Annual sales are 15.2 times the amount of receivables. A receivables turnover of 15.2 times per year indicates that receivables are paid off on the average in less than a month. This is the same information that was derived by computing the ACP, since 23.7 days is approximately 15 times a year (= 360/23.7 = 15.2). CCS generated $3.90 in sales for every $1 invested in plant and equipment (i.e., fixed assets) and $1.38 for every $1 in total assets.

Profitability ratios are measures of performance that indicate the amount the firm is earning relative to some base, such as sales, assets, or equity. The **gross profit margin** is:

$$Gross\ Profit\ Margin = \frac{Sales\ -\ Cost\ of\ goods\ sold}{Sales}$$ **11-10**

The **operating profit margin** is operating income divided by sales:

$$Operating\ Profit\ Margin = \frac{Operating\ earnings}{Sales}$$ **11-11**

Operating income is often defined as earnings before interest and taxes (EBIT), and in most cases that is sufficient unless the firm has extraordinary or nonrecurring items included in EBIT. While management will report these items as a separate entry, they may be included in income before interest and taxes. If operating income does include nonrecurring items, it isn't indicative of operating income.

The **net profit margin** is the ratio of net income after taxes to sales. That is,

$$Net\ Profit\ Margin = \frac{Earnings\ after\ taxes}{Sales}$$ **11-12**

Although the computation of all three profit margin ratios may seem unnecessary, they tell the analyst different things about profitability. The gross profit margin is sensitive only to changes in the cost of goods sold. The operating profit margin is affected by all operating expenses. Changes in advertising or depreciation affect the operating but not the gross profit margin. By computing both ratios, the financial analyst can determine whether changes in the cost of goods sold or changes in other operating expenses are affecting operating income.

The net profit margin adds the impact of financing expenses and taxes on profitability. A change in income tax rates affects net profits but not operating profits. This impact may be important for stockholders who are concerned with the bottom line (net income) but not for bondholders whose interest is paid before income tax. Bondholders may be concerned with expenses that affect operating income but not those that affect net income.

Other profitability ratios measure the **return on assets** and the return on equity. The return on assets is net earnings divided by assets. That is,

$$Return\ on\ Assets = \frac{Earnings\ after\ taxes}{Total\ assets}$$ **11-13**

This ratio measures the return on the firm's resources (i.e., its assets). It is an all-encompassing measure of performance that indicates the total that management can achieve on all the firm's assets. This return on assets considers the profit margin and the

gross profit margin
Percentage earned on sales after deducting the cost of goods sold.

operating profit margin
Percentage earned on sales before adjusting for nonrecurring items, interest, and taxes

net profit margin
The ratio of earnings after interest and taxes to sales

return on assets
The ratio of earnings to total assets

rate at which the assets are turned over (e.g., the rate at which the firm sells its inventory and collects its accounts receivable) as well as taxes and extraordinary items.

Although return on assets gives an aggregate measure of the firm's performance, it doesn't tell how well management is performing for the stockholders. This performance is indicated by the **return on equity**. The return on equity uses earnings after taxes, which are the earnings available to the firm's stockholders.

return on equity
The ratio of earnings to equity

$$Return\ on\ Equity = \frac{Earnings\ after\ taxes}{Equity} \qquad \textbf{11-14}$$

Equity is the sum of stock, additional paid-in capital (if any), and retained earnings (if any). The return on equity measures the amount that the firm is earning on the stockholders' investment.

Many stockholders may be concerned not with the return on the firm's total equity but with the return earned on the equity attributable to the common stock. To determine this return on common stock, adjustments must be made for any preferred stock the firm has outstanding. First, the dividends that are paid to preferred stockholders must be subtracted from earnings to obtain earnings available to common stockholders. Second, the contribution of the preferred stock to the firm's equity must be subtracted to obtain the investment in the firm by the common stockholders. Thus, the return to common stockholders is

$$Return\ on\ Common\ Equity = \frac{Earnings\ after\ taxes - Preferred\ stock\ dividends}{Equity - Preferred\ stock} \qquad \textbf{11-15}$$

Of course, if the firm has no preferred stock, the return on equity and the return on the common equity are identical.

11-2d Leverage Ratios

How can a firm magnify the return on its stockholders' investment? One method is the use of **financial leverage**. By successfully using debt financing, management can increase the return to the owners: the common stockholders. The use of financial leverage may be measured by capitalization ratios, which indicate the extent to which the firm finances its assets by debt. These ratios are also referred to as **debt ratios**.

Because debt financing can have such impact on the firm, each of these ratios is extremely valuable in analyzing the financial position of the firm. The most used capitalization ratios are the **debt-to-equity ratio** and the **debt-to-total assets ratio**. These ratios are:

financial leverage
The use of borrowed funds to acquire an asset

debt ratio
The ratio of debt to total assets, which measures the use of debt financing

debt-to-equity ratio
The ratio of debt to equity that evaluates a company's financial leverage

debt-to-total assets ratio
The ratio of debt to total assets that measures the proportion of the firm financed with debt

$$Debt\ to\ Equity = \frac{Debt}{Equity} \qquad \textbf{11-16}$$

$$Debt\ to\ Total\ Assets = \frac{Debt}{Total\ assets} \qquad \textbf{11-17}$$

Excel Expert 11-5

Profitability Ratios

Compute the profitability ratios for Chloe's Coats (CCS).

	A	B	C	D	E	F	G	H
1		**20X1**		**20X0**	**20X1**		**20X0**	
2	**ASSETS**				**Gross Profit Margin**			
3	Total assets	$4,412.20		$4,272.70	41.6%		42.6%	=(D7-D8)/D7
4	**LIABILITIES AND STOCKHOLDERS' EQUITY**				**Operating Profit Margin**			
5	Total stockholders' equity	872.60		937.60	17.3%		16.0%	=D9/D7
6	**INCOME STATEMENT**				**Net Profit Margin**			
7	Net sales	$6,080.80		$5,671.60	10.3%		9.0%	=D10/D7
8	Cost of good sold	3,548.90		3,255.80	**Return on Assets**			
9	Earnings before interest and ta	1,055.00		905.30	14.3%		11.9%	=D10/D3
10	Net income	$628.90		$509.80	**Return on Equity**			
11					72.1%		54.4%	=D10/D5
12					**Return on Common Equity**			
13					72.1%		54.4%	=(D10-0)/(D5-0)

The gross profit margin for 20X1 was 41.6%, which indicates the firm earned $0.416 on every dollar of sales before considering administrative expenses, depreciation, and financing costs. The operating profit margin was 17.3%, which was up slightly from the year before. The net profit margin of 10.3% indicates that CCS earned $0.103 on every $1 of sales.

For CCS, the return on assets was 14.3%, which is an improvement from the prior year. The return on equity of 72.0% is exceptionally high. For this reason, it is desirable to compute the ratio over a period of time to establish a more accurate indication of the continuing return that management is able to earn for stockholders. Lastly, the return on common equity is the same as the return on equity because CCS has no preferred stock.

For CCS, the values for these ratios for 20X1 were 4.06 and 0.802, respectively. The debt-to-equity ratio indicates that there was $4.06 in debt for every $1 of stock. The ratio of debt-to-total assets indicates that debt was used to finance 80.2% of the firm's assets.

Since these ratios measure the same thing (i.e., the use of debt financing), you may wonder which is preferred. Actually, either is acceptable. The debt-to-equity ratio expresses debt in terms of equity, while the debt-to-total assets ratio gives the proportion of the firm's total assets that are financed by debt. Financial analysts or investors should choose the one for which they feel most comfortable.

These capitalization ratios are aggregate measures. They both use total debt and hence do not differentiate between short-term and long-term debt. The debt-to-equity ratio uses total equity and doesn't differentiate between the financing provided by preferred and common stock. The debt-to-total assets ratio uses total assets and thus doesn't differentiate between current and long-term assets.

The debt ratios measure the extent to which assets are financed by creditors. The smaller the proportion of total assets financed by creditors, the larger the decline in the value of assets that may occur without threatening the creditors' position. Capitalization ratios thus give an indication of financial risk. Firms that have a small amount of equity capital are considered to involve greater risk because there is less cushion to protect creditors if the value of the assets deteriorates. For example, the ratio of debt-to-total assets for CCS was 80.2%. This indicates that the value of the assets may decline by 19.8% (100% − 80.2%) before only enough assets remain to pay off the debt. If the debt ratio had been 60%, it would take a decline of 40% in the value of the assets to endanger the creditors' position.

Capitalization ratios indicate risk as much to investors as they do to creditors, because firms with a high degree of financial leverage are riskier investments. If the value of the assets declines or if the firm experiences declining sales and losses, the equity deteriorates more quickly for firms that use financial leverage than for those that don't use debt financing. Hence, the debt ratios are an important measure of risk for both investors and creditors.

That capitalization ratios differ among firms is illustrated in **Table 11-3**. The debt-to-total assets range is large. Berkshire Hathaway and Salesforce.com have used very little debt in their capitalization. At the other extreme, Amgen, Ford, and United Airlines use debt financing for over half their capital. In general, firms in industries that need large amounts of fixed assets, like for manufacturing, tend to use more debt.

Financial theory suggests that there is an optimal combination of debt and equity financing that maximizes the value of a firm. The optimal use of financial leverage benefits common stockholders by increasing the per-share earnings of the company and by permitting faster growth and larger dividends. If, however, the firm uses too much financial leverage, creditors will require a higher interest rate to compensate them for the higher risk. Investors will invest their funds in a corporation with a large amount of financial leverage only if the anticipated return is higher. Thus, the debt ratio, which measures the extent to which a firm uses financial leverage, is one of the most important ratios that managers, creditors, and you may calculate.

11-2e Coverage Ratios

Although leverage ratios measure the firm's use of debt financing, coverage ratios measure the ability of the firm to service its debt and preferred stock. For debt, the ratios indicate to creditors and bondholders how much the firm is earning from its operations

Table 11-3: Debt-to-Total Assets Ratio for Selected Firms, December 2021

Company	Debt-to-Total Assets Ratio	Company	Debt-to-Total Assets Ratio
Alcoa	17.1%	IBM	42.6%
Amazon	26.3%	Merck	41.3%
American Express	23.4%	Microsoft	20.3%
Amgen	52.4%	Netflix	41.5%
Apple	25.6%	Salesforce	9.5%
Berkshire Hathaway	7.9%	Tesla	25.5%
Caterpillar	47.5%	United Airlines	55.0%
Chevron	18.5%	Verizon	47.6%
Disney	28.3%	Visa	25.3%
Ford	61.0%	Walmart	25.1%

relative to what is owed. The coverage for interest payments is called **times interest earned**. Times interest earned is the ratio of earnings that are available to pay the interest (i.e., operating income) divided by the amount of interest:

$$\text{Times Interest Earned} = \frac{\textit{Earnings before interest and taxes}}{\textit{Annual interest expense}} \quad \textbf{11-18}$$

times interest earned
Ratio of EBIT divided by interest expense, which measures the safety of debt

A ratio of two indicates that the firm has $2 after meeting other expenses to pay $1 of interest charges. The larger the times interest earned ratio, the more likely it is that the firm will be able to meet its interest payments.

For CCS, times interest earned is $1,055.00 ÷ $92.20 = $11.44, which indicates the firm has operating income of $11.44 for every $1 of interest expense.

The ability to cover the interest expense is important, for failure to meet interest payments as they become due may throw the firm into bankruptcy. A decline in the times interest earned ratio indicates declining income relative to debt, or stable income but increased use of debt. It serves as an early warning to creditors and investors, as well as to management, of a deteriorating financial position and the increased probability of default on interest payments.

11-2f Analysis of Cash Flow

The previous sections have been devoted to the analysis of a firm's income statement and balance sheet, with emphasis placed on profitability and earnings available to the common stockholder. Because earnings may be affected by nonrecurring items or need not represent cash, many financial analysts place more emphasis on cash flow. The argument is that the cash flow generated by a firm's operations is a better indication of its profitability and value. Instead of isolating income, these analysts determine the capacity of the firm to generate cash and use this information for their valuation of the firm.

The increased emphasis on the generation of cash has led to the creation of the statement of cash flows. This statement determines changes in the firm's holding of cash and cash equivalents (i.e., short-term liquid assets, such as Treasury bills). The emphasis is not on income or the firm's assets and liabilities but on the inflows and outflows of cash from the firm's operations, investments, and financing decisions.

A simplified statement of cash flows for CCS is presented in **Table 11-4**. The statement is divided into three sections: (1) operating activities, (2) investment activities, and (3) financing activities. Each section enumerates the inflow and outflow of cash. The cash inflows are the following:

1. A decrease in an asset
2. An increase in a liability
3. An increase in equity

The cash outflows are the following:

1. An increase in an asset
2. A decrease in a liability
3. A decrease in equity

The statement of cash flows starts with a firm's earnings and works through various entries to determine the change in the firm's cash and cash equivalents. As is illustrated in **Table 11-4**, CCS starts with earnings of $628.9. Since earnings are not

Table 11-4: Simplified Statement of Cash Flows for Chloe's Coats for Year End

	20X1	
Net income	$628.90	
Depreciation	176.60	
Cash flow	805.50	
Changes in operating assets and liabilities		
Accounts receivable	(9.50)	Outflow
Inventories	(115.30)	Outflow
Accounts payable	9.30	Inflow
Accruals	18.90	Inflow
Net cash provided by (used by) operating activities	(96.60)	Net outflow
Investing activities		
Purchase of plant and equipment	(122.00)	Outflow
Other	23.90	Inflow
Net cash provided by (used by) investing activities	(98.10)	Net outflow
Financing activities		
Short-term borrowing	(153.20)	Outflow
Long-term borrowing	206.80	Inflow
Repurchases of stock	(445.80)	Outflow
Additional paid-in capital	56.00	Inflow
Dividends paid	(358.00)	Outflow
Net cash provided by (used by) financing activities	(694.20)	Net outflow
Cash at beginning of year	$1,081.60	
Cash at end of year	998.20	
Change in cash	(83.40)	

synonymous with cash, adjustments must be made to determine the change in cash. The first adjustment is to add back all noncash expenses and deduct noncash revenues. The most important of these adjustments is usually depreciation—the noncash expense that allocates the cost of plant and equipment over the period. Other noncash expenses may include depletion of raw materials and amortization of intangible assets such as goodwill. In this illustration, depreciation expense is $176.6, which is added to the firm's earnings.

The next set of entries refers to changes in the firm's current assets and liabilities resulting from operations. Some of these generate cash while others consume it. If accounts receivable increase, that means the firm experienced a net increase in credit sales. These credit sales do not generate cash until the receivables are collected. If the receivables had declined, the firm would have experienced an increase in collections, which would be a cash inflow. In 20X1, CCS's receivables increased by $9.5, which is an outflow.

An increase in inventory, like an increase in accounts receivable, is a cash outflow. More inventory is purchased than is sold, so there is a cash outflow. If the firm's inventory declines, it experiences a cash inflow. A reduction in inventory indicates that less inventory was purchased than was sold. This cash inflow would be added to determine cash generated by operations. During 20X1, inventory increased by $115.3, and this cash outflow is subtracted to determine cash generated by operations.

These effects on cash by changes in accounts receivable and inventory also apply to other current assets. An increase in a current asset, other than cash or cash equivalents, is a cash outflow, while a decrease is a cash inflow. For example, if the firm prepays an insurance policy or makes a lease or rent payment at the beginning of the month, these payments are cash outflows. However, they are also increases in the asset prepaid expense; thus, the increase in the asset represents a cash outflow.

In addition to changes in current assets, normal day-to-day operations will alter the firm's current liabilities. Wages will accrue and other trade accounts may rise. An increase in the firm's payables is a cash inflow, because the cash has not yet been paid. A decrease in payables results when the accounts are paid, thus becoming a cash outflow. CCS experienced an increase of $9.3 in accounts payable and other accrued expenses ($18.9).

The sum of all the adjustments to income and the changes in operating current assets and current liabilities is the net cash provided by operating activities. CCS experienced a net cash outflow from operations of $96.6 during 20X1.

After the adjustments to income and the changes in current assets and current liabilities from operations, the statement of cash flows considers cash generated by investment activities. The acquisition of plant and equipment requires a cash outflow, whereas the sale of plant and equipment generates cash (an inflow). Expanding firms often need additional investments in plant and equipment, which consume cash. A stagnating firm with excess capacity may sell plant and equipment, which generates cash. CCS purchased plant and equipment ($122.0), which is a cash outflow. The net effect of its investment decisions was a cash outflow of $98.1.

The third part of the statement of cash flows covers the firm's financing decisions. Financing activities can be for either the long or the short term. Issuing new debt produces a cash inflow, so an increase in short-term liabilities (such as a bank loan) or long-term liabilities (such as a bond) is a source of cash. A reduction in bank loans or outstanding bonds requires a cash outflow. Issuing new stock (an increase in equity) generates a cash inflow, while redeeming stock or paying cash dividends are cash outflows.

The cash inflows and outflows from CCS financing decisions include a decrease in short-term borrowing ($153.2) and an increase ($206.8) of long-term debt. The firm repurchased stock (an outflow of $445.8) and paid $358.0 in dividends.

The bottom line in the statement of cash flows indicates the firm's cash position at the end of the accounting period. If the sum of the cash inflows from operations, investments, and financing is positive, the firm experienced a cash inflow. If the sum is negative, the result is a cash outflow. For CCS, outflows exceeded inflows by $83.4, which decreased the cash and cash equivalents from $1,081.6 to $998.2.

What does the statement of cash flows add to the financial analyst's knowledge? By placing emphasis on inflows and outflows, the statement highlights where the firm generated cash and how the funds were used. While CCS generated cash flow ($805.5), it was used to buy plant and equipment, pay cash dividends, and repurchase stock. These outflows exceeded the cash inflows, so the net effect was to reduce the firm's cash position.

11-3 Stock Valuation

Fundamental analysis and valuation follow a logical process from the general to the specific. The valuation of a stock starts with the economic environment, including estimates of economic growth, employment, inflation, and the geopolitical environment in which firms operate (Chapter 10). You should then proceed to more specific questions, such as regulatory issues and the impact of government policy and intervention. The incursion of government is not limited to regulation, since subsidies and tax policy are often designed to stimulate demand for specific products, such as more fuel-efficient cars. Public policy often shifts the demand and supply for specific goods and services and may also affect pricing and funds that firms divert to investments in specific products and services.

fundamental analysis
A method of determining a stock's current value.

After considering the macroeconomy and regulatory environment, you should move to the various sectors of the economy. Sectors are broad divisions of the economy, such as energy or technology or health. The economic impact on the various sectors will differ. Firms classified as producing consumer staples (e.g., Coca-Cola) may be less affected by the economic environment than firms producing consumer discretionary products (e.g., Ford). Sectors are subdivided into industries. For example, "health" includes pharmaceuticals, health providers such as hospitals, and producers of medical devices. "Energy" encompasses oil and natural gas drillers, refiners, distributors, and retailers. Within each industry, you need to be aware of the degree of competition, cost structures, the pricing environment, and anticipated growth. Such background is necessary prior to analyzing an individual firm.

After considering the macroeconomy, the sector, and the industry, you can progress to consider specific firms. The product mix, management, sources of funds, measures of performance such as return on assets and equity, and the capacity to generate cash are all part of the process of valuing a company. Ultimately, your purpose is to determine if the firm's securities (i.e., its stocks and bonds) are undervalued and should be purchased for inclusion in an individual's or investment company's portfolio. That valuation process constitutes the remainder of this chapter.

11-3a Investor Expected Return

Investors purchase stock with the anticipation of a total return consisting of a dividend yield and a capital gain. The dividend yield is the flow of dividend income paid by the stock. The capital gain is the increase in the value of the stock that is related to the growth in earnings. If the firm can achieve growth in earnings, then dividends can be increased, and over time the shares should grow in value.

The expected return on an investment, which was discussed in Chapter 5 and expressed algebraically in **Equation 5-6**, is reproduced here:

$$E(r) = \frac{E(D_1)}{P_0} + E(g)$$

The expected return, $E(r)$, is the sum of the dividend yield, which is the expected dividend $E(D_1)$ divided by the price of the stock (P_0) plus the expected growth rate $E(g)$. If a firm's $0.93 dividend is expected to grow at 7% to $1.00 and the price of the stock is $25, the anticipated annual return on an investment in the stock is

$$E(r) = \frac{\$1}{\$25} + 0.07 = 11\%$$

For an investment to be attractive, the expected return must be equal to or exceed your required return. If you require an 11% return on investments in common stock of comparable risk, then this stock meets your requirement. If, however, your required rate of return is greater than 11%, the anticipated yield on this stock is inferior, so you will not purchase the shares. Conversely, if the required rate of return on comparable investments in common stock is 10%, this stock is an excellent purchase because the anticipated return exceeds the required rate of return.

In a world of no-commission fees and in which the tax on dividends is the same as on capital gains, investors would be indifferent to the composition of their return. If you're seeking an 11% return, you should be willing to accept a dividend yield of zero if the capital gain is 11%. Conversely, a capital growth rate of zero should be acceptable if the dividend yield is 11%. Of course, any combination of growth rate and dividend yield with an 11% return should be acceptable.

However, because of commissions and taxes, you may be concerned with the composition of the return. To realize the growth in the value of the shares, you must sell the security and pay commissions. This cost suggests a preference for dividend yield. In addition, capital gains occur in the future and may be less certain than the flow of current dividends. The uncertainty of future capital gains versus the likelihood of current dividends also favors dividends over capital appreciation.

Are capital gains and dividends treated the same for tax purposes? Generally, the answer is no. But tax laws are always changing. The Tax Cuts and Jobs Act (TCJA) included sweeping changes to the tax laws in 2018, affecting both the tax rates and the brackets they apply to for ordinary personal income (including capital gains). The tax rate on long-term capital gains (investment held longer than one year), remained at the 0, 15, or 20% levels depending on your income bracket. Short-term capital gains (investment held less than a year) and dividends are treated as ordinary income.

Regardless of whether tax rates on dividends and capital gains are equivalent or not, there remains a tax argument favoring long-term capital gains. The tax on capital gains may be deferred until the gains are realized, while the tax on dividends cannot be deferred. (Because the federal income tax laws change frequently, you need to keep abreast of tax regulations and reconsider their impact on the composition of your portfolio.)

11-3b Stock Valuation: The Present Value of Dividends

Value investing focuses on what an asset is worth—its intrinsic value. Discounted cash flow methods value a stock by determining the present value of future cash inflows (e.g., dividends) using the appropriate discount factor. The discount factor is the required return, which is the return you demand to justify purchasing the stock. This return includes what you may earn on a risk-free security (e.g., a Treasury bill) plus a risk premium for bearing the risk associated with investments in common stock (Chapter 7).

Future cash inflows are discounted back to the present at the required rate of return. The resulting valuation (P_0) is then compared with the stock's current price to determine its attractiveness:

- P_0 < price, overvalued
- P_0 = price, fairly valued
- P_0 > price, undervalued

While this interpretation is straightforward, finding the value of a stock can be complicated. Value is the present value of the expected cash flows. What are the cash flows? The cash flows are dividends and sometimes an estimate of a future price. Note that dividends often change over time. Also, how far into the future should the analysis go? The following scenarios capture all the cases you might imagine.

Same Dividend, Infinite Time Period

The first case is a stock that pays a fixed dividend of $1 that is not expected to change. That is, the anticipated cash inflow is

Year	1	2	3	4	...	∞
Dividend	$1	$1	$1	$1	...	$1

The current value (P_0) of this indefinite flow of payments (i.e., the dividend, D) depends on the discount rate (i.e., the investor's required rate of return). This discounting process is expressed in the following equation:

$$P_0 = \frac{D}{(1+r)^1} + \frac{D}{(1+r)^2} + \frac{D}{(1+r)^3} + \cdots + \frac{D}{(1+r)^\infty}$$

Note that this implies an infinite number of computations. That would take a long time. However, if the required return is positive ($r > 0$), then the present value of those dividends far into the future will become very small. Thus, we are adding smaller and smaller numbers that eventually approach zero as the time approaches infinity. Mathematicians have solved this problem as one version of a power series. Fortunately, the complex equation collapses to the simple equation for the same dividend discounted with a positive interest rate over an infinite number of years, called the **perpetuity model**:

perpetuity model
A dividend discount model in which all future dividends are the same

$$P_0 = \frac{D}{r}$$ **11-19**

Chapter 12 illustrates some cases (e.g., preferred stock) in which this equation is appropriate.

Constant Growing Dividend, Infinite Time Period

Companies that pay dividends typically try to grow those dividends over time, as discussed in the first sections of this chapter. Thus, it is likely that each (annual) dividend in the future might be different. The exercise of discounting these dividends is illustrated in this equation.

$$P_0 = \frac{D_1}{(1+r)^1} + \frac{D_2}{(1+r)^2} + \frac{D_3}{(1+r)^3} + \cdots + \frac{D_\infty}{(1+r)^\infty}$$

Again, this implies an infinite number of computations. However, there is a simple equation that can find the value for you if you can determine how the dividends change each year. Specifically, if the dividends grow at a constant growth rate and that growth rate is smaller than the discount rate ($g < r$), then another power series helps reduce the equation to the **constant growth model**:

constant growth model
A valuation model that uses constant growing dividends and discounts them to the present

$$P_0 = \frac{D_1}{r-g} = \frac{D_0 \times (1+g)}{r-g}$$ **11-20**

There are two forms of the equation. The first shows that the year 1 dividend is divided by the difference between the required return and the growth rate. The second form shows the year 1 dividend being replaced by the current dividend that is multiplied by one plus the growth rate. Note that the future time value of money equation shows $D_1 = D_0 \times (1 + g)$. That is, the year 1 dividend is simply the year 0 dividend that grew one year at the growth rate. So, the two forms of the equation are equal.

This model is useful for valuing mature companies that have settled into a constant rate of growth. In addition, later models require a future value, like a predicted future price. The constant growth model is one method for estimating that future value.

Finite Time Periods

Making the assumption that a company will have a constant growth rate forever may be too limiting for many stocks. These common examples do not fit the assumptions of the previous models:

- Young, fast-growing company
- Firm not paying a dividend now, but is expected to pay one later
- Company using a constant earnings payout ratio dividend policy
- Company in decline

Excel Expert 11-6

Perpetuity and Constant Growth Models

Consider a company that paid a $2.50 per share dividend. Your required return is 10.5%. If the company's dividend is expected to grow at 0% per year, what is the value of the stock? What if the growth rate were 5%, 9%, or 12%?

	A	B	C	D	E	F	G
1	Current Dividend	Required Rate	Growth Rate	Dividend:	Year 1	Year 2	
2	$2.50	10.50%	0%		$2.50	$2.50	
3			5%		$2.63	$2.76	=$A$2*(1+C3)^2
4			9%		$2.73	$2.97	
5			12%		$2.80	$3.14	=$A$2*(1+C5)^2
6							
7		Value with g =	0%	=	$23.81	=A2/B2	
8		Value with g =	5%	=	$47.73	=$A$2*(1+C8)/($B$2-C8)	
9		Value with g =	9%	=	$181.67	=$A$2*(1+C9)/($B$2-C9)	
10		Value with g =	12%	=	($186.7)	=$A$2*(1+C10)/($B$2-C10)	

Although you don't need to estimate any future dividends when using these models, you will in other models. Thus, future dividends at each potential growth rate are shown in columns E and F. The 0% growth rate case is solved as a value of $23.81 in cell E7 using the perpetuity model. A 5% growth rate requires the use of the constant growth model, and its value is $47.73. The value of the 9% growth rate is $181.67. Notice that higher growth rates lead to higher valuations! Lastly, the constant growth model seems to have failed for the 12% growth case. Why? The reason is that the growth rate is larger than the required rate, which violates an important condition for the model. You can't use the constant growth model for the 12% growth case when the required rate is only 10.5%.

In addition, experienced investors know that making predictions longer than five years can be very precarious. Thus, a five-year holding period is common for fundamental analysis. The general form of the **dividend discount model** for a finite period of n years is:

dividend discount model
A valuation model that discounts future cash flows to the present

$$P_0 = \frac{D_1}{(1+r)^1} + \frac{D_2}{(1+r)^2} + \frac{D_3}{(1+r)^3} + \cdots + \frac{D_n}{(1+r)^n} + \frac{P_n}{(1+r)^n} \quad \textbf{11-21}$$

This model allows for varying dividends over the period. In the past year (n), there are two cash flows, the dividend, and the price you estimate for selling the stock. Note that you don't have to actually sell the stock in n years, you just need an ending (or sometimes called a terminal) value for the analysis. To use this model to estimate the value of a stock, you will need the following:

- Required rate
- Holding period
- Method for estimating the future dividends
- Method for estimating the year n price

The required return for a given level of risk is the topic of Chapters 7 and 8. The length of the holding period is your personal choice.

There are several ways to estimate future dividends. One method is to *project the recent trend* of the company's dividends. For example, **Excel Expert 11-1** shows the Coca Cola's dividend was $1.68 per share last year. It also shows that the dividend was increased by 4 cents per share in each of the past three years. Thus, it would be a reasonable estimate to predict the next five years of dividends to be $1.72, $1.76, $1.80, $1.84, and $1.88. Another method is to compute the past five years of dividend growth rate to use for predicting the next five years. For Coke, the 2016 dividend was $1.40. Thus, the annualized five-year growth rate for the dividend to grow from $1.40 to $1.68 was 3.7%. (Solve for the interest rate when PV = −1.40, PMT = 0, FV = 1.68, and N = 5.) Growing the current $1.68 dividend by 3.7% each year yields dividends during the next five years of $1.74 (= $1.68 × (1 + 0.037)), $1.81, $1.87, $1.94, and $2.01. Note that these estimates are much different than simply projecting a 4-cent increase.

Future Price

PE model
A model to estimate a future price using the future PE ratio, earnings, and growth

price target
An analysts' estimate of the future stock price

To complete the dividend discount model, you need the stock price in the future. There are two main methods for estimating the future price: the constant growth model estimated in the future year and the **PE model**. In addition to estimating a future price for the dividend discount model, securities analysts also use them to provide a **price target**.

Earlier, the constant growth model equation (11-20) was used to estimate today's value of a stock using today's dividend and a growth rate for the future. However, you could also use the same equation to estimate the stock value in year n using the dividend in year n and a growth rate. This method works well for companies that don't have a constant growth rate now but may be expected to in the future. For example, a young company may be growing too fast to assume that rate far into the future. These companies tend to experience slower growth as they get larger and their industry matures. You could estimate dividends each year until the mature growth rate starts and then estimate the future price at that year. The generic form of the constant growth rate equation is:

$$P_n = \frac{D_{n+1}}{r - g} = \frac{D_n \times (1 + g)}{r - g} \qquad \textbf{11-22}$$

An illustration of using the constant growth model in the dividend discount model to estimate future price is shown in **Figure 11-2**.

Then consider the price-to-earnings (PE) ratio, which is the price per share of the stock divided by the earnings per share. This is an important ratio in the investment industry and will be discussed further later in the chapter. In the context of a stock's price, the PE ratio is often referred to as the **PE multiple** because it is multiplied by earnings to compute stock price. That is, the price is set as a multiple of the earnings. So, if you knew the PE multiple of a stock five years from now and knew the company earnings, you could compute the stock's price. The PE model is:

PE multiple
The PE ratio used for valuing a company

$$P_n = \left(\frac{P}{E}\right)_n \times E_n = \left(\frac{P}{E}\right)_n \times (1 + g)^n \times E_0 \qquad \textbf{11-23}$$

The equation shows that the PE multiple n years from now is multiplied by the earnings per share n years from now to obtain the price n years from now. The earnings in the future are stated as the current earnings (E_0) that grew at the growth rate, g.

One difficulty with using the PE model is that the PE multiple is not constant over time for the stock market itself, and certainly not for individual companies. For individual companies, the PE ratio can be very volatile from year to year because earnings can fluctuate. For example, **Table 11-5** shows the PE ratios for various firms. United Airlines is missing because it had negative earnings that year. Some have absurdly high

Figure 11-2: Constant Growth Model in Year n

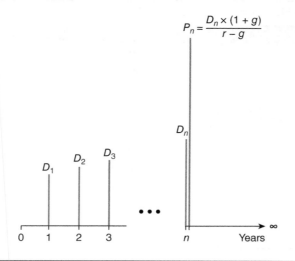

PE ratios because the stock prices were very high in spite of very low earnings (Disney, Salesforce, and Tesla). As a comparison, note that during this time, the S&P 500 Index PE ratio was 28.9, which was down from 39.9 the previous year.

Another difficulty is that the growth rate used in the PE model is the growth of earnings. Previously, the growth rate of dividends was used. Theoretically, they should be the same in the long run. But they can be quite different in the short run. Financial analysts report their estimated growth for the firms they follow. You can find them on Yahoo! Finance. After finding your company on the website, click the "Analysis" link on the menu. At the bottom of the page, Yahoo! reports the average next year and next five years' growth reported by the analysts. **Table 11-6** shows the next five years (per annum) for various firms.

Some of these estimates seem reasonable, like the earnings growth of Apple, Merck, and Microsoft being about 16% per year. The decline in Chevron earnings is likely more about the price of oil than their managers' ability to run the company. The United Airlines large negative number seems odd until you realize that its earnings were negative. Thus, a -129% change would make the earnings positive again.

Table 11-5: PE Ratios for Selected Companies

Company	PE Ratio	Company	PE Ratio
Alcoa	13.8	IBM	25.1
Amazon	66.9	Merck	27.0
American Express	17.2	Microsoft	38.2
Amgen	23.3	Netflix	55.0
Apple	32.0	Salesforce	140.7
Berkshire Hathaway	8.0	Tesla	357.2
Caterpillar	22.1	United Airlines	-
Chevron	23.0	Verizon	9.9
Disney	141.9	Visa	38.8
Ford	29.2	Walmart	50.3

Source: Yahoo! Finance, December 2021

Table 11-6: Next Five Years (Per Annum) for Selected Companies

Company	Growth	Company	Growth
Alcoa	199.7%	IBM	6.9%
Amazon	36.0%	Merck	15.3%
American Express	43.3%	Microsoft	16.5%
Amgen	5.9%	Netflix	42.6%
Apple	15.7%	Salesforce	10.0%
Berkshire Hathaway	−14.5%	Tesla	73.1%
Caterpillar	32.2%	United Airlines	−129.1%
Chevron	−4.9%	Verizon	3.8%
Disney	37.8%	Visa	17.7%
Ford	77.7%	Walmart	8.1%

Source: Yahoo! Finance, December 2021

Excel Expert 11-7 illustrates the valuation of a **multi-growth firm**. After the initial period of faster growth, the firm matures and is expected to grow more slowly. Note that to estimate the firm's value, you divide the flow of dividends into two stages: a period of high growth (years one through five) and a period of normal growth (from the end of year five and on). This strategy for valuing a firm is useful for many cases you may see. For example, the first and second stages could be as follows:

multi-growth firm
A firm that experiences periods of different growth rates

- Fast-growing dividends followed by normal dividend growth
- Constant dividends followed by normal dividend growth
- Negative dividend growth followed by normal dividend growth
- Zero dividends followed by dividend initiation with normal growth

Analyst Forecasts

Many investors turn to securities analysts to see what they forecast for firms of interest. As illustrated by **Excel Expert 11-7**, using different valuation models can lead to different valuations. Because of this, securities analysts often offer a range of values instead of one unique value. Also, there may be a large range among analysts.

It is important to understand that securities analysts tend to be divided into two groups. These two types of analysts have different roles, and thus different incentives.

Excel Expert 11-7 ⟩⟩

Dividend Discount Models

Consider a company that paid a $2.50 per share dividend. Your required return is 10.5%. The company's dividend is expected to grow at 8% per year for five years. What is the value of the stock using two methods for estimating price in five years?

(1) After the first five years, the growth rate slows to 5% indefinitely.
(2) The earnings per share was $4 and is expected to grow by 8% for five years. The current PE ratio is 15 and is expected to be 10% lower in five years.

	A	B	C	D	E	F	G	H	I	J	K
1	Current Dividend	Required Rate	Growth Rate	Dividend:	Year 1	Year 2	Year 3	Year 4	Year 5		
2	$2.50	10.50%	8%		$2.70	$2.92	$3.15	$3.40	$3.67	=H2*(1+$C$2)	
3			5%								
4					Using Constant Growth Model						
5	EPS	PE Ratio	PE Change					Future Price =	$70.13	=I2*(1+C3)/(B2-C3)	
6	$4.00	15	-10%	Cash flow =	$2.70	$2.92	$3.15	$3.40	$73.80	=I2+I5	
7								Value =	$54.24	=NPV(B2,E6:I6)	
8					Using PE Model						
9								Future Price =	$79.34	=B6*(1+C6)*((1+C2)^5)*A6	
10				Cash flow =	$2.70	$2.92	$3.15	$3.40	$83.02	=I2+I9	
11								Value =	$59.84	=NPV(B2,E10:I10)	

The first five dividends are estimated using the 8% growth rate. For the constant growth model, the price at year five, $70.13, is estimated using a 5% growth rate into the future. The next step is to add the year five dividend and the year five price. You can do that because they occur in the same year. The present value of the five dividends and future price estimates that the current value of the stock is $54.24. For the PE model, the year five price, $79.34, is estimated using the PE ratio that declined 10%, the current earnings of $4, and the 8% growth rate. The present value of these cash flows show the stock value to be $59.84.

The purpose of this exercise is to determine whether this stock is under- or overvalued. For that, we need a current stock price. Since the current EPS is $4 and the PE ratio is 15, the price must be $60 (= $4 × 15). Thus, the constant growth model technique suggests the stock is overvalued ($54.24 < $60), while the PE model technique suggest the stock is fairly valued ($59.84 ≈ $60).

sell-side analyst
A person who communicates to the public about their stock recommendations and forecasts

Sell-side analysts work for investment banks and brokerage firms. Their purpose is to generate interest in stocks that leads to trading through their employer. This type of analyst is commonly seen on CNN and other business outlets, and their forecasts are reported publicly. They commonly report a price target, earnings estimates, growth estimates, and a recommendation as to whether to buy, sell, or hold. The typical sell-side analyst focuses on one or two industries to become an expert in those firms. Sell-side analysts have been criticized as a group for having a positive bias. The criticisms come because they work for investment banks, who have a business relationship with the companies being examined. Because of that business relationship, the analysts will often stop providing forecasts rather than recommend a "sell" type rating. The Sarbanes–Oxley Act of 2002 attempted to eliminate the incentives for biased analyst recommendations, which has helped but not solved the problem.

buy-side analyst
A person who gives buy/sell advice and forecasts to the institutional firms for which they work

The **buy-side analyst** works for an institutional investor, like a mutual fund, hedge fund, or pension fund. The forecasts of this type of analyst are private recommendations to the fund about what they should buy, sell, or hold. You will not see their recommendations. Therefore, all the analyst forecasts publicly reported are from sell-side analysts.

Yahoo! Finance reports the aggregate sell-side analyst forecasts for earnings, growth, price targets, buy recommendations, and more. **Exhibit 11-1** shows the buy

Exhibit 11-1: Analyst Recommendations for Netflix, December 2021

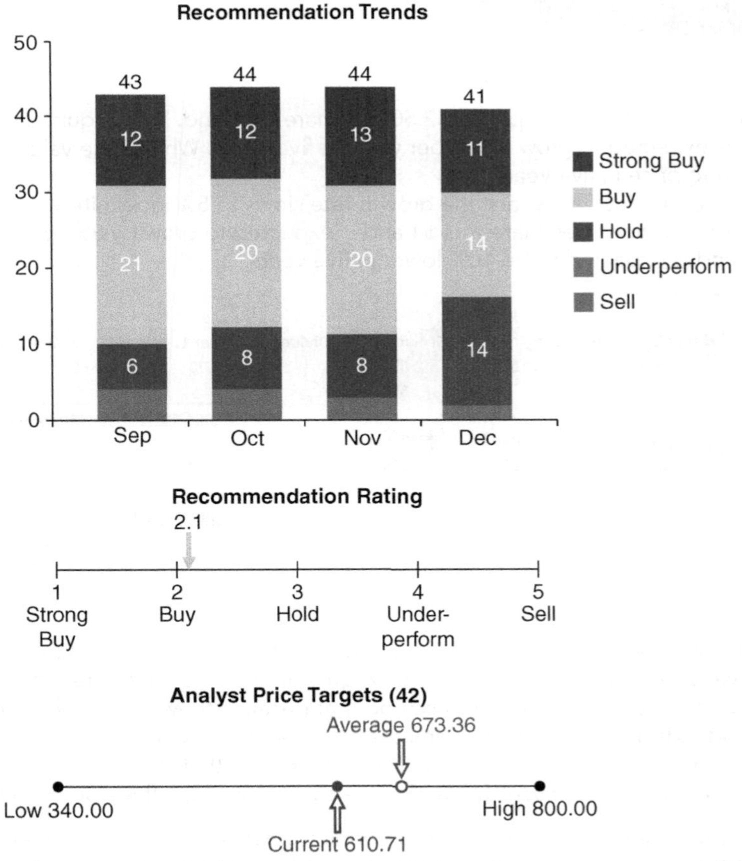

Source: Yahoo! Finance

recommendations and price target for Netflix in December 2021. The buy recommendation chart is delineated into Strong Buy, Buy, Hold, Underperform, and Sell. Not all analysts use this lexicon. Some use variations on Overweight, Market Weight, and Underweight. Note that between September and December, the positive recommendation for Netflix seems to be diminished. In addition, three analysts have dropped out. This is an example of them preferring to not report forecasts at all if those forecasts are not positive. This causes the average recommendation of analysts to be positive.

The recommendations are presumably the results of estimating the company's value and comparing it to the current price. As a part of that process, a future price, or price target, is estimated and reported. The exhibit shows that the price target range from the 42 analysts is quite wide, $340 to $800. The average of $673.36 is higher than the current price of $610.71.

11-4 Price Multiple Analysis

Dividend discount models are theoretically sound. However, they can be challenging to implement because of the many parameters that must be included. Many of those parameters, like future growth, appropriate discount rate, future PE multiple, dividend forecast, etc., are educated guesses at best. As a result, relative valuation assessments that compare a firm's stock price to its various profitability or value measures are common. Many of these use financial statement data. The PE ratio was mentioned earlier in the chapter and is the most common price multiple.

11-4a Price Multiples

PE Ratios

An alternative approach to discounted cash flow analysis is to use financial statements and develop price multipliers to assess a stock's relative value to other stocks. As mentioned earlier, one of the most common measures is the ratio of a stock's price-to-earnings per share, commonly referred to as the **PE ratio**. Unless otherwise stated, the earnings are measured from the past 12 months. The value of a stock is the product of the earnings per share and the PE multiple.

PE ratio
The ratio of stock price to the earnings per share

The PE multiple is a relative measure of value in the sense that it is typically compared to that company's historical multiple and the multiples of other firms in the same industry. For example, the current PE ratio for Coca-Cola is 29.04, while PepsiCo's PE ratio is 29.45. Thus, the two companies seem fairly valued compared to each other. Shoe and clothes maker, Nike, has a PE ratio of 44.44. That may seem overvalued compared to publicly traded competitors Adidas (23.98), Under Armour (19.08), and V.F. Corporation (23.35).

There are two other popular forms of the PE ratio. Note that discounted cash flow analysis is forward looking. That is, it is a valuation based on expectations for the future. A future expectations PE ratio is also popular. The **forward PE ratio** is the current price divided by the expected earnings in the next 12 months.

forward PE ratio
The ratio of stock price to the next 12 months of earnings per share

One criticism of the PE ratio is that earnings per share can be a volatile measure. A firm may have stable earnings for a couple of years and then, due to accounting write-offs, have a year of negative earnings. In order to provide a more stable measure, Nobel laureate Robert Shiller popularized a ratio in which earnings are averaged over the past 10 years. Because of the long period, the price and earnings are adjusted for inflation. This ratio is

Shiller PE ratio
A version of the PE ratio that uses ten years of earnings adjusted for inflation

usually referred to as the **Shiller PE ratio** or the CAPE ratio (cyclically adjusted price to earning):

$$Shiller\ PE\ Ratio = \frac{Share\ Price}{10\text{-}year\ average\ of\ inflation\ adjusted\ earnings} \qquad \textbf{11-24}$$

The Shiller PE ratio is generally applied to the stock market itself via major indexes like the S&P 500 Index to assess whether it is undervalued or overvalued from a historical context. You can obtain the Shiller PE ratio data at Shiller's Yale University website (http://www.econ.yale.edu/~shiller/data.htm). **Figure 11-3** graphs the monthly data from 2000 to 2021. The average for this sample is 26.6. The average since 1980 is 22.7 and since 1950 is 19.9. Note that the majority of the 2000s has been higher than the long-term and medium-term averages, indicated the market has been highly valued. The Shiller PE ratio in 2000 appears overvalued. That was followed by a steep market decline. The low for the period comes in 2008/2009 during the credit crisis. The market became relatively undervalued during the crisis. The COVID-19 pandemic decline in March of 2020 was so short that it appears as a small blip in the figure.

price-to-cash flow ratio
A measure of relative value that divides the price by the cash flow per share

Price-to-Cash Flow

An alternative to using earnings is to use cash flow as measured by the **price-to-cash flow ratio**. For growing firms, the ability to generate cash may be initially as important as earnings, since generating cash implies the firm is able to grow without requiring

Figure 11-3: Shiller PE Ratio, 2000 to 2021

Data Source: Robert Shiller's website at Yale University, http://www.econ.yale.edu/~shiller/data.htm

external financing. After the initial period of operating at a loss but producing positive cash flow, the firm may grow into a prosperous and profitable operation.

The valuation process using cash flow is essentially the same as is used with PE ratios, except cash flow is substituted for earnings and emphasis is placed on the growth in cash flow rather than the growth of earnings.

Price-to-Sales (PS) Ratio

A third valuation ratio is the ratio of the **price-to-sales ratio**. The PS ratio offers one advantage over the PE ratio. If a firm has negative earnings, the PE ratio has no meaning, and the ratio breaks down as a tool for valuation and comparisons. The PS ratio, however, can be computed even if the firm is operating at a loss, thus permitting comparisons of all firms, including those that are not profitable. This is very useful for young, fast-growing firms. For example, Uber went public in May 2019 but didn't record its first profitable quarter until the end of 2021. Thus, measuring its valuation progress through sales is useful.

Even if the firm has earnings and thus a positive PE ratio, the PS ratio remains a useful analytical tool. Earnings are ultimately related to sales. A low PS ratio indicates a low valuation; the stock market isn't placing a large value on the firm's sales. Even if the firm is operating at a loss, a low PS ratio may indicate an undervalued investment. A small increase in profitability may translate these sales into a large increase in the stock's price. When the firm returns to profitability, the market may respond to the earnings, and both the PE and PS ratios increase. Thus, a current low PS ratio may suggest that there is considerable potential for the stock's price to increase. Such potential wouldn't exist if the stock were selling for a high PS ratio.

price-to-sales ratio
A measure of relative value that divides the price by the sales per share

Price-to-Book Ratio

While the PE ratio may receive the most coverage in the financial press, financial analysts often use it in combination with other ratios, such as the **price-to-book ratio**. "Book" is the per-share book value of the firm derived as the sum of stock, additional paid-in capital, and retained earnings on a firm's balance sheet. Essentially, the application is the same as with the PE ratio. A low ratio may suggest that the stock is undervalued while a high ratio suggests the opposite. Determining what constitutes a "low" or a "high" ratio is left to the discretion of the analyst. Often, if a stock is selling for less than its book value (i.e., less than 1), it is considered undervalued.

The PE ratio and PB ratio are commonly used in the relative valuation approach for security selection. Value investing emphasizes stocks that are anticipated to grow more slowly than average but may be selling for low prices (i.e., are undervalued). These stocks often have low PE and PB ratios, and the firms often operate in basic or low-tech industries. The essence of this approach is that the market has overlooked these stocks. A value strategy is obviously opposite to a growth strategy, which emphasizes the selection of stocks with greater-than-average growth potential. The value and growth investment strategies are examined in a later section of this chapter.

price-to-book ratio
A measure of relative value that divides the price by the book value per share

The PEG Ratio

The PE, PS, and PB ratios value a stock relative to its earnings, sales, and book value. However, if you compare two firms in the same industry, and one has a higher PE ratio, you might consider that firm overvalued. However, that firm might also be growing much faster and thus deserves a higher PE multiple. For further analysis, adding the growth rate to the PE ratio provides some insight.

PEG ratio
The PE ratio divided by the growth rate of earnings

The **PEG ratio** is defined as PE ratio ÷ earnings growth rate.

The PEG ratio standardizes PE ratios for growth. It gives a relative measure of value and facilitates comparing firms with different growth rates. If the growth rate exceeds the PE ratio, the numerical value is less than 1.0 and suggests that the stock is undervalued. If the PE ratio exceeds the growth rate, the PEG ratio is greater than 1.0. The higher the numerical value, the higher the valuation and the less attractive is the stock. A PEG of 1.0 to 2.0 may suggest the stock is reasonably valued, and a ratio greater than 2.0 may suggest the stock is overvalued.

Because the PEG ratio standardizes for growth, it offers one major advantage over PE ratios. The PEG ratio facilitates comparisons of firms in different industries that are experiencing different rates of growth. Rapidly growing companies may now be compared to companies experiencing a lower rate of growth. The low PEG and the low PE ratios may be a good starting point but are probably not sufficient to conclude that stock is a good purchase. You should investigate why the ratios are low.

You can find many of the ratios described here online. For example, Yahoo! Finance provides the ratios shown in **Table 11-7** in the "Statistics" menu. The PE ratio column was presented in **Table 11-5**. The additional ratios add important context. For example, the firms with very high PE ratios, like Disney, Salesforce.com, and Tesla, have more reasonable forward PE ratios. This is likely due to nonrecurring accounting adjustments to earnings last year that are not expected to occur next year. United Airlines has no PE ratio or PEG ratio because its earnings are negative. Therefore, the forward PE ratio provides some guidance. The PS ratio for Tesla and Visa are very high. This suggests their price is overvalued compared to their sales. On the other hand, the

Table 11-7: Price Ratios for Selected Companies, December 2021

Company	PE Ratio	Forward PE	PS Ratio	PB Ratio	PEG Ratio
Alcoa	13.80	6.91	0.82	2.35	–
Amazon	66.90	53.78	3.86	14.49	2.05
American Express	17.20	17.33	3.32	5.30	0.66
Amgen	23.30	11.72	4.73	14.46	1.59
Apple	32.00	32.05	8.27	46.67	3.85
Berkshire Hathaway	8.00	20.88	1.92	1.37	9.08
Caterpillar	22.10	16.39	2.31	6.60	1.08
Chevron	23.00	12.02	1.69	1.68	–
Disney	141.90	33.22	4.14	3.13	1.11
Ford	29.20	10.45	0.64	2.34	0.19
IBM	25.10	10.86	1.50	5.01	2.15
Merck	27.00	10.10	3.50	5.12	1.16
Microsoft	38.20	37.45	14.75	16.92	2.91
Netflix	55.01	47.17	9.73	17.69	1.49
Salesforce	140.70	57.80	10.21	4.59	3.51
Tesla	357.20	121.95	24.67	37.75	2.67
United Airlines	–	12.35	0.70	2.63	–
Verizon	9.90	9.29	1.55	2.73	2.85
Visa	38.80	29.94	19.37	13.44	1.56
Walmart	50.30	21.23	0.70	4.75	3.20

Source: Yahoo! Finance, December 2021

small PS ratios of Alcoa, Berkshire Hathaway, Chevron, Ford, IBM, United Airlines, Verizon, and Walmart indicate they are relatively undervalued. PB ratios less than one indicates the firm is undervalued, which doesn't apply to these selected firms. However, several firms, such as Amazon, Amgen, Apple, Microsoft, Netflix, Tesla, and Visa, have very high PB ratios, suggesting they are overvalued. This may not be a surprise, given that the Shiller PE is showing the stock market is overvalued and many of these firms have led the bull market. Lastly, a PEG less than one indicates an undervalued firm, which applies to only American Express and Ford, though Caterpillar and Disney are close. PEG ratios greater than two indicate the firm is overvalued. This applies to Amazon, Berkshire Hathaway, IBM, Microsoft, Salesforce.com, Tesla, Verizon, and Walmart. In some cases, the ratios tell the same story, Apple, Microsoft, and Tesla are overvalued. Ford and Merck are likely undervalued.

11-5 Growth and Valuing Investing

There are many investment strategies you can follow. For example, you can form an optimal portfolio using the portfolio techniques described in Chapters 6 and 7. Many investors use index funds and index ETFs to either actively trade in and out of the market or sector, or passively match the market. Some investors follow momentum or other indicators from technical analysis described in Chapter 17. Investors may seek income, local firms, or socially responsible companies. However, one of the primary professional delineations comes from the growth versus value spectrum. Note from Chapter 4 that Morningstar categorizes the degree to which mutual funds have a growth or value orientation. Thus, growth versus value investing is very important in the investment industry.

Value investing involves focusing on securities considered to be undervalued or unpopular for various reasons. Another popular approach, **growth-stock investing**, involves focusing on companies expected to have above average rates of growth in sales and earnings. In both cases, investors seek bargains selling at prices below their actual value. In value investing, bargains are typically described in terms of a market price that is below its value of assets in place or future discounted cash flows. In growth-stock investing, bargains are defined in terms of securities selling for prices below the value of future growth opportunities.

Value investors argue that overly emotional investors sometimes cause stock prices to be moved by "fear" and "greed" to levels that are too low or too high based on the economic fundamentals. As a result, value investors adopt a contrarian investment philosophy based on the premise that they can profit by betting against the overly emotional crowd. Traditional value investors seek out-of-favor stocks selling at a discount to the overall market, measured in terms of low PE ratios, low PB ratios, and/or high dividend yields. Value investors like to find companies with good businesses whose stock is priced so low that its PE ratio is lower than the market average.

The concept of value investing was laid out in 1934, when Benjamin Graham and David L. Dodd published the book *Security Analysis*. Together, Graham and Dodd laid down the essential standards for value investing, an investment approach aimed at identifying stock market bargains. For the past several decades, value investing has been championed by Warren Buffett, the chairman of Berkshire Hathaway. Each year, near the first of May, Mr. Buffett preaches the value principles at the annual meeting of Berkshire Hathaway, Inc., in Omaha, Nebraska. Thousands of value investors make the

value investing
A stock strategy that seeks firms that are undervalued

growth-stock investing
A stock strategy that seeks firms with high earnings and sales growth

pilgrimage to hear the "Oracle of Omaha." His annual letter to shareholders is eagerly anticipated. In it, he drops value investing quips, such as these:

- "Price is what you pay, value is what you get."
- "Be fearful when others are greedy. Be greedy when others are fearful."
- "If you aren't willing to own a stock for 10 years, don't even think about owning it for 10 minutes."
- "It's far better to buy a wonderful company at a fair price than a fair company at a wonderful price."
- "Never invest in a business you cannot understand."
- "Our favorite holding period is forever."
- "The best chance to deploy capital is when things are going down."

Growth investors look to the future. They look for companies that are apt to deliver ever-higher revenue, earnings, and dividends. Each growth-stock investor might use different criteria to identify attractive candidates for purchase. Some look for companies with three or more consecutive years of above-average growth in both per-share earnings and revenues. Others look for firms with high profit margins and projected earnings increases of 10 to 15% (or more) for three to five years. Still others look for earnings growth at a rate that is at least twice that of the average company represented by the S&P 500 Index. A complete fundamental analysis is useful. However, growth-stock investors also look beyond earnings-per-share numbers to gauge whether a company can prudently sustain rapid growth.

Growth-stock investors favor aggressive companies that may sell at premium valuations when value is measured in terms of PE ratios. Dividend income is typically a secondary consideration, if relevant at all, because fast-growing companies need to reinvest their capital. Characteristics of a growth stock might include the firm using a disruptive technology, operating in a fast-growing industry, or dominating a lucrative niche. Such investors may be willing to accept larger-than-typical levels of risk in the pursuit of above-average long-term investment results.

The World of Investing

Socially Responsible Investing

During the past half century, socially responsible investing (SRI) has moved into the mainstream as more investors recognize its potential for attractive financial performance coupled with societal benefits. Investing can be more than putting money somewhere and hoping to get more back in the future. You may want to avoid investing in companies that do objectionable things like exploiting workers, customers, or the environment. Some people are even willing to sacrifice some returns to sleep better, if necessary.

The terminology describing trying to do well while doing right with your investments has evolved to include such labels as "ethical investing"; "environmental, social, and corporate governance (ESG)"; "responsible investing"; "socially responsible investing"; "sustainable investing"; "values-based investing"; "green investing"; "impact investing"; and "community investing."

SRI's popularity continues to grow, and thus the number of mutual fund and ETF offerings has greatly expanded. The number of tools to help you assess the sustainability of funds and firms has also expanded. Morningstar shows a mutual fund's scores for the three ESG pillars and a combined sustainability score. Yahoo! Finance has a Sustainability tab for each company. The site shows the company's ESG risk rankings provided by Sustainalytics. You can also go directly to https://www.sustainalytics.com/esg-ratings to obtain ratings.

Some investors incorporate their personal values into their investment and portfolio choices.

A growth stock may appear to be overvalued to a value investor. However, good growth-stock investors don't blindly buy highly valued stocks just because they have high expected growth. Indeed, many are looking for **growth-at-a-reasonable-price (GARP)**. For this, the PEG ratio is useful. GARP investors pick a maximum PEG ratio for which stocks with higher PEG ratios aren't deemed to be reasonably priced.

So, which is better, value or growth investing? The answer is that over the years, each has experienced dominance over the other for some time. For example, you can group many of the S&P 500 companies into growth and value categories based on using the three fundamental measures of PE ratio, PS ratio, and PB ratio. Consider the two exchange-traded funds (ETFs) that track S&P 500 growth and value stocks; iShares S&P 500 Value ETF (ticker: IVE) and iShares S&P 500 Growth ETF (ticker: IVW). Both were started in May 2000. **Figure 11-4** shows the performance of these two ETFs. The initial price has been scaled to $1 for each for easy comparison.

During the 21-year period, the value ETF climbed from an adjusted $1 to $4.33, while the growth ETF grew to $5.03. Note that for the period 2003 to mid-2007, value outperformed growth. However, for the next two years, growth greatly outperformed value. It is interesting to note that value stocks performed worse than growth stocks during the COVID pandemic.

growth-at-a-reasonable-price (GARP)
A stock strategy that seeks growth stocks that are not overvalued

Figure 11-4: Growth Versus Value ETFs, Scaled to Start at $1

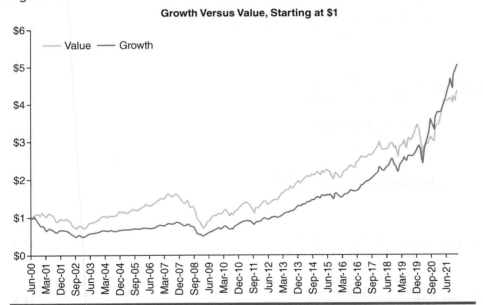

Source: Data for ETFs IVE and IVW from Yahoo! Finance

Conclusion

Fundamental analysis is a highly quantitative endeavor. However, it is also an art form. This chapter reveals the importance of dividends, financial statement analysis, discounted cash flow analysis, price ratio analysis, and growth versus value investing. The sheer volume of equations may seem daunting. However, many of the inputs to these equations are vague and open to interpretation. Fundamental analysis is difficult, and that is why analysts in the investment industry get paid very well.

This chapter reviews three approaches to fundamental analysis. The analysis of financial statements employs a variety of accounting measures, such as the return on equity, to examine the business operations of the firm. Discounted cash flow models require estimating cash flow, which is characterized as dividends and a future price, and expressing these values in the present (i.e., discounting future cash flows). This present value is compared to the current price of the stock to make a buy or sell decision. Price ratios, like the price-to-earnings (PE) ratio provide a good relative value measure. The purpose of all these methods is to determine if the stock should be bought or sold.

Chapter Equations

$$Payout\ Ratio = \frac{Dividends}{Earnings}$$
11-1

$$Retention\ Ratio = 1 - Payout\ Ratio = \frac{Earnings - Dividends}{Earnings}$$
11-2

$$Current\ Ratio = \frac{Current\ assets}{Current\ liabilities}$$
11-3

$$Quick\ Ratio = \frac{Current\ assets - Inventory}{Current\ liabilities}$$

$$= \frac{Cash + Cash\ equivalents + Accounts\ Receivable}{Current\ liabilities}$$
11-4

$$Inventory\ Turnover = \frac{Sales}{Average\ inventory}$$

$$or\ = \frac{Cost\ of\ goods\ sold}{Average\ inventory}$$
11-5

$$Average\ Collection\ Period\ (ACP) = \frac{Receivables}{Sales\ per\ day}$$
11-6

$$Receivables\ Turnover = \frac{Annual\ credit\ sales}{Accounts\ receivables}$$
11-7

$$Fixed\text{-}\ Asset\ Turnover = \frac{Annual\ sales}{Fixed\ assets}$$
11-8

$$Total\ Asset\ Turnover = \frac{Annual\ sales}{Total\ assets}$$
11-9

$$Gross\ Profit\ Margin = \frac{Sales - Cost\ of\ goods\ sold}{Sales}$$
11-10

$$Operating\ Profit\ Margin = \frac{Operating\ earnings}{Sales}$$ **11-11**

$$Net\ Profit\ Margin = \frac{Earnings\ after\ taxes}{Sales}$$ **11-12**

$$Return\ on\ Assets = \frac{Earnings\ after\ taxes}{Total\ assets}$$ **11-13**

$$Return\ on\ Equity = \frac{Earnings\ after\ taxes}{Equity}$$ **11-14**

$$Return\ on\ Common\ Equity = \frac{Earnings\ after\ taxes - Preferred\ stock\ dividends}{Equity - Preferred\ stock}$$ **11-15**

$$Debt\ to\ Equity = \frac{Debt}{Equity}$$ **11-16**

$$Debt\ to\ Total\ Assets = \frac{Debt}{Total\ assets}$$ **11-17**

$$Times\ Interest\ Earned = \frac{Earnings\ before\ interest\ and\ taxes}{Annual\ interest\ expense}$$ **11-18**

$$P_0 = \frac{D}{r}$$ **11-19**

$$P_0 = \frac{D_1}{r - g} = \frac{D_0 \times (1 + g)}{r - g}$$ **11-20**

$$P_0 = \frac{D_1}{(1 + r)^1} + \frac{D_2}{(1 + r)^2} + \frac{D_3}{(1 + r)^3} + \cdots + \frac{D_n}{(1 + r)^n} + \frac{P_n}{(1 + r)^n}$$ **11-21**

$$P_n = \frac{D_{n+1}}{r - g} = \frac{D_n \times (1 + g)}{r - g}$$ **11-22**

$$P_n = \left(\frac{P}{E}\right)_n \times E_n = \left(\frac{P}{E}\right)_n \times (1 + g)^n \times E_0$$ **11-23**

$$Shiller\ PE\ Ratio = \frac{Share\ Price}{10\text{-}year\ average\ of\ inflation\ adjusted\ earnings}$$ **11-24**

Excel Functions

AVERAGE(number1, [number2], ...)   NPV(rate, value1, [value2], ...)
INT(number)

Key Terms

average collection period – The number of days required to collect accounts receivable

buy-side analyst – A person who gives buy/sell advice and forecasts to the institutional firms for which they work

bylaw – A document specifying the relationship between a corporation and its stockholders

charter – A document specifying the relationship between a firm and the state in which it is incorporated

common stock – A security representing ownership in a corporation with voting rights

constant growth model – A valuation model that uses constant growing dividends and discounts them to the present

cross-sectional analysis – An analysis of several firms in the same industry at one point in time

cumulative voting – A system that permits each stockholder to cast all their votes for one candidate

current ratio – A measure of liquidity: current assets divided by current liabilities

date of record – The day on which an investor must own shares to receive the dividend payment

days sales outstanding – The number of days required to collect accounts receivable

debt-to-equity ratio – The ratio of debt to equity that evaluates a company's financial leverage

debt-to-total assets ratio – The ratio of debt to total assets that measures the proportion of the firm financed with debt

debt ratio – The ratio of debt to total assets, which measures the use of debt financing

dilution – A reduction in earnings per share due to the issuing of new securities

director – A person who is elected by stockholders to determine the firm's goals and policies

distribution date – The date on which a dividend is paid to stockholders

dividend – A payment to stockholders that is usually in cash but may be in stock

dividend discount model – A valuation model that discounts future cash flows to the present

dividend reinvestment plan (DRIP) – A program that permits stockholders to have cash dividends reinvested in stock shares

ex-dividend – Stock that trades exclusive of any dividend payment

ex-dividend date – The day on which a stock trades exclusive of any dividends

extra dividend – Cash paid in addition to the firm's regular dividend

financial leverage – The use of borrowed funds to acquire an asset

fixed-asset turnover – Ratio of sales to fixed assets, which tells how many fixed assets are needed to generate sales

forward PE ratio – The ratio of stock price to the next 12 months of earnings per share

fundamental analysis – A method of determining a stock's current value.

gross profit margin – Percentage earned on sales after deducting the cost of goods sold.

growth-at-a-reasonable-price (GARP) – A stock strategy that seeks growth stocks that are not overvalued

growth-stock investing – A stock strategy that seeks firms with high earnings and sales growth

inventory turnover – The speed with which inventory is sold

irregular dividend – Dividend payments that either don't occur in the regular intervals or vary in amount

liquidated – A company sells all its assets, pays creditors, and ceases operations

multi-growth firm – A firm that experiences periods of different growth rates

net profit margin – The ratio of earnings after interest and taxes to sales

operating profit margin – Percentage earned on sales before adjusting for nonrecurring items, interest, and taxes

payout ratio – The ratio of dividends to earnings

PE model – A model to estimate a future price using the future PE ratio, earnings, and growth

PE multiple – The PE ratio used for valuing a company

PE ratio – The ratio of stock price to the earnings per share

PEG ratio – The PE ratio divided by the growth rate of earnings

perpetuity model – **A dividend discount model in which all future dividends are the same**

price target – **An analysts' estimate of the future stock price**

price-to-book ratio – **A measure of relative value that divides the price by the book value per share**

price-to-cash flow ratio – **A measure of relative value that divides the price by the cash flow per share**

price-to-sales ratio – **A measure of relative value that divides the price by the sales per share**

preemptive right – **The right of current stockholders to maintain their proportionate ownership in the firm**

proxy battle – **A group of shareholders trying to gather enough shareholder proxy votes to win a company vote**

quick ratio (acid test) – **A measure of liquidity: current assets excluding inventory divided by current liabilities**

ratio analysis – **A method of gaining insight into a company's operation through examining its financial statements**

recapitalization – **A modification in a firm's sources of financing, such as the substitution of long-term debt for equity**

receivables turnover – **The speed with which a firm collects its accounts receivable**

regular dividend – **Steady dividend payments that are distributed at regular intervals**

repurchase – **A company purchasing its own shares of stock**

retention ratio – **The ratio of earnings not distributed to total earnings**

return on assets – **The ratio of earnings to total assets**

return on equity – **The ratio of earnings to equity**

rights offering – **Sale of new securities to existing stockholders**

sell-side analyst – **A person who communicates to the public about their stock recommendations and forecasts**

Shiller PE ratio – **A version of the PE ratio that uses ten years of earnings adjusted for inflation**

statement of cash flows – **An accounting statement that specifies a firm's cash inflows and cash outflows**

stock dividend – **A dividend paid as stock instead of cash**

stock split – **Company proportionally changes the number of shares outstanding, which affects their par value, earnings per share, and price**

time-series analysis – **An analysis of a firm over a period of time**

times interest earned – **Ratio of EBIT divided by interest expense, which measures the safety of debt**

total asset turnover – **Ratio of sales to total assets, which tells the amount of sales generated by total assets**

value investing – **A stock strategy that seeks firms that are undervalued**

voting rights – **The rights of stockholders to vote their shares**

Questions

1. **Distribution of Dividends.** Describe the timing dynamics of a company announcing and paying a cash dividend. (LO 11-1).

2. **Dividend Payments.** How do stock dividends differ from cash dividends? How do stock dividends differ from stock splits? (LO 11-2).

3. **Ratio Analysis.** What do the liquidity ratios, activity ratios, profitability ratios, leverage ratios, and coverage ratios tell you about a firm? (LO 11-3).

4. **Statement of Cash Flows.** What does the statement of cash flows add to the analyst's knowledge of the firm? (LO 11-4).

5. **Future Price.** Under what circumstances might you use the constant growth rate model compared to the PE model to estimate a future price? (LO 11-5).

6. **Dividend Discount Model.** What inputs are needed to value a stock using the dividend discount model? (LO 11-6).

7. **Analysts.** Why do you see sell-side analyst forecasts but not buy-side analyst forecasts? What incentives may each offer? (LO 11-7).

8. **PE ratios.** What are the differences between the PE ratio, forward PE ratio, and Shiller PE ratio? (LO 11-8).

9. **PEG ratio.** What does a PEG ratio tell you? (LO 11-9).

10. **PEG ratio.** What are the value and growth investment strategies? Which is better? (LO 11-10).

Problems

1. **Payout.** What are the payout ratio and retention ratio of the three companies? (LO 11-2).

	A	B	C
1		Earnings	Dividends
2		per share	per share
3	Company A	$ 0.52	$ 0.76
4	Company B	$ 2.66	$ 1.64
5	Company C	$ 3.65	$ 1.60

2. **Stock Splits.** You own 200 shares of a stock priced at $80 per share. How many shares of stock would you own and what is the stock price after each of these scenarios? (LO 11-2).

    a. 2-for-1 stock split.
    b. 4-for-1 stock split.
    c. 1-for-4 stock split.

3. **DRIPs.** You own 350 shares of a stock priced at $75 per share. If the stock has a dividend reinvestment program and pays a $0.45 per share dividend, how many shares of stock would you get and how much cash would be remaining? (LO 11-2).

    Use the balance sheet and income statement, provided in the data file, **ch11_pr04_10.xlsx** *to answer Problems 4 to 10:*

4. **Liquidity Ratios.** Given the balance sheet and income statement, compute the current ratio and the quick ratio for 20X1 and 20X0. Which year is better for each? (LO 11-3)

5. **Activity Ratios.** Given the balance sheet and income statement, compute the inventory turnover for 20X1 using both net sales and COGS. Also compute the average collection period and receivables turnover for 20X1 and 20X0. Which year is better for each? (LO 11-3)

6. **Activity Ratios.** Given the balance sheet and income statement, compute the fixed-asset turnover and total asset turnover for 20X1 and 20X0. Which year is better for each? (LO 11-3)

7. **Profitability Ratios.** Given the balance sheet and income statement, compute the gross profit margin, operating profit margin, and net profit margin for 20X1 and 20X0. Which year is better for each? (LO 11-3)

8. **Profitability Ratios.** Given the balance sheet and income statement, compute the return on assets and return on equity for 20X1 and 20X0. Which year is better for each? (LO 11-3)

9. **Leverage Ratios.** Given the balance sheet and income statement, compute the debt to equity and debt to total assets for 20X1 and 20X0. Which year is riskier for each? (LO 11-3)

10. **Coverage Ratios.** Given the balance sheet and income statement, compute the times interest earned for 20X1 and 20X0. Which year is better? (LO 11-3)

11. **Cash Flow.** Do each of the following activities lead to a net outflow or inflow of the cash position? (LO 11-4)

    a. Increase in accounts receivables
    b. Increase in accounts payables
    c. Purchase of plant and equipment
    d. Pay dividends
    e. Repurchase shares

12. **Perpetuity Model.** If a security pays a dividend of $2.40 per share per year that will not change over time and the required rate of return is 7%, what is the value of the security? If the required rate changes to 7.5%, what is the price change? (LO 11-5)

13. **Constant Growth Model.** A security paid a dividend of $1.25 per share for the year. Its required rate is 9.8%. If the dividend is expected to grow at the constant rates shown below, what is the value of the security? A new announcement is made that changes the growth expectation. If the growth changes as noted, what is the price change? (LO 11-5)

    a. Growth at 7%, then increases by 0.5%
    b. Growth at 7%, then decreases by 0.5%
    c. Growth at 6%, then increases by 0.5%
    d. Growth at 8%, then decreases by 0.5%

14. **Future Price Constant Growth Model.** A security paid a dividend of $2.75 per share for the year. The dividend is expected to grow by $0.05 per year for five years. Afterwards, the dividend will grow at a constant 4% forever. Its required rate is 8.8%. What is the expected price in five years? (LO 11-5)

15. **PE Model.** A security earned $4.16 per share for the year and has a price of $75 per share. Earnings are expected to grow at 12% annually for the next five years. If the PE multiple is expected to increase 10% between now and five years, what is the forecasted price of the stock in five years? (LO 11-5)

16. **Dividend Discount Model.** In three years, a company is expected to pay its first dividend of $1.44 per share per year. At that point, the dividend is expected to grow at 7% per year indefinitely. If the required rate of return is 9.4%, what is the value of the stock? (LO 11-6)

17. **Dividend Discount Model.** A company will pay a $0.88 per-share-per-year dividend next year. It is expected to increase that dividend by $0.04 each year for three years (to year four). In year four, the PE ratio of the firm is expected to be 21. Earnings were $2.10 per share last year and are expected to grow at 8% each year to year four. If the required rate of return is 8.7%, what is the value of the stock? (LO 11-6)

18. **Dividend Discount Model.** A company paid a $1.78 per-share-per-year dividend last year. It is expected to increase at an annual 9% growth rate to year five. After year five, the dividend will grow at 6% per year indefinitely. If the required rate of return is 10.2%, what is the value of the stock? (LO 11-6)

19. **Price Multiples.** Consider the data below from the financial statements. If the stock price of the company is $75 per share, what are the PE ratio, price-to-cash flow ratio, PS ratio, and PB ratio? (LO 11-8)

	(in 000)
Net Sales	$ 6,157.20
Net Income	$ 639.80
Cash Flow	$ 711.95
Book Value	$ 997.30
# Shares	220

20. **PEG ratio.** Compute the PEG ratio for the three firms below. Which is a more attractive PEG ratio to a GARP investor? (LO 11-9)

	Price	EPS	Growth (%)
Company A	$ 85.00	$ 2.56	11.0
Company B	$ 75.00	$ 2.75	8.0
Company C	$ 90.00	$ 0.56	15.0

Case Study

Fundamental Analysis

Conduct a fundamental analysis on Appaloosa, a clothes man-ufacturer. Appaloosa specializes in preteen clothes and pro-duces only a modest amount of clothes for other age groups. Its sales of preteen clothes account for one-third of the total preteen market, both domestic and abroad. Appaloosa's bal-ance sheets and income statements for the past two years are presented in Exhibit 1. Appaloosa's per-share earnings and div-idends are given in Exhibit 2. Except for the most recent year, 20X9, and 20X8, per-share earnings have steadily increased, and dividends have risen every year for the past 10 years. This pattern of earnings and dividend growth is impressive.

For Appaloosa to be a good investment, it should have strong fundamentals and be financially sound. Analyze Appa-loosa using ratios to analyze the firm's financial statements. You can compare the two years and compare to the industry averages given in Exhibit 3.

Currently, Appaloosa's stock sells for $50. You could invest in U.S. Treasury bills that yield 3.5%, but the stock market is expected to earn an annual 9.5%. The data are in the file, **ch11_case_study.xlsx**. Should you buy Appaloosa stock? Answer the following questions:

1. Compute the ratios shown in Exhibit 3 for both years of Appaloosa. What is your conclusion?
2. What is the firm's current payout ratio compared to its his-torical payout ratio?
3. What are the annual growth rates in the earnings per share and the dividend per share? Why is the growth rate in the dividend *not* sustainable?
4. Is there any reason to believe that the firm has changed its dividend policy?
5. Compute the PE ratio, PS ratio, and PB ratio. (Note that you can infer the number of outstanding shares from net income/EPS.) Does Appaloosa's PE, PS, and PB ratios suggest the firm is undervalued?
6. If a dividend growth rate of 4% can be sustained, is the stock a good purchase if the required return is 9.5%?

Valuing Preferred Stock

After completing this chapter, you should be able to:

LO 12-1 Define the main characteristics of preferred stock.

LO 12-2 Identify the differences in valuation between perpetual and finite-lived preferred shares.

LO 12-3 Differentiate between convertible and callable preferred shares.

LO 12-4 Describe and implement the valuation approach used to price floating preferred shares.

LO 12-5 Contrast the valuation of cumulative and noncumulative preferred shares.

LO 12-6 Explain how participating preferred shares offer investors additional income potential over otherwise identical nonparticipating preferred shares.

LO 12-7 Describe and calculate the differential tax treatment of preferred share dividends encountered by corporate and individual investors in preferred stock issues.

When investors think of equity ownership in a firm, they are normally thinking of common stock, which owns the majority of the equity control rights of the firm, and the valuation of which we discussed in the last chapter. However, as mentioned in Chapter 2, there is another type of stock, "preferred stock," that some firms issue in addition to their common stock. As the name implies, preferred stock holds a superior position to common stock in some aspects: preferred stockholders have the right to receive dividend payments before common stockholders do and, in the case of liquidation, they are also compensated before common stockholders get anything.

Although preferred stock is legally equity and hence represents ownership, many of its features are more similar to the characteristics of debt than of common stock. For example, preferred stock usually does not have any control rights and generally pays a fixed-dividend amount. Because of the latter, preferred stock is often lumped into the category of **fixed-income securities**, along with bonds. However, the decision to do so ignores the facts that many preferred share issues are **convertible** (meaning they include an option for the holder to convert the shares into a fixed number of common shares after a predetermined date); that they are usually issued in the early stages

fixed-income security
a security that promises to pay a fixed income stream in the form of fixed dividends or bond interest payments

convertible
a security that can be converted into shares of common stock upon the decision of the holder

London InterBank Offer Rate (LIBOR)
the benchmark interest rate at which major global banks lend to each other

perpetual
a feature of a security where it never matures

cumulative dividend
a feature of preferred stock wherein a "skipped" dividend has to be made up before the issuing firm can pay any dividends to common shareholders

TRuPS
hybrid securities that are included in regulatory tier 1 capital for Bank Holding Companies and whose dividend payments are tax deductible for the issuer

Bank for International Settlements (BIS)
an international organization tasked with supporting countries' central banks' pursuit of monetary and financial stability and acting as a bank for central banks

Tier 1 capital
the core capital held in a bank's reserves

participating
a feature of a preferred share or bond where a promised amount is paid each period, but also can possibly receive "extra" payments from the firm if some financial benchmark is met

of a firm's growth, when earnings are more uncertain and getting a "first claim" against them vis-à-vis other equity claimants is an important benefit; and that the **intent** of the preferred shareholders with regard to that conversion option is important: that is, do they view exercising it as an unlikely sort of "back up" plan or insurance against the firm getting into trouble, or do they view the exercise of that option as more-or-less inevitable once the firm has grown to a more stable, mature point?

Preferred stock may also have other important features that differentiate them from bonds:

1. Although most preferred share issues carry no voting rights, some have special voting rights to approve extraordinary events (such as the issuance of new shares or approval of the acquisition of a company). Other preferred shares gain voting rights when the preferred dividends are in arrears for a substantial time. This is all dependent on the rights assigned to the preferred shares at the time of incorporation.

2. Almost all preferred shares have a negotiated fixed-dividend amount, usually specified as a percentage of the par value or as a fixed amount (for example, Pacific Gas & Electric 6% Series A Preferred). As we will discuss in the next section of the textbook, this fixed payment is analogous to the obligated interest payment on debt. However, sometimes dividends on preferred shares may be set as floating; they may change according to a benchmark interest-rate index (such as the **London InterBank Offer Rate [LIBOR]**).

3. Most preferred stock is **perpetual**, meaning that there is no fixed date on which invested capital will be returned to the preferred shareholder (although there are redemption privileges held by the corporation), though there are a few with finite maturities. By contrast, almost all commercial debt has a maturity date, where the capital is returned to the lender.

4. Unlike debt interest payments, most preferred stock issues offer **cumulative dividends**, in that if the dividend is not paid, it will accumulate for future payment. There are, however, some types of preferred stock where dividends do *not* accumulate if they are unpaid; this is very common in **Trust Preferred Securities (TRuPS)** and bank preferred stock, since under **Bank for International Settlements (BIS)** rules, preferred stock must be noncumulative if it is to be included in **Tier 1 capital**. Note that one fundamental difference between preferred stock and debt is that while dividends on preferred stock must be paid on preferred shares prior to any common share dividends being paid, the firm's failure to do so does not constitute a contractual breach as it would if they had failed to pay debt interest when due.

5. Some shares of preferred stock are also said to be **participating**, meaning that these preferred issues offer holders the opportunity to receive extra dividends if the company achieves predetermined financial goals. Investors who purchased these stocks receive their regular dividend regardless of company performance (assuming the company does well enough to make its annual dividend payments), but if the company achieves predetermined sales, earnings or profitability goals, the investors receive an additional dividend.

6. Some preferred share issues have a call provision, meaning that the firm may buy back the shares (usually at a premium) when they so choose past a certain date. As discussed in the next chapter, bonds may also be similarly callable by the issuing firm.
7. Unlike bond interest, dividends paid to preferred shareholders are not tax-deductible for the issuing firm; however, if a corporation owns preferred shares in another corporation, the receiving corporation can deduct, within certain limits, 50% of the dividends received if the corporation receiving the dividend owns less than 20% of the corporation distributing the dividend. If the corporation owns 20% or more of the distributing corporation's stock, it can, subject to certain limits, deduct 65% of the dividends received. Because of this preferential treatment of dividends paid from one corporation to another, many preferred share issues are owned primarily by other corporations.

It's also important to realize that a company may issue more than one **class** of preferred shares. Each class can have a different dividend payment, a different redemption value, a different redemption date, and different attributes, such as those discussed earlier.

So, yes, if we had a completely "vanilla" preferred stock issue that carried no voting rights, had a fixed dividend that could be expected to be paid consistently at every period in the future, had no conversion option, and had sold preferred stock only to individual investors, then valuing such shares would be the equivalent of valuing a perpetual, fixed, **consol** bond. We will cover doing so in the next section.

However, valuing preferred shares that have any of those special attributes that we've mentioned is a bit trickier and requires more sophisticated calculations. As such, it makes sense to devote time and space in the form of their own chapter to the discussion of preferred shares.

The remainder of this chapter will do so, first discussing the valuation of "vanilla" preferred shares and then adding in a discussion of the additional possible features' impact on cash flows and the valuation of such impacts for finite, convertible, floating, noncumulative, and participating preferred share issues as well as the tax implications for preferred shares owned by other corporations, respectively.

class
a subcategory of stocks or bonds having different features than other classes of the same type of security for the same issuer

consol
a British government debt security having an infinite maturity

12-1 Valuing Vanilla Preferred Shares

The process of valuing vanilla preferred stock is essentially the same as that used to price bonds, because this kind of preferred stock is a fixed-income security. The future payments are brought back to the present at the appropriate discount rate. If the preferred stock does not have a required **sinking fund** or **call provision**, it may be viewed as a perpetual debt instrument. The fixed dividend (D) will continue indefinitely. These dividends must be discounted by the yield being earned on newly issued preferred stock (k). The process for determining the present value of the preferred stock (P) is as follows:

$$P_0 = \frac{D}{(1 + k)^1} + \frac{D}{(1 + k)^2} + \frac{D}{(1 + k)^3} + \cdots + \frac{D}{(1 + k)^\infty}$$

As in the case of the perpetual consol bond covered in the next chapter, this equation is reduced to

sinking fund
a pool of money required by an issuing firm to be accumulated over time in preparation of the buyback or settlement of a security issue

call provision
a feature of a security that allows the issuer to retire the security early, usually by paying a premium over the par value

$$P_0 = \frac{D}{K}$$ **12-1**

This is the same as Equation 12-1 used to value a perpetual bond except for the notation used. For example, if a newly issued preferred stock pays an annual dividend of $4 and the appropriate discount rate is 8%, the present value of the preferred stock is

$$P_0 = \frac{4}{(1+.08)^1} + \frac{4}{(1+.08)^2} + \frac{4}{(1+.08)^3} + \cdots + \frac{4}{(1+.08)^\infty}$$

$$= \frac{4}{.08}$$

$$= \$50.00$$

If an investor buys this preferred stock for $50.00, they can expect to earn 8% ($50.00 × 0.08 = $4) on the investment as long as they own it. Of course, the realized rate of return on the investment will not be known until the investor sells the stock and adjusts this 8% return for any capital gain or loss. However, at the current price, the preferred stock is selling for an 8% dividend yield.

After the preferred stock is first issued by the company, note that the dividend will remain the same but that it is entirely likely for the "going" rate of return to change, due to changes in the company's prospects or in the underlying economic environment. For example, if, one year later, the appropriate discount rate changes to 7%, then the price of the preferred stock if sold would be

$$P_0 = \frac{4}{.07}$$

$$= \$57.14$$

If the investor had bought the preferred stock for $50, held it for one year, and then sold it for that price of $57.14, then their total return would have been equal to

$$\text{Return} = \text{Dividend Yield} + \text{Capital Gains Yield}$$

$$= k + \frac{P_1 - P_0}{P_0}$$ **12-2**

Excel Expert 12-1

As shown in Equation 12-1, to calculate the present value of the perpetuity of fixed dividend payments, we simply divide the dividend amount by the appropriate discount rate:

	A	B	C
1	Dividend	$ 4.00	
2	Discount rate	8.00%	
3	Price	$ 50.00	=B1/B2

So, the price of the preferred stock should be $50.

Or, in this case

$$Return = k + \frac{P_1 - P_0}{P_0}$$

$$= .08 + \frac{\$57.14 - \$50.00}{\$50}$$

$$= .2229 \text{ or } 22.29\%$$

In reality, most preferred shares don't pay annual dividends, but instead, just as with most common shares, pay quarterly dividends. Further complicating this is that, as per our previous discussion concerning nominal versus effective rates, dividend rates, yields, and/or appropriate rates of return are quoted on a nominal annual basis, but based on quarterly compounding. This makes converting the quoted rates to the effective periodic rate(s) necessary in a problem straightforward but implies that annual rates derived from them can be a little more complicated.

For example, let's go back to our original example. However, instead of paying $4 per year, let's assume that the preferred shares pay $1 per quarter. In line with that, let's also convert the quoted annual yield of 8% by dividing it by 4 to get an effective quarterly yield of 2%. Our price calculation still gives a valuation of $50:

$$P_0 = \frac{\$1}{.02}$$

$$= \$50.00$$

Extending our example to calculate the rate of return from buying, holding the preferred share for a year, and then selling it when the rate of interest changes to 7%

Excel Expert 12-2

To calculate the total return, we will need the price paid (P_0) and the price sold at (P_1):

	A	B	C
1	Dividend	$ 4.00	
2	Discount rate at time 0	8.00%	
3	P_0	$ 50.00	=B1/B2
4			
5	Discount rate at time 1	7.00%	
6			
7	P_1	$ 57.14	=B1/B5
8			
9	Return	22.29%	=B2+(B7-B3)/B3

So, the total return will be 22.29%.

Excel Expert 12-3

Just as before, we need the price paid (P_0) and the price sold at (P_1):

	A	B	C
1	Dividend	$ 1.00	
2	Dividends per year	4	
3	Discount rate at time 0	2.00%	
4	P_0	$ 50.00	=B1/B3
5			
6	Discount rate at time 1	1.75%	=0.07/4
7			
8	P_1	$ 57.14	=B1/B6
9			
10	Return	22.53%	=((1+B3)^B2-1)+(B8-B4)/B4

But because the effective rates and the dividends are now quarterly, the total return will be 22.53%.

requires that we convert the effective quarterly dividend yield to an effective annual yield before adding it to the capital gains yield component:

$$\text{Return} = \left[(1.02)^4 - 1\right] + \frac{\$57.14 - \$50.00}{\$50}$$

$$= .2253 \text{ or } 22.53\%$$

The fact that this total return calculation is higher than what we previously calculated illustrates two important points: first, that "2% per quarter" is not the same as "8% per year," meaning that there is enhanced value to getting $3 of the $4 dividend paid earlier than the end of the year; and, secondly, that we should never add two rates that are both effective rates, but for different lengths of time. Instead, as we just illustrated, you need to convert one of the rates to the same time-basis as the other before adding them.

Please note that, though most preferred shares do pay dividends quarterly, we will revert to the assumption of annual dividends for the remainder of the chapter for the sake of simplicity.

12-2 Valuing Finite-Lived Preferred Shares

If the preferred stock has a finite life, this must be considered in determining the stock's value. As with the valuation of long-term debt, the amount that is repaid when the preferred stock is retired must be discounted back to the present value. This amount, denoted P_n below, is often set higher than the price at issue to assure capital gains for the purchaser, which often have preferential tax treatment over dividends. Thus, when preferred stock has a finite life, the valuation equation becomes

$$P_0 = \frac{D}{(1+k)^1} + \frac{D}{(1+k)^2} + \frac{D}{(1+k)^3} + \cdots + \frac{D}{(1+k)^n} + \frac{P_n}{(1+k)^n}$$

Excel Expert 12-4 ⟩

Excel includes a PV() function that allows us to value a stream of constant payments that end at the same point in time as the lump sum:

	A	B	C
1	Dividend	$ 4.00	
2	n	20	
3	Discount rate at time 0	8.00%	
4	P_n	$ 100.00	
5			
6	P_0	$60.73 =-PV(B3,B2,B1,B4)	

The only notable aspect of using this function is that, due to the way Excel implements its time value of money functions such as PV(), the payments to the annuity and the lump sum must have the same sign, and the PV the opposite sign. Since we are inputting positive values for both the annuity payments and the lump sum price at the end of n periods, we put a "-" sign in front of the function to have it display a positive number.

where P_n represents the amount that is returned to the stockholder when the preferred stock is retired after n number of periods. As this is simply the present value of an annuity plus the present value of a lump sum, both received at time n, this is usually simplified as

$$P_0 = D \times \frac{1 - \frac{1}{(1 + k)^n}}{k} + \frac{P_n}{(1 + k)^n} \qquad \text{12-3}$$

Continuing our previous example, let's assume the 8% annual dividend shares are callable in 20 years at a price of $100. The price today should then be

$$P_0 = \$4 \times \frac{1 - \frac{1}{(1.08)^{20}}}{.08} + \frac{\$100}{(1 + .08)^{20}}$$

$$= \$39.273 + \$21.455$$

$$= \$60.73$$

Except for the variable names, this is the same as Equation 12-2, which is used to value a bond with a finite life.

12-3 Valuing Convertible Preferred Shares

Convertible preferred shares offer their owners the right to turn them in for a certain number of shares of the company's common stock after a predetermined time span or on a specific date. The fixed-income component offers a steady income stream and some protection of the invested capital due to the priority of preferred dividends over common share dividends, while the option to convert these securities into stock gives the investor the opportunity to gain from a rise in the share price.

conversion ratio
the number of shares of common stock received for converting a preferred share or bond into common stock

conversion price
the effective price per share paid when converting a share of preferred stock or a bond into common stock

The **conversion ratio** represents the number of common shares that shareholders may receive for every convertible preferred share and is set by management prior to the original issue of the preferred shares, typically with guidance from an investment bank. The conversion ratio can be used to determine what price the common stock needs to be trading at for the shareholder of the preferred shares to make money on the conversion. This price, known as the **conversion price**, is equal to the purchase price of the preferred share, divided by the conversion ratio.

$$\text{Conversion Price} = \frac{P_0}{\text{Conversion Ratio}} \qquad \textbf{12-4}$$

For example, suppose that the preferred shares used in our previous example are convertible and have a conversion ratio of 6.5. The conversion price of the preferred shares would then be

$$\text{Conversion Price} = \frac{P_0}{\text{Conversion Ratio}}$$

$$= \frac{\$50}{6.5}$$

$$= \$7.69$$

Once the market price of the company's common stock rises above the conversion price, it may be worthwhile for the preferred shareholders to convert and realize an immediate profit, dependent upon transaction costs and the investor's expectation of future common share prices. It is important to remember, however, that after a preferred shareholder converts their shares, they give up their rights as a preferred shareholder and become a common shareholder.

From a valuation perspective, convertible preferred shares can be modeled in two ways: first, as a vanilla preferred stock with an embedded option to purchase the issuer's common stock at the conversion price; and second, as a bundle of common shares carrying the right to additional current income over some time horizon. Either way, the value of the convertible preferred share would be equal to the value of a vanilla preferred share plus the value of the embedded option, V_0.

$$P_{\text{Convertible},0} = \frac{D}{k} + V_0 \qquad \textbf{12-5}$$

Excel Expert 12-5

The conversion price is simply the purchase price of the preferred shares divided by the conversion ratio:

	A	B	C
1	P_0	$ 50.00	
2	Conversion Ratio	6.5	
3			
4	Conversion Price	$7.69	=B1/B2

We will defer the actual calculation of V_0 until we have a chance to go over option pricing in Chapter 15. We will also defer the discussion of callable preferred to the same time, as the approach for valuing them is very similar but with investors in callable preferred in the position of providing (rather than receiving, as they do with a convertible preferred) an option to buy back the preferred to the issuing firm.

12-4 Valuing Floating Preferred Shares

Variable-rate, or **floating**, preferred shares have dividend payments that adjust at certain points over their life. These issuances can typically structure their dividend payments as floating from-the-start or to convert from a fixed-to-float after a certain amount of time or dividends have been paid. In either case, once the dividend rate is set to float, it is typically adjusted on a quarterly or semi-annual basis, with the adjustment determined by adding an interest rate benchmark, like three-month LIBOR, to a predetermined credit spread.

Fixed-to-float preferreds are more common than floating rate. They offer a coupon payment that is fixed for a certain number of years, most commonly 5 or 10, before transitioning to a floating rate preferred with regular coupon resets.

Whether floating or fixed-to-float, these variable-rate preferreds can play an important role in investors' portfolios as a low-**duration**, income-oriented asset class. As we will discuss in the next chapter, when we cover bonds, investments with lower durations carry less interest rate risk, so including them in an investor's portfolio can reduce the average interest rate risk of the portfolio. This can be a particularly important feature during a rising interest rate environment, where investors are likely looking to reduce their portfolio's duration.

Vanilla, fixed-rate preferreds, on the other hand, tend have higher duration due to their often perpetual nature and are a good investment to have when rates are expected to fall.

Since the dividends of floating preferreds adjust to match changes in the going yield on equivalent securities, their price tends to remain close to the issue price. The exact valuation can be done using a special case of Equation 12-3, where n is set equal to the length of time until the next dividend adjustment. and where P_n is set equal to the issue price. For example, consider again the example of preferred shares with a quarterly dividend of $1. Now assume that the dividend rate is floating and will be reset to the three-month LIBOR plus 5% when the next dividend is paid. In the interest rate environment at the time of the writing of this text, the three-month LIBOR rate is at about 13%, so let's assume that the appropriate interest rate is 50% + 13% = 63%. The current price of the preferred share would be

floating
a security whose payments to purchasers adjust based on some variable market rate of return

duration
the weighted average time to maturity of a security's cash flows

$$P_0 = \$1 \times \frac{1 - \frac{1}{(1.0063)^1}}{.0063} + \frac{\$50}{(1 + .0063)^1}$$

$$= \$50.68$$

As we would expect, the price of the shares of this preferred are going to stay fairly close to $50, the initial issue price.

Excel Expert 12-6

The price of the floating preferred set to reset in one quarter will be:

	A	B	C
1	Dividend	$ 1.00	
2	n	1	
3	Discount rate at time 0	0.63%	
4	P_n	$ 50.00	
5			
6	P_0	$50.68	=-PV(B3,B2,B1,B4)

12-5 Valuing Noncumulative Preferred Shares

Most preferred stock issues have cumulative dividend requirements, meaning that the firm is required to make up any skipped dividends to the preferred shares before any dividends can be paid out to common shareholders. However, there are some preferred issues that specify **noncumulative dividends**, permitting the issuing firm to choose not to pay dividends to the preferred stockholders during periods where the firm's board of directors so chooses. The one mitigating factor in such a situation is that, if the issuing company skips paying noncumulative preferred stockholders dividends, it also isn't allowed to pay a dividend to the common shareholders, either.

noncumulative dividend
a feature of preferred stock allowing for a dividend on the stock to be skipped by the issuer with no penalty or repayment necessary

Such an arrangement obviously benefits the company, as skipping preferred stock dividend payments may help the company if it is in financial distress or unable to achieve desirable financial benchmarks. For instance, let's assume that Company AFS is not able to pay dividends to its noncumulative preferred shareholders this year. The shareholders have no right to claim for the missed dividends in the future years, and the company has no obligation of paying the skipped dividends to the holders of noncumulative preferred stock in the future. However, in the case of cumulative preferred shareholders, the company has an obligation of ensuring that such shareholders receive all their pending dividends. The same shareholders have a right to claim any pending dividend payment the issuing company owes them.

So, what's in it for the preferred shareholders? Why would they agree to purchase noncumulative preferred shares? Well, first, they don't expect dividends to be consistently skipped, but instead for it to be an occasional thing, mitigated by common shareholders' desires to receive their dividends, and driven primarily by the good of the company in the long run. If it *were* expected to be consistent and frequent, then, no one would want to invest in those shares.

As it is, predicting whether any particular one or few dividends will be skipped is going to be difficult, so investors normally treat the dividend stream as if they are going to get the quoted dividends with certainty, but discounting them at a slightly higher rate to offset the risk that some may be skipped.

For example, let's go back to our previous example of a $4 annual dividend but now assume that the dividends are noncumulative. In that case, the preferred shareholders would require a higher yield, perhaps as much as 9%, and the preferred stock valuation would be

Excel Expert 12-7

The price of the noncumulative preferred will be:

	A	B	C
1	Dividend	$ 4.00	
2	Discount rate	9.00%	
3	Price	$ 44.44	=B1/B2
4			

Note that this is less than the price ($50) of an otherwise equivalent cumulative preferred.

$$P_0 = \frac{4}{.09}$$

$$= \$44.44$$

Note that this is less than the price of $50 that we calculated investors would be willing to pay for an otherwise equivalent cumulative preferred share. The difference lies in the certainty with which the investor can count on receiving the stream of dividends: if they feel they can count on getting $4 every year, they'll pay $50, but if they feel that sometimes the $4 annual dividend might not be such a sure thing, then they'll require a higher return to offset that risk. Since the dividends for both the cumulative and noncumulative shares in our examples are set at $4 per year, requiring a higher return translates into being only willing to pay a lower price for the noncumulative shares.

12-6 Valuing Participating Preferred Shares

Participating preferred stock gives the holder the right to receive dividends equal to the customarily specified rate that preferred dividends are paid to preferred shareholders, as well as an additional dividend based on some predetermined condition. The additional dividend ensures that these shareholders receive an equivalent dividend as common shareholders under the specified conditions.

For example, suppose Company ILW issues participating preferred shares with a dividend rate of $1 per share. The preferred shares also carry a clause on extra dividends for participating preferred stock, which is triggered whenever the dividend for common shares exceeds that of the preferred shares. If during its current quarter, Company ILW announces that it will release a dividend of $1.05 per share for its common shares, the participating preferred shareholders will receive a total dividend of $1.05 per share ($1.00 + 0.05) as well.

Participating preferred stock can also receive preferential treatment upon a liquidation event, with participating preferred shareholders often having the right to receive the stock's purchasing price back as well as a pro-rata share of any remaining proceeds that the common shareholders receive.

Continuing our example, let's us assume that ILW is facing a liquidation event. The company has $10 million of preferred participating stock outstanding, representing 20% of the company's capital structure and the other 80%, or $40 million, made up of common stock. If ILW liquidates, it will receive $60 million from the sale of its assets. The participating preferred shareholders would receive $10 million but also would be entitled to 20% of the remaining proceeds, $10 million in this case (20% × ($60 million − $10 million)). Nonparticipating preferred shareholders would not receive additional consideration but would instead receive only their liquidation value and any dividends in arrears if applicable.

Participating preferred stock is not common, but we do see it issued fairly frequently in response to a hostile takeover bid as part of a **poison pill** strategy.

poison pill
a defense mechanism used mainly in hostile takeover situations

Similar to the situation with noncumulative preferred shares, predicting whether any particular one or few dividends will be enhanced with "extra" dividend payments is going to be difficult and the product of a lot of different factors, so investors normally treat the "extra" dividend stream as having much more uncertainty than the guaranteed dividends. They accordingly are willing to accept a lower promised yield on participating preferred stocks than they would on an otherwise equivalent vanilla issue.

For example, let's go back yet again to our previous example of a $4 annual dividend but now assume that the shares are participating and that the shareholders are therefore willing to accept a promised yield of only 6%. In such a case, the preferred stock valuation would be

$$P_0 = \frac{4}{.06}$$
$$= \$66.67$$

Note that this is more than the price of $50 that we calculated investors would be willing to pay for an otherwise equivalent nonparticipating, cumulative preferred share. The difference lies in the expected amounts and probability of receiving the "extra" dividends above $4: they'll pay $50 for the stream of guaranteed dividends, but the price difference $66.67 − $50.00 = $16.67 must be the expected value of the possible "extra" future dividends.

Excel Expert 12-8

The price of the participating preferred will be:

	A	B	C
	A	B	C
1	Dividend	$ 4.00	
2	Discount rate	6.00%	
3	Price	$ 66.67	=B1/B2

Note that this is more than the price ($50) of an otherwise equivalent cumulative preferred.

12-7 Valuing More Exotic Preferred Shares

Each of the features we've previously discussed can also be combined to create more unique issues based on the needs and situation of the firm. For example, a startup firm that was very concerned about its ability to make consistent dividend payments in the first few years after an issue might choose to issue noncumulative shares but might also seek to "sweeten" the pot by making the shares participating and convertible: the noncumulative feature would lower the issue's selling price, but the other two features would have a countervailing effect. Which effect would be stronger would depend on expectations concerning how likely/often the noncumulative feature would be exercised by the firm, the conversion ratio and resulting conversion price, the likely timing and amount of the participating feature kicking in, etc.

Assuming that this startup firm was going to set the dividend on such preferred shares at $7 per year, that the net yield—taking into account the impacts of both the noncumulative and participating features—is 6.5%, and that the value of the option to convert, V_0, is $12.37, the value of the shares at issuance would be

$$P_{Convertible,0} = \frac{\$7}{.065} + \$12.37$$
$$= \$120.06$$

12-8 After-Tax Returns to Preferred Shareholders

Though some preferred shares are owned by individual investors, many of them are issued by startup firms to other corporations to raise their initial capital, particularly when those startups are spun off from another, more mature, corporation.

In the United States, at the time of the writing of this text, the corporate tax rate remains a flat 21%, while personal tax rates range from 10% up to 37%, depending upon income tax bracket. To further complicate matters, dividends received by one corporation from another benefit from a **dividend received deduction (DRD)** on the amount of dividends that taxes must be paid on, amounting to at least 50% (or 65%, if the recipient of the dividend distribution owns at least 20% but less than 80% of the distributing corporation) of dividends received.

dividend received reduction (DRD) a policy of the U.S. Internal Revenue Service (IRS) allowing corporations to only pay taxes on between 35% and 50% of dividends received from other corporations

Excel Expert 12-9

The price of the noncumulative, participating convertible preferred will be:

	A	B	C
1	Dividend	$ 7.00	
2	Discount rate	6.50%	
3	V_0	$ 12.37	
4			
5	Price	$ 120.06	=B1/B2+B3

Taking into account the already existing differential between tax rates faced by corporations and those faced by individuals, the effective after-tax dividend yield for corporations investing in preferred stock can range from

$$\text{after-tax corporate yield if ownership} \geq 20\% \text{ and} < 80\% = k \times (1 - .21$$
$$\times [1 - .65]) = .9265k$$

to

$$\text{after-tax corporate yield if ownership} < 20\% \text{ or} \geq 80\% = k \times (1 - .21$$
$$\times [1 - .50]) = .895k$$

While the effective after-tax yields to individuals investing in preferred stock can range from

$$\text{after-tax individual yield if tax rate is } 10\% = k \times (1 - .10) = .9k$$

to

$$\text{after-tax individual yield if tax rate is } 37\% = k \times (1 - .37) = .63k$$

Obviously, between the relatively low tax rate of 21% and the impact of the DRD, corporations have a significant tax advantage over most individual investors when investing in preferred stock.

However, certain types of dividends are excluded from the DRD and corporations cannot claim a deduction for them. For example, corporations cannot take a deduction for dividends received from a real estate investment trust (REIT), or if the company distributing the dividend is exempt from taxation under section 501 or 521 of the Internal Revenue Code for the tax year of the distribution or the preceding year.

Conclusion

Although vanilla preferred stock mimics many of the characteristics of fixed-coupon debt, we have seen that even it exhibits several characteristics (cumulative dividends, the possibility to defer dividends if necessary, and potential voting rights in certain situations) that differentiates it from debt. When we add other, unique additional features, such as convertibility, noncumulative dividends, and participation, preferred stock starts to much more closely resemble common stock. As such, investing in preferred shares, if they are chosen correctly, can provide a good deal of flexibility and diversification to a portfolio.

While more exotic preferreds, such as convertibles, require sophisticated option-pricing formulas to value them,

most of the other types of preferred stock with special features merely require adjustment to the dividends or interest rates in the Gordon Growth Pricing Model used to value stocks covered in Chapter 11.

The tax implications of preferred issues also require special attention, as the size and use of convertible issues often involve them representing a sizeable portion of the startup capital of new firms. This means that the percentage ownership of one corporation by another corporation that receives preferred stock can easily fall in the "sweet" spot between 20% and 80% ownership necessary to take full advantage of the DRD.

Chapter Equations

$$P_0 = \frac{D}{k}$$ 12-1

$$Return = k + \frac{P_1 - P_0}{P_0}$$ 12-2

$$P_0 = D \times \frac{1 - \dfrac{1}{(1 + k)^n}}{k} + \frac{P_n}{(1 + k)^n}$$ 12-3

$$Conversion\ Price = \frac{P_0}{Conversion\ Ratio}$$ 12-4

$$P_{Convertible,0} = \frac{D}{k} + V_0$$ 12-5

Excel Functions

PV(rate, nper, pmt, [fv], [type])

Key Terms

Bank for International Settlements (BIS) – an international organization tasked with supporting countries' central banks' pursuit of monetary and financial stability and acting as a bank for central banks

call provision – a feature of a security that allows the issuer to retire the security early, usually by paying a premium over the par value

class – a subcategory of stocks or bonds having different features than other classes of the same type of security for the same issuer

consol – a British government debt security having an infinite maturity

conversion price – the effective price per share paid when converting a share of preferred stock or a bond into common stock

conversion ratio – the number of shares of common stock received for converting a preferred share or bond into common stock

convertible – a security that can be converted into shares of common stock upon the decision of the holder

cumulative dividend – a feature of preferred stock wherein a "skipped" dividend has to be made up before the issuing firm can pay any dividends to common shareholders

dividend received reduction (DRD) – a policy of the U.S. Internal Revenue Service (IRS) allowing corporations to only pay taxes on between 35% and 50% of dividends received from other corporations

duration – the weighted average time to maturity of a security's cash flows

fixed-income security – a security that promises to pay a fixed income stream in the form of fixed dividends or bond interest payments

floating – a security whose payments to purchasers adjust based on some variable market rate of return

London InterBank Offer Rate (LIBOR) – the benchmark interest rate at which major global banks lend to each other

noncumulative dividend – a feature of preferred stock allowing for a dividend on the stock to be skipped by the issuer with no penalty or repayment necessary

participating – a feature of a preferred share or bond where a promised amount is paid each period, but also can possibly receive "extra" payments from the firm if some financial benchmark is met

perpetual – a feature of a security where it never matures

poison pill – a defense mechanism used mainly in hostile takeover situations

sinking fund – a pool of money required by an issuing firm to be accumulated over time in preparation of the buyback or settlement of a security issue

tier 1 capital – the core capital held in a bank's reserves

TRuPS – hybrid securities that are included in regulatory tier 1 capital for Bank Holding Companies and whose dividend payments are tax deductible for the issuer

Questions

1. **Preferred Stock.** Why would someone invest in preferred stock? What features would appeal to them, and why? (LO 12-1)
2. **Change in Yield.** What effect would an increase in the required rate of return have on the price of an existing share of preferred stock? Why? (LO 12-1)
3. **Finite Lives.** Would a finite-lived preferred stock sell for more or less than a perpetual preferred stock? Why? (LO 12-2)
4. **Conversion Ratio.** What effect should you expect a common stock split to have on the conversion ratio for convertible preferred shares? Why? (LO 12-3)
5. **Floating Preferred Shares.** Why do floating preferred shares generally sell for close to par? (LO 12-4)
6. **Noncumulative Preferred Shares.** What would keep firms from permanently skipping dividends on noncumulative preferred shares? (LO 12-5)
7. **Participating Preferred Shares.** Explain how participating preferred shares could be used as part of a poison pill strategy. (LO 12-6)
8. **Preferred Share Options.** Intuitively, how would you value callable, puttable preferred shares? (LO 12-3)
9. **DRD.** Explain how a change in the DRD to only allow corporations to exclude 35% of dividends from other corporations would affect the price of preferred shares. (LO 12-7)
10. **Non-Preferred Shares.** If we wanted to create a class of common stock that could be called "non-preferred shares," how would we go about doing so? What features discussed in this chapter would such shares have? (LO 12-1)

Problems

1. **Stock price.** If a newly issued preferred stock will have an annual dividend of $3 and a dividend yield of 7%, what will the price of each share be? (LO 12-1)
2. **Dividend yield.** If a newly issued preferred stock will have an annual dividend of $1.23 and a price of $25.25, what will the dividend yield be? (LO 12-1)
3. **Stock price.** If a newly issued preferred stock will have a quarterly dividend of $1.05 and a dividend yield of 4.23%, what will the price of each share be? (LO 12-1)
4. **Quarterly dividend.** If a company wants to price a new preferred stock issue at $50 and needs to offer an effective annual yield of 5.5%, what should they set the quarterly dividend to? (LO 12-1)

5. **Preferred stock price.** Suppose that a preferred stock is paying an annual dividend of $4.25, has a 6% rate of return, and is callable in 10 years at a price of $250. What should the price of each share be? (LO 12-2)

6. **Preferred stock price.** Suppose that a preferred stock is paying a quarterly dividend of $1.27, has a 5.5% effective annual rate of return, and is callable in 15 years at a price of $75. What should be the price of each share? (LO 12-2)

7. **Conversion price.** If a preferred share is selling for $31.30 and has a conversion ratio of 1.5, what is the conversion price? (LO 12-3)

8. **Conversion price.** If a preferred share is selling for $125 and has a conversion ratio of 5, what is the conversion price? (LO 12-3)

9. **Floating preferred.** You are considering buying a floating preferred share slated to pay an annual dividend of $2.50 one year from now. The preferred's dividends will reset to LIBOR + 2.3%, and the current LIBOR rate is .7%. If the shares have a par value of $25, what price should you expect to pay today? (LO 12-4)

10. **Floating preferred.** You are considering buying a floating preferred share slated to pay a quarterly dividend of $.75 one quarter from now. The preferred's dividends will reset to LIBOR + 1.5%, and the current LIBOR rate is .7%. If the shares have a par value of $50, what price should you expect to pay today? (LO 12-4)

11. **Floating preferred.** You are considering buying a floating preferred share slated to pay a quarterly dividend of $.50 each quarter over the next year. The preferred's dividends will reset to LIBOR + 3.25%, but only annually and, in this case, at the end of the coming year. If the current LIBOR rate is .5% and the shares have a par value of $37.50, what price should you expect to pay today? (LO 12-4)

12. **Noncumulative preferred.** You own a floating, noncumulative preferred share that normally pays dividends quarterly. The firm has announced that, due to current economic conditions, it will not be paying dividends for the next year but expects to restart dividends one quarter into next year, paying the promised rate of LIBOR + 2.2%. If the current LIBOR rate is .5% and the shares have a par value of $37.50, what price should you expect to pay today? (LO 12-5)

13. **Noncumulative preferred.** You own a share of noncumulative preferred stock that normally pays a quarterly dividend of $1. If the appropriate rate of return is 6% per year, but the company has announced that it will be suspending dividends for the next two quarters, what price should the stock be selling for right now? (LO 12-5)

14. **Preferred interest rate.** A share of noncumulative preferred stock that normally pays a dividend of $1.25 per quarter but which has had its dividend halted for the next year is selling for a price of $33.45. What is the appropriate interest rate for this stock? (LO 12-5)

15. **Participating preferred.** A share of participating preferred stock offers a guaranteed $5 annual dividend and has an appropriate rate of return of 8%. What should the stock be selling for? (LO 12-6)

16. **Participating preferred.** A share of participating preferred stock offers a guaranteed $1.50 quarterly dividend and has an appropriate rate of return of 5%. What should the stock be selling for? (LO 12-6)

17. **Conversion option.** Suppose a share of convertible preferred stock was selling for $27.50 when an otherwise equivalent share of preferred stock for the same company was selling for $19.73. What would be the value of the conversion option? (LO 12-3)

18. **Conversion option.** Suppose a share of convertible preferred stock was selling for $10.50 when an otherwise equivalent share of preferred stock for the same company was selling for $13.00. What would be the value of the conversion option? (LO 12-3)

19. **Preferred after-tax yield.** A corporation owning preferred shares in another corporation earns a before-tax dividend yield of 6.7% on those shares. If the receiving corporation faces a corporate tax rate of 21%, what is the effective after-tax yield on those shares if the corporation owns 35% of the dividend-paying firm? (LO 12-7)

20. **Preferred after-tax yield.** An individual owning preferred shares in another corporation earns a before-tax dividend yield of 8.2% on those shares. If they face a personal tax rate of 22%, what is their effective after-tax yield on those shares? (LO 12-7)

Case Study

Preferred share issue

On June 22, 2021, LifeMD filed a prospectus with the U.S. Securities and Exchange Commission (SEC) for an issue of preferred shares. That prospectus is available at https://www .sec.gov/Archives/edgar/data/948320/000149315221024380 /form424b5.htm. You may also find current pricing information on these shares at Yahoo! Finance by searching for "LFMDP" on http://finance.yahoo.com. Refer to these sources to answer the following questions:

a. Using the prospectus, what are the details of the preferred issue (how many shares, par value, etc.) and which, if any, of the special features discussed in this chapter does this issue have?

b. How much will the dividends be, and how often will they be paid?

c. Based on the current market price, what is the dividend yield on these shares?

Part 4

Investing in Debt

Part 4 focuses on particular types of securities that pay a fixed annual income: corporate bonds and bonds issues and backed by federal, state, and municipal governments. Chapter 13 covers on (1) the characteristics and risks common to all corporate debt instruments, (2) the mechanics of purchasing bonds, (3) the variety of types of bonds available by varying their characteristics, (4) the retirement of debt, (5) bond pricing, and (6) how variations in risk and yields affect their pricing. Chapter 14 takes a similar approach with government debt, covering (1) the variety of federal government debt securities, (2) types of state and local government debt securities, and (3) the debt of foreign governments.

Chapter 13

Valuing Corporate Bonds

Learning Objectives

After reading this chapter, you should be able to:

LO 13-1   Identify and discuss the implications of the general characteristics of bonds.
LO 13-2   Explain how risk is rated in bonds, and how those ratings affect firms' borrowing terms.
LO 13-3   Describe the mechanics of purchasing bonds.
LO 13-4   Detail the types and attributes of corporate bonds and high-yield securities.
LO 13-5   Explain how interest is accrued and taxed with bonds.
LO 13-6   Illustrate how debt is retired.
LO 13-7   Demonstrate how to price bonds.
LO 13-8   Calculate and explain the various measures of bond yield.
LO 13-9   Estimate and give examples of the use of duration and convexity to measure the impact of changes in yield on bond price.
LO 13-10 Construct strategies for managing bond portfolios.

bond
a debt security that matures in longer than a year

covenant
the terms of agreement between a bond issuer and the bondholder

Benjamin Franklin once recommended, "If you would know the value of money, go and try to borrow some." Even though the terms of a loan can be burdensome corporations and governments do borrow, often under disadvantageous terms, to finance investments in plant, equipment, or inventory or for the construction of roads and schools. Internally generated funds are often insufficient to finance such investments on a pay-as-you-go basis. **Bonds**, defined as debt securities that mature at the end of a term longer than one year, permit firms and governments to acquire assets now and pay for them over a period of years. This long-term debt is then retired for corporations by the cash flow that is generated by plant and equipment and for governments by the fees or tax revenues that are collected.

If you are not familiar with bonds, they probably sound a lot like the loans consumers take out to acquire large material assets, such as car loans or home mortgages. In terms of the borrower using the funds to invest in an asset, they are very similar; however, but bonds' **covenants** and their cash flows to pay back the loan can exhibit an amazingly wide variety. This chapter will delve into that variety, building up from a discussion of the characteristics common to all debt instruments and the risks and mechanics of investing in them. We will then discuss the pertinent attributes of the different major types of corporate bonds, including how they are paid off. The chapter will end with pricing bonds and how to measure and deal with the **price sensitivity** associated with holding bonds in your portfolio.

Like stock, bonds may initially be purchased by financial institutions in a **private placement** or by investors through a **public offering**. Once the bonds have been sold to the general public, these debt securities may subsequently be bought and sold through organized exchanges or in the over-the-counter markets. There is an active secondary market for many debt securities, so the investor may readily increase or liquidate positions in bonds.

> **price sensitivity**
> the variance in bond price caused by changes in yield

> **private placement**
> an issue of securities that are sold to pre-selected investors and institutions rather than on the open market

> **public offering**
> an issue of securities that are sold on the open market

13-1 General Features of Bonds

13-1a Interest and Maturity

All bonds (i.e., long-term debt instruments) have similar characteristics. They represent the indebtedness (liability) of their issuers in return for a specified sum, which is called the **principal**. Virtually all debt has a **maturity date**, which is the particular date by which it must be paid off. When debt is issued, the length of time to maturity is set; it may range from one day to 20 or 30 years or more. (As an example, Disney has an outstanding bond that matures in 2093.) If the maturity date falls within a year of the date of issuance, the debt is referred to as short-term debt. Long-term debt matures more than a year after it has been issued. (Debt that matures in 1 to 10 years is sometimes referred to as "intermediate-term" debt.) The owners of debt instruments receive a flow of payments, which is called **interest**, in return for the use of their money. Interest should not be confused with other forms of income, such as the cash dividends that are paid by common and preferred stock. Dividends are distributions from earnings, whereas interest is an expense of borrowing.

> **principal**
> the amount borrowed in a bond issue

> **maturity date**
> the date that the final repayment of principal is made on a bond issue

> **interest**
> money paid by a borrower in compensation for the use of the lender's funds

When a debt instrument such as a bond is issued, the rate of interest to be paid by the borrower is established. This rate is frequently referred to as the bond's **coupon rate**. The amount of interest is usually fixed over the lifetime of the bond. (There are exceptions; for example, see the section on variable interest rate bonds later in this chapter.) The return earned by the investor, however, need not be equal to the specified rate of interest, because bond prices change. They may be purchased at a discount (a price below the face amount or principal) or at a premium (a price above the face amount of the bond). The return that is actually earned depends on the interest received, the purchase price, and what the investor receives upon selling or redeeming the bond.

> **coupon rate**
> the interest rate paid on a bond, expressed as a percentage of the face value of the bond

The potential return offered by a bond is referred to as the **yield**. Yield is frequently expressed in two ways: the current yield and the yield to maturity. **Current yield** refers only to the annual flow of interest or income. The **yield to maturity (YTM)** refers to the yield that the investor will earn if the debt instrument is held from the moment of purchase until it is redeemed at par (face value) at maturity. The difference between the current yield and the yield to maturity is discussed in the section on the pricing of bonds.

> **yield**
> the return offered by a bond

> **current yield**
> the annual flow of interest on a bond, expressed as a percentage of the price paid

Generally, the longer the term to maturity, the higher the interest rate will be. This relationship is illustrated in **Figure 13-1**, which plots the yield of various U.S. government securities as of April 2004, March 2012, and October 2021.

> **yield to maturity (YTM)**
> the yield that an investor will earn if the bond is held until it is redeemed at face value at maturity

Figure 13-1: Positively Sloped Yield Curves

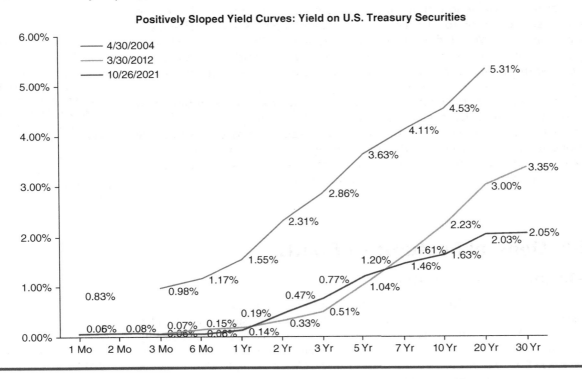

This figure, which is frequently referred to as a **yield curve**, indicates that bonds with the longest time to maturity have the highest interest rates. For example, in April 2004, the short-term securities with three months to maturity had a yield of 0.92%; one-year bonds paid 1.19%, and the bonds that mature in 20 years paid almost 4.8%. The figure also illustrates the large decline in interest rates that followed the financial crises of 2008–2009 and the aftermath of the COVID-19 pandemic. In both cases, the yields on the 1- through 12-month securities were virtually nonexistent (less than 0.15%). While yields on the longer-term bonds were higher than the short-term securities, the spread between the long- and short-term bonds was much smaller; i.e., the slope of the yield curve was a lot flatter.

yield curve
a plot of bond yield against bond maturity

The positive relationship between yields and the term to maturity makes intuitive sense. The longer the term, the longer the investor must tie up their funds. To induce investors to lend their funds for lengthier periods, it is usually necessary to pay them more interest. Also, there is more risk involved in purchasing a bond with a longer term to maturity, as both the future financial condition of the issuer and the spending power of the interest received are less certain. This means that investors will generally require additional compensation to bear the risk associated with long-term debt.

Although such a positive relationship between time and yield does usually exist, there have been periods when the opposite has occurred (i.e., when short-term interest rates exceeded long-term interest rates). This happened from 1978 to 1979, again in 1981, and yet again right before the COVID-19 pandemic in 2019, as illustrated in **Figure 13-2**. In each case, the yield curves had a negative slope, indicating that as the length of time to maturity increased, the interest rates declined.

Figure 13-2: Negatively Sloped Yield Curves

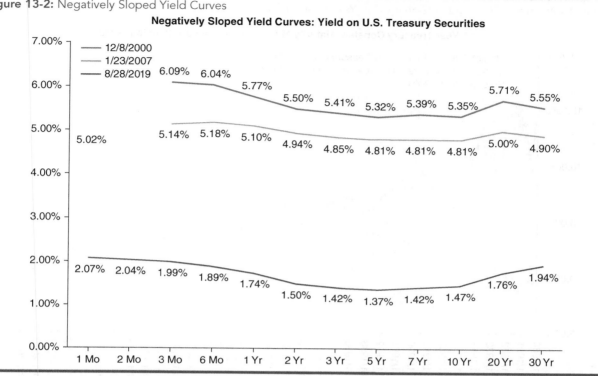

Negatively Sloped Yield Curves: Yield on U.S. Treasury Securities

Such a yield curve can sometimes be explained by inflation, which exceeded 10% in 1981 to 1982. The Board of Governors of the Federal Reserve was pursuing a tight monetary policy in order to fight inflation. It sold short-term government securities (i.e., Treasury bills) in an effort to reduce the capacity of commercial banks to lend. These sales depressed the prices of all fixed-income securities, which resulted in higher yields. (As is explained later in this chapter, yields on debt instruments rise as their prices fall.) The yields on short-term securities rose more than those on long-term securities, and this, coupled with other events in the money and capital markets, resulted in the negatively sloped yield curve. When the rate of inflation abated during the mid-1980s, the yield curve returned to the positive slope that it maintains during most periods.

Figures 13-1 and 13-2 also illustrate that interest rates do change. (You should remember that the interest rate is the current rate paid for credit. That rate should not be confused with the coupon rate, which is fixed when the debt is issued.) Although all interest rates fluctuate, short-term rates fluctuate more than long-term rates. These differences in fluctuations are illustrated in **Figure 13-3**, which plots the yields on a 2-year Treasury bond and a 30-year Treasury bond, as well as the difference or "spread" between them, since 1980. As may be seen in the figure, the fluctuations for the short-term debt are greater than for the 30-year bond. For example, the yields on the two-year Treasury bond decreased from 7% in late 1990 to below 4% in early 1992, while the yield on the bond declined from 8.5 to 7.9% during the same period. Figure 13-3 also illustrates how quickly rates can change. Short-term rates rose from 10.1 to 15% in only three months during 1980 in response to change in the demand and supply of short-term credit.

Figure 13-3: Rates and Spread on 2-Year vs. 10-Year Treasury Bonds

10-Year Treasury Constant Maturity Minus 2-Year Treasure Constant Maturity

Legend:
— Market Yield on 10-Year US Treasury Constant Maturity
— Market Yield on 2-Year US Treasury Constant Maturity
— Spread (10 Yr - 2 Yr)

13-1b The Indenture

Each debt agreement has terms that the debtor must meet. These are stated in a legal document called the indenture. (For publicly held corporate bond issues, the indenture is filed with the Securities and Exchange Commission.) These terms include the coupon rate, the date of maturity, and any other conditions required of the debtor. One of the more frequent of these requirements is the pledging of collateral, which is property that the borrower must offer to secure the loan. For example, the collateral for a mortgage loan is the building. Any other assets owned by the borrower, such as securities or inventory, may also be pledged to secure a loan. If the borrower defaults on the debt, the creditor may seize the collateral and sell it to recoup the principal. Default occurs when the borrower fails to meet not only the payment of interest but any of the terms of the indenture. The other conditions of the indenture are just as important as meeting the interest payments on time, and often they may be more difficult for the debtor to satisfy.

Examples of common loan restrictions include (1) limits on paying dividends, (2) limits on issuing additional debt, and (3) restrictions on merging or significantly changing the nature of the business without the prior consent of the creditors. In addition, loan agreements usually specify that if the firm defaults on any other outstanding debt issues, this debt issue is also in default, in which case the creditors may seek immediate repayment. Default on one issue, then, usually puts all outstanding debt in default.

These examples do not exhaust all the possible conditions of a given loan. Since each loan is separately negotiated, there is ample opportunity for differences among loan agreements. During periods of scarce credit, the terms of a loan agreement will be stricter, whereas during periods of lower interest rates and more readily available credit, the restrictions will tend to be more lenient. The important point, however, is that if any part of the loan agreement is violated, the creditor may declare that the debt is in default and may seek a court order to enforce the terms of the indenture.

13-1c The Role of the Trustee

Many debt instruments are purchased by individual investors who may be unaware of the terms of the indenture. To protect their interests, a trustee is appointed for each publicly held bond issue. It is the trustee's job to see that the terms of the indenture are upheld and to take remedial action if the company defaults on the terms of the loan. For performing these services, the trustee receives compensation from the issuer of the debt.

Trustees are usually commercial banks that serve both the debtor and the bondholders. They act as transfer agents for the bonds when ownership is changed through sales in the secondary markets. These banks receive from the debtor the funds to pay the interest, and this money is then distributed to the individual bondholders. It is also the job of the trustee to inform the bondholders if the firm is no longer meeting the terms of the indenture. In case of default, the trustee may take the debtor to court to enforce the terms of the contract. If there is a subsequent reorganization or liquidation of the company, the trustee continues to act on behalf of the individual bondholders to protect their principal.

13-1d Forms of Debt

Debt instruments are issued in one of two forms: (1) registered bonds or (2) bearer bonds to which coupons are attached (therefore, they are also called **coupon bonds**). Registered bonds are similar to stock certificates; the bonds are registered in the owner's name. Delivery of the bonds is made to the registered owner, who also receives the interest payments from the trustee bank. When the bond is sold, it is registered in the name of the new owner by the transfer agent.

coupon bond
a bond that pays a coupon payment

While bonds may be registered in the name of the owner, most registered bonds are issued in book form. No actual bonds are printed; instead, a computer record of owners is maintained by the issuer or the issuer's agent, such as a bank. If a bond is sold only in book form, the investor cannot take delivery, and the bond must be registered in the street name of the investor's brokerage firm or whoever is holding the bond for the investor. Such a system is obviously more efficient than physically issuing the bond.

Bearer bonds are entirely different. Ownership is evidenced by mere possession and is transferred simply by passing the bond from the seller to the buyer. No new certificates are issued. Securities in this form are easy to transfer. They are like currency if lost, so the possibility of theft has to be a real concern. If the bonds are stolen, they may not be traceable. For this reason, many brokerage firms will not accept bearer bonds for sale or to put on an account unless the individual has proof of purchase.

Because the issuer of bearer bonds does not know the names of the owners of the securities, coupons are attached to the bond. The owner detaches the coupon and sends it in for payment to collect the interest. In the past, most bonds were issued in this form. Investors who relied on fixed-income payments for their livelihood were frequently called "coupon clippers," and the term "coupon" continues to mean the interest payment made by a bond.

Under current federal law, all newly issued corporate and municipal bonds must be registered in the name of the owner or whoever holds the bond for the owner (e.g., a brokerage firm). The primary reason for this ban on issuing bearer bonds with coupons attached is that they are an easy means to evade taxes. When the coupons are cashed, there may be no record of the interest payment, so income taxes may not be paid. Since possession is indication of ownership, the bonds may also be used to evade estate taxes. When the owner dies, the bonds may pass to an heir without being included in the estate. Since the transfer of ownership through the estate is avoided, the value of the bonds may not be reported for purposes of estate taxation. Given the ease with which these bonds facilitate tax evasion, it should hardly be surprising that the federal government outlawed bearer bonds.

13-2 Risk

An important characteristic of all debt is risk: risk that the interest will not be paid (i.e., risk of default); risk that the principal will not be repaid; risk that the price of the debt instrument may decline; risk that inflation will reduce the purchasing power of the interest payments and of the principal when it is repaid; risk that the bond will be retired (i.e., called) prior to maturity, thereby denying the investor the interest payments for the term of the bond; and risk that interest rates will fall, resulting in lower interest income when the proceeds are reinvested. These risks vary with different types of debt. For example, even with the credit downgrade in 2011, the general belief is that there is no risk of default on the interest payments and principal repayments of the debt of the federal government. The reason for this absolute safety is that the federal government has the power to tax and to create money. The government can always issue the money that is necessary to pay the interest and repay the principal. (A decline in the value of the dollar in foreign countries may reduce the attractiveness of federal obligations. Fluctuations in the value of the dollar impose an additional risk for foreigners who invest in federal government securities.)

The procedure is more subtle than just printing new money. The federal government issues new debt and sells it to the Federal Reserve Board. With the proceeds of these sales, the federal government retires the old debt. The money supply increases because newly created money is used to pay for the debt. The effect of selling debt to the Federal Reserve Board and then using the proceeds to retire existing debt (or to finance a current deficit) is no different from printing and spending new money. The money supply expands in either case. Thus, the federal government can always pay its interest expense and retire its debt when it becomes due.

Even though the federal government can refund its debt and is thus free of the risk of default, the prices of the federal government's bonds can and do fluctuate. In addition, the purchasing power of the dollar may decline as a result of inflation, and, therefore, the purchasing power of funds invested in debt also may decline. Thus, investing in federal government securities is not free of risk, as the investor may suffer losses from price fluctuations of the debt or from inflation.

The debt of firms, individuals, and state and local governments involves even greater risk, for all these debtors may default on their obligations. To aid buyers of debt instruments, several companies have developed credit rating systems. The most important of these services are Moody, Dun & Bradstreet, and S&P's. Although these firms do not rate all debt instruments, they do rate the degree of risk of a significant number. (The word credit is derived from the Latin word *credo*, which means "I believe." The implication is that creditors believe the borrower will pay the interest and repay the principal.)

Exhibit 13-1 gives the risk classifications presented by Moody and S&P's. The rating systems are quite similar, for each classification of debt involving little risk (high-quality debt) receives a rating of triple A, while debt involving greater risk (poorer-quality debt) receives progressively lower ratings. Bonds rated triple B or better are considered investment grade, while bonds with lower ratings are often referred to as junk bonds or high-yield securities. The growth in this poor-quality debt was one of the phenomena within the financial markets during the 1980s. (The variety of features found in junk bonds is covered later in this chapter.)

Even within a given rating, both Moody and S&P's fine-shade their rankings. Moody adds the numbers 1 through 3 to indicate degrees of quality within a ranking, with 1 representing the highest rank and 3 the lowest. Thus, a bond rated A1 has a higher rating than a bond rated A3. Standard & Poor's uses + and − to indicate shades of quality. Thus, a bond rated A+ has a higher rating than an A bond, which, in turn, has a better rating than an A− bond.

Because the rating services analyze the comparable data, their ratings of specific debt issues should be reasonably consistent. This consistency is illustrated in **Exhibit 13-2**, which gives the ratings for several different bond issues. Generally, both S&P's and Moody assigned comparable ratings such as the AA+ and Aa1 ratings for the Apple bond. When the ratings differ, the discrepancies are small.

Exhibit 13-1: Bond Ratings

Moody's Bond Ratings*			
Aaa	Bonds of highest quality	B	Bonds that lack characteristics of a desirable investment
Aa	Bonds of high quality		
A	Bonds whose security of principal and interest is con sidered adequate but may be impaired in the future	Caa	Bonds in poor standing that may be defaulted
Baa	Bonds of medium grade that are neither highly protected nor poorly secured	Ca	Speculative bonds that are often in default
		C	Bonds with poor prospects of any investment value (lowest rating)
Ba	Bonds of speculative quality whose future cannot be considered well assured		

For rating Aa through B, 1 indicates the high, 2 indicates the middle, and 3 indicates the low end of the rating class.

S&P's Bond Rating†			
AAA	Bonds of highest quality	BBB	Bonds of lower-medium grade with few desirable investment characteristics
AA	High-quality debt obligations	B	Primarily speculative bonds with great uncertainties and major risk if exposed to adverse conditions
A	Bonds that have a strong capacity to pay interest and principal but msy be susceptible to adverse effects	CCC	Income bonds on which no interest is being paid
		C	
BBB	Bonds that have an adequate capacity to pay interest and principal but are move vulnerable to adverse economic conditions or changing circumstances	D	Bonds in default

Plus(+) and minus (−) are used to show relative strength and weakness within a rating category.

*Source: Adapted from *Moody's Bond Record*.
†Source: Adapted from *Standard & Poor's Bond Guide*.

Exhibit 13-2: Ratings for Selected Bond Issues

Issuer	Coupon Rate of Interest Moody's Rating	S&P's Rating
3M	3.05% A1	A+
Apple	1.65% Aa1	AA+
Bank of America	4.25% A2	A–
Conagra	8.25% Baa3	BBB–
Dollar General	3.50% Baa2	BBB
Kellogg	2.10% Baa2	BBB
Proctor & Gamble	1.20% Aa3	AA–
Target	2.35% A2	A

Source: E^TRADE

These ratings play an important role in the marketing of debt obligations. Because the possibility of default may be substantial for poor-quality debt, some financial institutions and investors will not purchase debt with a low credit rating. Many financial institutions, especially commercial banks, are prohibited by law from purchasing bonds with a rating below Baa. Thus, if the rating of a bond issued by a firm or a municipality is low or declines from the original rating, the issuer may have difficulty selling its debt. Corporations and municipal governments try to maintain good credit ratings because high ratings reduce the cost of borrowing and increase the marketability of the debt.

Although the majority of corporate and municipal bonds are rated, there are exceptions. If a firm or municipality believes it will be able to market the securities without a rating, it may choose not to incur the costs necessary to have the securities rated. Unrated securities tend to be small issues and, because they lack the approval implied by a rating, probably should be viewed as possessing considerable risk.

Besides the risk of default, creditors are also subject to the risk of price fluctuations. Once debt has been issued, the market price of the debt will rise or fall depending on market conditions. If interest rates rise, the price of existing debt must fall so that its fixed interest payments relative to its price become competitive with the higher rates. In the event that interest rates decline, the opposite is true. The higher fixed-interest payments of the bond make the debt more attractive than comparable newly issued bonds, and buyers will be willing to pay more for the debt issue. Why these fluctuations in the price of debt instruments occur is explained in more detail later in the chapter.

There is, however, one feature of debt that partially compensates for the risk of price fluctuations. The holder knows that the debt ultimately matures: the principal must be repaid. If the price of the bond decreases and the debt instrument sells for a discount (i.e., less than the face value), the value of the debt must appreciate as it approaches maturity, because on the day of maturity, the full amount of the principal must be repaid.

Since interest rates fluctuate, bondholders may also bear reinvestment rate risk. This risk does not apply if the investor is spending payments as they are received, but that is often not the case. Instead, the payments are reinvested, and lower interest rates imply that the individual will earn less and accumulate a lower terminal value. The converse would also apply if interest rates were higher. The reinvested payments would earn more, and the investor would accumulate a larger terminal value.

Bondholders and creditors also endure the risk associated with inflation, which reduces the purchasing power of money. During periods of inflation, the debtor repays the loan in money that purchases less. Creditors must receive a rate of interest that is at least equal to the rate of inflation to maintain their purchasing power. If lenders anticipate inflation, they will demand a higher rate of interest to help protect their purchasing power. For example, if the rate of inflation is 3%, the creditors may demand 6%. Although inflation still causes the real value of the capital to decline, the higher interest rate partially offsets the effects of inflation.

If creditors do not anticipate inflation, the rate of interest may be insufficient to compensate for the loss in purchasing power. Inflation, then, hurts the creditors and helps the debtors, who are repaying the loans with money that purchases less.

The supposed inability of creditors to anticipate inflation has led to a belief that it is better to be a debtor during inflation. However, creditors invariably make an effort to protect their position by demanding higher interest rates. There is a transfer of purchasing power from creditors to debtors only if the creditors do not fully anticipate the inflation and do not demand sufficiently high interest rates. A transfer of purchasing power from debtors to creditors will occur in the opposite situation. If inflation is anticipated but does not occur, many debtors may pay artificially high interest rates, which transfers purchasing power from them to their creditors. Debtors may seek to protect themselves from the anticipated inflation that is not occurring by having the bond be callable. The call feature is discussed later in this chapter. Hence, the transfer of purchasing power can go either way if one group inaccurately anticipates the future rate of inflation.

If the investor acquires bonds denominated in a foreign currency, there is the additional risk that the value of the currency will decline relative to the dollar. Payments received in yen, euros, or pounds have to be converted into dollars before they may be spent in the United States, so fluctuations in the value of the currency affect the number of dollars the investor will receive. Of course, the value of the foreign currency could rise, which means the investor receives more dollars, but the value could also fall.

All the sources of risk to bondholders (default, fluctuations in bond prices from fluctuations in interest rates, reinvestment rate risk, loss of purchasing power from inflation, and foreign exchange rate risk) are essentially the same as the sources of risk to investors in stock. While a diversified bond portfolio reduces the risk identified with a specific asset (i.e., the risk of default), the risks associated with bond investments in general are not reduced by diversification. Even diversified bond investors must still bear the risks of fluctuations in interest and reinvestment rates, loss of purchasing power from inflation, and declining exchange rates.

13-3 The Mechanics of Purchasing Bonds

Bonds may be purchased in much the same way as stocks. The investor can buy them through a brokerage firm, and some bonds (e.g., federal government securities) can be purchased through commercial banks. The various purchase orders that may be used to buy stock (e.g., the market order or the limit order with a specified price) also apply to the purchase of bonds. Bonds may be bought with cash or through the use of margin. After the debt has been purchased, the broker sends a confirmation statement. **Exhibit 13-3** presents simplified confirmation statements for the purchase and subsequent sale of $10,000 in face value of Tesoro Petroleum bonds. In addition to a description of the securities, the confirmation statements include the price, commission, accrued interest, and net amount due.

Bonds earn interest every day, but the firm distributes the interest payments only twice a year. Thus, when a bond is purchased, the buyer owes the previous owner **accrued interest** for the days that the owner held the bond. In the case of the first transaction, the purchase was made after the last interest payment, so the accrued interest amounted to $54.00. This interest is added to the purchase price that the buyer must pay. When the bond is sold, the seller receives the accrued interest. The second transaction occurred soon after the interest payment, and in this case, the accrued interest was only $12.00, which was added to the proceeds of the sale.

accrued interest
interest owed but not yet paid out

Interest on bonds accrues daily. At 5.25%, the interest on $10,000 is $525, or approximately $1.44 a day. If the purchase of the bond occurs 37 days after the payment date, the accrued interest owed is $53.28. If the sale occurs eight days after the interest payment, the accrued interest received is $11.52. Accrued interest amounts in Exhibit 13-3 are rounded to facilitate the calculation of gains (or losses) in **Exhibit 13-4**.

Exhibit 13-3: Simplified Confirmation Statements for the Purchase and Sale of a Bond

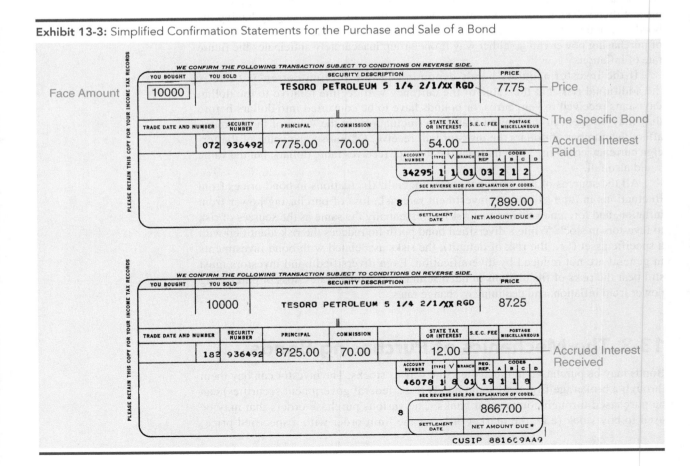

Exhibit 13-4: Determination of Profit or Loss on the Sale of a Bond

Cost basis of the bond:	$7,899.00
Amount due	−54.00
Less accrued interset	$7,845.00
Revenue from the sale:	$8,667.00
Preceeds of the sale	−12.00
Less accrued interest	$8,655.00
Profit (or loss) on the investment:	
Return from the sale of the bond	$8,655.00
Cost basis of the bond	7,845.00
Profit (or loss) on the investment	$810.00

The profit or loss from the investment cannot be figured as the difference between the proceeds of the sale and the amount that is due after the purchase (i.e., $8,667.00 − $7,899.00). Instead, an adjustment must be made for the accrued interest. This procedure is illustrated in Exhibit 13-4. First, the accrued interest must be subtracted from the amount due to obtain the cost of the bond. Thus, $7,899.00 minus $54.00 is the cost ($7,845.00) of this purchase. Second, the accrued interest must also be subtracted from the proceeds of the sale. Thus, $8,667.00 minus $12.00 yields the revenues from the sale. To determine the profit or loss, the cost basis is subtracted from the sale value. In this particular instance, that is $8,655.00 (the sale value) minus $7,845.00 (the cost basis), which represents a gain of $810.00.

A few bonds trade without accrued interest. These bonds are currently in default and are not paying interest. Such bonds are said to trade flat, and an F is placed next to them in the transactions reported by the financial press. These bonds are of little interest except to speculators. The risk in buying them is substantial, but some do resume interest payments that can result in substantial returns.

13-4 Variety of Corporate Bonds

Corporations issue many types of bonds: mortgage bonds, equipment trust certificates, debenture bonds and subordinated debentures, income bonds, convertible bonds, variable interest rate bonds, and zero coupon bonds. These corporate debt instruments are either secured or unsecured. If a debt instrument is secured, the debtor pledges a specific asset as collateral. In case of default, the creditor may seize this collateral (through a court proceeding). Bonds that are not collateralized by specific assets are unsecured. If the debtor were to default, there would be no specific assets the creditors could seize to satisfy their claims on the borrower. Such unsecured debt instruments are supported by the general capacity of the firm to service its debt (i.e., pay the interest and repay the principal). Thus, the capacity of the borrower to generate operating income (i.e., earnings before interest and taxes) is crucial to the safety of unsecured debt obligations.

13-4a Mortgage Bonds

mortgage bond
a bond issued to purchase specific assets and that is secured by that asset

Mortgage bonds are issued to purchase specific fixed assets, which are then pledged to secure the debt. This type of bond is frequently issued by utility companies. The proceeds that are raised by selling the debt are used to build power plants, and these plants secure the debt. As the plants generate revenues, the firm earns the cash flow that is necessary to service (pay interest on) and retire the debt. If the firm defaults on the interest or principal repayment, the creditors may take title to the pledged property. They may then choose to hold the asset and earn income from it (to operate the fixed asset) or to sell it. These options should give investors cause for thought: How many creditors could operate a power plant? If the investors choose to sell it, who would buy it?

These two questions illustrate an important point concerning investing in corporate debt. Although property that is pledged to secure the debt may decrease the lender's risk of loss, the creditor is not interested in taking possession of and operating the property. Lenders earn income through interest payments and not through the operation of the fixed assets. Such creditors are rarely qualified to operate the assets should they take possession of them. If they are forced to seize and sell the assets, they may find few buyers and may have to sell at distress prices. Despite the fact that pledging assets to secure debt increases the safety of the principal, the lenders prefer the prompt payment of interest and principal.

13-4b Equipment Trust Certificates

equipment trust certificate
a mortgage bond secured by assets with substantial resale value

Not all collateral has questionable resale potential. Unlike the mortgage bonds that are issued by utility companies, **equipment trust certificates** are secured by assets with substantial resale value. These certificates are issued to finance specific equipment, which is pledged as collateral. Equipment trust certificates are primarily issued by railroads and airlines to finance rolling stock (railroad cars) and airplanes. As the equipment is used to generate cash flow, the certificates are retired. The collateral supporting these certificates is generally considered to be of excellent quality, for, unlike some fixed assets (e.g., the aforementioned utility plants), this equipment may be readily moved and sold to other railroads and airlines in the event that the firm defaults on the certificates.

Investors, however, should realize that while equipment may be more readily sold than power plants, these investors could still suffer losses. For example, when Eastern, Pan Am, and several small airlines went bankrupt, they dumped a large number of aircraft on the market, so prices for used aircraft declined. This, of course, meant that even the secured creditors did not receive all their principal owed from the proceeds of the sales of the planes.

13-4c Other Asset-Backed Securities and Securitization

While equipment trust certificates are secured by equipment such as railroad cars and mortgages are secured by real estate, other assets may also be used as collateral for a debt issue. For example, a firm may issue and sell debt securities backed by its accounts receivable. (The firm may also sell the receivables outright to a financial institution or factor, who, in turn, issues debt instruments secured by the assets.) As the accounts are collected, the funds are used to retire the securities and pay the interest. The advantage to the issuing firm is simple. It obtains the funds immediately and does not have to wait for the collection of the receivables. The advantage to the investors, especially large pension plans, is that they receive an interest-paying security that is relatively safe since it is secured by the underlying assets.

The process of converting illiquid assets such as accounts receivable into liquid assets is called **securitization**. Textron, a manufacturer of Bell helicopters, Cessna aircraft, automotive products, and fastening systems, sells a variety of products, which generates accounts receivable. In its 2014 Form 10-K, Textron reported that it securitized over $172 million in assets. The proceeds of the sales were then used to retire debt previously issued by Textron.

securitization
the process of turning illiquid assets such as accounts receivable into liquid assets which can be sold

13-4d Debentures

Debentures are unsecured promissory notes that are supported by the general creditworthiness of the firm. This type of debt involves more risk than bonds that are supported by collateral. In the case of default or bankruptcy, the unsecured debt is redeemed only after all secured debt has been paid off. Some debentures are subordinated, and these involve even more risk, for they are redeemed after the other general debt of the firm has been redeemed. Even unsecured debt has a position superior to the subordinated debenture. These bonds are among the riskiest debt instruments issued by firms and usually have higher interest rates or other attractive features, such as convertibility into the stock of the company, to compensate the lenders for assuming the increased risk.

debenture
an unsecured bond or note supported by the general creditworthiness of the firm

Financial institutions, such as commercial banks or insurance companies, prefer a firm to sell debentures to the general public. Because the debentures are general obligations of the company, they do not tie up its specific assets. Then, if the firm needs additional funds from a commercial bank, it can use specific assets as collateral, in which case the bank will be more willing to lend the funds. If the assets had been previously pledged, the firm would lack this flexibility in financing.

Although the use of debentures may not decrease the ability of the firm to issue additional debt, default on the debentures usually means that all senior debt is in default as well. A common indenture clause states that if any of the firm's debt is in default, all debt issues are also in default, and in this case the creditors may declare that all outstanding debt is due. For this reason, a firm should not overextend itself through excessive amounts of unsecured debt.

13-4e Income Bonds

Income bonds are the riskiest bonds issued by corporations. Interest is paid only if the firm earns it. If the company is unable to cover its other expenses, it is not legally obligated to pay the interest on these bonds. Owing to the great risk associated with them, income bonds are rarely issued by corporations. One notable exception is an issue of Disney bonds that could pay as much as 13.5% annually if a package of 20 Disney movies grossed over $800 million. If, however, the gross were less, the bonds could yield as little as 3%.

income bond
a bond that pays interest during a period only if the company makes a certain amount of money during that period

Although income bonds are rarely issued by firms, a similar type of security is often issued by state and municipal governments. These are revenue bonds, which are used to finance a particular capital improvement that is expected to generate revenues (e.g., a toll road or a municipal hospital). If the revenues are insufficient, the interest is not paid.

There is, however, one significant difference between income bonds and revenue bonds. Failure to pay interest does not result in default for an income bond, but it does mean that a revenue bond is in default. Most projects financed by revenue bonds have generated sufficient funds to service the debt, but there have been notable exceptions. Perhaps the most famous default was the multibillion-dollar default by the Washington Public Power Supply System, whose defaulted bonds became virtually worthless.

13-4f Convertible Bonds

Convertible bonds are a hybrid-type security. Technically they are debt: the bonds pay interest, which is a fixed obligation of the firm, and have a maturity date. But these bonds have a special feature: The investor has the option to convert the bond into a specified number of shares of common stock. For example, the Omnicare Inc. 3.75%bond due in 2025 may be converted into 36.4409 shares of Omnicare common stock. The market price of convertible bonds depends on both the value of the stock and the interest that the bonds pay. If the price of the common stock rises, then the value of the bond must rise. The investor thus has the opportunity for capital gain should the price of the common stock rise. If, however, the price of the common stock does not appreciate, the investor still owns a debt obligation of the company and therefore has the security of an investment in a debt instrument.

Convertible bonds have been popular with some investors, and thus firms have issued these bonds as a means to raise funds. However, since convertible bonds are a hybrid-type security, they are difficult to analyze. For this reason, a detailed discussion is deferred until Chapter 16, which follows the discussion of nonconvertible debt and precedes the discussion of options.

13-4g Variable Interest Rate Bonds

Generally, the interest that a bond pays is fixed at the date of issuance; however, some corporations issue **variable interest rate bonds**. Citicorp was the first major American firm to offer bonds with variable interest rates to the general public. Two features of the Citicorp bond were unique at the time it was issued: (1) a variable interest rate that was tied to the interest rate on Treasury bills and (2) the right of the holder to redeem the bond at its face value.

The interest rate to be paid by the Citicorp bond was set at 1% above the average Treasury bill rate during a specified period. This variability of the interest rate means that if short-term interest rates rise, the interest rate paid by the bond must increase. The bond's owner participates in any increase in short-term interest rates. Of course, if the short-term interest rates decline, the bond earns a lower rate of interest.

The second unique feature of the Citicorp bond was that two years after it was issued, the holder had the option to redeem the bond for its face value or principal. This option recurred every six months. If the owner needed the money more quickly, the bond could have been sold in the secondary market, for it was traded on the New York Stock Exchange. An important implication of the variable coupon is that the market price of the bond fluctuates less than the price of a fixed coupon bond. As is explained later in the chapter, the price of a fixed coupon bond fluctuates inversely with interest rates. Such price changes will not occur with a variable rate bond because the interest paid fluctuates with interest rates in general. Hence, these bonds avoid one of the major sources of risk associated with investing in bonds: higher interest rates driving down the bond's market value.

13-4h Zero Coupon Bonds

In 1981, a new type of bond was sold to the general public. These bonds pay no interest and are sold at a discount. The pathbreaking issue was the J.C. Penney **zero coupon bond**. This bond was initially sold for a discount ($330) but paid $1,000 at maturity in 1989. The investor's funds grew from $330 to $1,000 after eight years. The annual rate of growth (i.e., the yield on the bond) was 14.86%.

After the initial success of this issue, other firms, including IBM Credit Corporation (the financing arm of IBM) and ITT Financial, issued similar bonds. In each case the firm pays no periodic interest. The bond sells for a discount, and the investor's return accrues from the appreciation of the bond's value as it approaches maturity.

Because the return on an investment in a zero coupon bond depends solely on the firm's capacity to retire the debt, the quality of the firm is exceedingly important. Zero coupon bonds issued by such firms as IBM Credit Corporation are of excellent quality and should be retired at maturity. In these cases the investor will earn the expected return that accrues when the bond approaches maturity. If, however, the investor purchases low-quality zero coupon bonds, these bonds may never be redeemed. If the firm were to go bankrupt, the investor might receive nothing. Thus, it is possible for the individual who buys zero coupon bonds to lose the entire investment and never receive a single interest payment.

13-4i Eurobonds

Many U.S. firms also issue bonds in foreign countries to raise funds for foreign investments (e.g., plant and equipment). These bonds fall into two basic types, depending on the currency in which they are denominated. U.S. firms can sell bonds denominated in the local currency (e.g., British pounds or European euros). For example, Exxon-Mobil reported in its 2010 10-K report that $617 million of its $11.610 billion of long-term debt (5.3%) was denominated in foreign currencies. The firm can also sell abroad bonds denominated in U.S. dollars called **Eurobonds**. This term applies even though the bonds may be issued in Asia instead of Europe.

When a firm issues a Eurobond, the U.S. firm promises to make payments in dollars. This means that the U.S. investor does not have to convert the payments from the local currency (e.g., British pounds) into dollars. As is explained in Chapter 5, fluctuation in the value of one currency relative to another is a major source of risk that every individual who acquires foreign securities must bear. By acquiring Eurobonds, the U.S. investor avoids this currency risk. However, foreign investors do bear this risk. They have to convert the dollars into their currency, so the yields on Eurobonds tend to be higher than on comparable domestic securities. The higher yield is a major reason some investors find Eurobonds attractive.

Eurobond
a bond issued by a U.S. company that is denominated in U.S. dollars but sold abroad in foreign markets

13-4j LIBOR

The London InterBank Offer Rate (LIBOR) is established daily by the British Bankers' Association and is the interest rate at which large international banks are willing to lend to each other for periods ranging from one day (referred to as "overnight") to one year. Generally, LIBOR is about half a percentage point above the rate on U.S. federal government securities with the same maturities. This differential increases during periods of financial strife such as the last quarter of 2008.

LIBOR is important for two fundamental reasons: (1) it is calculated in 10 currencies and has become the global benchmark for global lending and interest rates; and (2) although LIBOR is not the rate paid on a particular type of debt instrument, it plays an important role in the determination of borrowing costs and hence yields. Many debt instruments have variable rates of interest that are tied to LIBOR. Thus, increases in LIBOR are transferred throughout the world to all debt instruments tied to that rate. These instruments include the corporate high-yield bonds covered in the next section, small business loans, student loans, and adjustable-rate mortgages. The rates on these loans are often several percentage points above the LIBOR rate; this means that if LIBOR rises from 2 to 3%, an adjustable mortgage set 5 percentage points above LIBOR will rise from 7 to 8%.

13-5 High-Yield Securities

high-yield security
any debt of low quality and high risk

High-yield securities (sometimes referred to as junk bonds) are not a particular type of bond but refer to any debt of low quality (i.e., bonds rated below triple B). These bonds have the same general features associated with investment-grade debt. In addition to the interest payment (the coupon) and the maturity date, junk bonds often have call features and sinking funds. Although junk bonds are usually debentures and may be subordinated to the firm's other debt obligations, some do have collateral (i.e., they are mortgage bonds). As is subsequently discussed, some high-yield securities have variations on the basic features associated with all bonds.

The poor quality of junk bonds requires that they offer high yields, at least relative to investment-grade debt. Generally, triple B or better is considered investment grade, and many financial institutions, such as trust departments of commercial banks, are allowed to purchase only investment-grade bonds. Anything with a lower credit rating is not an acceptable risk.

Junk bonds (and high-yield preferred stock) are often issued to finance takeovers and mergers or to finance start-up firms with little credit history. The bonds are purchased by financial institutions and individuals who are accustomed to investing in poor-quality debt and who are willing and able to accept the larger risk in order to earn the higher yields. These investors may treat the bonds as if they are equity instruments that will generate their potential return if the firm generates cash flow and survives. In many cases, the additional return may be 3 or 4 percentage points greater than the yield on investment-grade debt.

High-yield securities may be divided into two classes. First are the bonds that were initially investment grade but whose credit ratings were lowered as the issuing firms developed financial problems. This type of high-yield bond is often referred to as a **fallen angel**. When RJR Nabisco was purchased and taken private, the surviving firm issued substantial new debt that resulted in the downgrading of outstanding RJR Nabisco bonds. The prices of what were previously high-quality debt declined dramatically, and the issues became high-yield securities. Of course, the high yields were to be earned by new buyers and not by the original investors who suffered losses when the prices of the previously issued bonds declined.

fallen angel
a formerly investment-grade bond that has become a high-yield security because of lowered credit ratings

Some fallen angels ultimately go bankrupt. Manville, Public Service of New Hampshire, and Texaco all went bankrupt and defaulted on their debts. However, bonds in default continue to trade, and there is always the possibility that the firm will recover and the price of the bonds will rise. This did occur in the case of Texaco. One of the attractions of the high-yield security market is the possibility that the financial condition of the issuing firm will improve. A higher credit rating should be beneficial to the holders of the firm's debt, because the bonds' prices should increase as the firm's financial condition improves.

The second class of high-yield securities is composed of bonds and preferred stock issued by firms with less than investment-grade credit ratings. The maturities of these securities can range from short term (i.e., high-yield commercial paper) to long term (i.e., bonds and preferred stock).

13-5a Split Coupon Bonds

split coupon bond
a bond that initially pays not coupon, but which starts paying a fixed coupon after a set number of years

A split coupon bond combines the features of zero coupon and high coupon bonds. During the first three to five years, the bond pays initially no (or a small amount of) interest. The interest accrues like a zero coupon bond. After this initial period, the bond pays a high coupon. For example, Dr Pepper issued a split coupon bond that paid no interest for the first four years and then paid a coupon of 11.5% for the next six years, until the bond matured.

The advantage to the firm issuing split coupon bonds is that debt service is eliminated during the initial period. Split coupon bonds conserve cash, but the accrual of interest is tax deductible to the issuing firm. Split coupon bonds are often issued in leveraged buyouts and other recapitalizations that result in the firm issuing substantial amounts of debt.

Split coupon bonds tend to be very costly to the firm issuing them. The high yield to investors means a high cost of funds to the issuers. There is an incentive for the firm to retire the securities as soon as possible. Thus, most split coupon bonds have call features that permit the firm to retire the securities before their maturity. For example, Safeway Stores called half of its issue of junior subordinated debentures only 11 months after the bonds were originally issued.

13-5b Reset Securities and Increasing Rate Bonds

Although the coupons are fixed when most high-yield securities are issued, there are exceptions. With a **reset bond**, the coupon is adjusted at periodic intervals, such as six months or every year. The coupon is usually tagged to a specified rate, such as the six-month Treasury bill rate plus 5%, and there is often a minimum and a maximum coupon. For example, American Shared Hospital Service issued a reset note whose coupon can range from 14 to 16.5%.

reset bond
a bond with a coupon that is readjusted at set intervals

Because the coupon is permitted to change, price fluctuations associated with changes in interest rates are reduced. The minimum coupon, however, means that if interest rates fall on comparably risky securities, the price of the bond will rise, as the coupon becomes fixed at the lower bound. The same applies when interest rates rise. If the coupon reaches the upper limit, further increases in comparable yields will decrease the bond's price. However, within the specified range, the changing coupon should stabilize the price of the bond. Of course, if the firm's financial condition changes, the price of the bond will change independently of changes in interest rates.

An **increasing rate bond** is a debt security whose coupon increases over time. For example, RJR Holdings issued $5 billion of increasing rate notes. One issue had an initial coupon of 14.5625%, but future coupons were to be the higher of 13.4375% or 4% plus the three-month LIBOR rate. Subsequent coupons would increase by 0.5% quarterly for two years and 0.25% quarterly for years three and four. Unless yields declined dramatically so that 13.4375% became the coupon, the yield on this bond would rise over time. Obviously, increasing rate securities are an expensive means for any firm to raise funds, so the investor can anticipate that the issuer will seek to retire the debt as rapidly as possible. This is precisely what occurred, as RJR Holdings refinanced after interest rates fell and its financial position improved.

increasing rate bond
a bond whose coupon increases over time

13-5c Extendible Securities

In the previous discussion, the high-yield securities had differing coupons but fixed maturity dates. Split coupon bonds have periods during which interest accrues but is not paid. Reset and increasing rate notes and bonds have coupons that vary. Each of these types of high-yield securities has a fixed maturity date. However, a firm may issue an **extendible security** in which the term to maturity may be lengthened by the issuer. For example, Mattel issued a bond with an initial maturity date in 1990, but the company could extend the bond for one-, two-, or three-year periods with a final maturity in 1999. Thus, the investor who acquired this bond did not know if the bond would be outstanding for one year or six years or longer. Only the final maturity in 1999 was known.

extendible security
a bond where the term to maturity may be extended at the option of the issuer

The ability to extend the maturity date is, of course, beneficial to the issuer. If the firm does not have the capacity to retire the debt at the initial maturity date, the date may be extended. This buys time for the firm to find the funds or to refinance the debt. Failure to retire the debt at the final maturity, of course, throws the bond into default.

13-5d Spreads and Returns

The coupons on high-yield securities are promised or anticipated yields. In many cases, the promised return will be realized as the firm makes timely payments and retires the securities on schedule. However, securities markets and firms are dynamic entities. Change is always occurring, so the returns actually earned by investors often differ from the expected yields. The actual returns could be higher, especially if interest rates decline or the firm's financial condition improves. In either case, the price of the high-yield security should rise, so that the investor earns a higher return.

While earning higher returns is possible, the greater concern is usually that something will go wrong and that the investor will earn a lower return. Firms that issue high-yield securities are obviously not financially strong, and some will not survive. If the investor is unfortunate enough to select those firms, they could lose a substantial amount of money—perhaps all the funds invested. Avoiding such an outcome is obviously desirable and is the purpose of analyzing the issuer's financial condition and determining the quality of its debt.

Analysis of investment-grade debt revolves around the firm's current and future capacity to service the debt. This analysis may start with such ratios as the debt ratio or times-interest-earned. For high-yield securities, the emphasis is often placed on cash flow (operating income plus noncash expenses, such as depreciation), as interest is paid with funds from operations and not with earnings. Even if the firm is operating at an accounting loss, it may still generate sufficient cash to service its debt.

spread
the difference between rates on high-yield and investment-grade bonds

basis point
one one-hundredth of a percent, or 0.01%

The spread in yields (i.e., the difference) between high-yield and investment-grade debt can be substantial. This difference is usually expressed in terms of basis points. A basis point is 0.01%, so that a difference of 50 basis points is 0.5%. If the yield on AAA-rated bonds is 4.6% and the yield on a B-rated bond is 5.2%, the difference is 60 basis points. If the yields were 4.6 and 7.2%, the difference is 260 basis points (2.6%).

During December 2008, the spread between high-yield junk bonds and AAA-rated bonds reached over 2,100 basis points. In other words, if high-quality debt yielded 4%, junk bonds were yielding over 25%. Eighteen months earlier the spread was about 200 basis points (2%). Even as the financial crisis appeared to abate, the spread still exceeded 1,000 basis points in June 2009. The spread continued to shrink and in January 2015, the yield on junk bonds approximated 7% based on the S&P High Yield Corporate Bond Index and 3.8% for AAA-rated bonds. This difference of 3.2%, however, still exceeded the spread prior to the financial crisis.

Investors may use the spread as a guide for an investment strategy. When the spread increases, the investor sells the quality debt and purchases the lower-quality debt. The process would be reversed when the spread diminished. Essentially, the spread must be sufficient to compensate for the additional risk. Even if only 5% of the bonds were to default, the total loss on each bond may offset a substantial proportion of the yield advantage.

Studies have concluded that returns on portfolios of high-yield debt generate higher returns than investment-grade bonds. Even after adjusting for defaults, the returns were higher. Of course, this would be expected, as the investor bears more risk. If the returns were consistently lower, no one would buy poor-quality debt. The surprise, however, was that high-yield bonds were less volatile. During periods of changing interest rates, their prices did not fluctuate as much.

This lower volatility seems inconsistent with the concept of risky high-yield bonds. However, as is discussed later in the chapter, the prices of bonds with higher coupons tend to fluctuate less than the prices of bonds with lower coupons. Higher-yield bonds have higher coupons than investment-grade bonds, so their prices are less sensitive to changes in interest rates. It is the firm-specific risk (i.e., the unsystematic risk) and not the market or interest rate that is the primary source of risk. The firm-specific source of risk is reduced, if not eliminated, by the construction of a well-diversified portfolio of high-yield securities.

Even though studies concluded that high-yield bonds have done well and exhibit less price volatility, you should realize that historical returns are not future returns. Even if there have been periods when high-yield securities produced greater returns than investment-grade debt, you should not conclude these bonds will continue to do well. Many firms that issue junk bonds ultimately default. Some will be reorganized and survive, but many will not and their bonds will become worthless. During 2007–2009, many firms did default and filed for bankruptcy. Their bonds sold for mere pennies on the dollar. Such valuations suggest that the market did not anticipate the companies and their bonds would survive.

13-6 Accrued Interest, Zero Coupon Bonds, Original-Issue Discount Bonds, and Income Taxation

Bonds accrue interest every day, and that reality affects income taxation. Taxation, of course, affects financial planning and portfolio management. As was illustrated in the section on the mechanics of purchasing a bond, you pay the prior owner accrued interest. In Exhibit 13-3, the accrued interest paid was $54.00. When you receive the six-month $262.50 interest payment (($10,000 \times 0.0525)/2 = $262.50), only $208.50 is subject to income taxation. When you sell the bond, the accrued interest that you receive ($12.00 in Exhibit 13-3) is subject to income taxation.

Zero coupon bonds are initially sold for less than their face value and do not annually pay interest. Instead the interest accrues daily and is received when the bond matures. Tax on the accrued interest, however, occurs every year as if the interest were received. Consider a four-year $1,000 zero coupon bond that sells for $683. The interest rate is 10% and the interest is paid annually. (Bond pricing is discussed below.) After one year, the price of the bond is $751 if interest rates do not change. The appreciation from $683 to $751 ($68) is the accrual of interest, and that $68 is subject to income taxation. At the end of the second, third, and fourth years, the bond's values are $826, $909, and $1,000. The accrued interest earned in each year is $75, $83, and $91.

Notice that the interest earned each year is not an average of the discount: ($1,000 − $683)/4 = $79.25. Each year the accrued interest is determined on the principal and added to the prior year's principal. Thus, the $68 earned in year one is added to $683, which becomes the principal owed ($751) at the end of the first year. This process is repeated until the bond is redeemed at maturity for $1,000. The accrued interest, however, continues to be taxed each year.

The prices in the previous example were determined assuming that interest rates do not change and that the value of the bond increases with the accrual of interest. After the first year, the bond could sell for more or less than $751. If the bond is sold for $773 instead of $751, there is a gain of $90 ($773 − $683). The appreciation, however, is not a capital gain because $68 is the result of the accrued interest. The $68 is taxed as income and the $22 is taxed at the appropriate capital gains tax rate if the bond were sold.

If the price of the bond is $723 and the investor sells the bond, the appreciation is only $723 − $683 = $40. The accrued interest, however, remains $68, so the investor experiences a capital loss of $40 − $68 = ($28). This loss is applied against other capital gains and ordinary income. (The use of capital losses to offset capital gains and ordinary income is discussed in Chapter 4.)

Original-issue discount bonds combine the features of a zero coupon and a coupon bond. When they are issued, the coupon is less than the yield on comparable debt, so the bond sells for a discount. Because the bond does pay some interest, the amount of the discount is less than the discount associated with a zero coupon bond. Over time, the discount disappears as the interest accrues and the bond is redeemed for its face value at maturity. The taxation of the accrual for an original-discount bond is the same as the taxation of a zero coupon bond.

The taxation of the accrued interest that is earned but not received until maturity suggests investors may have little reason to purchase zero coupon bonds. There is, however, one major exception: tax-deferred pension plans. The tax on the accrued interest is deferred until the funds are withdrawn from the account. So the primary reason for acquiring zero coupon bonds is to use them as part of a tax-deferred retirement account.

13-7 Retiring Debt

Debt issues must ultimately be retired, and this retirement must occur on or before the maturity date of the debt. When the bond is issued, a method for periodic retirement is usually specified, for very few debt issues are retired in one lump payment at the maturity date. Instead, part of the issue is systematically retired each year. This systematic retirement may be achieved by issuing the bond in a series or by having a sinking fund.

13-7a Serial Bonds

serial bond
a bond issue where a portion of the issue is scheduled to be retired each year until maturity

In an issue of serial bonds, some bonds mature each year. (Preferred stock may also be issued in series.) This type of bond is usually issued by corporations to finance specific equipment, such as railroad cars, which is pledged as collateral. As the equipment depreciates, the cash flow that is generated by profits and depreciation expense is used to retire the bonds in a series as they mature.

The advertisement presented in **Exhibit 13-5** is for equipment trust certificates issued by Union Pacific Railroad Company. These equipment trust certificates were designed so that one-fifteenth of the securities matured each year. Thus, the firm retired $2,337,000 of the certificates annually as each series within the issue matured. At the end of 15 years, the entire issue of certificates had been retired.

Few corporations, however, issue serial bonds. They are primarily issued by state and local governments to finance capital improvements, such as new school buildings, or by ad hoc government bodies, such as the Port Authority of New York, to finance new facilities or other capital improvements. The bonds are then retired over a period of years by tax receipts or by revenues generated by the investment (e.g., toll roads).

13-7b Sinking Funds

sinking fund
a fund into which periodic payments on a bond issue's principal is made in order to ensure orderly retirement of the debt issue

Sinking funds are generally employed to ease the retirement of long-term corporate debt. A sinking fund is a periodic payment to retire part of the debt issue. One type of sinking fund requires the firm to make payments to a trustee, who invests the money to earn interest. The periodic payments plus the accumulated interest retire the debt when it matures.

Exhibit 13-5: Example of a Serial Bond Issue

This announcement is under no circumstances to be construed as an offer to sell or as a soliciation of an offer to buy any of these securities. The offering is made only by the Offering Circular Supplement and the Offering Circular to which it relates.

NEW ISSUE   July 17, 1985

$35,055,000

Union Pacific Railroad Company

Equipment Trust No. 1 of 1985

Serial Equipment Trust Certificates
(Non-callable)

Price 100%

(Plus accrued dividends, if any, from the date of original issuance.)

MATURITIES AND DIVIDEND RATES.

(To mature in 15 equal annual installments
of $2,337,000, commencing July 15, 1987.)

1987	6.500%	1992	7.500%	1997	7.800%
1988	7.000	1993	7.600	1998	7.800
1989	7.125	1994	7.700	1999	7.875
1990	7.300	1995	7.700	2000	7.875
1991	7.375	1996	7.750	2001	7.875

These Certificates are offered subject to prior sale, when, as and if issued and received by us, subject to approval of the Interstate Commerce Commission.

Merrill Lynch Capital Markets

Thomson McKinnon Securities Inc.

Source: Reprinted with permission of the Union Pacific Railroad Company

Another type of sinking fund requires the firm to set aside a stated sum of money and to randomly select the bonds that are to be retired. The selected bonds are called and redeemed, and the holder surrenders the bond because it ceases to earn interest once it has been called. This type of sinking fund is illustrated in **Exhibit 13-6** by an advertisement taken from the *Wall Street Journal*. The specific bonds being retired are selected by a lottery. Once they are chosen, these bonds are called. The owners must surrender the bonds to obtain their principal. If the bonds are not presented for redemption, they are still outstanding and are obligations of the company, but the debtor's obligation is limited to refunding the principal, since interest payments cease at the call date.

Since each debt issue is different, there can be wide variations in sinking funds. A strong sinking fund retires a substantial proportion of the debt before the date of maturity. For example, if a bond issue is for $10 million and it matures in 10 years, a strong sinking fund may require the firm to retire $1 million, or 10%, of the issue each year. Thus, at maturity, only $1 million is still outstanding. With a weak sinking fund, a substantial proportion of the debt is retired at maturity. For example, a sinking fund for a debt issue of $10 million that matures in 10 years may require annual payments of $1 million commencing after five years. In this example, only $5 million is retired before maturity. The debtor must then make a lump sum payment to retire the remaining $5 million. Such a large final payment is called a balloon payment.

Two bonds issued by GT&E illustrate these differences in sinking funds. (GT&E merged with Bell Atlantic to form Verizon.) A 9% issue required the company to retire $12,500,000 of the bonds each year so that at maturity only 5% of the issue was still outstanding. However, a 7.9% issue that is due in 2027 does not have a sinking fund. Unless the company takes steps to retire the bonds (e.g., the call feature discussed later in this chapter), the entire issue will come due in 2027.

The strength of a sinking fund affects the element of risk. A strong sinking fund requirement means that a substantial amount of the debt issue is retired during its lifetime, which makes the entire debt issue safer. The sinking fund feature of a debt issue, then, is an important factor in determining the amount of risk associated with investing in a particular debt instrument.

13-7c Repurchasing Debt

If bond prices decline and the debt is selling for less than face value (i.e., at a discount), the firm may try to retire the debt by purchasing it on the open market. The purchases may be made from time to time, in which case the sellers of the bonds need not know that the company is purchasing and retiring the debt. The company may also offer to purchase a specified amount of the debt at a certain price within a particular period. Bondholders may then tender their bonds at the offer price; however, they are not required to sell their bonds and may continue to hold the debt. If more bonds are tendered than the company offered to buy, the firm prorates the amount of money that it had allocated for the purchase among the number of bonds being offered.

The advantage of repurchasing debt that is selling at a discount is the savings to the firm. If a firm issued $10 million in face value of debt and the bonds are currently selling for $0.60 on $1, the firm may reduce its debt by $1,000 with a cash outlay of only $600, resulting in a $400 savings for each $1,000 bond that is purchased. This savings is translated into income and is reported under the heading "other gains and losses." For example, General Cinema reported a gain of $419.6 million from the purchase of Harcourt Brace Jovanovich's debt at a discount as part of the acquisition of the publisher. The low interest rates of the 2000s caused bond prices to rise. (See later in the chapter for an explanation of changes in interest rates and their impact on bond prices.) The increase in bond prices meant the opportunity to repurchase bonds at a discount had disappeared.

Exhibit 13-6: Example of a Sinking Fund Retiring Debt

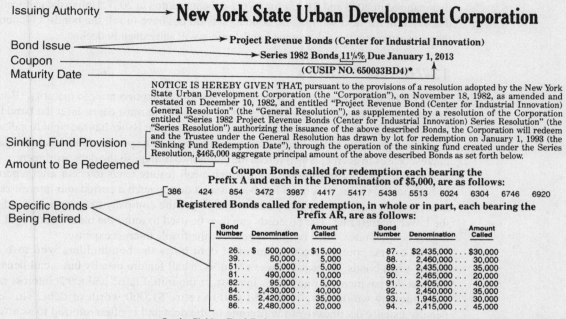

NOTICE OF REDEMPTION
To the Holders of

Issuing Authority ──────→ # New York State Urban Development Corporation

Bond Issue ──────→ **Project Revenue Bonds (Center for Industrial Innovation)**
Coupon ──────→ **Series 1982 Bonds 11⅛% Due January 1, 2013**
Maturity Date ──────→ **(CUSIP NO. 650033BD4)***

NOTICE IS HEREBY GIVEN THAT, pursuant to the provisions of a resolution adopted by the New York State Urban Development Corporation (the "Corporation"), on November 18, 1982, as amended and restated on December 10, 1982, and entitled "Project Revenue Bond (Center for Industrial Innovation) General Resolution" (the "General Resolution"), as supplemented by a resolution of the Corporation entitled "Series 1982 Project Revenue Bonds (Center for Industrial Innovation) Series Resolution" (the "Series Resolution") authorizing the issuance of the above described Bonds, the Corporation will redeem

Sinking Fund Provision ─┐ and the Trustee under the General Resolution has drawn by lot for redemption on January 1, 1993 (the "Sinking Fund Redemption Date"), through the operation of the sinking fund created under the Series

Amount to Be Redeemed ── Resolution, $465,000 aggregate principal amount of the above described Bonds as set forth below.

Coupon Bonds called for redemption each bearing the
Prefix A and each in the Denomination of $5,000, are as follows:

386   424   854   3472   3987   4417   5417   5438   5513   6024   6304   6746   6920

Registered Bonds called for redemption, in whole or in part, each bearing the
Prefix AR, are as follows:

Bond Number	Denomination	Amount Called	Bond Number	Denomination	Amount Called
26...	$ 500,000	... $15,000	87...	$2,435,000	... $30,000
39...	50,000	... 5,000	88...	2,460,000	... 30,000
51...	5,000	... 5,000	89...	2,435,000	... 35,000
81...	490,000	... 10,000	90...	2,465,000	... 20,000
82...	95,000	... 5,000	91...	2,405,000	... 40,000
84...	2,430,000	... 40,000	92...	2,450,000	... 35,000
85...	2,420,000	... 35,000	93...	1,945,000	... 30,000
86...	2,480,000	... 20,000	94...	2,415,000	... 45,000

On the Sinking Fund Redemption Date, there shall become due and payable on each of the above mentioned Bonds to be redeemed, the sinking fund redemption price, namely 100% of the principal amount thereof. Interest accrued on such Bonds to said Sinking Fund Redemption Date will be paid in the usual manner. From and after the Sinking Fund Redemption Date, interest on the Bonds described above shall

Interest Will Cease ──┐ cease to accrue.
to Accrue   └   IN ADDITION THE CORPORATION HAS ELECTED TO REDEEM ON JANUARY 1, 1993 (THE "REDEMPTION DATE") ALL REMAINING OUTSTANDING BONDS NOT HERETOFORE CALLED FOR SINKING FUND REDEMPTION AT A REDEMPTION PRICE EQUAL TO 103% OF THE PRINCIPAL AMOUNT THEREOF. INTEREST ACCRUED ON SUCH BONDS TO THE REDEMPTION DATE WILL BE PAID IN THE USUAL MANNER. FROM AND AFTER THE REDEMPTION DATE, INTEREST ON THE BONDS SHALL CEASE TO ACCRUE.

The Bonds specified herein to be redeemed shall be redeemed on or after both the Sinking Fund Redemption Date and the Redemption Date upon presentation and surrender thereof, together, in the case of coupon Bonds, with all appurtenant coupons attached, if any, maturing after January 1, 1993, to Bankers Trust Company, as Trustee and Paying Agent, in person or by registered mail (postage prepaid) at the following addresses:

IN PERSON:

Bankers Trust Company
Corporate Trust and Agency Group
First Floor
123 Washington Street
New York, New York

BY MAIL:

Bankers Trust Company
Corporate Trust and Agency Group
P.O. Box 2579
Church Street Station
New York, NY 10008
Attn: Bond Redemption

If any of the Bonds designated for redemption are in registered form, they should be accompanied by duly executed instruments of assignment in blank if payment is to be made to other than the registered holder thereof.

Coupons maturing January 1, 1993 appertaining to the coupon Bonds designated for redemption should be detached and presented for payment in the usual manner. Interest due January 1, 1993 on registered Bonds designated for redemption will be paid to the registered holders of such registered Bonds in the usual manner.

 NEW YORK STATE URBAN DEVELOPMENT CORPORATION
By: BANKERS TRUST COMPANY, *as Trustee*

Source: Empire State Development Corporation

Even if interest rates decline and bond prices increase, firms may still repurchase outstanding debt. If the firm is able to issue debt with a lower rate, it may be advantageous to pay the premium necessary to repurchase the existing bonds with the higher interest cost. In 2014, Merck offered to repurchase a variety of outstanding debt at prices that exceeded the principal amount. For example, Merck offered $1,297 for a 6.3% debenture that matured in 2028 and $1,394 for 5.76% debentures due in 2037. Unlike the call feature discussed in the next section, the bondholders do not have to sell the bonds. Of course, these investors run the risk that the bonds' prices will subsequently decline.

13-7d Call Feature

Some bonds may have a call feature that allows for redemption prior to maturity. (Bonds that lack a call feature may be referred to as "bullets.") In most cases, after the bond has been outstanding for a period of time (e.g., five years), the issuer has the right to call and retire the bond. The bond is called for redemption as of a specific date. After that date, interest ceases to accrue, which forces the creditor to relinquish the debt instrument.

Such premature retiring of debt through a call feature tends to occur after a period of high interest rates. If a bond has been issued during such a period and interest rates subsequently decline, it may be advantageous for the company to issue new bonds at the lower interest rate. The proceeds can then be used to retire the older bonds with the higher coupon rates. Such refunding reduces the firm's interest expense.

Of course, premature retirement of debt hurts the bondholders who lose the higher-yield bonds. To protect these creditors, a call feature usually has a call penalty, such as the payment of one year's interest. If the initial issue had a 9% interest rate, the company would have to pay $1,090 to retire $1,000 worth of debt. This call penalty usually declines over the lifetime of the debt and is often referred to as a "call premium" (which it is, from the viewpoint of bond investors). **Exhibit 13-7** illustrates the call penalty associated with the CoreCivic 8.25% of 2025. In 2024, the penalty will be $41.25 per $1,000 but declines to zero in 2025. Such a call penalty does protect bondholders, and the debtor has the right to call the bond and to refinance debt if interest rates fall sufficiently to justify paying the call penalty.

Exhibit 13-7: Bond Offering Detail Showing Call Penalty

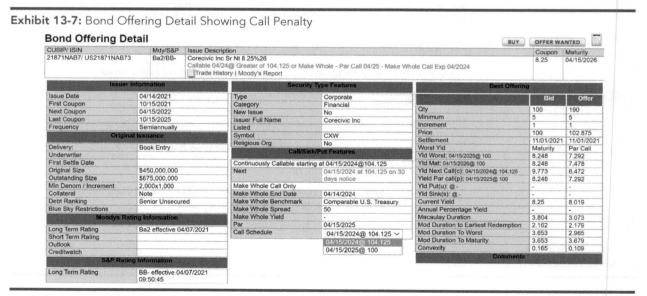

Several such refinancings occurred during the 2000s, when interest rates fell to lows that had not been seen in 20 to 40 years. Bell Atlantic retired $125 million of bonds with 7.5% coupons. The company paid $101.5 per bond (i.e., $1,015 per $1,000) for a penalty of $15 per bond. Texas Instruments retired $200 million of its 12.7% bonds. It paid $1,047 to retire $1,000 in face value of debt (i.e., a premium of $47 per bond). These refinancings sufficiently reduced the companies' interest expense to justify paying the call penalty.

13-7e Escrowed to Maturity

As is explained in the previous section, many firms and state and local governments that had previously issued debt when interest rates were higher will refund the bonds after interest rates decline. Such a refunding is essentially issuing new debt to retire old debt. The option to refund is, of course, one reason to have the call feature, but calling the debt is not necessarily a refunding. The firm can have funds from other sources, such as earnings or a new issue of stock, and may use those funds to retire the debt. (Some bond indentures permit the firm to call and retire the bond prior to maturity but do not permit a refunding in which new bonds are issued to retire an existing issue.)

While refunding may be profitable when interest rates decline, there is the possibility that interest rates will decline before the bond is callable. Suppose, for example, a company issued a bond in 2006 that matures in 2026 and is callable in 2016. Interest rates declined perceptibly during 2007–2011, so management wanted to refund the initial bond. Since the bonds cannot be called until 2016, there is the risk that interest rates will subsequently increase and the opportunity to save on interest expense will vanish.

Management may avoid this risk by issuing new bonds at the current and lower rate of interest and using the proceeds from the sale to purchase U.S. government securities with the same maturity date as the call date. In the above example, management would invest the proceeds in Treasury bonds that mature in 2016. When the Treasury bonds mature, the proceeds will then be used to call the old bonds. This original issue will now be referred to as having been "escrowed to maturity," since funds have been separated and earmarked for the bonds' retirement. The interest earned on the U.S. securities may offset all or at least part of the interest expense on the old bonds, so that there may be a net interest savings to the firm.

Does this strategy increase the perception that the firm is using more financial leverage? It now has two debt issues: the original bonds and the new bonds. The answer to that question is no. Since the old bonds are escrowed to maturity, they are considered to have been retired and are removed from the issuer's balance sheet. Even though the actual retirement will occur in the future, from an accounting perspective, the bonds are retired and any appearance that the firm is more financially leveraged is avoided.

13-8 Obtaining Information on Bonds

Obtaining information on bonds by using the Internet is as easy as obtaining information on stocks. A variety of sites offer data such as bond pricing, financial analysis, tutorials, and commentary. For example, the FINRA Bond Center (https://finra-markets.morningstar.com/BondCenter/Default.jsp) provides yields and news and lets you screen for specific types of bonds. Investing in Bonds (www.investinginbonds.com) is sponsored by the Bond Market Association, which is the bond market's trade association and is part of the Securities Industry and Financial Markets Association.

In addition to data, it provides current information concerning bonds. Other possibilities include Bonds Online (www.bondsonline.com) and Briefing.com (www.briefing.com), though most of the information on Briefing requires a subscription. And your brokerage firm should also be able to provide you with sufficient information to buy and sell the various debt securities available to meet your financial objectives.

13-9 Bond Pricing

13-9a Perpetual Securities

Some securities have an indefinite life. A corporation and its common stock may exist for centuries. Many issues of preferred stock have no maturity dates and are perpetual. There are even a few debt issues that are perpetual. The issuer never has to retire the principal; it only has to meet the interest payment and the other terms of the indenture. The British government issued perpetual bonds called **consols** to refinance (i.e., consolidate) the debt issued to support the Napoleonic Wars. These bonds will never mature, but they do pay interest, and there is an active secondary market in them.

Although there are few perpetual bonds, they facilitate illustrating the process of the valuation of debt instruments. Bond valuation is essentially the same as common stock valuation: future cash inflows are discounted back to the present, while the discount rate is the return that the investor can earn on comparable securities. (That is, the perpetual interest payments are brought back to the present at the current rate paid by bonds with the same degree of risk.) For example, a perpetual bond pays the following interest payment annually:

Year 1	Year 2	...	Year 20	...	Year 100	...	Year 1000	...
$80	$80		$80		$80		$80	

consol
a perpetual bond issued by the British government to finance the Napoleonic Wars and that never matures

How much are these interest payments currently worth? To answer the question, the investor must know the rate of interest that may be earned on alternative investments. If the investor can earn 10% elsewhere, the present value or price (P) is

$$P = \frac{\$80}{(1+0.10)^1} + \frac{\$80}{(1+0.10)^2} + \cdots + \frac{\$80}{(1+0.10)^{20}} + \cdots + \frac{\$80}{(1+0.10)^{100}} + \cdots + \frac{\$80}{(1+0.10)^{1000}} + \cdots$$

$$= \$80(0.9091) + \$80(0.8264) + \cdots + \$80(0.1486) + \cdots + \$80(0.0001) + \cdots + \$80(0.0000)$$

$$= \$800$$

The $80 interest payments received in the near future contribute most to the present value of the bond. Dollars received in the distant future have little value today. The sum of all of these present values is $800, which means that if alternative investments yield 10%, an investor would be willing to pay $800 for a promise to receive $80 annually for the indefinite future.

This is the same situation we faced in Chapter 12, when valuing a vanilla preferred stock, though the terminology is a little different. Here, we're valuing payments on a bond at the risk-appropriate interest rate for that bond, so we can express this relationship more formally as:

$$P = \frac{PMT}{(1+i)^1} + \frac{PMT}{(1+i)^2} + \frac{PMT}{(1+i)^3} + \cdots$$

This is a geometric series, and its sum may be expressed as

$$P = \frac{PMT}{i}$$ 13-1

Equation 13-1 gives the current value of an infinite stream of equal interest payments. If this equation is applied to the previous example in which the annual interest payment is $80 and alternative investments can earn 10%, then the present value of the bond is

$$P = \frac{\$80}{0.10} = \$800$$

Note that bond prices and bond interest rates are inversely related: if market interest rates of alternative investments were to increase to 20%, the value of this perpetual stream of interest payments would decline; if market interest rates were to fall to 8%, the value of the bond would rise. These changes occur because the bond pays a fixed flow of income; that is, the dollar amount of interest paid by the bond is constant. Lower interest rates mean that more money is needed to purchase this fixed stream of interest payments, and with higher interest rates, less money is needed to buy this fixed flow of income.

The inverse relationship between interest rates and bond prices is illustrated in **Figure 13-4**, which presents the value of the preceding perpetual bond at different interest rates. As may be seen from the exhibit, as current market interest rates rise, the present value of the bond declines. Thus, if the present value is $1,000 when interest rates are 8%, the value of this bond declines to $400 when interest rates rise to 20%.

A simple example may show why this inverse relationship between bond prices and interest rates exists. Suppose two investors offered to sell two different bond issues. The first is the perpetual bond that pays $100 per year in interest. The second is also a perpetual bond, but it pays $120 per year in interest. If the offer price in each case is $1,000, which bond would be preferred? If they are equal in every way except in the amount of interest, a buyer would prefer the second bond that pays $120. What could the seller of the first bond do to make the bond more attractive to a buyer? The obvious answer is to lower the asking price so that the yield the buyer receives is identical for both bonds. Thus, if the seller were to ask only $833 for the bond that pays $100

Excel Expert 13-1

As shown in Equation 13-1, the price of a perpetuity is simply the periodic cash flow divided by the interest rate:

	A	B	C
1	Coupon	$ 80	
2	i	10.00%	
3			
4	P$_B$	$800.00	=B1/B2

So the price of the bond should be $800.

Figure 13-4: Relationship Between Interest Rates and Bond Price

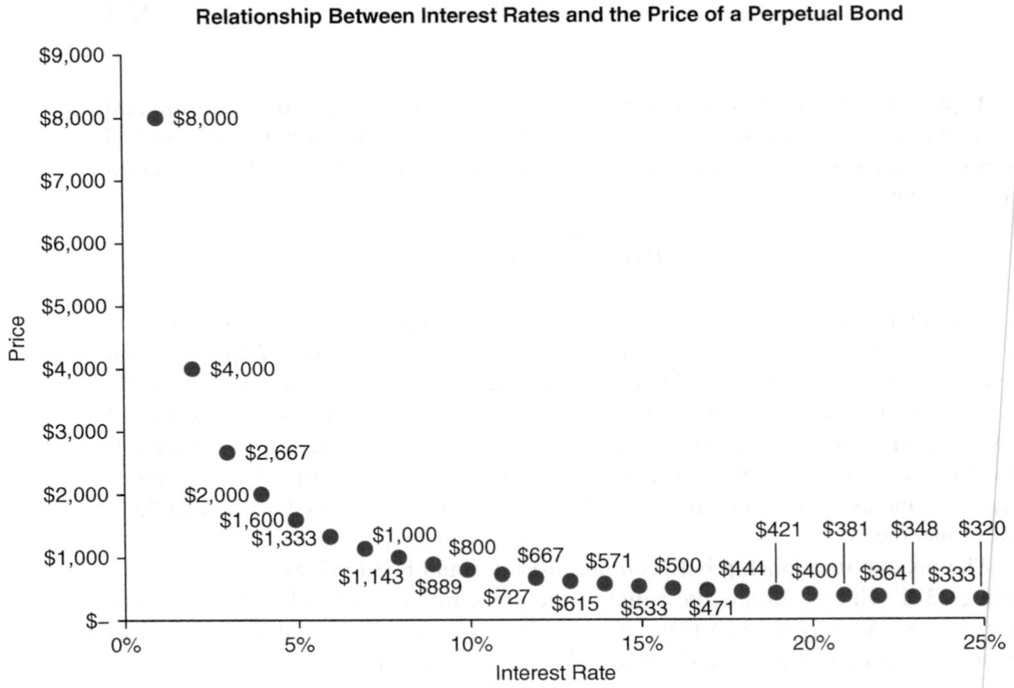

Relationship Between Interest Rates and the Price of a Perpetual Bond

annually, the buyer should be indifferent as to which to purchase. Both bonds would then offer a yield of 12% (i.e., $100 ÷ $833 for the first bond and $120 ÷ $1,000 for the second bond).

13-9b Bonds with Maturity Dates

face value
the principal to be repaid on the maturity of a bond

The majority of bonds are not perpetual but have a finite life, similar to finite-lived preferred shares covered in the last chapter. They mature, and this fact must affect their valuation. A bond's price is related not only to the interest that it pays but also to its **face value** (i.e., the principal). The current price of a bond equals the present value of the interest payments plus the present value of the principal to be received at maturity. Although most bonds pay interest semiannually, this initial discussion uses annual compounding to simplify the explanation. Semiannual compounding is illustrated in the next section. A few bonds pay interest quarterly, and there are examples of bonds that pay monthly.

The value of a bond with a finite life is the present value of its cash flows (interest and principal repayment). This value is expressed algebraically in **Equation 13-2** as the sum of the present value of the annuity of interest payments, PMT, plus the present value of the lump sum face value, FV:

$$P_B = PMT \times \frac{1 - \dfrac{1}{(1+i)^n}}{i} + \frac{FV}{(1+i)^n}$$ **13-2**

Excel Expert 13-2

Equation 13-2 can be calculated using a single instance of the PV() function in Excel:

	A	B	C
1	FV	$ 1,000.00	
2	Coupon	$ 100	
3	n	3	
4	i	10.00%	
5			
6	P$_B$	$1,000.00	=-PV(B4,B3,B2,B1)

So, the price of the bond should be $1,000.

For example, suppose a firm has a $1,000 bond outstanding that matures in three years with a 10% coupon rate ($100 annually). All that is needed to determine the price of the bond is the current interest rate, which is the rate being paid by newly issued competitive bonds with the same length of time to maturity and the same degree of risk. If the competitive bonds yield 10%, the price of this bond will be par, or $1,000, for

$$P_B = \$100 \times \frac{1 - \frac{1}{(1 + 0.10)^3}}{0.10} + \frac{\$1,000}{(1 + 0.10)^3} = \$1,000$$

If competitive bonds are selling to yield 12%, this bond will be unattractive to investors. They will not be willing to pay $1,000 for a bond yielding 10% when they could buy competing bonds at the same price that yield 12%. For this bond to compete with the others, its price must decline sufficiently to yield 12%. In terms of Equation 13-2, the price must be

Excel Expert 13-3

	A	B	C
1	FV	$ 1,000.00	
2	Coupon	$ 100	
3	n	3	
4	i	12.00%	
5			
6	P$_B$	$951.96	=-PV(B4,B3,B2,B1)

So. the price of the bond should drop to $951.96 when yields rise to 12%.

Excel Expert 13-4

	A	B	C
1	FV	$ 1,000.00	
2	Coupon	$ 100	
3	n	3	
4	i	8.00%	
5			
6	P_B	$1,051.54	=-PV(B4,B3,B2,B1)

So, the price of the bond should rise to $1,051.54 when yields drop to 8%.

$$P_B = \$100 \times \frac{1 - \dfrac{1}{(1 + 0.12)^3}}{0.12} + \frac{\$1,000}{(1 + 0.12)^3} = \$951.96$$

discount
a bond selling for less than face value

The price of the bond must decline to approximately $952; that is, it must sell for a **discount** (a price less than the stated principal) in order to be competitive with comparable bonds. At that price, investors will earn $100 per year in interest and approximately $50 in capital gains over the three years, for a total annual return of 12% on their investment. The capital gain occurs because the bond is purchased for $952.20, but when it matures, the holder will receive $1,000.

If comparable debt were to yield 8%, the price of the bond in the previous example would have to rise. In this case, the price of the bond would be

$$P_B = \$100 \times \frac{1 - \dfrac{1}{(1 + 0.08)^3}}{0.08} + \frac{\$1,000}{(1 + 0.08)^3} = \$1,051.54$$

premium
used to refer to a bond selling for more than face value

The bond, therefore, must sell at a **premium** (a price greater than the stated principal). Although it may seem implausible for the bond to sell at a premium, this must occur if the market interest rate falls below the coupon rate of interest stated on the bond.

These examples illustrate the same general conclusion that was reached earlier concerning bond prices and changes in interest rates. They are inversely related. When the current rate of interest rises, the prices of existing bonds decline. When the market rate of interest falls, bond prices rise. This relationship is illustrated in **Figure 13-5**, which shows the prices of the $1,000 bond with a 10% coupon that matures after three years for various interest rates. As may be seen in the exhibit, higher interest rates depress the bond's current value. Thus, the bond's price declines from $1,000 to $952.20 when interest rates rise from 10 to 12%; the price rises to $1,051.70 when interest rates decline to 8%. (Factors that affect the amount of the price change are covered later in this chapter.)

The inverse relationship between the price of a bond and the interest rate suggests a means to make profits in the bond market. All investors need to know is the direction of future changes in the interest rate. If investors anticipate that

Figure 13-5: Relationship Between Interest Rates and Price

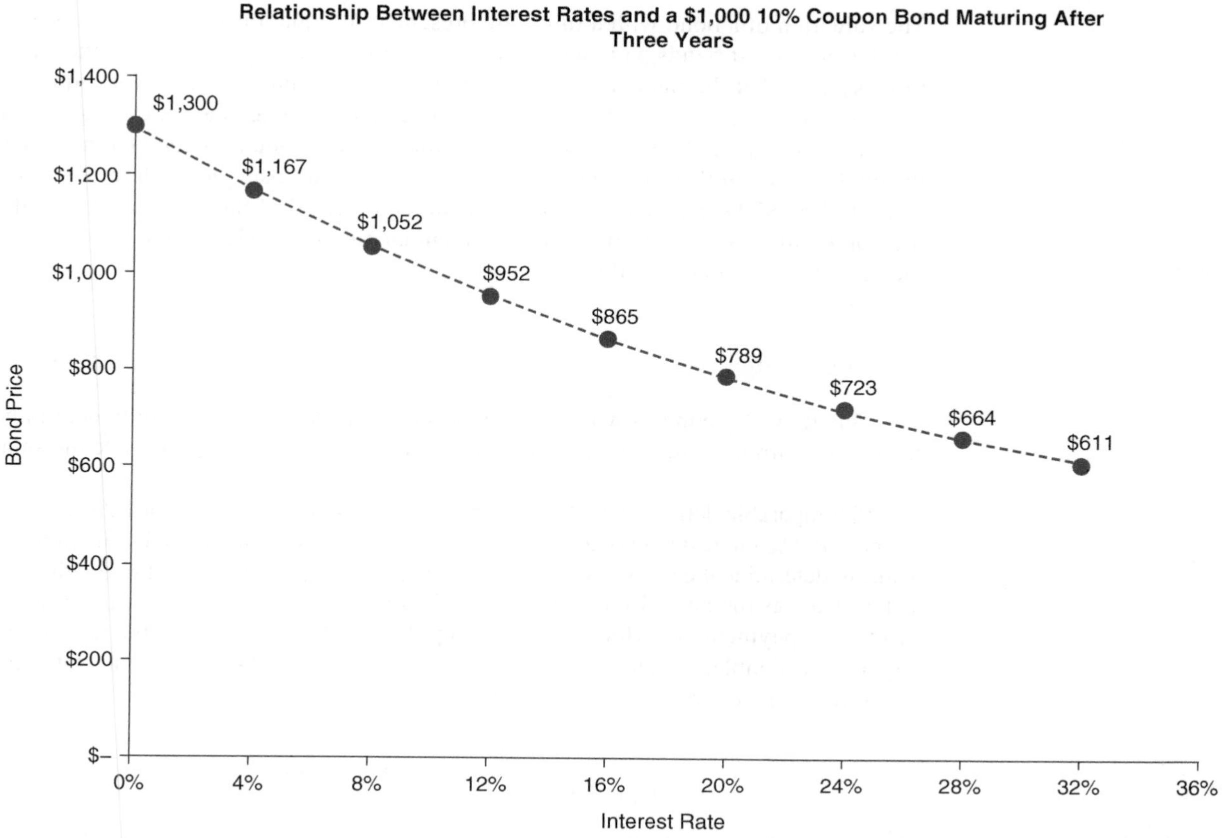

Relationship Between Interest Rates and a $1,000 10% Coupon Bond Maturing After Three Years

interest rates will decline, then they are expecting the price to rise for previously issued bonds with a given number of years to maturity and of a certain risk. This price increase must occur in order for previously issued bonds to have the same yield as currently issued bonds. The reverse is also true, if investors anticipate that interest rates will rise, they are also anticipating that the price of currently available bonds will decline. This decline must occur for previously issued bonds to offer the same yield as currently issued bonds. Therefore, if investors can anticipate the direction of change in interest rates, they can also anticipate the direction of change in the price of bonds.

Investors, however, may anticipate incorrectly and thus suffer losses in the bond market. If they buy bonds and interest rates rise, then the market value of their bonds must decline, and the investors suffer capital losses. These individuals, however, have something in their favor: The bonds must ultimately be retired. Since the principal must be redeemed, an investment error in the bond market may be corrected when the bond's price rises as the bond approaches maturity. The capital losses will eventually be erased. The correction of the error, however, may take years, during which time the investors have lost the higher yields that were available on bonds issued after their initial investments.

13-9c Semiannual Compounding

The valuation of a bond with a finite life presented in Equation 13-2 is a bit misleading, because most bonds pay interest twice a year (i.e., semiannually), and the equation assumes that the interest payments are made only annually. However, Equation 13-2 may be readily modified to take into consideration semiannual (or even quarterly or weekly) compounding. This is done by adjusting the amount of each payment and the total number of these payments. To adjust the previous example, each interest payment will be $50 if payments are semiannual, and instead of three annual payments, the bond will make a total of six $50 semiannual payments. Hence, the flow of payments that will be made by this bond is

Year 1			Year 2			Year 3		
$50	$50		$50	$50		$50	$50	$1,000

This flow of payments would then be discounted back to the present to determine the bond's current value. The question then becomes, what is the appropriate discount factor?

If comparable debt yields 12%, the appropriate discount factor is not 12%; it is 6% per period. 6% interest paid twice a year yields 12% interest compounded semiannually. Thus, to determine the present value of this bond, the comparable interest rate is divided in half (just as the annual interest payment is divided in half). However, the number of interest payments to which this 6% is applied is doubled (just as the number of payments is doubled). Hence, the current value of this bond, which pays interest twice a year (is compounded semiannually), is

$$P_B = PMT \times \frac{1 - \dfrac{1}{(1 + i)^n}}{i} + \frac{FV}{(1 + i)^n}$$

$$= \$50 \times \frac{1 - \dfrac{1}{(1 + 0.06)^6}}{0.06} + \frac{\$1,000}{(1 + 0.06)^6}$$

$$= \$950.83$$

With semiannual compounding, the current value of the bond is slightly lower (i.e., $950.83 versus $952.20) because the effective annual yield on the debt is slightly higher with semiannual compounding (6% every six months versus 12% a year). The bond's price must decline more to compensate for the more frequent compounding. Thus, if interest rates rise, causing bond prices to fall, the decline will be greater if the interest on bonds is paid semiannually than if it is paid annually.

Equation 13-2 may be altered to include semiannual compounding. This is done in **Equation 13-3**. Only one new variable, c, is added, which represents the frequency of compounding (i.e., the number of times each year that interest payments are made).

$$P_B = \frac{PMT}{c} \times \frac{1 - \dfrac{1}{\left(1 + \dfrac{i}{c}\right)^{n \times c}}}{\dfrac{i}{c}} + \frac{FV}{\left(1 + \dfrac{i}{c}\right)^{n \times c}} \qquad \textbf{13-3}$$

$$P_B = \frac{80}{2} \times \frac{1 - \dfrac{1}{\left(1 + \dfrac{0.065}{2}\right)^{8 \times 2}}}{\dfrac{0.065}{2}} + \frac{1000}{\left(1 + \dfrac{0.065}{2}\right)^{8 \times 2}} = 1092.43 \qquad \textbf{13-3}$$

Note that when we have annual compounding (i.e., when $c = 1$), Equation 13-3 simplifies to Equation 13-2, so we really only need Equation 13-3.

13-10 Fluctuations in Bond Prices

As the preceding examples illustrate, a bond's price depends on the interest paid, the maturity date of the bond, and the yield currently earned on comparable securities. The illustrations also demonstrate that when interest rates rise, bond prices fall, and when interest rates fall, bond prices rise.

The amount of price fluctuation depends on (1) the amount of interest paid by the bond, (2) the length of time to maturity, and (3) risk. The smaller the amount of interest, the larger the relative price fluctuations will tend to be. The longer the term, or time to maturity, the greater the price fluctuations will be. Riskier bonds may also experience greater fluctuations in price.

This section is concerned with the first two factors that affect price fluctuations—the amount of interest and the term to maturity. The impact of risk is covered in a subsequent section. The effect of the amount of interest and term to maturity may be seen by the following illustrations. In the first case, consider two bonds with equal lives (i.e., 10 years to maturity) but unequal coupons. Bond A pays $80 a year (an 8% coupon), and bond B pays $140 annually (a 14% coupon). **Figure 13-6** gives the prices of each bond at various rates of interest. For example, if interest rates rise from 10 to 14%, the price of bond A declines from $877 to $687. Bond B's price falls from $1,246 to $1,000. These are 22 and 20% declines, respectively. If interest rates continue to rise, the bonds' prices decline further. At 20%, the values of the bonds are $497 and $748. The percentage declines in the bond with the lower coupon are greater. (The extreme case would be a zero coupon bond whose price depends solely on the repayment of the principal.)

The length of time to maturity also affects the fluctuation in a bond's price. Consider the two bonds in **Figure 13-7**. Both bonds pay $100 interest annually (a 10% coupon), but bond A matures after 1 year, and bond B matures after 10 years. If interest rates are 10%, each bond sells for its principal value ($1,000). If interest rates rise to 12%, the prices of the bonds decline to $982 and $887. The short maturity of bond A, however, cushions the impact of the change in interest rates. At the extreme case of 20%, the price of bond A declines only to $917, while the price of bond B declines to $581.

If interest rates fall, the prices of both bonds will rise, but the price of the bond with the longer term will rise more. For this reason, individuals who are speculating on a decline in interest rates will favor bonds with a longer term to maturity, but investors who are concerned with both interest income and safety of principal will prefer short-term debt. These investors will accept less interest income for safety and liquidity. Of course, the extreme form of such investments is the money market mutual fund, which invests solely in short-term investments (e.g., commercial paper and Treasury bills), for such investments offer liquidity that cannot be obtained through investments in longer-term debt.

Figure 13-6: Relationship Between Interest Rates and Bond Prices Across Coupons

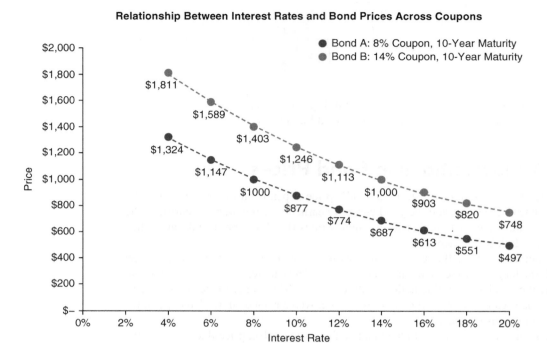

Relationship Between Interest Rates and Bond Prices Across Coupons

● Bond A: 8% Coupon, 10-Year Maturity
● Bond B: 14% Coupon, 10-Year Maturity

Bond B values: $1,811 / $1,589 / $1,403 / $1,246 / $1,113 / $1,000 / $903 / $820 / $748

Bond A values: $1,324 / $1,147 / $1000 / $877 / $774 / $687 / $613 / $551 / $497

Figure 13-7: Relationship Between Interest Rates and Bond Prices Across Term

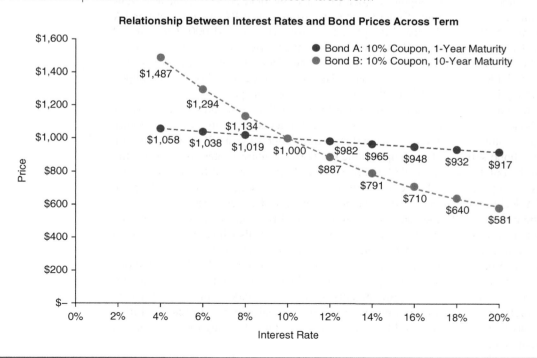

Relationship Between Interest Rates and Bond Prices Across Term

● Bond A: 10% Coupon, 1-Year Maturity
● Bond B: 10% Coupon, 10-Year Maturity

Bond B values: $1,487 / $1,294 / $1,134 / $1,000 / $887 / $791 / $710 / $640 / $581

Bond A values: $1,058 / $1,038 / $1,019 / $1,000 / $982 / $965 / $948 / $932 / $917

13-10a Bond Valuation Applications to Nontraditional Bonds

In the previous examples of valuation, all the bonds paid interest annually and were retired at maturity. However, as previously discussed, bond features are not limited to a fixed payment and maturity date. For example, zero coupon bonds accrue interest but do not distribute it. Several high-yield securities (e.g., the split coupon bond, the reset bond, or the extendable bond) have features that differ from the traditional bond.

Although bonds can have these varying features, their valuations remain the same: the present value of future cash flows. For example, what would an investor pay for a $1,000 zero coupon bond that matures after 10 years? The answer has to be the present value of the $1,000—that is, the present value of the future cash flow. If the investor requires a return of 7%, then the value is

$$P_B = PMT \times \frac{1 - \frac{1}{(1 + i)^n}}{i} + \frac{FV}{(1 + i)^n}$$

$$= \$0 \times \frac{1 - \frac{1}{(1 + 0.07)^{10}}}{0.07} + \frac{\$1,000}{(1 + 0.07)^{10}}$$

$$= \$508.35$$

If the required return had been 10%, the value of the bond would be

$$P_B = PMT \times \frac{1 - \frac{1}{(1 + i)^n}}{i} + \frac{FV}{(1 + i)^n}$$

$$= \$0 \times \frac{1 - \frac{1}{(1 + 0.10)^{10}}}{0.10} + \frac{\$1,000}{(1 + 0.10)^{10}}$$

$$= \$385.54$$

Excel Expert 13-5

	A	B	C
1	FV	$ 1,000.00	
2	Coupon	$ -	
3	n	10	
4	i	7.00%	
5			
6	P$_B$	$508.35	=-PV(B4,B3,B2,B1)

Note that the coupon here is set to 0 (zero).

Excel Expert 13-6

	A	B	C
1	FV	$ 1,000.00	
2	Coupon	$ -	
3	n	10	
4	i	10.00%	
5			
6	P_B	$385.54	=-PV(B4,B3,B2,B1)

The valuation of split coupon and reset bonds is essentially the same. Consider the Dr Pepper bond in a previous example that illustrated a split coupon bond. That bond paid $0 in interest during the first 4 years, $115 annually for the next 6 years, and matured after 10 years. How much would an investor pay if the required return were 15%? The answer can be calculated using a variety of NPV equations, but the most straightforward way to is to use Equation 13-2 to value it one year before the first coupon (i.e., when the bond will have six years left to maturity, and then treat that value as a future value lump sum to be moved from time 4 to time 0:

$$P_4 = \$115 \times \frac{1 - \dfrac{1}{(1 + 0.15)^6}}{0.15} + \frac{\$1,000}{(1 + 0.15)^6}$$

$$= \$867.54$$

Excel Expert 13-7

This valuation will involve two uses of the PV() function: one to value the stream of cash flows one period before the coupons start (i.e., at time 4), and the other to move that value from time 4 to time 0:

	A	B	C
1	FV	$ 1,000.00	
2	Coupon	$ 115	
3	n	6	
4	i	15.00%	
5			
6	P_4	$867.54	=-PV(B4,B3,B2,B1)
7			
8	P_B	$496.02	=PV(B4,4,0,-B6)

So, the value of the bond today should be $496.02.

$$P_B = \frac{\$867.54}{(1.15)^4}$$

$$= \$496.02$$

If interest rates declined (or the firm's financial condition improved) so the comparable rate is 12%, the bond's price would rise to

$$P_4 = \$115 \times \frac{1 - \dfrac{1}{(1 + 0.12)^6}}{0.12} + \frac{\$1,000}{(1 + 0.12)^6}$$

$$= \$979.44$$

$$P_B = \frac{\$979.44}{(1.12)^4}$$

$$= \$622.45$$

for a 25.5% increase. Of course, the converse is also true; higher yields would cause the price of the split coupon bond to decline.

As we've seen, the valuations of zero coupon and split coupon bonds are essentially no different from the valuation of a regular coupon bond since the payments (their amounts and timing) are known. With a reset bond or an extendable bond, the payments and their timing are not known. The interest payments or the maturity date or both are permitted to vary. While the valuation process remains the present value of future cash inflows, the investor must make assumptions concerning these inflows. For example, in the case of an extendable bond, the investor must assume a particular repayment date. If the investor expects the bond's maturity date to be extended, then the longer term is used to value the bond. Using a shorter term may result in the bond receiving a higher valuation, in which case the investor would pay too much and realize a smaller return if the maturity is extended.

Excel Expert 13-8

	A	B	C
1	FV	$ 1,000.00	
2	Coupon	$ 115	
3	n	6	
4	i	12.00%	
5			
6	P_4	$979.44	=-PV(B4,B3,B2,B1)
7			
8	P_B	$622.45	=PV(B4,4,0,-B6)

So, the value of the bond today at a yield of 12% should be $622.45.

13-11 Bond Yields

yield to call (YTC)
the yield that an investor will earn if the bond is held until it is called before maturity

The word *yield* is frequently used with regard to investing in bonds. There are three important types of yields with which the investor must be familiar: the current yield, the yield to maturity, and the yield to call. This section will differentiate among these three yields.

13-11a The Current Yield

The current yield is the percentage that the investor earns annually. It is simply

$$\text{Current Yield} = \frac{\text{Annual Interest Payment}}{\text{Price of the Bond}} \qquad \textbf{13-4}$$

The discounted bond discussed previously has a coupon rate of 10%. Thus, when the price of the bond is $952, the current yield is

$$\text{Current Yield} = \frac{\$100}{\$952}$$

$$= 0.105 \text{ or } 10.5\%$$

The current yield is important because it gives the investor an indication of the current return that will be earned on the investment. Investors who seek high current income prefer bonds that offer a high current yield.

However, the current yield can be misleading, for it fails to consider any change in the price of the bond that may occur if the bond is held to maturity. Obviously, if a bond is bought at a discount, its value must rise as it approaches maturity. The opposite occurs if the bond is purchased for a premium, because its price will decline as maturity approaches. For this reason, it is desirable to know the bond's yield to maturity.

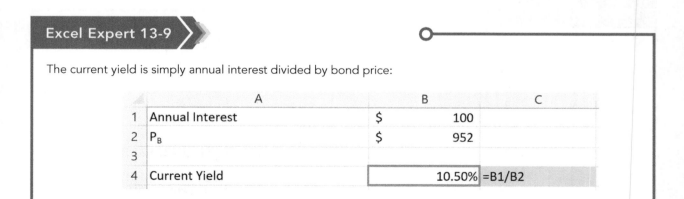

Excel Expert 13-9

The current yield is simply annual interest divided by bond price:

	A	B	C
1	Annual Interest	$ 100	
2	P$_B$	$ 952	
3			
4	Current Yield	10.50% =B1/B2	

13-11b The Yield to Maturity

The yield to maturity considers the current income generated by the bond as well as any change in its value when it is held to maturity. If the bond referred to earlier is purchased for $952 and is held to maturity, after three years, the investor will receive a return of 12%. This is the yield to maturity, because this return considers not only the current interest return of 10.5% but also the price appreciation of the bond from $952 at the time of purchase to $1,000 at maturity. Since the yield to maturity considers both the flow of interest income and the price change, it is a more accurate measure of the return offered to investors by a particular bond issue.

The yield to maturity may be determined by using Equation 13-2 and solving it for *i*. That equation is

$$P_B = PMT \times \frac{1 - \dfrac{1}{(1 + i)^n}}{i} + \frac{FV}{(1 + i)^n}$$

The yield to maturity is a specific application of the internal rate of return discussed in corporate finance books. In an efficient market, the *i* will be the current rate of interest paid by newly issued bonds with the same term to maturity and the same degree of risk. If the investor buys a bond and holds it to maturity, the yield that is being paid by newly issued bonds (*i*) will also be the yield to maturity.

Determining the yield to maturity when the coupon rate of interest, the bond's price, and the maturity date are known is possible without the use of a financial calculator or Excel, but it is neither simple nor fast, as doing so involves guessing an interest rate, adjusting it downward (upward) if the price of the bond using that interest rate is too low (high), then repeating again and again until you narrow your guesses down to the rate that makes the price you get from the formula equal to the price you see in the market. It is much easier to do so using Excel, where the IRR() function does that guessing and adjusting for you.

Excel Expert 13-10

To calculate the YTM, simply detail out each of the cash flows and apply the IRR() function to them:

	A	B	C	D	E	F	G	H
1	P_B	$ 952		YTM	12.00%	=IRR(B8:B18)		
2	Annual Interest	$ 100						
3	FV	1000						
4	Call Penalty	0						
5	n	3						
6								
7	Time	CF						
8	0	-$952.00 =-B1						
9	1	$100.00 =IF(A9>$B$5,"",IF(A9=$B$5,$B$2+$B$3+$B$4,IF(A9<$B$5,$B$2)))						
10	2	$100.00 =IF(A10>$B$5,"",IF(A10=$B$5,$B$2+$B$3+$B$4,IF(A10<$B$5,$B$2)))						
11	3	$1,100.00 =IF(A11>$B$5,"",IF(A11=$B$5,$B$2+$B$3+$B$4,IF(A11<$B$5,$B$2)))						

13-11c A Comparison of the Current Yield and the Yield to Maturity

The current yield and the yield to maturity are equal only if the bond sells for its principal amount, or par. If the bond sells at a discount, the yield to maturity exceeds the current yield. This may be illustrated by the bond in the previous example. When it sells at a discount (e.g., $952), the current yield is only 10.5%. However, the yield to maturity is 12%. Thus, the yield to maturity exceeds the current yield.

If the bond sells at a premium, the current yield exceeds the yield to maturity. For example, if the bond sells for $1,052, the current yield is 9.5% ($100 ÷ $1,052) and the yield to maturity is 8%. The yield to maturity is less in this case because the loss that the investor must suffer when the price of the bond declines from $1,052 to $1,000 at maturity has been included in the calculation.

Figure 13-8 presents the current yield and the yield to maturity at different prices for a bond with an 8% annual coupon that matures in 10 years. As may be seen in the graph, the larger the discount (or the smaller the premium), the greater are both the current yield and the yield to maturity. For example, when the bond sells for $850, the yield to maturity is 10.49%, but it rises to 12.52% when the price declines to $750.

Discounted bonds offer investors attractive opportunities for financial planning. For example, a person who is currently 60 years old may purchase discounted bonds that mature after five years to help finance retirement. This investor may purchase several bonds that mature five, six, seven years, and so on, into the future. This portfolio will generate a continuous flow of funds during retirement as the bonds mature.

Figure 13-8: Current Yield and YTM as a Function of Bond Price

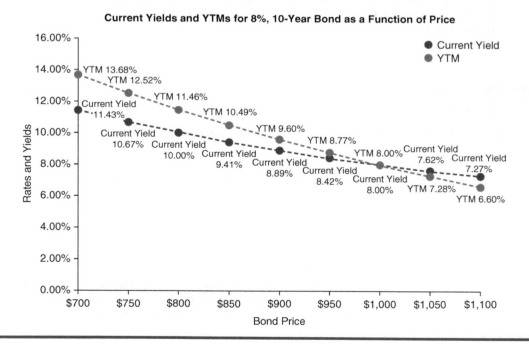

Figure 13-9: Price vs. Cash Flow for a Portfolio of Zero Coupon Bonds

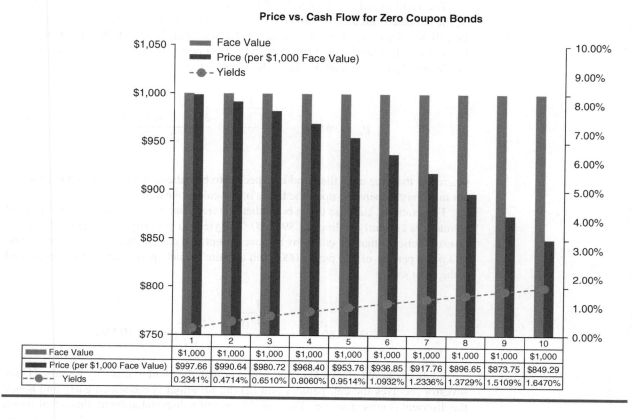

Price vs. Cash Flow for Zero Coupon Bonds

	1	2	3	4	5	6	7	8	9	10
Face Value	$1,000	$1,000	$1,000	$1,000	$1,000	$1,000	$1,000	$1,000	$1,000	$1,000
Price (per $1,000 Face Value)	$997.66	$990.64	$980.72	$968.40	$953.76	$936.85	$917.76	$896.65	$873.75	$849.29
Yields	0.2341%	0.4714%	0.6510%	0.8060%	0.9514%	1.0932%	1.2336%	1.3729%	1.5109%	1.6470%

Discounted bonds generally result from an increase in interest rates. If interest rates fall, bonds would sell for a premium, so the previous strategy cannot be executed. An alternative but similar strategy uses zero coupon bonds, which always sell for a discount. This strategy is illustrated in **Figure 13-9**, in which the individual needs funds for next 10 years and buys a series of zero coupon bonds with 1 to 10 years to maturity. For a total outlay of $9,365.47, the investor will receive $1,000 for each of the 10 years.

Although the two strategies illustrated are similar, there are differences. First, as was previously explained, bonds with higher coupons experience less price fluctuation with changes in interest rates, so the zero coupon bond strategy subjects the investor to more price volatility. Such price fluctuations are relevant only if interest rates rise and the investor needs to sell the bonds before their maturity dates. Second, the discounted bonds pay some interest each year, while the zero coupon bonds pay nothing. If the investor wants cash flow each year prior to the bonds' maturity dates, the discounted bonds may be the better choice.

13-11d The Yield to Call

Some bonds will never reach maturity but are retired before they become due. In some cases, the issuer may call the bonds before maturity and redeem them. In other cases, the sinking fund will randomly call selected bonds from the issue and retire them.

For these reasons, the yield to call may be a more accurate estimate of the return actually earned on an investment in a bond that is held until redemption.

The yield to call is calculated in the same way as the yield to maturity except that (1) the expected call date is substituted for the maturity date and (2) the principal plus the call penalty (if any) is substituted for the principal. Note that the anticipated call date is used. Unlike the maturity date, which is known, the date of a call can only be anticipated. In such a situation, the yield to call is the i that solves

$$P_B = PMT \times \frac{1 - \dfrac{1}{(1 + i)^t}}{i} + \frac{FV + \text{Call Penalty}}{(1 + i)^t} \qquad \textbf{13-5}$$

where t is the time until the bond is expected to be called, and the call penalty may or not may exist depending upon the terms of the call provision.

For example, suppose that a bond that matures after 10 years and pays 8% interest annually is currently selling for $935.00. The yield to maturity is 9%. However, if the investor believes that the company or government will call the bond after five years and will pay a penalty of $50 per $1,000 bond to retire the debt permanently, the yield to call is the i that solves

$$\$935 = 80 \times \frac{1 - \dfrac{1}{(1 + i)^5}}{i} + \frac{\$1,050}{(1 + i)^5} \Rightarrow i = 10.55\%$$

In this example, the yield to call is higher than the yield to maturity because (1) the investor receives the call penalty and (2) the principal is redeemed early and hence the discount is erased sooner. Thus, in the case of a discounted bond, the actual return the investor earns exceeds the yield to maturity if the bond is called and retired before maturity.

Excel Expert 13-11 ⟩

The yield to call is calculated similarly to the YTM, but with the inclusion of the call penalty in the cash flows, and with the term set equal to the time to expected call:

	A	B	C	D	E	F	G	H
1	P_B	$ 935		YTM	10.55%	=IRR(B8:B18)		
2	Annual Interest	$ 80						
3	FV	1000						
4	Call Penalty	50						
5	n	5						
6								
7	Time	CF						
8	0	-$935.00	=-B1					
9	1	$80.00	=IF(A9>$B$5,"",IF(A9=$B$5,$B$2+$B$3+$B$4,IF(A9<$B$5,$B$2)))					
10	2	$80.00	=IF(A10>$B$5,"",IF(A10=$B$5,$B$2+$B$3+$B$4,IF(A10<$B$5,$B$2)))					
11	3	$80.00	=IF(A11>$B$5,"",IF(A11=$B$5,$B$2+$B$3+$B$4,IF(A11<$B$5,$B$2)))					
12	4	$80.00	=IF(A12>$B$5,"",IF(A12=$B$5,$B$2+$B$3+$B$4,IF(A12<$B$5,$B$2)))					
13	5	$1,130.00	=IF(A13>$B$5,"",IF(A13=$B$5,$B$2+$B$3+$B$4,IF(A13<$B$5,$B$2)))					

However, if this bond were selling for a premium such as $1,147 with a yield to maturity of 6% and the firm were to call the bond after five years, the yield to call would become

$$\$1,147 = 80 \times \frac{1 - \frac{1}{(1+i)^5}}{i} + \frac{\$1,050}{(1+i)^5} \Rightarrow i = 5.46\%$$

This return is less than the anticipated yield to maturity of 6%. The early redemption produces a lower return for the investor because the premium is spread out over fewer years, reducing the yield on the investment. If an investor expected the bond to be called for $1,050 after five years and wanted to earn 6%, the price would have to be $1,122.

Which case is more likely to occur? If a firm wanted to retire debt that was selling at a discount before maturity, it would probably be to its advantage to purchase the bonds instead of calling them. (See the section on repurchasing debt earlier in the chapter.) By doing so, the firm would avoid the call penalty and might even be able to buy the bonds for less than par. If the firm wanted to retire debt that was selling at a premium, it would probably be advantageous to call the bonds and pay the penalty. If the bonds were selling for more than face value plus the call penalty, this would obviously be the chosen course of action.

Remember, however, that call provisions on bonds are exercised at the discretion of the issuing firm, so an investor should not expect a firm to prematurely call a bond issue that is selling at a discount, as the bond would only sell at a discount if the current going rate of interest was higher than what had been the prevailing rate when the bond was issued. However, if interest rates fall and bond prices rise, the firm may refinance the debt. It will then issue new debt at the lower (current) interest rate and use the proceeds to retire the older and more costly debt. In this case, the yield to the anticipated call is probably a better indication of the potential return offered by the bonds than is the yield to maturity.

The preceding example also illustrates the importance of the call penalty. If an investor bought the bond in anticipation that it would yield 6% at maturity (i.e., the

Excel Expert 13-12

	A	B	C	D	E	F	G	H
1	P_B	$ 1,147		YTM		5.46%	=IRR(B8:B18)	
2	Annual Interest	$ 80						
3	FV	1000						
4	Call Penalty	50						
5	n	5						
6								
7	Time	CF						
8		0	-$1,147.00	=-B1				
9		1	$80.00	=IF(A9>$B$5,"",IF(A9=$B$5,$B$2+$B$3+$B$4,IF(A9<$B$5,$B$2)))				
10		2	$80.00	=IF(A10>$B$5,"",IF(A10=$B$5,$B$2+$B$3+$B$4,IF(A10<$B$5,$B$2)))				
11		3	$80.00	=IF(A11>$B$5,"",IF(A11=$B$5,$B$2+$B$3+$B$4,IF(A11<$B$5,$B$2)))				
12		4	$80.00	=IF(A12>$B$5,"",IF(A12=$B$5,$B$2+$B$3+$B$4,IF(A12<$B$5,$B$2)))				
13		5	$1,130.00	=IF(A13>$B$5,"",IF(A13=$B$5,$B$2+$B$3+$B$4,IF(A13<$B$5,$B$2)))				

investor paid $1,147) and the bond is redeemed after five years for the principal amount ($1,000), the return on the investment is only 4.6%. Although the $50 call penalty does not restore the return to 6%, the investor does receive a yield of 5.46%, which is considerably better than 4.6%.

13-12 Risk and Fluctuations in Yield

Stock investors will bear risk only if they anticipate a sufficient return to compensate for the risk, and a higher anticipated return is necessary to induce them to bear additional risk. This principle also applies to investors who purchase bonds. Bonds involving greater risk must offer higher yields to attract investors. Therefore, the lowest yields are paid by bonds with the highest credit ratings, and low credit ratings are associated with high yields.

Because interest rates change over time, the anticipated yields on all debts vary. However, the yields on debt involving greater risk tend to fluctuate more. This is illustrated in **Figure 13-10**, which plots the yields on Moody's Baa-rated bonds in the top line and the yields on its Aaa-rated bonds in the bottom line for the period 1986–2021.

Though the yields on Baa-rated and Aaa-rated bonds tended to track together during the 1990s, both the financial crisis of 2008 and the financial impact of the COVID-19 pandemic motivated investors to move from poorer-quality debt into higher-quality debt, driving prices of Baa-rated bonds down and their yields up, thereby increasing the spread between Baa-rated and Aaa-rated bonds.

Figure 13-10: Fluctuations in Yield to Maturity for Moody's Aaa- and Baa-Rated Corporate Bonds

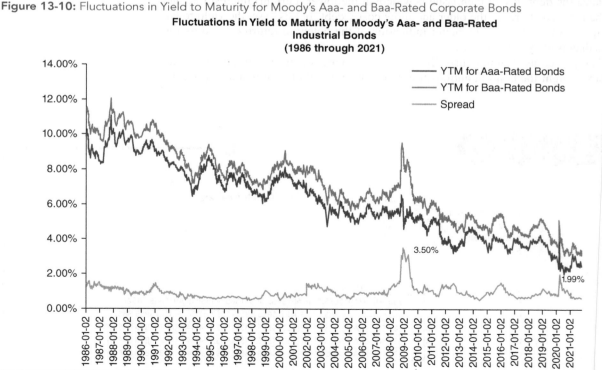

In the 2008 financial crisis, this "flight to safety" caused the spread, which had been averaging less than 1.0% (less than 100 basis points) during the 1990s to peak at 3.50% (338 basis points) in December 2008. The uncertainty surrounding the COVID-19 pandemic caused a similar, though smaller, peak of 1.99% (199 basis points) in April 2020. It is also important to note that, since 2008, the spread has tended to be "spikier," exhibiting the tendency to stay above the previous average of less than 1.0% a good deal of the time. This is taken to mean that investors have been appropriately leery of jumps in yields ever since the 2008 financial crisis.

Also, please note that the data in Figure 13-10 use average yields. There were numerous examples of bonds with Baa ratings that sold for much higher yields.

13-12a Changes in Risk

Previous sections demonstrated that when interest rates change, bond prices fluctuate in the opposite direction. If interest rates rise after a bond is issued, it will sell for a discount as the price adjusts so that the yield to maturity will be comparable with bonds being currently issued. If interest rates fall after the bond is issued, it will sell for a premium so that once again the yield to maturity is comparable to current interest rates.

The amount of price change depends on the coupon, the term of the bond, and the risk. The smaller the coupon, the greater the price fluctuation for a given maturity and level of risk. The longer the term of the bond, the greater the price fluctuation for a given coupon and level of risk. For given coupons and maturity dates, the prices of riskier bonds tend to fluctuate more.

The coupons and maturity dates of a bond are set when the bond is issued. However, the risk of default on a bond may vary over time as the financial condition of the issuer varies. Firms that were financially sound when their bonds were issued may fall on hard times. Their credit ratings deteriorate. Other firms' financial positions may improve. These changes in risk will, of course, affect the value of outstanding bonds.

13-12b Duration

In the (very) short term, the risk of a bond is unlikely to change, so we can model the volatility in the price of a bond as being dependent upon the coupon amount and the term to maturity. For a given risk class and coupon amount, the price of the bond with the longer term to maturity should be more volatile. Bonds with equal maturities but different coupons may be compared on the basis of the interest payments. Again, for a given risk class, the price of the bond with the smaller coupon will tend to be more volatile.

In reality, however, even bonds of the same risk class may have different coupons and different maturity dates at the same time, usually because they were issued at different times and in differing economic conditions. Computing the yield to maturity is one method for comparing two bonds in that situation, but the yield to maturity does not indicate which bonds' prices will tend to be more volatile.

An alternative calculation that may be used to compare bonds with different coupons and different terms to maturity is called the bond's **duration** (more formally, the "Macaulay duration") and seeks to compare bonds with different coupons and different maturity dates by determining each bond's price sensitivity to changes in interest rates.

duration
the weighted-average length of time to receive a bond's cash flows

To put it simply, duration is defined as the weighted average time it takes the bondholder to receive the interest and the principal of the bond. To illustrate how duration is determined, consider a $1,000 bond with three years to maturity and a 9% coupon. The annual payments are as follows:

Year	Payment
1	$ 90
2	90
3	1,090

Currently, the yield on comparable bonds is 12%, so this bond's price is $927.95. The bond's duration is the sum of the present value of each payment weighted by the time period in which the payment is received, with the resulting quantity divided by the price of the bond. Thus, for this bond, the duration is determined as follows:

Term of Each Payment		Amount of Payment		Present Value of Each Dollar at 12%		
1	×	$ 90	×	0.893	=	$ 80.37
2	×	90	×	0.797	=	143.46
3	×	1,090	×	0.712	=	2,328.24
						$2,552.07

$$\text{Duration} = \frac{\$2,552.07}{\$927.95} = 2.75 \text{ years}$$

A duration of 2.75 years means that the bondholder collects, on an average, all the payments in 2.75 years. Obviously, all the payments are not made exactly at 2.75 years into the future. Ninety dollars is received at the end of year one, $90 is received at the end of year two, and $1,090 is received at the end of year three. But the weighted average of all these payments is 2.75 years.

Excel Expert 13-13

Excel's built in DURATION(*settlement, maturity, coupon, yld, frequency, [basis]*) function requires the *settlement* and *maturity* values to be dates. In this case, as all we care about is the term and not the actual dates, we can make use of the TODAY() function to set the settlement date to the current date, and then add the term of the bond to TODAY() to get the maturity date:

	A	B	C	D	E	F
1	Annual coupon rate	9%		Duration	2.75	=DURATION(B3,B5,B1,B2,B6,B7)
2	Yield	12%				
3	Settlement date	11/23/2021	=TODAY()			
4	n	3				
5	Maturity date	11/23/2024	=DATE(YEAR(B3)+B4,MONTH(B3),DAY(B3))			
6	Payments per year	1				
7	Basis	0				

Duration may also be computed when payments are semiannual, in which case the annual payment and interest rate on comparable debt are divided by two and the number of payments is multiplied by two. If this example had used semiannual compounding, the bond's price would be $926.24, and the computation of duration is

Term of Each Payment (in Six-Month Periods)		Amount of Payment		Present Value Interest Factor at 6%		
1	×	$ 45	×	0.943	=	$ 42.44
2	×	45	×	0.890	=	80.04
3	×	45	×	0.840	=	113.40
4	×	45	×	0.792	=	142.56
5	×	45	×	0.747	=	168.08
6	×	1,045	×	0.705	=	4,420.35
						$4,966.87

$$\text{Duration} = \frac{\$4,966.87/2}{\$926.24} = 5.3624/2 \text{ years} = 2.68 \text{ years}$$

Note that the duration is slightly smaller with semiannual coupons because the cash inflows are received slightly faster as the result of semiannual compounding.

The calculation of duration (D) may be formally expressed as follows:

$$\text{Duration} = \frac{\sum_{t=1}^{m} PVCF_t \times t}{P_B} \qquad \textbf{13-6}$$

The numerator states that the cash flow in each year (CF_t) is stated in present value terms (PV) and weighted by the number of the period (t) in which the payment is received. The individual present values are summed from $t = 1$ to $t = m$ (maturity), and the resulting amount is divided by the current price of the bond (P_B).

Excel Expert 13-14

Calculating duration with semiannual payments simply involves changing the *frequency* argument:

	A	B	C	D	E	F
1	Annual coupon rate	9%		Duration	2.68	=DURATION(B3,B5,B1,B2,B6,B7)
2	Yield	12%				
3	Settlement date	11/23/2021	=TODAY()			
4	n	3				
5	Maturity date	11/23/2024	=DATE(YEAR(B3)+B4,MONTH(B3),DAY(B3))			
6	Payments per year	2				
7	Basis	0				

Notice that duration is not the sum of the present value of each payment. (That sum is the price of the bond.) Duration takes the present value of each payment and weighs it according to when the payment is received. Payments that are to be received farther into the future have more weight in the calculation. If two bonds pay the same coupon but the term of one bond is 10 years while the term of the other is 20 years, the weights given to the payments in years 11 through 20 result in a larger weighted average. The duration, or the weighted average of when all the payments will be received, is longer for the second bond.

The preceding manual calculation of duration can be tedious. Luckily, Excel includes a DURATION() function to calculate this for us.

By making this calculation for bonds with different coupons and different maturities, the investor standardizes the sensitivity of the bonds' prices to fluctuations due to changes in interest rates from current levels. Bonds with the same duration will experience similar price fluctuations, while the prices of bonds with a longer duration will fluctuate more.

For example, consider the following two bonds, priced when their YTM is 10%. Bond A has a 10% coupon, matures in 20 years, and currently sells for $1,000. Bond B has a 7% coupon and matures after 10 years with a current price of $815.66. (In this illustration, it is assumed that the bonds sell for the same yield to maturity. While generally the long-term bond should offer a higher yield, this assumption facilitates comparisons for a given change in interest rates.) If interest rates rise, the price of both bonds will fall, but which bond's price will fall more? Since the bonds differ with regard to maturity date and coupon, the investor does not know which bond's price will be more volatile.

In general, the longer the term to maturity, the more volatile the bond's price. By that reasoning, bond A will be more volatile. However, lower coupons are also associated with greater price volatility, and by that reasoning bond B's price should be more volatile. Thus, the investor cannot tell on the basis of term and coupon which of these two bonds' prices will be more volatile. However, once their durations have been determined (9.36 and 7.22, respectively), the investor knows that the price of bond A will decline more in response to an increase in interest rates. That is, comparing the duration of two different bonds will tell us the relative impact of a given change in rates on the prices of the two bonds: the bond with the larger duration will be affected more by a given change in rates than the bond with the small duration. For example, if interest rates rise to 12% from 10%, the prices of the two bonds become $850.61 and $717.49, respectively. Bond A's price will decline by 15%, while bond B's price will fall by 12%, implying that Bond A's price was more volatile.

For extremely small changes in interest rates, duration may also be used to determine the *amount* by which a bond's price will fluctuate. The percentage change in a bond's price for a change in the yield to maturity is

$$\frac{\Delta P_B}{P_B} = -D \times \frac{\Delta y}{1 + y}$$

in which P_B is the current price of the bond, D is the bond's duration, and y is the current yield to maturity while Δy is the change in yield. By rearranging terms, the change in the price of a bond is

$$\Delta P_B = -D \times \frac{\Delta y}{1 + y} \times P_B \qquad \text{13-7}$$

The equation may be illustrated by using bond A above, which sold for $1,000 when the yield to maturity was 10%, and whose duration was 9.36. If interest rates rise to 10.2%, the change in the price of bond A is

$$\Delta P_B = -9.36 \times \frac{0.002}{1 + 0.10} \times \$1,000 = -\$17$$

The increase in interest rates from 10 to 10.2% causes the price of the bond to decline from $1,000 to $983. If interest rates were to fall from 10 to 9.8% (−0.002), the price of the bond would similarly rise to $1,017.

The usefulness of duration to forecast a bond's price change due to a given change in interest rates diminishes as the change in interest rates increases. For example, if interest rates had increased from 10 to 12%, Equation 13-7 would indicate that bond A's price would have declined by $170, whereas the actual bond valuation would show that the new price would be $850.61, a decline of $149.39. This difference occurs because, while Equation 13-7 expresses ΔP_B as being a *linear* function of Δy, it is actually a *convex* function, as shown in **Figure 13-11**.

So, if estimating changes in bond price using duration via Equation 13-7 only gives an approximation, why use it at all? Why not use Equation 13-2 instead? Two reasons: First, even though using duration only gives an approximation for changes in price due to changes in interest rates, it's a very good approximation for small changes in rates. And since rates tend to change over time, but not usually instantaneously, using duration to estimate price changes due to rate changes actually does a pretty good job of preparing you for what's likely to happen in the near future.

Secondly, using the bond pricing formula in Equation 13-2 to price a bond at a new, changed interest rate would require you to know what the new rate will be, and

Figure 13-11: Calculating Bond Prices Using Valuation vs. Duration

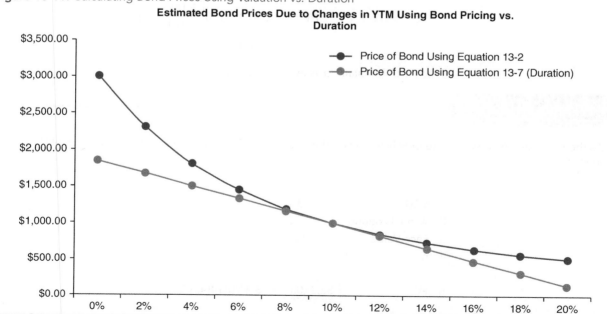

Estimated Bond Prices Due to Changes in YTM Using Bond Pricing vs. Duration

Legend:
- Price of Bond Using Equation 13-2
- Price of Bond Using Equation 13-7 (Duration)

the valuation from Equation 13-2 will be different for each of the different possible new future interest rates. Using Equation 13-7, on the other hand, only involves the calculation of one statistic, duration, which is much more tractable.

Using duration in this manner does involve a trade-off, however: to the extent that yields are constantly changing, the duration for a bond that you calculate at one yield gets outdated pretty quickly. So any strategy that depends on predicting sensitivity in prices due to changes in interest rates using duration, such as portfolio immunization discussed below, requires you to recalculate duration fairly often.

13-12c Duration and Portfolio Immunization

immunization
matching the duration of a portfolio to the timing of the investor's need for funds

Pension plan managers and some portfolio managers (e.g., managers of a life insurance company's bond portfolio) use duration as a tool of risk management. These professional investors know reasonably well the time and the amount of funds needed for distributions. They then match the duration of their portfolios with the timing of the need for funds. This strategy is often referred to as **immunization**, because it reduces the risk associated with interest rate fluctuations and the reinvestment of interest payments.

Consider a portfolio manager who needs $2,200 at the end of seven years and purchases at par a high-yield 12% coupon bond that matures at the end of seven years. If interest rates remain at 12%, the investor will have $2,210.68 because the coupons are reinvested at 12%. The terminal value is equal to the $1,000 FV of the bond plus the future value of the reinvested coupons:

$$FV = \$1,000 + \$120\left[\frac{1.12^7 - 1}{0.12}\right]$$
$$= \$2,210.68$$

If interest rates rise and the portfolio manager reinvests at 14%, the terminal value is

$$FV = \$1,000 + \$120\left[\frac{1.14^7 - 1}{0.14}\right]$$
$$= \$2,287.66$$

and the portfolio manager is even better off.

Excel Expert 13-15

As the FV is already at time 7, we only have to find the future value of the coupon payments using the FV() function:

	A	B	C	D
1	YTM	0.12		
2	Annual coupon	120		
3	Face Value	1000		
4	n	7		
5				
6	FV	$2,210.68	=B3+FV(B1,B4,-B2)	

Excel Expert 13-16

	A	B	C	D
1	YTM	0.14		
2	Annual coupon	120		
3	Face Value	1000		
4	n	7		
5				
6	FV	$2,287.66 =B3+FV(B1,B4,-B2)		

A problem arises when interest rates fall and the coupons are reinvested at a lower rate. For example, if interest rates decline to 8%, the terminal value is

$$FV = \$1,000 + \$120\left[\frac{1.08^7 - 1}{0.08}\right]$$

$$= \$2,070.74$$

and the portfolio manager does not have the required $2,200. The lower reinvestment of the interest payments resulted in an insufficient terminal value.

The portfolio manager could have avoided the shortage by acquiring a bond whose duration (and not its term) is equal to seven years. For example, if the portfolio manager purchases a bond with a 12% coupon that matures in 12 instead of 7 years, that bond has a duration of 6.9 years that almost matches when the $2,200 is needed. (The 12% 7-year bond has a duration of 5.1 years.) As will be subsequently illustrated, the purchase of the 12-year bond instead of the 7-year bond eliminates the reinvestment risk.

Since the 12-year bond will have to be sold at the end of 7 years, the obvious question is: At what price? The price could rise (if interest rates fall) or decline (if interest rates rise). Should the portfolio manager be concerned with interest rate risk (i.e., the fluctuation in the bond's price), which would not apply if the bond matured

Excel Expert 13-17

	A	B	C	D
1	YTM	0.08		
2	Annual coupon	120		
3	Face Value	1000		
4	n	7		
5				
6	FV	$2,070.74 =B3+FV(B1,B4,-B2)		

at the end of seven years? The answer is no. The bond's price of course will change, but the impact of the price fluctuation is offset by the change in the reinvestment of the interest payments. The effect, then, of both reinvestment rate risk and interest rate risk is eliminated.

Suppose interest rates immediately rise to 14% after the portfolio manager buys the bond. The portfolio manager holds the bond for seven years and reinvests the interest payments at 14%. How much will this investor have at the end of seven years? Assuming that rates stay at 14% until the portfolio manager needs to sell the bond, the answer is the sum of the interest payments reinvested at 14% for seven years [$120(10.730) = $1,287.66] plus the sale price of the bond. Since the bond has five years to maturity, its price is

$$P_B = \$120 \times \frac{1 - \dfrac{1}{(1 + 0.14)^5}}{0.14} + \frac{\$1,000}{(1 + 0.14)^5} = \$931.34$$

Thus, the portfolio manager has $1,287.66 + $931.34 = $2,219, which meets the desired amount ($2,200). The loss on the sale of the bond is offset by the increased interest earned when the annual interest payments are reinvested at the higher rate.

Suppose interest rates immediately decline to 8% after the bond is purchased. The portfolio manager holds the bond for seven years and reinvests the interest payments at 8%. How much will the investor have at the end of seven years? The answer in this case is the sum of the interest payments reinvested at 8% for seven years [$120(8.923) = $1,070.74] plus the sale price of the bond. Since the bond has five years to maturity, its price is

$$P_B = \$120 \times \frac{1 - \dfrac{1}{(1 + 0.08)^5}}{0.08} + \frac{\$1,000}{(1 + 0.08)^5} = \$1,159.71$$

Thus, the portfolio manager has $1,070.74 + $1,159.71 = $2,230.45, which once again meets the desired amount ($2,200). The gain on the sale of the bond offsets the reduction in interest earned when the interest payments are reinvested at the lower rate.

Excel Expert 13-18

	A	B	C
1	FV	$ 1,000.00	
2	Coupon	$ 120	
3	n	5	
4	iYTM	14.00%	
5			
6	P_B	$931.34	=-PV(B4,B3,B2,B1)

Excel Expert 13-19

	A	B	C
1	FV	$ 1,000.00	
2	Coupon	$ 120	
3	n	5	
4	YTM	8.00%	
5			
6	P$_B$	$1,159.71	=-PV(B4,B3,B2,B1)

Notice that in both cases the individual achieves the investment goal of $2,200 at the end of seven years. Lower reinvestment income from a decline in interest rates is offset by the increase in the price of the bond, while higher reinvestment income from an increase in interest rates is offset by the decline in the price of the bond. Thus, the impact of reinvestment rate risk and interest rate risk is eliminated. Of course, the portfolio manager has lost the opportunity to earn a higher return, but the purpose of the strategy is to ensure a particular amount in the future.

As this discussion indicates, the concept of duration is exceedingly important for any investor who knows when funds will be needed and in what amount. Pension managers know both when payments must be made and their amount. Mortality tables help establish the same information for life insurance companies. Portfolio managers immunize their risk exposure and ensure that the desired funds are available when needed. (These portfolio managers, of course, still have the risk of default or incorrect forecasts, such as changes in a mortality table.)

Individual investors will probably find duration less useful. For example, even if parents know when their children will attend college, they do not necessarily know the cost—hence the future value is unknown. In addition, the duration of each bond is not readily available and, as is explained in the next section, the value changes with each change in the bond's price. Thus, individual investors who want to apply this concept will have to perform the calculation themselves and frequently adjust their portfolios as the duration of each bond in the portfolio fluctuates.

13-12d Modified Duration

As discussed above, Macaulay duration refers to the weighted average time before repayment or the time when cash flow is received. When we are particularly interested in estimating the impact of changes in YTM on bond prices, you will tend to hear professionals refer to **modified duration**, which explicitly refers to the percentage change in price for a unit change in yield. To calculate modified duration, denoted as D^*, you simply divide duration by 1 plus the YTM:

$$D^* = \frac{D}{1 + YTM}$$

13-8

modified duration duration divided by one plus the YTM that measures the price sensitivity of the bond to interest rate changes

Excel Expert 13-20

Modified duration can be calculated in Excel using the *MDURATION()* function:

	A	B	C	D	E	F
1	Annual coupon rate	10%		Duration	8.51	=MDURATION(B3,B5,B1,B2,B6,B7)
2	Yield	10%				
3	Settlement date	11/23/2021	=TODAY()			
4	n	20				
5	Maturity date	11/23/2041	=DATE(YEAR(B3)+B4,MONTH(B3),DAY(B3))			
6	Payments per year	1				
7	Basis	0				

For bond A shown in Figure 13-11, this would be equal to:

$$D^* = \frac{9.36}{1 + 0.10} = 8.51$$

And, if we were using modified duration, we would rewrite Equation 13-7 as:

$$\Delta P_B = -D^* \times \Delta YTM \times P_B \qquad \textbf{13-9}$$

As shown in **Figure 13-12**, **Equations 13-7** and **13-9** will give us the same estimated prices in response to changes in YTM:

Figure 13-12: Calculating Bond Prices Using Valuation vs. Duration and Modified Duration

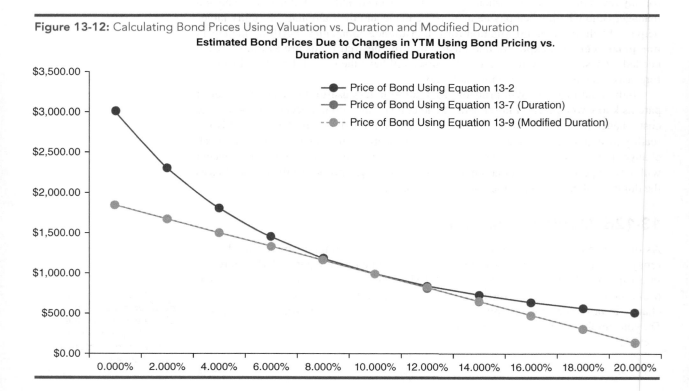

Estimated Bond Prices Due to Changes in YTM Using Bond Pricing vs. Duration and Modified Duration

13-12e Bond Price Convexity

While duration may be used to rank-order bonds with regard to their price volatility and to determine their price change for a given change in interest rates, the accuracy of the estimated price change predicted using duration varies with the amount of the fluctuation in interest rates, with the error between duration-predicted prices (using Equations 13-7 and 13-9) and valuation prices (i.e., using Equation 13-2) increasing as the yield moves further and further from the yield at which duration was calculated.

The source of this is that duration predicts the same price change for each 1% movement in the interest rate, but the actual price change varies. As seen in Figure 13-12, the actual price of the bond will move along a curve that is convex to the origin, while the

Excel Expert 13-20

There is no built-in convexity function in Excel, but it can be calculated by replicating the mathematical steps in the formula:

	A	B	C	D	E
1	FV	$ 1,000.00			
2	Coupon	$ 100			
3	n	20			
4	YTM	10.00%			
5					
6	Convexity	116.22	=1/(B1*(1+B4)^2)*SUM(E9:E39)		
7					
8	t	CF	PV(CF)	t^2+t	PV(CF)x(t2+t)
9	1	100	$90.91	2	181.82
10	2	100	$82.64	6	495.87
11	3	100	$75.13	12	901.58
12	4	100	$68.30	20	1,366.03
13	5	100	$62.09	30	1,862.76
14	6	100	$56.45	42	2,370.79
15	7	100	$51.32	56	2,873.69
16	8	100	$46.65	72	3,358.85
17	9	100	$42.41	90	3,816.88
18	10	100	$38.55	110	4,240.98
19	11	100	$35.05	132	4,626.52
20	12	100	$31.86	156	4,970.64
21	13	100	$28.97	182	5,271.89
22	14	100	$26.33	210	5,529.96
23	15	100	$23.94	240	5,745.41
24	16	100	$21.76	272	5,919.51
25	17	100	$19.78	306	6,054.05
26	18	100	$17.99	342	6,151.17
27	19	100	$16.35	380	6,213.30
28	20	1100	$163.51	420	68,673.36

duration-predicted price moves along the straight line. For a given change in interest rates (e.g., 8 to 9% or 9 to 10%), the amount of actual price change varies, while the duration–predicted price change has a constant slope, so the forecasted error increases for larger changes in yield.

convexity
refers to both a measure of and an adjustment for the curvature in the relationship between bond prices and yields

This **convexity** of the actual price change decreases the practicality of using a unique value of duration to forecast price changes. In order to adjust our forecast for that convexity, we can use the following measure of convexity:

$$Convexity = \frac{1}{P_B \times (1 + YTM)^2} \sum_{t=1}^{n} \left| \frac{CF_t}{(1 + YTM)^t}(t^2 + t) \right| \qquad \textbf{13-10}$$

This can, in turn, be used to estimate changes in bond prices as a function of changes in YTM:

$$\Delta P_B = \left(-D^* \times \Delta YTM + \frac{1}{2} \times Convexity \times \Delta YTM^2 \right) \times P_B \qquad \textbf{13-11}$$

For example, returning to Bond A used in previous examples, *Convexity* would be measured as:

$$Convexity = \frac{1}{\$1,000 \times (1 + 0.10)^2} \left(\sum_{t=1}^{19} \left| \frac{\$100}{(1 + 0.10)^t}(t^2 + t) \right| + \frac{\$1,100}{(1 + 0.10)^{20}}(20^2 + 20) \right)$$

$$= 116.22$$

Figure 13-13: Bond Prices Using Valuation, Duration, and Convexity

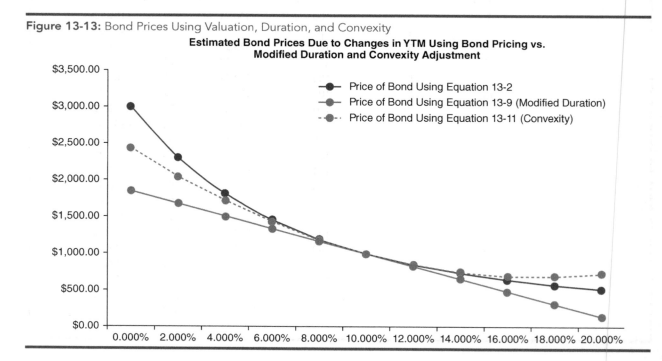

If, as also previously discussed, the YTM on the bond increased to 12%, the convexity-adjusted estimate would be:

$$\Delta P_B = \left(-8.51 \times 0.02 + \frac{1}{2} \times 116.22 \times 0.02^2\right) \times \$1{,}000$$

$$= -\$146.96$$

which is much closer to the valuation decline of $149.39 previously noted.

In fact, using *convexity* and Equation 13-11 results in much less overall forecasting error than just using duration. This is shown in **Figure 13-13**.

As you can see, the average error between the gray convexity-adjusted forecast and the blue actual valuation line is much less than when using just duration.

13-13 Management of Bond Portfolios

Since bonds pay a fixed income and mature at a specified date, they are conducive to passive management. The investor may acquire a portfolio of bonds and simply hold them to maturity (i.e., a buy-and-hold strategy). Each year the interest is received and at maturity the principal is repaid. During the interim, the value of the portfolio could rise (i.e., interest rates fall) or the value of the portfolio could fall (i.e., interest rates rise). Such fluctuations in the value of the portfolio may have little meaning to the investor who is passively holding the portfolio and collecting the interest until the bonds mature. Of course, if the individual had to sell the bonds for any reason, their prices would become crucial since the investor would receive only what the bonds were currently worth.

Not all bondholders, however, are passive investors. As was explained in the previous section, using duration for the management of reinvestment rate risk requires frequent trading of bonds. A strategy designed to take advantage of an expected change in rates paid by one type of bond relative to a different type requires the swapping of one bond for another. A strategy designed to reduce interest rate risk may require the construction of a portfolio with many bonds with different maturity dates. A strategy designed to match the timing of a bond portfolio's cash flows with when the funds are needed may require frequent trading of bonds. None of these constitutes passive management of a bond portfolio.

13-13a Management of Interest Rate Risk

Since interest rates change daily, the value of a bond portfolio fluctuates daily. Of course, the investor could avoid these fluctuations by acquiring only short-term debt obligations. This strategy generates less income since shorter maturities generally have lower yields than bonds with longer maturities. The opposite strategy (i.e., to purchase long-term bonds) will increase income but also increases the risk associated with changes in interest rates.

The investor could construct a portfolio of bonds with maturities distributed over a period of time. Such a strategy is sometimes referred to as a laddered approach. For example, a $1,000,000 portfolio could acquire $100,000 worth of bonds that mature for each of the next 10 years. If interest rates change, the prices of the bonds with the shorter terms (i.e., the bonds with one to five years to maturity) will fluctuate less than the prices of the bonds with the longer terms (i.e., years 6 through 10). Hence, such a portfolio reduces the impact of changes in interest rates.

In addition to reducing the impact on the value of the portfolio from fluctuating interest rates, a laddered portfolio offers two important advantages. First, since the structure of yields is generally positive, the interest earned on the bonds will tend to be greater than would be earned on a portfolio of short-term debt instruments. (Correspondingly, it would be smaller than the interest earned on a portfolio consisting solely of bonds with long terms to maturity.) Second, some of the bonds mature each year. If the individual needs the funds, they are available; if the individual does not need the funds, they may be reinvested. If the funds are reinvested each year in bonds with a 10-year maturity, the original structure of the portfolio is retained.

The previous example illustrates a **straight ladder**. The width of each step is the same and the distance between each step is the same. But both the width and the distance may vary. For example, suppose the investor anticipates needing more funds further into the future. The top of the ladder could be expanded and the base could be narrowed. The 10-year $1,000,000 ladder could be constructed so that $50,000 matures in the first year and that amount increases each year ($75,000 in year two, $100,000 in year three, $125,000 in year four, and so on). This strategy will increase annual income if the yield curve is positively sloping, but it also exposes the investor to more interest rate risk. If interest rates do rise, the value of the bonds with the longest maturity will decline more. Investing a larger proportion in the longer-term bonds may produce a larger loss if the interest rates rise and the investor must sell the ladder.

The possibility of an increase in interest rates suggests the opposite strategy: widen the ladder at the base. The investor may allocate the $1,000,000 ladder so that $200,000 matures in the first year, $175,000 in the second year, $150,000 in the third year, and so on. If interest rates do rise, the funds received when the shorter-term bonds mature can be reinvested at the higher rates. Of course, if interest rates do not rise, this strategy generates less income than the ladder with more invested further into the future. Certainly, the investor's need for funds or expectation of an increase in interest rates affects the construction of the shape of the ladder.

One disadvantage associated with a ladder strategy is that if the investor wants to (or needs to) alter the portfolio, virtually all the bonds have to be liquidated. If the investor anticipates lower interest rates, then a portfolio consisting of only long maturities is desirable. All the bonds with short to intermediate terms would have to be sold and reinvested in bonds with long maturities. The opposite would occur if the individual anticipates higher rates. In that case, the individual wants only short-term securities, so all the bonds with intermediate to long terms would have to be sold.

This lack of flexibility and the need to change a large proportion of the portfolio if the investor seeks to take advantage of anticipated changes in interest rates has led to an entirely different strategy for management of a bond portfolio. In this strategy, which is sometimes referred to as a barbell, the investor acquires a portfolio consisting of very long and very short maturities. If the individual has $1,000,000 to invest, $500,000 may be used to purchase bonds with short maturities (e.g., six months to a year) and $500,000 to purchase 20-year bonds. If the investor then anticipates a change in interest rates, only half of the portfolio needs to be changed. Expectation of lower rates would imply selling the short-term bonds and investing the proceeds in long-term bonds. If the investor anticipated higher interest rates, they would do the opposite: sell the long-term bonds and move into the short-term bonds.

A **barbell strategy** will reduce the impact of fluctuating interest rates if the investor anticipates correctly. It will magnify the impact if the investor is incorrect. A movement into long-term bonds just prior to an increase in interest rates could inflict a substantial loss on the value of the portfolio. The strategy also has a second major

straight ladder
a bond investment strategy where an equal amount of face value of bonds is purchased with different, but equally spaced over time, maturities

barbell strategy
a bond investment strategy consisting of very long and very short maturities

disadvantage: With the passage of time, the short-term bonds will mature, and the maturities of the long-term bonds will diminish. Thus, this bond strategy requires active management, as the proceeds of the maturing bonds will have to be reinvested and some of the longer bonds may have to be sold and the proceeds invested in bonds with even longer maturities. Failure to take these steps means that the investor's cash position will increase and the term of the remaining bonds will decrease.

13-13b Matching Strategies

The "barbell strategy" is designed to facilitate swapping bonds of different terms to benefit from anticipated changes in interest rates. The "immunized portfolio" discussed earlier matches the duration of the bond portfolio with the investor's cash needs. This particular strategy requires the investor to monitor the portfolio and adjust it should the duration differ from the time when the funds will be needed.

An alternative to the immunized portfolio is the **dedicated bond portfolio**, which matches the receipt of cash flows with the need for the funds. The interest payments and principal repayments are matched with when the investor anticipates needing these cash inflows to make payments. For example, a parent may construct a portfolio of zero coupon bonds, each of which matures when the child's tuition is due. While this is perhaps an exceptionally obvious example, the strategy would also apply to the trustees of a pension plan. In that case, the timing and amount of the payments to the retirees are known. The trustees then acquire bonds such that the interest payments and principal repayments match the required payments.

An individual could follow a similar strategy with funds in an individual retirement account (IRA). While the investor will not know exactly when the funds will be needed, they can estimate cash requirements. For example, suppose a retiree owns a house with no mortgage, a new car, and supplementary medical insurance. That individual may not know how much each payment will be in the future, but they know when property taxes and insurance payments are due. The retiree may also have an estimate of annual maintenance requirements for the house and the car and when the car would be replaced. Acquiring bonds that pay interest or mature at the same time these payments fall due should facilitate making the payments.

Interest rate risk is irrelevant for both immunized and dedicated bond portfolios. By matching the duration of the portfolio with the duration of the investor's liabilities or by timing the cash received with cash needs, the impact of fluctuations in interest rates is minimized. Such strategies are better than a simple buy-and-hold strategy because they seek to match the portfolio with the need for funds. Since a simple buy-and-hold does not consider when the funds will be needed, the investor will be subject to interest rate risk. The funds may possibly be needed during a period of higher interest rates, in which case the investor will not realize the value of the initial investment.

dedicated bond portfolio
an investment strategy that matches the receipt of cash flows with the investor's need for funds

13-13c Interest Rate Swaps

Interest rate swaps have emerged as one of the major recent innovations in finance for managing risk and basically involve swapping the future cash flows of the bonds you have for those of bonds where the future cash flows more closely resemble your future liabilities.

Many financial institutions have mismatched assets and liabilities. For example, the primary assets of a mortgage real estate investment trust or a savings and loan may be long-term mortgages, while its primary liabilities are short to intermediate term (i.e., deposits and certificates of deposit). When interest rates rise, a savings and loan institution loses on two counts: The higher interest rate reduces the value of its assets and increases the interest it must pay to attract depositors. To reduce this risk, the savings and loan needs a flow of payments that will vary with changes in interest, so the savings and loan swaps the flow of fixed-interest payments it will receive on the mortgages for a series of variable payments.

The swap is made with a corporation that has the need to make fixed payments. For example, suppose a utility has a large number of fixed-coupon bonds outstanding. The utility agrees to make variable payments to the savings and loan in exchange for the fixed-interest payments. Now the utility will have the funds coming in to make the interest payments. In effect, the utility is substituting variable-interest payments to the savings and loan for the fixed-interest payments that it would have to make to its bondholders, while the savings and loan substitutes the receipt of variable-interest payments for fixed-interest payments from the mortgages. The swap helps both firms better match their receipts and disbursements and manage their assets and liabilities.

Conclusion

As we have seen, bonds are actually very complex financial instruments, and their relatively long maturity and the tendency to have the majority of their principal repaid at maturity makes their prices very susceptible to changes in yields. We've also seen that such changes happen frequently, and that cumulative changes in rates can add up significantly in a short period of time, implying that bond prices will be equally volatile.

Given such an environment, it just makes sense that the investor should always be anticipating that such changes are going to happen and be planning a strategy to deal with them when they occur. This chapter has given us the basic tools for measuring the risk and likelihood of that happening as well as some basic strategies for minimizing the impact of that risk as much as possible.

Chapter Equations

$$P = \frac{PMT}{i} \tag{13-1}$$

$$P_B = PMT \times \frac{1 - \frac{1}{(1+i)^n}}{i} + \frac{FV}{(1+i)^n} \tag{13-2}$$

$$P_B = \frac{PMT}{c} \times \frac{1 - \frac{1}{\left(1+\frac{i}{c}\right)^{n \times c}}}{\frac{i}{c}} + \frac{FV}{\left(1+\frac{i}{c}\right)^{n \times c}} \tag{13-3}$$

$$Current\ Yield = \frac{Annual\ Interest\ Payment}{Price\ of\ the\ Bond} \tag{13-4}$$

$$P_B = PMT \times \frac{1 - \frac{1}{(1+i)^t}}{i} + \frac{FV + Call\ Penalty}{(1+i)^t} \tag{13-5}$$

$$Duration = \frac{\sum_{t=1}^{m} PVCF_t \times t}{P_B} \tag{13-6}$$

$$\Delta P_B = -D \times \frac{\Delta y}{1+y} \times P_B \qquad \text{13-7}$$

$$D^* = \frac{D}{1+y} \qquad \text{13-8}$$

$$\Delta P_B = -D^* \times \Delta y \times P_B \qquad \text{13-9}$$

$$Convexity = \frac{1}{P_B \times (1+y)^2} \sum_{t=1}^{n} \left| \frac{CF_t}{(1+y)^t}(t^2+t) \right| \qquad \text{13-10}$$

$$\Delta P_B = \left(-D^* \times \Delta y + \frac{1}{2} \times Convexity \times \Delta y^2 \right) \times P_B \qquad \text{13-11}$$

Excel Functions

DATE(year, month, day)
DAY(serial_number)
DURATION(settlement, maturity, coupon, yld, frequency, [basis])
FV(rate, nper, pmt, [pv], [type])
IF(logical test, [value_if_true], [value_if_false])
IRR(values, [guess])

MDURATION(settlement, maturity, coupon, yld, frequency, [basis])
MONTH(serial_number)
PV(rate, nper, pmt, [fv], [type])
SUM([number1], [number2],...)
YEAR(serial_number)

Key Terms

accrued interest – interest owed but not yet paid out

barbell strategy – a bond investment strategy consisting of very long and very short maturities

basis point – one one-hundredth of a percent, or 0.01%

bond – a debt security that matures in longer than a year

consol – a perpetual bond issued by the British government to finance the Napoleonic Wars and that never matures

convertible bond – a bond that may be exchanged for a certain number of shares in the issuing company

convexity – refers to both a measure of and an adjustment for the curvature in the relationship between bond prices and yields

coupon bond – a bond that pays a coupon payment

coupon rate – the interest rate paid on a bond, expressed as a percentage of the face value of the bond

covenant – the terms of agreement between a bond issuer and the bondholder

current yield – the annual flow of interest on a bond, expressed as a percentage of the price paid

debenture – an unsecured bond or note supported by the general creditworthiness of the firm

dedicated bond portfolio – an investment strategy that matches the receipt of cash flows with the investor's need for funds

discount – a bond selling for less than face value

duration – the weighted-average length of time to receive a bond's cash flows

equipment trust certificate – a mortgage bond secured by assets with substantial resale value

Eurobond – a bond issued by a U.S. company that is denominated in U.S. dollars but sold abroad in foreign markets

extendible security – a bond where the term to maturity may be extended at the option of the issuer

face value – the principal to be repaid on the maturity of a bond

fallen angel – a formerly investment-grade bond that has become a high-yield security because of lowered credit ratings

high-yield security – any debt of low quality and high risk

immunization – matching the duration of a portfolio to the timing of the investor's need for funds

income bond – a bond that pays interest during a period only if the company makes a certain amount of money during that period

increasing rate bond – a bond whose coupon increases over time

interest – money paid by a borrower in compensation for the use of the lender's funds

LIBOR – the London InterBank Offer Rate, the interest rate at which large international banks lend to each other

maturity date – the date that the final repayment of principal is made on a bond issue

modified duration – duration divided by one plus the YTM that measures the price sensitivity of the bond to interest rate changes

mortgage bond – a bond issued to purchase specific assets and that is secured by that asset

premium – used to refer to a bond selling for more than face value

price sensitivity – the variance in bond price caused by changes in yield

principal – the amount borrowed in a bond issue

private placement – an issue of securities that are sold to pre-selected investors and institutions rather than on the open market

public offering – an issue of securities that are sold on the open market

reset bond – a bond with a coupon that is readjusted at set intervals

securitization – the process of turning illiquid assets such as accounts receivable into liquid assets which can be sold

serial bond – a bond issue where a portion of the issue is scheduled to be retired each year until maturity

sinking fund – a fund into which periodic payments on a bond issue's principal is made in order to ensure orderly retirement of the debt issue

split coupon bond – a bond that initially pays not coupon, but which starts paying a fixed coupon after a set number of years

spread – the difference between rates on high-yield and investment-grade bonds

straight ladder – a bond investment strategy where an equal amount of face value of bonds is purchased with different, but equally spaced over time, maturities

variable interest rate bond – a bond that pays a coupon rate that varies based on market rates

yield – the return offered by a bond

yield curve – a plot of bond yield against bond maturity

yield to call (YTC) – the yield that an investor will earn if the bond is held until it is called before maturity

yield to maturity (YTM) – the yield that an investor will earn if the bond is held until it is redeemed at face value at maturity

zero coupon bond – a bond that pays no periodic interest coupons; all interest is paid at maturity

Questions

1. **Interest and Maturity.** Explain why interest and maturity are the two most important attributes of a bond driving its valuation. (LO 13-1)
2. **Bond Risk.** Explain what would cause the spread between different rankings of bonds to increase. How would this affect your portfolio investment strategy? (LO 13-2)
3. **Purchasing Bonds.** Why would you buy a flat bond? (LO 13-3)
4. **Corporate Bond Types.** What types of firms would be able to sell debentures? Why would they want to do so versus selling some type of secured bond issue? (LO 13-4)
5. **Accrued Interest.** Why are zero coupon bonds taxed on interest accrual instead of interest payment? (LO 13-5)
6. **Bond Retirement.** Why does a sinking fund make a bond safer for investors? (LO 13-6)
7. **Bond Pricing.** Why might some argue that bonds are easier to price than stocks? (LO 13-7)
8. **Yields.** When would an investor want to focus on current yield instead of YTM? Why? (LO 13-8)
9. **Duration and Convexity.** Why is a convexity-adjusted calculation of bond price changes in response to changes in interest rate more accurate than one done using only duration? (LO 13-9)
10. **Bond Portfolio Management.** Suppose you expected bond rates to go up in the next few years. What type of strategy would you want to adopt regarding your bond portfolio? Why? (LO 13-10)

Problems

1. **Consol bond.** What price would a consol bond paying $75 per year trade for if the YTM were 5%? (LO 13-7)

2. **Annual coupon.** What price would a 10% annual coupon bond with maturity of 17 years and a face value of $1,000 sell for if the current YTM were 12.3%? (LO 13-7)

3. **Seminannual coupon.** What price would an 8% semiannual coupon bond with maturity of eight years and a face value of $1,000 sell for if the current YTM were 6.5%? (LO 13-7)

4. **Zero coupon.** How much would a zero coupon bond with a face value of $10,000 and eight years to maturity sell for if the YTM were 7%? (LO 13-7)

5. **Split coupon.** A split coupon bond with a face value of $1,000 pays $0 in interest during the first 10 years, then $200 annually for the next 10 years, and matures after 20 years. How much would an investor pay if the required return were 13%? (LO 13-7)

6. **Current yield.** What would the current yield on an 8% annual coupon bond with maturity of 14 years and a face value of $1,000 be if it were selling for $1,137? (LO 13-8)

7. **Current yield.** What would the current yield on a 7% semiannual coupon bond with maturity of four years and a face value of $1,000 be if it were selling for $987? (LO 13-8)

8. **YTM.** What would the YTM yield on a 8.5% annual coupon bond with maturity of 12 years and a face value of $1,000 be if it were selling for $987? (LO 13-8)

9. **YTM.** What would the YTM yield on a 7.25% semiannual coupon bond with maturity of 16 years and a face value of $1,000 be if it were selling for $1,034? (LO 13-8)

10. **YTC.** What would the YTC on an 8.5% annual coupon bond with maturity of 12 years and a face value of $1,000 be if it were selling for $987, carried a call penalty of $85, and you expected it to be called in three years? (LO 13-8)

11. **Macaulay duration.** What would the Macaulay duration of a bond be with an annual 6% coupon rate, seven years until maturity, and a YTM of 7.3%? (LO 13-9)

12. **Macaulay duration.** What would the Macaulay duration of a bond be with a semiannual 5% coupon rate, 17 years until maturity, and a YTM of 5.3%? (LO 13-9)

13. **Portfolio future value.** Consider a portfolio manager who needs $1,200 at the end of three years and purchases at par a 6% annual coupon bond that matures at the end of three years. If the yield immediately changes to 8.5%, how much will the investor have at the end of three years if he can reinvest the coupons at 8.5%? (LO 13-9)

14. **Modified duration.** What would the modified duration of a bond be with an annual 7% coupon rate, 12 years until maturity, and a YTM of 4%? (LO 13-9)

15. **Modified duration.** What would the modified duration of a bond be with a semiannual 4% coupon rate, 12 years until maturity, and a YTM of 7%? (LO 13-9)

16. **Convexity.** Calculate the convexity of a 15-year, 8.2% annual coupon bond with a YTM of 8.8%. (LO 13-9)

17. **Expected price change.** What would the expected price change be using a convexity-adjusted estimate if the YTM on a 10-year, 7% annual coupon bond changed from 6.5 to 7.2%? (LO 13-9)

18. **Straight ladder.** Suppose you use a $500,000 bond portfolio to construct a straight ladder over the next 10 years. How much would you invest in bonds maturing in each year of the ladder? (LO 13-10)

19. **Barbell.** Suppose you use a $250,000 bond portfolio to construct a barbell strategy over the next 20 years. How much would you invest in bonds maturing in year 20? (LO 13-10)

20. **Expected price.** What would the expected new price be using a convexity-adjusted estimate if the YTM on a 30-year, 6% annual coupon bond selling at par increased by one basis point? (LO 13-9)

Case Study

Changes in Yield

On March 18, 2020, the yield on Moody's Aaa-rated bonds with maturities from 20 years and longer went from 3.40 to 3.92%, the largest jump since the Federal Reserve started tracking such ranked yields in 1983.

Using this 3.92% figure as the YTM for a 20-year bond issue that was selling at par the day before, graph expected bond prices as a function of future YTMs on that date using the convexity adjustment.

Chapter

14

Valuing Government Securities

Learning Objectives

After reading this chapter you should be able to:

LO 14-1 Distinguish among the types of federal government debt.
LO 14-2 Explain STRIPS and how they are used in retirement accounts.
LO 14-3 Illustrate how TIPS are adjusted for changes in the CPI.
LO 14-4 Differentiate between the types of assets backing the different federal agencies' debt issues.
LO 14-5 Isolate the primary advantage of state and local debt.
LO 14-6 Illustrate how to equalize yields on corporate and state and local debt.
LO 14-7 List and explain the risks associated with investment in foreign government debt securities.
LO 14-8 Explain how government securities are offered by investment companies.

During the 2012 election, one of the political issues in Washington was the size of the federal government's deficit, which had risen to over $1.4 trillion in the aftermath of the 2008 financial crisis and, which at the end of 2012, had only sunk to slightly over $1 trillion. The Obama administration managed to chip away at it, bringing it down to just under $442 billion by the end of 2015, while the activities of the Trump administration caused it to grow to just under $1 trillion again by the end of 2019.

As shown in **Figure 14-1**, all such previous budget deficits paled next to those incurred during the COVID-19 pandemic. In 2020, the budget ballooned to over $3.129 trillion; it is estimated to grow further to over $3.668 trillion in 2021.

Government deficits such as this occur when disbursements (expenditures) exceed receipts (revenues). Whenever a deficit occurs, someone must finance it. In order to raise funds to cover its deficit, the federal government issues a variety of debt instruments. This variety helps tap different sources of funds that are available in the money and capital markets.

Figure 14-1: U.S. Federal Budget Deficits

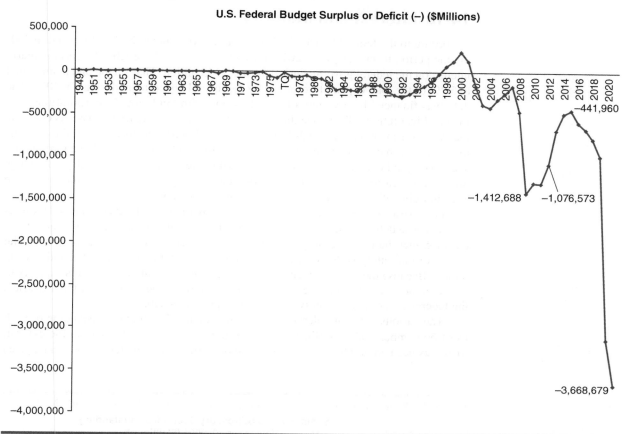

U.S. Federal Budget Surplus or Deficit (–) ($Millions)

Chapter 13 discussed a variety of corporate debt securities. This chapter extends the discussion to debt securities issued by the federal government, its agencies, and state and municipal governments. Many of the features associated with corporate debt (e.g., interest payments, maturity dates, and call features) apply to government securities, so we won't repeat that specific material; instead, this chapter will emphasize the features that differentiate government securities from corporate bonds.

The chapter begins with a discussion of the various types of debt securities issued by the federal government. These debt instruments range from **EE bonds** issued in small denominations to short-term **Treasury bills** and long-term bonds. The federal government also has created agencies such as the **Government National Mortgage Association (GNMA)**. These agencies also issue debt securities, whose interest rates generally exceed the rate paid by the bonds of the federal government. The chapter ends with coverage of the debt issued by state and local governments. These bonds, often referred to as municipal bonds, or munis, offer a real alternative to corporation and federal government bonds because they pay interest that is exempt from federal income taxation.

EE bond
a low-risk savings product that pays interest until it reaches 30 years or you cash it in, whichever comes first

Treasury bill (T-bill)
a short-term U.S. government debt obligation backed by the Treasury Department with a maturity of one year or less

Government National Mortgage Association (GNMA, or "Ginnie Mae")
a government agency that guarantees timely payments on mortgage-backed securities, providing liquidity in the market for home loans

14-1 The Variety of Federal Government Debt

14-1a Interest and Maturity

According to the federal budget for fiscal year 2020 (denoted by FY 2020 and including the period from October 1, 2019, through September 30, 2020), the current yearly interest on the federal government's debt was $345 billion. That's a lot, and it amounted to 5.2% of the total expenditures made by the federal government during FY 2020. The debt was financed by a variety of investors, including individuals, corporations, and financial institutions. To induce this diverse group of investors to purchase its debt, the federal government has issued different types of debt instruments that appeal to the various potential buyers. (Information concerning the public debt is available through the Treasury's public debt website, www.treasurydirect.gov, and includes yields on savings bonds and Treasury bills [as of the auction date] and how the investor may buy these Treasury obligations directly from the federal government.)

For investors, the unique advantage offered by the federal government's debt is its safety. These debt instruments are the safest of all possible investments, for there is no question that the U.S. Treasury is able to pay the interest and repay the principal. The source of this safety is the federal government's constitutional right to tax and to print money. Because there is no specified limitation on the federal government's capacity to create money, only Congress can enact legislation (e.g., the debt ceiling) that restricts the federal government's ability to retire or refinance its debt.

The various types of federal government debt and the amount outstanding of each as of November 2021 are illustrated in **Figure 14-2**. As may be seen in the exhibit, there has been an emphasis on the use of short-term T-bills (maturity less than a year)

Figure 14-2: Summary of U.S. Federal Government Debt on November 30, 2021

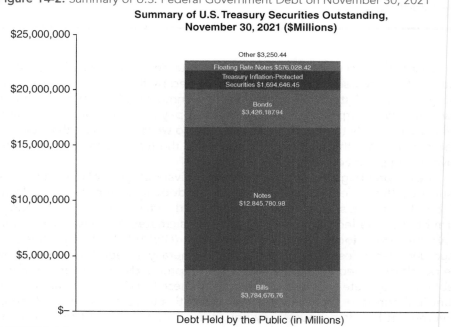

and intermediate-term Treasury notes (maturities between 2 and 10 years) rather than longer-term Treasury bonds. This emphasis is partially explained by interest costs, as interest rates on short-term debt are usually lower than those on long-term debt. Hence, the use of short-term financing reduces the Treasury's interest expense. Furthermore, Congress restricts the interest rate that the Treasury may pay on long-term debt, but it does not restrict the interest rate on short-term securities. Thus, during periods of high interest rates, the Treasury may not be permitted to sell long-term securities even if it desires to do so.

14-1b Nonmarketable Federal Government Debt

Perhaps the most widely held federal government debt is the Series EE bonds. Their predecessors, the original Series E bonds, were issued in 1941 to help finance World War II. They were sold at a discount in small denominations, such as $25, $50, and $100, so virtually every person could save and contribute to the war effort.

On January 2, 1980, the Treasury started to issue Series EE bonds to replace the Series E bonds. In November 1982, the Treasury changed the method for computing interest on EE bonds from a fixed rate to a variable rate, which is changed every six months. The variable rate permits the small investor to participate in higher yields when interest rates rise, but does earn less when interest rates fall.

EE bonds mature after 17 years. If the bonds are not redeemed at maturity, they will continue to earn interest for an additional 13 years, for a total of 30 years. EE bonds issued from May 1997 through April 2005 earn a variable rate of return. The interest rate is announced every May 1 and November 1 and applies for the following six months. The new rate is 90% of an average of the rate paid by five-year Treasury securities for the preceding three months. Interest is added to the value of the bonds every six months after they are purchased. EE bonds issued in May 2005 and later earn a fixed rate of return.

An important difference between Series EE bonds and other bonds is the lack of a secondary market. If the investor needs immediate cash, the bonds cannot be sold. Instead, they are redeemed at a financial institution, such as a commercial bank. Nor can the bonds be transferred as a gift, although they can be transferred through an estate. The Treasury also forbids using EE bonds to secure a loan. Although corporate bonds can be used as collateral, EE bonds cannot.

As the EE bonds were transitioned from variable- to fixed-rate interest, the Treasury introduced Series I bonds. Series I bonds are sold in denominations ranging from $50 to $10,000, and the interest rate is set by the Treasury every May and November for the next six months. The interest payment combines a fixed rate and an additional amount based on the consumer price index (CPI). Thus, I bonds offer a guaranteed minimum rate plus an adjustment for inflation. The maturity date is 20 years after date of issue but may be extended for an additional 10 years, after which interest payments cease. Interest is exempt from state income taxation and may be excluded from federal income tax if the interest is used to pay qualified higher education expenses.

E bond
a war bond issued by the U.S. government in 1941 to finance World War II, with face amounts between $18.75 to $10,000 and a maturity of 10 years

I bond
a security that earns interest based on both a fixed rate and a rate that is set twice a year based on inflation. The bond earns interest until it reaches 30 years or you cash it in, whichever comes first

14-1c Treasury Bills

Short-term federal government debt is issued in the form of Treasury bills (T-bills). These bills are sold in denominations of $10,000 to $1,000,000 and mature in 3 to 12 months. Like Series EE bonds, they are sold at a discount; however, unlike Series EE bonds, the discounted price is not set. Instead, the Treasury continually auctions off the bills, which go to the highest bidders. For example, if an investor bids $9,700 and obtains the bill, they will receive $10,000 when the bill matures, which is a yield of 3.1% ($300 ÷ $9,700) for the holding period. If the bid price had been higher, the interest cost to the Treasury (and the yield to the buyer) would have been lower.

Once Treasury bills have been auctioned, they may be bought and sold in the secondary market. They are issued in **book-entry form**, meaning that no physically engraved certificate is given to investors, and that ownership is tracked electronically. They are easily marketed, as there is an active secondary market in these bills. For Treasury bills quotes are given in the following form:

book-entry form
a method of tracking ownership of securities where no physically engraved certificate is given to investors

Maturity	Days to Maturity	Bid	Asked	Ask Yield
12/06/2X	126	3.49	3.47	3.56

These quotes indicate that for a Treasury bill maturing on December 6, 202X, buyers were willing to bid a discounted price that produced a discount yield of 3.49%. Sellers, however, were willing to sell (offer) the bills at a smaller discount (higher price) that returned a **discount yield** of 3.47%. The **annualized yield** on the bill based on the asked price is 3.56%.

discount yield
a yield calculated on the basis of the face amount of the bill and using a 360-day year

The reason for the difference between the discount yield and the annualized yield is that Treasury bills are sold at a discount and are quoted in terms of the discount yield. The discount yield is not the same as (nor is it comparable to) the annualized yield on the bill or the yield to maturity on a bond. The discount yield is calculated on the basis of the face amount of the bill and uses a 360-day year. The annualized yield, which is sometimes referred to as the **bond-equivalent yield**, depends on the price of the bill and uses a 365-day year.

annualized yield
the annual yield interest earned by a bond, calculated by dividing the discount amount by the price of the bond, annualized using 365 days in a year

The difference between the two calculations may be seen in the following example. Suppose a three-month $10,000 Treasury bill sells for $9,800. The discount yield (i_d) is

bond-equivalent yield
see annualized yield

$$i_d = \frac{Par\ value - Price}{Par\ value} \times \frac{360}{Number\ of\ days\ to\ maturity}$$

$$= \frac{\$10,000 - \$9,800}{\$10,000} \times \frac{360}{90}$$

$$= 8\%$$

14-1

Again, the best way to get the discount yield in Excel is to implement Equation 14-2:

	A	B	C
1	Par Value	$ 10,000	
2	Price	$ 9,800	
3	Number of days to maturity	90	
4			
5	i_a	8.277%	=(B1-B2)/B2*365/B3

The annualized yield (i_a) is

$$i_a = \frac{Par\ value - Price}{Price} \times \frac{365}{Number\ of\ days\ to\ maturity}$$

$$= \frac{\$10,000 - \$9,800}{\$9,800} \times \frac{365}{90}$$

$$= 8.277\% \qquad \textbf{14-2}$$

Because the discount yield uses the face amount and a 360-day year, it understates the yield the investor is earning. The discount yield may be converted to the annualized yield by the following equation:

$$i_a = \frac{365 \times i_d}{360 - (i_d \times Days\ to\ maturity)} \qquad \textbf{14-3}$$

Thus, if the discount rate on a three-month Treasury bill is 8%, the annualized yield is

$$i_a = \frac{365 \times .08}{360 - (.08 \times 90)} = 8.277\%$$

which is the same answer derived using the annual yield equation.

The annualized yield is a simple rate and should not be confused with the annual compound return. If you earn a simple, annualized rate of 8.277%, the compound rate is higher, as the interest earned in the first period is put to work to earn interest in subsequent periods. The calculation of the compound rate (i_c) is

$$i_c = \sqrt[n]{\frac{Par\ value}{Price}} - 1 \qquad \textbf{14-4}$$

Using Equation 14-3:

	A	B	C
1	i_d	8.00%	
2	Number of days to maturity	90	
3			
4	i_a	8.277%	=(365*B1)/(360-(B1*B2))

Excel Expert 14-4

Using Equation 14-4:

▲	A	B	C
1	Par Value	$ 10,000	
2	Price	$ 9,800	
3	Number of days to maturity	90	
4			
5	i_c	8.54%	=(B1/B2)^(365/B3)-1

where n is the percentage of 365 represented by the days to maturity. For our example, this would be

$$i_c = \sqrt[\frac{90}{365}]{\frac{\$10,000}{\$9,800}} - 1 = .0854 \text{ or } 8.54\%$$

Preference for a particular rate may depend upon the investor's usage. If you are acquiring the bill for only three months, the simple annualized yield is sufficient. However, if you are rolling over the bills as they come due (i.e., reinvesting the proceeds), the compound rate may be preferred.

Treasury bills may be purchased through brokerage firms, commercial banks, and any Federal Reserve bank. These purchases may be new issues or bills that are being traded in the secondary market. Bills with one year to maturity are auctioned once a month. Shorter-term bills are auctioned weekly. If the buyer purchases the bills directly through the Federal Reserve bank, there are no commission fees. Brokers and commercial banks do charge commissions, but the fees are modest compared with those charged for other investment transactions, such as the purchase of stock.

Treasury bills are among the best short-term debt instruments available to investors who desire safety and some interest income. The bills mature quickly, and there are many issues from which the investor may choose. Thus, the investor may purchase a bill that matures when the principal is needed. For example, an individual who has ready cash today but who must make a payment after three months may purchase a bill that matures at the appropriate time. In doing so, the investor puts the cash to work for three months.

Perhaps the one feature that differentiates Treasury bills from all other investments is risk. These bills are considered the safest of all possible investments. There is no question concerning the safety of principal when investors acquire Treasury bills. The federal government always has the capacity to refund or retire Treasury bills because it has the power to tax and the power to create money.

The primary buyers of Treasury bills are corporations with excess short-term cash, commercial banks with unused lending capacity, money market mutual funds, and foreign investors seeking a safe haven for their funds. Individual investors may also purchase them. However, the minimum denomination of $10,000 excludes many savers. Individual investors who desire such safe short-term investments may purchase shares in money market mutual funds that specialize in buying short-term securities, including Treasury bills.

14-1d Treasury Notes and Bonds

Intermediate-term federal government debt is in the form of Treasury notes. These notes are issued in denominations of $1,000 to more than $100,000 and mature in 1 to 10 years. Treasury bonds, the government's debt instrument for long-term debt, are issued in denominations of $1,000 to $1,000,000 and mature in more than 10 years from the date of issue. These bonds are among the safest intermediate- and long-term investments available and are purchased by pension funds, financial institutions, or savers who are primarily concerned with moderate income and safety. Since these debt instruments are safe, their yields are generally lower than that which may be obtained with high-quality corporate debt, such as IBM bonds. For example, in March 2019, ExxonMobil bonds that were rated triple A yielded 2.73%, while Treasury bonds with approximately the same time to maturity yielded 2.52%.

U.S. Treasury notes and bonds pay a fixed rate of interest. In January 2013, the U.S. Treasury issued its first-ever floating-rate notes. Unlike the inflation-indexed bonds explained later in this chapter, these floating-rate notes (referred to as **floaters**) pay interest that is set weekly and tied to the most recent 13-week Treasury bill rate. If the bill rate were to increase, the rate on the floaters would also increase, but the converse is also true. Lower Treasury bill rates will decrease the interest paid by the floaters. Hence, these securities would appeal to investors who anticipate an increase in the short-term rate of interest.

floater
a floating-rate note that pays interest that is set weekly and tied to the most recent 13-week Treasury bill rate

New issues of Treasury bonds may be purchased through commercial banks and brokerage firms. These firms will charge commissions, but the individual may avoid such fees by purchasing the securities from any of the Federal Reserve banks or their branches. Payment, however, must precede purchase. Unless the individual investor submits a competitive bid, the purchase price is the average price charged by institutions that buy the bonds through competitive bidding. By accepting this noncompetitive bid, the individual ensures matching the average yield earned by financial institutions, which try to buy the securities at the lowest price (highest yield) possible.

Once the bonds are purchased, they may be readily resold, as there is an active secondary market in U.S. Treasury bonds. Price quotes, however, are different from the quotes for stock, as Treasury bonds are quoted in 32nds. If a bond were quoted 107:13–107:15, that means the bid price is 107 13/32 and the ask price is 107 15/32. These amounts are $10,740.63 and $10,746.88 per $10,000 face amount of debt.

While Treasury bonds are among the safest investments available to investors, there are ways in which the holder of Treasury notes and bonds can suffer losses. These debt instruments pay a fixed amount of interest, which is determined when the notes and bonds are issued. The fixed interest means the bonds are subject to **interest rate risk**. If interest rates subsequently rise, existing issues will not be as attractive, and their market prices will decline. If an investor must sell the debt instrument before it matures, the price will be lower than the principal amount and the investor will suffer a capital loss.

interest rate risk
the risk that increase in prevailing rates will drive the price of a fixed-coupon bond down

Interest rates paid by Treasury debt have varied over time. The extent of this variation was illustrated by Figure 13-3 in Chapter 13, which showed the yields on 10- and 2-year Treasury bonds. Yields also can fluctuate rapidly. For example, yields on three-month Treasury bills changed from a high of 15% in March 1980 to 8.7% only two months later. These fluctuations in yields are due to variations in the supply of and demand for credit in the money and bond markets. As the demand and supply vary, so will the market prices and the yields on all debt instruments, including the debt of the federal government. When demand for bonds becomes strong and exceeds supply at the old prices, bond prices will rise and yields will decline. The reverse occurs when supply exceeds demand: bond prices decline and yields rise.

An investor may also sustain a loss in spending power on an investment in Treasury debt when the rate of inflation exceeds the interest rate earned on the securities. For example, in 1974, the yield on government bonds rose to 7.3%, but the rate of inflation for consumer goods exceeded 10%. In 2014, inflation was almost nonexistent, but the rate (0.8%) continued to exceed the rate paid by short-term Treasury bills (0.1%). Only the longer-term debt (e.g., the 30-year Treasury bond) offered a yield (2.8%) that exceeded the rate of inflation. Obviously, individuals who acquired the short-term debt sustained a loss, since the yield was insufficient to compensate for inflation.

These two factors, fluctuating yields and inflation, illustrate that investing in federal government debt, like all types of investing, subjects the investor to interest rate risk and purchasing power risk. Therefore, although federal government debt is among the safest of all investments with regard to payment of interest and principal, some element of risk still exists.

Foreign investors have the additional risk associated with exchange rates when they purchase U.S. federal government securities. If the value of their currency rises relative to the dollar, then the interest and principal repayment is reduced when the dollars are converted into their currency. However, the value of the dollar could rise, in which case the return on the investment is enhanced. During periods of economic uncertainty in other countries, foreign investors will buy dollars both as a safe haven and for the enhanced return that will occur if their currency declines and the value of the dollar rises.

14-1e The Variability of Federal Government Bond Returns

Over the past 100 years, returns to both stock and bonds have been very variable, as illustrated in **Figure 14-3**.

Overall, returns on stock (proxied here by returns on the S&P 500, which tends to be fairly representative of the stock market as a whole) tended to be more volatile, with "higher highs" and "lower lows" than bonds, but there have been several periods during which bond returns exceeded those of stocks. For example, during the early 1980s,

Figure 14-3: Annual Returns on S&P 500 and 10-Year U.S. Treasury Bonds

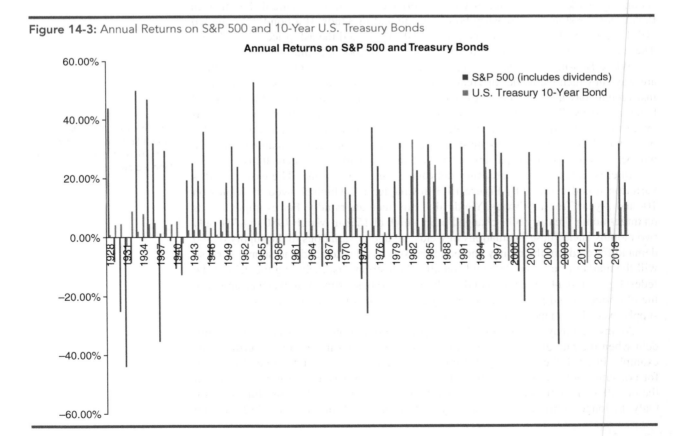

when inflation went down dramatically, bond yields followed suit and, as previously discussed, when bond yields go down, prices of existing bonds go up. We can see this illustrated in 1981–1982, 2000–2002, 2007–2008, 2011, and 2018, all periods when T-bonds outperformed stocks. This seems like a lot of times, but, remember, the rest of the time, stocks outperform bonds, sometimes significantly.

It is easier to see the nuances of the relationship between return and risks on stock and bonds if we look at histograms of their returns. As you can see in **Figure 14-4**, the returns on T-bonds have a "tighter" distribution, meaning that they have been more consistent over time, but the S&P 500 average return is more than twice that of the average T-bonds return.

This observation leads to one of the axioms of investments: if your investment horizon is relatively soon, you should be invested more in bonds than in stocks, as the relatively low volatility of the returns on bonds will make it more likely that you will have the amount you need when you reach that investment horizon. But if you have a longer investment horizon, one where you can weather possible downturns in the stock market, you should probably invest more of your portfolio in stocks, as their much higher rates of average return will help you accumulate more wealth.

Of course, "shorter" and "longer" investment horizons are a relative matter, dependent upon the financial situation of the investor and the financial goal they are pursuing, but, in general, investing more in stocks when you have a longer investment horizon and more in bonds when you have a shorter horizon is still a good recommendation, and one that you will see throughout the investment industry.

For example, consider the question of retirement portfolio allocation. Many brokers and financial advisors advocate using some rough type of "age calculation" as a guide to how much to invest in stocks versus bonds. Three common such calculations, based on an assumption of an investment goal of retiring at age 60, are as follows:

Figure 14-4: Histograms of S&P 500 and T-Bond Returns

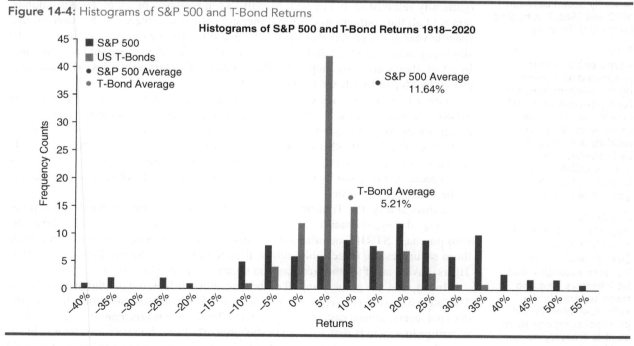

1. "Age in bonds." A 20-year-old would have 20% in bonds, a 40-year-old would have 40%, and so forth. While this may have been an appropriate guideline decades ago, when bond rates were relatively high and life expectancies were relatively low, most financial advisors today feel that this is far too conservative, as it would mean a beginner investor at 20 years old would already have 20% bonds right out of the gate, and a 60-year-old retiree, with possible decades of retirement to fund, would have the majority (60%) of their retirement funds in bonds.

2. "Age minus 20 in bonds." Here, a 20-year-old would have nothing in bonds, a 40-year-old would have 20% in bonds, and so forth. This calculation is much more in line with expert recommendations and would result in the often-suggested 60/40 stock/bond portfolio for a retiree at age 60.

3. "[(Age – 40)*2]." Here, bonds don't show up in the portfolio until age 40, allowing for maximum growth while early accumulation is more important, then accelerating the shift to prioritizing capital preservation nearing retirement age. This calculation seems to most closely follow the glide paths of the top target date funds, and would also result in the suggested 60/40 stock/bond portfolio at age 60.

Generally speaking, it could be said that these three formulas coincide with low-, moderate-, and high-risk tolerances, respectively.

14-2 STRIPS

14-2a Zero Coupon Treasury Securities

individual retirement account (IRA)
an account set up at a financial institution that allows an individual to save for retirement using before-tax income

Treasury Investment Growth Receipt (TIGR, or Tigers)
the first zero coupon bonds derived from regular Treasury bonds

Certificate of Accrual on Treasury Securities (CATS)
a zero-coupon bond, privately issued between 1982 and 1986, but backed by the U.S. Treasury

Treasury receipts (TRs)
a type of bond that is purchased at a discount by the investor in return for a payment of its full face value at its date of maturity. Treasury receipts are created by brokerage firms but are collateralized by underlying U.S. government securities

Separate Trading of Registered Interest and Principal Securities (STRIPS)
Treasury securities that let investors hold and trade separately the individual interest and principal components of eligible Treasury notes and bonds

With the advent of **individual retirement accounts (IRAs)**, corporations started issuing zero coupon bonds. Because the Treasury did not issue such bonds at that time, selected brokerage firms created their own zero coupon Treasury securities. For example, Merrill Lynch created the **Treasury Investment Growth Receipt (TIGR)** (generally referred to as **Tigers**). Merrill Lynch bought a block of Treasury bonds, removed all the coupons, and offered investors either the interest to be received in a specific year or the principal at the bonds' maturity. Since payment was limited to the single payment at the specified time in the future, these Tigers were sold at a discount. In effect, they were zero coupon bonds backed by Treasury securities originally purchased by Merrill Lynch and held by a trustee.

Other brokerage firms created similar securities by removing coupons from existing Treasury bonds. Some of these zero coupon Treasury securities were given clever acronyms, such as Salomon Brothers' **Certificates of Accrual on Treasury Securities (CATS)**. In other cases, they were just called **Treasury receipts (TRs)**. In each case, however, the brokerage firm owns the underlying Treasury securities. The actual security purchased by the investor is an obligation of the brokerage firm and not of the federal government.

Subsequently, the Treasury introduced its own zero coupon bonds, **Separate Trading of Registered Interest and Principal Securities (STRIPS)**. Investors who purchase STRIPS acquire a direct obligation of the federal government. Since these securities are direct obligations, they tend to have slightly lower yields than Tigers, CATS, and the other zero coupon securities created by brokerage firms.

In any case, the primary appeal of these securities is their use in retirement accounts. The interest earned on a zero coupon bond is taxed as it accrues, even though the holder does not receive annual cash interest payments. Thus, there is little reason to acquire these securities in accounts that are not tax sheltered. They are, however, excellent vehicles for retirement accounts, since all the funds (i.e., principal and accrued interest) are paid in one lump sum at maturity. Because any tax on a retirement account is paid when the funds are withdrawn, the tax disadvantage of zero coupon bonds is circumvented. The investor can purchase issues that mature at a desired date to meet retirement needs. For example, a 40-year-old investor could purchase zero coupon government securities that mature when they reach the age of 65, 66, and so on. Such a laddered bond strategy would ensure that the funds were received after retirement, at which time they would replace the individual's earned income that ceases at retirement.

If the investor does acquire zero coupon bonds, that individual should be aware that these securities have the most price volatility of all federal government bonds. As was discussed in Chapter 13, changing interest rates generate fluctuations in bond prices. The longer the term or the smaller the coupon, the greater the price fluctuation. Zero coupon bonds make no periodic interest payments; thus, for a given term to maturity, their prices are more volatile than coupon bonds with the same maturity. For example, if interest rates were 4% compounded annually, a 10-year zero coupon bond would sell for $675.56, while a 10-year 4% coupon bond would sell for $1,000. If interest rates rose to 8%, the price of the zero coupon bond would fall to $463.19 for a decline of approximately 31%. The price of the 4% coupon bond would fall to $731.60 for a decline of approximately 26.8%.

The reason for a zero coupon bond's increased price volatility in response to changes in interest rates is that the entire return falls on the single payment at maturity. Since the current price of any bond is the present value of the interest and principal payments, the price of a zero coupon bond is solely the result of the present value of the single payment received at maturity: that is, all the zero's cash flows are "hanging out at the end" of the bond's life. Since no interest payments will be received during the early years of the bond's life, this increases the responsiveness of the bond's price to changes in interest rates over that of a bond that *does* pay periodic coupon payments between purchase and maturity.

This price volatility suggests that zero coupon bonds may well serve a laddered bond strategy and may be excellent candidates for purchase in anticipation of lower interest rates. In the laddered strategy, there is no intention to sell the bond prior to maturity. Instead, the investor expects to collect the payment at the bond's maturity, so price volatility is unimportant. Bond purchases made in anticipation of lower interest rates are made to take advantage of the price increase that would accompany lower rates.

laddered bond strategy
a strategy involving investing in bonds with different maturities

14-3 Inflation-Indexed Treasury Securities

In addition to traditional marketable debt instruments, the federal government also issues inflation-indexed securities, sometimes referred to as Treasury Inflation Protected Securities (TIPS). There are two basic types of marketable federal government inflation-indexed debt. The first is notes, which are issued annually on January 15 and July 15 and mature after 10 years. The second is the inflation-indexed bond, which is a 30-year security issued every October 15.

Inflation-indexed notes and bonds pay a modest rate of interest plus make an adjustment for changes in the consumer price index (CPI) (i.e., the rate of inflation). The interest rate is the "real yield" earned by the investor. The adjustment occurs by altering the amount of principal owed by the federal government; no adjustment is made in the semiannual interest rate. The amount of the change in the principal depends on the current CPI relative to the CPI when the securities were issued. For example, assume the 10-year notes have a real interest rate of 3.875% and the CPI is 164. Two years later, the CPI is 174, so the principal is increased by a factor of 1.06098 (174/164). A $1,000 note is increased to $1,060.98. The investor would then receive interest of $41.075

Treasury Inflation Protected Services (TIPS)
a Treasury bond whose principal value is indexed to an inflationary gauge to protect investors from the decline in the purchasing power of their money

inflation-indexed bond
a bond whose interest payments are tied to the costs of consumer goods as measured by an inflation index, such as the consumer price index (CPI)

($1,060.98 × 0.03875) instead of the $38.75, which was the amount initially earned when the note was issued. Since the principal and the amount of interest received are increased with the rate of inflation, the investor's purchasing power is maintained.

Inflation-indexed bonds appeal to individuals who are primarily concerned that the rate of inflation will increase so that an investment in a traditional, fixed-rate bond will result in a loss of purchasing power. If, for example, the rate of inflation is 2%, and an investor purchases a 5% 10-year bond, and the rate of inflation rises to 6%, the interest is insufficient to cover the higher rate of inflation. The purchasing power of the investor's principal is also eroded. If that investor had acquired an inflation-indexed security, the principal owed and the interest earned would rise sufficiently to cover the increased inflation and provide a modest return.

While federal government inflation-indexed notes and bonds are a means to manage purchasing power risk, there are risks associated with an inflation-indexed bond. The fixed, real rate paid by the bonds is less than the nominal rate that could be earned by an investment in a traditional bond. For example, the rate of interest on 20-year bonds in 2015 was 2.24%, which exceeded the rate on the inflation-indexed 20-year bond. Of course, if the rate of inflation were to increase, the real return on the traditional note would diminish while the inflation-indexed bond would earn a higher rate that maintains the investor's purchasing power. If, however, inflation does not increase, the inflation-indexed security produces an inferior return.

Inflation-indexed federal government notes and bonds are, of course, illustrative of an important trade-off investors must accept. To obtain protection and reduce the risk from inflation, investors may acquire the indexed bonds. If, however, the rate of inflation does not increase, this strategy earns a lower rate of interest. Investors can earn a higher rate by not acquiring the indexed bonds, but then they bear the risk associated with inflation. Although the traditional bond may generate more current interest income, the investors who acquire them in preference to the indexed bond bear the risk associated with the loss of purchasing power from inflation.

The possibility also exists that the CPI may decline. If deflation were to occur, the inflation-indexed principal would be reduced, which decreases the periodic interest payments. If the inflation-adjusted principal were less than the original par value at maturity of the security, the federal government would repay the initial par value. The buyer is assured of receiving the initial amount invested in inflation-indexed securities (when they are issued) if they are held to maturity. Only the periodic interest payments would be reduced.

In addition to these risks, there is a tax disadvantage associated with the federal government's inflation-indexed debt securities. The addition to the principal is considered taxable income even though it is not received until the instrument matures (or is sold). In the preceding example, the principal amount rose from $1,000 to $1,060.89. The $60.89 is taxable income during the two years in which the accretion occurred even though the investor received only interest of 3.875% of the principal value. This tax treatment of the accretion in the principal value may reduce the attractiveness of inflation-indexed notes and bonds except for usage in tax-deferred retirement accounts.

14-4 Federal Agencies' Debt

In addition to the debt issued by the federal government, certain agencies of the federal government and federally sponsored corporations issue debt. These debt instruments encompass the entire spectrum of maturities, ranging from short-term securities to long-term bonds. Like many U.S. Treasury debt issues, there is an active secondary market in some of the debt issues of these agencies, and price quotations for many of the bonds are given daily in the financial press.

Several federal agencies have been created to fulfill specific financial needs. For example, the **Banks for Cooperatives** were organized under the **Farm Credit Act**. These banks provide farm business services and make loans to farm cooperatives to help purchase supplies. The **Student Loan Marketing Association (Sallie Mae)** was created in 1972 to provide liquidity to the insured student loans made under the **Guaranteed Student Loan Program** by commercial banks, savings and loan associations, and schools that participate in the program. This liquidity should expand the funds available to students from private sources. (In 2004, Sallie Mae became an independent publicly traded company.)

Federal agency bonds are not issued by the federal government and are not the debt of the federal government. Hence, they tend to offer higher yields than those available on U.S. Treasury debt. However, the bonds are extremely safe because they have government backing. In some cases, this is only moral backing, which means that in case of default, the federal government does not have to support the debt (i.e., to pay the interest and meet the terms of the indenture). Some of the debt issues, however, are guaranteed by the U.S. Treasury. Should these issues go into default, the federal government is legally required to assume the obligations of the debt's indenture.

The matter of whether the bonds have the legal or the moral backing of the federal government is probably academic. All these debt issues have high credit quality, because it is doubtful that the federal government would let the debt of one of its agencies go into default. Since these bonds offer slightly higher yields than those available on U.S. Treasury debt, the bonds of federal agencies have become attractive investments for conservative investors seeking higher yields. This applies not only to individual investors who wish to protect their capital but also to financial institutions, such as commercial banks, insurance companies, or credit unions, which must be particularly concerned with the safety of the principal in making investment decisions.

Federal agency debt can be purchased by individuals; however, few individual investors own these bonds, except indirectly through pension plans, mutual funds, and other institutions that own the debt. Many individual investors are probably not even aware of the existence of this debt and the potential advantages it offers. Any investor who wants to construct a portfolio with an emphasis on income and the relative safety of the principal should consider these debt instruments.

14-4a Ginnie Mae Securities

One of the most important and popular debt securities issued by a government agency and supported by the federal government is the **Ginnie Mae**, a debt security issued by the **Government National Mortgage Association (GNMA)** or (Ginnie Mae), a division of the Department of Housing and Urban Development (HUD). The funds raised through the sale of Ginnie Mae securities are used to acquire a pool of FHA/VA guaranteed mortgages. (FHA and VA are the Federal Housing Administration and Department of Veterans Affairs, respectively.) The mortgages are originated by private lenders, such as savings and loan associations and other savings institutions, and packaged into securities that are sold to the general public and guaranteed by GNMA. The minimum size of the individual Ginnie Mae securities sold to the public is $25,000. Individuals with less to invest may acquire shares in a mutual fund that invests in mortgage-backed securities. Since Ginnie Maes convert an illiquid asset (a mortgage loan) into a marketable security, they are an illustration of **securitization**. Few investors are willing to hold a mortgage because mortgage notes are difficult to sell. A Ginnie Mae, however, may be readily sold. The effect, then, is to convert an illiquid asset into a marketable asset. (See the discussion of securitization in Chapter 13.)

Banks for Cooperatives
a government-sponsored bank responsible for providing credit and other financial services to the American agricultural sector

Farm Credit Act
legislation passed during the Great Depression in the United States offering short-term loans for agricultural production as well as extended low interest rates for farmers threatened by foreclosure. Small farmers were able to refinance their mortgages with the aid of twelve district banks, called Banks for Cooperatives

Student Loan Marketing Association (Sallie Mae)
a publicly traded U.S. corporation that provides private student loans

Guaranteed Student Loan Program
a provision of the Higher Education Act of 1965, which had taxpayers guaranteeing loans made by private lenders to students

securitization
the process in which certain types of assets are pooled so that they can be repackaged into interest-bearing securities

To understand how a Ginnie Mae (or any mortgage-backed bond) works, it is necessary to understand the payments generated by a mortgage. This process is illustrated in **Exhibit 14-1**. The individual buys a house with a down payment and finances the balance of the cost of the house through a mortgage. The homeowner makes periodic equal payments that cover the interest and retire the principal. The amount of the payment is fixed when the mortgage is granted. In Exhibit 14-1, the mortgage loan is $150,000, the interest rate is 8%, and the term of the mortgage is 25 years (300 months). Each monthly payment is $1,157.72, which consists of an interest payment and a principal repayment. The first column of the table gives the number of payment. These range from 1 to 300 because the loan requires 12 monthly payments for 25 years for a total of 300 payments. The second column presents the interest payment, and the third column gives the amount of principal repayment. The balance of the loan is given in the last column. Since the amount of interest is determined on the balance owed, the amount of interest remitted with each payment declines, and the amount of the payment used to retire the principal rises. For example, the amount of interest in the third payment is $997.89, but in payment number 148, interest is $738.84. Since the amount of interest declines, the principal repayment increases from $159.83 in payment number 3 to $418.89 in payment number 148. Payments during the early years of the mortgage loan primarily cover the interest owed, but payments near the end of the life of the loan primarily reduce the balance of the loan.

If the interest rate had been 4%, the monthly payment would be reduced to $791.76. This amount is perceptibly less than $1,157.72, but the total amount owed ($150,000) remains the same. Lower interest rates do not affect the principal owed, but they do affect the interest, which causes the monthly payment to decline. Higher interest rates, of course, would have the opposite impact as they would increase the interest payment and the required monthly payment.

Exhibit 14-1: Repayment Schedule for a $150,000 Mortgage

Number of Payment	Interest Payment	Principal Repayment	Balance of Loan
1	$1,000.00	$157.72	$149,842.28
2	998.95	158.78	149,683.50
3	997.89	159.83	149,523.67
—	—	—	—
—	—	—	—
—	—	—	—
148	738.84	418.89	110,407.01
149	736.05	421.68	109,985.33
150	733.24	424.49	109,560.84
—	—	—	—
—	—	—	—
—	—	—	—
298	22.85	1,134.88	2,292.50
289	15.28	1,142.44	1,150.06
300	7.67	1,150.06	0.00

Selected Payments from a Repayment Schedule for a $150,000 Mortgage Loan at 8% for 25 years (Monthly Payment: $1,157.72)

Excel Expert 14-5

Calculating a repayment schedule in Excel simply involves the use of the PMT() function and then calculating how much of that payment goes toward interest on the remaining balance and principal for each payment (i.e., row):

	A	B	C	D	E	F	G	H
1	Loan Amount	$ 150,000						
2	Interest Rate	8.00%						
3	Term (Years)	25						
4	Payment	$ 1,157.72	=PMT(B2/12,B3*12,-B1)					
5								
6	Number of Payment		Interest Payment		Principal Repayment		Balance of Loan	
7	1		$ 1,000.00	=B2/12*B1	$ 157.72	=B4-$C$7	$ 149,842.28	=B1-E7
8	2	=A7+1	$ 998.95	=$B$2/12*G7	$ 158.78	=$B$4-C8	$ 149,683.50	=G7-E8
9	3	=A8+1	$ 997.89	=$B$2/12*G8	$ 159.83	=$B$4-C9	$ 149,523.67	=G8-E9
154	...							
155	148	=A153+1	$ 738.84	=$B$2/12*G153	$ 418.89	=$B$4-C155	$ 110,407.01	=G153-E155
156	149	=A155+1	$ 736.05	=$B$2/12*G155	$ 421.68	=$B$4-C156	$ 109,985.33	=G155-E156
157	150	=A156+1	$ 733.24	=$B$2/12*G156	$ 424.49	=$B$4-C157	$ 109,560.84	=G156-E157
305	...							
306	298	=A304+1	$ 22.85	=$B$2/12*G304	$ 1,134.88	=$B$4-C306	$ 2,292.50	=G304-E306
307	299	=A306+1	$ 15.28	=$B$2/12*G306	$ 1,142.44	=$B$4-C307	$ 1,150.06	=G306-E307
308	300	=A307+1	$ 7.67	=$B$2/12*G307	$ 1,150.06	=$B$4-C308	$ (0.00)	=G307-E308

Ginnie Mae securities serve as a conduit through which the interest and principal repayments are received from the homeowners and distributed to investors. The investor acquires part of the Ginnie Mae pool. As interest and principal repayments are made to the pool, the funds are channeled to the Ginnie Mae's owners. The investor receives a monthly payment that is their share of the principal and interest payments received by the pool. Since payments to the pool vary from month to month, the amount received by the investors also varies monthly. Thus, a Ginnie Mae is one example of a long-term debt instrument whose periodic payments are not fixed.

Ginnie Mae securities have become popular with investors financing retirement or accumulating funds in retirement accounts. The reason for their popularity is safety, as the federal government insures the payment of principal and interest. Thus, if a mortgage payer were to default, the federal government would make the required payments. This guarantee virtually assures the timely payment of interest and principal to the holder of the Ginnie Mae.

In addition to safety, Ginnie Maes offer higher yields than federal government securities. Since the yields are ultimately related to the mortgages acquired by the pool, they depend on mortgage rates rather than on the yields of federal government bills and bonds. This yield differential can be as great as 2 percentage points (usually referred to as 200 basis points) over the return offered by long-term federal government bonds.

Ginnie Mae securities are also useful to investors seeking a regular flow of payments, as interest and principal repayments are distributed monthly. The mortgage repayment schedules define the minimum amount of the anticipated payments. However, if the homeowners speed up payments or pay off their loans before the full term of the mortgage, the additional funds are passed on to the holder of the Ginnie Mae securities.

These securities are supported by the full faith and credit of the federal government, but there are risks associated with Ginnie Maes. One is the loss of purchasing power through inflation. Of course, investors will not purchase Ginnie Maes if the anticipated yield is less than the anticipated rate of inflation.

Even if the anticipated return is sufficient to justify the purchase, investors could still lose if interest rates rise. All the mortgages in a particular pool have the same interest rate, and because Ginnie Maes are fixed-income debt securities, their prices fluctuate with interest rates. Higher interest rates will drive down their prices. Thus, if an investor were to seek to sell the security in the secondary market (and there is an active secondary market in Ginnie Maes), they could sustain a capital loss resulting from the rise in interest rates. Of course, the investor could experience a capital gain if interest rates were to decline, thus causing the security's value to rise.

The last source of risk concerns the reinvestment rate, which reduces the certainty of the monthly payments. Homeowners can (and do) repay their mortgage loans prematurely. This occurs when individuals move and sell their homes and when interest rates fall. Lower rates encourage homeowners to refinance their mortgages (i.e., obtain new mortgages at the current, lower rate and pay off the old, higher-rate mortgages). Since the old loans are retired, the owners of the Ginnie Mae receive larger principal repayments but can relend the funds only at the current, lower rate of interest. The opposite would occur if interest rates rose. Homeowners will not refinance and prepayments will decline, so the holder of the Ginnie Mae receives lower principal repayments.

This uncertainty of the timing of payments affects the valuation of Ginnie Mae securities. Pricing Ginnie Maes is essentially the same as any other bond: the interest and principal repayments are discounted back to the present at the current rate of interest. Because of reinvestment rate risk, the amount of each principal payment is not certain. If a large number of homeowners rapidly pay off their mortgages, the payments will quickly retire the Ginnie Maes. (This disadvantage associated with Ginnie Maes may be reduced by acquiring **collateralized mortgage obligations [CMOs]**, which are discussed later.)

collateralized mortgage obligations [CMOs]
A type of mortgage-backed security that contains a pool of similar mortgages bundled together and sold as an investment

This uncertainty of future payments can lead to differences in the estimated yields. Consider a Ginnie Mae that has an expected life of 12 years and is currently selling for a discount (which could result if interest rates rose after this Ginnie Mae pool had been assembled and sold). In such a case, the price of the Ginnie Mae would decline so that the anticipated yield is comparable with securities currently being issued. For the Ginnie Mae selling at a discount, the yield would depend on the flow of interest payments and how rapidly the mortgage loans are paid off.

If the mortgages are paid off more rapidly than expected (i.e., if the life of the pool is less than the expected 12 years), the realized return will be higher because the discount will be erased more rapidly. However, if the mortgages are retired more slowly, the realized return will be less than the expected return. Thus, it is possible that the actual yield may differ from the yield assumed when the security was purchased. This makes it possible for two dealers to assert different yields for the same Ginnie Mae sold at the same discounted price. If one dealer assumes that the mortgage loans will be retired more quickly, a higher yield is anticipated. However, another dealer may make a more conservative assumption as to the rate at which the mortgages will be retired.

The speed with which the mortgages are paid off depends in part on the interest rates being paid on mortgage loans. If the Ginnie Mae mortgage loans have relatively high rates, homeowners will seek to refinance these loans when rates decline, so the original mortgages are retired rapidly. The opposite holds when the rates on the Ginnie Maes' mortgage loans are lower than current interest rates. In this case, there is little incentive for early retirement, which will tend to extend the life of the mortgage pool. Thus, a Ginnie Mae that sells for a discount because the mortgage loans have lower interest rates will tend to have a longer life than a Ginnie Mae selling at a premium because its mortgage loans have a higher rate of interest.

The investor who purchases a Ginnie Mae security should be aware that the payment received represents both earned interest income and return of invested funds. If the investor spends all the payment, that individual is depleting their principal. Thus, the investor should be fully aware that the individual payments received are composed of both interest and principal repayment and that the latter should be spent only if there is reason for the investor to consume the principal.

14-4b Collateralized Mortgage Obligations (CMOs)

While Ginnie Maes are supported by the federal government so the investor knows that the interest and principal will be paid, the amount of each monthly payment is unknown. Because principal repayments vary as homeowners refinance their homes, the amount of principal repayment received by the investor changes every month. This variation in the monthly cash flow may be a disadvantage to any individual (e.g., a retiree) seeking a reasonably certain flow of monthly cash payments.

A collateralized mortgage obligation (CMO) reduces, but does not erase, this uncertainty. CMOs are backed by a trust that holds Ginnie Mae and other federal government-supported mortgages. When a CMO is created, it is subdivided into classes (called **tranches**). For example, a $100 million CMO may be divided into four tranches of $25 million each. The principal repayments received by the CMO are initially paid to the first class until that tranche has been entirely retired. Once the first tranche has been paid off, mortgage principal repayments are directed to the holders of the CMOs in the second tranche. This process is repeated until all the tranches have been repaid.

Within a tranche, principal repayments may be made on a *pro rata* basis, or by lottery. Whether a *pro rata* or a lottery system is used to determine repayment is specified in the CMO's indenture; thus, investors know which system applies to a particular CMO. In either case, no principal repayments are made to the next tranche until all the funds owed by the first tranche are paid.

This pattern of payment is illustrated by the following CMO with four tranches. Each tranche consists of a $200,000 loan ($800,000 total outstanding), $100,000 of which is retired each year. Interest is paid annually on the amount of the loan outstanding in each tranche. The rate of interest varies with the expected life of each tranche. The interest rates start at 7% for tranche A and rise to 10 percent for tranche D. For accepting later repayment of principal, the investor can expect to earn a higher interest rate. The tranche with the shortest expected life earns the lowest interest rate, while the one with the longest expected life earns the highest rate.

The annual payments to each tranche are applicable as shown in **Exhibit 14-2** if the anticipated payment schedules are made.

tranche
an issue of bonds that is a portion of a pooling of like obligations (such as securitized mortgage debt), where the parts of that portion have the same maturity or rate of return

Exhibit 14-2: Tranche Payments

Year	A Interest	A Principal	B Interest	B Principal	C Interest	C Principal	D Interest	D Principal
1	$14,000	$100,000	$16,000	$0	$18,000	$0	$20,000	$0
2	7,000	100,000	16,000	0	18,000	0	20,000	0
3	0	0	16,000	100,000	18,000	0	20,000	0
4	0	0	8,000	100,000	18,000	0	20,000	0
5	0	0	0	0	18,000	100,000	20,000	0
6	0	0	0	0	9,000	100,000	20,000	0
7	0	0	0	0	0	0	20,000	100,000
8	0	0	0	0	0	0	10,000	100,000

This schedule indicates that tranche D is a loan for $200,000 at 10%, so the annual interest payment is $20,000 for the first seven years and $10,000 in year eight. Repayment of principal does not occur until all the preceding tranches are retired. Under the anticipated schedule, the principal repayments of $100,000 occur in years seven and eight, which is why the interest payment is $10,000 instead of $20,000 in year eight.

Over the eight years, the borrower pays a total of $326,000 in interest for the use of the funds and retires the $800,000 loan. While the owners of the different tranches receive different interest rates, the borrower pays the same rate on the entire loan. The trustee structures the tranches to coincide with the loan payments. In this illustration, the borrower's repayment schedule is shown in **Exhibit 14-3**.

The rate of interest on the loan is 9.056% on the declining balance. (The 9.056% is a forced number. Generally, the terms of the loan are established and the trustee constructs the tranches to match the borrower's payments. Since the purpose of this example is to illustrate the payments to the tranches, the loan is being forced to approximate the payments to the investors.)

The total interest paid by the borrower is $326,016, and the interest payments approximate those received by the tranches. Notice that the borrower's interest rate of 9.056% applies to the entire $800,000 loan, while each tranche receives a different rate of interest. In effect, the early tranches subsidize the later tranches. Investors in the early tranches accept a lower rate for a more rapid repayment of principal, while the investors who acquire the longer tranches accept later payments in order to earn a higher rate of interest. The borrower's payments, however, do not make this distinction. The trustee who makes the loan to the borrower establishes the tranches and converts the borrower's debt obligation into a series of securities that different investors with different financial needs find acceptable.

When an investor purchases a CMO, an estimated principal repayment window is known. As in the preceding illustration, the schedule gauges when the investor can expect to receive principal repayments and when a particular tranche will be entirely redeemed. As with Ginnie Mae payments, the CMO payment schedule is based on historical repayment data, but the actual timing of the repayments cannot be known with certainty. Lower interest rates will tend to speed up payments as homeowners refinance, while higher interest rates will tend to retard principal repayments.

Since the actual timing of principal repayment is not known, CMOs reduce but do not erase this source of risk. However, less timing risk exists with a CMO than with a Ginnie Mae. When the investor acquires a Ginnie Mae, the repayments are spread over

Exhibit 14-3: Payment Components of Loan

Year	Principal Owed at the End of the Year	Interest Payment	Principal Repayment
0	$800,000		
1	700,000	$ 72,448	$100,000
2	600,000	63,392	100,000
3	500,000	54,336	100,000
4	400,000	45,280	100,000
5	300,000	36,224	100,000
6	200,000	27,168	100,000
7	100,000	18,112	100,000
8	0	9,056	100,000
		$326,016	

the life of the entire issue. With a CMO, the repayments are spread over each tranche. The investor who acquires a CMO can better match the anticipated need for cash. For example, a 65-year-old retiree may have less immediate need for cash than an 80-year-old. The latter may acquire the first tranche, while the former acquires the third tranche within a CMO. The 65-year-old would receive the current interest component, but the principal repayment would be deferred until the first and second tranches were entirely retired.

14-4c Tranches Based on Risk

A variation on tranches based on principal repayments is tranches based on risk. Suppose a $100,000,000 pool of mortgages ranges from very safe to very risky mortgages. Tranches could be constructed and sold to investors based on risk. Tranche A is composed of the safest mortgages, B and C encompass the next riskiest, and D is composed of the riskiest mortgages. The anticipated interest rates that investors would be paid increase with the risk associated with each tranche (e.g., A has a rate of 6%, while B, C, and D have rates of 7%, 8%, and 9%). A is obviously the least risky tranche and should receive the anticipated interest and principal repayment, but an additional feature increases their safety: all required interest and principal payments must be made to A before any payments are made to B. And that pattern continues through C and D, so defaults initially fall solely on the investors who purchased D.

This structure is consistent with investors' bearing risk and their anticipated return. The housing crises in the late 2000s, however, led to many defaults. Individuals, investment companies, and retirement funds that had purchased the D tranche in anticipation of the higher yields sustained large losses and in some cases they, too, subsequently declared bankruptcy. There were, however, individual investors who perceived the risks and identified specific mortgages they anticipated would default. These individuals sold the securities short and made fortunes. Their success is documented in Michael Lewis, *The Big Short* (New York: W. W. Norton, 2010), which is one of the most fascinating books to emerge from the financial crisis.

14-5 State and Local Government Debt

State and local governments also issue debt to finance capital expenditures, such as schools or roads. The government then retires the debt as the facilities are used. The funds used to retire the debt may be raised through taxes (e.g., property taxes) or through revenues generated by the facilities themselves.

Unlike the federal government, state and local governments do not have the power to create money. These governments must raise the funds necessary to pay the interest and retire the debt, but the ability to do so varies with the financial status of each government. Municipalities with wealthy residents or valuable property within their boundaries are able to issue debt more readily and at lower interest rates because the debt is safer. The tax base in these communities is larger and can support the debt.

14-5a The Tax Exemption

The primary factor that differentiates state and local government debt from other forms of debt is the tax advantage that it offers to investors. The interest earned on state and municipal government debt is exempt from federal income taxation. Hence, these bonds are frequently referred to as tax-exempt or municipal bonds. Although state and local governments may tax the interest, the federal government may not. The rationale for this tax exemption is legal and not financial. The U.S. Supreme Court ruled that the federal government does not have the power to tax the interest paid by the debt of state and municipal governments. Since the interest paid by all other debt, including corporate bonds, is subject to federal income taxation, this exemption is advantageous to state and local governments, for they are able to issue debt with substantially lower interest rates.

Investors are willing to accept a lower return on state and local government debt because the after-tax return is equivalent to higher yields on corporate debt. For example, if an investor is in the 24% federal income tax bracket, the return after taxes is the same for a corporate bond that pays 10% as for a state or municipal government bond that pays 7.6%: The after-tax return is 7.6% in either case.

The willingness of investors to purchase state and local government debt instead of corporate and U.S. Treasury debt is related to their income tax bracket. If an investor's federal income tax rate is 24%, a 4.75% nontaxable municipal bond gives the investor the same yield after taxes as a 6.25% corporate bond, the interest of which is subject to federal income taxation. The individual investor may determine the equivalent yields on tax-exempt bonds and nonexempt bonds by using the following equation:

$$i_c(1 - t) = i_m \qquad \textbf{14-5}$$

in which i_c is the interest rate paid on corporate debt, i_m is the interest rate paid on municipal debt, and t is the individual's tax bracket (i.e., the marginal tax rate). This equation is used as follows. If an investor's tax bracket is 24% and tax-exempt bonds offer 4.75%, then the equivalent corporate yield is

$$i_c(1 - .24) = 0.0475$$

$$i_c = \frac{0.0475}{0.76} = .0626 \text{ or } 6.25\%$$

If the investor lives in a state that taxes income, **Equation 14-5** may be modified to include the impact of the local tax. **Equation 14-6** includes the impact of the federal income tax rate (t_f): and the state and/or local income tax rate (t_s):

$$i_c(1 - t_f - t_s) = i_m \qquad \textbf{14-6}$$

If the investor's federal income tax bracket is 24% and the state income tax bracket is 6%, then a high-yield, low-quality bond offering 10% has an inferior after-tax yield to a local municipal bond offering more than 7.0% (10% [1 − 0.24 − 0.06] = 7.0%).

Exempting the interest on these bonds from federal income taxation has been criticized because it is an apparent means for the "rich" to avoid federal income taxation. Because the minimum denomination for municipal bonds is $5,000, and dealers may require larger purchases (e.g., $25,000), individuals with modest amounts to invest may be excluded from this market except through investing in investment companies (mutual funds and ETFs) that invest in tax-exempt bonds. The exemption does, however, reduce the interest cost for the state and municipal governments that issue debt, which in effect subsidizes those governments. From an economic point of view, the important question is whether the exemption is the best means to aid state and local governments. Other means, such as federal revenue sharing, could be used for this purpose. Thus, the interest exemption is primarily a political question. Changes in the legal structure may alter the tax exemption in the future. Until that time, however, the interest on state and municipal debt remains exempt from federal income taxation, with the effects being that (1) state and local governments can issue debt with interest rates that are lower than those individuals and corporations must pay, and (2) these bonds offer the wealthier members of our society a means to obtain tax-sheltered income.

Although state and local government debt interest is tax-exempt at the federal level, it may be taxed at the state level. States do exempt the interest paid by their own local governments but tax the interest paid by other states and their local governments. Interest earned on New York City obligations is not taxed in New York, but it is taxed in New Jersey. While New Jersey taxes the interest earned on New York City obligations, it exempts interest earned on New Jersey municipal bonds.

It should also be noted that state and local governments cannot tax the interest paid by the federal government. While interest earned on series EE bonds and Treasury bills, notes, and bonds is taxed by the federal government, this interest cannot be taxed by state and local governments. In states with modest or no income taxes, this exemption is meaningless. However, in states with high income taxes, such as Massachusetts or New York, this tax exemption may be a major reason for acquiring U.S. Treasury securities. For example, the yield on a Treasury bill on an after-tax basis may exceed the yield on a federally insured certificate of deposit or the yield offered by a money market mutual fund. In such cases, the tax laws will certainly encourage the investor to acquire the federal security, because that investor has both a higher after-tax yield and less risk (i.e., the full faith and credit of the federal government).

14-5b Yields on Municipal Bonds

Like the yields on other debt securities, the yields on tax-exempt bonds have varied over time. However, due to the tax exemption that such bonds enjoy, such bonds normally yield slightly less than equivalent-maturity treasury bonds. In fact, yields on munis are often expressed using the **municipal/Treasury (M/T) ratio**, a comparison of the current yield of municipal bonds to U.S. Treasuries calculated by comparing the yield on an index of AAA-rated municipal bonds vs. the yield on the equivalent Treasury Note. For example, if AAA 10-year municipal bonds were yielding 1.4% and 10-Year Treasuries were yielding 2.2%, then the M/T ratio would be 64% (1.40%/2.20%= 0.64).

The M/T ratio historically hovers near 80% to 90%, with anything over 100% suggesting that munis are a good deal, as they're yielding more than equivalent Treasury securities. During the COVID-19 pandemic, however, muni investors apparently feared that state and local government revenues would fall and spending would increase, hurting governments' ability to service their debt.

In March 2020, investors sold a record $45 billion from muni funds. Municipal bond prices dropped, and the yield on muni bonds rose sharply above the yield on comparable U.S. Treasuries, driving the M/T ratio above 300%.

To support the muni market, the Federal Reserve in March 2020 made municipal securities eligible for its **Commercial Paper Funding Facility (CPFF)** (meaning that the Fed was willing to buy short-term muni debt directly from state and local governments) and for the **Money Market Mutual Fund Liquidity Facility (MMLF)** (meaning that the Fed would make loans to banks secured by municipal securities bought from money market mutual funds). Together, both actions successfully stabilized the muni market, bringing the M/T ratio back below 1.0 by August 2020. Both actions were intended to stabilize municipal bond prices and state and local governments' ability to borrow through the public health crisis. Both the MMLF and CPFF expired on March 31, 2021.

As of December 2021, the M/T ratio for 10-year munis was 79%.

municipal/Treasury (M/T) ratio the yield on a municipal bond index divided by the yield on an equivalent-maturity Treasury note or bond. In general, this ratio should be less than 1.0 due to the tax exemption on munis

Commercial Paper Funding Facility (CPFF) a special purpose vehicle (SPV) created by the Federal Reserve to purchase commercial paper to ensure that commercial paper markets remained liquid

Money Market Mutual Fund Liquidity Facility (MMLF) a mechanism set up by the Federal Reserve to allow prime money market funds to take out secured loans against their assets rather than having to redeem them during runs on money market funds

14-5c Types of Tax-Exempt Securities

State and local governments issue a variety of debt instruments; these can be classified either according to the means by which the security is supported or according to the length of time to maturity (i.e., short or long term). State and municipal debt is supported by either the taxing power of the issuing government or the revenues generated by the facilities that are financed by the debt. If the bonds are secured by the taxing power, the debt is a **general obligation bond** of the government.

A bond supported by the revenue generated by the project being financed with the debt is called a **revenue bond**. Revenue bonds are issued to finance particular capital improvements, such as a toll road that generates its own funds. As these revenues are collected, they are used to pay the interest and retire the principal.

General obligation bonds are safer than revenue bonds, as the government is required to use its taxing authority to pay the interest and repay the principal. General obligation bonds may have to be approved by popular referendum, and public approval of the bonds may be difficult to obtain. These characteristics associated with issuing the debt reduce the risk of investing in general obligation bonds. Revenue bonds are supported only by funds generated by the project financed by the sale of the bonds. If the project does not generate sufficient revenues, the interest cannot be paid and the bonds go into default. For example, the Chesapeake Bay Bridge and Tunnel did not produce sufficient toll revenues, so its publicly held bonds went into default. The default, of course, caused the price of the bonds to fall. Since the bondholders could not foreclose on the bridge, their only course of action was to wait for a resumption of interest payments. After several years elapsed, toll revenues rose sufficiently, such that interest payments to the bondholders were resumed.

In addition to general obligation and revenue bonds and notes issued in anticipation of taxes and other revenues, some municipalities have sold **certificates of participation (COPs)**. COPs are issued to finance specific projects (e.g., equipment such as police vehicles, correction facilities, or administrative buildings) that are subsequently leased to the municipality. The rental payments cover the debt-service payments to the holders of the certificates. The municipal government is not responsible for payments to the investors who purchase the COPs; the municipality only makes the lease or rental payments.

COPs are often issued by governments seeking to circumvent limits on their ability to issue debt or to avoid having to obtain voter approval to sell debt. Since the government makes lease payments and not interest and principal repayments, the debt is not considered an obligation of the government. This exclusion of the debt from the municipality's balance sheet understates its obligations.

The removal also increases the investor's risk. Unlike the required interest and principal repayment of general obligation bonds, there is no assurance the government will allocate the funds to make the lease payments. Legislative bodies in Brevard County, Florida, and Florence, South Carolina, have threatened to withhold the lease payments. Without such appropriations, payments to the investors would not be made and the COPs would go into default. Any default on a specific certificate could affect all COPs and lead to their downgrading by the rating services. This increased risk associated with COPs results in their offering higher yields (from 0.1 to 0.5 percentage points) than are available through traditional municipal bonds of the same credit rating.

Tax-exempt bonds are issued in minimum denominations of $5,000 face value. Although a secondary market exists for this debt, small denominations tend to lack

general obligation bond
a municipal bond backed solely by the credit and taxing power of the issuing jurisdiction rather than the revenue from a given project

revenue bond
a category of municipal bond supported by the revenue from a specific project, such as a toll bridge, highway, or local stadium

certificates of participation (COPs)
a type of financing in which an investor purchases a share of the lease revenues of a program

marketability. That does not mean you cannot sell one $5,000 bond issued by a small municipality, but the market is exceedingly thin. The spread between the bid and ask prices may be substantial. (One municipal bond salesperson referred to the $5,000 muni bond as a roach motel. Once you are in, you can't get out. The unit is just too small for bond dealers to buy it. If you do acquire municipal securities in small units, you had best plan to hold the bond until it is retired.)

Although most corporate bonds are issued with a maturity date and a sinking fund requirement, many tax-exempt bonds are issued in a series. With a serial issue, a specific amount of the debt falls due each year. Serial bonds offer advantages to both the issuer and the buyer. In contrast to corporate debt, in which a random selection of the bonds may be retired each year through the sinking fund, the buyer knows when each bond will mature. The investor can then purchase bonds that mature at the desired time, which helps in portfolio planning. Because a portion of the issue is retired periodically with serial bonds, the issuing government does not have to make a large, lumpsum payment. Since these bonds are scheduled to be retired, there is no call penalty. If the government wants to retire additional debt, it can call some of the remaining bonds.

Although most of the debt sold to the general public by state and local governments is long term, there are two exceptions: tax or revenue anticipation notes. A tax or revenue anticipation note is issued by a government anticipating certain receipts in the future—it issues a debt instrument against these receipts. When the taxes or other revenues are received, the notes are retired. The maturity date is set to coincide with the timing of the anticipated receipts so that the notes may be easily retired.

14-5d Tax-Exempt Securities and Risk

Although the sources of risk associated with investing in tax-exempt bonds were alluded to in the preceding discussion, it is helpful to summarize them. First, there is the market risk associated with changes in interest rates. Higher interest rates will drive down the prices of existing bonds. The investor may reduce this source of risk by purchasing bonds of shorter maturity, because the prices of bonds with longer terms to maturity fluctuate more. If the investor is concerned with price fluctuations and the preservation of capital, then shorter-term tax-exempt bonds should be preferred to long-term bonds. The investor, however, should realize that shorter-term bonds generally pay less interest.

The second source of risk is the possibility that the government might default on the interest and principal repayment. While the number of defaults is small, Stockton, California, defaulted on its debt in 2012, and Detroit filed for bankruptcy in 2013. Unfortunately, finding information on particular bond issues can be difficult for the individual investor. Municipal bonds are not registered with the Securities and Exchange Commission (SEC) prior to their sale to the general public, and state and local governments do not publish annual reports and send them to bondholders. However, the Municipal Securities Rulemaking Board has recently developed a database on municipal bonds that is available to the general public. The Electronic Municipal Market Access (EMMA) is available at www.emma.msrb.org; individual investors can easily access the information by entering the municipality's or agency's name or the individual bond's CUSIP number.

If the investor wants to locate specific information concerning individual issues, several firms, such as Standard & Poor's (S&P) and Moody's, rate many of the tax-exempt bonds that are sold to the general public. These ratings are based on a substantial amount of data, for the rating services require the municipal and state governments to provide them with financial and economic information. Since failure of the bond issue to receive a favorable rating will dissuade many potential buyers, the state and local governments supply the rating services with the required information.

The investor can take several steps to reduce the risk associated with default. The first is to purchase a diversified portfolio of tax-exempt bonds, which spreads the risk associated with any particular government. Second, the investor may limit purchases to debt with high credit ratings. If the investor purchases only bonds with AAA or AA credit ratings, there is little risk (perhaps no real risk) of loss from default.

A third means by which the investor may limit the risk of default is to purchase municipal bonds that are insured. Several insurance companies guarantee the payment of interest and principal of the municipal bonds they insure. For example, Garden State (NJ) Preservation Trust bonds are insured by Assured Guaranty Municipal Corporation and have an AAA rating by S&P's. Other municipal bond insurers include Municipal Bond Insurance Association (MBIA), which is traded on the NYSE (MBI), and Financial Guaranty Insurance Co. (FGIC), which is part of GE Capital.

prerefunded municipal bond
a debt security that is issued in order to fund a municipal bond

A fourth means to limit risk is to acquire **prerefunded municipal bonds**. Bonds are often issued with terms of 15, 20, or 25 years with fixed rates of interest. If interest rates subsequently decline, the municipality may issue new bonds. The proceeds are then used to acquire U.S. Treasury bonds that mature when the original municipal bonds mature. The interest earned on the Treasury bonds is then used to pay the interest on the original bonds. In effect, the municipality pays interest only on the new bonds. Once the municipal government (or authority) issues the new bonds, segregates the proceeds, and acquires the Treasury securities, the original issue is referred to as prerefunded. From the investor's perspective, any uncertainty concerning default on interest payments and the repayment of principal is eliminated. Although prerefunded municipal debt continues to have interest rate and reinvestment rate risk, these tax-free bonds are as safe as Treasury securities.

The existence of risk does not imply that an investor should avoid tax-exempt bonds. The return offered by these bonds is consistent with the amount of risk the investor must bear. If a particular bond were to offer an exceptionally high return, it would be readily purchased and its price driven up so that the return was in line with comparably risky securities. Tax-exempt bonds should be purchased by investors with moderate-to-high incomes who are seeking tax-free income and who do not need liquidity. Like any investment, tax-exempt bonds may fit into an individual investor's portfolio and offer a return (after tax) commensurate with the risk the investor must endure.

14-5e Authority Bonds

authority
a government body created for a single purpose, such as the building of an industrial complex

In addition to general obligation and revenue bonds, some local and state governments have created industrial authorities that issued bonds, built facilities, and leased them to firms. Local governments sold these industrial revenue bonds to stimulate economic growth or obtain a desired facility, such as a hospital. Since the local government authority and not the user issued the debt, the interest is tax-exempt. (An **authority** is a government body created for a single purpose, such as the building of an industrial complex. The authority then leases the facility to a corporation. Authorities are also created to build and operate toll roads, bridges, tunnels, ports, and airports. Examples include the New York Port Authority and the New Jersey Turnpike Authority.) The interest payments are the responsibility of the industrial authority and not the local or state government that created the authority (i.e., the bonds are revenue bonds of the authority and not general obligations of the state or its municipalities). If the firm using the facilities fails to make the required payments, the industrial authority would be unable to make the interest payments to the bondholders. Although this suggests industrial revenue bonds can be risky investments, many are among the safest municipal securities because the payments are supported by major corporations. For example, the Waynesboro, Virginia, Industrial Authority bonds are supported by DuPont.

While municipal bonds are generally exempt from federal income taxation, the interest on some nontaxable bonds may be subject to the **alternative minimum tax (AMT)** that some individuals must pay. This alternative tax is designed to ensure that individuals who may not be subject to federal income tax under the regular tax laws will be required to make some federal income tax payments. Hence, tax-exempt interest may be subject to the alternative taxation.

An example of tax-exempt debt subject to the AMT was the issue of bonds sold by the Richmond, Virginia, Redevelopment and Housing Authority. The funds raised by the issue were used to develop condominiums, apartments, and retail space. Part of the financing, which included both private and public participation, was a $100 million issue of authority bonds. Although the interest was exempt from regular federal income taxation, it was subject to the AMT.

> **alternative minimum tax (AMT)**
> an alternative calculation of income tax that, effectively, places a minimum "floor" on the tax rate that must be paid

14-6 Foreign Government Debt Securities

American investors are not limited to the securities issued by the federal government, its agencies, the states, and their political subdivisions. Investors can also purchase the debt of foreign governments. These foreign securities may offer a higher yield because they have additional risk, such as the risks associated with changes in exchange rates and with default.

Investments in foreign government securities have exchange rate risk—that is, the currency in which the debt is denominated. Unless the debt is denominated in dollars, the American investor bears the risk associated with fluctuations in exchange rates. Since the value of the dollar relative to other currencies changes daily, higher promised yields in the local currency may translate into modest or even negative returns once the local currency is converted into dollars.

The second source of risk is the risk of default. It is unlikely that the governments of world financial powers such as the United Kingdom would fail to pay the interest and redeem the bonds. The risk of default, however, is perceptibly greater for other governments. For example, Greece defaulted on its euro debt on June 30, 2015. Default could also be the result of political events. For example, when Castro came to power, Cuba nationalized assets held by U.S. firms and repudiated debts the government owed. (Cuban bonds continued to trade in the United States even though interest was not paid and their maturity had passed.)

14-7 Government Securities and Investment Companies

Investment companies are tailor-made for investing in government securities. Although investment companies are available for equities, some individuals prefer to manage their own portfolios. There is no denying the potential excitement or satisfaction of acquiring a stock and then having its price rise. (The converse would be true if the individuals sold the stock short and its price subsequently declined.) Even if the investor does not outperform the market over a period of time (and efficient markets suggest that the individual will not outperform the market on a risk-adjusted basis), there is satisfaction from the process of security selection and personal management of the portfolio.

Even these individuals, however, may prefer to use mutual funds for the acquisition of government securities. Several reasons have been alluded to throughout this chapter, two of which are the lack of marketability of some government securities and the lack of readily available information on which to base an investment decision. A third reason is the size of the unit of trading, and a fourth is diversification.

While federal government securities have active secondary markets, it is not true for many tax-exempt securities. Even if the investor is able to acquire the bonds, the spread between the bid and ask prices can be substantial, especially for small issues or if the individual acquires small denominations, such as a $5,000 face amount.

The inability of the investor to obtain financial information concerning the issuing government authority is also related to the size of the issue. Municipal bonds are not registered with the SEC. Information on many issues is not readily available. Prices are not quoted, and though bond values may be provided by brokers on the investor's monthly statements, the values are at best approximations and are not indicative of actual trades or available bid prices.

A third disadvantage is the size of the unit of trading, and that minimum size has implications for diversification. For example, Ginnie Mae bonds are sold in units of $25,000, and municipal bonds are sold in units of $5,000. The large unit for trading in buying Ginnie Maes suggests that investors may prefer to buy shares in a mutual fund that specializes in these mortgage-backed bonds. Certainly, the unit of trading is small, but the funds offer an additional advantage. The fund's portfolio would encompass many issues, which increases diversification. Since Ginnie Maes are supported by the federal government, the need to diversify the risk of default is minimal. What a diversified portfolio of Ginnie Maes accomplishes is an increase in the certainty of monthly payments. Since these payments are a combination of interest and principal repayment, prepayments and refinancings imply that monthly cash flows are uncertain. The greater variety of issues of Ginnie Maes that the investor owns, the more certain the monthly payments will be. Repayments and refinancing cannot be the same for each issue; hence, a portfolio of Ginnie Mae bonds should have a more certain flow of monthly cash payments than the monthly payments from a single issue of Ginnie Mae bonds.

Diversifying a municipal government bond portfolio also requires purchasing a variety of issues. However, diversifying may not be important if the investor limits the bonds to those with investment-grade ratings, as bonds with these ratings should not default. (Of course, the investor still must bear the risk associated with changes in interest rates, as all bond prices will change with an increase or a decrease in the rate of interest.) Diversifying a bond portfolio will require a variety of issues, whose features would differ in order for their returns not to be perfectly correlated. Diversification would obviously be important if the investor constructed a portfolio of less-than-investment-grade municipal bonds or a portfolio of foreign government debt issues. Such a diversified portfolio will require a substantial investment, since the minimum unit of trading increases the total cost of diversifying the portfolio.

These disadvantages associated with managing an individual government bond portfolio are avoided by acquiring shares in investment companies. The shares are easily bought and redeemed (in the case of mutual funds) or bought and sold (in the case of closed-end investment companies and ETFs). Information is, of course, readily available on the investment company, such as its size, past performance, management, and fees. Information on the specific securities held by the investment company may be irrelevant to the individual investor. Instead, the information is relevant to the fund's professional managers.

The size of the unit is also not a problem for the investor. Presumably, the fund has the resources to buy and sell the individual debt security using a cost-efficient unit of trading. The investor then buys the shares of the closed-end investment company or ETF on the open market or buys the shares directly from the open-end mutual fund. The amount of the purchase can be as small as the investor wishes, subject to minimum size of purchase from the fund (e.g., $1,000) or the minimum amount to be cost-effective to acquire the publicly traded shares of the closed-end investment company.

Last, diversification is one of the advantages offered by investment companies. Unless the individual acquires shares solely in specialized investment companies, the individual has a piece of a diversified portfolio. Even if the investor acquires a position in a specialized fund, that portfolio is diversified within the specialization.

14-7a Specialized Government Investment Companies

Many investment companies have portfolios that specialize in particular debt instruments. Although many money market mutual funds hold a cross section of short-term debt instruments, some hold only Treasury bills and other short-term securities guaranteed by the U.S. government. These funds pay the lowest rates available from money market funds, but they are also the absolute safest of all the money market funds.

Other mutual funds specialize in intermediate-term federal government bonds, while others hold long-term bonds. The latter funds may move into intermediate-term bonds if the portfolio manager anticipates higher interest rates. Such a movement would protect investors if long-term rates did rise. This portfolio manager would follow an opposite strategy in anticipation of lower rates, since the prices of the longest-term bonds would increase the most in response to lower rates. Other portfolio managers may follow a more passive strategy, which emphasizes the collection of interest and the repayment of principal, not the timing of interest rate changes.

Among the most important government securities funds are those specializing in municipal bonds. These include (1) money market mutual funds that acquire short-term municipal debt, (2) general bond funds that hold a cross section of municipal bonds, and (3) state municipal bond funds with portfolios devoted entirely to the government bonds issued in a particular state. The short-term municipal bond funds are always open-end mutual investment companies, but the general bond funds and the specialized state funds can be either open-end or closed-end investment companies whose shares are traded on the secondary markets.

The appeal of the general municipal bond funds is primarily directed to investors seeking income that is exempt from federal income taxation. For example, Dreyfus Muni Bond Fund (DRTAX) holds 100 percent of its assets in municipal bonds issued in various states. In 2014, this fund distributed $0.403 a share for a yield of 3.32 percent. All the income was exempt from federal income taxation. The distributions, however, were subject to state income taxes, but if the individual lived in a state with no income tax, then the distribution was not taxed at the state level.

Individuals who live in states with high state income taxes may prefer the specialized municipal bond funds. These specialized funds are obviously designed to attract the funds of investors who live in the particular state. For example, Nuveen New Jersey Dividend Advantage Municipal Fund (NXJ) is a closed-end investment company that owns investment-grade municipal bonds issued by the state of New Jersey and its political subdivisions. NXJ's shares are traded on the New York Stock Exchange, and, although any investor may acquire the stock, its primary appeal is to residents of New Jersey, who pay both federal and state income tax. For residents in the top bracket, the total tax rate is 43.97% (35% federal plus 8.97% state). If the investor in the top bracket acquires the shares of NXJ and earns 3.50%, that is the equivalent of 6.22% on a taxable investment.

Conclusion

In order to tap funds from many sources, the federal government issues a variety of debt instruments. These range from Series EE and I bonds, which are sold in small denominations, to short-term Treasury bills and long-term bonds, which are sold in large denominations.

Because there is little possibility of default, federal government debt is among the safest of all possible investments. However, the investor still bears the risk of loss through fluctuations in interest rates and (except for indexed bonds) inflation. If interest rates rise, the prices of federal government bonds decline. If the rate of inflation exceeds the yield on debt instruments, the investor experiences a loss of purchasing power.

In addition to the debt issued by the federal government itself, bonds are issued by its agencies. These bonds tend to offer slightly higher yields but are virtually as safe as the direct debt of the federal government. In some cases, the agency's debt is even secured by the full faith and credit of the U.S. Treasury.

One example of a federal government agency security is the mortgage pass-through bonds issued by the GNMA, or Ginnie Mae. These bonds serve as a conduit through which interest and principal repayments are made from homeowners to the bondholders. Payments are made monthly, so Ginnie Mae bonds are popular with individuals desiring a flow of cash receipts. These bonds expose investors to risk of loss from fluctuating interest rates or from inflation, but the interest payments and principal repayments are guaranteed by an agency of the federal government.

An alternative to the Ginnie Mae is the CMO, which is issued by a trust that holds mortgages guaranteed by the federal government. CMOs are sold in series, or tranches, with the obligations in the shortest tranche being retired before any of the CMOs in the next series are retired.

State and local governments issue long-term debt instruments to finance capital improvements, such as schools and roads. The debt is retired over a period of time by tax receipts or revenues. Some of these bonds are supported by the taxing authority of the issuing government, but many are supported only by the revenues generated by the facilities financed through the bond issues.

State and municipal debt differs from other investments because the interest is exempt from federal income taxation. These bonds pay lower rates of interest than taxable securities (e.g., corporate bonds), but their after-tax yields may be equal to or even greater than the yields on taxable bonds. The nontaxable bonds are particularly attractive to investors in high income tax brackets because the bonds provide a means to shelter income from taxation.

Tax-exempt bonds can be risky investments, as the capacity of state and local governments to service the debt varies. Moody's and S&P's rating services analyze this debt based on the government's ability to pay the interest and retire the principal. Such ratings indicate the risk associated with investing in a particular debt issue. In addition, investors must bear the risks associated with fluctuations in securities prices and the lack of liquidity associated with tax-exempt bonds.

Chapter Equations

$$i_d = \frac{Par\ value - Price}{Par\ value} \times \frac{360}{Number\ of\ days\ to\ maturity} \qquad \text{14-1}$$

$$i_a = \frac{Par\ value - Price}{Price} \times \frac{365}{Number\ of\ days\ to\ maturity} \qquad \text{14-2}$$

$$i_a = \frac{365 \times i_d}{360 - (i_d \times Days\ to\ maturity)} \qquad \text{14-3}$$

$$i_c = \sqrt[n]{\frac{Par\ value}{Price}} - 1 \qquad\qquad \textbf{14-4}$$

$$i_c(1 - t) = i_m \qquad\qquad \textbf{14-5}$$

$$i_c(1 - t_f - t_s) = i_m \qquad\qquad \textbf{14-6}$$

Excel Functions

$PMT(rate, nper, pv, [fv], [type])$

Key Terms

alternative minimum tax (AMT) – an alternative calculation of income tax that, effectively, places a minimum "floor" on the tax rate that must be paid

annualized yield – the annual yield interest earned by a bond, calculated by dividing the discount amount by the price of the bond, annualized using 365 days in a year

authority – a government body created for a single purpose, such as the building of an industrial complex

Banks for Cooperatives – a government-sponsored bank responsible for providing credit and other financial services to the American agricultural sector

bond-equivalent yield – see annualized yield

book-entry form – a method of tracking ownership of securities where no physically engraved certificate is given to investors

Certificate of Accrual on Treasury Securities (CATS) – a zero-coupon bond, privately issued between 1982 and 1986, but backed by the U.S. Treasury

certificates of participation (COPs) – a type of financing in which an investor purchases a share of the lease revenues of a program

collateralized mortgage obligation (CMO) – a type of mortgage-backed security that contains a pool of similar mortgages bundled together and sold as an investment

Commercial Paper Funding Facility (CPFF) – a special purpose vehicle (SPV) created by the Federal Reserve to purchase commercial paper to ensure that commercial paper markets remained liquid

discount yield – a yield calculated on the basis of the face amount of the bill and using a 360-day year

E bond – a war bond issued by the U.S. government in 1941 to finance World War II, with face amounts between $18.75 to $10,000 and a maturity of 10 years

EE bond – a low-risk savings product that pays interest until it reaches 30 years or you cash it in, whichever comes first

Farm Credit Act – legislation passed during the Great Depression in the United States offering short-term loans for agricultural production as well as extended low interest rates for farmers threatened by foreclosure. Small farmers were able to refinance their mortgages with the aid of twelve district banks, called Banks for Cooperatives

floater – a floating-rate note that pays interest that is set weekly and tied to the most recent 13-week Treasury bill rate

general obligation bond – a municipal bond backed solely by the credit and taxing power of the issuing jurisdiction rather than the revenue from a given project

Government National Mortgage Association (GNMA, or "Ginnie Mae") – a government agency that guarantees timely payments on mortgage-backed securities, providing liquidity in the market for home loans

Guaranteed Student Loan Program – a provision of the Higher Education Act of 1965, which had taxpayers guaranteeing loans made by private lenders to students

I bond – a security that earns interest based on both a fixed rate and a rate that is set twice a year based on inflation. The bond earns interest until it reaches 30 years or you cash it in, whichever comes first

inflation-indexed bond – a bond whose interest payments are tied to the costs of consumer goods as measured by an inflation index, such as the consumer price index (CPI)

individual retirement account (IRA) – an account set up at a financial institution that allows an individual to save for retirement using before-tax income

interest rate risk – the risk that increase in prevailing rates will drive the price of a fixed-coupon bond down

investment horizon – the length of time until an investor needs to cash out their investment

laddered bond strategy – a strategy involving investing in bonds with different maturities

Money Market Mutual Fund Liquidity Facility (MMLF) – a mechanism set up by the Federal Reserve to allow prime money market funds to take out secured loans against their assets rather than having to redeem them during runs on money market funds

municipal bond (muni) – debt securities issued by states, cities, counties, and other governmental entities whose interest is generally exempt from federal income tax

municipal/Treasury (M/T) ratio – the yield on a municipal bond index divided by the yield on an equivalent-maturity Treasury note or bond. In general, this ratio should be less than 1.0 due to the tax exemption on munis

prerefunded municipal bond – a debt security that is issued in order to fund a municipal bond

revenue bond – a category of municipal bond supported by the revenue from a specific project, such as a toll bridge, highway, or local stadium

securitization – the process in which certain types of assets are pooled so that they can be repackaged into interest-bearing securities

Separate Trading of Registered Interest and Principal Securities (STRIPS) – Treasury securities that let investors hold and trade separately the individual interest and principal components of eligible Treasury notes and bonds

Student Loan Marketing Association (Sallie Mae) – a publicly traded U.S. corporation that provides private student loans

tranche – an issue of bonds that is a portion of a pooling of like obligations (such as securitized mortgage debt), where the parts of that portion have the same maturity or rate of return

Treasury bill (T-bill) – a short-term U.S. government debt obligation backed by the Treasury Department with a maturity of one year or less

Treasury Inflation Protected Services (TIPS) – a Treasury bond whose principal value is indexed to an inflationary gauge to protect investors from the decline in the purchasing power of their money

Treasury Investment Growth Receipt (TIGR, or Tigers) – the first zero coupon bonds derived from regular Treasury bonds

Treasury receipts (TRs) – a type of bond that is purchased at a discount by the investor in return for a payment of its full face value at its date of maturity. Treasury receipts are created by brokerage firms but are collateralized by underlying U.S. government securities

Questions

1. **Government Bonds.** What distinguishes Series EE bonds from Treasury bills? (LO 14-1)
2. **STRIPS.** Explain why STRIPS are well suited to be held in retirement accounts. (LO 14-2)
3. **TIPS.** How are TIPS adjusted for inflation? (LO 14-3)
4. **Asset-Backed Bonds.** What different types of assets back the debt of the government agencies discussed in this chapter? What were the objectives behind the creation of such agencies? (LO 14-4)
5. **CMOs.** Explain the advantage of CMOs over Ginnie Maes for investors. (LO 14-4)
6. **Munis.** Munis offer tax advantages to investors. Is this advantage of equal value to all investors? Why or why not? (LO 14-5)
7. **M/T Ratio.** Why might the M/T ratio go close to or even over 1.0? (LO 14-5)
8. **State Tax Exemption.** Is Equation 14.6 assuming that munis in a given state are exempt from state taxes, or not exempt? (LO 14-6)
9. **Exchange Rate Risk.** If an investor invests in the debt of a foreign government that uses the U.S. dollar as the basis of their currency, will there still be exchange rate risk? Why or why not? (LO 14-7)
10. **Mutual Funds.** Explain why individual investors may wish to invest in government securities through a mutual fund rather than purchasing such securities themselves. (LO 14-8)

Problems

1. **Bid vs asked.** Suppose a $10,000 T-bill is quoted with bid and asked prices of 2.37 and 2.34, respectively. At what price would you be able to buy a bond for? (LO 14-1)

2. **Bid vs asked.** Suppose a $10,000 T-bill is quoted with bid and asked prices of 2.75 and 2.73, respectively. At what price would you be able to sell a bond for? (LO 14-1)

3. **Discount yield.** What will the discount yield of a five-month $10,000 Treasury bill selling for $9,800 be? (LO 14-1)

4. **Annualized yield.** What will the annualized yield of a seven-month $10,000 Treasury bill selling for $9,550 be? (LO 14-1)

5. **Annualized yield.** Suppose the discount yield on a four-month T-bill is 3.40%. What will the annualized yield be? (LO 14-1)

6. **Annual compound return.** If you earn a simple annualized rate of 6.3%3 on a four-month $10,000 T-bill selling for $9,723, what will the annual compound return be? (LO 14-1)

7. **Bond quotes.** If a $10,000 Treasury bond is quoted as 105:09–105:12, what price would you pay to buy the bond? (LO 14-1)

8. **Bond quotes.** If a $10,000 Treasury bond is quoted as 95:09–95:11, at what price would you be able to sell the bond at? (LO 14-1)

9. **Age in bonds.** According to the "age in bonds" calculation, what percentage of their portfolio should a 57-year-old have invested in stocks? (LO 14-1)

10. **Age minus 20.** According to the "age minus 20 in bonds" calculation, what percentage of their portfolio should a 43-year-old have invested in stocks? (LO 14-1)

11. **(Age minus 40)*2.** According to the "[(age-40)*2]" calculation, what percentage of their portfolio should a 53-year-old have invested in stocks? (LO 14-1)

12. **Yield change.** Suppose you buy both a $1,000, 4% annual coupon bond with a maturity of eight years and a zero coupon bond with a maturity of eight years. The yield is 6.25% when you buy them but changes to 5.50%. What will the new prices of the bonds be? (LO 14-2)

13. **Yield change.** Suppose you buy both a $1,000, 4% annual coupon bond with a maturity of 10 years and a zero coupon bond with a maturity of 10 years. The yield is 4% when you buy them but changes to 5%. How much more or less will the price of the zero go down than the price of the coupon bond? (LO 14-2)

14. **Inflation-indexed.** Assume you buy a 10-year inflation-indexed bond having a real interest rate of 3.625% when the CPI was 260.229. If, one year later, the CPI has risen to 277.948, how much interest will you receive? (LO 14-3)

15. **Mortgage interest.** If you purchase a $290,000 30-year mortgage carrying an interest rate of 3.697%, how much interest will you receive during the first year (i.e., from the first 12 payments)? (LO 14-4)

16. **CMO.** Suppose a CMO has five tranches. Each tranche consists of a $200,000 loan ($1,000,000 total outstanding), $100,000 of which is retired each year. Interest is paid annually on the amount of the loan outstanding in each tranche. The rate of interest varies with the expected life of each tranche. The interest rates start at 5% for tranche A and rise to 9% for tranche E. How much total interest across all tranches will be paid in year 5? (LO 14-4)

17. **Equivalent municipal yield.** An investor faces a federal tax rate of 24% and can buy a corporate bond yielding 2.71%. What would the equivalent municipal yield be? (LO 14-6)

18. **Equivalent corporate yield.** An investor faces a federal tax rate of 24% and can buy a muni bond yielding 4.08%. What would the equivalent corporate yield be? (LO 14-6)

19. **Equivalent municipal yield.** An investor lives in a state that taxes income and faces a state tax rate of 6% and a federal tax rate of 24%. If they can buy a corporate bond yielding 2.71%, what would the equivalent municipal yield be? (LO 14-6)

20. **Equivalent corporate yield.** An investor lives in a state that taxes income and faces a state tax rate of 6% and a federal tax rate of 24%. If they can buy a muni bond yielding 4.25%, what would the equivalent corporate yield be? (LO 14-6)

Case Study

M/T Ratio

In 2021, M/T ratios hit a historic low. Explain what factors were behind it. What does this mean for yields on munis?

Part 5

Investing in Derivative Securities

Part 5 is devoted to derivative securities. As their name implies, derivatives are based on another asset, and a derivative's value is dependent on the value of that underlying asset. Chapter 15 provides intuitive explanation of the use of the two most popular types of derivative securities, futures contracts and options. Chapter 16 covers the actual valuation of derivative securities and the strategies for using them to leverage purchasing power or to hedge risk. Because futures and options offer the possibility of a large return, those investors who are willing to bear the risk may find this material to be the most fascinating in the text.

Chapter

15

An Introduction to Futures Contracts and Options

Learning Objectives

After reading this chapter you should be able to:

LO 15-1   Define the word *option* as it applies to securities and differentiate between an option's market value and its intrinsic value.

LO 15-2   Identify the risks associated with purchasing or selling an option and the factors affecting an option's time premium.

LO 15-3   Differentiate the profit and loss from writing a covered call option versus a naked call option.

LO 15-4   Explain the relationship between the price of a stock and a put option.

LO 15-5   Identify the advantages offered by stock index options, currency options, and interest rate options.

LO 15-6   Differentiate warrants from call options.

LO 15-7   Define a futures contract and differentiate between the long and short positions in a futures contract.

LO 15-8   Contrast the role of margin in the stock market with its role in the futures markets.

LO 15-9   Distinguish speculators from hedgers and describe the role played by each in the futures markets.

LO 15-10 Identify the forces that determine the price of a futures contract.

LO 15-11 Demonstrate how speculators may earn profits or suffer losses in financial and currency futures.

LO 15-12 Demonstrate how futures and swaps help manage risk.

All of the securities we've dealt with so far have been pretty straightforward to value: you figure out the expected future cash flows and then use TVM principles to figure out what the worth of those cash flows is at the expected time of purchase. There is risk and uncertainty in those future cash flows, but once you've purchased the security, you've more or less "locked in" those risks and uncertainties, and if the realized future cash flows are different from what was expected, the purchaser bears the brunt of/rejoices at (depending upon whether the uncertainties were resolved against or in their favor, respectively) the unexpected deviations of the cash flows from what was expected.

However, in this chapter and Chapter 16, we're going to talk about securities that are fundamentally different because they're **derivative securities**: securities that derive their value from an underlying asset or security and that bear only a specific portion of the risk of that underlying asset while allowing the holder of the derivative security to forgo other risks.

There are four basic types of derivative securities: options, futures, forwards, and swaps. All of these types of derivative securities allow you to either hedge your bets about the future uncertainties inherent in the underlying assets, or to use the particular risks that you've taken on through holding the derivative security to offset risks arising from other portions of your portfolio. Futures and forward contracts allow you to lock in today the future price of an underlying asset while still committing you to purchase or sell the asset at a certain price on a certain date in the future; swaps allow you to enter into an agreement to exchange the payments or cash flows from one asset that you own for those of another asset that someone else owns; and options allow you the choice of buying or selling the underlying asset at a set price, up to a certain expiration date in the future.

Because of these aspects, derivative securities can be very instrumental in mitigating risk: for example, if you already own a particular stock and would like to hold on to it, but there is a chance you might have to sell it in the (relatively near) future to cover some unexpected expenses, you could purchase a **put option**, allowing you the right but not the obligation to sell the stock at a certain price. Effectively, the put option would act as insurance against the price of the stock going down and your having to sell it at a lower price, though the insurance would only last as long as the put were in effect.

Likewise, if you are a corn farmer and are planning on harvesting your crop in three months, you could enter into a futures or forward contract in which you contract to sell your harvest at a certain price in three months. You would still face uncertainties about the yield of your harvest but would have insured yourself against a drop in the going price of corn.

Finally, if you were a U.S.-based firm with investors expecting dividends in U.S. dollars but future revenues from a Chinese subsidiary will be in yuan, you could enter into a yuan-for-dollars swap with another U.S. firm that planned on investing in assets in China in the future (and, hence, *needed* yuan), thereby eliminating the **exchange rate risk** associated with converting your future yuan revenues to U.S. dollars.

In the real world, however, many participants in the options and futures markets aren't buying or selling options to mitigate risk; instead, they're buying to *speculate* on the prices of the underlying assets. If they "go long" (i.e., purchase) an option or a futures contract, and the price of the underlying stock or commodity goes up, then they can turn around and liquidate their position at a higher price than what they paid for it. This tendency to speculate is further encouraged by two facts: (a) since derivatives don't convey ownership of the entire underlying asset and last for only a finite time, purchasing a derivative that "controls" just a particular type and amount of that asset is relatively cheap, allowing you to effectively gain control of the portion of the underlying assets you want for a fraction of those assets' current market prices; and (b) both options and futures contracts are able to be purchased on **margin**, where the buyer can borrow a large percentage of their price.

derivative security
a security that derives its value from an underlying asset or security

put option
an option contract that gives you the right, but not the obligation, to sell an underlying asset at a certain price

exchange rate risk
the risk that exchange rates may go against your favor when you are scheduled to receive one currency in the future and will need to convert it to another

margin
when purchasing assets on margin, the money borrowed from a broker to purchase an investment and the difference between the total value of the investment and the loan amount; when entering into a futures contract, the amount each party is required to keep on account against future movements of the underlying asset's price against them

This chapter will lay the groundwork for understanding how options and futures contracts work, including how they are created and by whom, how they react to changes in the values of their respective underlying assets, and how they are liquidated upon termination. The following chapter will cover how they are valued while "in play."

15-1 Call Options

15-1a Interest and Maturity

option
a derivative contract giving the right to buy or sell an underlying asset for a pre-specified price at the owner's discretion over a predetermined time period

call option
an option contract that gives you the right, but not the obligation, to buy an underlying asset at a certain price

intrinsic value
the value of an option at the current market price of the underlying asset if the option were to expire now

An **option** is the right to buy or to sell stock at a specified price within a specified time period. At the end of the time period, the option expires on its expiration date. A **call option** is the right to *buy* (*call forth*) a specified number of shares (usually 100). The opposite option, known as a **put option**, grants the right to *sell* a specified number of shares (usually 100) at a specified price within a specified time period. A put option, then, is the right to *place* or put the *shares* with someone else. (Puts are discussed later in this chapter.)

Notice the phrase "within a specified time period." *American* put and call options may be exercised at any time prior to expiration, but *European* options may be exercised only at expiration. This difference means that an investor can exercise a call option prior to a dividend payment and receive the dividend. Such is not the case with a European option. Although few American options are exercised prior to expiration, this increased flexibility makes American options more valuable than otherwise equivalent European options.

The minimum price that a call option will command is its **intrinsic value** as an option. For a call option, this intrinsic value is the difference between the price of the stock and the per-share exercise (strike) price of the option:

$$\text{Intrinsic Value of Call} = \max(P_s - P_e, 0) \qquad \textbf{15-1}$$

where P_s = the current stock price and P_e = the exercise price of the option. For a put option, the intrinsic value will be equal to:

$$\text{Intrinsic Value of Put} = \max(P_e - P_s, 0) \qquad \textbf{15-2}$$

Intuitively, this would be the value of the option, right before expiration, when there isn't really time for the stock price to move any further, but when there's still time to exercise the option and reap any profits. (Think of this as sort of a "use it or lose it" situation for the option.) If a call option gives the right to buy stock at $30 a share and the stock is selling for $40, then the intrinsic value of the call is $10 ($40 − $30 = $10).

However, if the stock is selling for only $25, then the intrinsic value is zero (0). Exercising the option in such a situation would actually result in a loss, as you would pay $30 per share for the stock through the option and only be able to sell it at the market price of $25, resulting in a loss of $25 − $30 = −$5 per share. But remember why it's called an "option": the owner of the call doesn't have to exercise it, and won't, if they are going to lose money.

payoff diagram
a graphical depiction of the value of a derivative at expiration as a function of the value of the underlying asset

It can be a little difficult to envision this in our heads, which is why we often make use of a **payoff diagram**, a graph of the value of the derivative at the time of expiration as a function of the value of the underlying asset. For financial assets such as stocks, we normally graph the value of a derivative based on a single share or bond against the value of that stock or bond. (Even though, as we'll discuss later, such derivatives normally sell in contracts of 100 shares.) For example, if we take a little liberty and treat a share of stock as both the underlying asset and as a "derivative" on itself, then the payoff diagram of holding a stock that we paid $50 for would look like **Figure 15-1**.

Figure 15-1: Payoff Diagram for Stock

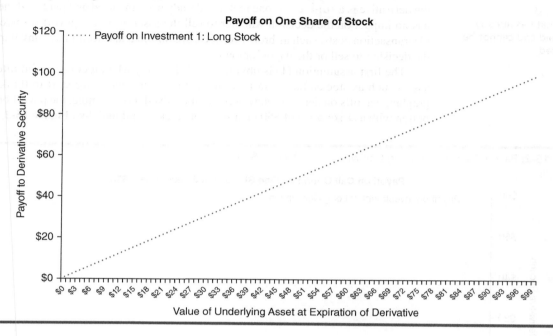

Excel Expert 15-1

Graphing option payoffs and profits is straightforward but tedious, so rather than showing you how to build an Excel spreadsheet from basic elements, as we have done in previous chapters, here we provide you with a template that will allow you to graph up to two derivates at the same time, showing their individual payoffs and profits in addition to the totals for the combined position.

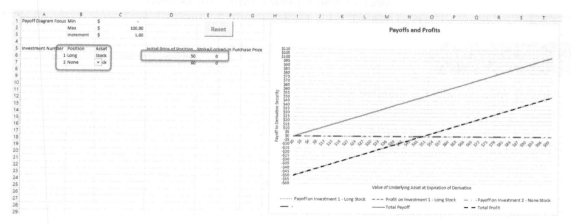

Note that we have set the second position to "none" and the first position to a long stock position with an initial price of $50. To replicate the graph seen in **Figure 15-1**, simply delete the lines that are not relevant (including the lines for total payoff and total profit).

This template will be provided on the book's website.

sunk cost
a cost that has already
been paid and cannot be
recovered

Notice that the payoff diagram makes two big assumptions: (1) the investment in the derivative is a **sunk cost**, one that has already been incurred and paid, and therefore has no impact on the decision whether to sell the asset or on the payoff received; and (2) transaction costs, such as brokerage fees, are minimal and won't have any impact on the decision to sell or the payoff amount.

The first assumption (1) is obviously a little shaky when it comes to infinite-lived assets such as stocks, but it starts to make more sense when we start to think about graphing payoffs on derivatives, which *are* finite-lived. For example, the payoff on a call option with a strike price of $50 on a share of stock would look like **Figure 15-2**.

Figure 15-2: Payoff Diagram for Long Call with Strike Price of $50

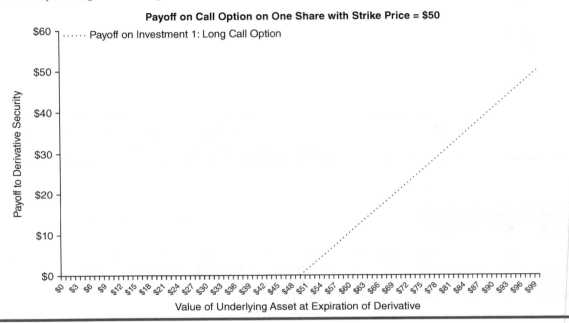

Excel Expert 15-2

Use *Payoff Grapher.xlsx* with the indicated inputs:

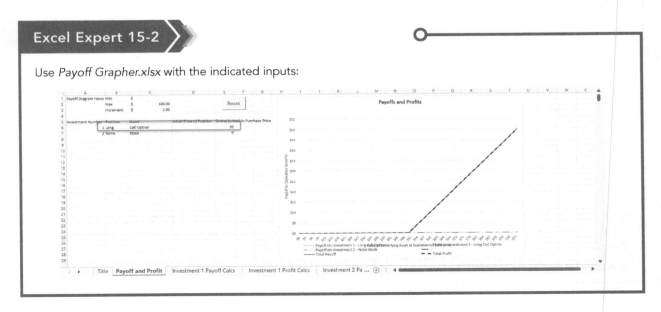

Suppose that we had originally paid $3 to purchase this call. If the option is about to expire, and the stock is trading at $51, we could purchase at $50 by exercising the call and then turn right around and sell the share for $51, realizing a payoff of $51 − $50 = $1. Yes, the $1 payoff is less than the $3 cost of the option, but we're never getting that $3 back: it's been paid and can't be recouped. But if we go ahead and exercise the option, our profit on the call (including the initial purchase price) will be −$3 + $1 = −$2, which is better than the −$3 we'll be stuck with if we don't exercise the option. So yes, we'll exercise and minimize our losses.

In terms of assumption (2) above, remember that call contracts don't actually trade on just one share: the contract is usually on at least 100 shares, and, while there may be transaction fees associated with exercising the option and then selling the shares to get your payoff, the per-share transaction fees will usually be fairly low (especially if we consider that most such option exercises take place among large or corporate investors, which enjoy economies of scale on such transaction fees).

If we were considering the possible rewards to entering into a derivative position *before* we had actually purchased it, then, yes, the purchase price of the derivative (frequently referred to as the option's **premium**) would matter, and we might want to take a look at the potential profit in addition to the payoff. For the call option we just discussed, this would look like **Figure 15-3**.

premium
for options, the purchase price

If we look at this diagram as a tool for analyzing whether we should purchase this option to start with, we can see that we would only do so if we expected the share price to be above $53 (i.e., the strike price of $50 plus the purchase price of $3), though, if we did purchase it, we would still exercise the call as long as the stock price went above $50.

Using both profit and payoff like this also helps illustrate why someone would sell a call option in the first place **Figure 15-4**.

Figure 15-3: Payoff and Profit Diagrams for Long Call with Strike Price of $50

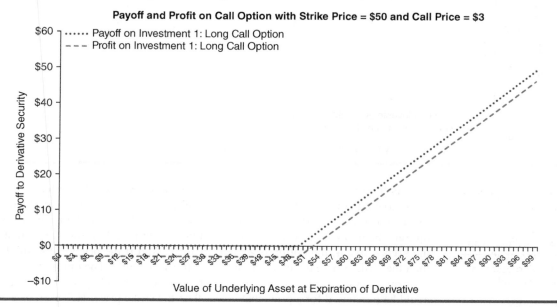

Payoff and Profit on Call Option with Strike Price = $50 and Call Price = $3

⋯⋯ Payoff on Investment 1: Long Call Option
− − − Profit on Investment 1: Long Call Option

Excel Expert 15-3

Use *Payoff Grapher.xlsx* with the indicated inputs:

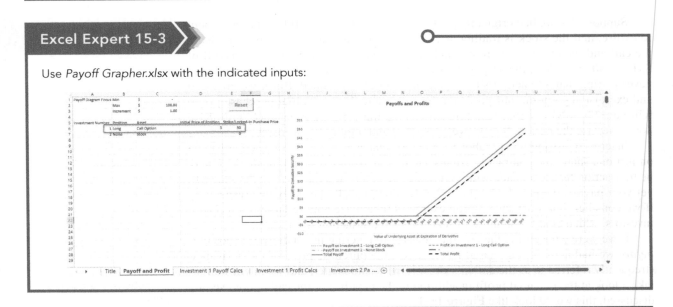

Figure 15-4: Payoff and Profit Diagrams for Short Call with Strike Price of $50

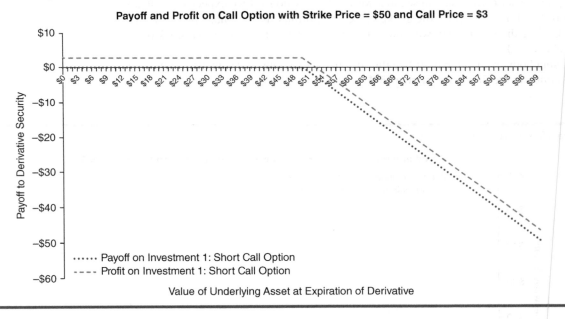

in the money
an option having positive intrinsic value

strike price
the price specified in an options contract at which the underlying asset can be bought or sold at

at the money
an option selling when the strike price equals the current market price of the underlying security

As long as the underlying stock price stays below $53, the seller of the call is going to come out ahead. If the stock is selling for a price greater than the per-share exercise price, the call has positive intrinsic value. This may be referred to as the option's being **in the money**. If the common stock is selling for a price that equals the **strike price**, the option is **at the money**. And if the price of the stock is less than the strike price, the call option has no intrinsic value. The option is **out of the money**. No one would purchase and exercise an option to buy stock when the stock could be purchased for a price that is less than the strike price. However, as explained subsequently, such options may still trade.

Before the call is close to expiration, there is still a chance that the price of the underlying asset can move, and therefore a chance that the call can move further into

Excel Expert 15-4

Use *Payoff Grapher.xlsx* with the indicated inputs:

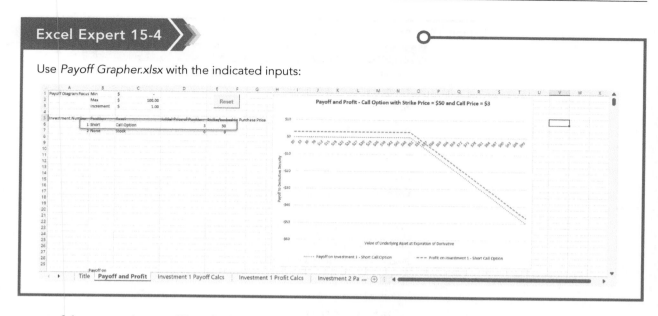

or out of the money. As we will see in the next chapter, the volatility of the underlying asset, and hence, the chance and possible magnitudes of such movements, plays an important part in valuing a call option. But the market price of a call must approach its intrinsic value as the option approaches its expiration date, as time and possibility are running out on such possible moves. On the day that the option is to expire, the market price can be only what the option is worth as stock. It can be worth only the difference between the market price of the stock and the exercise price of the option. This fact means that the investor may use the intrinsic value of a call as an indication of the "floor" of the option's future price, for the investor knows that the market price of the option must approach its intrinsic value as the option approaches expiration.

Because of arbitrage, the intrinsic value sets the minimum price that the security will command. As explained previously, arbitrage is the act of simultaneously buying and selling a commodity or security in two different markets to make a profit from the different prices offered by the markets. In the case of an option, the two markets are the market for the stock and the market for the option. The essence of the arbitrage position is a short sale in the stock and a long position (i.e., a purchase) in the option. After these transactions are enacted, the arbitrageur will exercise the option. Then the shares acquired by exercising the call will be used to cover the short position in the stock.

For example, let's assume that the price of the stock is $60 and the strike price of the option is $50, so the option's intrinsic value is $10. If the current market price of the option is $6, an investor can buy the option and exercise it to acquire the stock. By doing so the investor saves $4, for the total cost of the stock is $56 (i.e., $6 for the option and $50 to exercise the option). The investor then owns stock that has a market value of $60, but only paid $56 for it.

If the investor continues to hold the stock, the $4 saving can evaporate if the stock's price falls. However, if the investor simultaneously buys the call and sells the stock short, the $4 profit is guaranteed. In other words, the investor uses arbitrage, with the steps (shown in **Exhibit 15-1**) necessary to act on the arbitrage opportunity.

In this strategy, the investor sells the stock short at $60 and purchases the call for $6 (step 1). The stock is borrowed from the broker and delivered to the buyer. Then the investor exercises the option (step 2) and covers the short position with the stock acquired by exercising the option (step 3). This set of transactions locks in the $4 profit

out of the money
an option having zero intrinsic value

Exhibit 15-1: Arbitrage Strategy

Current situation		
Price of the stock		$60
Per-share strike price of the option		50
Price of the option		6
Step 1		
Buy the call for $6		
Sell the stock short for $60		
Step 2		
Exercise the option, acquiring the stock for $50		
Step 3		
Cover the short position (i.e., surrender the stock)		
Determination of profit or loss		
Proceeds from shorting the stock		$60
Cost of the stock		
Cost of the call	$6	
Cost to exercise the option	50	
Total cost		$56
Net Profit		$4

because the investor sells the stock short at $60 per share and simultaneously purchases and exercises the option for a combined cost of $56 per share. By selling the stock short and purchasing the call at the same time, the investor ensures that they will gain the difference between the intrinsic value of the option and its price. Through arbitrage the investor guarantees the profit.

Of course, the act of buying the option and selling the stock short will drive up the option's price and put pressure on the price of the stock to fall. Thus, the opportunity to arbitrage will disappear, because arbitrageurs will bid up the price of the option to at least its intrinsic value. Once the price of the call has risen to its intrinsic value, the opportunity for a profitable arbitrage disappears. However, if the price of the call were to fall again below its intrinsic value, the opportunity for arbitrage would reappear, and the process would be repeated. Thus, the intrinsic value of an option becomes the minimum price that the option must command, for arbitrageurs will enter the market as soon as the price of an option falls below its intrinsic value as an option.

If the price of the option were to exceed its intrinsic value, arbitrage would offer no profit, nor would an investor exercise the option. If the call to buy the stock in the previous examples were to sell for $5 when the price of the common stock was $50, no one would exercise the option. The cost of the stock acquired by exercising the call would be $55 (i.e., $50 + $5). The investor would be better off buying the stock outright than purchasing the call and exercising it.

Actually, the opportunity for the typical investor to execute a profitable arbitrage is exceedingly rare. Market makers are cognizant of the possible gains from arbitrage and are in the best possible position to take advantage of any profitable opportunities that may emerge. Hence, if the opportunity to purchase the call for a price less than its intrinsic value existed, the purchases would be made by the market makers, and the opportunity to arbitrage would not become available to the general public. For the general investor, the importance of arbitrage is not the opportunity for profit that it offers but the fact that it sets a floor on the price of an option, and that floor is the minimum or intrinsic value. As explained in the next chapter on the Black-Scholes option valuation model, the minimum price must exceed the option's intrinsic value prior to expiration.

15-2 Leverage

As discussed above, options offer investors the advantage of **leverage**. The potential return on an investment in a call may exceed the potential return on an investment in the underlying stock (i.e., the stock that the option represents the right to purchase). Like the use of margin, this magnification of the potential gain is an example of leverage.

Exhibit 15-2, which illustrates the relationship between the price of a stock and a call's intrinsic value, also demonstrates the potential leverage that call options offer. For example, if the price of the stock rose from $60 to $70, the intrinsic value of the option would rise from $10 to $20. The percentage increase in the price of the stock is 16.67 percent ([$70 − $60] ÷ $60), whereas the percentage increase in the intrinsic value of the option is 100 percent ([$20 − $10] ÷ $10). The percentage increase in the intrinsic value of the call exceeds the percentage increase in the price of the stock. If the investor purchased the option for its intrinsic value and the price of the stock then rose, the return on the investment in the call would exceed the return on an investment in the stock.

Leverage, however, works in both directions. Although it may increase the investor's potential return, it may also increase the potential loss if the price of the stock declines. For example, if the price of the stock in Exhibit 15-2 fell from $70 to $60 for a 14.2% decline, the intrinsic value of the call would fall from $20 to $10, for a 50% decline. As with any investment, the investor must decide if the increase in the potential return offered by leverage is worth the increased risk.

15-2a The Time Premium Paid for a Call

If an option offers a greater potential return than does the stock, investors may prefer to buy the option. In an effort to purchase the option, investors will bid up its price, so the market price will exceed the option's intrinsic value. Since the market price of an option is frequently referred to as the premium, the extent to which this price exceeds

leverage
the ability to pay a relatively small premium for market exposure in relation to the contract value

Exhibit 15-2: Relationship Between Stock Price, the Value of a Call, and the Hypothetical Market Price of the Option

		Option		
Price of Stock	Per-Share Strike Price	Intrinsic Value	Hypothetical Market Price	Time Premium
$10	$50	$0	$0	$0.00
20	50	0	0.02	0.02
30	50	0	0.25	0.25
40	50	0	1	1.00
50	50	0	6	6.00
60	50	10	15	5.00
70	50	20	23	3.00
80	50	30	32	2.00
90	50	40	41	1.00
100	50	50	50	0.00

the option's intrinsic value is referred to as the time premium or time value. Investors are willing to pay this time premium for the potential leverage the option offers. This time premium, however, reduces the potential return and increases the potential loss.

The time premium for a call is illustrated in Exhibit 15-2, which adds a hypothetical set of prices in column 4 and the time premium in column 5. The hypothetical market prices are greater than the intrinsic values of the call because investors have bid up the prices. To purchase the call, an investor must pay the market price and not the intrinsic value. Thus, in this example when the market price of the stock is $60 and the intrinsic value of the option is $10, the market price of the call is $15. The investor must pay $15 to purchase the call, which is $5 more than the option's intrinsic value.

The relationships in Exhibit 15-2 between the price of the stock and the call's intrinsic value and hypothetical price are illustrated in **Figure 15-5**. The time premium is easily seen in the graph, for it is the shaded area indicating the difference between the line representing the market price of the call (line DE) and the line representing its intrinsic value (line ABC). Thus, when the price of the stock and call are $60 and $15, respectively, the time premium is $5 (the price of the option, $15, minus its intrinsic value, $10).

As may be seen in Figure 15-5, the amount of the time premium varies at the different price levels of the stock. However, the amount of the time premium declines as the price of the stock rises above the option's strike price. Once the price of the stock has risen considerably, the call may command virtually no time premium over its intrinsic value. At $100 per share, the option is selling at approximately its intrinsic value of $50. The primary reason for this decline in the time premium is that as the price of the stock and the intrinsic value of the option rise, the potential leverage is reduced. In addition, at higher prices the potential price decline in the call is greater if the price of the stock falls. For these reasons investors become less willing to bid up the price of the call as the price of the stock rises, and hence the amount of the time premium diminishes.

The time premium decreases the potential leverage and return from investing in options. If, for example, this stock's price rose from $60 to $70 for a 16.7% gain, the call's price would rise from $15 to $23 for a 53.3% gain. The percentage increase in the price of the option still exceeds the percentage increase in the price of the stock; however, the difference between the two percentage increases is smaller, since the call sells for more than its intrinsic value. The time premium has substantially reduced the potential leverage that the call offers investors.

Figure 15-5: Call Option Price vs. Intrinsic Value

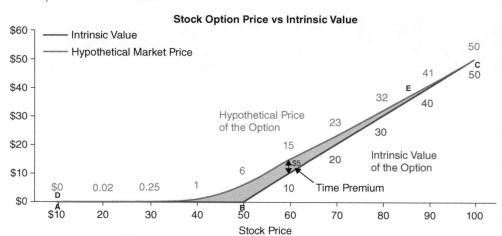

Investors who are considering purchasing calls should ask themselves what price increase they can expect in the option if the price of the underlying stock should rise. For the call to be attractive, its anticipated percentage increase in price must exceed the anticipated percentage increase in the price of the stock. The call must offer the investor leverage to justify the additional risk. Obviously, an investor should not purchase the call if the stock's price is expected to appreciate in value more rapidly than the option's price. The previous example illustrates that the time premium paid for an option may substantially decrease the potential leverage. Thus, recognition of the time premium that an option commands over its intrinsic value is one of the most important considerations in the selection of an option for investment.

The valuation of a call determines the amount of the time premium (i.e., valuation determines where line DE in Figure 15-5 lies in the plane relating the price of the stock and the option's value). Several factors affect an option's value; since these factors differ among companies, time premiums commanded by options on their stocks also differ. While a detailed discussion of option valuation (and hence the time premium) is deferred until the next chapter, the following gives an overview of the determinants of an option's time premium.

As an option approaches expiration, its market price must approach the option's intrinsic value. On the expiration date, a call cannot command a price greater than its intrinsic value based on the underlying stock. Thus, as an option nears expiration, it will sell for a smaller time premium, and that premium disappears at the option's expiration.

Other determinants of an option's time premium include the payment of cash dividends, the volatility of the underlying stock, and interest rates. Options of companies that pay cash dividends tend to sell for smaller time premiums. There may be two possible explanations for this relationship. First, companies that retain (do not distribute) earnings will have more funds available for investments. By retaining and reinvesting earnings, a company may grow more rapidly, and this growth may be reflected in the price of its stock. Hence, the potential gain in the price of the call may be greater if the firm retains its earnings and does not pay a cash dividend. Second, if a company pays a dividend, the owner of the option does not receive the cash payment unless they exercise the option prior to the ex-dividend date. The call will be less attractive relative to the common stock, for the owner of the option must forgo the dividend. Therefore, investors will not be willing to pay as much for the call and it will sell for a smaller time premium.

Another factor that affects the time premium paid for an option is the price volatility of the common stock. (In the next chapter this volatility will be measured by the variability of the stock's return as measured by the standard deviation of the return.) If the stock's price fluctuates substantially, the option may be more attractive and command a higher time premium. Since the price of the call follows the price of the underlying stock, fluctuations in the price of the stock will be reflected in the option's price. The more volatile the price of the stock, the more opportunity the option offers for a price increase. Thus, options on volatile stocks tend to be more attractive (at least to speculators) and command a higher time premium than options on stocks whose prices are more stable and less volatile.

Interest rates affect options by their impact on the present value of the funds necessary to exercise the option. Since options are exercised in the future, higher interest rates imply that the investor must set aside a lower amount of money to exercise the call. Since a call's intrinsic value is the price of the stock minus the strike price, a lower strike price must increase the value of the option. In effect, higher interest rates reduce the present value of the strike price, which makes the call option more valuable.

15-2b Purchasing Calls

Calls may be purchased by investors who want to leverage their position in a stock. Should the price of the stock rise, the price of the call will also rise. Since the cost of the call is less than the cost of the stock, the percentage increase in the call may exceed that of the stock, so the investor earns a greater percentage return on the call option than on the underlying stock. If the price of the stock declines, the value of the call also falls, so the investor sustains a larger percentage loss on the option than on the stock. However, since the cost of the call is less than the stock, the absolute loss on the investment in the call may be less than the absolute loss on the stock.

The potential payoff and profit at expiration on the purchase of a call for $15 when the stock sells for $60 are illustrated in **Figure 15-6**. As long as the price of the stock is

Figure 15-6: Payoff and Profit for Call with Strike Price of $50 and Cost of $15

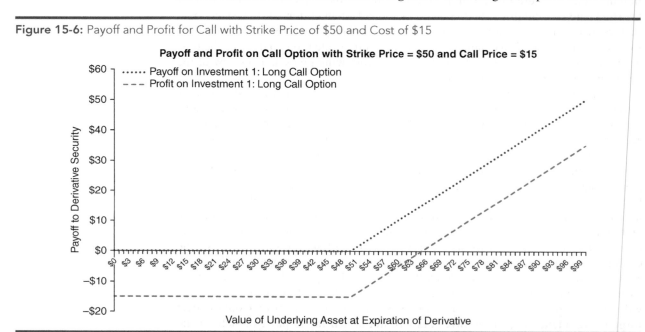

Excel Expert 15-5

Use *Payoff Grapher.xlsx* with the indicated inputs:

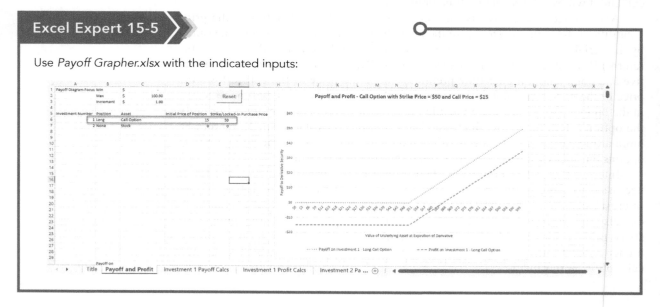

$50 or less, the entire investment in the call ($15) is lost. As the price of the stock rises above $50, the loss is reduced. The investor breaks even at $65, because the intrinsic value of the call is $15—the cost of the option. The investor earns a profit as the price of the stock continues to rise above $65. (Remember that in this illustration the starting price of the stock was $60. The price has to rise only by more than $5 to assure the investor of a profit on the position in the call.)

Figure 15-7 replicates the payoff to the option from Figure 15-6 and adds the profits and losses from buying the stock at $60. Both involve purchases and therefore are long positions in the securities. If the price of the stock rises above or declines below $60, the investor earns a profit or sustains a loss. The important difference between the lines indicating the profit and losses on the long positions in the

Figure 15-7: Potential Profits on Stock and Call when Stock Price = $60, Call with Strike Price of $50 and Price of $15

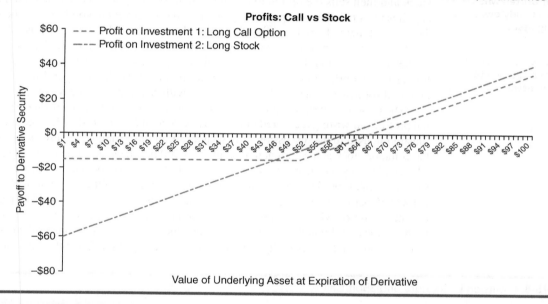

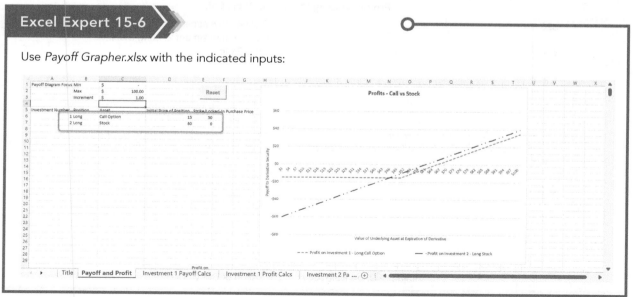

Excel Expert 15-6

Use *Payoff Grapher.xlsx* with the indicated inputs:

two securities is the possible large dollar loss from buying the stock compared to the limited dollar loss on the call. In the worst-case scenario, the investor could lose $60 on the stock but only $15 on the call.

15-2c Writing Calls

The preceding section considered purchasing call options to obtain leverage; this section will cover the opposite: selling call options. In the jargon of options, the act of issuing and selling a call is referred to as "writing" the option. While a long position in a call gives the investor an opportunity to profit from the leverage the option offers, the short position (i.e., writing and selling calls) produces revenues from their sale.

There are two ways to write options. The first is the less risky strategy, which is called **covered option** writing. The investor buys (or already owns) the underlying stock and then sells the option to buy that stock. If the option is exercised, the investor supplies the stock that was previously purchased (i.e., covers the option with the stock). The second method entails selling the call without owning the stock. This is referred to as **naked option** writing, for the investor is exposed to considerable risk. If the price of the stock rises and the call is exercised, the option writer must buy the stock at the higher market price in order to supply it to the buyer. With naked option writing the potential for loss is considerably greater than with covered option writing.

The reason for writing options is the income to be gained from their sale. The potential profit from writing a covered option may be seen in **Figure 15-8**, which continues the illustration used in the discussion of buying a call. In this example, the investor purchases the common stock at the current market price of $60 per share and simultaneously sells for $15 a call to buy the shares at the strike price of $50. As may be seen in Figure 15-8, the sale of the call is profitable to the investor as long as the price of the common stock remains below $65 per share; as long as the price of the common stock stays above $45 per share, the entire position will yield a profit before commission fees. The maximum amount of this profit, however, is limited to $5. Thus, by selling the call, the investor forgoes the possibility of large gains but helps partially immunize themselves against a fall in the stock price. For

covered option
an option written when the seller already owns the underlying asset

naked option
an option written when the writer does not own the underlying asset

Figure 15-8: Profits on Long Stock and Short Call

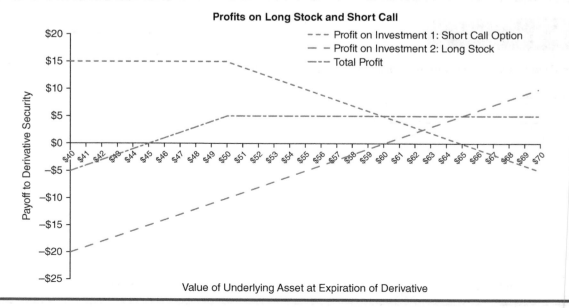

Excel Expert 15-7

Use *Payoff Grapher.xlsx* with the indicated inputs:

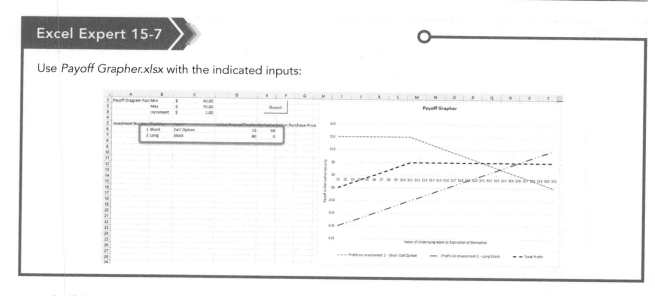

example, if the price of the stock were to rise to $70 per share, the holder of the call would exercise it and purchase the 100 shares from the seller at $50 per share. The seller would then net $5 ($50 from the stock + $15 from the sale of the call − $60 cost of the stock).

If the price of the stock were to fall below $45, the entire position would result in a loss to the seller. For example, if the price of the common stock fell to $40, the investor would lose $20 on the purchase of the stock. However, $15 was received from the sale of the call. Thus, the net loss is only $5. The investor still owns the stock and may now write another call on that stock. As long as the investor owns the stock, the same shares may be used over and over to cover the writing of options. Thus, even if the price of the stock does fall, the investor may continue to use it to write more options. The more options that can be written, the more profitable the shares become. For individuals who write options, the best possible situation would be for the stock's price to remain stable. In that case, the investors would receive the income from writing the options and never suffer a capital loss from a decline in the price of the stock on which the option is being written.

The relationship between the price of the stock and the profit or loss on writing a covered call is illustrated in Figure 15-8. As may be seen from the figure, the sale of the covered option produces a profit (before commissions) for all prices of the stock above $45. However, the maximum profit (before commissions) is only $5.

Option writers do not have to own the common stock on which they write calls. Although such naked or uncovered option writing exposes the investor to a large amount of risk, they do stand to reap the entire premium if the option stays out of the money. If the writer of the preceding option had not owned the stock and had sold the option for $15, the position would have been as shown in **Figure 15-9**, and would have been profitable as long as the price of the common stock remained below $65 per share at the expiration of the call.

The potential loss, however, is theoretically infinite, for the naked option loses $100 for every $1 increase in the price of the stock above the call's exercise price. For example, if the price of the stock were to rise to $90 per share, the call would be worth $4,000 ($40 per share × 100 shares). The owner of the call would exercise it and purchase the 100 shares for $5,000. The writer of the call would then have to purchase the shares on the open market for $9,000. Since the writer received only $1,500 when the call was sold and $5,000 when the call was exercised, the loss would be $2,500. Therefore, uncovered option writing exposes the writer to considerable risk if the price of the stock rises. (This risk may be reduced by an order to purchase the stock at $65. If the price of the stock rises, the order is executed so that the option writer buys the stock and the position in the call is no longer naked.)

Figure 15-9: Potential Profits on Selling Naked Call

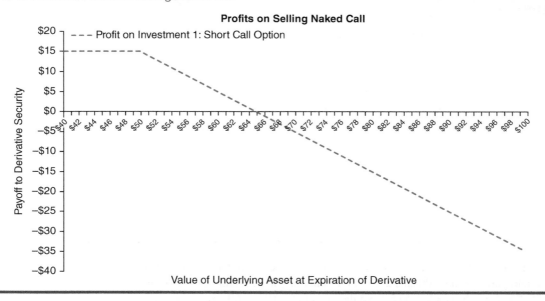

Excel Expert 15-8

Use *Payoff Grapher.xlsx* with the indicated inputs:

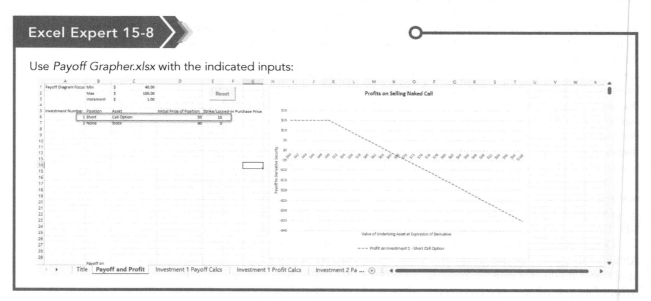

Investors should write naked call options only if they anticipate a decline (or at least no increase) in the price of the stock. These investors may write covered call options if they believe the price of the stock may rise but are not certain of the price increase. And they may purchase the stock (or the option) and not write calls if they believe there is substantial potential for a price increase.

15-3 Puts

A put is an option to sell stock (usually 100 shares) at a specified price within a specified time period. As with a call, the time period is short: three, six, or nine months. Like all options, a put has an intrinsic value, which is the difference between the strike price of

Figure 15-10: Payoff of a Long Put with a Strike Price of $30

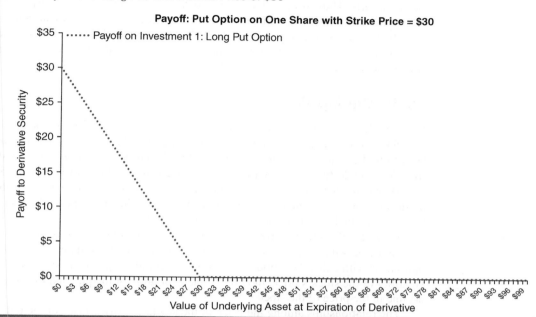

Payoff: Put Option on One Share with Strike Price = $30

the put and the price of the stock. Notice that the intrinsic value of a put is the reverse of the intrinsic value of an option to buy (e.g., a call). Compare Figures 15-2 and 15-10.

The relationship between the price of a stock and the intrinsic value of a put is illustrated in **Figure 15-10**. This put is an option to sell a share at $30 per share.

If the price of the stock is less than the strike price, the put has a positive intrinsic value and is said to be in the money. If the price of the stock is greater than the strike price, the put has no intrinsic value and is said to be out of the money. If the price of the stock equals the strike price, the put is at the money. As with call options, the market price of a put is called the premium.

As may be seen in Figure 15-10, when the price of the stock declines, the intrinsic value of the put rises. Since the owner of the put may sell the stock at the

Excel Expert 15-9

Use *Payoff Grapher.xlsx* with the indicated inputs:

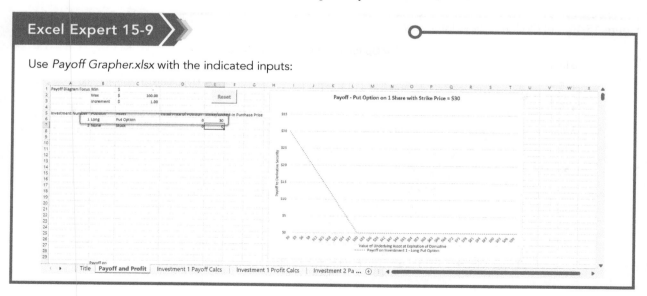

price specified in the option agreement, the value of the option rises as the price of the stock falls. Thus, if the price of the stock is $15 and the exercise price of the put is $30, the put's intrinsic value as an option contract (i.e., for 100 shares) must be $1,500. The investor can purchase the 100 shares of stock for $1,500 on the stock market and sell them for $3,000 to the person who issued the put. The put, then, must be worth the $1,500 difference between the purchase and sale prices.

15-3a Buying Puts

Why should an investor purchase a put? The reason is the same for puts as it is for other speculative options: the put offers potential leverage to the investor. Such leverage may be seen in the example presented in Figure 15-10. When the price of the stock declines from $25 to $20 (a 20% decrease), the intrinsic value of the put rises from $5 to $10 (a 100 percent increase). In this example, a 20 percent decline in the price of the stock produces a larger percentage increase in the intrinsic value of the put. It is this potential leverage that makes put options attractive to investors.

As with call options, investors are willing to pay a price that is greater than the put's intrinsic value: the put commands a time premium above its intrinsic value as an option. As with calls, the amount of this time premium depends on such factors as the volatility of the stock's price, the time to the expiration of the put, and the potential for decline in the price of the stock.

The relationships among the price of the stock, the strike price of the put, and the hypothetical prices for the put are illustrated in **Figure 15-11**. As we saw with the call, the hypothetical price of the put exceeds the intrinsic value, for the put commands a time premium over its intrinsic value as an option.

This figure also shows the inverse relationship between the price of the stock and the put's intrinsic value. As the price of the stock declines, the intrinsic value of the put increases (e.g., from $5 to $10 when the stock's price declines from $25 to $20). The figure also readily shows the time premium paid for the option, which is the difference between the price of the put and the option's intrinsic value. If the price of the put is $7.50 and the intrinsic value is $5, the time premium is $2.50.

Also note that the hypothetical market price of the put converges with the put's intrinsic value as the price of the stock declines. If the price of the stock is sufficiently high (e.g., $50 in Figure 15-11), the put will not have any market value because the price

Figure 15-11: Put Option Price vs Intrinsic Value

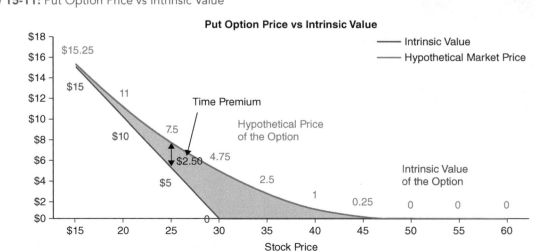

of the stock must decline substantially for the put to have any intrinsic value. At the other extreme, when the price of the stock is low (e.g., $15), the price of the put is equal to the put's intrinsic value as an option. There are two reasons for this convergence. First, if the price of the stock rises, the investor may lose the funds invested in the put. As the price of the stock declines below the strike price of the put, the potential risk to the investor if the price of the stock should start to rise becomes greater. Thus, put buyers are less willing to pay a time premium above the put's intrinsic value. Second, as the intrinsic value of a put rises when the price of the stock declines, the investor must spend more to buy the put; therefore, the potential return on the investment is less. As the potential return declines, the willingness to pay a time premium diminishes.

The potential profit and loss from purchasing a put is illustrated in **Figure 15-12**. If the price of the stock is $25 and the strike price of the put is $30, the intrinsic value

Figure 15-12: Potential Profits on Put with Strike = $30, Premium = $8

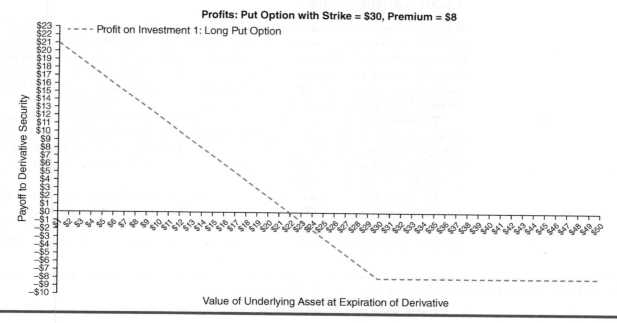

Profits: Put Option with Strike = $30, Premium = $8

- - - Profit on Investment 1: Long Put Option

Payoff to Derivative Security

Value of Underlying Asset at Expiration of Derivative

Excel Expert 15-10

Use *Payoff Grapher.xlsx* with the indicated inputs:

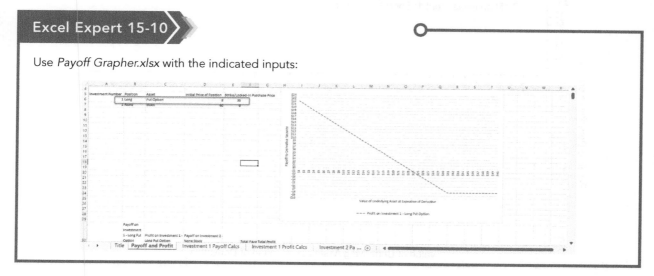

is $5 (i.e., the put is in the money). Suppose the price of the put is $8, so it commands a time premium of $3. As may be seen in Figure 15-12, the purchase of the put is profitable as long as the price of the stock is less than $22, and the profit rises as the price of the stock declines. In the unlikely case that the price of the stock were to fall to $0, the maximum possible profit is $22 (the strike price minus the cost of the put).

If the price of the stock rises, the position sustains a loss. As long as the price of the stock is $30 or greater, the put has no intrinsic value (the put is out of the money). No one would exercise an option to sell at $30 if the stock could be sold for a higher price elsewhere. The option would have no value and expire. In this case the investor loses the entire cost of the option ($8). This is, of course, the worst-case scenario, but it emphasizes that the most the investor can lose is the cost of the option. As explained when comparing purchasing a put to selling a stock short, the latter strategy can generate greater losses.

15-3b Writing Puts

Whereas the previous section discussed buying a put, this section will consider its opposite—selling a put. As with call options, investors may either buy or sell a put (i.e., they may write a put). The investor buys a put in anticipation of a fall in the price of the stock. The investor who writes a put, on the other hand, believes that the price of the stock will not fall. The price of the stock could rise, which is certainly acceptable from the writer's perspective, but the emphasis is on the stock's price not falling.

The writer may be either naked or covered. If the investor only sells the put, the position is naked. If the writer simultaneously shorts the stock, the writer is covered. If the put is exercised and the writer buys the stock, the writer could then use the stock to cover the short position. However, since covered put writing is rare, the following discussion is limited to naked put writing.

The possible profits and losses from writing a put may be seen by continuing the example in Figure 15-12. In that illustration, the investor purchased the put for $8 to sell stock at $30 when the stock was selling for $25. In the opposite case, the investor writes the put to sell the stock at $30, and receives the $8 proceeds. The

Figure 15-13: Profits on Short Put Option with Strike Price = $30 and Premium = $8

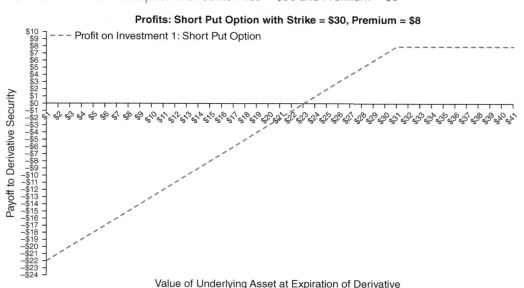

Excel Expert 15-11

Use *Payoff Grapher.xlsx* with the indicated inputs:

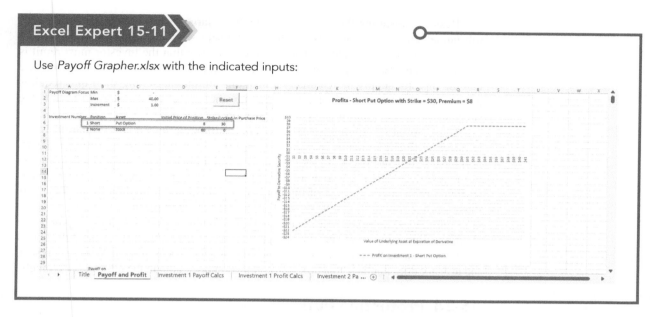

writer's possible profits and losses are shown in **Figure 15-13**. As long as the price of the stock exceeds $22, the position generates a profit. The profit rises along with the price of the stock and reaches a maximum of $8 when the price of the stock is $30. The position sustains a loss if the price of the stock is less than $22, and the loss increases as the price of the stock declines. The maximum possible loss is $22 if the price of the stock were to fall to $0.

15-3c Puts Compared with Short Sales

Investors purchase put options when they believe that the price of the stock is going to decline. Purchasing puts, however, is not the only method investors can use to profit from falling securities prices. As was explained previously, an investor who believes that the price of a stock is going to fall may profit from the decline by selling short. Buying a put is another form of a short position. However, the put option offers the investor two major advantages over selling short. First, the amount of potential loss is less; second, puts may offer a greater return on the investor's capital because of their leverage.

In order to execute a short position, the investor must sell the stock, deliver the borrowed stock, and later purchase the stock to cover the position. The profit or loss is the difference between the price at which the borrowed stock was sold and the price at which the stock is purchased to repay the loan. If the price of the stock declines, the investor reaps a profit, but if the price of the stock rises, the investor suffers a loss. This loss may be substantial if the stock's price rises significantly. For example, if 100 shares are sold short at $30 and later purchased at $50, the investor loses $2,000 plus commissions on the investment. The higher the price of the stock rises, the greater is the loss that the short position inflicts on the investor. (Notice that once again the investor may limit this potential loss by establishing an order to purchase the stock should the price rise to some predetermined level.)

Purchasing a put option does not subject the investor to a large potential capital loss. If the investor purchases for $300 a put that is the option to sell 100 shares at $30, the maximum amount that the investor can lose is $300. If the price of the common stock rises from $30 to $50, the maximum that can be lost with the put is still only $300. However, the loss on the short position is $2,000 when the price of the stock rises from $30 to $50. Puts reduce the absolute amount that the investor may lose.

Besides subjecting the investor to potentially large losses, the short sale ties up a substantial amount of capital. When the investor sells short, the broker will require that they put up funds as collateral. The minimum amount that the investor must remit is the margin requirement set by the Federal Reserve, and individual brokers may require that the investor supply more collateral than this minimum. Selling short thus requires the investor to tie up capital, and the larger the amount that the investor must remit, the smaller the potential return on the short position.

Less capital is required to invest in a put. Although the amount of margin varies at different time periods, it certainly will not be as low as the price of the put. Thus, purchasing the put instead of establishing the short position ties up a smaller amount of the investor's funds. The potential return is greater if the price of the stock declines sufficiently to cover the cost of the put because the amount invested is smaller. Puts thus offer the investor more leverage than does the short position.

Short sales, however, offer one important advantage over puts. Puts expire, but a short position can be maintained indefinitely. If an investor anticipates a price decline, it must occur during the put's short life for the investment to be profitable. With a short sale, the investor does not have this time constraint and may maintain the position indefinitely.

15-3d Protective Puts

Purchasing put options may be viewed as a speculative investment strategy. The buyer profits as the value of the underlying stock declines, which causes the value of the put to rise. Since the long-term trend in stock prices is to increase as the economy expands, purchasing a put seems to be betting against the natural trend in a stock's price.

Although purchases of puts by themselves may be speculative, they may, when used in conjunction with the purchase of stock, reduce the individual's risk exposure. Such a strategy—the simultaneous purchase of the stock and a put—is called a **protective put** because it conserves the investor's initial investment while permitting the investor to maintain a long position in a stock so the profit can grow.

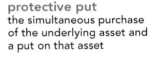
protective put
the simultaneous purchase of the underlying asset and a put on that asset

Suppose an individual buys a stock for $40 but does not want to bear the risk associated with a decline in the price of the stock. This investor could purchase a put, whose

Figure 15-14: Profits on Long Stock and Long Put with Strike Price of $40 and Premium of $2.50

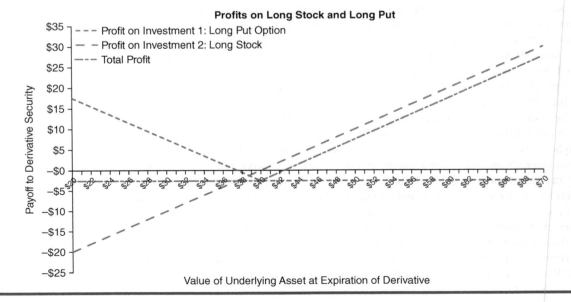

Excel Expert 15-12

Use *Payoff Grapher.xlsx* with the indicated inputs:

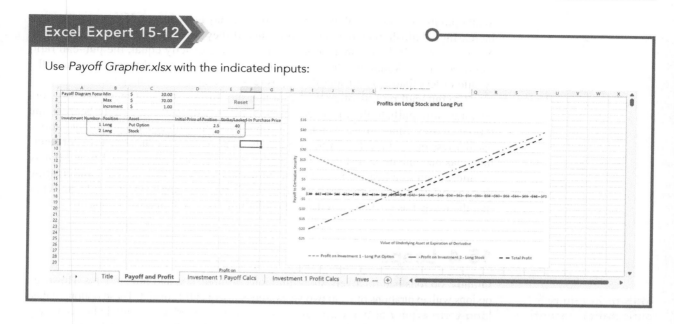

value would rise if the price of the stock were to decline. Suppose there is a six-month put with a strike price of $40 that is currently selling for $2.50. **Figure 15-14** presents the benefit of buying the put in combination with the stock.

Notice that the worst-case scenario is a loss of $2.50. No matter how low the price of the stock falls, the maximum loss to the investor is $2.50. If the price of the stock rises, the maximum possible profit is unlimited. The only effect, then, is that the potential profit is reduced by $2.50, the price of the put. Basically, the investor has bought insurance against the fall of the stock price by paying $2.50 for the put.

This protective put strategy may be viewed as an alternative to placing a **stop-loss order** to sell the stock at $37.50. The advantage of the protective put is that the investor is protected from the price of the stock falling, the stock being sold, and the price subsequently rising. Day-to-day fluctuations in the price of the stock have no impact on the protective put strategy. The disadvantage is that the put ultimately expires, whereas the limit order may be maintained indefinitely. Once the put expires, the investor no longer has the protection and would once again be at risk from a decline in the price of the stock. To maintain the protection, the investor could buy another put. In the previous example, the cost of the put was $2.50. If the put were in existence for six months, expired, and the investor bought another put for the same price, the annual cost of the protection is $5. The protective put is similar to buying car or home insurance. The individual must renew the policy in order to maintain the coverage. The limit order, however, has no costs—although the investor may periodically have to instruct the broker to reinstate the limit order.

There is no clear answer as to whether the limit order or the protective put is the better strategy. The limit order involves no cost but does subject the investor to being sold out on a dip in the price of the stock. The protective put avoids the risk of being sold out by a temporary price decline but requires the investor to pay the cost of the option, which reduces the potential profit from the position in the stock.

15-3e The Put–Call Ratio

The number of options in existence (the **open interest**, as it's sometimes called) is not static. Initially, the number rises as new options are created and diminishes as the options approach expiration and positions are closed. While this general pattern applies

stop-loss order
a standing order to sell an asset owned when the price goes down to a specified level

open interest
the number of a particular derivative contracts in existence

to all options, the number of puts relative to calls may also change. If investors become increasingly bullish, they may buy more calls. If they become more bearish, they may buy more puts. If the number of puts and calls were exactly equal, the put–call ratio would equal 1.0. A ratio greater than 1.0 indicates the existence of more puts than calls. A ratio of less than 1.0 indicates the opposite—more calls exist than puts.

The put–call ratio is often used as a measure of investor sentiment. As investors become more bullish, the ratio decreases, but if investors become more bearish, the ratio increases. Since investors tend to be optimistic, the numerical value of the ratio is usually less than 1.0. If, however, the ratio rises above 1.0, that suggests investor sentiment has become pessimistic, at least on that stock. A put–call ratio of 1.6 or 2.0 may be interpreted as a bearish indicator of future stock prices. Investors are anticipating that the price of a specific stock will decline (if the ratio applies to a single stock) or that the market as a whole will decline (if the ratio is based on a stock index).

15-4 Leaps

long-term equity anticipation securities (LEAPS)
options that are typically longer than nine months in duration

Initially, options had relatively short durations of three, six, and nine months. However, options with expirations of up to two years were subsequently created. These options, called **long-term equity anticipation securities (LEAPS)**, work essentially in the same way as traditional puts and calls, but since the term is longer, LEAPS command a larger time premium. For example, when Cisco was trading for $23.48, a 5-month call to buy the stock at $25 sold for $3, but the 19-month call sold for $7.10. The same price relationships hold for puts. The Cisco 5-month put and the 19-month put sold for $4.10 and $7.10, respectively.

Investors who anticipate that the price of Cisco will increase have several alternatives. They could buy the stock or they could buy an option. If these investors decide to buy an option, they may prefer the LEAPS to the short-term option because the LEAPS offers additional time for the price of Cisco to rise. They are, however, paying a higher price for the additional time. (The option writer may also prefer to sell the longer-term call because the premium is larger.) Of course, for the LEAPS to be profitable, the price of Cisco must rise sufficiently to cover the cost of the option. And if that price increase does occur, the writer of the option will sustain a loss.

15-5 Price Performance of Puts and Calls

The prices of puts and calls depend on what happens to the price of the underlying stock. This is illustrated in **Figures 15-15** and 15-16 for puts and calls on United States Steel (USX) and Teledyne. Figure 15-15 clearly illustrates the impact of the decline in USX's stock price. The stock continuously declined during the time period, causing the price of the call to fall while the price of the put rose. The call, which initially traded for $2.50, was worthless at expiration, but during the same time period the price of the put rose from less than $1 to $5.

Figure 15-16 illustrates what happens when the price of the stock fluctuates, but at the options' expiration, the price was virtually unchanged. Initially, Teledyne's stock was $34. During the next three and a half months, it fell to below $31, then rose to $36. At the option's expiration, the price was trading for $35, which was the option's strike price. As may be seen in the figure, the price of the put rose rapidly at first (i.e., its price doubled in January); however, the price fell almost as rapidly in February, and the option was worthless at expiration. The price of the call initially fell and then rose in late February in response to the increase in the stock's price. However, in late March the price of the call fell and at expiration the call was worthless.

Figure 15-15: Price of USX Stock and April Put and Call at $25

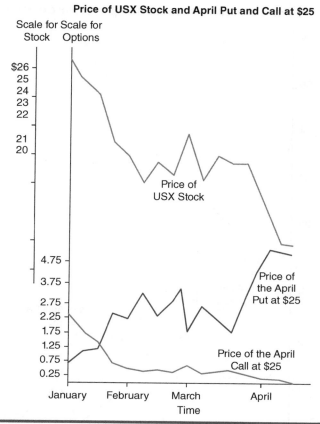

Perhaps what is most striking about Figure 15-16 is the fact that the ending price of Teledyne's stock was only $1 above the starting price. This small increase of less than 3% from January to mid-April caused the value of the put to fall from $1.62 to $0, for a 100% decline and the value of the call to fall from $2.12 to $0, also for a 100% decline. Even though the price of the stock did rise from $34 to $35, the increase was insufficient to offset the time premium the call initially commanded, so the price of the call fell.

It should be obvious from these illustrations that there can be large variations in the returns from investments in options. Since there are many options for a given stock, the investor has a mind-boggling array of possible strategies. No particular strategy can be expected to yield consistently superior results. If such a strategy existed, many investors would seek to use it, which would reduce the strategy's potential profit. As with investments in other securities (such as stocks and bonds), profits from investments in options should not tend to exceed the return consistent with the risk borne by the investor.

15-6 The Chicago Board Options Exchange

Prior to the formation of the Chicago Board Options of Exchange (CBOE) (www.cboe.com), calls were purchased from an options dealer. Each option sold was different, because the exercise price and the expiration date were negotiated with each sale. Once the option was purchased, the investor who desired to sell it had difficulty because there was no secondary market in options.

Chicago Board Options Exchange (CBOE)
an organized market for puts and calls

Figure 15-16: Prices of Teledyne Stock and the April Put and Call at $35

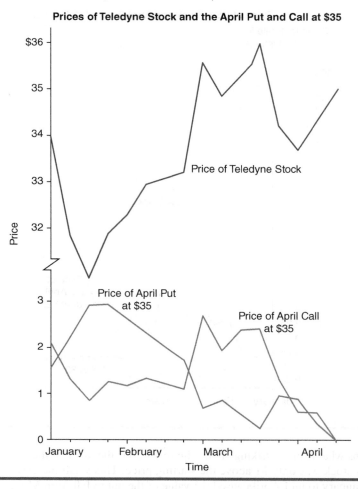

With the advent of the CBOE, an organized market in put and call options was created. For the first time, investors could buy and sell call and put options through an organized exchange. An investor purchasing a call on the CBOE knew that there would be a secondary market for that option. This ability to sell options that had been purchased gave a degree of marketability to options that previously did not exist.

The creation of a secondary market in options led to a large increase in option trading. This initial success of the CBOE exceeded expectations, and soon after its formation, other exchanges started to list options.

Transactions are continuously reported, and investors can easily obtain price quotes for puts and calls. While the formats differ, **Exhibit 15-3** illustrates the type of information that is reported. The first column gives the price of the stock (63). Next come the strike prices and the expiration dates, which are the third Friday in each of the given months (e.g., the option with a strike price of 65 expires on the third Friday in August). The last entries are the volume of trades and the prices for the calls and puts. For the August call at 65, 600 calls traded, with the last one selling for 0.60 ($60). For the August put, 350 options traded, with the last trade at 2.60 ($260). There are no entries for the February puts, which means either there were no trades or the option does not exit. The number of trades should not be confused with the number of contracts in existence, which is called the *open interest*, and which we discussed previously.

Exhibit 15-3: Option Trading Reporting

| | | | The Reporting of Option Trading | | | |
| | | | Call | | Put | |
Stock Price	Strike Price	Expiration Date	Volume	Last	Volume	Last
$63	60	Aug	1,000	$3.60	148	0.55
63	60	Sept	500	4.50	20	1.50
63	65	Aug	600	0.60	350	2.60
63	70	Feb	1,200	2.90	—	—
63	75	Feb	1,400	1.60	—	—

Exhibit 15-3 also shows price relationships between options. For example, if you compare options with the same strike price but different expiration dates, the option with the longer life commands the higher price. Both the September call and the September put with the 60 strike price traded for a higher price than the call and the put with the August expiration date ($4.50 versus $3.60 for the call). This is intuitively obvious, as there is more time for the price of the stock to move and cause the value of the option to change. If you compare options with the same expiration date but different strike prices, there is also a relationship between the option prices. For calls, the option with the lower strike price is more valuable (e.g., $3.60 versus $0.60 for the August calls at 60 and 65). For puts, the pricing relationship is the opposite. The August put at 65 sold for $2.60 while the put at 60 sold for $0.55. These relationships hold because as the price of the stock rises, call options with lower strike prices become more valuable but put options with lower strike prices become less valuable. (Option valuation is covered in more detail in the next chapter on the Black-Scholes option valuation model.)

15-7 Stock Index Options

Although put and call options were initially created for individual stocks, **stock index options** have developed in response to demand. Stock index options are similar to options based on individual stocks, but the index option is based on an aggregate measure of the market, such as the S&P's 500 stock index. In addition to puts and calls based on the aggregate market, there are options based on subsets of the market, such as computer technology stocks or pharmaceutical stocks. A sample of index, sector, and industry options and their ticker symbols is provided in **Exhibit 15-4**. These options have proved to be particularly popular and account for a substantial proportion of the daily transactions in options.

stock index option
option on an aggregate measure of the market, such as the S&P 500

Index options are popular because they permit the investor to take a position in the market or a sector without having to select specific companies. For example, suppose an investor anticipates that the stock market will rise. What does this individual do? They cannot buy every stock but must select individual stocks. (The investor could buy an index mutual fund or exchange-traded fund, as such funds construct portfolios that mirror aggregate measures of the stock market.) Remember from the previous discussion of risk that there are two sources of risk associated with the individual stock: non-diversifiable systematic risk and diversifiable unsystematic risk. One source of systematic risk is the tendency of a stock's price to move with the market. Unsystematic risk results from price movements generated by the security that are independent of the market (e.g., a takeover announcement, dividend cut, or large increase in earnings).

Exhibit 15-4: Selected Index Options and Their Ticker Symbols

Selected Index Options and Their Ticker Symbols
Index Options
Dow Jones Industrials (DJX)
S&P 100 (OEX)
S&P 500 (SPX)
Nasdaq 100 (NDX)
NYSE (NYA)
Russell 2000 (RUT)
Value Line (VAY)
Industry Options
Bank (BKW)
Biotech (BTK)
Gold/Silver (XAU)
Pharmaceuticals (DRG)
Oil Service (OSX)
SemiConductors (SOX)

Index options offer the investor an alternative to creating diversified portfolios as a means to earn the return associated with movements in the market. For example, if the investor anticipates that the market will rise in the near future, they may purchase a call option based on an index of the market as a whole (such as the S&P's 500 stock index). If the market does rise, the value of the call option also increases. The investor has avoided the unsystematic risk associated with the individual stock. In addition, the investor has avoided the commission costs necessary to construct a diversified portfolio.

If the investor anticipates the market will decline, they will purchase a stock index put. If the investor is correct and the market does fall, the value of the stock index put rises. Of course, if the market does not decline but rises instead, the investor loses the amount invested in the put option, but the maximum that the investor can lose is the cost of the option. An investor who sells stocks short instead of purchasing stock index put options may be exposed to a larger loss if stock prices rise.

Stock index options also give investors a means to manage existing portfolios. This is particularly important for portfolio managers with large holdings or individuals who want to improve the tax and risk management of these holdings. Consider a substantial stock portfolio that has appreciated in value. If the investor anticipates declining stock prices and sells the shares, this is a taxable transaction. Instead of selling the stocks, the investor may sell stock index calls or purchase stock index puts (i.e., construct a protective put using stock index puts). Then if the market declines, profits in these positions will help offset the losses on the individual stocks.

If the investor were to sell stock index call options, the value of these options would decline as the market decreased. The gain on the sale would then offset the loss in individual stocks. If the investor were to purchase stock index put options, the value of the options would increase if the market declined. The loss on the portfolio would be offset by the gain on the put option. (The amount offset would depend on how many put options the investor purchased. The number of options necessary to hedge a portfolio is discussed in the next chapter in the section addressing the hedge ratio.) As these two cases illustrate, stock index options offer the investor a means to hedge existing portfolios against a decline in the market without having to liquidate the positions and thus incur the capital gains tax liability. By buying or selling the appropriate stock index option, the investor achieves protection of capital without selling the appreciated securities.

There is one major difference between stock index options and put and call options on specific stocks. With a call option to buy shares of IBM, the owner may exercise the option and buy the stock. With a put option to sell shares of IBM, the owner may exercise the option by delivering shares of IBM stock. Such purchases or deliveries are not possible with a stock index option. The owner of the call cannot exercise it and receive the index. Instead, stock index options are settled in cash. For example, suppose the owner of a call based on the S&P's 500 index does not sell the option prior to expiration (i.e., does not close the position). At expiration the intrinsic value of the option is determined and that amount is paid by the seller of the option to the buyer (the owner). Of course, if the option has no intrinsic value at expiration, it is worthless and expires. The seller of the option then has no further obligation to the option's owner. In that case the premium paid for the option (i.e., its price) becomes profit for the seller.

15-8 Currency and Interest Rate Options

While most investors may think of options as the right to buy and sell stock, puts and calls are not limited to equities. There are also options to buy and sell currencies and debt securities (interest rate options). The principles that apply to the options to buy and sell stock also apply to currency and interest rate options.

Individuals may buy or sell these options in anticipation of price movements or to generate income from the sales. Suppose an investor expects the price of the British pound to rise. That investor purchases a call option to buy pounds at a specified price within a specified time period. If the price of the pound did rise, the value of the option would also increase. If the investor expects the price of the British pound to fall, they purchase a put option to sell pounds at a specified price within a specified time period. If the price of the pound did fall, the value of the option would increase. In both cases the price of the option is its intrinsic value plus the time premium.

In order for the investor to purchase a currency option, someone has to be selling the put or call. As in the case of options to buy stock, the seller can be naked or covered. The naked seller of the call option is anticipating that the price of the currency will not rise, and the naked seller of the put options is anticipating that the value of currency will not decline. Obviously, both the buyer and the seller of the option cannot be correct. If the price of the currency does rise, the buyer of the call profits at the expense of the seller, while the seller of the put option profits at the expense of the buyer.

Currency options, however, are not just used to speculate on an anticipated change in the price of a currency. They are also used to help manage risk. If an investor has a position in a currency, that individual may take the opposite position in a currency option. For example, suppose an investor owns several British stocks (e.g., has a long position in the stocks) and wants to reduce the risk from a decline in the value of the pound. If that investor purchases a put option on the pound, then the value of the option rises when the currency declines, which helps offset any loss the investor might experience from the value of the currency declining.

interest rate option
an option to buy and sell debt securities

Interest rate options work essentially the same way, except the investor has to think of them in reverse. If an investor expects interest rates to fall, that individual buys a call option. This may seem backward because the investor is buying the call option in anticipation of interest rates declining. However, since lower interest rates will increase the price of the underlying bond, buying a call option is the correct strategy. If an investor expects interest rates to rise and bond prices to fall, the investor would buy a put. If this individual is right and interest rates do fall, the value of the option increases, since the investor has an option to sell the bond at the price specified in the option.

Individuals who own bonds may use these options to reduce interest rate risk. If the investor were to purchase a put option and interest rates were to rise, the increase in the value of the put would offset some (perhaps all) of the decline in the bonds' value. The investor would continue to collect the interest paid by the bonds, and, in the event the bonds had to be sold, the loss on the bonds would be offset by the gain on the option. This offsetting of loss means that the investor has reduced the risk associated with changes in interest rates.

15-9 Warrants

warrant
a call option issued by firms on their own shares

The preceding material covered calls and puts on stocks that are created by third parties, independent of the firms that issued shares. However, firms may also issue options in the form of **warrants**. Like a call, a warrant is an option issued by a company to buy its stock at a specified price within a specified time period, but warrants tend to be much longer-lived than typical call options offered by third parties and may have some unique attributes. For example, the specified exercise price may rise at predetermined intervals (e.g., every five years) or the firm may have the right to extend the expiration date or to call the warrant.

Most warrants are an option, or right, to buy one share of common stock. Some warrants, however, are the option to buy more or less than one share. Such terms may be the result of stock dividends, stock splits, or a merger. For example, a warrant that is the option to buy 0.4 share may have evolved through a merger. The warrant initially represented the option to purchase one share of the company. However, when the company subsequently merged into another firm, the terms of the merger were 0.4 share of the acquiring firm (i.e., the surviving company) for each share of the company being acquired. The warrant then became an option to buy one share that had been converted into 0.4 share of the surviving company.

If a warrant is an option to buy more or less than one share, the strike price and the market price of the warrant can be readily converted to a per-share basis. Such conversion is desirable to facilitate comparisons among warrants. Consider, for example, an option that gives the right to buy 0.4 share at $10 and is currently selling for $4. The warrant's strike price and market price are divided by the number of shares that the warrant is an option to buy. Thus, the per-share strike price is $25 ($10 ÷ 0.4), and the per-share market price is $10 ($4 ÷ 0.4). Stated differently, 2.5 warrants are necessary to buy one share for $25.

Warrants are usually issued by firms in conjunction with other financing. They are attached to other securities, such as debentures or preferred stock, and are a sweetener to induce investors to purchase the securities. For example, AT&T and Chrysler Corporation issued bonds and preferred stock with warrants attached, where the warrants were an added inducement to purchase the securities.

When a warrant is exercised, the firm issues new stock and receives the proceeds. For this reason, most warrants usually have a finite life. The expiration date ultimately forces the holder to exercise the option if the strike price is less than the current market price of the stock. However, if the strike price exceeds the stock's price at expiration (i.e., if the warrant has no intrinsic value), the warrant will not be exercised and will expire. After the expiration date, the warrant is worthless. This was the case with the Berkshire Realty warrant, which was the option to buy the stock at $11.79. The stock sold for $9.625 on the expiration date. No one would exercise a warrant to buy stock at $11.79 that could be bought for $9.625, so the warrant expired.

Other than those few idiosyncratic attributes, warrants are very similar to calls; their definitions are essentially identical. They offer speculators potential leverage because the price of a warrant moves with the price of the underlying stock. Since the warrant sells for a lower price than the underlying stock, the percentage increase in the price of the warrant tends to exceed the percentage increase in the price of the stock. The converse is also true: The percentage decline in the price of the warrant will exceed the percentage decline in the price of the stock. Again, leverage works both ways.

15-10 Futures and Forward Contracts

While calls and puts represent claims against underlying shares of stock, **futures contracts** and **forward contracts** allow you to speculate on those shares as well as on contracts of commodities, or the raw materials used in industry, such as oil, pork bellies, corn, etc. It should be noted, though, these futures contracts are among the riskiest investments available, as prices can change rapidly and produce sudden losses or profits.

There are two participants in the futures markets: the speculators who establish positions in anticipation of price changes, and the hedgers who employ futures contracts to reduce risk. The hedgers are growers, producers, and other users of commodities. They seek to protect themselves from price fluctuations, and by hedging they pass the risk of loss to the speculators. The price of a futures contract ultimately depends on the demand for and supply of these contracts by the hedgers and speculators.

Although futures contracts are not appropriate assets for the vast majority of investors, many individuals indirectly participate in these markets. Some corporate financial managers use futures contracts to reduce risk from commodity price fluctuations, changes in interest rates, and changes in currency prices. Portfolio managers also employ futures contracts to reduce risk from fluctuations in securities prices. This usage is often disclosed in the financial statements investors receive from corporations and mutual funds. So, while individual investors may never personally participate in futures markets, they will have a better understanding of financial statements if they have a basic knowledge of these contracts and how the contracts are used for speculating and for hedging.

futures contract
an agreement traded on an organized exchange to buy and sell an underlying asset at a particular date in the future for a locked-in price

forward contract
a *customized* agreement to buy and sell an underlying asset at a particular date in the future for a locked-in price that is not traded on an organized exchange

15-10a Investing in Commodity Futures

Individuals participate in many markets for goods and services in which they may be buyers or sellers. You may buy or sell a house or car; any number of restaurants may sell you a hamburger or slice of pizza. Markets exist for many products and services, but these are not futures markets. Futures markets have developed for specific commodities, such as corn, oil, or gold. Of course, you may buy items such as corn or gasoline, but these are consumer goods and not investments. Even purchasing gold jewelry is rarely considered solely an investment. Acquiring futures contracts for corn or oil or gold, however, is a type of investment, even if the investment is considered a risky speculation. What differentiates buying gold jewelry from buying a gold futures contract?

The answer lies in the fact that certain goods, those that are suited for trading through futures contracts, are perfect substitutes for each other. The assets are "fungible." Gold that is mined in North America is no different than gold mined in South Africa, provided it has the same purity. The same concept applies to all commodities that trade through the futures markets. There is no difference in oil, wheat, or orange juice, provided the commodity meets the specifications associated with the particular contract. And the same concept applies to currencies and debt instruments. A euro acquired in Berlin is no different than a euro acquired in Paris. A 30-year federal government bond purchased in New York is no different than one purchased in Chicago. These assets are fungible, and this substitutability is a necessary condition for the development of futures markets.

15-10b Futures Markets

A commodity such as corn may be purchased for current delivery or for future delivery. Investing in futures refers to a contract to buy or to sell (deliver) a commodity in the future. For this reason, these contracts are often referred to as *futures*. A futures contract is a formal agreement between a buyer or seller and a commodity exchange. In the case of a purchase contract, the buyer agrees to accept a specific commodity that meets a specified quality in a specified month. In the case of a sale, the seller agrees to deliver the specified commodity during the designated month.

Investing in commodity futures is considered to be very speculative. For that reason, investors should participate in this market only after their financial obligations and primary financial goals have been met. There is a large probability that the investor will suffer a loss on any particular purchase or sale of a commodity contract. Individuals who buy and sell commodity contracts without wanting to deal in the actual commodities are generally referred to as *speculators*, which differentiates them from the growers, processors, warehousers, and other dealers who also buy and sell commodity futures but really wish to buy or sell the actual commodity.

As discussed previously in the context of options, the primary appeal of commodity contracts to speculators is the potential for a large return on the investment resulting from the leverage inherent in commodity trading. This leverage exists because (1) a futures contract controls a substantial amount of the commodity, and (2) the investor must make only a small payment to buy or sell a contract (i.e., there is a small margin requirement). These two points are discussed in detail later in this chapter.

Like stocks and bonds, commodity futures are traded in several markets. One of the most important is the Chicago Mercantile Exchange (CME, or "the MERC"), which acquired the Chicago Board of Trade (www.cmegroup.com) and formed the CME Group Inc. CME Group subsequently acquired the New York Mercantile Exchange (NYMEX). The CME Group trades a variety of commodity futures, such as corn and soybeans, and futures for currencies and for debt and equity instruments. Other commodities (e.g., coffee and cocoa and energy resources, such as oil and natural gas) trade through the Intercontinental Exchange (www.theice.com).

Individuals acquire commodity futures through brokers who act on behalf of the investor by purchasing and selling the contracts through a commodity exchange. The investor opens an account by signing an agreement that requires the contracts to be guaranteed. Since trading commodity contracts is considered to be speculative, brokers will open accounts only after the investor has proved the capacity both to finance the account and to withstand the losses.

Once the account has been opened, the individual may trade commodity contracts. These are bought and sold in much the same way as stocks and bonds; however, the use of the words *buy* and *sell* is misleading. The individual does not buy or sell a contract, but enters a contract to buy or sell. A buy contract specifies that the individual will *accept* delivery and hence "buy" the commodity. A sell contract specifies that the individual will *make* delivery and hence "sell" the commodity.

A commodity order specifies whether the contract is a buy or a sell, the type of commodity and the number of units, and the delivery date (i.e., the month in which the contract is to be executed and the commodity is bought or sold). The investor can request a market order and have the contract executed at the current market price, or they may place orders at specified prices. Such orders may be for a day or until the investor cancels them (i.e., the order is good till canceled). Once the order is executed, the broker provides a confirmation statement for the sale or purchase and charges a commission for executing the order. This fee covers both the purchase and the sale of the contract.

Although a futures contract appears to involve a buyer and a seller, the actual contract is made between the individual and the exchange. If an individual buys a contract, the exchange guarantees the delivery (the sale). If an individual sells a contract, the exchange guarantees to take delivery (the purchase). When a contract is created, the exchange simultaneously makes an opposite contract with another investor. While the exchange has offsetting buy and sell contracts, the effect is to guarantee the integrity of the contracts. If one of the parties were to default (e.g., the buyer), the seller's contract is upheld by the exchange.

15-10c Commodity Positions

The investor may purchase a contract for future delivery. This is the long position, in which the investor will profit if the price of the commodity and hence the value of the contract rise. The investor may also sell a contract for future delivery. This is the short position, in which the seller agrees to make good the contract (i.e., to deliver the goods) sometime in the future. This investor will profit if the price of the commodity and hence the value of the contract decline. These long and short positions are analogous to the long and short positions that the investor takes in the securities market. Long positions generate profits when the value of the security rises, whereas short positions result in profits when the value of the security declines.

The way in which each position generates a profit can be seen in a simple example. Assume that the **futures price** of wheat is $3.50 per bushel. If a contract is purchased for delivery in six months at $3.50 per bushel, the buyer will profit from this long position if the price of wheat *rises*. If the price increases to $4.00 per bushel, the buyer can exercise the contract by taking delivery and paying $3.50 per bushel. The speculator then sells the wheat for $4 per bushel, which produces a profit of $0.50 per bushel.

futures price
the price agreed to in a futures contract

The opposite occurs when the price of wheat declines. If the price of wheat falls to $3.00 per bushel, the individual who bought the contract for delivery at $3.50 suffers a loss. But the speculator who sold the contract for the delivery of wheat (i.e., who took the short position) earns a profit from the price decline. The speculator can then buy wheat at the market price (which is referred to as the **spot price**) of $3.00, deliver it for the contract price of $3.50, and earn a $0.50 profit per bushel.

spot price
the current market price of a commodity for immediate delivery

If the price rises, the short position will produce a loss. If the price increases from $3.50 to $4.00 per bushel, the speculator who sold a contract for delivery suffers a loss of $0.50 per bushel, because they must pay $4.00 to obtain the wheat that will be delivered for $3.50 per bushel.

For speculators, the preceding losses and profits are generated without the goods being delivered. Of course, when a speculator enters a contract to accept future delivery, there is always the possibility that this individual will receive the goods. Conversely, if the speculator enters a contract to make future delivery, there is the possibility that the goods will have to be supplied. However, such deliveries occur infrequently because the speculator can offset the contract before the delivery date. This is achieved by buying back a contract that was previously sold or selling a contract that is owned.

This process of offsetting existing contracts is illustrated in the following example. Suppose a speculator has a contract to buy wheat in January. If the individual wants to close the position, they can enter a contract for the delivery of wheat (to sell) in January. The two contracts cancel (i.e., offset) each other, as one is a purchase and the other is a sale. (This process is analogous to the writer of an option buying back the option. In both cases, the investor's position is closed.) If the speculator actually received the wheat by executing the purchase agreement, they could pass on the wheat by executing the sell agreement. However, since the two contracts offset each other, the actual delivery and subsequent sale are not necessary. Instead, the speculator's position in wheat is closed, and the actual physical transfers do not occur.

Correspondingly, if the speculator has a contract for the sale of wheat in January, it can be canceled by entering a contract for the purchase of wheat in January. If the speculator were called upon to deliver wheat as the result of the contract to sell, the individual would exercise the contract to purchase wheat. The buy and sell contracts would then cancel each other, and no physical transfers of wheat would occur. Once again the speculator has closed the initial position by taking the opposite position (i.e., the sales contract is offset by a purchase contract).

Because these contracts are canceled and actual deliveries do not take place, it should not be assumed that profits or losses do not occur. The two contracts need not be executed at the same price. For example, the speculator may enter a contract for the future purchase of wheat at $3.50 per bushel. Any contract for the future delivery of comparable wheat can cancel the contract for the purchase. But the cost of the wheat for future delivery could be $3.60 or $3.40 (or any conceivable price). If the price of wheat rises (e.g., from $3.50 to $3.60 per bushel), the speculator with a long position earns a profit. However, if the speculator has a short position (i.e., a contract to sell wheat), this individual sustains a loss. If the price declines (e.g., from $3.50 to $3.40 per bushel), the short seller earns a profit, but the long position sustains a loss.

However, when it comes to growers, processors, warehousers, and other dealers who also buy and sell commodity futures but really wish to buy or sell the actual commodity, they often enter into a futures contract because they either expect to have and need to sell (on the part of producers) or expect to need to buy (on the part of manufacturers, warehousers, etc.) the underlying commodities. For these participants in the futures markets, futures contracts allow them to "lock in" the price they will get/pay for the underlying commodities. Rather that adding risk to their business operations, futures allow them to reduce risks of positions they already hold, similar in effect to our previous discussion of the owner of a share buying a put to immunize themselves against dips in the stock price.

The key difference here, however, is that these participants, rather than paying an option premium to insure themselves against "one side" of the risk (e.g. the share price going down, as previously discussed), immunize themselves against prices shifting against them (down for commodity producers, or up for commodity purchasers) by giving up the potential that prices may shift in their favor. A farmer, for example, may lock in a price of $2.50 per bushel for corn they expect to harvest in July; if the spot price for corn when July gets here is below that price, they will be glad they did so, but if corn is selling for, say, $2.80 a bushel in July, they may regret entering into the futures contract. But they gave up the opportunity to earn more than $2.50 in exchange for insuring that they wouldn't earn less than $2.50.

15-10d The Units of Commodity Contracts

To facilitate trading, contracts must be uniform. For a particular commodity, the contracts must be identical. Besides specifying the delivery month, the contract must specify the grade and type of the commodity (e.g., a particular type of wheat) and the units of the commodity (e.g., 5,000 bushels). Thus, when an individual buys or sells a contract, there can be no doubt as to the nature of the obligation. For example, if the investor buys wheat for January delivery, there can be no confusion with a contract for the purchase of wheat for February delivery. These are two different commodities in the same way that AT&T common stock, AT&T preferred stock, and AT&T bonds are all different securities. Without such standardization of contracts there would be chaos in the commodity (or any) markets.

The units of trading vary with each commodity. For example, if the investor buys a contract for corn, the unit of trading is 5,000 bushels. If the investor buys a contract for lumber, the unit of trading is 110,000 board feet. Although the novice investor may not remember the units for a contract, the experienced investor is certainly aware of them. As will be explained later, because of the large units of many commodity contracts, a small change in the price of the commodity produces a considerable change in the value of the contract and in the investor's profits or losses.

15-10e Reporting of Futures Trading

Commodity futures prices and the number of contracts in existence are reported in the financial press. Typical reporting is as follows:

	Open	High	Low	Settle	Change	LIFETIME High	Low	Open Interest
Corn 5,000 bu; cents per bushel								
Jan	233.0	233.5	230.5	230.50	−3.00	243	210.75	36,790
Mar	240.0	241.5	236.5	237.25	—	270	205.0	10,900
May	244.5	244.5	241.0	241.75	+0.25	286	221.0	5,444

The unit of trading is 5,000 bushels (bu), and prices are quoted in cents. The opening price for January delivery was 233.0 ($2.330) per bushel. The high, low, and closing (settle) prices were 233.5¢, 230.5¢, and 230.5¢, respectively. This closing price was 3 cents below the closing price on the previous day. The high and low (prior to the reported day of trading) for the lifetime of the contract were 243¢ and 210.75¢, respectively. The open interest, which is the number of contracts in existence, was 36,790.

This open interest varies over the life of the contract. Initially, the open interest rises as buyers and sellers establish positions. It then declines as the delivery date approaches and the positions are closed. This changing number of contracts is illustrated in **Figure 15-17**, which plots the spot and futures prices and the open interest for a September contract to buy Kansas City wheat. When the contracts were initially traded in November, there were only a few contracts in existence. By June the open interest had risen to over 10,000 contracts. Then, as the remaining life of the contracts declined, the number of contracts fell as the various participants closed their positions. By late September, only a few contracts were still outstanding.

As is explained in the section on pricing, futures prices tend to exceed spot prices. If speculators anticipate higher prices, they will buy contracts for future delivery.

Figure 15-17: Spot and Futures Prices and Open Interest for a September Contract for Kansas City Wheat

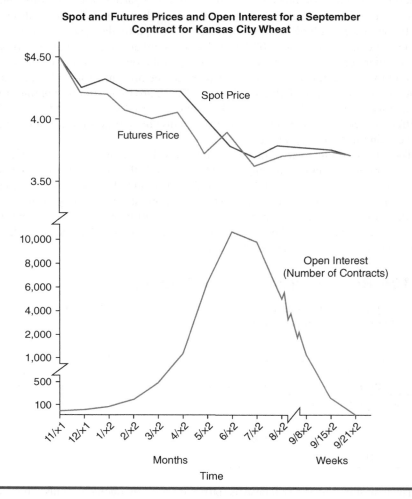

Spot and Futures Prices and Open Interest for a September
Contract for Kansas City Wheat

This anticipation of inflation and the cost of storing commodities usually drive up futures prices relative to the spot price, so the futures price exceeds the current price.

Figure 15-17, however, illustrates that this relationship does not always hold. The figure gives the futures price and the spot price of Kansas City wheat, and, except for a brief period, the spot price exceeds the futures price. This inversion of the relationship occurs if speculators believe the price of the commodity will decline. These speculators sell contracts now to lock in the higher prices so they may buy back the contracts at a lower price. This selling of the futures contracts drives their price down below the spot price.

The futures price must converge with the spot price as the expiration date of the contract approaches. As with options such as puts and calls, the value of the futures contract can be worth only the value of the underlying commodity at the expiration date. This pattern of price behavior is also illustrated in Figure 15-17. In March, April, and May, there was a considerable differential between the two prices. However, in late September, the futures and spot prices converged and erased the differential.

15-10f The Regulation of Commodity Markets

The commodity exchanges, like stock exchanges, are subject to regulation. Until 1974, federal laws pertaining to commodity exchanges and commodity transaction laws were enforced by the Commodity Exchange Authority, a division of the Department of Agriculture. In 1974, Congress created the Commodity Futures Trading Commission (www.cftc.gov) to control entry into and operation of the futures markets. As with the regulation of securities transactions, the regulations do not protect investors or speculators from their own folly. Instead, the regulations establish uniform standards for each commodity. The regulatory authority also has control over trading procedures, the hours of trading, and the maximum allowable daily price movements.

15-10g Forward Contracts

In addition to futures contracts, there are also forward contracts. These are essentially the same as futures contracts, with a couple of important different features. A futures contract is a standardized contract between two parties that specifies the amount of the commodity and the delivery date. Since the contract is standardized, futures may be bought and sold through organized futures markets. On the other hand, a forward contract is a contract between two parties but is tailor-made for each transaction. The uniqueness of each forward contract makes it adaptable to the specific needs of the respective parties.

Forward contracts are common in the normal course of business. Any contract for the future delivery of a commodity or service is a forward contract. For example, a magazine subscription or an airline ticket illustrates a forward contract. In each case, one party contracts to deliver a commodity (the magazine) or service (the plane ride) at specified future dates and for a specified amount of money. The money may be paid when the contract is executed or upon delivery.

Many businesses could not exist without forward contracts in which one party agrees to provide something in the future for a specified price and the other party agrees to take delivery and pay the specified price. Firms, governments, and households enter such contracts, and each contract creates legal obligations on both parties.

Although a forward contract specifies the amount and delivery date, the uniqueness of its features reduces the marketability of the contract. When the contract is written, the intention is to maintain the contract until delivery, so there are no organized forward markets. In effect, forward contracts are illiquid futures contracts. There is, however, some trading of forward contracts over-the-counter among financial institutions. In addition, if a firm has a forward contract to buy a commodity, it may enter into another contract to deliver the commodity. In effect, the two forward contracts cancel each other.

In addition to the lack of liquidity, the other important difference between forward and futures contracts is daily settlement, which applies to futures contracts but not to forward contracts. Forward contracts are not marked to the market daily, and funds are not transferred between the two parties. Final settlement thus occurs when the commodity is delivered and paid for as specified in the contract.

15-11 Leverage of Futures and Forward Contracts

Commodities are paid for on delivery. Thus, a contract for future delivery means that the goods do not have to be paid for when the individual enters the contract. Instead, the investor (either a buyer or a seller) provides an amount of money, which is called margin, to protect the exchange and the broker and to guarantee the contract. This margin should not be confused with the margin that is used in the purchase of stocks and bonds. In the trading of stocks and bonds, margin represents the investor's equity in the position, whereas margin for a commodity contract is a deposit to show the investor's good faith and to protect the broker against an adverse change in the price of the commodity.

In the stock market, the amount of margin required varies with the price of the security, but in the commodity markets, the amount of margin does not vary with the dollar value of the transaction. Instead, each contract has a fixed minimum margin requirement. These margin requirements are established by the commodity exchanges but cannot be below the minimums established by the U.S. Commodity Futures Trading Commission. Individual brokers may require more, especially for small accounts.

The margin requirements are only a small percentage of the value of the contract. For example, the $1,400 margin requirement for cocoa gives the owner of the contract a claim on 10 metric tons of cocoa. If cocoa is selling for $1,400 a metric ton, the total value of the contract is $14,000. The margin requirement as a percentage of the value of the contract is only 10% ($1,400/$14,000). This small amount of margin is one reason why a commodity contract offers so much potential leverage.

The potential leverage from speculating in commodity futures may be illustrated in a simple example. Consider a contract to buy wheat at $3.50 per bushel. Such a contract controls 5,000 bushels of wheat worth a total of $17,500 (5,000 × $3.50). If the investor buys this contract and the margin requirement is $1,000, they must remit $1,000. An increase of only $0.20 per bushel in the price of the commodity produces an increase of $1,000 in the value of the contract. This $1,000 is simply the product of the price change ($0.20) and the number of units in the contract (5,000). The profit on the contract if sold is $1,000.

What is the percentage return on the investment? With a margin of $1,000 the return is 100%, because the investor put up $1,000 and then earned an additional $1,000. An increase of less than 6% in the price of wheat produced a return on the speculator's money of 100%. Such a return is the result of leverage that comes from the small margin requirement and the large amount of the commodity controlled by the contract.

Leverage, of course, works both ways. In the previous example, if the price of the wheat declines by $0.10, the contract will be worth $17,000. A decline of only 2.9% in the price reduces the investor's margin from $1,000 to $500. To maintain the position, the investor must deposit additional margin with the broker. The request for additional funds is referred to as a **margin call**. Failure to meet the margin call will result in the broker closing the position. Since the contract is supported only by the initial margin, further price declines will mean that there is less collateral to support the contract. Should the investor (i.e., the buyer or the seller) default on the contract, the exchange becomes responsible for its execution. The margin call thus protects the exchange.

Actually, there are two margin requirements. The first is the minimum initial deposit, and the second is the **maintenance margin**. The maintenance margin specifies when the investor must deposit additional funds with the broker to cover a decline in the value of a commodity contract. For example, the margin requirement for wheat is $1,000 and the maintenance margin is $750. If the investor owns a contract for the purchase of wheat and the value of the contract declines by $250 to the level of the maintenance margin ($750), the broker makes a margin call. This requires the investor to deposit an additional $250 into the account, which restores the initial $1,000 margin.

margin call
a requirement for a party to a futures contract to put more funds into the contract

maintenance margin
the minimum amount that a party to a futures contract must keep on account to cover shifts in the underlying asset that cause them to owe money to the other party

Maintenance margin applies to both buyers and sellers. If, in the previous example, the price of wheat were to rise by $250, the speculators who had sold short would see their margin decline from the initial deposit of $1,000 to $750. The broker would then make a margin call, which would require the short sellers to restore the $1,000 margin. Once again this protects the exchange, as the value of the contract has risen and the short sellers has sustained the loss.

These margin adjustments occur daily. After the market closes, the value of each account is totaled. In the jargon of futures trading, each account is **marked to the market**. If a position has gained in value, funds are transferred into the account. If a position has lost value, funds are transferred out of the account. The effect is to transfer the funds from the accounts that have sustained losses to those accounts that have experienced gains. If, as a result of the transfer of funds, the account does not meet the maintenance margin requirement, the broker issues a margin call that the individual must meet or the broker will close the position.

marked to the market refers to the action of calculating the gain in value to a futures contract due to changes in the underlying spot price; is usually performed once a day at the close of trading

The process of marking to the market and daily cash flows may be seen in the following example for a futures contract for 5,000 bushels of a commodity (e.g., wheat or corn). The futures price is $3.00, the margin requirement is $1,500, and the maintenance margin requirement is $800. There are two speculators, one who expects the price to rise and enters the contract to buy (i.e., is long) and the other who is short and enters the contract to sell. Both make the initial $1,500 margin payment, so at the end of the first day, their respective positions are as follows:

Day 1   Futures price: $3.00

Value of the contract: $15,000

Margin positions:

Speculator Long	Speculator Short
$1,500	$1,500

During the second day, the futures price rises to $3.05 and the margin accounts are as follows:

Day 2   Futures price: $3.05

Value of the contract: $15,250

Margin positions:

	Speculator Long	Speculator Short
Beginning balance	$1,500	$1,500
Change in balance	+250	−250
Required deposits	—	—
Voluntary withdrawals	250	—
Ending balance	$1,500	$1,250

Notice that Speculator Long has gained $250 while Speculator Short has lost $250, and the appropriate adjustments are made at the end of the day as each account is marked to the market. Since both accounts have more than $800, both meet the maintenance margin requirement, so no deposits of additional funds are needed. Speculator Long, however, may remove $250, as the account exceeds the initial margin requirement. These funds may be invested (e.g., in a money market account) to earn interest.

During the third day, the futures price continues to rise to $3.20 a bushel, so the value of the contract is $16,000. The positions for each account are now as follows:

Day 3   Futures price: $3.20

Value of the contract: $16,000

Margin positions:

	Speculator Long	Speculator Short
Beginning balance	$1,500	$1,250
Change in balance	+750	−750
Ending balance	$2,250	$500

Speculator Long may remove an additional $750, as the account again exceeds the margin requirement. Speculator Short's position is now less than the maintenance margin requirement. They will have to restore the account to the initial margin ($1,500), which will require an additional $1,000. After these changes, the accounts will be as follows:

	Speculator Long	Speculator Short
Beginning balance	$1,500	$1,250
Change in balance	+750	−750
Balance	2,250	500
Required deposits	—	1,000
Voluntary withdrawals	−750	—
Closing balance	$1,500	$1,500

Notice that Speculator Long's $1,000 gain equals Speculator Short's $1,000 loss. If the futures price had declined from $3.00 to $2.80, the cash flows would have been reversed. Speculator Short would have $2,500 in the account and could remove $1,000, while Speculator Long would have only $500. Speculator Long would receive a margin call for $1,000 to restore the account to $1,500.

Whether the speculator chooses to meet the margin call is, of course, that person's decision, but a primary purpose of daily marking all positions to the market is to let the process of transferring funds occur. If a participant fails to meet a margin call, the broker closes the position so that losses will not continue to increase (and put the brokerage firm at risk). Since speculators are highly aware of their risk exposure and often rapidly close positions, the probability they will receive a margin call is small. Such speculators rapidly close losing positions in order to limit their losses.

Although commodity prices can and do fluctuate, limits are imposed by the markets on the amount of price change permitted each day. The **daily limit** establishes the maximum permissible price increase or decrease from the previous day. The purpose of these limits is to help maintain orderly markets and to reduce the potentially disruptive effects from large daily swings in the price of the futures contract. (The daily limit applies to many futures prices but not all, especially financial futures based on federal government debt and stock index futures.)

Once the price of the futures contract rises by the permissible daily limit, further price increases are not allowed. This does not necessarily mean that trading ceases, because transactions can still occur at the maximum price or below should the price of the commodity weaken. The same applies to declining prices. Once the daily limit has been reached, the price cannot continue to fall, but transactions can still occur at

daily limit
the maximum amount of allowed daily price change on a futures contract.

the lowest price or above should the price strengthen. For example, when the 1992 Florida orange crop came in at the higher end of expectations, orange juice futures prices quickly fell. Contracts for January, February, and March delivery declined by the 5¢ daily limit. Although trading could have continued at the lowest price, trading ceased because no one was willing to buy at that level and speculators anticipated further price declines. The same result occurred during the 2003 mad cow disease scare. Even though the Chicago Mercantile Exchange *increased* the daily limit, the futures price of beef declined to the new daily limit and trading ceased. The same principle applies to price increases. In 2011, the flooding in Thailand threatened the rice crops. The expectation that the price of the commodity would increase caused rice futures to rise dramatically. The price reached the daily limit and trading ceased.

15-12 Hedging with Futures and Forward Contracts

As with the growth of options, one major reason for the development of commodity futures markets was the desire of producers to reduce the risk of loss through price fluctuations. The procedure for this reduction in risk is called **hedging** and consists of taking opposite positions at the same time. In effect, a hedger simultaneously takes the long and the short position in a particular commodity.

hedging
the use of derivative contracts to immunize against risk in an underlying asset that the party already has a stake in

Hedging is best explained by illustrations. In the first example, a wheat farmer expects to harvest a crop at a specified time. Since the costs of production are determined, the farmer knows the price that is necessary to earn a profit. Although the price that will be paid for wheat at harvest time is unknown, the current price of a contract for the future delivery of wheat is known. The farmer can then enter a contract for future delivery. Such a contract is a hedged position because the farmer takes a long position (the wheat in the ground) and a short position (the contract for future delivery).

Such a position reduces the farmer's risk of loss from a price decline. Suppose the cost to produce the wheat is $2.50 per bushel and September wheat is selling in June for $2.75. If the farmer *sells* wheat for September delivery, a $0.25 per bushel profit is assured, because the buyer of the contract agrees to pay $2.75 per bushel on delivery in September. If the price of wheat declines to $2.50, the farmer is still assured of $2.75. However, if the price of wheat rises to $3.10 in September, the farmer still gets only $2.75. The additional $0.35 gain goes to the owner of the contract who bought the wheat for $2.75 but can now sell it for $3.10.

Is this transaction unfair? Remember that the farmer wanted protection against a decline in the price of wheat. If the price had declined to $2.40 and the farmer had not hedged, the farmer would have suffered a loss of $0.10 (the $2.40 price minus the $2.50 cost) per bushel. To obtain protection from this risk of loss, the farmer accepted the modest profit of $0.25 per bushel and relinquished the possibility of a larger profit. The speculator who entered the contract to buy bore the risk of loss from a price decline and received the reward from a price increase.

Users of wheat hedge in the opposite direction. A flour producer desires to know the future cost of wheat in order to plan production levels and the prices that will be charged to distributors. However, the spot price of wheat need not hold into the future, so this producer *enters* a contract for future delivery and thereby hedges the position. This is hedging because the producer has a long position (the contract for the future delivery of wheat) and a short position (the future production of flour, which requires the future delivery of wheat).

If the producer enters a contract in June for the delivery of wheat in September at $2.75 per bushel, the future cost of the grain becomes known. The producer cannot be hurt by an increase in the price of wheat from $2.75 to $3.10, because the contract is for delivery at $2.75. However, the producer has forgone the chance of profit from a decline in the price of wheat from $2.75 to $2.40 per bushel.

Instead, the possibility of profit from a decline in the price of wheat rests with the speculator who owns the contract to sell. If the price of wheat were to decline, the speculator could buy the wheat in September at the lower price, deliver it, and collect the $2.75 that is specified in the contract. However, this speculator would suffer a loss if the price of September wheat rose over $2.75. The cost would then exceed the delivery price specified in the contract.

These two examples illustrate why growers and producers hedge. They often take the opposite side of hedge positions. If all growers and producers agree on prices for future delivery, there would be no need for speculators; but this is not the case. Speculators buy or sell contracts when there is an excess or an insufficient supply. If the farmer in the preceding example could not find a producer to buy the contract for the future delivery of wheat, a speculator would buy the contract and accept the risk of a price decline. If the producer could not find a farmer to supply a contract for the future delivery of wheat, the speculator would sell the contract and accept the risk of a price increase.

Of course, farmers, producers, and speculators are simultaneously entering contracts to buy and sell. No one knows who buys and who sells at a specific moment. However, if there is an excess or a shortage of one type of contract, the futures price of the commodity changes, which induces a certain behavior. For example, if September wheat is quoted at $2.75 per bushel, but no one is willing to buy at that price, the price declines. This induces some potential sellers to withdraw from the market and some potential buyers to enter the market. By this process, an imbalance of supply and demand for contracts for a particular delivery date is erased. It is the interaction of the hedgers and the speculators that establishes the price of each contract.

15-13 The Selection of Commodity Futures Contracts

As with the selection of securities, there are two basic methods for the selection of commodity futures contracts: the technical approach and the fundamental approach. The technical approach uses the same methods that are applied to the selection of securities. Various averages, point-and-figure charts, and bar graphs and their patterns are constructed for various commodities and are used to identify current price movements and to predict future price movements. Since this material was covered earlier in the book, it is not repeated here.

The fundamental approach is primarily concerned with those factors that affect the demand for and the supply of the various commodities. Although the approach is similar to the selection of securities in that it uses economic data, the specifics are different. The price of a commodity depends on the supply of that commodity relative to the demand. Since the commodities are produced (e.g., wheat) or mined (e.g., silver), there are identifiable sources of supply. Correspondingly, there are identifiable sources of demand. However, a variety of exogenous factors may also affect the supply of or the demand for a particular commodity, and these factors can have a powerful impact on the price of a specific commodity.

To illustrate these points, consider a basic commodity such as wheat. It takes several months for wheat to be produced. It has to be planted, grown, and harvested. The amount of wheat that is planted is known because statistics are kept by the U.S. Department of Agriculture. Such statistics are necessary for government forecasts of the economy, and this information is certainly available to those firms and individuals concerned with the size of the wheat crop.

The size of the crop that is planted and the size that is harvested, however, may be considerably different. The actual harvest depends on other factors. Particularly important is the weather, which can increase or decrease the yield. Good weather at the appropriate time can result in a bountiful harvest. A larger than anticipated supply of wheat should depress its price. On the other hand, bad weather, be it drought or excess rain, will significantly reduce the anticipated supply. A reduction in supply should increase the price of wheat.

Demand, like supply, depends on both predictable and unpredictable forces. The demand for wheat depends on the needs of the firms that use the grain in their products. The producers of flour and cereals are obvious potential customers for wheat. However, the total demand also includes exports. If a foreign government enters the market and buys a substantial amount of wheat, this may cause a significant increase in its price.

Such government intervention in the market is not limited to foreign governments. The U.S. government also buys and sells commodities. Sometimes it buys to absorb excess supplies of a commodity and thus supports the commodity's price. In other cases, the federal government may sell from its surplus stocks of a given commodity. This, of course, has the opposite impact on the price of the commodity. The increased supply tends to decrease the price or at least to reduce a tendency for the price to rise. These exogenous forces in the commodity markets are just another source of risk with which the speculator must contend.

Obviously, the speculator needs to identify shifts in demand or supply *before* they occur in order to take the appropriate position. Anticipation of a price increase indicates the purchase of a futures contract, whereas an anticipated price decline indicates the sale of a futures contract. Unfortunately, the ability to consistently predict changes in demand and supply is very rare. This should be obvious! If an individual could predict the future, they would certainly make a fortune not just in the commodity futures markets but in any market. Mortals, however, lack such clairvoyance, which leaves them with fundamental and technical analysis as means to select commodity futures for purchase.

Whether an investor uses technical or fundamental analysis, there is an important strategy for trading futures. The speculator should limit losses and permit profits to run. Successful commodity futures trading requires the speculator's ability to recognize bad positions and to close them before they generate large losses. Behavioral finance suggests that many speculators, especially novices, do the exact opposite by taking small profits as they occur but maintaining positions that sustain losses. Then, when price changes produce margin calls, the speculator is forced either to close the position at a loss or to put up additional funds. If the speculator meets the margin call by committing additional funds, that individual is violating the strategy. Instead of taking the small loss, this investor is risking additional funds in the hope that the price will recover.

15-13a Managed Futures and ETFs

Investing in futures involves considerable risk and requires active portfolio management and specialized knowledge. Can individuals participate in these specialized markets and perhaps contribute to the diversification of their portfolios? Can these investors avoid the risk associated with margin calls and reduce their need for active management? The answer is yes, by acquiring positions in investment companies that specialize in commodities.

One possible solution is managed futures. Managed futures refers to an investment company administered by professional money managers (commodity trading advisors, or CTAs). These advisors select the specific futures contracts to be bought and sold. CTAs have specializations in specific commodities and extensive knowledge of futures contracts. Managed futures thus allow individual investors to avoid actively managing a futures portfolio and making investment decisions concerning buy and sell decisions of specific commodities.

An alternative to managed futures is an exchange-traded fund (ETF) with a portfolio based on a commodity index. For example, Barclays iShares CGSI Commodity-Indexed Trust (GSG) tracks a basket of 24 commodities. The DB Commodity Tracking Fund (DBC) tracks commodities ranging from corn and wheat to oil, silver, and gold. The values of GSG and DBC shares fluctuate with changes in the price of the underlying commodities in each index.

managed future
a futures contract managed by a professional management company

commodity trading advisors
an individual or firm that provides individualized advice regarding the buying and selling of futures contracts

exchange-traded fund (ETF)
a traded portfolio based on a commodity index

15-14 The Pricing of Futures

Several factors may affect a futures contract's price. For example, expectations have frequently been discussed as motivating speculators. The expectation of higher prices leads speculators to take long positions, and the expectation of lower prices results in their establishing short positions. Thus, the futures price mirrors what speculators anticipate prices will be in the future. In addition, the futures price and the spot price are not independent of each other. Such factors as the cost of carrying the commodity link the spot and futures prices. The pricing of futures contracts is an involved topic. The following material covers only the basics so an investor can have an understanding of the pricing of a futures contract. More detailed discussions may be found in texts devoted solely to derivatives.

The following discussion is based on a commodity whose spot price is $100; the futures contract is for delivery after one year. Suppose individuals expect the price of the commodity to be $110 after one year. What should be the current price of a one-year futures contract? The answer is $110. Consider how individuals would react if the price were $108. They would buy the futures contract and, after one year, when the price of the commodity was $110, they would exercise the contract to buy the good for $108 and promptly sell it for $110, making a $2 profit. If the futures price exceeded $110 (e.g., $113), they would reverse the procedure and sell the futures contract. After one year, they would buy the commodity for $110, deliver it for the contract price of $113, and clear $3. For any futures price other than $110, speculators would take positions in the futures contracts. Only if the futures price equals the expected price in the future will the market be in equilibrium, and speculators will take no action.

For this reason, futures prices are often considered to be measures of what investors, speculators, and other market participants currently expect the price of the commodity to be in the future. That is, the current futures prices are an indication of what the future holds. In fact, the process of using futures prices as a forecasting tool is sometimes referred to as price disclosure. The current futures price discloses what market participants believe the future price will be.

If expectations concerning future prices were to change, then the futures price must also change. A major failure of the coffee crop would be expected to increase the future price of coffee, so the expectation of high prices would drive up the current futures price.

price disclosure
the practice of using futures prices as an indicator concerning expectations of future spot prices

Of course, if the price of coffee did not rise, those speculators who bought in anticipation of the price increase would lose, while those who sold in anticipation that the price increase would not occur would win.

An additional factor that affects futures prices is the cost of carrying the commodity. In the previous examples, the speculator took only one side, that is, they entered a contract to buy or sell in anticipation of a price change, and the futures price mirrored the speculator's expected price change. Suppose the individual could buy the commodity now for $100 *and* sell the futures contract at $110. If the price rises to $110, the investor wins because the commodity that cost $100 can be delivered for $110. If the price exceeds $110, this individual still gets $110 and earns the $10. If the price is less than $110, the profit remains $10 because the price is set in the contract at $110. What is the catch?

The problem is the cost of carrying the commodity. If the individual buys the commodity for $100, those funds will not be earning interest (if the investor uses their own money) or will be requiring interest payments if the funds were borrowed. Suppose the interest rate is 8%. Now the individual can borrow $100, buy the commodity for $100, enter into a contract to deliver the commodity after a year for $110, and clear a $2 profit. Thus, *if the futures price exceeds the spot price plus the cost of carry*, then an opportunity for a risk-free arbitrage exists. The arbitrageurs will buy the commodity and sell the futures; they would long the commodity and short the futures. The act of executing these positions will drive up the spot price of the commodity and drive down the futures price. Speculators who anticipate a price of $110 in the future will gladly enter the futures contract for less than $110, since they anticipate earning the difference between $110 and whatever amount they buy the contract for.

If the interest rate were 12%, the arbitrageurs would reverse the procedure. They would sell the commodity at the current spot price (receiving the $100) and buy a contract for future delivery at $110. That is, the arbitrageurs would short the commodity and long the futures. Next they would invest (lend) the money received from the sale at 12%. At the end of the year, the arbitrageurs would receive the commodity that previously had been sold and make $2 on the transaction. Although the cost of the commodity was $110 and the arbitrageurs received only $100 from the sale, they earned $12 on the sale proceeds and netted $2 on the set of transactions.

Once again the act of executing these positions affects the prices of the commodity. Selling the commodity in the spot market will decrease its price, and buying the futures contract will increase its price. As the futures price increases, the speculators, who anticipate the price will be $110, gladly supply (i.e., sell) the contracts as the futures price rises above $110.

In the previous illustration, the cost of carry was limited to the rate of interest. Although that limitation may apply to a financial contract, it does not apply to a contract for a commodity. For commodities, the cost of carry includes interest expense and warehouse expenses, insurance, and shipping.

Consider the preceding case in which the spot price was $100, the futures price was $110, and the interest rate was 8%; the arbitrageurs bought the commodity with borrowed funds and sold the futures contract. Now, however, add a $9 cost of warehousing and shipping the commodity. These additional expenses alter the potential for an arbitrage profit. The futures price must exceed $117 for the arbitrageurs to earn a profit. If they sell the futures contract for $120, they can buy the commodity today for $100 with borrowed funds, pay the $8 interest, cover the $9 in other expenses, and earn a $3 profit without bearing any risk. However, now the futures price must greatly exceed the spot price for the arbitrage opportunity to exist.

15-15 Financial Futures and Currency Futures

financial future
a contract for the future delivery of securities, such as stocks

currency future
a contract for the future exchange of currencies

In the previous discussion, commodity contracts meant futures contracts for physical goods. However, there are also financial and currency futures. Financial futures are contracts for the future delivery of securities such as stocks, Treasury bills, and bonds. Currency futures are contracts for the future delivery of currency, such as the British pound or the European euro. The markets for these contracts, like the market for commodity futures, have two participants: the speculators and the hedgers. It is the interaction of these two parties (i.e., the demand and supply of each contract) that determines the futures price.

15-15a Stock Market Futures

stock index futures
a futures contract based on an index of the market

Stock index futures are futures contracts based on an index of the stock market (e.g., the S&P 500 stock index or the NYSE Composite Index). These contracts offer speculators and hedgers opportunities for profit or risk reduction that are not possible through the purchase of individual securities. For example, the S&P 500 stock index futures contracts have a value that is 250 times the value of the index. Thus, if the S&P 500 stock index is 1,000, the contract is worth $250,000. By purchasing this contract (i.e., by establishing a long position), the holder profits if the market rises. If the index were to rise to 1,100, the value of the contract would increase to $275,000. The investor would then earn a profit of $25,000. Of course, if the S&P 500 Index should decline, the buyer would experience a loss. ("Mini" contracts that are worth 50 times the S&P 500 stock index are also available.)

The sellers of these contracts also participate in the fluctuations of the market. However, their positions are the opposite of the buyers' positions (i.e., they are short). If the value of the S&P 500 stock index were to fall from 1,000 to 900, the value of the contract would decline from $250,000 to $225,000, and the short seller would earn a $25,000 profit. Of course, if the market were to rise, the short seller would suffer a loss. Obviously, if the individual anticipates a rising market, that investor should buy the futures contract. Conversely, if the investor expects the market to fall, that individual should sell the contract.

S&P 500 stock index futures contracts are similar to other futures contracts. The buyers and sellers must make good-faith deposits (i.e., margin payments). As with other futures contracts, the amount of this margin (approximately 7% of the value of the contract) is modest relative to the value of the contract. Thus, these contracts offer considerable leverage. If stock prices move against the investor and their equity in the position declines, the individual will have to place additional funds in the account to support the contract. Since there is an active market in the contracts, a speculator may close a position at any time by taking the opposite position. Thus, if the speculator had entered a contract to buy, that long position would be closed by entering a contract to sell. If the speculator had entered a contract to sell, that short position would be closed by entering a contract to buy.

There is one important difference between stock market index futures and commodity futures contracts. Settlement at the expiration or maturity of the contract occurs in cash. There is no physical delivery of securities, as could occur with a futures contract to buy or sell wheat or corn. Instead, gains and losses are totaled and are added to or subtracted from the participants' accounts. The long and short positions are then closed.

One reason for the development of commodity futures markets was the need by producers and users of commodities to hedge their positions against price fluctuations.

Stock index futures (and other financial and currency futures) developed in part for the same reason. Portfolio managers buy and sell stock index futures in order to hedge against adverse price movements. For example, suppose a portfolio manager has a well-diversified portfolio of stocks. If the market rises, the value of this portfolio rises. However, there is risk of loss if the market were to decline. The portfolio manager can reduce the risk of loss by entering a contract to sell the NYSE Composite Index. If the market declines, the losses experienced by the portfolio will be at least partially offset by the appreciation in the value of the short position in the futures contract.

To execute such a hedge, the portfolio manager uses a futures contract that matches the composition of the portfolio. The NYSE Composite Index contract is suitable for a well-diversified stock portfolio but would not be appropriate for a specialized portfolio. Instead, the portfolio manager who is responsible for a portfolio of smaller companies would more likely use futures on the S&P Midcap index, which gives more weight to smaller companies.

To hedge using stock index futures, the portfolio manager divides the value of the portfolio by the value of the contract to determine the number of contracts to sell. For example, if the value of the portfolio is $1,000,000 and the futures contracts are worth $85,000, the individual would sell 11 to 12 contracts ($1,000,000/$85,000 = 11.76). It may not be possible to exactly hedge the portfolio, as the futures contracts may be unavailable in the desired units. In this example, the portfolio manager would not be able to sell 11.76 futures contracts, but would have to sell either 11 or 12 contracts. This question of units is less of a problem for managers of large portfolios. If the portfolio's value had been $100,000,000, the number of contracts would be 1,176 ($100,000,000/$85,000 = 1,176.47), and the difference between 1,176 and 1,177 is immaterial. The problem facing this portfolio manager will be the market's ability to absorb such a large number of contracts. Is there sufficient demand at current prices to absorb $100,000,000 worth of futures contracts? If the answer is no, then prices will change (which changes the required number of contracts) or the portfolio manager will not be able to completely hedge the long position in the stocks.

In addition to the number of contracts, the portfolio manager must consider the volatility of the portfolio relative to the market. The preceding illustration implicitly assumes that the value of the portfolio exactly follows the index on which the futures contract is based. In effect, the example assumes that the portfolio's beta equals 1.0. If the beta is greater than 1.0, more contracts must be sold to hedge against a price decline, as the value of the contracts sold short will decline less than the value of the portfolio. If the portfolio's beta is less than 1.0, fewer contracts must be sold, as the value of the market will decline more than the value of the portfolio.

Besides selling the index futures contract (establishing a short position in futures), the portfolio manager could have hedged by writing an index call option (establishing a covered call position) or by purchasing an index put option (establishing a protective put position). Each of these strategies is designed to protect against a decline in the market as a whole. Each offers potential advantages and has disadvantages, so there is no clear argument to use one exclusively. Entering a futures contract to sell is an easy position to establish and tends to have low transaction costs. If, however, the market were to rise, the loss on the futures contract will offset the gain on the market. Selling the futures eradicates the upside potential.

Selling the call generates income from the sale, but the downside protection is limited. If the market were to decline sufficiently to offset the proceeds of the sale of the call, the portfolio will sustain a loss. In addition, if the market rises, the value of the call will increase, which offsets the gain in the portfolio. The protective put does not limit the upside potential. If the market were to rise, the increase in the value of the portfolio is not offset by an equal decrease in the value of the put. But buying the put requires a cash outlay, and the process must be repeated (and cash outlays increased) if the portfolio manager wants to retain the protection from a market decline.

15-15b Programmed Trading and Index Arbitrage

Programmed trading arose after the creation of stock index futures and has become a major link between the stock market and the futures market. Through programmed trading and index arbitrage, price changes in one market are transferred to the other and vice versa as the participants move funds between the markets to take advantage of price differentials.

programmed trading
automated trading of portfolios of securities initiated by computer when certain circumstances occur

The term **programmed trading** refers to the coordinated purchases or sales of an entire portfolio of securities. The managers of mutual funds or financial institutions cannot physically place individual orders to buy and sell large quantities of stocks. Instead, large orders are placed through computers that are programmed (hence the name *programmed trading*) to enter the trades if certain specifications are met.

As explained earlier in this text, arbitrage refers to the simultaneous establishment of long and short positions to take advantage of price differentials between two markets. If, for example, the price of the British pound were $2.46 in Paris and $2.50 in Bonn, the arbitrageur would buy pounds in Paris and simultaneously sell them in Bonn. The pounds bought in Paris could be delivered in Bonn; hence, the individual is assured of a $0.04 profit on the transaction. This riskless arbitrage position ensures that the price of the pound will be approximately the same in Paris and Bonn with minute differentials being explained by transactions costs.

Conceptually, index arbitrage is no different, except the arbitrageur is buying or selling index futures and securities instead of pounds. The principle is the same. If prices deviate in different markets, an opportunity for arbitrage is created. Arbitrageurs will seek to take advantage of the price differentials, and through their actions the differentials are erased. This type of arbitrage is frequently done by mutual funds with large holdings of securities that duplicate the various indexes of stock prices. These funds shuffle money between stocks and futures to take advantage of price differentials.

Programmed trading index arbitrage combines the two concepts: Computers are programmed to enter orders to sell or buy blocks of securities designed to take advantage of arbitrage opportunities that exist in the securities and futures markets. If stock index futures prices rise, the arbitrageurs will short the futures and buy the stocks in the index. If futures prices decline, the arbitrageurs do the opposite. They go long in the futures contracts and short the stocks in the index.

Three potential problems arise: (1) There are some transactions costs that must be covered, so the difference between the value of the futures contracts and the underlying securities must be sufficient to cover this cost. (2) There is an obvious problem with buying or shorting all the securities in a broad-based index. Since the S&P 500 stock index uses 500 different stocks, positions would have to be taken in all 500. To get around this problem, the arbitrageurs have developed smaller portfolios called *baskets* that mirror the larger index. The price performance of these stock baskets then mimics the price movements in the index. (3) For arbitrage to be riskless, both positions must be made simultaneously. If they were not, there would be a period when the investor is either long or short (i.e., has only one position) and thus would be at risk. This need for simultaneous executions led to the use of computers that are programmed to coordinate the purchases or sales of the baskets. It is the use of the computers that permits the arbitrageur to enter simultaneous orders to buy or sell large quantities of many individual stocks.

We discussed earlier why an option's intrinsic value sets a floor on the option's price. If the price were to decline below the intrinsic value, an opportunity for arbitrage would exist. The same concept applies to stock index futures, except in this case the option is replaced by the index futures and the individual stock by the stock basket.

The idea may be explained by a simple example. Suppose the S&P stock index stands at 300 and the futures contract is trading for 301.5. Assume that the contract has a value of 500 times the index, so the value of each contract is $150,750. The arbitrageur shorts the futures and buys the $150,000 worth of the stocks in the index (or the shares in the basket). In effect, the arbitrageur has paid $150,000 for $150,750 worth of stock, because the arbitrageur has already entered into a contract for the sale of the stock at $150,750 through the short position in the futures.

If, after executing the position, the futures price declines or the prices of the stocks in the index rise, the arbitrageur will close both positions (referred to as *unwinding*) and make a profit. For example, suppose the prices of the stocks rise sufficiently that the index is 301.50 and the futures contract has only risen to 302. The arbitrageur may now sell the stocks and repurchase the futures contract. The loss on the futures is $250 (301.5 × $500 − 302 × $500), while the gain on the stocks is $750 (301.5 × $500 − 300 × $500). Since all the transactions can occur in a matter of minutes, the cost of carrying the positions is negligible. The arbitrageur need only cover the transaction cost associated with the trades.

If the differential between the values of the futures and index is not rapidly erased, the arbitrageur can maintain the positions until the expiration date of the futures contracts. As the expiration date approaches, the futures price must converge with the current (i.e., spot) price. Options can be worth only their intrinsic value at expiration, and futures prices must equal the spot prices when the contracts expire. Thus, the arbitrageur knows that the differential between the value of the futures contract and the index must disappear and thus assure the profit. The only difference between this and the previous situation is the cost of carrying the stocks, which may be partially offset by income generated by the securities.

If the prices had been reversed (e.g., the futures were trading at 298.5 when the index was 300), so would the procedure. The arbitrageur goes long in the futures and short in the stocks. The simultaneous long and short positions lock in the differential and assure the arbitrageur of the profit. If the price differential rapidly disappears, the positions are unwound and the profit realized. Even if the differential persists, the arbitrageur knows that at expiration the differential must be erased.

This process of index arbitrage is illustrated in **Figure 15-18**, which presents the differential between the value of the futures contract and the underlying stocks in the index during a trading day. The line at zero represents no differential, and the lines at +0.1 and −0.1 represent the transaction costs of executing index arbitrage. Once the differential between the futures and the index exceeds +0.1 or −0.1, the opportunity for a profitable arbitrage exists.

The computers are then programmed to enter the appropriate buy and sell orders when the differential is sufficient to cover the costs associated with the transactions. For example, at 10:15 am, the differential is sufficient on the plus side that the arbitrageur would short the futures and buy the stocks. By 11:45, the differential has vanished, so the positions are closed and the profits are realized. At 2:00 pm, the differential has once again sufficiently increased (on the negative side) so that the arbitrageur goes long in the futures and shorts the stocks. By 3:30, the differential is again erased and the arbitrageur unwinds the positions.

Of course, as the differentials are erased, the impact is felt in the various markets. Increased demand for futures contracts relative to the underlying stocks generates demand

Figure 15-18: Differential Between the Value of a Stock Index Futures Contract and the Underlying Stocks

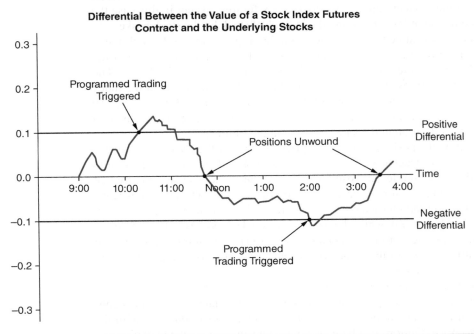

Differential Between the Value of a Stock Index Futures Contract and the Underlying Stocks

by the arbitrageurs for the stocks and hence their prices rise. In a similar way, an increase in stock prices would be transferred to the futures markets. The converse would also be true: a decline in stock prices would tend to drive down the futures prices.

It is important to realize that index arbitrage-programmed trading does *not* depend on the level of stock prices or the level of futures prices. Instead, it depends on (1) spot prices relative to futures prices and (2) synchronized trading. Index arbitrage-programmed trading does not depend on technical analysis, fundamental analysis of a firm's financial statements, changes in information such as an increase in earnings or dividends, or forecasts of the economy.

Programmed trading can distort a stock's price. An individual stock can be fairly valued based on fundamental analysis but experience a large swing in its price if it becomes caught up in programmed trading. As arbitrageurs seek to establish long positions in stocks, the prices of individual securities included in the index or basket can rise rapidly and dramatically. Of course, the converse would be true if arbitrageurs sought to unwind long positions in the stocks or establish short positions. Thus, it is possible for the prices of individual securities to be whipsawed during a trading day in response to the establishing or unwinding of arbitrageurs' positions. Such price volatility can create buying (or shorting) opportunities in individual stocks if their prices deviate from their values as indicated by fundamental analysis.

This price volatility may be particularly noticeable near the expiration dates and especially on the four days during the year that are referred to as the *triple witching hour*. On these days, the S&P 500 stock index futures contract, the S&P 100 stock index options contract, and individual option contracts expire. This convergence of expirations can lead to large volatility in the prices and the volume of the securities traded.

On the triple witching day, the time period is so short that even small differentials can create arbitrage opportunities. The various participants in the markets (i.e., the owners and writers of option contracts and the speculators and hedgers with futures contracts) seek to close their positions, so price differentials can develop and computers can spot them. If, for example, the futures price becomes marginally higher than the value of the underlying stocks, the arbitrageurs immediately short the futures and buy the stocks knowing that the differential must disappear in a matter of hours. Conversely, if the values of the stocks rise, the arbitrageurs sell the stocks and buy the futures because any difference between the futures contracts and the underlying stocks must disappear at the expiration of the contracts and the options. The possibility of such arbitrage profits, of course, has the effect of increasing the volume of transactions and driving prices so that any disparity is erased.

The large swings in stock prices may create buying (or shorting) opportunities in individual stocks if they become under- or overvalued. Evidence exists that large price changes in individual stocks on the triple witching day are quickly erased during trading on the day after the expiration date. This is, of course, consistent with efficient markets. If, for some reason, an individual stock were to be mispriced, investors would buy or sell the security so that its price would be indicative of what the market believed the security was worth. The unwinding of stock index arbitrage positions can create, albeit briefly, such opportunities.

The volatility of securities prices has raised the question of the desirability of programmed trading. The answer partially revolves around whether programmed trading and index arbitrage are viewed as a cause or as a reaction to other events that are occurring in the securities and futures markets. Consider the case in which speculators believe that the Federal Reserve will ease credit and interest rates will fall. These speculators seek to take long positions and purchase stock index call options and futures contracts. The prices of these contracts rise above the value of the underlying stocks, which triggers programmed selling of futures contracts and large purchases of securities. Stock prices rise dramatically.

The converse applies if speculators expect securities prices to fall. They sell futures contracts that will be transferred to the securities markets. The decline in the futures price would result in programmed trading taking long positions in the futures and short positions in the stocks (i.e., selling stocks). These illustrations, of course, suggest that it is not programmed trading and index arbitrage that are the cause of the changes in stock prices. Instead, it is the speculators who initiated the changes; the programmed trading was only in response to the initial cause.

The existence of index arbitrage is one reason why index futures are followed prior to the opening of the stock market. If index futures are trading higher, that means the stock market will open higher. If the futures are lower, the stock market will open lower. Unfortunately, just because you know that futures are trading higher does not mean that you will be able to take advantage of the information. The market makers will adjust the stocks' prices as trading starts in response to the increased demand resulting from the increase in the futures price. The existence of index arbitrage assures that you will not be able to profit by the price differentials and is another illustration of why financial markets are considered so efficient.

15-16 Futures for Debt Instruments

The previous section covered stock index futures. Futures also exist for debt instruments such as Treasury bills and long-term bonds. Changes in interest rates affect the cost of borrowing and the yields from lending. To reduce the loss from fluctuations in interest rates, borrowers and lenders establish a hedge position to lock in a particular interest rate. Speculators, of course, are not seeking to reduce the risk but to reap large returns from taking risks. The speculators are bearing the risk that the hedgers are seeking to avoid. These speculators try to anticipate the direction of change in interest rates and take a position that will yield profits. The return they earn (if successful) is magnified by the leverage resulting from the small margin requirement necessary to establish the positions.

How financial futures may produce profits for speculators can be illustrated with an example using an interest rate futures contract for the delivery of U.S. Treasury bonds. Suppose a speculator expects interest rates to fall and bond prices to rise. This individual would *enter* a contract to buy Treasury bonds in the future. The individual establishes a *long* position. (Do not confuse yourself; it is easy to get the positions backward because you anticipate a *decline in interest rates* and the word "decline" implies taking a short position.) If interest rates do fall and bond prices rise, the value of this contract increases because the speculator has the contract for the delivery of bonds at a lower price (i.e., higher yield). If, however, interest rates rise, bond prices fall and the value of this contract declines. The decline in the value of the contract inflicts a loss on the speculator who entered the contract when yields were lower.

If the speculator expects interest rates to rise, that individual *enters* a contract to sell Treasury bonds (i.e., establishes a *short* position). If interest rates do rise and the value of the bonds declines, the value of this contract must decline, but the speculator earns a profit. This short seller can buy the bonds at a lower price and deliver them at the price specified in the contract. Or the speculator may simply enter a contract to buy at the lower value, thereby closing out the position at a profit. Of course, if this speculator is wrong and interest rates fall, the value of the bonds increases, inflicting a loss on the speculator, who must now pay more to buy the bonds to cover the contract.

15-17 Currency Futures

Currency futures are contracts for the sale and delivery of a foreign currency, such as the British pound. Speculators take positions in anticipation of change in the price of one currency relative to another. Hedgers use the contracts to reduce the risk of loss from the price change. Essentially, currency contracts perform the same role as the contracts for commodities, stock indexes, and debt instruments.

Suppose the dollar price of the British pound is $2. A speculator who anticipates that the price of the pound will rise establishes a long position in the pound. This individual enters a contract to buy pounds. The futures price may be $2.02 or $1.96. It need not necessarily equal the current, or spot, price. (If many speculators expect the price of the pound to rise, they will bid up the futures price so that it exceeds the current price. If speculators expect the price of the pound to fall, they will then drive down the futures price.) If this speculator enters the futures contract for $2.02 and is correct (i.e., the price of the pound rises), that individual makes a profit. If, for example, the price of the pound were to rise to $2.20, the value of the contract may rise by $0.18 per pound, that is, $2.20 − $2.02. (At expiration the futures and spot prices must be equal. Thus, if the pound is $2.20 on the expiration date, the value of the contract must be $2.20 per pound.) Of course, if the speculator is wrong and the price of the pound declines to $1.80, the value of the contract also declines, and the speculator suffers a loss.

A speculator who anticipated a decline in the value of the pound would establish a short position and enter a contract to sell. If the speculator is right and the value of the pound declines, they may close the position for a profit. Since pounds are now worth less, the speculator may buy the cheaper pounds and deliver them at the higher price specified in the contract. (Actually the speculator would close the short position by buying an offsetting contract for the future delivery of pounds.) If the speculator had been wrong and the price of the pound had risen, that individual would have suffered a loss, as it would have cost more to buy the pounds to make the future delivery required by the contract.

15-17a Currency Futures and Risk Reduction Through Hedging with Currency Futures

Currency futures offer individuals a means to speculate on price changes, but their use as a means to hedge exchange rate fluctuations is probably more important. American investors who acquire foreign securities and American firms that invest abroad have to bear the risk associated with fluctuations in exchange rates. Currency futures offer a means to manage that risk.

If the prices of currencies were stable, there would be little risk associated with investing in another country. Such is not the case illustrated in **Figure 15-19**, which plots the price of the British pound from 1980 through 2014. Consider the price decline experienced in 2008. The pound fell from $2.00 to less than $1.50, a decline in excess of 25%. A decline of that magnitude would easily wipe out most positive returns earned on assets denominated in British pounds. If the investors or firms that held the assets established hedged positions, the gains on the hedges would offset (or at least partially offset) the losses from the decline in the dollar value of the pound.

To see how such a hedge works, consider the following example. You purchase 100 shares of stock for £50 a share (£5,000). The pound is currently worth $2.00, so the dollar value of the stock is $10,000. Since you are long in the stock (and hence long in the pound), you need to be short in the futures if you want to hedge against a decline in the pound (i.e., you short pounds). The futures price of the pound is $2.02, that is, $1.00 = £0.4951. (In this example, the futures price exceeds the current or spot price. The converse, in which the futures price is less than the spot price, is also possible.) To establish the short position, you enter into a contract to deliver £5,000 at $2.02. The value of this contract is 5,000 × $2.02 = $10,100, which is almost the same as the value of stock.

Figure 15-19: Dollar Value of the British Pound, 1980–2014

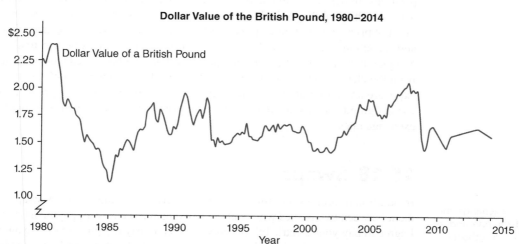

Suppose the price of the stock does not change, but the price of the pound declines to $1.90. You have lost nothing on the stock; its price remains £50, but £5,000 are now worth $9,500 (5,000 × $1.90). If you were to sell the stock and convert the pounds back to dollars, you would lose $500. The value of the futures contract, however, must have also declined. If the price of the pound is $1.90, the contract is worth $9,500. You could purchase £5,000 for $9,500, deliver them for $2.02 a pound ($10,100), and make $600 on the transaction. The gain on the short in the futures more than offsets the loss from the decline in the dollar value of the pound.

Suppose the price of the stock does not change, but the price of the pound rises to $2.20. You have lost nothing on the stock; its price remains £50, but £5,000 are worth $11,000 (5,000 × $2.20). If you were to sell the stock and convert the pounds back to dollars, you would gain $1,000. The value of the futures contract, however, would have also risen. If the price of the pound is now $2.20, the contract is worth $11,000. You would have to pay $11,000 to purchase £5,000, but receive only $10,100 ($2.02 × 5,000). You would lose $900 on the futures contract. The loss on the short in the futures consumes most of the gain from the appreciation in the value of the pound.

A British investor who acquires American stock would follow the opposite strategy. Suppose this investor buys 200 shares of a $50 stock ($10,000). If the price of the dollar is £0.50, the cost of the stock is £5,000 ($10,000 × 0.5). They will sustain a loss if the value of the pound rises (dollar declines). For example, suppose the price of the stock remains $50, but the pound rises from $2.00 to $2.20. The value of the dollar declines from £0.50 (1/$2) to £0.4545 (1/$2.20). The 200 shares are now worth £4,545 [(200 shares × $50)/2.20]. The British investor sustains a loss of £455 (£4,545 − £5,000) when the dollars are converted back to pounds.

To hedge against this loss, the investor enters into a futures contract. This individual has a long position in U.S. securities and enters into a short position in dollars (a long position in pounds). That is, the investor enters into a contract to purchase pounds (deliver dollars). Such a contract rises if the value of the dollar declines. If the investor enters into a contract to sell $10,000 when the future price is £1.00 × $2.02, the value of the contract is £4,950 ($10,000/2.02). If the value of the dollar declines to £1.00 = $2.20, the stock is worth £4,545 [(200 shares × $50)/2.20]. The British investor, however, may buy $10,000 for £4,545 ($10,000/2.2) and deliver them for £4,950. The £405 gain almost offsets the £455 loss from the decline in the value of the dollar.

You should notice that in these examples, the investors did not completely hedge their positions. In the first example, the investor had a net gain, and in the second there was a net loss. This inability to hedge completely may result from (1) the difference between the spot price and the futures price or (2) the difference between the size of the contract and the amount invested in the foreign security. Even if investors are unable to hedge completely and to offset exactly the potential loss, the hedge reduces the potential loss from the change in the exchange rate. Many portfolio managers with foreign exchange exposure and corporate financial managers whose firms have foreign operations often use hedging to reduce a substantial amount of the risk associated with fluctuations in exchange rates.

15-18 Swaps

swap
a contract to exchange the cash flows from one underlying security with those from another

In addition to options and futures, another derivative is the **swap**. A swap is an agreement between two parties who contract to exchange (i.e., swap) payments. For example, I agree to pay your electric bill if you will agree to pay my phone bill. We agree to trade payments. Individuals rarely, if ever, swap payments, but firms and financial institutions often participate in the swap market. Firms make their profits through operations and not from speculating on anticipated price changes. To reduce the risk of loss from price changes, management may enter into a swap agreement. Since accounting disclosure requires swaps to be discussed in annual reports, the investor needs to understand swaps and how corporations use these derivatives to manage the firm's risk exposure.

15-18a Currency and Interest Rate Swaps

There are a variety of swap agreements between firms. For example, two firms may swap payments in different currencies (a currency swap). In another case, one firm swaps a series of fixed payments for a series of variable payments. The opposing firm (called the *counterparty*) swaps the variable payments and receives the fixed payments.

The large increase in foreign investments and foreign operations by global firms has greatly increased the use of swap agreements to manage exchange rate risk. Consider a U.S. firm with operations in the United Kingdom that is required to make payments in British pounds. The dollar value of the payments will rise if the pound increases (dollar declines), but the dollar value declines if the pound decreases (dollar increases). The converse is true for a British firm with American operations that must make payments in dollars. Earnings, however, can be increased or *decreased* by fluctuations in the value of the foreign currencies.

One means to reduce the risk of loss is to hedge using the currency futures discussed earlier in this chapter. Swapping payments is another means to reduce the foreign exchange risk. The British firm agrees to make the American firm's required payments in pounds, and the American firm agrees to make the British firm's dollar payments. Since both firms are now making the payments in their native currency, neither has the risk associated with changes in the exchange rate. If the dollar rises (pound falls), the effect on both firms is immaterial.

Swaps involving funds borrowed abroad may also reduce interest expense. Suppose an American firm can borrow in the United States under favorable terms but needs the funds in England where the cost of the loan will be greater. A British firm can borrow in England at a lower rate but needs the funds in the United States. In both cases, the firm saves interest expense if it borrows in the domestic market. However, since the funds are needed abroad, they will have to be converted into the local currency. Once converted, the firm now faces exchange rate risk when the funds are exchanged back to retire the loans.

If the American firm could borrow in the United States and the British firm could borrow in England and then agree to swap the liabilities, each firm would have a loan denominated in its currency. To accomplish this swap, the firms use a swap dealer (usually a large financial institution, such as a major commercial bank) who charges a fee for the service. The American firm issues dollar-denominated debt and passes the funds to the dealer. The dealer, in turn, passes the funds to the British firm. Simultaneously, the British firm issues debt denominated in pounds and passes the funds to the dealer, who passes the funds to the American firm.

The British firm now pays interest in pounds, and the American firm pays interest in dollars. The net effect is that the American firm has a dollar-denominated debt on its balance sheet but is able to use pounds. Since the debt is denominated in dollars by the swap agreement, there is no exchange rate risk. In addition, the interest expense may actually be lower if the firm is able to issue debt domestically at a lower interest rate. The converse is true for the British firm, which has borrowed in pounds but can use dollars.

For this swap to occur, both parties must perceive a benefit, and the amounts must be comparable. The potential benefits are (1) potential savings in interest expense, (2) reduction in exchange rate risk, or (3) a combination of both. By acting as an intermediary, the swap dealer facilitates the creation of the swap. For this service, the dealer receives a fee.

The potential benefits may be seen by the following simple example in which an American firm needs £625,000 and a British firm needs $1,000,000. A pound costs $1.60. (Conversely, $1.00 buys £0.625.) Given this exchange rate, $1,000,000 equals £625,000. The American firm can borrow $1,000,000 from a domestic bank at 6% but must pay 7% if it borrows £625,000 from a British bank. The interest payment will be £43,750, and the loan will be denominated in pounds. The British firm can borrow £625,000 for 6% in the United Kingdom but must pay 8% for $1,000,000 in the United States. The interest cost will be $80,000, and the loan will be denominated in dollars.

In this case, there is an interest savings if the two firms swap obligations. A swap dealer arranges the swap in which each firm borrows the funds in the domestic market and exchanges the obligations. The American firm has the use of £625,000 with an interest cost of £37,500. The interest savings is £6,250, which is $10,000 at the current exchange rate. The British firm has the use of $1,000,000 with an interest cost of $60,000. The interest savings is $20,000, which is £12,500 at the current exchange rate. There is a net interest savings to both firms from the swap.

The previous example illustrates the potential interest savings if each party can borrow at a lower interest cost in a particular market. The next example illustrates the reduction of exchange rate risk. Assume the amounts borrowed and the exchange rate are the same as in the previous example, and the interest rate is 6% for both parties in both markets. (Equal interest rates remove the savings from interest payments, so the impact of changing exchange rates is highlighted.) Under these assumptions, the American firm borrows $1,000,000 at 6% ($60,000 interest payment), and the British firm borrows £625,000 at 6% (£37,500 interest payment). The firms swap the funds so both get the use of the money in the foreign currency.

After a year, the loans have to be repaid, but the exchange is now $1.00 = £0.50 (£1.00 = $2.00). The dollar cost of the pound has risen from $1.60 to $2.00, for a 25% increase. If the American firm had to buy pounds, their cost has risen dramatically. If the firm had borrowed £625,000, it would owe £625,000 + (0.06) × (£625,000) = £625,000 + £37,500 = £662,500. The dollar cost of the pounds is $2 × 662,500 = $1,325,000. The savings from the swap is $1,325,000 − $1,060,000 = $265,000.

The British firm pays £625,000 + (0.06) × (£625,000) = £662,500. If the firm had borrowed $1,000,000, it would have to pay $1,060,000 to retire the loan. Since the loan is denominated in dollars, $1,060,000 would cost £530,000 ($1,060,000/2). The British firm has lost an opportunity to gain £662,500 − £530,000 = £132,500 from the increased value of the pound. The British firm, however, has avoided the possible loss that would have occurred if the dollar had risen in value against the pound. (And the American firm has lost the opportunity to gain from a decline in the cost of the pound.)

Since firms are generally in business to generate profits from operations and not from speculating on changes in exchange rates, many firms with international operations participate in currency swap agreements. For example, in 2011, Coca-Cola reported to its stockholders that it uses futures contracts, swaps, and other derivatives to reduce risk associated with exchange rates and other sources of risk, such as changes in interest rates and commodity prices. Without the existence of these derivatives, a firm's exposure to fluctuations in foreign exchange rates, interest rates, and commodity prices would be increased.

15-18b Equity Swaps

In addition to interest rate swaps and currency swaps, there are equity swaps in which investors swap payments based on a stock index. Consider Investor A, with a substantial portfolio of stocks. Investor A expects their prices to decline and would like to move into debt securities. The sale of the stocks may generate taxable gains and will involve transaction costs (commissions). Investor B has substantial holdings of debt securities and anticipates that stock prices will rise. Investor B would like to sell the bonds and purchase stocks. However, the bonds may be illiquid (especially if they are nontaxable municipal bonds) and the sales will involve transaction costs. These two investors could execute a swap agreement that meets each investor's needs.

To see how this equity swap works, assume an amount such as $1,000,000 (the notational principal). If the interest rate is 10%, the $1,000,000 earns $100,000 annually. Investor A, who wants the bonds, agrees to pay Investor B the return on the S&P 500 stock index. If the index rises by 5%, A pays $50,000 ($1,000,000 × 0.05). Investor B, who wants the stocks, agrees to pay Investor A $100,000 annually. For each year during which the swap agreement is in effect, Investor A receives $100,000 from Investor B and pays B an amount based on the S&P return. If the S&P 500 rises by 10%, A pays B $100,000 and B pays A $100,000, so the amounts cancel. The following table sets out other possible cash flows between the two investors based on the return on the stock index.

Cash Flows Investor A

S&P 500 Return	Payment to B	Payment from B	Net
15%	$150,000	$100,000	($50,000)
4	40,000	100,000	60,000
−3	−30,000	100,000	130,000

Cash Flows Investor B

S&P 500 Return	Payment to A	Payment from A	Net
15%	$100,000	$150,000	$50,000
4	100,000	40,000	(60,000)
−3	100,000	−30,000	(130,000)

If the S&P return is 15%, A receives $100,000 but must pay $150,000, so there is a net cash outflow of $50,000 to B. If the S&P return is 4 percent, A receives $100,000 but has to pay only $40,000, so A nets $60,000. In the case when the S&P return is −3%, A receives $100,000 from B plus an additional $30,000 because the index return is negative.

Investor B's cash flows are, of course, the mirror image of A's. When the return on the S&P index exceeds 10%, Investor A's payments to B exceed the $100,000 B has agreed to make. B then receives a net cash inflow. If the S&P return is less than 10%, B's payments to A exceed the cash received, and B experiences a net cash outflow. Actually, only the net cash flow payments are made. If the return on the market is 15%, there is no need for A to pay B $150,000 and for B to pay A $100,000. Only the net cash flow payment is made, which in this case would be the $50,000 payment from A to B.

What advantage does this swap offer each investor? The answer is that the swap approximates what would have happened if the parties had made their portfolio changes. Suppose A had sold $1,000,000 worth of stock to buy the 10% bonds, and the market rose 15%. The investor would have earned $100,000 in interest but had an opportunity loss of $150,000 in capital appreciation. By entering the swap, the investor experiences a cash outflow of $50,000, so the end result is essentially the same, except the investor avoided all the transaction costs associated with securities sales and subsequent purchases and avoided all the tax consequences of the sales.

From B's perspective, selling the bonds would have resulted in forgoing $100,000 in interest, but the stock purchases would have generated $150,000 in appreciation. The net difference is the $50,000, which is essentially the same as the $50,000 cash inflow from the swap. By executing the swap, Investor B avoided the transaction costs and any marketability or illiquidity problems associated with selling the debt instruments.

In this illustration, the swap occurred when two investors wanted to alter their portfolios from equity to debt (and vice versa). Other possible equity swaps may occur if investors want to move from one sector to another or to alter their exposure to foreign securities. For example, one investor wants to reduce holdings of large cap stocks in favor of small cap stocks, while another investor wants fewer small cap stocks in favor of large cap stocks. In this case, a swap is based on indexes of large and small cap stocks. The investor who wants the large cap stocks would receive payments based on the large cap index and make payments based on the performance of the small cap index. The investor wanting greater exposure to small cap stocks would make and receive the opposite payments (i.e., receive payments based on the small cap index and make payments based on the large cap index).

The same basic principle applies to equity swaps involving foreign securities. Consider an American investor who wants to diversify by including foreign securities. Simultaneously, a foreign investor wants to diversify by owning American securities. Instead of each investor acquiring foreign securities, a swap is arranged. The American investor receives payment based on an index of foreign securities and makes payments based on an index of American securities. The foreign investor makes payments based on their domestic index and receives payments based on the performance of the index of American securities. The American investor will receive a net cash inflow if the foreign index generates the higher return but will have to make payments if the foreign index has the lower return. That is essentially the same result that would have occurred if American stocks had been sold to buy foreign stocks. Higher returns abroad would have resulted in an increased return to the American investor, while lower returns abroad would have produced lower returns. The swap agreement achieves a similar result without having to buy and sell individual stocks.

15-18c Credit Default Swaps

You purchase a house and then purchase insurance. In effect, you enter into a contract with an insurance company. You agree to make periodic payments, and the insurance company agrees to make payments if an insured event were to occur. The buyer of the policy will receive compensation from the seller, the insurance company, if an event such as a fire were to occur.

Credit default swaps are analogous to your home insurance. It is a contract in which one party, the buyer, makes periodic payments to the seller, the supplier, for protection against the loss from a lender defaulting. For example, you purchase $10,000 face value of 10% bonds. The bonds should pay you $1,000 a year, but there is the risk that the issuer will default. To reduce the impact of the loss, you enter into a contract with a third party and agree to pay $300. If the bonds were to default, you would receive the $1,000 from the supplier of the swap. This payment pattern is analogous to your home insurance: you have "swapped" payments. By giving up some of the interest (the cost of the swap), you will be compensated if the event (default) were to occur. In effect, the swap is another version of a hedging. You have accepted a lower return to reduce the risk of loss. The risk has been transferred to the firm that agrees to make the payment if the original debtor were to default.

Individuals rarely participate in the market for swaps, but investment companies, endowments, or pension plans may use them. Such institutions purchase debt obligations to generate income but have to bear the risk associated with the investments. To reduce the risk, they enter a swap agreement with a third party, such as a bank or insurance company. By making the payments to the third party, the pension plan transfers the risk to the insurance company or bank. The pension plan accepts a lower return because the payments reduce the cash flow generated by the investment. The price the pension plan pays for the swap is one measure of the perceived risk. As risk increases, the amount of the payment also increases as the seller (e.g., the insurance company) demands increased compensation for bearing the additional risk. Such swaps were at center stage of the financial crisis of 2008–2009, when significant numbers of borrowers did default on loans, such as mortgages, and the sellers of the swaps were unable to meet the obligations of their swap agreements.

While investors acquire credit default swaps as a hedging tool, they may be bought or sold as a speculative tool. Suppose you anticipate a default: you could buy a swap. You *do not have to own the underlying security* on which the swap is based. Consider the $10,000 bond in the previous example. You anticipate the company will default and agree to pay the $300 but will receive the $1,000 if the issuer were to default. Since you do not own the bond, the position is not a hedge but rather a speculation on the default. You pay $300 in anticipation of receiving $1,000 if the borrower defaults. Of course, if you anticipate that the borrower will *not* default, you could *sell* the swap and collect the payment from the buyer. Both parties to the swap cannot be correct: the default either does or does not occur. One of the parties has to sustain a loss.

Once created, a secondary market can develop in swap agreements. If one investor buys the swap, that speculator can subsequently sell the contract to another speculator. The second buyer now assumes the payments and receives the compensation if the borrower were to default. The creator of the swap may also sell the agreement, in which case the seller no longer receives the payments but is no longer at risk. The prices of these secondary sales should mirror the perceived risks at the time of the sale, and that price may not be the price that existed when the credit default swap was initially created.

If all the payments are made, there is no problem. The seller of the credit default swap receives payments from the buyer. The buyer's net return is lower, but that is to be expected because risk is reduced. If the borrower does default, the party that sold the "insurance" makes the payment to the buyer (the owner of the debt instrument), and the system works. A major problem occurs when the seller of the swap does not make the required payment. The party that bought the swap to reduce the risk of loss now sustains two losses. Not only does that party not receive the interest payment from the lender, but they do not receive compensation from the seller of the swap. Because the seller of the swap fails to make the required payment and the original borrower fails to make the interest payments, the lender loses on both sides.

Conclusion

As we have seen, derivative securities have an important part to play in allowing market participants to hedge risk. The leverage they provide can also be attractive to speculators, but that leverage comes at the risk of large potential losses. While individual investors, presumably having no inside or advance notice concerning stock moves, interest rate shifts, and the like, would be well advised not to speculate in the derivative markets, they are handy for constructing carefully selected hedging strategies to help immunize investor portfolios from potential risks.

Chapter Equations

$$Intrinsic\ Value\ of\ Call = max\ (P_s - P_e,\ 0) \qquad \textbf{15-1}$$

$$Intrinsic\ Value\ of\ Put = max\ (P_e - P_s,\ 0) \qquad \textbf{15-2}$$

Key Terms

at the money – an option selling when the strike price equals the current market price of the underlying security

call option – an option contract that gives you the right, but not the obligation, to buy an underlying asset at a certain price

Chicago Board Options Exchange (CBOE) – an organized market for puts and calls

commodity trading advisors – an individual or firm that provides individualized advice regarding the buying and selling of futures contracts

covered option – an option written when the seller already owns the underlying asset

currency future – a contract for the future exchange of currencies

daily limit – the maximum amount of allowed daily price change on a futures contract

derivative security – a security that derives its value from an underlying asset or security

exchange rate risk – the risk that exchange rates may go against your favor when you are scheduled to receive one currency in the future and will need to convert it to another

exchange-traded fund (ETF) – a traded portfolio based on a commodity index

financial future – a contract for the future delivery of securities, such as stocks

forward contract – a *customized* agreement to buy and sell an underlying asset at a particular date in the future for a locked-in price that is not traded on an organized exchange

futures contract – an agreement traded on an organized exchange to buy and sell an underlying asset at a particular date in the future for a locked-in price

futures price – the price agreed to in a futures contract

hedging – the use of derivative contracts to immunize against risk in an underlying asset that the party already has a stake in

in the money – an option having positive intrinsic value

interest rate option – an option to buy and sell debt securities

intrinsic value – the value of an option at the current market price of the underlying asset if the option were to expire now

long-term equity anticipation securities (LEAPS) – options that are typically longer than nine months in duration

leverage – the ability to pay a relatively small premium for market exposure in relation to the contract value

managed future – a futures contract managed by a professional management company

margin – when purchasing assets on margin, the money borrowed from a broker to purchase an investment and the difference between the total value of the investment and the loan amount; when entering into a futures contract, the amount each party is required to keep on account against future movements of the underlying asset's price against them

marked to the market – refers to the action of calculating the gain in value to a futures contract due to changes in the underlying spot price; is usually performed once a day at the close of trading maintenance margin – **the minimum amount that a party to a futures contract must keep on account to cover shifts in the underlying asset that cause them to owe money to the other party**

margin call – **a requirement for a party to a futures contract to put more funds into the contract**

naked option – **an option written when the writer does not own the underlying asset**

open interest – **the number of a particular derivative contracts in existence**

option – **a derivative contract giving the right to buy or sell an underlying asset for a pre-specified price at the owner's discretion over a predetermined time period**

out of the money – **an option having zero intrinsic value**

payoff diagram – **a graphical depiction of the value of a derivative at expiration as a function of the value of the underlying asset**

premium – **for options, the purchase price**

price disclosure – **the practice of using futures prices as an indicator concerning expectations of future spot prices**

programmed trading – **automated trading of portfolios of securities initiated by computer when certain circumstances occur**

protective put – **the simultaneous purchase of the underlying asset and a put on that asset**

put option – **an option contract that gives you the right, but not the obligation, to sell an underlying asset at a certain price**

spot price – **the current market price of a commodity for immediate delivery**

stock index futures – **a futures contract based on an index of the market**

stock index option – **option on an aggregate measure of the market, such as the S&P 500**

stop-loss order – **a standing order to sell an asset owned when the price goes down to a specified level**

strike price – **the price specified in an options contract at which the underlying asset can be bought or sold at**

sunk cost – **a cost that has already been paid and cannot be recovered**

swap – **a contract to exchange the cash flows from one underlying security with those from another**

warrant – **a call option issued by firms on their own shares**

Questions

1. **Options.** What is an option? How is an option's minimum (or intrinsic value) determined? How does arbitrage ensure that the price of an option will not be less than the option's intrinsic value? If you saw that the price of a share of stock was $20, the exercise price of an option to buy the stock was $10, and the price of the option was $5, what would you do? (LO 15-1)

2. **Leverage.** What is the source of leverage in a call option? Why may an option be considered a speculative investment? (LO 15-2)

3. **Covered vs naked calls.** What is the difference between covered and naked call writing? Why do some individuals buy call options while others write calls? (LO 15-3)

4. **Put vs short sale.** When would you use a put versus a short sale? Why? (LO 15-4)

5. **Term premium.** Why is an option "worth more alive than dead"? That is, why is the premium for an option always more than its intrinsic value as long as there is time left on the option until expiration? (LO 15-5)

6. **Warrants vs calls.** Suppose warrants and call options both exist on a certain share of stock. What is the major difference between warrants and call options? (LO 15-6)

7. **Futures vs forwards.** What are the differences between futures contracts and forwards? Who might prefer a forward contract, and why? (LO 15-7)

8. **Margin call.** If you were a farmer who had entered into a futures contract to sell your wheat harvest, what changes in the spot price of wheat would generate a margin call for you? Why? (LO 15-8)

9. **Naked call vs futures.** How are the positions of a naked call writer and the seller in a futures contract different? (LO 15-9)

10. **Hedging.** Suppose you have a futures contract to exchange U.S. dollars for euros in six months. What aspect(s) of your business would have led you to enter into this contract as a hedge? (LO 15-11)

Problems

1. **Put exercising.** Suppose you buy a long put on a stock with a strike price of $37 and a premium of $3. What is the highest stock price at which you would exercise the put? (LO 15-1)

2. **Call exercising.** Suppose you buy a long call on a stock with a strike price of $23 and a premium of $2.50. What is the lowest stock price at which you would exercise the call? (LO 15-1)

3. **Call intrinsic value.** You bought a call with a strike price of $20 for $2, and the underlying asset is now selling for $15. What is the intrinsic value of the call? (LO 15-1)

4. **Call intrinsic value.** You bought a call with a strike price of $10 for $2, and the underlying asset is now selling for $18. What is the intrinsic value of the call? (LO 15-1)

5. **Put intrinsic value.** You bought a put with a strike price of $20 for $2, and the underlying asset is now selling for $15. What is the intrinsic value of the put? (LO 15-1)

6. **Put intrinsic value.** You bought a put with a strike price of $10 for $2, and the underlying asset is now selling for $18. What is the intrinsic value of the put? (LO 15-1)

7. **Call profit.** You bought a call with a strike price of $27 for $2.50. At what price of the underlying stock will you start to make a profit on your investment? (LO 15-1)

8. **Put profit.** You bought a put with a strike price of $27 for $2.50. At what price of the underlying stock will you start to make a profit on your investment? (LO 15-1)

9. **Call premium.** Suppose you buy a call option with a $27 strike price on a stock that is currently trading for $30. What is the minimum premium you would expect to have to pay to purchase this option? (LO 15-1)

10. **Call exercising.** You bought a call with a strike price of $27 for $2.50. At what price of the underlying stock would the call go out of the money? (LO 15-1)

11. **Call profit.** You can purchase a three-month call option that gives you the right to buy stock at $20. Currently, the stock is selling for $22 and the call is selling for $5. You are considering buying 100 shares of the stock ($2,200) or one call option ($500, giving you the right to buy 100 shares). If the price of the stock rose to $29 within three months, what would the profits or losses be on each position? (LO 15-1)

12. **LEAPS time premium.** A LEAPS call with an expiration date of two years is an option to buy stock at $24. The current market price of the stock is $35, and the market price of the LEAPS is $15. What is the time premium paid for the LEAPS? (LO 15-3)

13. **Warrant conversion.** You have a warrant that gives you the right to buy .75 shares of a stock for $25 that is currently selling for $3. How many such warrants are necessary to buy one share of stock? (LO 15-6)

14. **Per-share strike price.** You have a warrant that gives you the right to buy .25 shares of a stock for $25 that is currently selling for $3. What is the per-share strike price? (LO 15-6)

15. **Futures profit or loss.** Assume that you buy a futures contract on corn at $4.00 a bushel for 5,000 bushels. If the spot price of corn at the settlement of the contract is $3.75, how much will you make or lose? (LO 15-7)

16. **Futures margin.** You expect the stock market to decline, but instead of selling stocks short, you decide to sell a stock index futures contract based on an index of NYSE common stocks. The index is currently 700, and the contract has a value that is $250 times the amount of the index. The margin requirement is $2,000, and the maintenance margin requirement is $1,000. When you sell the contract, how much must you put in the margin account? (LO 15-8)

17. **Price discovery.** One use for futures markets is "price discovery"; that is, the futures price mirrors the current consensus of the future price of the commodity. The current price of gold is $1,827, but you expect the price to rise to $2,000. If the futures price were $1,990 per ounce for a contract for 100 ounces, what would you do? If your expectation is fulfilled, what is your profit? (LO 15-10)

18. **Swap cash flows.** Two institutional investors execute a swap agreement for $10,000,000 in which party A agrees to remit payments to counterparty B based on the EAFE, an index of European, Australasian, and Far Eastern stocks. Counterparty B agrees to remit payments based on the return on the S&P 500 to party A. During the next four time periods, the returns on the two indexes are as follows. What are the cash flows between the two parties for each time period? (LO 15-12)

Period	S&P 500	EAFE
1	4%	10%
2	−3	8
3	15	0
4	2	−5

19. **Position investment.** An investor buys a stock for $37. At the same time, a six-month put option to sell the stock for $34 is selling for $2. If the investor also purchases the put (i.e., constructs a protective put), what is the combined cash outflow? (LO 15-3)

20. **Position profits.** Suppose you buy a call with a strike price of $25 for $3 and a put with a strike price of $20 for $2, both on the same underlying stock. At what price(s) will you start making a profit on this position? (LO 15-2)

Case Study

Options Quotes Versus Intrinsic Values

Go to the CBOE options page for AMD stock and obtain the quotes for the calls and puts on AMD that are expiring the soonest. Compare the intrinsic values of these calls and puts with the premiums ("asks") being quoted. What patterns do you see?

Chapter

16

Derivative Valuation and Strategies

Learning Objectives

After reading this chapter you should be able to:

LO 16-1 Determine the relationship between the value of an option and the variables specified in the Black–Scholes option valuation model.

LO 16-2 Calculate the value of calls and puts using the Black–Scholes option valuation model and put–call parity.

LO 16-3 Explain the intuition of alternative option pricing models.

LO 16-4 Explain how the hedge ratio is used to reduce the risk associated with a position in a stock.

LO 16-5 Determine the potential profits and losses from option strategies.

LO 16-6 Explain how incentive-based stock options may affect a firm's earnings.

The previous chapter presented the basics concerning options. It described their features, the reasons why investors may purchase or sell them, and how they are used as speculative investments or as a means to reduce risk. The chapter also explained how an option sells for a time premium that disappears with the passage of time, so that the option sells for its intrinsic value on the day it expires.

This chapter develops the material on options by (1) discussing two alternative option pricing models, the Black–Scholes option valuation model and the binomial option pricing model; (2) explaining how stock, bond, and option markets are interrelated, so that changes in one are transmitted to the other markets; and (3) illustrating several strategies using options. Options are a very involved topic that can be approached from a sophisticated mathematical perspective. The approach used in this chapter seeks to reduce the abstractions while liberally illustrating the concepts so that the individual investor can understand the fundamentals and importance of option valuation even if they never intend to apply them.

16-1 Black–Scholes Option Valuation

Valuation is a major theme in finance and investments. The valuation of bonds, preferred stock, and common stock composes a substantial proportion of the chapters that we've devoted to those securities; however, in every case, the approach we used was the same: estimate the future expected cash flows to a security and then use TVM concepts to value the security today.

We're going to apply the same basic approach to valuing options, but with a bit of a "plot twist" caused by two fundamental differences between stocks and bonds and options. First, even though we didn't explicitly point it out at the time, when we valued common and preferred shares and bonds, we were primarily focusing on their potential expected returns in the long-term, their future coupon payments, dividends, etc. For stocks and bonds, these cash flows occur in discrete "chunks": that is, we find out what a dividend payment will be on the ex-dividend date, whether the next coupon payment on a bond will be paid when it is due, etc. Realized cash flows, and implicitly also revised information about later, future potential cash flows, comes out of firms like drips from a consistently leaky faucet. Because of the discrete nature of these cash flows, we've been using discrete mathematical models and formulas, based on the fluid concepts of the "time period" between cash flows, to value the relevant securities.

With options, the cash flows don't come out in a steady, consistent pattern. Instead, as we saw in the last chapter, options move into and out of the money based on the valuation of the underlying assets, not on those assets' cash flows. Particularly if those underlying assets take the form of publicly traded stocks or bonds, valuation revision on those underlying assets is occurring continuously, every minute of every day that the stocks and bonds are being traded. So discrete math doesn't work so well in valuing options; instead, we have to use a *continuous-time* version of TVM, one that allows for the possibility/probability that changes in the underlying asset valuation can happen any time, and with a continuous range of such changes possible.

The other fundamental difference between stocks/bond and options is that while stocks/bonds are (usually) relatively long-lived, options aren't. "Surprises" that affect the next few dividends or coupon payments may have a relatively small impact on the relevant stock/bond, as the "next few" dividends or coupon payments probably represent a rather minor portion of all of the expected cash flows that the stock/bond owner stands to receive over time. But for options, which are relatively short-lived, the "next few" dividends or coupon payments are likely to be the *only* cash flows to the underlying assets that might possibly affect the option owner.

To put it another way: in the last chapter, we defined *leverage* as the ability to purchase the potential to reap rewards from possible changes in the value of the underlying asset more cheaply than if we were investing the same dollars in the underlying asset itself. Or, to put it another way: $X dollars invested in options on a stock can *magnify* the potential gains with respect to those possible if we invested the same $X in the stock itself. That magnification comes about because, due to their short-lived nature, option prices tend to be more sensitive to changes/surprises than do the changes to the prices of the underlying assets of those options.

The continuous-time option valuation formula we will use is known as the Black–Scholes option valuation model. (The derivation of the model is much more complex than the derivation of the discrete-time TVM formulas, so is not covered here. You will just have to take the model on faith.) The question of valuation of an option is illustrated in **Figure 16-1**, which essentially reproduces Figure 15-5. Looking at

Black–Scholes option valuation model
a differential equation-based model for pricing call contracts

Figure 16-1: Black–Scholes Valuation vs. Intrinsic Value for a Call Option

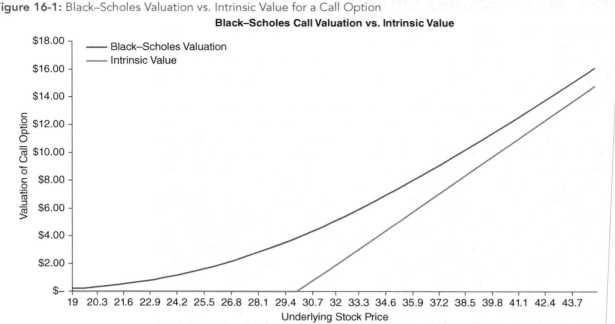

Black–Scholes Call Valuation vs. Intrinsic Value

Figure 16-1, several questions come to mind: Why is the Black–Scholes valuation above the intrinsic value? Why isn't it more/less above the intrinsic value? What variables cause the line to shift up or down? As we'll see, the Black–Scholes model determines the value of the option *given the time to expiration, the standard deviation of the returns to the underlying stock, and risk-free rate of return*, for each price of the stock, and it's the value of those given variables that determine where the Black–Scholes valuation line lies relative to the intrinsic values at each stock price.

In Black–Scholes, the value of a call option (V_o) depends on all of the following:

- P_s, the current price of the stock
- P_e, the option's exercise or strike price (i.e., the price at which the underlying asset may be purchased under the call option)
- T, the time in years to the option's expiration date (i.e., if expiration is 3 months, $T = 0.25$)
- σ, the standard deviation of the stock's annual rate of return
- r, the annual risk-free rate of interest on an asset (e.g., Treasury bill) with a term equal to the time to the option's expiration.

Both theory and empirical examination of actual option prices indicate that the relationships between the value of a call (the dependent variable) and each of these independent variables (assuming the remaining variables are held constant) are as follows:

- An increase in the price of the stock (an increase in P_s) increases the value of a call option (V_o). This is true since the intrinsic value of the option rises as the price of the stock rises.
- An increase in the strike price (an increase in P_e) decreases the value of a call option. Higher strike prices reduce the option's intrinsic value for a given price of the stock.
- An increase in the time to expiration (an increase in T) increases the value of a call option. As time diminishes and the option approaches expiration, its value

declines. (Note that T is normally expressed as a percentage of year, so that three months is expressed as 25%, etc.; however, for more precision, we can also use that fact that there are an average of 252 trading days per year on the U.S. stock and option markets.)

- An increase in the variability of the stock (an increase in σ) increases the value of a call option. A speculator will find an option on a volatile stock more attractive than an option on a stock whose price tends to be stable. Decreased variability decreases the value of an option.
- An increase in interest rates (an increase in r) increases the value of a call option. Higher interest rates are associated with higher call option valuations.

Most of the relationships between the independent variables and an option's value seem reasonable with the exception of a change in the interest rate. Throughout the rest of this text, an increase in interest rates decreases the value of the asset. Higher interest rates reduce the present value of a bond's interest payments and principal repayment, thus reducing the value of the bond. Higher interest rates increase the required return for a common stock, thus decreasing the valuation of the common stock. This negative relationship between changes in interest rates and a security's value does not hold for call options. Higher interest rates increase the value of an option to buy stock. Intuitively, this is because with a call option, you're basically locking in the rate you will have to pay in the future (if you decide to exercise) instead of paying for the stock today, thus allowing you to invest the money you would have used to buy the stock today until you need it to exercise the call in the future. So, higher rates allow you to earn more return while you're waiting to exercise the call.

It should be noted that dividends are excluded from the Black–Scholes model. In its initial formulation, the valuation model was applied to options on stocks that did not pay a dividend. Hence, the dividend played no role in the determination of the option's value. The model has been extended to dividend-paying stocks. Since the extension does not significantly change the basic model, this discussion will be limited to the original presentation.

Black–Scholes puts the variables together in the following equation for the value of a call option (V_o):

$$V_o = P_s \times N(d_1) - \frac{P_e}{e^{rT}} \times N(d_2) \qquad \textbf{16-1}$$

The value of a call depends on two pieces: the price of the stock times a function, $N(d_1)$; and the strike price, expressed in present value terms, times a function, $N(d_2)$. While the price of the stock (P_s) presents no problem, the strike price (P_e) expressed as a present value (P_e/e^{rT}) needs explanation. The strike price is divided by the number $e = 2.71828$ raised to rT, the product of the risk-free interest rate and the option's time to expiration. The use of $e = 2.71828$ expresses compounding on a continuous basis instead of discrete (e.g., quarterly or monthly) time periods.

$N(x)$ represents the cumulative standard normal function, where mean is 0 and standard deviation is 1, and which returns the probability that a value will be less than or equal to x standard deviations from the mean. The two values that we will pass through the cumulative standard normal function are

$$d_1 = \frac{\ln\left(\dfrac{P_s}{P_e}\right) + \left(r + \dfrac{\sigma^2}{2}\right)T}{\sigma\sqrt{T}} \qquad \textbf{16-2}$$

and

$$d_2 = d_1 - \sigma\sqrt{T} \qquad\qquad \textbf{16-3}$$

The ratio of the price of the stock and the strike price (P_s/P_e) is expressed as a natural logarithm (ln). The numerical values of d_1 and d_2 represent the area under the normal probability distribution. Applying Black–Scholes requires a table of the values for the cumulative normal probability distribution. Such a table is readily available in statistics textbooks, and one is provided in **Exhibit 16-1** for convenience. Once d_1 and d_2 have been determined and their values from the cumulative standard normal probability distribution located, it is these values that are used in the Black–Scholes model [i.e., substituted for $N(d_1)$ and $N(d_2)$ in **Equation 16-1**].

How the model is applied may be seen by the following example. The values of the variables are as follows:

- Stock price (P_s) $52
- Strike price (P_e) $50
- Time to expiration (T) 0.25 (three months)
- Standard deviation (σ) 0.20
- Interest rate (r) 0.10 (10% annually)

Thus, the values of d_1 and d_2 are

$$d_1 = \frac{\ln\left(\dfrac{P_s}{P_e}\right) + \left(r + \dfrac{\sigma^2}{2}\right)T}{\sigma\sqrt{T}}$$

$$= \frac{\ln\left(\dfrac{\$52}{\$50}\right) + \left(0.10 + \dfrac{0.20^2}{2}\right)0.25}{0.20\sqrt{.25}}$$

$$= 0.6922$$

and

$$d_2 = d_1 - \sigma\sqrt{T}$$

$$= 0.6922 - 0.20\sqrt{.25}$$

$$= 0.5922$$

The values from the cumulative normal distribution are:

$$N(0.6922) \approx 0.755$$

$$N(0.5922) \approx 0.722$$

The probability distribution seeks to measure the probability of the option being exercised. If there is a large probability that the option will have positive intrinsic value at expiration, the numerical values of $F(d_1)$ and $F(d_2)$ approach 1, and the option's value will approach the price of the stock minus the present value of the strike price:

$$V_o = P_s \times 1 - \frac{P_e}{e^{rT}} \times 1 = P_s - \frac{P_e}{e^{rT}}$$

Exhibit 16-1: Cumulative Normal Distribution

d	N(d)	d	N(d)	d	N(d)	d	N(d)	d	N(d)	d	N(d)	d	N(d)	d	N(d)	d	N(d)	d	N(d)	d	N(d)
−3.09	0.001	−2.51	0.0060	−1.93	0.0268	−1.35	0.0885	−0.77	0.2207	−0.19	0.4247	0.39	0.6517	0.94	0.8264	14.9	0.9319	2.04	0.9793	2.59	0.9952
−3.08	0.001	−2.50	0.0062	−1.92	0.0274	−1.34	0.0901	−0.76	0.2236	−0.18	0.4286	0.40	0.6554	0.95	08289	1.5	0.9332	265	0.979B	2.6	0.9953
−3.07	0.0011	−2.49	0.0064	−1.91	0.0281	−1.33	0.0918	−0.75	0.3266	−0.17	0.4325	0.41	0.6591	0.96	0.8315	1.51	0.9345	266	0.9B03	2.61	0.9955
−3.06	0.0011	−2.48	0.0066	−1.90	0.0287	−1.32	0.0934	−0.74	0.2297	−0.16	0.4364	0.42	0.6623	0.97	0.834	1.52	0.9357	267	0.9808	262	0.9956
−3.05	0.0011	−2.47	0.0068	−1.89	0.0294	−1.31	0.0951	−0.73	0.3327	−0.15	0.4404	0.43	0.6664	0.98	0.8365	1.53	0.937	2.08	0.9812	2.63	0.9957
−3.04	0.0012	−2.46	0.0069	−1.88	0.0301	−1.30	0.0965	−0.72	0.2358	−0.14	0.4443	0.44	0.67	0.99	0.B359	1.54	0.9382	209	0.9817	2.64	0.9959
−3.03	0.0012	−2.45	0.0071	−1.87	0.0307	−1.39	0.0985	−0.71	0.2389	−0.13	0.4483	0.45	0.6736	1.00	0.84T3	1.55	0.9394	2.1	0.9821	2.65	0.996
−3.02	0.0013	−2.44	0.0073	−1.86	0.0314	−1.38	0.1003	−0.70	0.342	−0.12	0.4522	0.46	0.6772	1.01	0.8438	1.56	0.9406	2.11	0.9826	2.66	0.9961
−3.01	0.0013	−2.43	0.0075	−1.85	0.0322	−1.37	0.102	−0.69	0.2451	−0.11	0.4562	0.47	0.6808	1.02	0.8461	1.57	0.9418	2.12	0.983	2.67	0.9962
−3.00	0.0013	−2.42	0.0078	−1.84	0.0329	−1.26	0.1038	−0.68	0.2483	−0.10	0.4602	0.4B	0.6844	1.03	0.8485	1.58	0.9429	213	0.9834	2.68	0.9963
−2.99	0.0014	−2.41	0.0080	−1.83	0.0336	−1.25	0.1057	−0.67	0.2514	−0.09	0.4641	0.49	0.6879	1.04	0.8508	1.59	0.9441	214	0.9838	2.69	0.9964
−2.98	0.0014	−2.40	0.0082	−1.82	0.0344	−1.34	0.1075	−0.66	0.2546	−0.08	0.4681	0.50	0.6915	1.05	0.8531	1.6	0.9452	2.15	0.9842	2.7	0.9965
−2.97	0.0015	−2.39	0.0084	−1.81	0.0351	−1.33	0.1093	−0.65	0.2578	−0.07	0.4721	0.51	0695	1.06	0.8554	1.61	0.9463	2.16	0.9846	2.71	0.9966
−2.96	0.0015	−2.38	0.0087	−1.80	0.0359	−1.32	0.1112	−0.64	0.2611	−0.06	0.4761	0.52	0.6985	1.07	0.8577	1.62	0.9474	217	0.985	2.72	0.9967
−2.95	0.0016	−2.37	0.0089	−1.79	0.0367	−1.21	0.1131	−0.63	0.2643	−0.05	0.4801	0.53	0.7019	168	0.8599	1.63	0.9484	218	0.9854	2.73	0.9968
−2.94	0.0016	−2.36	0.0091	−1.78	0.0375	−1.30	0.1151	−0.62	0.2676	−0.04	0.484	0.54	0.7054	169	0.8621	1.64	0.9495	2.19	0.9857	2.74	0.9969
−2.93	0.0017	−2.35	0.0094	−1.77	0.0354	−1.19	0.117	−0.61	0.2709	−0.03	0.488	0.55	0.7088	1.10	08643	1.65	0.9505	2.2	0.9861	2.75	0.997
−2.92	0.0018	−2.34	0.0096	−1.76	0.0392	−1.18	0.119	−0.60	0.2743	−0.02	0.492	0.56	0.7123	1.11	0.8665	166	0.9515	221	0.9564	2.76	0.9971
−2.91	0.0018	−2.33	0.0099	−1.75	0.0401	−1.17	0.121	−0.59	0.2776	−0.01	0.496	0.57	0.7157	1.12	08686	1.67	0.9525	222	0.9868	2.77	0.9972
−2.90	0.0019	−2.32	0.0102	−1.74	0.0409	−1.16	0.123	−0.58	0.281	0.00	0.5	0.58	0.719	1.13	0.8708	1.68	0.9535	223	0.9871	2.78	0.9973
−2.89	0.0019	−2.31	0.0104	−1.73	0.0418	−1.15	0.1251	−0.57	0.2843	0.01	0.504	0.59 $d_2\rightarrow$	0.7224	1.14	0.6729	169	0.9545	224	0.9875	2.79	0.9974
−2.88	0.002	−2.30	0.0107	−1.72	0.0427	−1.14	0.1271	−0.56	0.2877	0.02	0.508	0.60	0.7257	1.15	0.8749	1.7	0.9554	225	0.9878	2.8	0.9974
−2.87	0.0021	−2.29	0.0110	−1.71	0.0436	−1.13	0.1292	−0.55	0.2912	0.03	0.512	0.61	0.7291	1.16	0.877	1.71	0.9564	226	0.9881	2.81	0.9975
−2.86	0.0021	−2.28	0.0113	−1.70	0.0446	−1.12	0.1314	−0.54	0.2946	0.04	0.516	0.62	0.7324	1.17	0879	1-72	0.9573	227	0.9884	2.82	0.9976
−2.85	0.0022	−2.27	0.0116	−1.69	0.0455	−1.11	0.1335	−0.53	03981	0.05	0.5199	0.63	0.7357	1.1B	0.881	1.73	0.9582	228	0.9887	2.83	0.9977
−2.34	0.0023	−2.26	0.0119	−1.68	0.046S	−1.10	0.1357	−0.52	0.3015	0.06	0.5239	0.64	0.7389	1.19	0.883	1.74	0.9591	229	0.989	2.84	0.9977
−2.83	0.0023	−2.25	0.0122	−1.67	0.0475	−1.09	0.1379	−0.51	0.305	0.07	0.5279	0.65	0.7422	1.20	0.8849	1.75	0.9599	2.3	0.9893	2.85	0.9978
−2.82	0.0024	−2.24	0.0125	−1.66	0.0485	−1.05	0.1401	−0.50	0.3085	0.08	0.5319	0.66	0.7454	1.21	0.8869	1.76	0.9608	231	0.9896	2.86	0.9979
−2.81	0.0025	−2.23	0.0129	−1.65	0.0495	−1.07	0.1423	−0.49	0.3121	0.09	0.5359	0.67	0.7486	1.22	0.8888	1.77	0.9616	232	0.9898	2.87	0.9979
−2.80	0.0026	−2.22	0.0132	−1.64	0.0505	−1.06	0.1446	−0.48	0.3156	0.1	0.5398	0.68	0.7517	1.23	0.8907	1.78	0.9625	2.33	0.9901	2.88	0.998
−2.79	0.0026	−2.21	0.0136	−1.63	0.0516	−1.05	0.1469	−0.47	0.3192	0.11	0.5 438	0.69 $d_1\rightarrow$	0.7549	1.24	0.8925	179	0.9633	23 4	0.9904	2.89	0.9981
−2.78	0.0027	−2.20	0.0139	−1.62	0.0526	−1.04	0.1492	−0.46	0.32 28	0.12	0.5478	0.7	0.758	1.25	0.8943	1.8	0.9641	235	0.9906	2.9	0.9981

(Continued)

Exhibit 16-1: *(Continued)*

d	N(d)	d	N(d)	d	N(d)	d	N(d)	d	N(d)	d	N(d)	d	N(d)	d	N(d)	d	N(d)	d	N(d)	d	N(d)
-2.77	0.0028	-2.19	0.0143	-1.61	0.0537	-1.03	0.1515	-0.45	0.3264	0.13	0.5517	0.71	0.7611	1.26	0.8962	1.81	0.9649	2.36	0.9909	2.91	0.9982
-2.7b	0.0029	-2.18	0.0146	-1.60	0.0548	-1.02	0.1539	-0.44	0.33	0.14	0.5557	0.72	0.7642	1.27	0.898	1.82	0.9656	2.37	0.9911	2.92	0.9982
-2.75	0.003	-2.17	0.0150	-1.59	0.0559	-1.01	0.1562	-0.43	0.3336	0.15	0.5596	0.73	0.7673	1.28	0.8997	1.83	0.9664	2.38	0.9913	2.93	0.9983
-2.74	0.0031	-2.16	0.0154	-1.58	0.0571	-1.00	0.1587	-0.42	0.3372	0.16	0.5636	0.74	0.7703	1.29	0.9015	1.84	0.9671	2.39	0.9916	2.94	0.9984
-2.73	0.0032	-2.15	0.0158	-1.57	0.0582	-0.99	0.1611	-0.41	0.3409	0.17	0.5675	0.75	0.7734	1.30	0.9032	1.85	0.9678	2.4	0.9918	2.95	0.9984
-2.72	0.8033	-2.14	0.0162	-1.56	0.0594	-0.98	0.1635	-0.40	0.3446	0.18	0.5714	0.76	0.7764	1.31	0.9049	1.86	0.9686	2.41	0.992	2.96	0.9985
-2.71	0.0034	-2.13	0.0166	-1.55	0.0606	-0.97	0.166	-0.39	0.3483	0.19	0.5753	0.77	0.7793	1.32	0.9066	1.87	0.9693	2.42	0.9922	2.97	0.9985
-2.7	0.8035	-2.12	0.0170	-1.54	0.0618	-0.96	0.1685	-0.38	0.352	0.2	0.5793	0.78	0.7823	1.33	0.9082	1.88	0.9699	2.43	0.9925	2.98	0.9986
-2.69	0.8036	-2.11	0.0174	-1.53	0.063	-0.95	0.1711	-0.37	0.3557	0.21	0.5832	0.79	0.7852	1.34	0.9099	1.89	0.9706	2.44	0.9927	2.99	0.9986
-2.68	0.8037	-2.10	0.0179	-1.52	0.0643	-0.94	0.1736	-0.36	0.3594	0.22	0.5871	0.80	0.7881	1.35	0.9115	1.9	0.9713	2.45	0.9929	3	0.9987
-2.67	0.0038	-2.09	0.0183	-1.51	0.0655	-0.93	0.1762	-0.35	0.3632	0.23	0.591	0.81	0.791	1.36	0.9131	1.91	0.9719	2.46	0.9931	3.01	0.9987
-2.66	0.0039	-2.08	0.0188	-1.50	0.0668	-0.92	0.1788	-0.34	0.3669	0.24	0.5948	0.82	0.7939	1.37	0.9147	1.92	0.9726	2.47	0.9932	3.02	0.9987
-2.65	0.004	-2.07	0.0192	-1.49	0.0681	-0.91	0.1314	-0.33	0.3707	0.25	0.5987	0.53	0.7967	1.38	0.9162	1.93	0.9732	2.48	0.9934	3.03	0.9988
-2.64	0.0041	-2.06	0.0197	-1.48	0.0694	-0.90	0.1841	-0.32	0.3745	0.26	0.6026	0.84	0.7995	1.39	0.9177	1.94	0.9738	2.49	0.9936	3.04	0.9988
-2.63	0.0043	-2.05	0.0202	-1.47	0.0708	-0.89	0.1867	-0.31	0.3783	0.27	0.6064	0.85	0.8023	1.40	0.9192	1.95	0.9744	2.5	0.9938	3.05	0.9989
-2.62	0.0044	-2.04	0.0207	-1.46	0.0721	-0.88	0.1894	-0.88	0.3821	0.28	0.6103	0.86	0.8051	1.41	0.9207	1.96	0.975	2.51	0.994	3.06	0.9989
-2.61	0.0045	-2.03	0.0212	-1.45	0.0735	-0.87	0.1922	-0.29	0.3859	0.29	0.6141	0.87	0.8078	1.42	0.9222	1.97	0.9756	2.52	0.9941	3.07	0.9989
-2.60	0.0047	-2.02	0.0217	-1.44	0.0749	-0.86	0.1949	-0.28	0.3897	0.3	0.6179	0.88	0.8106	1.43	0.9236	1.98	0.9761	2.53	0.9943	3.08	0.999
-2.59	0.0048	-2.01	0.0222	-1.43	0.0764	-0.85	0.1977	-0.27	0.3936	0.31	0.6217	089	0.8133	1.44	0.9251	1.99	0.9767	2.54	0.9945	3.09	0.999
-2.58	0.0049	-2.00	0.0228	-1.42	0.0778	-0.84	0.2005	-0.26	0.3974	0.32	0.6255	0.30	0.8159	1.45	0.9265	2	0.9772	2.55	0.9946		
-2.57	0.0051	-1.99	0.0233	-1.41	0.0793	-0.83	0.2033	-0.25	0.4013	0.33	0.6293	0.31	0.8186	1.46	0.9279	281	0.9778	2.56	0.9948		
-2.56	0.0052	-1.98	0.0239	-1.40	0.0808	-0.82	0.2061	-0.24	0.4052	0.34	0.6331	0.32	0.8212	1.47	0.9292	282	0.9783	2.57	0.9949		
-2.55	0.0054	-1.97	0.0244	-1.39	0.0823	-0.81	0.209	-0.23	0.409	0.35	0.6368	0.93	0.8238	1.48	0.9306	283	0.9788	2.58	0.9951		
-2.54	0.0055	-1.96	0.0250	-1.38	0.0838	-0.80	0.2119	-0.22	0.4129	0.36	0.6406										
-2.53	0.0057	-1.95	0.0256	-1.37	0.0853	-0.79	0.2148	-0.21	0.4168	0.37	0.6443										
-2.52	0.0059	-1.94	0.0262	-1.36	0.0869	-0.78	0.2177	-0.20	0.4207	0.38	0.648										

	Critical Values of z for		
Significance Level	Two Tails	Lower Tail	Upper Tail
0.10	±1.65	-1.28	+1.28
0.05	±1.96	-1.65	+1.65
0.01	±2.58	-2.33	+2.33

Excel Expert 16-1

Luckily, Excel has a NORMSDIST() function that calculates the cumulative normal distribution for us, so calculating Black–Scholes option valuation is straightforward:

	A	B	C	D
1	Current Stock Price (P_s)	$ 52.00		
2	Exercise Price (P_e)	$ 50.00		
3	Time Until Expiration (% of Year) (T)	25.00%		
4	Continuously Compounded Risk-Free Rate (r)	10.00%		
5	Standard Deviation of Underlying Stock Returns (σ)	20.00%		
6				
7	d_1	0.69221	= d1	=(LN(Ps/Pe)+(_r_+σ^2/2)*T)/(σ*SQRT(T))
8	d_2	0.59221	= d2	=B7-(σ*SQRT(T))
9				
10	V_0	$ 4.03	=(Ps*NORMSDIST(_d1_))-(Pe*EXP(-_r_*T)*NORMSDIST(_d2_))

Note that we have named the input cells to make readability of the final formula easier (with the requirement that we had to put underscores on some names to avoid conflicts with Excel cell naming conventions).

Also note that the option value, $4.03, is slightly different than the value calculated previously by hand. This is due to the increased precision possible by using Excel, so this Excel solution is correct.

If there is little probability that the option will have positive intrinsic value at expiration, the numerical values of $N(d_1)$ and $N(d_2)$ will approach 0, and the option will have little value:

$$V_o = P_s \times 0 - \frac{P_e}{e^{rT}} \times 0 = 0$$

Given the values for $N(d_1)$ and $N(d_2)$ determined from the normal distribution, the value of the call option is

$$V_o = \$52 \times 0.755 - \frac{\$50}{e^{0.10 \times 0.25}} \times 0.722 = \$4.05$$

If the call is selling for more than $4.03, it is overvalued. If it is selling for less, it is undervalued.

If the price of the stock had been $60, the Black–Scholes model determines the value of the option to be $11.27. If the price of the stock were $40, the value of the option is $0.04. By altering the price of the stock, the various values of the option are determined. To see this graphically, we can use Excel to create both the intrinsic values and the Black–Scholes option valuations for a series of stock values, as demonstrated in **Excel Expert 16-2**.

As shown in Excel Expert 16-2, the different prices of the stock generate the general pattern of option values illustrated in **Figure 16-2**.

One of the other handy aspects of using Excel to calculate and graph multiple Black–Scholes calculations like this is that we can easily use the resulting spreadsheet to perform "what-if" analyses. If we change one of the other variables (i.e., T, σ, P_e, and r) while holding the price of the stock constant, we can see how the curve representing the Black–Scholes valuations at different prices would shift. For example, if the life of the option had been nine months instead of three months, the curve would shift up.

Excel Expert 16-2

As demonstrated below (and as you may download from the book's website), the hardest part of graphing the Black–Scholes option valuations across a series of prices is creating a table to be graphed in a manner that makes it easiest to graph the results. It turns out to be easiest to do so in Excel if the calculations for d_1 and d_2 are performed "in stream"; that is, within the same cell containing the calculation for V_0:

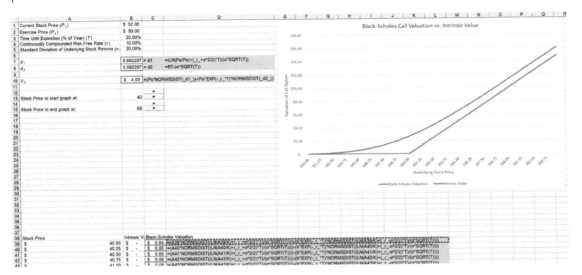

Understandably, that makes the resulting equations, such as those shown listed in cell D39 and below, rather complicated.

Note that we have also used Excel spin buttons in cells C12/13 and C14/15 to allow you to zoom in our out to better see the Black–Scholes and intrinsic valuations at prices you may be interested in.

Figure 16-2: Option Valuation When $T = 75\%$

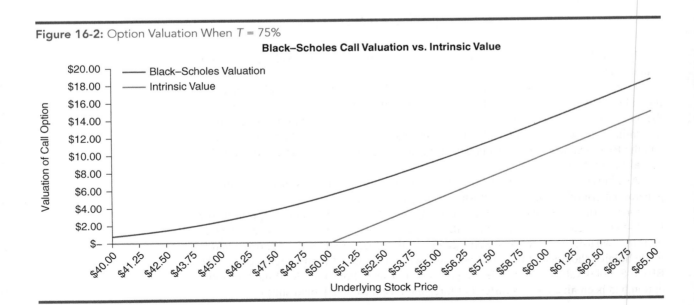

As you can see by experimenting with the spreadsheet yourself, increased price volatility, a lower strike price, or higher interest rates would also shift the Black–Scholes option valuation curve upward, while a shorter time to expiration, a lower interest rate, a higher strike price, or smaller volatility would shift the curve downward.

Although Black–Scholes may appear formidable, it is easily applied when we use Excel or one of many other computer programs to handle the calculations for us. All the variables but standard deviation are readily observable on the options markets. However, calculating *expected* future standard deviation in the underlying stock returns is not as straightforward as simply calculating the standard deviation of the stock's historic returns: just because that standard deviation was true in the past, it doesn't mean that changes in expectations concerning the firm's prospects, the economic environment, etc., won't cause the expected value to differ from the historic value.

One method to overcome that problem is to reverse the equation and solve for the standard deviation. If the individual knows the price of the stock, the strike price, the price of the option, the term of the option, and the interest rate, Black–Scholes may be used to solve for the standard deviation of the returns. Historical data are then used in Black–Scholes to determine the implied historical variability of the underlying stock's returns. If it can be assumed that the variability has not changed, then that value for the standard deviation is assumed to be the correct measure of the stock's current variability and is used to determine the present value of an option.

16-1a Alternative Option Pricing Models

The Black–Scholes option pricing model is not perfect, because some of its assumptions simply do not strictly hold in the real world. We know, for example, that stock returns are *not* normally distributed, because shareholders' limited liability implies that returns to stock can never be less than 100% of the purchase price. Similarly, as we already discussed, we can infer and approximate the expected standard deviation in the underlying stock's returns but can never actually observe it, so our estimate will be inexact.

Because of this, several alternative option pricing models have been developed that align slightly better with reality and tend to perform, on average, a little bit better at pricing options than the Black–Scholes model. One of the most popular of these alternative models is the binomial Cox–Ross–Rubinstein model that, like other similar binomial pricing models, models movement in the underlying stock price using a binomial "tree," dividing the time until option maturity into discrete intervals and presuming that the price of the underlying asset follows a binomial process during each of these intervals, moving from its initial value P_s up to price P_{su} (with probability p) or down to price P_{sd} (with probability $1-p$).

Binomial Cox–Ross–Rubinstein model
a binomial pricing model used to price options

The actual mechanics of doing so are relatively simple, but using a binomial option pricing model correctly requires the re-computation of the value every time the underlying stock price changes. That said, we will leave discussion of this model to a derivatives class.

16-2 Expensing Employee Stock Options and Option Valuation

Many firms grant stock options to select employees as a type of deferred compensation or "incentive-based compensation." For example, Pactiv reported that management and the board of directors receive 25 to 55% of their compensation in stock and options.

The strike price is set equal to or greater than the market price of the stock. Since there is no positive intrinsic value, the recipient has no immediate tax obligation. (If the strike price were less than the market price of the stock, the option would have positive intrinsic value, which would be taxable.) If the company does well and the price of its stock rises, the value of these incentive options also increases, and the employee will have been compensated for contributing to the firm's success. (The gain on the option may be taxed at the long-term capital gains tax rate, which will be lower than the employee's marginal tax rate.)

Since many firms grant top management incentive-based stock options, a question arises: Does this practice have a cost to the firm? That is, are these options expenses? The initial answer may seem to be no. The option has no intrinsic value and the firm has no cash outflow when the options are issued.

Even if the options have no positive intrinsic value and even if the firm has no cash outflow, that is not the same as stating that out-of-the-money options have no value. The Black–Scholes option valuation model indicates that the value of an option depends not only on the price of the stock and the strike price but also on the risk-free rate, the time to expiration, and the volatility of the underlying stock. Out-of-the-money options have value because of the difference between the price of the stock and the present value of the strike price. Since incentive options often have 5 to 10 years to expiration, the present value of the strike price is often considerably lower than the current stock price. Because the recipient receives this value, the option has a cost to the issuing firm. (Another approach to concluding that incentive-based options are an expense is to use the following reasoning: instead of granting the option, the firm sells the option and uses the proceeds to compensate the employee. The firm now has a cash outflow, which is an obvious expense.)

Why is the conclusion that incentive stock options have value and should be expensed by the issuing firm important? The answer is the potential impact on the firm's earnings. If the present value of the option were expensed, the firm's earnings would be decreased. Expensing the options lowers the firm's reported earnings. Since incentive-based options are a form of compensation, they are a cost that should be currently recognized and deducted from current earnings. The accounting profession has acknowledged that incentive-based compensation involves a cost. Under current reporting requirements, a firm must estimate the cost of incentive-based compensation and provide the impact on earnings on its income statement.

Since the options must be expensed, the question becomes how to determine the value of the options. Currently, Black–Scholes is the model most accepted by U.S. firms for valuing options. However, the model does have its weaknesses. For example, applying the model requires an assumption concerning the stock's future price volatility. Also, the recipient may exercise an incentive-based option prior to expiration. The Black–Scholes model requires using a specific date. (The expiration date is generally used because it is known, while the actual date the option will be exercised cannot be known.) These problem areas decrease the model's attractiveness for valuing employee stock options. (An alternative model, the *binomial option pricing model*, is discussed in the appendix to this chapter.)

16-3 Put–Call Parity

At this point, we've developed a valuation formula for calls, but what about for puts? Well, consider a portfolio consisting of a long put plus a long stock, where the purchase price of the stock is the same as the strike price of the put, graphed with our Payoff diagram from Chapter 15 (refer **Figure 16-3**).

Figure 16-3: Profits on Long Stock and Long Put

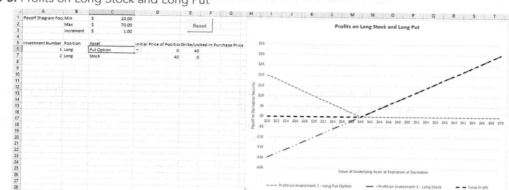

Figure 16-4: Profit on Long Call

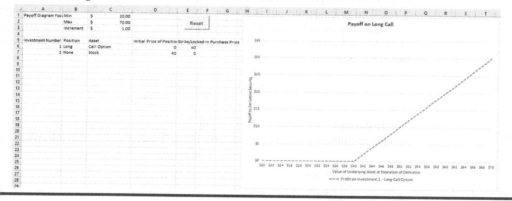

As you can see, the total payoff, shown in black, looks identical to the payoff of a call option at the same strike price (refer **Figure 16-4**).

Once the value of a call has been determined, so has the value of a put with the same strike price and term to expiration, because the price of the stock, put, and call are interrelated. A change in the value of one must produce a change in the value of the others. If such a change did not occur, an opportunity for a riskless arbitrage would exist. As investors sought to take advantage of the opportunity, prices would change until the arbitrage opportunity ceased to exist.

The relationship between the prices of a put and a call, the price of the underlying stock, and the option's strike price is referred to as put–call parity. In effect, put–call parity says a pie may be cut into pieces of different sizes, but the total pie cannot be affected. Taking into account the difference in timing between the strike prices of the options and purchase of the stock, put, and call today, this relationship can be expressed as the price of a stock plus the price of a put is equal to the price of the call plus the present value of the strike price:

$$P_s + P_p = P_c + \frac{P_e}{(1+i)^n} \qquad \textbf{16-4}$$

Fairly often, this equation is rearranged to allow for solving for the value of a put option as a function of the other parts:

$$P_p = P_c + \frac{P_e}{(1 + i)^n} - P_s \qquad \text{16-5}$$

In the previous example, the price of the stock was $52, the strike price of the call was $50, and the value of the call was $4 when the annual rate of interest was 10% and the option expired in three months. The values imply that the price of a three-month put to sell the stock at $50 must be:

$$P_p = \$4.00 + \frac{\$50}{(1.10)^{0.25}} - \$52$$

$$= \$0.82$$

If the equation does not hold, an opportunity for arbitrage exists. Consider the following example: A stock sells for $105; the strike price of both the put and call is $100. The price of the put is $5, the price of the call is $20, and both options are for one year. The rate of interest is 11.1% (11.1% is used because the present value of $100 at 11.1% is $100/1.111 = $90, which is easier to work with in this illustration). Given these numbers, the equation holds:

$$\$5.00 = \$20.00 + \frac{\$100}{(1.111)^1} - \$105$$

If the call sold for $25, then an opportunity for arbitrage would exist. The investor (or the computer) perceives the disequilibrium and executes the following trades:

1.	Buy the stock	Cash outflow	$105
2.	Buy the put	Cash outflow	5
3.	Sell the call	Cash inflow	25
4.	Borrow $90 at 11.1%	Cash inflow	90

(Notice there is an important assumption that the investor can either lend funds and earn 11.1% or borrow funds at that rate.) There is a net cash inflow of $5 ($25 + $90 − $105 − $5), so the investor has committed no cash and has actually received funds at the time they enter into these trades. At expiration, if the call is in the money, they will sell the stock at the $100 strike price of the call and use the proceeds to pay off the loan, so their net cash flow will be zero; if the call is out of the money, the put will be in the money, and they will be able to exercise the put and receive $100, also allowing them to pay off the loan, and again receiving net cash flow of zero.

Put–call parity may also be used to show interrelationships among financial markets and why a change in one must be transferred to another. Suppose the Federal Reserve uses open market operations to lower interest rates. The Fed buys short-term securities, which drives up their prices and reduces interest rates. This means the equilibrium prices in the preceding example will no longer hold. The lower interest increases the present value of the strike price. At the existing prices, investors would borrow funds at the new lower rate, buy the stock, sell the call, and buy the put. Executing these transactions generates a net cash inflow and ensures the individual of a profitable riskless arbitrage. Of course, the act of simultaneously trying to buy the stock and the put and to sell the call alters their respective prices until the arbitrage opportunity is negated. The effect of the Federal Reserve's action in one market will then have been transferred to the other financial markets.

16-4 The Hedge Ratio

In addition to option valuation and the development of put–call parity, the Black–Scholes model provides useful information to investors seeking to hedge positions. Hedged positions occur when the investor takes one position in the stock and the opposite in the option (e.g., a long in the stock and a short in the option). Unfortunately, as discussed before, the differential leverage inherent in options and stock implies that the price movement in an option and the underlying stock are not equal. This was illustrated in the previous chapter, in Figure 15-5, in which the price of the call option increased from $15 to $23 when the price of the stock rose from $60 to $70. The percentage increase in the call exceeded the percentage increase in the price of the stock, and the absolute price changes were not equal. Since absolute price changes are not equal, the investor cannot use one call option to exactly offset price changes in the stock. Thus, a hedge position of one call option cannot exactly offset the price movement in 100 shares of the stock.

To exactly offset a stock's price change, the investor must know the hedge ratio of the option. This is the ratio of the change in the price of the call option to the change in the price of the stock. The hedge ratio is also referred to as an option's **delta**. For a call option, the delta must be a positive number. (For a put, the delta is a negative number.) If the delta is 0.5, this means that the per-share price of the option will rise $0.50 for every $1.00 increase in the price of the stock. Thus, if the investor owns 100 shares of the stock and has written two calls (for 100 shares each), a $1.00 increase in the stock should generate a $1.00 per-share loss in the options (i.e., a $50 increase in the value of each option, which produces a total loss of $100 for the individual who has written two options). The $100 gain in one position (e.g., the long position in the stock) is exactly offset by the $100 loss in the other position (e.g., the short position in the option). The entire position is completely hedged.

> **delta**
> an option's hedge ratio, which is the rate of change of an option's price for changes in the value of the underlying asset

If an investor or a portfolio manager wants to exactly offset price changes by using options, the hedge ratio is crucial information. The reciprocal of the hedge ratio, which is

$$\text{Number of call options to hedge 100 shares} = \frac{1}{\text{Hedge ratio}} \qquad \textbf{16-6}$$

defines the number of call options that should be sold for each 100 shares purchased. (For short positions in the stock, the ratio indicates the number of calls the individual must buy for every 100 shares sold short.) Thus, in the previous example, the number of call options sold to construct a complete hedge is

$$\frac{1}{0.5} = 2$$

The portfolio manager must sell two call options for every 100 shares purchased to have a perfectly hedged position.

The **hedge ratio** may also be viewed as the number of shares of stock that must be purchased for each option sold. In the preceding example, the hedge ratio of 0.5 implies that 50 shares purchased for every call option sold is a completely hedged position. Both views of the hedge ratio are essentially the same. One view determines

> **hedge ratio**
> the number of shares that must be purchased for each option sold to have a perfectly hedged position

the number of shares to buy per call option, while the other determines the number of call options to sell per 100 shares of stock.

Fortunately, the hedge ratio is easy to obtain. The numerical value of $F(d_1)$ in the Black–Scholes option valuation model is the hedge ratio. In the preceding illustration of the valuation model, $N(d_1)$ was determined to equal 0.755. Thus at a price of the stock of $52, the number of call options necessary to completely hedge a position in the stock is $1/0.755 = 1.325$ options. Since the investor cannot buy or sell 1.325 call options, the hedge could be expressed as follows: For every call option, the investor takes the opposite position in shares of the stock. Thus, one call option hedges 76 shares of the stock.

While the hedge gives the number of call options that must be bought (or sold) for every 100 shares of stock, the numerical value of the ratio frequently changes. This is due to the value of the call being nonlinear in the value of the stock: when the current stock price changes, the value of the option changes, but it does so at different "slopes" depending upon the shape of the Black–Scholes valuation curve. As we saw in Figure 16-1, the slope of the line changes from being relatively flat for low prices of the stock to being parallel with the line representing the option's intrinsic value. Because the slope of the line increases with a rise in the stock's price, the numerical value of the hedge ratio also increases. This implies that fewer call options must be sold to construct a perfectly hedged portfolio. To maintain a perfectly hedged position, the individual must frequently adjust the positions in the call options or in the underlying securities.

The prior discussion focused on the use of call options and the hedge ratio to reduce the risk associated with a position in a particular stock. Investors, however, may wish to reduce the risk associated with their entire portfolios and may use stock index options to hedge their portfolios. To hedge a portfolio using stock index options, the investor must consider (1) the value of the portfolio, (2) the volatility of the portfolio, (3) the implied value of the option, and (4) the option's hedge ratio.

The value of the portfolio is the sum of the value of all the securities in the portfolio. The volatility of the portfolio is measured by the portfolio's beta. (Failure to include the beta assumes that the portfolio moves exactly with the market [i.e., that the beta $= 1.0$].) The implied value of the option is the product of the option's strike price and $100. [If a Standard & Poor's (S&P) 500 index option's strike price is 560, the implied value of the option is $560 \times \$100 = \$56,000$.] The hedge ratio is derived from the Black–Scholes option valuation model.

The number of index options necessary to hedge a portfolio is given in **Equation 16-7**:

$$\text{Number of index options} = \frac{\text{Value of the portfolio}}{\text{Implied value of the option}} \times \text{Portfolio's beta} \times \frac{1}{\text{Hedge ratio}} \qquad \textbf{16-7}$$

Exhibit 16-2 illustrates how an investor may hedge a $200,000 portfolio by writing index call options. The S&P 500 stock index stands at 550, and an out-of-the-money index stock call with a strike price of 560 sells for $800. (The price would be reported as $8 in the financial press, but the cost to the buyer and the proceeds to the seller are 8×100.) The stock index call option's hedge ratio is 0.4.

Equation 16-7 indicates that the investor should write 6.7 calls. Since fractional sales are not possible, the investor sells six calls for $800 each and receives $4,800 before commissions. In case 1, the market declines by 2% (the S&P 500 declines from 550 to 539). The decline in the market causes the price of the index option to fall from $8 to $3.50. The investor repurchases the six options for $2,100 and earns a profit of $2,700, which almost offsets the $3,000 loss on the portfolio. In case 2, the S&P 500 rises by 2% from 550 to 561, and the price of the call rises from $8 to $11. The investor loses $1,800 on the sale of the index options and earns a net profit of $1,200.

As these examples illustrate, using stock index options in hedged positions can reduce the risk of loss, but hedging also reduces and may erase the potential gain from the portfolio. Unlike covered call writing, which seeks to take advantage of the time premium disappearing as the option approaches expiration, the purpose of hedging is to reduce the impact of price fluctuations. This example illustrates the reduction in loss if the market were to decline, but the hedge reduces any gain when the market rises because the option is not at expiration and still commands a time premium. (The call's intrinsic value is $56,100 − $56,000 = $100, but it costs $1,100 to repurchase the option. The profit would be even smaller if the option commanded a larger time premium and the option price had been higher. At a cost of $1,400, the position would have generated a $200 loss even though the market rose.)

Exhibit 16-2: Using Stock Index Call Options to Hedge a $200,000 Portfolio

Givens

Value of portfolio: $200,000

Beta: 0.75

Value of S&P 500 stock index call: 550

Strike price of S&P 500 stock index call: 560

Implied value of S&P 500 stock index option: $100 × 560 = $56,000

Price of the stock index option: $8($800)

Hedge ratio: 0.4

Number of calls necessary to hedge: ($200,000/$56,000)(0.75)(1/0.4) = 6.7

Number of call index options sold: 6

Proceeds from the sale of one option: $800

Total received: 6 × $800 = $4,800

Market declines by 2% to 539

Price of one option: $350

Cost of the repurchase of options: $350 × 6 = $21,00

Gain on call options sold: $4,800 − $2,100 = $2,700

Loss on portfolio: $200,000(1 − 0.02) − $200.000(0.75) = −$3,000

Net loss: $2,700 − $3,000 = − $300

Market declines by 2% to 561

Price of one option: $1,100

Cost of the repurchase of options: $1,100 × 6 = $6,600

Loss on call options sold: $4,800 − $6,600 = −$1,800

Gain on portfolio: $200,000(1 + 0.02) − $200,000(0.75) = $3,000

Net loss: $3,000 − $1,800 = − $1,200

Constructing this hedge requires active portfolio supervision. The data necessary to construct a hedge include the portfolio's beta, which changes with the composition of the portfolio, and the option's hedge ratio. As was discussed earlier, the hedge ratio changes as the price of the option responds to changes in the underlying stock.

Maintaining a well-hedged portfolio requires continuous supervision and frequent rebalancing of the number of index options in the hedge. For the individual investor, using stock index options to hedge a portfolio can be both time-consuming and costly (when commissions are considered) and simply may be impractical. However, using stock index options in hedge positions could be a viable means to reduce the risk of loss for short periods of time when the investor is no longer bullish and does not want to liquidate the portfolio. (Another possibility for hedging a stock or a portfolio is the "collar" strategy considered in the next section on additional option strategies. For the individual investor, a collar may be more practical, as it avoids rebalancing and is a passive strategy.)

16-4a Delta and Other Greeks

An option's delta is the first derivative (the slope of the line) relating changes in the value of an option to changes in the price of the underlying stock. All the other variables in the Black–Scholes option valuation model are held constant. But these variables can change, and their first derivatives may also be important. Like delta, these slopes may be referred to by letters of the Greek alphabet. You may never use these Greeks, but knowing them should increase your ability to comprehend material that you may encounter in the literature on investments and portfolio management.

vega
change in the value of an option with respect to a change in volatility in the underlying asset

theta
change in the value of an option with respect to changes in time to expiration

rho
a change in the value of an option with respect to changes in the interest rate

gamma
the change in delta to the changes in the value of the underlying asset; the second derivative with respect to the price of the underlying asset

Vega refers to the change in the value of the option with respect to change in volatility. That is, an increase in the standard deviation of the stock's returns causes what change in the value of the option? Theta refers to the rate of change in the value of the option with respect to changes in time. As the option approaches expiration, how rapidly does the value of the option decline? Rho refers to the rate of change in the option's value with respect to a change in the interest rate. As the interest rate increases, what is the increase in the value of a call option?

Delta, vega, theta, and rho are first derivatives. You may encounter gamma, which is the second derivative relating the change in the price of an option to the change in the price of the stock. The line representing the value of a call option with respect to the price of the stock is a curve. Its slope changes as the price of the stock changes. Gamma measures the rate of change in that slope.

The hedge ratio is derived from the slope relating the price of the option to the price of the stock. This change in the slope means that an investor who uses the delta to hedge a position will have to readjust the number of options as the price of the stock changes. Because gamma measures the rate of change in the delta, sophisticated investors may use it to adjust the number of options. Such adjustments should facilitate their risk management strategies.

16-5 Additional Option Strategies

Even if arbitrage drives option markets toward an equilibrium so that the investor cannot take advantage of mispricings, fairly priced options may still be used in a variety of strategies. For example, in the previous chapter, the protective put was illustrated as a means to reduce potential loss. The investor bought a put when buying a stock, so if the value of the stock were to fall, the value of the put would rise and at least partially offset the loss on the stock.

This section covers several other strategies involving options. These include the **covered put** and the **protective call**. Next follow the **straddle**, which combines buying (or selling) both a put and a call, and the spreads, which involve the simultaneous purchase and sale of options with different strike prices on the same stock. The last strategy, the **collar**, which involves the stock and both a put and a call, is a means to limit the impact of a decline in the price of the stock. Although these additional strategies do not exhaust all the possible strategies using options, they do give an indication of the variety of possible alternatives available that employ puts and calls.

covered put
selling a stock short while selling a put on the stock

protective call
combining a short in a stock with a long call

straddle
the purchase of a put and call with the same exercise price and expiration date

collar
a protective position constructed by selling a call at one strike price and buying a put at a lower strike price

16-5a The Covered Put

The covered put is the opposite of the covered call. To construct a covered put, the investor sells the stock short and sells the put. If the put is exercised (forcing the investor to buy the stock), that individual may use the shares to cover the short in the stock. This is, of course, the opposite of the covered call, in which the writer supplies the previously purchased stock if the call option is exercised.

As with the covered call, the covered put limits the potential profit, but it also reduces risk. An investor constructs this position in anticipation of a stable stock price. If the investor anticipates a large change in the price of the stock, an alternative strategy

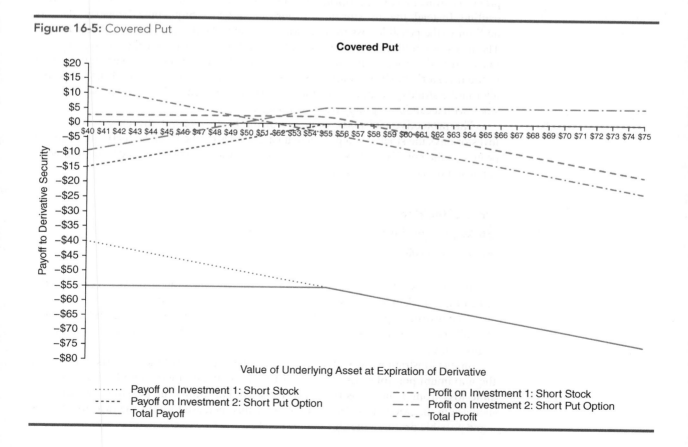

Figure 16-5: Covered Put

is superior to the covered put. For example, if the investor anticipates a large price decline, selling the stock short or buying the put offers more potential gain if the stock's price were to fall. To see the potential profit and loss from the covered put, consider the following example:

Price of the stock (P_s)	$52
Strike price of the put (P_e)	$55
Price of the put	$5.50

The put is in the money, since it has a positive intrinsic value ($P_e - P_s =$ $55 − $52 = $3). It is also selling for a time premium ($5.50 − $3 = $2.50). Because the investor expects the price of the stock to remain stable or decline modestly, a covered put is constructed by selling the stock short at $52 and selling the put for $5.50. The potential profit and loss at the expiration of the put from this position at various prices of the stock are shown in **Figure 16-5**.

As long as the price of the stock remains below $57.50, the position generates a profit, but the maximum possible net profit is $2.50 (the time premium of the put).

16-5b The Protective Call

Obviously, if the investor anticipates a large decline in the price of the stock, the previous strategy is inappropriate because it limits the potential profit from a price decline. Instead, the investor would short the stock (or buy a put). However, there is no limit to the possible loss from a short position if the price of the stock were to rise. The investor could limit the loss by entering a limit order to buy the stock and cover the short if the price of the stock were to rise. A limit order, however, could result in the investor's position being closed by a brief run-up in the price of the stock. An alternative strategy would be for the investor to buy a call. Combining a short in the stock with a call is the protective call strategy.

The protective call is the opposite of the protective put strategy, in which the investor buys the stock and a put. In that case, losses on the stock are partially offset by profits on the put. To see how the protective call strategy works, consider the following extension of the previous illustration:

Price of the stock	$52
Strike price of the call	$55
Price of the call	$1.50

In this illustration, the call is out of the money since the strike price exceeds the price of the stock. The option sells for a time premium of $1.50.

To construct a protective call, the investor shorts the stock at $52 and purchases the call for $1.50. The possible profits and losses from the position are as shown in **Figure 16-6**.

In this illustration, the worst case occurs when the price of the stock rises; however, the maximum possible loss is $4.50. Since theoretically there is no limit to the possible loss from a short position, the protective call limits the possible loss from an increase in the price of the stock. To achieve this increased safety, the investor forgoes some possible profit on the short in the stock.

Figure 16-6: Covered Put

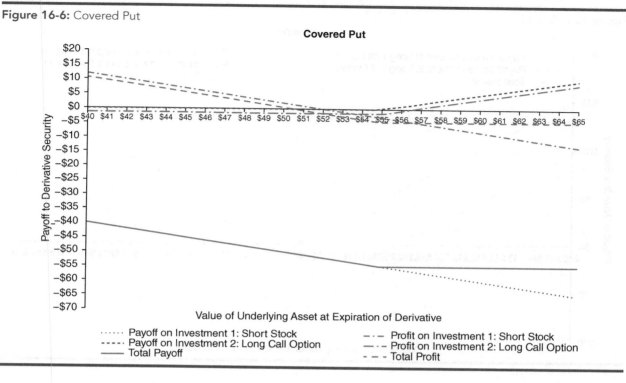

16-5c The Straddle

A straddle consists of a purchase (or sale) of a put and a call with the same exercise price and the same expiration date. If the investor buys both options, it is possible to earn a profit if the price of the stock rises or falls. The price increase may generate a profit on the call, and the price decline may generate a profit on the put.

Investors construct straddles if they expect the stock's price to move but are uncertain as to the direction. Consider a stock that is trading for $50 as the result of takeover rumors. If the takeover does occur, the price of the stock should rise. That argues for a long position in the stock. If the anticipated takeover does not occur and the rumors abate, the price of the stock will probably decline. That argues for a short position.

A long or a short position by itself may inflict losses if the investor selects the wrong position. To avoid this, the investor purchases both a put and a call. A price movement in either direction generates a profit (if the price movement covers the two premiums), and the maximum possible loss is the cost of the two options.

To see these potential profits and losses, consider the stock and the two options used in the previous illustrations:

Price of the stock	$52
Price of a call at $55	$1.50
Price of a put at $55	$5.50

Figure 16-7: Straddle

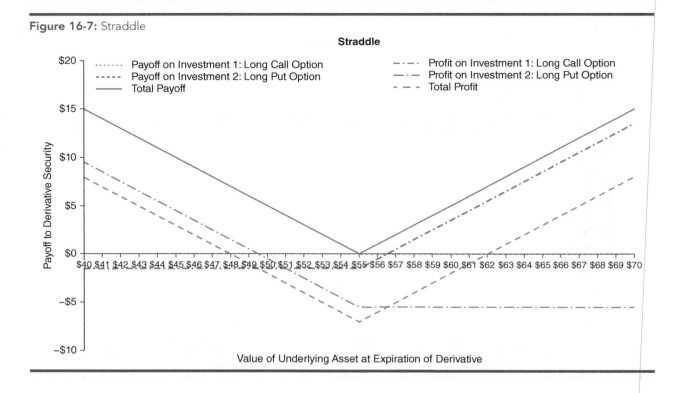

Instead of purchasing or shorting the stock, the investor buys both options. The possible profits and losses at the expiration of the options for various prices of the stock are shown in **Figure 16-7**.

The position generates a profit as long as the stock price exceeds $62 or is less than $48 (i.e., the range of stock prices that generates a loss is $48 $<P_s<$ $62). If the price of the stock moves either above $62 or below $48, the investor is assured of a profit. The maximum possible loss is $7, which occurs when the price of the stock equals the options' strike price at their expiration. At that price, neither option has any intrinsic value and both expire, so the investor loses the entire amount invested in both options.

Why would the investor construct a straddle in which it is possible to sustain a loss, even if the price fluctuates but does not fluctuate sufficiently to cover the cost of the two options? The answer is that the investor anticipates a large movement in the price of the stock but is uncertain as to the direction. This position offers potential profit if such a price change occurs and limits the loss if the anticipated change does not materialize.

If the investor expects the price of the stock to be stable, that individual *writes* a straddle. The investor sells a put and a call. This strategy is, of course, the opposite of buying a straddle and its profit/loss profile is the exact opposite.

16-5d The Bull Spread

The covered put, the protective call, and the straddle do not exhaust all the possible strategies using puts and calls. The investor can also construct spreads, using options with different strike prices and/or expiration dates. In this case, the investor takes a long position in one option and a short position in the other.

Consider the following:

Price of the stock	$52
Price of a call at $50	$5
Price of a call at $55	$1.50

The investor may construct a **bull spread** by purchasing the call with the lower strike price and selling the call with the higher strike price. In this illustration, the investor buys the $50s for $5 and sells (writes) the $55s for $1.50. The net cash outlay is $3.50 (the $5 cost of the call at $50 minus the $1.50 received from the sale of the call at $55). The profile of the possible profit and loss at the options' expiration for various prices of the stock is as shown in **Figure 16-8**.

The position generates a profit as long as the price of the stock exceeds $53.50, with a maximum possible profit of $1.50. The maximum possible loss is $3.50 (the net cash outlay). The amount of the profit may seem trivial, but since only $3.50 was at risk, the percentage return (before commissions) is 42.8 percent ($1.50/$3.50).

bull spread
a long position in a call with a lower strike price combined with a short position in a call on the same stock with a higher strike price

16-5e The Bear Spread

The investor could also reverse the preceding position and construct a **bear spread**. The investor buys the option with the higher strike price and sells the option with the lower strike price. In this illustration, the investor buys the option at $55 for $1.50 and sells the option at $50 for $5. This produces a net cash inflow; however, margin requirements will not permit the individual to remove the entire net proceeds.

bear spread
a long position in a call with a higher strike price combined with a short position in a call on the same stock with a lower strike price

Figure 16-8: Bull Spread

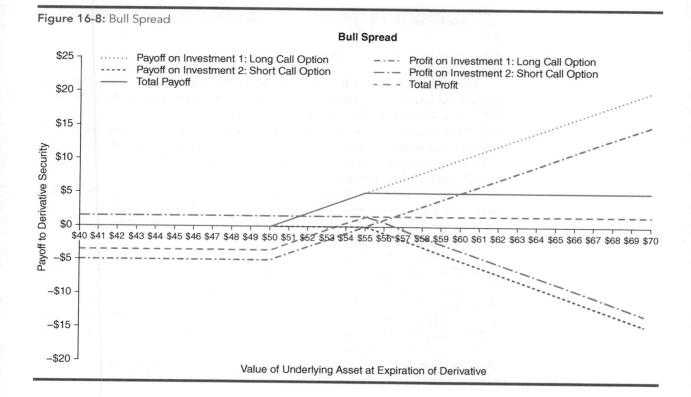

Both of these spreads are types of hedge positions because they combine a long position and a short position. The effect in both cases is to limit the possible loss, which has the corresponding effect of limiting the potential profit. Neither may be appropriate if the investor anticipates a large movement in the price of the stock in a particular direction. Instead, these spreads are appropriate when the investor anticipates modest price movements in a particular direction. If this expected price change is downward, the investor should sell the option with the lower strike price and buy the option with the higher strike price (i.e., construct the bear spread). Conversely, if a modest price increase is anticipated, the investor buys the option with the lower strike price and sells the option with the higher strike price (i.e., constructs the bull spread). In either case, if the price of the stock moves in the anticipated direction, the investor earns a modest profit on a small outlay. If the price of the stock moves against the investor, the spread protects the investor from a large loss.

16-5f Collars

In a shirt, there is an opening for the head and the cloth covers the shoulders. Both shoulders are protected, but there is room for the individual's head. A collar in investments is similar. The individual is protected on both sides from price movements.

A collar is constructed when an investor owns a stock and for some reason (possible reasons are considered later) wants to hedge against a movement in the stock's price. The investor constructs a collar by selling a call at one strike price and buying a put at a lower strike price. Since this strategy involves both a purchase and a sale, the cash flows offset each other, resulting in either a small cash inflow or, at worst, a modest cash outflow.

Consider the following options and their prices:

Strike Price	Price of a Call	Price of a Put
$45	NA	$2
50	$3	NA

The stock is currently selling for $48, and the investor owns 100 shares. The collar requires the investor to sell the call at $50, a $3 cash inflow, and purchase the put at $45, a $2 cash outflow. The result is a net cash inflow of $1. (This small inflow may cover the commissions, in which case the investor has no net cash outflow. No net cash outflow is one of the considerations when selecting options to establish the collar.) The investor now has three positions: (1) a long position in the stock, (2) a short position in the call, and (3) a long position in the put.

The profit/loss profile of the two option positions is shown in **Figure 16-9**. In this illustration, if the price of the stock rises, there is a modest gain. If the price of the stock declines, there is a modest loss. The investor's aim to avoid a possible large loss has been achieved.

The profit/loss profile for the collar is similar to the profit/loss profile for a bull spread. The positions, however, are different and serve different purposes. With a collar, the investor owns the stock and is attempting to avoid the impact of a price decline. Movements in the price of the stock in either direction have little or no effect. In a bull spread, the investor buys the call with the lower strike price and sells the call with the higher strike price. The investor does not own the stock. In a bull spread, the investor anticipates an increase in the price of the stock and wants to make a large percentage return on the modest amount invested. The purpose of the spread is to magnify the price increase while limiting the potential loss if the price of the stock declines.

Figure 16-9: Collar

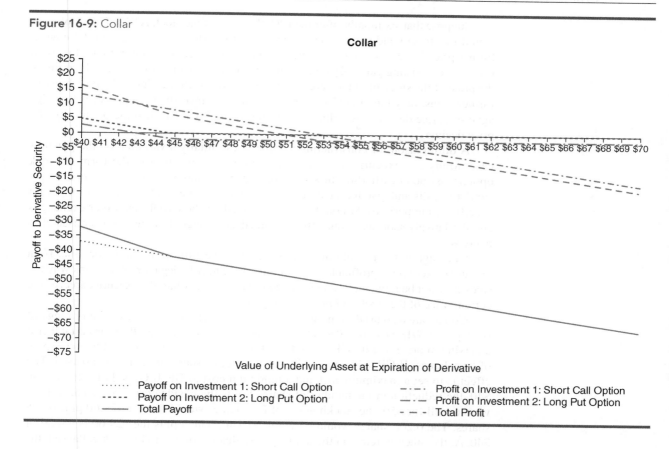

Collar

Payoff to Derivative Security / Value of Underlying Asset at Expiration of Derivative

.... Payoff on Investment 1: Short Call Option
----- Payoff on Investment 2: Long Put Option
——— Total Payoff

–·–· Profit on Investment 1: Short Call Option
——·— Profit on Investment 2: Long Put Option
– – – Total Profit

Why would an investor construct a collar? There are several reasons, which revolve around the timing of sales and limits on the investor's ability to sell. Consider the situation of an investor who bought the preceding stock at $20 and would like to sell at $48. The sale, however, produces a capital gain, which the investor would prefer to defer to the next taxable year. Constructing the collar locks in the price and the profit on the stock because if the price does change, the profits/losses on the various components cancel each other. The original appreciation in the stock from $20 to $48 is retained and the taxes are deferred until the positions are unwound, which could occur in the next taxable year.

Another, and more likely, reason for constructing the collar is to protect a gain when the investor is forbidden to sell the stock. Prior to an initial public offering (IPO), a firm may issue employees stock as compensation or grant employees options to buy the stock. For instance, a firm expects to go public and sell stock at $50 and grants current employees shares based on the following formula. Each employee is to receive stock based on 40% of that individual's prior year's compensation. That dollar value then will be divided by $50, the initial anticipated price of the IPO, to determine the number of shares that will be granted prior to the IPO. If an employee earned $80,000, the number of shares to be received is 640 shares (0.4[$80,000/$50]). The employee, however, cannot immediately sell the shares. Shares are restricted units, one-third of which may be sold on the anniversary dates of the IPO for the next three years. The employee can sell only 213 shares a year for the next three years. (The purpose of such restrictions is to avoid the dumping of stock right after an IPO, especially if the price of the stock rises. See the discussion of lock-ups in Chapter 2.)

Suppose that six months after the IPO, the price of the stock is $72. The employees would like to sell and realize the $22 profit, but the stock cannot be sold. Of course, further price increases would be welcome, but a price decline could inflict a loss or at least reduce existing gains. By constructing a collar, these employees are able to freeze the price of the stock until they are able to sell it. Although they forgo the possibility of further gains, they lock in existing profits. Since the investment objective is to hedge against a price decline, the collar protects these employees against the possibility of a price decline.

A third reason for constructing a collar is essentially a variation on the previous case. Many top executives receive additional compensation in the form of stock options instead of cash. (See the section on expensing options.) These stock options are similar to calls and give the executives the right to buy the stock at specified prices for specified time periods. Although the calls traded on the CBOE and other exchanges are of relatively short duration, options granted executives often may be exercised after many years.

Once again, the use of collars protects the investors from a price decline. If an executive exercises a profitable stock option, there may be legal or tax reasons why the stock may not be immediately sold. By constructing the collar, the executive freezes the current price of the stock and protects the gain.

Collars are also used in merger agreements to lock in a specified price or range of stock prices. When Georgia Pacific (GP) offered to buy Fort James, the terms established a maximum price of $40. GP offered $29.60 plus 0.2644 shares of GP for every share of Fort James. If GP sold above $40, the number of shares would be decreased. The effect is to set a maximum cost and a minimum cost to GP. If GP sold for more than $40, the reduction in the number of shares limits the upside cost to $40. Thus, if GP were to sell for $50, the stockholders of Fort James would receive $29.60 plus 0.208 shares. The 0.208 shares would be worth $10.40, which plus the $29.60 is a total of $40. At the other extreme, in the unlikely case that the price of GP stock collapsed, the stockholders of Fort James would receive $29.60. The effect is to guarantee Fort James stockholders $29.60 to $40 and to limit the cost to GP of the acquisition from $29.60 to $40. Such merger agreements, which guarantee a minimum but limit the upside price, are common when the acquiring firm offers to swap its stock for the other firm's stock.

Conclusion

While the previous chapter presented the basics concerning options, this chapter expanded that material by covering the Black–Scholes option valuation model; explaining how the stock, bond, and option markets are interrelated so that changes in one are transmitted to the others; and illustrating several strategies using options.

The Black–Scholes option valuation model specifies that the value of a call option is positively related to the price and to the volatility of the underlying stock. As the price of the stock rises, the value of the option rises. The same relationship holds for variability of returns, as options on volatile stocks command higher valuations. Call option values are also positively related to the life of the option. As the term of the option diminishes and the option approaches expiration, the option's value declines.

Although an increase in interest rates generally depresses the value of a financial asset, this negative relationship does not apply to options to buy stock. An increase in interest rates increases the value of the option, because higher rates reduce the present value of a call's strike price. The lower strike price then increases the value of the option to buy the stock.

In addition to being used to value publicly traded puts and calls, the Black–Scholes model may be applied to options issued by firms to selected employees, especially senior management. These options are part of incentive-based compensation packages. If the firm is successful and the value of its stock rises, the value of the options also increases. Since incentive options are part of the employee's compensation, an accounting question arises: Should the cost of the options be expensed? Expensing requires a valuation, and the Black–Scholes model is often used to value incentive options in order to determine their cost.

The Black–Scholes option valuation model also calculates the hedge ratio, which determines the number of options necessary to completely hedge a stock portfolio. A completely hedged portfolio means that any loss generated on one side (e.g., a long position in stocks) is offset by the gain on the opposite side (e.g., a short position in the options). Such a hedging strategy is executed by portfolio managers to reduce risk. Such risk reduction may not be available to individual investors, as the portfolio has to be rebalanced frequently as the hedge ratio changes.

Put–call parity explains the interrelationships among financial markets. In equilibrium, the price of the underlying stock, the price of the puts and calls on the stock, and the present value of the strike price (as affected by the rate of interest) must balance or an opportunity for a risk-free arbitrage would exist. As investors seek to execute the arbitrage, the prices of the various securities are affected. An implication of put–call parity is that any change in one of the markets (e.g., an increased demand for stocks) must be transmitted to the other markets.

Strategies using options include the covered put and the protective call, which are the reverse of the covered call and the protective put. Other possible option strategies are straddles, bull and bear spreads, and collars. Straddles and spreads involve buying or selling more than one option on the same stock. Straddles and spreads permit investors to take long, short, or hedged positions in stocks without actually owning or selling the stocks. Collars permit investors who own stock but cannot sell it to lock in the current price. All these strategies using options alter the individual's potential returns and risk exposure from investing in financial assets. Options, thus, are a means both to speculate on anticipated price movements in the underlying stocks and to manage the risk from actual price movements in the underlying stocks.

Chapter Equations

$$V_o = P_s \times N(d_1) - \frac{P_e}{e^{rT}} \times N(d_2) \tag{16-1}$$

$$d_1 = \frac{\ln\left(\frac{P_s}{P_e}\right) + \left(r + \frac{\sigma^2}{2}\right)T}{\sigma\sqrt{T}} \tag{16-2}$$

$$d_2 = d_1 - \sigma\sqrt{T} \tag{16-3}$$

$$P_s + P_p = P_c + \frac{P_e}{(1+i)^n} \tag{16-4}$$

$$P_p = P_c + \frac{P_e}{(1+i)^n} - P_s \tag{16-5}$$

$$\textit{Number of call options to hedge } 100 \textit{ shares} = \frac{1}{\textit{Hedge ratio}} \tag{16-6}$$

$$\textit{Number of index option} = \frac{\textit{Value of the portfolio}}{\textit{Implied value of the option}} \\ \times \textit{Portfolio's beta} \\ \times \frac{1}{\textit{Hedge ratio}} \tag{16-7}$$

Excel Functions

EXP(number)
LN(number)

NORMSDIST(z)
SQRT(number)

Key Terms

Binomial Cox–Ross–Rubinstein model – a binomial pricing model used to price options

Black–Scholes option valuation model – a differential equation-based model for pricing call contracts

bear spread – a long position in a call with a higher strike price combined with a short position in a call on the same stock with a lower strike price

bull spread – a long position in a call with a lower strike price combined with a short position in a call on the same stock with a higher strike price

collar – a protective position constructed by selling a call at one strike price and buying a put at a lower strike price

covered put – selling a stock short while selling a put on the stock

delta – an option's hedge ratio, which is the rate of change of an option's price for changes in the value of the underlying asset

gamma – the change in delta to the changes in the value of the underlying asset; the second derivative with respect to the price of the underlying asset

hedge ratio – the number of shares that must be purchased for each option sold to have a perfectly hedged position

protective call – combining a short in a stock with a long call

rho – a change in the value of an option with respect to changes in the interest rate

straddle – the purchase of a put and call with the same exercise price and expiration date

theta – change in the value of an option with respect to changes in time to expiration

vega – change in the value of an option with respect to a change in volatility in the underlying asset

Questions

1. **Black-Scholes sensitivity.** According to the Black–Scholes option valuation model, what is the relationship between the value of a call option and each of the following? (LO 16-1)
   a. Risk as measured by the variability of the underlying stock's return
   b. Interest rates
   c. The term of the option (i.e., the length of time to expiration)

2. **Put-call parity.** According to the Black–Scholes option valuation and put–call parity, what will happen to the value of a call option if interest rates decline? (LO 16-1)

3. **Risk inference.** How might the Black–Scholes option valuation model be used to determine the risk associated with the underlying stock? (LO 16-1)

4. **Straddle exposure.** An investor expects the price of a stock to remain stable and writes a straddle. What is this individual's risk exposure? How may the investor close the position? (LO 16-5)

5. **Bull spread.** Why would an investor use a bull spread instead of just buying a call? (LO 16-5)

6. **Put-call parity.** How would you use put–call parity to value a stock? (LO 16-2)

7. **Risk mitigation.** You sell a stock short. How can you use an option to reduce your risk of loss should the price of the stock rise? (LO 16-5)

8. **Straddle.** If you thought a stock was fairly valued and its price would not change, how could you use a straddle to take advantage of your valuation? (LO 16-5)

9. **Risk management.** How do collars, the hedge ratio, the protective call, and the protective put help investors manage risk? (LO 16-5)

10. **Volatility impact.** Explain what effect an increase on volatility in the underlying stock would have on a call option. (LO 16-1)

Problems

1. **Call valuation.** A stock sells for $28. What is the value of a one-year call option to buy the stock at $25, if debt currently yields 10% and the standard deviation of stock returns is 15%? (LO 16-2)

2. **Call valuation.** A stock sells for $32. What is the value of a three-month call option to buy the stock at $35, if debt currently yields 8% and the standard deviation of stock returns is 15%? (LO 16-2)

3. **Put valuation.** A stock sells for $28. What is the value of a one-year put option to buy the stock at $25, if debt currently yields 10% and the standard deviation of stock returns is 15%? (LO 16-2)

4. **Put valuation.** A stock sells for $32. What is the value of a three-month put option to buy the stock at $35, if debt currently yields 8% and the standard deviation of stock returns is 15%? (LO 16-2)

5. **Hedge ratio.** One useful piece of information derived from the Black–Scholes model for the valuation of a call option is the hedge ratio, which gives the slope of the line relating the change in the price of an option to the change in the price of the stock. If the delta is 0.7 and the investor owns 600 shares of stock, how may the investor use call options to hedge the position? (LO 16-4)

6. **Put-call parity.** Put–call parity basically says that the combination of a stock and a put produces the same return as the comparable position in a call and a risk-free bond. If not, at least one market is in disequilibrium. The resulting arbitrage alters the securities' prices until the value of the stock plus the put equals the prices of the call and the bond. However, put–call parity only holds at the current stock price: things will have to readjust if the stock price changes. If the price of a stock is currently $100 while the price of a call option at $100 is $9, the price of the put option at $100 is $3, and the price of a discounted bond is $94, show that put–call parity holds at the current stock price of $100 but *wouldn't* hold if all else remained the same but the stock price changed to $90, $95, $105, or $110. (LO 16-2)

7. **Put strategy.** Currently, a stock that sells for $57 has a put option at $55 and another at $60. The prices of the options are $6 and $3, respectively. What would you do? (LO 16-2)

8. **Call valuation.** A stock sells for $25. What is the value of a one-year call option to buy the stock at $28, if debt currently yields 10% and the standard deviation of stock returns is 15%? (LO 16-2)

9. **Hedge ratio.** One useful piece of information derived from the Black–Scholes model for the valuation of a call option is the hedge ratio, which gives the slope of the line relating the change in the price of an option to the change in the price of the stock. If the delta is 0.66 and the investor owns 1,300 shares of stock, how may the investor use call options to hedge the position? (LO 16-4)

10. **Position payoff.** Suppose an investor sells a stock short and sells a put on the stock with a strike price of $35. What will be the net payoff to their total position if the stock price is at $30 at option expiration? (LO 16-5)

11. **Position payoff.** You short shares of ABM at $20 and buy a call on ABM with an exercise price of $23. What will be your total payoff if the stock is selling for $25 at option expiration? (LO 16-5)

12. **Straddle payoff.** Suppose you enter into a straddle with an exercise price of $37. What will your payoff be at a price of $41? (LO 16-5)

13. **Straddle payoff.** Suppose you enter into a straddle with an exercise price of $21. What will your payoff be at a price of $18? (LO 16-5)

14. **Bull spread profit.** You enter into a bull spread by purchasing a call with a strike price of $79 and selling a call with a strike price of $90. If the first call costs $10 and the second call sells for $3, at what underlying stock price will you break even? (LO 16-5)

15. **Bull spread strategy.** You enter into a bull spread by purchasing a call with a strike price of $29 and selling a call with a strike price of $40. If the first call costs $7 and the second call sells for $3, what is the lowest price you will exercise the first call at? (LO 16-5)

16. **Bull spread profit.** You enter into a bull spread by purchasing a call with a strike price of $47 and selling a call with a strike price of $50. If the first call costs $7 and the second call sells for $3, what is the most profit you can make from this strategy? (LO 16-5)

17. **Bull spread strategy.** You enter into a bear spread by selling a call with a strike price of $47 and buying a call with a strike price of $50. If the first call sells for $7 and the second call costs $3, what is the most profit you can make from this strategy? (LO 16-5)

18. **Collar profit.** You enter into a collar by selling a call with a strike price of $47 for $4.00 and buying a put with a strike price of $35 for $3.00 when you already own the stock. What is the most profit you can make from this strategy? (LO 16-5)

19. **Implied standard deviation.** A stock sells for $28 and a one-year call option on the stock with a $37 exercise price sells for $5.70. If debt currently yields 10%, what is the implied annual standard deviation in stock returns? (LO 16-2)

20. **Implied standard deviation.** A stock sells for $67 and a three-month call option on the stock with a $73 exercise price sells for $3.70. If debt currently yields 8%, what is the implied annual standard deviation in stock returns? (LO 16-2)

Case Study

Option Valuation

Got to www.cboe.com and retrieve the latest ask price for the call option on Amazon (AMZN) with the highest strike price maturing the soonest. Download the last five years' worth of monthly prices for AMZN from www.finance.yahoo.com and use the adjusted closing prices to estimate annual standard deviation in returns. Use that standard deviation, along with other applicable information from the CBOE option quote, to calculate the Black–Scholes valuation for the option. How does it compare to the actual quoted ask price?

Part

6

Special Topics

Part 6 of this text explores the stock price and volume action known as Technical Analysis (Chapter 17)

Chapter 17

Technical Analysis

Traders often look at price and volume trends to guide short-term buy and sell decisions. While contrarian traders might hold off on buying when a stock price has spiked up on heavy volume, momentum players look to buy stocks that go up on rising volume. The interpretation of key signals obviously differs, but many contrarian and momentum players pay close attention to price and volume information. Even long-term investors using fundamental analysis to decide what stocks to buy may consult price and volume information to determine *when* to buy them. Both fundamental investors and growth-stock advocates often look to recent price and volume information to help guide their buy and sell decisions. Look at Yahoo! Finance or MSN Money and note the prominent role played by price and volume charts. The same is true in the print and broadcast media. The graphical display of price–volume information has obvious and widespread appeal.

Despite the pervasive popularity of eye-catching displays of price–volume information, many academics remain skeptical about the usefulness of **technical analysis**. As a result, some mainstream academics regard technical analysis as antiquated and simply ignore it in their investments classes. However, technical analysis is an interesting and useful part of a well-rounded study of investments for two reasons. First, part of becoming knowledgeable about investments involves becoming familiar with popular terms and methods of analysis. After all, technical analysis has a language of its own that's frequently used in the media. The analysis of price and volume information is certainly popular, and investors need to know what the buzz is about. Second, even if the effectiveness of technical analysis is doubtful, popular use of technical analysis is an interesting aspect of investor behavior. Why do investors consult charts?

This chapter is a brief introduction to technical analysis. It begins by describing several methods used in technical analysis. These techniques, such as charting and moving averages, may be applied to aggregate financial markets or to individual stocks.

technical analysis
The study of historical price and volume information to forecast future prices

17-1 The Technical Analysis Approach

17-1a Supply and Demand

Technical analysis involves the study of price and volume information and is based on a simple premise. Technical analysts believe that changes in the short-run supply and demand for a stock cause prices to change. Instead of focusing on the intrinsic or economic value of a stock, as fundamental analysts do, technical analysts try to understand, measure, and predict the forces of supply and demand. Technical analysts sometimes rely on charts for their analysis. Many profess to know nothing about the business operations of the stocks depicted on their charts and graphs. Others see technical analysis merely as a means for identifying attractive purchase or sale prices and a useful supplement to fundamental analysis.

To value a company, fundamental analysts strive to understand the underlying business. They determine the company's expected revenues, profits, and cash flows (see Chapter 11). Such detailed company-specific operating and valuation information is of much less interest to the technical analyst. In technical analysis, the relevant information is contained in past share price and trading volume information. This information can be communicated by summary data, sophisticated equations, or charts to express whether the optimism that drives buyer demand for a stock is mounting or fading. Technical analysts also look to charts to examine whether the pessimism for a stock that fuels seller supply is mounting or diminishing.

Technical analysts focus on understanding and predicting supply and demand relationships for stocks, bonds, and commodities. They also seek to assess *who* is buying and selling. This stems from the basic economic principles of supply and demand. Anyone who has taken a basic economics course remembers the supply versus demand graphs that determine price. Change supply and/or demand, and the price changes.

17-1b A Visual Approach

The New York Stock Exchange has always distributed stock price quotes and volume. Many decades ago, investors would literally sit at their local brokerage firms and watch stock price and volume information on what was referred to as the **ticker tape**. In those days, the ticker tape was paper. Today, financial institutions, markets, and even business schools have elaborate digital ticker tape displays.

ticker tape
A paper or electronic representation of stock prices appearing in a linear manner

Ticker tape information isn't useful for determining a firm's fundamental value but might be helpful in assessing short-term supply and demand conditions for a stock. Because price and volume information are a natural by-product of the trading process, it has been widely available since the start of organized trading. Indeed, early in the evolution of the stock market, prices and volumes were the only sound information available to investors. The sophisticated accounting data obtained today was either not available or not trustworthy at the time. Therefore, technical analysis is a much older profession than fundamental analysis. Since the beginning, technicians have used market price–volume information to develop measures of market activity that go beyond just the reporting of market index levels and overall trading volume information. Technicians want to know more than just whether the stock market went up or down today. Technicians study how many companies rose in price versus how many declined during the trading period. If the number of firms rising in price declines over time, this could lead to an interpretation that demand is weakening. That might indicate a market top is approaching. Conversely, if the number of firms falling in price declines over time, it could mean that supply is drying up and that a market bottom is approaching.

Modern proponents of technical analysis face the problem of having to efficiently condense and interpret widely available price–volume information. One method for doing this is to use a visual approach based on graphs of stock price and volume data. This process is called **charting** and is an important aspect of technical analysis.

Here are a few of the many websites with charting tools:

- Big Charts: bigcharts.marketwatch.com
- FINVIZ: finviz.com
- TradingView: tradingview.com
- Yahoo! Finance: finance.yahoo.com

charting
The use of two-dimensional price and volume graphs to analyze market behavior and anticipate future price movements

17-1c Theory and Practice

Technical analysis is an important part of the investment industry. Lots of traders seem to use technical trading rules to guide their trading decisions. Lots of individual investors also appear interested in technical analysis. Whenever a stock analyst discusses an investment opportunity on television, the discussion seems to always be accompanied by a price chart that depicts recent price and volume information.

However, according to the efficient market hypothesis (EMH) (Chapter 8), the current market price is the best available estimate of the intrinsic value of the firm. Moreover, short-run changes in price and volume information appear to be essentially random in nature. Trading rules based on historical price and volume information are fruitless in a perfectly efficient market. Thus, technical analysis is a controversial subject in academia and on Wall Street. If markets are highly efficient, technical trading tools will not enable investors to earn positive abnormal returns.

In an imperfectly efficient stock market in which investor psychology plays an important role, fundamental valuation is not all that matters. In an imperfectly efficient stock market, how investors react matters. If investment news and information make investors optimistic, their buying pressure on stocks will cause prices to rise. If investment news and information make investors pessimistic, prices will fall.

The CMT Association (cmtassociation.org) provides the industry with a technical analysis certification: the Chartered Market Technician® (CMT). To earn the CMT, you must pass three exams covering the totality of technical analysis subjects. The CMT Association is also a national association for market professionals interested in technical analysis. It sponsors national conferences, an academic journal, webinars, and local meetings.

17-2 Charting

17-2a Dow Theory

The Dow theory is one of the oldest technical methods for analyzing securities prices. It is an aggregate measure of securities prices and hence does not predict the direction of change in individual stock prices. What it purports to show is the direction that the general market will take. Thus, it is a method that tries to identify the top of a bull market and the bottom of a bear market.

The Dow theory developed from the work of Charles Dow (1851–1902). Dow founded Dow Jones and Company and was the first editor of the *Wall Street Journal*. Dow identified three movements in securities prices: primary, secondary, and tertiary.

- Primary trend price movements are related to the security's intrinsic value. Such values depend on the earning capacity of the firm and the distribution of dividends.
- Secondary trend price movements, or "swings," are governed by current events that temporarily affect value by the manipulation of stock prices. These price swings may persist for several weeks and even months.
- Tertiary trend price movements are daily price fluctuations to which Dow attributed no significance.

Although Charles Dow believed in fundamental analysis, the Dow theory evolved into a technical approach to the stock market. It asserts that stock prices demonstrate patterns over four to five years and that these patterns are mirrored by indexes of stock prices. The Dow theory employs two of the Dow Jones averages: the industrial average and the transportation average.

If one of the averages starts to decline after a period of rising stock prices, the two are at odds. For example, the industrial average may be rising while the transportation average is falling. This is referred to as a divergence. It suggests that the industrials may not continue to rise but may soon start to fall. Hence, the smart investor will use this signal to sell securities and convert to cash.

The converse occurs when, after a period of falling securities prices, one of the averages starts to rise while the other continues to fall. According to the Dow theory, this divergence suggests that the bear market is over and that securities prices in general will soon start to rise. The investor will then purchase securities in anticipation of the price increase.

Dow theory
The idea that market movements can be predicted by studying trends in the Dow Jones Industrial Average (DJIA) and Dow Jones Transportation Average (DJTA)

primary trend
A bull and bear market that lasts anywhere from less than one year up to several years

secondary trend
A short-term move in the market that runs contrary to the primary trend and usually last from three weeks to three months

tertiary trend
A very short-term stock market trend that reflects minor price moves

divergence
A disagreement between market direction between indicators

17-2b Demand Support and Supply Resistance

A basic tenet of technical analysis is that *trends in supply and demand tend to persist*. This explains the common phrase, "the trend is your friend." Another core belief is that momentum is to be expected in terms of changes in supply and demand. You should follow the current trend while looking for signs that the trend is ending and that a new trend is about to begin. When the trend changes, so must your strategy. Technical analysis is a trading tool used to guide short-term buy and sell decisions.

Consider two years of daily stock prices for Tesla, Inc., graphed in **Figure 17-1**. Also depicted is the 50-day price moving average (MA). Each point on a 50-day moving average shows the average price over the previous 50 trading days (roughly two calendar months). Use of the 200-day moving average is also popular among technicians, whose points show average prices over 200 trading days, roughly one year of trading activity. Notice that moving averages show much less volatility than the actual price graph. This makes it easier for technical analysts to surmise the underlying trend

50-day moving average
The average stock price over the previous 50 trading days (roughly two calendar months)

200-day moving average
The average stock price over the previous 200 trading days (roughly one year)

Figure 17-1: Tesla Stock Prices with Moving Averages and Support and Resistance Lines

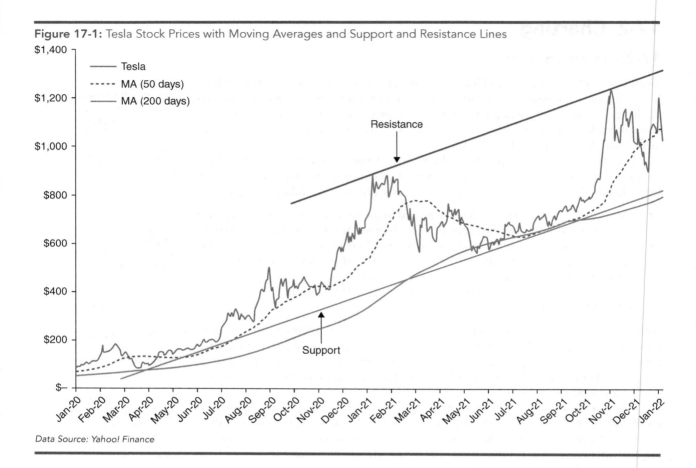

Data Source: Yahoo! Finance

in prices. From a visual perspective, technical analysts see that the price trend is reversing itself when the actual price line crosses over an important moving average. When the actual price line crosses from below to above its moving average, a bull trend has started, and a buy signal is generated. Similarly, when the actual price crosses the moving average from above to below, the new trend is bearish, and the signal is to sell. As shown in the figure, Tesla indicated a sell signal in February of 2021, when its price fell below the 50-day moving average (orange line). The price continued to fall through March and then traded mostly sideways through April. One problem with using a moving average with fewer days being averaged (like 50 days versus 200 days) is that there can be a lot of trading signals. The chart shows a buy signal in late April and then another sell signal in May. Frequent trading can lower profits. The 200-day moving average (gray line) has very few buy or sell signals except for the May to August 2021 period, in which the stock price crossed over the moving average several times.

In addition to the moving average lines, the chart depicts a **resistance line** and a **support line**. The resistance line (in purple) represents price points at which selling pressure (supply) has emerged in the past and can therefore limit a stock's upside potential. However, once the current stock price has risen through the resistance line, called a **breakout**, the price is predicted to continue rising. A price support line (in yellow) connects relatively low points on a stock price graph and represents prices at which additional demand for the stock has emerged in the past. The support line also represents price points at which buying pressure (demand) is expected to emerge in

resistance line
A graphical depiction of price points at which selling pressure (supply) has emerged in the recent past

support line
A graphical depiction of price points at which additional demand for the stock has emerged in the past

breakout
A change in trend out of the channel

the future to limit a stock's downside risk. Technical analysts believe that as the price increases to approach the resistance line, more investors want to sell, thereby increasing supply and limiting future price increases. On the other hand, as prices decline toward the support line, more investors want to buy, thereby increasing demand and limiting downside risk.

Taken together, the resistance line and the support line form a **channel** trend for the price. According to technical analysts, as prices bounce between the upper and the lower bounds of the channel, excess demand or supply will eventually get used up and the price will break out of the channel. A breakout through the support line is bearish, while a breakout to the upside of the resistance line is bullish. Whenever a channel breakout occurs, technical analysts say that a new trend is forming. Eventually, new support and resistance lines will be drawn to illustrate the channel of the new trend. The figure shows an *ascending channel* that rises over time. A *descending channel* represents a bear market trend. A *horizontal channel* moves laterally across time.

channel
The area between resistance and support lines that illustrates the direction of the trend

17-2c Types of Charts

Figure 17-1 displayed a typical line graph. However, using a daily line graph to present daily stock prices over time loses some data. The line graph connects the closing daily price for each day into a line. Note that the trading range during the day could also provide important information. A **bar graph** shows the high for the day, the low for the day, and the closing price. A vertical line represents the range of the stock's price (i.e., the high and the low prices), and the horizontal line represents the closing price.

Sometimes the bar graphs are expanded to candlesticks. A **candlestick graph** requires one additional piece of data: the opening price. Like the bar graph, a thin line connects the high and low prices. The body of the candlestick connects the opening and closing prices. If the opening price exceeds the closing price, indicating that the price fell, the body of the candlestick is filled in with black or red. If the opening price is less than the closing price (the price rose), the body is filled in as clear or with green. As perhaps would be expected, dark or red candlesticks (especially long sticks, which indicate a large decline from the opening to the closing price) are bearish indicators, while light or green candlesticks are bullish.

Yahoo! Finance can graph line, bar, and candlestick charts. As the purple circles show in **Exhibit 17-1** for Disney stock, the Chart link has this graphing capabilities with various options. This chart shows one day intervals, but there are options from one minute to 12-month intervals.

bar graph
A chart that depicts historical high, low, and closing security prices

candlestick graph
A chart that depicts historical open, high, low, and closing security prices

17-2d Price Patterns

Technical analysts believe that specific price patterns tend to emerge when the forces of supply and demand change. Changes in trend are due to a shift in supply or demand. As these shifts sort themselves over time, they create consistent patterns. Over the past 100 years, a variety of price patterns has been identified and categorized. Technical analysts look for these familiar patterns and use them to predict the future direction of price changes.

The **head and shoulders** chart price pattern is perhaps the most popular. Candlesticks may also be used to graph head and shoulder patterns and other configurations that technical analysts use to forecast the direction of stock prices. As its name implies, the head and shoulders pattern is made up of a left shoulder, head, right shoulder, and neckline. **Figure 17-2** illustrates the pattern. While still in an uptrend, the left shoulder forms a peak that marks the high point of the current trend. After making this

head and shoulders
A popular price chart pattern that signals a reversal to a bear market trend

Excel Expert 17-1

Moving Averages

Daily stock prices for The Walt Disney Company (DIS) are obtained for a 5-year period from Yahoo! Finance, then sorted so that the most recent prices appear at the top. Note that computing a moving average is easy. Simply average the past X days of prices, copy and paste. The Excel screenshot below shows the 50- and 200-day moving averages.

	A	B	C	D	E	F
1	Date	DIS	50-Day MA	200-Day MA		
2	1/14/2022	151.94	155.15	172.24	=AVERAGE(B2:B201)	
3	1/13/2022	155.44	155.51	172.42		
4	1/12/2022	157.8	155.80	172.57		
5	1/11/2022	157.89	156.05	172.70		
6	1/10/2022	156.6	156.27	172.84		
7	1/7/2022	157.83	156.54	172.99		
8	1/6/2022	156.9	156.77	173.13		
9	1/5/2022	155.19	157.07	173.27		

Graphing the DIS prices and both moving averages looks like this:

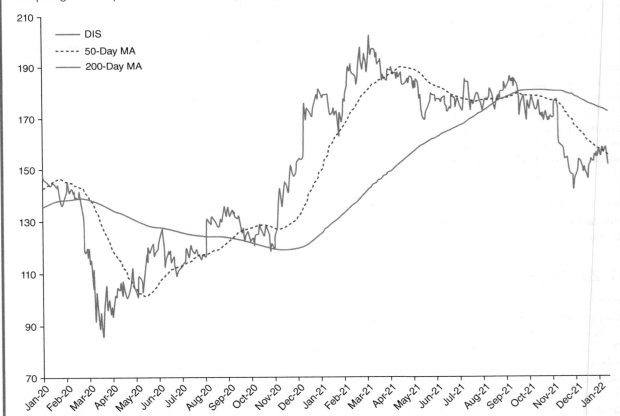

Note that the 50-day MA signaled many buy and sell trades through 2020. However, the last buy signal in November 2020 preceded a sharp increase in price. The 200-day MA signaled fewer trades. A longer moving average signals fewer trades but also often signals a buy or sell trade after the stock has already been rising or falling for some time. Thus, some profit opportunities are missed.

Exhibit 17-1: Yahoo! Finance Charting Options

Source: Yahoo! Finance

peak, a decline ensues to complete the formation of the shoulder. The low of the decline usually remains above the trend line, keeping the uptrend intact. From the low of the left shoulder, an advance begins that exceeds the previous high and marks the top of the head. After peaking, the low of the subsequent decline marks the second point of the neckline. The low of the decline usually breaks the uptrend line, putting the uptrend in jeopardy. The right shoulder peak is lower than the head (a lower high) and usually in line with the high of the left shoulder. While symmetry is preferred, sometimes shoulders can be out of whack. The decline from the peak of the right shoulder should break the neckline. The neckline forms by connecting low points from the formation of each shoulder prior to the formation of the head. Depending on the relationship between the two low points, the neckline can slope up, slope down, or be horizontal. The slope of the neckline will affect the pattern's degree of bearishness—a downward slope is more bearish than an upward slope. During a bull market trend, the formation of the head and shoulders pattern *signals a reversal to a bear market trend*. A sell signal occurs when the price falls below the neckline after the right shoulder forms.

While the head and shoulders price formation pattern is one of the most popular price formations studied by chartists, dozens of other price patterns also come under scrutiny. Examples of popular price patterns are shown in **Exhibit 17-2**. **Reversal patterns** that indicate an important change in trend include the head-and-shoulders top and the head-and-shoulders bottom. **Continuation patterns** that indicate a persistence of the underlying bullish or bearish trend include the flag, pennant, rectangle, and triangle. The study of reversal and continuation patterns is an interesting and colorful aspect of stock market lore, with pattern names like bump and run, double top,

reversal pattern
A change in trend signal

continuation pattern
The persistence of the underlying bullish or bearish trend

Excel Expert 17-2 ⟩⟩

Bar and Candlestick Charts

Weekly stock prices for The Walt Disney Company (DIS) are obtained from Yahoo! Finance, then sorted so that the most recent prices appear at the top. For the bar graph, you need the Date, High, Low, and Close prices. Highlight them for the period desired. The bar and candle graphs can be found in the Stock group of charts:

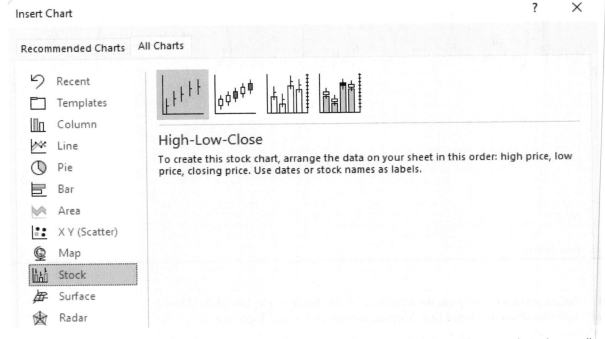

Insert Chart   ?   ×

Recommended Charts   All Charts

↺ Recent
▢ Templates
▥ Column
📈 Line
◔ Pie
⬛ Bar
◰ Area
⦂⦂ X Y (Scatter)
◉ Map
▥ Stock
⧗ Surface
✦ Radar

High-Low-Close

To create this stock chart, arrange the data on your sheet in this order: high price, low price, closing price. Use dates or stock names as labels.

The High-Low-Close graph is the bar chart. The one next to it, the Open-High-Low-Close graph, is the candle chart. The bar graph for one year of weekly returns is:

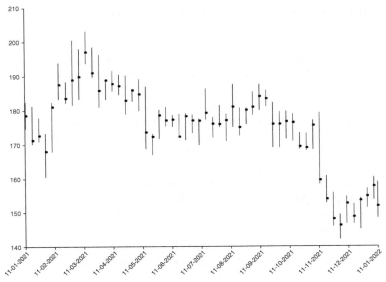

(Continued)

For the candlestick chart, you need the Date, Open, High, Low, and Close prices. Highlight them for the period desired.

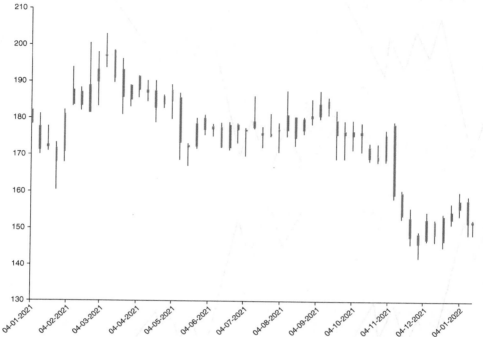

You can use the graph options to color the candlesticks green and red as shown here, or use any colors.

Figure 17-2: Head and Shoulders Pattern

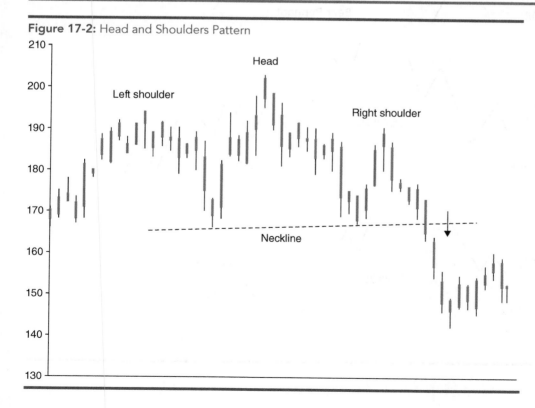

Exhibit 17-2: Popular Chart Patterns

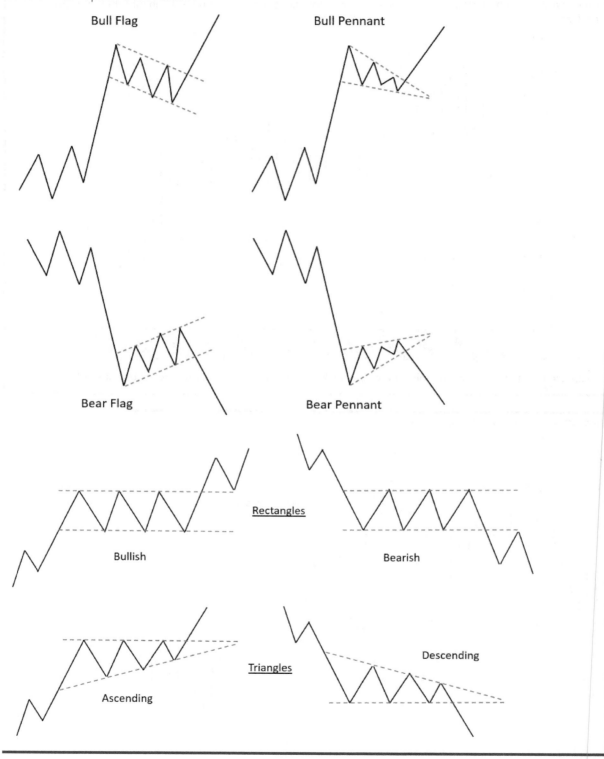

double bottom, falling wedge, rising wedge, rounding bottom, triple top, triple bottom, and cup with handle. These patterns reflect support and resistance between demand and supply trigger prices. If you are interested in this topic, there are entire books written about charts. Chartists use price patterns to make future price predictions but do not take such predictions as literal truth. Instead, they think of such forecasts in terms of probabilities. *If* the bearish prediction of a head-and-shoulders pattern is correct 66.7% of the time, investors making decisions based on this pattern would be correct twice as often as they are wrong. When dealing with the uncertainty of the stock market, charting is one tool that technical analysts believe provides investors with methods for profitably assessing the underlying forces of supply and demand.

17-3 Volume

While price information can be useful for identifying trends that are caused by changes in supply and demand, the volume of trading also has the potential to provide useful information. When investors are uncertain, they do nothing. That is why trading volume tends to diminish during periods of sideways movement or near a market reversal. Trading volume information can give you clues as to the possible future direction of prices by measuring the level of conviction among buyers and the sellers.

Technical analysts often interpret volume information alongside underlying price trends. For the primary trend to continue, volume should increase in the direction of that trend. Technical analysts believe that if the primary trend in prices is up, then volume should be higher on up days and lower on down days. Alternatively, if the primary price trend is down, volume should be higher on down days. It is often taken as a warning that the trend in place is losing steam and that a reversal could be ahead if volume starts to decline. In a bull market trend, when trading volume is higher on dips than on rallies, technicians typically believe that buying pressure is diminishing and sellers are becoming more aggressive. Any large divergence between the primary price trend and the trend in volume is typically taken as a warning of a pending reversal.

Technical analysts do more than simply contrast volume on up days with volume on down days. The most positive signal is a bullish price trend with increasing volume on up days. For a price trend to be bullish, price should climb on rising volume with minor setbacks. If a new high in price is not confirmed by a new high in volume, technical analysts regard this as a warning that the positive price trend may be close to reversing. **Figure 17-3** shows price and volume information for Meta Platforms Inc., known as Facebook (FB). Note that in phase 1 of the chart, both the price and the volume are increasing. This is a bullish signal. In phase 2, the volume and price diverge. The price keeps rising while the volume declines. The divergence increases in magnitude in phase 3, which signals a reversal in the price trend. Phase 4 shows the new downward price trend for FB. This is considered a strong new bear trend because volume is increasing.

Technical analysts believe that heavy volume on moderate price changes suggests that the market psychology is changing. Significant market bottoms are often characterized by heavy volume. If the overall market or an individual stock price rises slightly on heavy volume, an already established bear trend is thought to be in the process of reversing. A similar interpretation is given during bull trends. If a price trend seems to have stalled out in a long bull market, it is called a final **blow off** if volume continues to rise when prices have stalled. This is seen as a bearish signal.

blow off
A spike in volume when prices have stalled

Figure 17-3: Price and Volume Chart of Meta Platforms (Known as Facebook, FB)

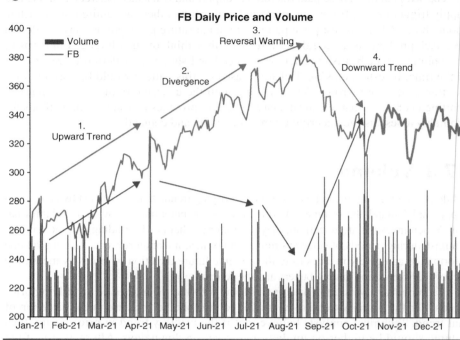

17-4 Technical Indicators

17-4a Market Breadth

market breadth
A measure of the number of issues that are rising relative to the number that are declining

Even during a rampant bull market, not all stocks rise in price. Individual stocks never rise in a straight line, and neither does the overall market. Some stocks and market sectors flourish during the early part of the business cycle, while others do best while an economic recovery is well under way. For the overall market to be classified as healthy, the bulk of stocks must be rising in price on rising volume. Market breadth measures how many issues are rising relative to the number of issues that are declining (see **Table 17-1**). If companies from only one sector of the market are driving the market higher, then such a rally suffers from bad breadth. Unless breadth increases, technical analysts worry that the bull market is aging or nearing an end.

advance–decline ratio
The number of firms that advanced in price divided by the number that declined on a given trading day

Some of the most widely used market breadth measures are based on advance–decline data. At the end of the trading day, each trading venue reports the number of stocks that advanced in value, declined, and remained unchanged. On January 14, 2022, the S&P 500 Index gained 0.08%, while the Nasdaq gained 0.59%. **Table 17-1** shows the number of stocks advancing and declining that day. For example, 2,106 NASDAQ stocks advanced in price while 2,491 declined in price. Nasdaq's advance–decline ratio for that trading day is the number of firms that advanced in price divided by the number that declined, or 0.845 (= 2,106/2,491). The advance–decline ratio is considered by technical analysts as good measure of the overall market's direction. Technicians consider it bullish if the advance–decline ratio is greater than 1 and bearish if the ratio is less than 1.

Table 17-1: Markets Diary for January 14, 2022, Wall Street Journal

	NYSE	NASDAQ
Issues		
Advancing	1,350	2,106
Declining	1,994	2,491
Unchanged	135	281
Total	3,479	4,878
Issues At		
New Highs	101	79
New Lows	199	685
Share Volume		
Total	4,478,992,869	4,438,787,247
Advancing	2,311,451,434	2,496,495,925
Declining	2,067,938,747	1,826,639,422
Unchanged	99,602,688	115,651,900

The **advance–decline line** is the ongoing sum of the number of advancing stocks minus the number of declining stocks. Like the advance–decline ratio, it is used as a measure of market strength because a rising advance–decline line reflects the fact that there are more advancing issues than declining issues. If the advance–decline line moves lower, there are more declining issues than advancing issues. If the advance–decline line is rising, advancing issues are dominating declining issues and the market is then said to be healthy. If the advance–decline line is falling, then the market is said to be unhealthy. Most of the time, the advance–decline line and the overall market move higher and lower together. At times, however, the overall market can continue to move higher despite a drop in the advance–decline line. This divergence is taken by technicians as a warning of a pending reversal in the underlying price trend.

advance–decline line
The ongoing sum of the number of advancing stocks divided by the number of declining stocks

17-4b Market Imbalance

The advance–decline line gives technical analysts a useful broad measure of daily changes in supply and demand. A common indicator of market imbalance is called the **trading index (TRIN) ratio**. The TRIN ratio is an indicator used to detect **overbought** and **oversold** levels in the market. The idea of the TRIN ratio is to detect market emotions on a small daily scale. Investor emotions like thrill and excitement are associated with bullish conditions. However, if such emotions get too strong, euphoria can result and signal a market top. The TRIN ratio uses terms like "overbought" to denote this situation in daily time intervals. Bearish emotions of fear, desperation, and panic can lead to market bottom emotions like capitulation and despondency—or, in TRIN terminology, oversold conditions. The TRIN ratio combines advance and decline data with upside and downside volume information. The ratio is computed as

trading index (TRIN) ratio
A common indicator of advancing and declining stock, and up and down volume, to measure market imbalance

overbought
An insufficient future demand at the market top

oversold
An insufficient future supply at the market bottom

$$TRIN = \frac{\#Advancing\ Stocks\ /\ \#Declining\ Stocks}{Up\ Volume\ /\ Down\ Volume}$$ **17-1**

The TRIN provides a look at the volume that is trading in the advancing and declining stocks. If the number of advancing issues equals the number of declining issues and total up volume equals total down volume, the TRIN ratio is 1.0. Ratios less than 1.0 are considered bullish, while ratios over 1.0 are considered bearish. Technical analysts consider a TRIN < 0.65 as very bullish, 0.65 < TRIN < 0.90 as bullish, 0.90 < TRIN < 1.10 as neutral, 1.10 < TRIN < 1.35 as bearish, and a TRIN > 1.35 as very bearish. On the other hand, technicians argue that TRIN ratios at the farthest extremes become contraindicative. A ratio of 1.80 might be argued as bullish because it indicates an extremely oversold condition, suggesting a market bottom. Most technical analysts use TRIN charts with 20-day moving averages as a short-term barometer for the market or individual stocks. A rising TRIN is bearish, and a falling TRIN is bullish. Unusually large volume among advancing issues will create a low TRIN ratio and is a sign of intense buying demand. Heavy volume among declining issues causes a high TRIN ratio and suggests intense selling pressure.

Excel Expert 17-3 ❯❯

Market Breadth and Imbalance

The Markets Diary from **Table 17-1** is shown here. What are the advance–decline ratio and TRIN ratio for each marketplace?

	A	B	C	D	E	F	G	H	I
1		**NYSE**	**NASDAQ**			**NYSE**	**NASDAQ**		
2		*Issues*			**A-D Ratio =**	0.677	0.845	=C3/C4	
3	Advancing	1,350	2,106						
4	Declining	1,994	2,491		**TRIN =**	0.606	0.619	=(C3/C4)/(C12/C13)	
5	Unchanged	135	281						
6	Total	3,479	4,878						
7		*Issues At*							
8	New Highs	101	79						
9	New Lows	199	685						
10		*Share Volume*							
11	Total	4,478,992,869	4,438,787,247						
12	Advancing	2,311,451,434	2,496,495,925						
13	Declining	2,067,938,747	1,826,639,422						
14	Unchanged	99,602,688	115,651,900						

The data show that more stocks declined in price than advanced in price for both the NYSE and NASDAQ markets. However, there were more shares traded for advancing firms than for declining ones. This is not consistent. Thus, the advance–decline ratio, at 0.677 and 0.845, respectively, is considered bearish, while the TRIN ratio of 0.606 and 0.619, respectively, is considered very bullish.

The World of Investing

2021 Breadth

The stock market had a great year in 2021, with the S&P 500 Index gaining 26.9%. However, the breadth was narrow.

- Just five of the largest stocks, Microsoft, Nvidia, Apple, Alphabet, and Tesla, accounted for about a third of the market's return.
- In December 2021, about 60% of the New York Stock Exchange stocks traded below their 200-day moving average. This means that more than half of the stocks were trading at a price that was less than their average price for the year.
- Less than a third of the Nasdaq stocks traded above their 200-day MA.
- Small companies didn't do as well: the Russell 2000 Index gained 14.8%.
- The S&P 1500 Index advance–decline line declined in the fourth quarter of 2021.

Narrow breadth has several risks for investors:

- Any reversal in the performance of the few stocks driving the market will have a negative impact on the market.
- Market volatility is likely to increase.

Technical analysts believe the market rally needs to broaden out or it could struggle in 2022.

17-4c Buy–Sell Indicators

Technical analysts often strive to measure actual investor behavior to infer their beliefs about the market or a stock. For example, some technical analysts follow various **odd-lot indicators**. Recall that in the stock market, a round lot is 100 shares. While individual investors sometimes buy shares in odd lots, say 35 shares or 88 shares, institutional investors typically deal in terms of thousands of shares, or tens of thousands of shares, per trade. Analysts who want to track what individual investors are doing look at odd-lot trading volume. If odd-lot purchases are greater than odd-lot sales, then individual investors are buying. If odd-lot sales are greater than odd-lot purchases, then individual investors are selling. Most technicians believe institutional investors represent "smart money," whereas individual investors symbolize the overly emotional crowd. Therefore, odd lots are considered a **contrary indicator**. Measures that focus on individual investors and regular consumers are contrary indicators. Measures that are based on professional investors are not considered to be contrary indicators. Many technical analysts suggest that savvy investors do just the opposite of the individual investor: sell in the face of net buying activity by odd-lot traders and buy in the face of net selling activity by odd-lot traders.

Other buy–sell indicators focus on mutual fund cash flows and brokerage account credit balances. Every month, the Investment Company Institute (www.ici.org) reports the amount of new money that is invested in equity and bond mutual funds. It also reports the amount of money that has been withdrawn from mutual funds. Because individual investors are the biggest investors in mutual funds, **mutual fund flow indicators** that show mutual fund inflows, outflows, and credit balance information illustrate the actions of individual investors. Similarly, **brokerage account credit balance indicators** focus on the amount of buying power that resides in the account balances of brokerage customers. Credit balance information is reported weekly in *Barron's* and other leading financial publications. Technical analysts regard high credit

odd-lot indicator
The number of trades using odd-lots to gauge individual investor buying and selling

contrary indicator
A measure that assesses what others are doing and suggests you should do the opposite

mutual fund flow indicator
A mutual fund inflow, outflow, and credit balance information

brokerage account credit balance indicator
A gauge of buying power that resides in the account balances of Wall Street brokerage customers

Confidence Index
An indicator of investor mood based on bond yields

balances as bullish because they represent potential buying power. Low credit balances reflect a lack of potential buying power.

Technicians also look to the bond and option markets for insight concerning the future direction of stock prices. If a weak economy and weak stock prices are expected, bond traders favor high-quality bonds because financial stress and the risk of bankruptcy increase during recessions. Traders are more likely to favor lower-rated bond issues if robust economic growth and a positive stock market environment are expected. The Barron's **Confidence Index** (0 to 100%) is measured by the ratio of the yield to maturity on Barron's best grade bonds (index of 10 bonds) to Barron's intermediate grade bonds (index of 10 bonds). The bond market Confidence Index will be low if a weak economy and a poor stock market environment are expected and high if a robust economy and favorable stock market are anticipated. For example, Barron's Market Lab shows that the Confidence Index to be:

- 76.8 (1.89% ÷ 2.46%) in the second week of January 2022
- 51.0 in the previous week
- 53.5 one year ago

These values suggest that bond traders believe the economy is strong, much better than a year ago.

put–call ratio
A ratio of the trading volume of put options to call options

In the option market (see Chapter 15), technicians know that optimists buy call options while pessimists buy put options. Put-option trading volume divided by call-option trading volume is the put–call ratio and is a useful contrarian indicator. **Put–call ratio** data is available at the Chicago Board Options Exchange (CBOE). There is put–call data for all options, index options, and more. It is the equity put–call ratio that is shown in **Figure 17-4**. A high put–call ratio indicates that option traders are pessimistic. A low

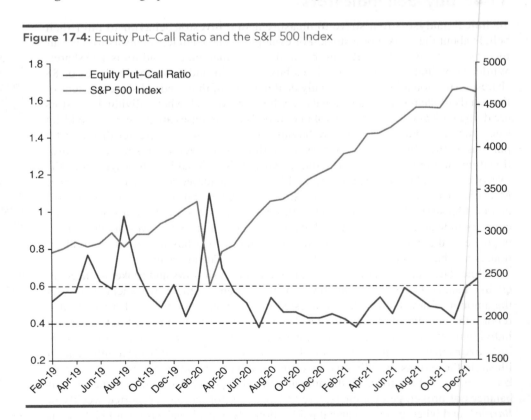

Figure 17-4: Equity Put–Call Ratio and the S&P 500 Index

put–call ratio means that option traders are optimistic. Typically, this ratio falls in a range between 0.6 and 0.4. When the put–call ratio moves outside this range, technicians take notice. The figure shows that this indicator was flashing a concern about the market in late 2019 and then again at the start of the pandemic in the United States.

Ownership Data

Technical analysts want to know the ownership structure of a firm because it has implications for future supply and demand. Specifically, you should look for the number of shares held by insiders and institutions, and the degree of short sales. Insider ownership is shares owned by people associated with the firm, like management. These shares are not sold very often, but when insiders do sell, that is an important sell signal for technicians. Institutional ownership is the shares held by institutional investors like pension funds, mutual funds, and hedge funds. The trend of institutional ownership is closely followed. As a group, institutions are the majority owner in the U.S. market. So, when institutions start buying a stock, there is potential for them to push up the stock price. Of course, pervasive institutional selling pushes down the price.

The degree of short sales for the firm can be important. Recall from Chapter 3 that a short sale is the sale of borrowed stock. This is done when you believe the stock price is going to decline. Short-sale interest has two interpretations. First, the investors that sell short a stock are typically sophisticated individual investors or institutions. If they believe the stock price is likely to decline, you should take notice. The second interpretation recognizes that every share sold short will have to be repurchased to close out the position. Thus, high short interest is a signal of high future demand.

The rise of the retail meme stock investors in 2021 shows another way to use short-sale interest. These investors identified stocks with very high short interest and then tried to squeeze the short sellers by buying the stock and pressuring it to rise in price. This is known as a short squeeze. As the price rises, short sellers lose money. Eventually, some of them will start buying the stock to close their short position, causing even further prices increases. That squeezes the remaining short seller even more. This cycle can create a dramatic, though usually temporary, price increase.

For example, in early 2021, meme investors identified GameStop, Inc., as a stock ripe for a short squeeze. **Exhibit 17-3** shows that in January 2021, 61.78 million shares were sold short. This hardly seem possible, as there were only 69.75 million shares outstanding and 46.89 million of float. Float is the shares outstanding less shares that are not available for trading. This high degree of short sales can occur by investors borrowing stock from their brokerage firms and subsequently selling the stock, which is the process for selling short. The investor who purchases the stock likely holds it through a brokerage firm. The buyer's broker then lends it out to another short seller. Thus, one share of stock may be sold short more than once. At 122%, the percentage held by institutions looks improbable during a normal situation but is possible with such a high degree of short selling.

The short squeeze worked very well. GameStop (GME) opened on January 4, 2021, with a price of $19.03 and more than doubled to $43.03 by January 21. That price increase put pressure on the short sellers. As the price kept rising, short sellers had to buy the shares back to cover their short positions. Note from the bottom line of the exhibit that there were 68.13 million shares sold short on December 15. By January 15, about 6.5 million shorted shares had already been covered. Investor buying and short covering sent the price even higher. The share price topped $483 in the morning of January 28. Some of the short sellers were hedge funds, which lost hundreds of

insider ownership
Shares owned by the company's management, directors, and anyone with access to the firm's key information

institutional ownership
Shares owned by financial firms, like pension funds, mutual funds, insurance companies, and hedge funds

short sale
The sale of borrowed stock used to profit from a falling stock price

short-sale interest
The number of shares sold short in a firm

short squeeze
When short sellers are pressured to cover their short position through buying stock when the price rises

Exhibit 17-3: Ownership Statistics of GameStop, Inc.

January 15, 2021		December 31, 2021	
Share Statistics		**Share Statistics**	
Avg Vol (3 month)[3]	25.58M	Avg Vol (3 month)[3]	2.8M
Avg Vol (10 day)[3]	115.8M	Avg Vol (10 day)[3]	4.35M
Shares Outstanding[5]	69.75M	Shares Outstanding[5]	76.35M
Float	46.89M	Implied Shares Outstanding[6]	76.49M
% Held by Insiders[1]	27.33%	Float[8]	62.52M
% Held by Institutions[1]	122.04%	% Held by Insiders[1]	18.01%
Shares Short (Jan 15, 2021)[4]	61.78M	% Held by Institutions[1]	28.39%
Short Ratio (Jan 15, 2021)[4]	2.81	Shares Short (Dec 31, 2021)[4]	8.45M
Short % of Float (Jan 15, 2021)[4]	226.42%	Short Ratio (Dec 31, 2021)[4]	3.17
Short % of Shares Outstanding (Jan 15, 2021)[4]	88.58%	Short % of Float (Dec 31, 2021)[4]	18.22%
Shares Short (prior month Dec 15, 2020)[4]	68.13M	Short % of Shares Outstanding (Dec 31, 2021)[4]	11.07%
		Shares Short (prior month Nov 30, 2021)[4]	6.42M

Source: Yahoo! Finance

millions of dollars. Individual investors coordinated their buying of GME through the social media platform Reddit, and much of the trading occurred through no-commission online brokerage platforms, such as Robinhood.

Nearly a year later, Exhibit 17-3 shows that GameStop's ownership structure appears more normal, with only 8.45 million shares sold short and 28.39% held by institutions. Although GameStop is still considered a meme stock, most of the trading action moved to AMC, the movie theater chain, and then Bed Bath & Beyond, Blackberry, Nokia, Palantir, and Virgin Galactic.

17-4d Sentiment Surveys

The previous buy–sell indicators attempt to discern whether certain groups of investors are more likely to buy or to sell. If we want to know investor plans, why don't we just ask them? We do. To track the mood of Wall Street and individual investors, regular surveys of investor **sentiment** are conducted. There are many surveys available. Among the more widely followed surveys used to gauge investor sentiment are the following:

sentiment
An investor mood of optimism or pessimism regarding the financial markets or economy

- **AAII Investor Sentiment Survey:** The American Association of Individual Investors (AAII) Sentiment Survey measures the percentage of individual investors who are bullish, bearish, and neutral on the stock market in the short term. People are polled on a weekly basis from the AAII website (www.aaii.com).
- **Consumer Confidence Index:** The Consumer Confidence Survey is based on a representative sample of thousands of U.S. households. It seeks to gauge consumer attitudes, buying intentions, vacation plans, and expectations for inflation, stock prices, and interest rates. The monthly survey is conducted by The Conference Board (www.conference-board.org).

- **University of Michigan Consumer Sentiment:** The Index of Consumer Sentiment (ICS) is based on consumer survey questions regarding spending and savings plans (www.sca.isr.umich.edu).
- **Bank of America Merrill Lynch Sell Side Indicator**: This monthly indicator gauges the bullishness on Wall Street by surveying strategists about what percentage of assets they recommend that clients allocate to equities.
- **Robert Shiller's Stock Market Confidence Indexes:** Yale University Professor Robert Shiller compiles four different indexes based on surveys of individual and institutional investors: One-Year Confidence Index, Buy on Dips Confidence Index, Crash Confidence Index, and Valuation Confidence Index.

Statistical studies of investor sentiment and stock returns document that sentiment and stock prices tend to move together—that is, until sentiment gets too extreme. Then technical analysts use sentiment as a contrary indicator. Excessive optimism on the part of the public and market professionals almost always coincides with market tops. Acute pessimism tends to coincide with market bottoms.

The American Association of Individual Investors Sentiment Survey measures the percentage of individual investors who are bullish, bearish, and neutral on the stock market. **Figure 17-5** shows the bullish percentage minus the bearish percentage each week. Positive values indicate individual investors are net bullish, while negative values indicate they are net bearish. Note that individual investors aren't very good at predicting the stock market movements. Their sentiment didn't turn bearish until the market had already started falling during the pandemic crash and sentiment remained bearish long after the market was already recovering. About halfway through the bull market run, investors finally turned bullish.

Figure 17-5: AAII Bullish Sentiment Minus Bearish Sentiment vs. the S&P 500 Index

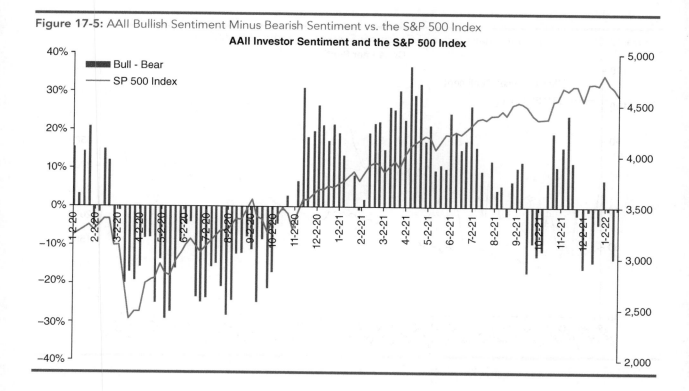

The monthly Index of Consumer Sentiment is shown in **Figure 17-6** versus the S&P 500 Index. The consumer sentiment index focuses on expectations for spending and savings. Note that it is very volatile since 2008 compared to the stock market. Sentiment plunged at the beginning of the COVID-19 pandemic. While the stock market quickly recovered, sentiment didn't.

17-4e Momentum

momentum
The speed, or velocity, of price changes

Momentum strategies based on the technical analysis of price and volume information have become increasingly popular with both retail investors and professionals, like hedge funds. Momentum is typically measured by the speed of price change. Advocates of momentum strategies consider momentum to be a leading indicator of change in a stock's price trend. In the stock market, momentum players believe stock price and volume trends behave much like a pendulum. Drop a pendulum and it starts down slowly, picking up speed as gravity pulls it down. After the pendulum swings through its lowest point, its speed slows until it stops and reverses direction. A momentum investor buys a stock that's in an upward trend and follows various momentum indicators to assess whether the trend may be ending soon. Several different indicators have been developed to track momentum.

momentum indicator
A popular indicator that includes rate of change, MACD, and Relative Strength Index

Momentum indicators are designed to identify the relative enthusiasm of buyers and sellers. Some momentum indicators compare the change in price over time, while others measure deviations from trend lines. The simplest momentum indicator is the **rate of change (ROC)** indicator. The ROC shows the amount prices have changed over the given period, often over 10 to 12 days. A rising ROC indicates expanding momentum, which is a bullish signal, while a falling ROC is a bearish signal of declining momentum. An extremely low ROC suggests the stock is oversold and a recovery

rate of change (ROC)
A comparison of the current price with a previous price, usually 10 or 12 days ago

Figure 17-6: University of Michigan's Index of Consumer Sentiment vs. the S&P 500 Index

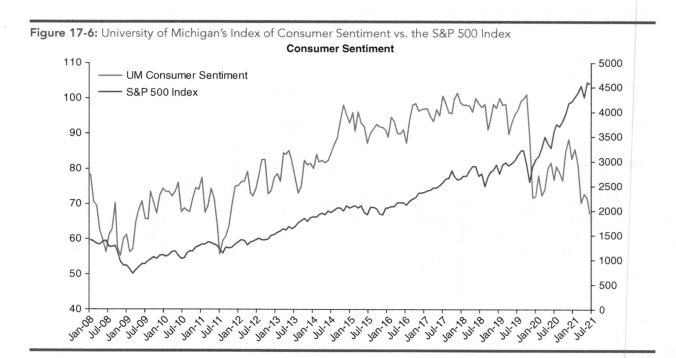

Consumer Sentiment

is likely. An extremely high ROC suggests that the market is overbought. ROC is interpreted as a leading indicator of a change in price trend. ROC is calculated with this formula:

$$ROC_N = \left(\frac{Current\ Price}{Price\ N\ Days\ Ago} - 1 \right) \times 100 \qquad \textbf{17-2}$$

One of the most popular momentum indicators is the **moving average convergence–divergence (MACD)** indicator. It has two aspects. The first, called the *MACD line,* is calculated by subtracting the value of a 26-period *exponential moving average* from the value of a 12-period exponential moving average. The second is determined by calculating a 9-day exponential moving average of the MACD. The MACD trading rule is to sell when the MACD line falls below its 9-day moving average and to buy when the MACD line rises above the 9-day moving average. Traders sometimes vary the calculation period of the moving average and may use different moving average lengths in calculating the MACD, depending on the security and trading strategy.

moving average convergence–divergence (MACD)
A trend-following momentum indicator that shows the relationship between two moving averages

What is an exponential moving average (EMA)? A simple average computes the average price of the past *N* days. It "moves" by computing the average on the next day and then the day after that. Each average includes N days. The simple average can change slowly to market changes because the next day's average includes the next price (tomorrow's price) and drops one price (the past $N + 1$ day's price). The exponential moving average is an attempt to react faster to price changes. The equation for the EMA is:

$$EMA_N = \frac{2}{N+1}(Closing\ Price - Previous\ EMA) + Previous\ EMA \quad \textbf{17-3}$$

The EMA illustrates how much the closing price deviates from the previous day's EMA, scaled by $2 \div (N + 1)$, and added to the previous day's EMA. To get started, the simple average is used for the first EMA. The procedure for the 9-day EMA is:

1. Compute the simple average for the first 9 days of the sample.
2. For day 10, subtract the new price from the simple average previously computed, multiply it by 0.2 ($= 2 \div 10$), and then add the simple average previously computed.
3. For day 11, subtract the new price from the EMA computed in step 2, multiply it by 0.2, and then add the EMA from step 2.
4. Proceed through all of the data.

The MACD line and its 9-day moving average can be shown, or just the difference can be illustrated. The MACD crossing above zero is considered bullish, while crossing below zero is bearish. Secondly, when the MACD turns up from below zero, it is considered bullish. When it turns down from above zero, it is considered bearish.

In addition to the ROC and MACD, common momentum indicators include stochastic momentum, Williams %R, the Relative Strength Index (RSI), the ultimate oscillator, and the price oscillator. There are different variations of each, as well as a host of others.

Each momentum indicator has specific characteristics, but they all share a few common methods of interpretation. Most momentum indicators are used to generate

Excel Expert 17-4

Computing MACD

One year of daily Disney stock prices are obtained. The 12-day and 26-day exponential moving averages are computed. From these, the MACD is calculated. Lastly, a 9-day moving average of the MACD is shown.

	A	B	C	D	E	F	G	H	I	J	K
1	Date	DIS	EMA-12	EMA-26	MACD	MACD 9-Day Ave					
2	1/4/2021	177.68									
3	1/5/2021	178.44						12-Day Average =	176.21	=AVERAGE(B2:B13)	
4	1/6/2021	179.12						26-Day Average =	175.65		
5	1/7/2021	178.58									
6	1/8/2021	178.69									
7	1/11/2021	179.09									
8	1/12/2021	175.99									
9	1/13/2021	176.12									
10	1/14/2021	173.43									
11	1/15/2021	171.44									
12	1/19/2021	172.26									
13	1/20/2021	173.64	176.21	=I3							
14	1/21/2021	171.28	175.45	=(2/(12+1))*(B14-C13)+C13							
15	1/22/2021	172.78	175.04								
16	1/25/2021	171.89	174.55								
17	1/26/2021	169.56	173.79								
18	1/27/2021	163.03	172.13								
19	1/28/2021	171.88	172.09								
20	1/29/2021	168.17	171.49								
21	2/1/2021	170.97	171.41								
22	2/2/2021	176.96	172.26								
23	2/3/2021	176.43	172.90								
24	2/4/2021	180.23	174.03								
25	2/5/2021	181.16	175.13								
26	2/8/2021	190	177.42								
27	2/9/2021	188.21	179.08	175.65	3.42	=C27-D27					
28	2/10/2021	189.63	180.70	176.69	4.01						
29	2/11/2021	190.91	182.27	177.74	4.53						
30	2/12/2021	187.67	183.10	178.48	4.62						
31	2/16/2021	186.35	183.60	179.06	4.54						
32	2/17/2021	186.44	184.04	179.61	4.43						
33	2/18/2021	183	183.88	179.86	4.02						
34	2/19/2021	183.65	183.84	180.14	3.70						
35	2/22/2021	191.76	185.06	181.00	4.06	4.15	=AVERAGE(E27:E35)				
36	2/23/2021	197.09	186.91	182.19	4.72	4.29					

The MACD analysis is typically shown in a graph with the stock price, MACD, and MACD moving average like this:

(*Continued*)

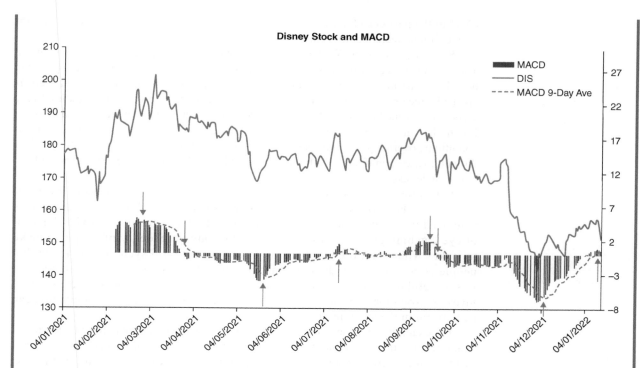

The MACD starts positive and starts to turn down in early March. This turning down is bearish. It then turns negative in early April, which is still bearish. However, in mid-May, the negative MACD peaks and turns up, which is bullish. It says near zero for several months. Another sell signal occurs in mid-September and is confirmed in late September. The signal remains bearish until early December, when the negative MACD turns upward.

overbought or oversold signals that warn of a price reversal to come. Sometimes, momentum indicators diverge from the underlying price trend and thereby give warning of an upcoming price-trend reversal. When a trend in momentum reverses but the price trend does not, a divergence is said to have occurred. According to momentum players, the longer a divergence is in effect, the more drastic the reversal is likely to be. However, when the trend in momentum reverses, the price trend does not always follow quickly. Not all divergences will lead to a reversal, and so supporting evidence is sought from other technical techniques, such as channel breakout, moving averages, price pattern recognition, and so on.

17-5 Is Technical Analysis Useful?

Technical analysis is a controversial subject in academia and on Wall Street due to the efficient market hypothesis (EMH) perspective (see Chapter 8). According to the EMH, the current market price is the best available estimate of the intrinsic value of the firm. Moreover, short-run changes in price and volume information appear to be essentially random in nature. Trading rules based on historical price and volume information are fruitless in a perfectly efficient market. If markets are highly efficient, technical trading tools will not enable investors to earn positive abnormal returns. Of course, if markets are perfectly efficient, or even semi-strong form efficient, most fundamental analysis would be fruitless as well. However, research has uncovered some limitations of the

EMH in the past decade, thus emboldening dedicated technicians. If markets are not fully efficient, technical tools may have merit.

Some academics and Wall Street professionals doubt the practical value of technical analysis. Such skepticism stems from the lack of convincing evidence that the application of technical trading rules can be consistently profitable. Proponents of technical analysis lay the blame on a lack of empirical evidence on the methods used in such studies. Many academics say the fault lies in the failure of technical analysis to give precise trading rules. Can traders make money when they place short-term bets based on breakouts, oversold conditions, overbought conditions, or strong market trends? Even when profitable, it is difficult to ascertain if any such trading profits adequately compensate traders for the level of risk undertaken.

Given the skepticism of many academics toward the value of technical analysis, it may be surprising to see the enthusiasm with which technical analysis is embraced in the financial media. This is partially due to the obvious visual appeal of eye-catching graphics. It is also due to the natural tendency of people to make mistakes when learning by observation and induction. Psychologists know that people commonly use inductive reasoning based on limited observation because it is a useful tool for interacting with the natural world. Unfortunately, many naïve investors lose money because inductive reasoning based on limited observation can be harmful in the stock market.

For example, suppose you eat an apple and get sick. You might believe that you will again get sick if you eat another apple. Such inductive reasoning works great when it identifies the outcome from an underlying process that is deterministic and always true. However, inductive reasoning based on limited experience can fail miserably when the underlying process is not deterministic. You might have gotten sick because of food you ate before eating the apple. You now have an unfounded fear of eating an apple and getting sick because you incorrectly extrapolated from limited experience. Investors often make the same type of mistake. Suppose an investor buys a stock after its price completes a flag pattern and ends up making a profit. Using inductive reasoning based on limited experience, the investor might assume that a profit will be made every time they buy a stock that has displayed a flag pattern. However, because short-term changes in stock prices have a large random component, inferences based on such technical trading rules will often be wrong. Many investors make the mistake of thinking that the market is more deterministic than it really is. This causes them to look for patterns that they believe are meaningful and that will repeat. Too often, investors lose money when such patterns inexplicably change.

Conclusion

Technical analysis is the study of past price movements and trading volume information to forecast future price movements in stock, bond, and commodity markets. Price trends and reversals are determined by supply and demand trends. Technicians adopt a visual approach based on two-dimensional graphs of stock price and volume information. This process often includes moving averages, support lines, and resistance lines to determine whether the price trend will continue or reverse. In addition, price patterns may be recognized, like the head-and-shoulders pattern, that may indicate a reversal or continuation of the trend.

Some technical indicators examine the health of the market. The number of stocks advancing or declining and the associated up and down volume give technical analysts a measure of the market breadth. Momentum is also widely followed to assess the trend and potential reversals for individual stocks.

Technical analysts are interested in supply and demand and who is driving the trading. Thus, there are technical indicators like odd-lot trades and mutual fund flow that try to assess what individual investors are doing. Institutional ownership and short sales help assess what more sophisticated investors are doing. Lastly, we try to measure the sentiment of investors by asking them their opinions and intentions through various surveys.

Skepticism of technical analysis stems from the lack of convincing evidence that technical trading rules can be consistently profitable. Nevertheless, technical analysis is popular because investors naturally want to *see* what an investment bargain looks like.

Chapter Equations

$$TRIN = \frac{\#Advancing\ Stocks / \#Declining\ Stocks}{Up\ Volume / Down\ Volume}$$

17-1

$$ROC_N = \left(\frac{Current\ Price}{Price\ N\ Days\ Ago} - 1\right) \times 100$$

17-2

$$EMA_N = \frac{2}{N+1}(Closing\ Price - Previous\ EMA) + Previous\ EMA$$

17-3

Excel Functions

AVERAGE(number1, [number2], …)
High-Low-Close Chart

Open-High-Low-Close Chart

Key Terms

50-day moving average – The average stock price over the previous 50 trading days (roughly two calendar months)

200-day moving average – The average stock price over the previous 200 trading days (roughly one year)

advance–decline line – The ongoing sum of the number of advancing stocks divided by the number of declining stocks

advance–decline ratio – The number of firms that advanced in price divided by the number that declined on a given trading day

bar graph – A chart that depicts historical high, low, and closing security prices

blow off – A spike in volume when prices have stalled

breakout – A change in trend out of the channel

brokerage account credit balance indicator – A gauge of buying power that resides in the account balances of Wall Street brokerage customers

candlestick graph – A chart that depicts historical open, high, low, and closing security prices

channel – The area between resistance and support lines that illustrates the direction of the trend

charting – The use of two-dimensional price and volume graphs to analyze market behavior and anticipate future price movements

Confidence Index – An indicator of investor mood based on bond yields

continuation pattern – The persistence of the underlying bullish or bearish trend

contrary indicator – A measure that assesses what others are doing and suggests you should do the opposite

divergence – A disagreement between market direction between indicators

Dow theory – The idea that market movements can be predicted by studying trends in the Dow Jones Industrial Average (DJIA) and Dow Jones Transportation Average (DJTA)

head and shoulders – A popular price chart pattern that signals a reversal to a bear market trend

insider ownership – Shares owned by the company's management, directors, and anyone with access to the firm's key information

institutional ownership – Shares owned by financial firms, like pension funds, mutual funds, insurance companies, and hedge funds

market breadth – A measure of the number of issues that are rising relative to the number that are declining

momentum – The speed, or velocity, of price changes

momentum indicator – A popular indicator that includes rate of change, MACD, and Relative Strength Index

moving average convergence–divergence (MACD) – A trend-following momentum indicator that shows the relationship between two moving averages

mutual fund flow indicator – A mutual fund inflow, outflow, and credit balance information

odd-lot indicator – The number of trades using odd-lots to gauge individual investor buying and selling

overbought – An insufficient future demand at the market top

oversold – An insufficient future supply at the market bottom

primary trend – A bull and bear market that lasts anywhere from less than one year up to several years

put–call ratio – A ratio of the trading volume of put options to call options

rate of change (ROC) – A comparison of the current price with a previous price, usually 10 or 12 days ago

resistance line – A graphical depiction of price points at which selling pressure (supply) has emerged in the recent past

reversal pattern – A change in trend signal

secondary trend – A short-term move in the market that runs contrary to the primary trend and usually last from three weeks to three months

sentiment – An investor mood of optimism or pessimism regarding the financial markets or economy

short sale – The sale of borrowed stock used to profit from a falling stock price

short-sale interest – The number of shares sold short in a firm

short squeeze – When short sellers are pressured to cover their short position through buying stock when the price rises

support line – A graphical depiction of price points at which additional demand for the stock has emerged in the past

technical analysis – The study of historical price and volume information to forecast future prices

tertiary trend – A very short-term stock market trend that reflects minor price moves

ticker tape – A paper or electronic representation of stock prices appearing in a linear manner

trading index (TRIN) ratio – A common indicator of advancing and declining stock, and up and down volume, to measure market imbalance

Questions

1. **Technical Analysis.** What is the purpose of technical analysis? What are the underlying forces it is trying to measure and assess? (LO 17-1)

2. **Moving Averages.** Explain the importance of moving averages and moving average crossovers in technical analysis. When is a moving average crossover bullish or bearish? (LO 17-2).

3. **Charts.** What are the different type of charts used by technicians, and what are they used for? (LO 17-3)

4. **Chart Patterns.** In technical analysis terms, what is a head and shoulders trading pattern? Is such a pattern bullish or bearish? (LO 17-4)

5. **Volume.** Why is trading volume important in technical analysis, and how is it used? (LO 17-5)

6. **Market Breadth and Imbalance.** What are the indicators for market breadth and imbalance, and how are they interpreted? (LO 17-6)

7. **Investor Demand.** Is an increase in odd-lot trading and mutual fund inflows considered bullish or bearish, and why? (LO 17-7)

8. **Sentiment.** What is investor sentiment, and why do technical analysts value it? How is it measured? (LO 17-8)

9. **Momentum.** What is price momentum, and how is it measured? (LO 17-9)

10. **Technical Analysis.** What are the major challenges to technical analysis validity? (LO 17-10)

Problems

1. **Moving Average.** Compute the 5-day moving average for days, 0, −1, and −2. (LO 17-2)

Date	Price
Today, T = 0	217.25
−1	221.72
−2	223.84
−3	220.01
−4	221.40
−5	225.83
−6	224.47

2. **Moving Average.** Compute the 10-day moving average for days, 0, −1, and −2. The data are in the file, **ch17_pr02.xlsx**. (LO 17-2)

Date	Price
Today, T = 0	228.86
−1	234.17
−2	231.95
−3	231.44
−4	231.91
−5	227.92
−6	224.91
−7	224.1
−8	221.01
−9	217.74
−10	220.07
−11	219.19

3. **Moving Average.** On what day does this stock price, provided in the file, **ch17_pr03.xlsx**, cross its 10-day moving average? Is it a cross from above or from below? (LO 17-2)

4. **Advance–Decline Ratio.** What is the advance–decline ratio for this day for the NYSE and the NASDAQ? Is this bullish or bearish for each market? The data are in the file, **ch17_pr04.xlsx**. (LO 17-6)

	NYSE	NASDAQ
Issues		
Advancing	2,461	3,204
Declining	892	1,444
Unchanged	141	263
Total	3,494	4,911
Issues At		
New Highs	96	45
New Lows	57	172
Share Volume		
Advancing	3,417,259	3,354,742
Declining	659,203	992,125

5. **Advance–Decline Ratio.** What is the advance–decline ratio for this day for the NYSE and the NASDAQ? Is this bullish or bearish for each market? The data are in the file, **ch17_pr05.xlsx**. (LO 17-6)

	NYSE	NASDAQ
Issues		
Advancing	1,218	1,597
Declining	2,133	3,126
Unchanged	178	267
Total	3,529	4,900
Issues At		
New Highs	95	87
New Lows	205	740
Share Volume		
Advancing	1,742,692	2,403,016
Declining	2,715,391	2,708,862

6. **Trading Index Ratio.** What is the TRIN for this day for the NYSE and the NASDAQ? Is this very bearish, bearish, neutral, bullish, or very bullish for each market? The data are in the file, **ch17_pr06.xlsx**. (LO 17-6)

	NYSE	NASDAQ
Issues		
Advancing	2,461	3,204
Declining	892	1,444
Unchanged	141	263
Total	3,494	4,911
Issues At		
New Highs	96	45
New Lows	57	172
Share Volume		
Advancing	3,417,259	3,354,742
Declining	659,203	992,125

7. **Trading Index Ratio.** What is the TRIN for this day for the NYSE and the NASDAQ? Is this very bearish, bearish, neutral, bullish, or very bullish for each market? The data are in the file, **ch17_pr07.xlsx**. (LO 17-6)

	NYSE	NASDAQ
Issues		
Advancing	1,218	1,597
Declining	2,133	3,126
Unchanged	178	267
Total	3,529	4,900
Issues At		
New Highs	95	87
New Lows	205	740
Share Volume		
Advancing	1,742,692	2,403,016
Declining	2,715,391	2,708,862

8. **Confidence Index.** Compute the Confidence Index for each week with the yields provided. Does the trend suggest a prediction of a stronger or weaker economy? The data are in the file, **ch17_pr08.xlsx**. (LO 17-7)

Week	Best Grade Bond	Interim Grade Bond
T=0	2.45	2.90
−1	1.89	2.46
−2	1.8	2.44
−3	1.69	2.48
−4	1.58	2.55
−5	1.55	2.65
−6	1.42	2.70

9. **Put–Call Ratio.** Using the put option volume and call option volume below, what day does the option market start signaling optimism for the stock market? The data are in the file, **ch17_pr09.xlsx**. (LO 17-7)

10. **Put–Call Ratio.** Using the put option volume and call option volume below, what day does the option market start signaling pessimism for the stock market? The data are in the file, **ch17_pr10.xlsx**. (LO 17-7)

11. **AAII Sentiment.** Using the monthly AAII sentiment survey results below for 12 months, in what month does the survey first show bullish optimism by individual investors? The data are in the file, **ch17_pr11.xlsx**. (LO 17-8)

12. **AAII Sentiment.** Using the monthly AAII sentiment survey results below for 12 months, in what month does the survey first show bearish pessimism by individual investors? The data are in the file, **ch17_pr12.xlsx**. (LO 17-8)

13. **Rate of Change.** Calculate the 10-day rate of change (ROC) for days 0, −1, −2, −3, −4, and −5. Do the results imply a bullish or bearish signal? The data is in the file, **ch17_pr13.xlsx**. (LO 17-9)

14. **Rate of Change.** Calculate the 12-day rate of change (ROC) for days 0, −1, −2, −3, and −4. Do the results imply a bullish or bearish signal? The data is in the file, **ch17_pr14.xlsx**. (LO 17-9)

15. **Exponential Moving Average.** Calculate the 12-period EMA for days 0, -1, -2, and -3. The data is in the file, **ch17_pr15.xlsx**. (LO 17-9)

16. **Exponential Moving Average.** Calculate the 5-period EMA for days 0 through -6. The data is in the file, **ch17_pr16.xlsx**. (LO 17-9)

Day	Price
T=0	174.45
−1	162.11
−2	159.63
−3	158.43
−4	158.83
−5	157.33
−6	155.58
−7	154
−8	154.16
−9	151.03
−10	151.34

17. **MACD.** Calculate the MACD for this day when the price is $149.10, EMA(12) is $150.95, and EMA(26) is 154.71. (LO 17-9)

18. **MACD.** Calculate the MACD for each day. On what day is there a trade signal, and what is the signal? The data is in the file, **ch17_pr18.xlsx**. (LO 17-9)

19. **MACD** Calculate the 9-day moving average MACD for days 0, -1, and -2. The data is in the file, **ch17_pr19.xlsx**. (LO 17-9)

20. **MACD** Given the six months of price data provided in the file, **ch17_pr20.xlsx**, compute the EMA(12), EMA(26), MACD, and MACD 9-day moving average. Report these four statistics for the last day, January 21. (LO 17-9)

Case Study

Charts

Use an online financial website, like Yahoo! Finance, to obtain specific charts for Amazon.com, Inc. (AMZN).

Use the one-year date range of January 22, 2021, to January 21, 2022, of daily data.

Perform the following analysis:

a. Obtain and interpret a candlestick chart.
b. Obtain a line graph with 50-day MA and 200-day MA and assess the crossovers.
c. Obtain a line graph with the MACD and evaluate momentum signals.

Glossary

A

10-K report A required annual report filed with the SEC by publicly held firms

10-Q report A required quarterly report filed with the SEC by publicly held firms

12b-1 fees Marketing expenses charged to the mutual fund shareholder

13-D report A document filed with the SEC by an individual who acquires 5% of a publicly held firm's stock

200-day moving average The average stock price over the previous 200 trading days (roughly one year)

50-day moving average The average stock price over the previous 50 trading days (roughly two calendar months)

8-K report A document filed with the SEC that describes a change in a firm that may affect the value of its securities

abnormal return Same as alpha

accredited investor A sophisticated investor requiring a minimum $1 million in net worth and $200,000 in annual income

accrued interest Interest owed but not yet paid out

active investment strategy Actively buying and selling assets to try to outperform a benchmark or index

actively managed An investment strategy in which the portfolio manager chooses securities to outperform an index

adjusted close An end-of-day stock price that is adjusted for subsequent dividends and stock splits

advance–decline line The ongoing sum of the number of advancing stocks divided by the number of declining stocks

advance–decline ratio The number of firms that advanced in price divided by the number that declined on a given trading day

agency auction Brokers represent buyers and sellers, and prices are determined by supply and demand

allocation effects Returns generated by how the portfolio weights allocate capital to sectors or asset classes

alpha Abnormal return measured from an asset pricing model

alternative minimum tax (AMT) An alternative calculation of income tax that, effectively, places a minimum "floor" on the tax rate that must be paid

American depositary receipts (ADRs) Domestic shares issued to represent ownership in foreign securities held by a trustee

annual percentage rate (APR) A nominal rate consisting of the periodic effective rate multiplied by the number of payments per year

annualized yield The annual yield interest earned by a bond, calculated by dividing the discount amount by the price of the bond, annualized using 365 days in a year

anomalies Security prices that deviate from the efficient market hypothesis

arbitrage Simultaneous buying and selling of the same asset at different markets to capture a mispricing

arithmetic average The sum of a set of numbers divided by the number of observations

ask The lowest price at which a dealer is willing to sell shares

asset allocation The process of diversifying an investment portfolio across various asset categories, such as stocks, bonds, and cash

asset-based fee A fee charged as a percentage of the assets under management

asset pricing theory Models of expected return expressed as risk-free rates, risks, and risk premiums

asset-specific risk The chance that problems with an individual asset will reduce the value of the portfolio

at the money An option selling when the strike price equals the current market price of the underlying security

attribution analysis Evaluation of how active management decisions explain a portfolio's performance against a benchmark

authority A government body created for a single purpose, such as the building of an industrial complex

average collection period The number of days required to collect accounts receivable

B

back-end load Commissions paid when a fund is sold

back testing Backward-looking analysis

Bank for International Settlements (BIS) An international organization tasked with supporting countries' central banks' pursuit of monetary and financial stability and acting as a bank for central banks

banker's acceptance A short-term debt issued by a corporation but guaranteed by a bank

Banks for Cooperatives A government-sponsored bank responsible for providing credit and other financial services to the American agricultural sector

bar graph A chart that depicts historical high, low, and closing security prices

barbell strategy A bond investment strategy consisting of very long and very short maturities

basis point One one-hundredth of a percent, or .01%

bear spread A long position in a call with a higher strike price combined with a short position in a call on the same stock with a lower strike price

benchmark Diversified portfolio of similar risk or investment style used as a comparison

best-efforts agreement An agreement with an investment banker who does not guarantee the sale of a security but who agrees to make the best effort to sell it

beta Measure of the market risk of an asset or portfolio

bid The highest price at which a dealer is willing to buy shares

bid–ask spread The difference between the bid and the ask prices, which represents a cost to traders

Binomial Cox–Ross–Rubinstein model A binomial pricing model used to price options

Black–Scholes option valuation model A differential equation-based model for pricing call contracts

blended fund a fund that buys stocks and debt instruments

blow off A spike in volume when prices have stalled

blue chips A large-cap company with a sterling business reputation

bogey Industry slang for the benchmark

bond A debt security that matures in longer than a year

bond fund a fund that buys debt instruments

book-entry form A method of tracking ownership of securities where no physically engraved certificate is given to investors

bond-equivalent yield See annualized yield

book-to-market ratio Accounting book value per share divided by the stock price

breakout A change in trend out of the channel

broker An agent who handles buy and sell orders for an investor.

brokerage account credit balance indicator A gauge of buying power that resides in the account balances of Wall Street brokerage customers

bull spread A long position in a call with a lower strike price combined with a short position in a call on the same stock with a higher strike price.

buy-and-hold strategy A strategy that minimizes transactions by holding investments for long periods of time

buy-side analyst A person who gives buy/sell advice and forecasts to the institutional firms for which they work

bylaw A document specifying the relationship between a corporation and its stockholders

C

call option an option contract that gives you the right, but not the obligation, to buy an underlying asset at a certain price

call provision a feature of a security that allows the issuer to retire the security early, usually by paying a premium over the par value

candlestick graph A chart that depicts historical open, high, low, and closing security prices

capital allocation Line Most efficient portfolios for some risky assets and the risk-free asset

capital appreciation The increase in value of an investment

capital asset pricing model A pricing model used often to describe the relationship between systematic risk and expected return for stocks

capital gain An increase in the value of a capital asset, such as a stock

capital gains distribution Payment of realized capital gains

capital gains yield A measure of an investment's return based solely on the capital appreciation

capital market line Most efficient portfolios with *all* risky assets and the risk-free asset

Carbon Risk Ratings A measure of how consistent a firm's activities and products are related to the transition to a low-carbon economy

CDs Negotiable certificates of depot issued by commercial banks

Certificate of Accrual on Treasury Securities (CATS) A zero-coupon bond, privately issued between 1982 and 1986, but backed by the U.S. Treasury

certificates of participation (COPs) A type of financing in which an investor purchases a share of the lease revenues of a program

channel The area between resistance and support lines that illustrates the direction of the trend

charter A document specifying the relationship between a firm and the state in which it is incorporated

charting The use of two-dimensional price and volume graphs to analyze market behavior and anticipate future price movements

Chicago Board Options Exchange (CBOE) An organized market for puts and calls

class A subcategory of stocks or bonds having different features than other classes of the same type of security for the same issuer

closed-end fund A mutual fund that trades as a security on an exchange

collar A protective position constructed by selling a call at one strike price and buying a put at a lower strike price

collateralized mortgage obligation (CMO) A type of mortgage-backed security that contains a pool of similar mortgages bundled together and sold as an investment

commercial paper A short-term debt issued by a corporation

Commercial Paper Funding Facility (CPFF) A special purpose vehicle (SPV) created by the Federal Reserve to purchase commercial paper to ensure that commercial paper markets remained liquid

commodity A basic good used in commerce that is interchangeable with other goods of the same type

common stock A security representing ownership in a corporation with voting rights

compound interest Interest earned on both principal and earlier interest

Confidence Index An indicator of investor mood based on bond yields

consol A perpetual bond issued by the British government to finance the Napoleonic Wars and that never matures

constant growth model A valuation model that uses constant growing dividends and discounts them to the present

consumer confidence index (CCI) An indicator providing an indication of expected future developments of households' consumption and saving, based upon answers to a survey regarding their expected financial situation, their sentiment about the general economic situation, unemployment, and capability of savings

consumer price index (CPI) A measure of the average change over time in the prices paid by urban consumers for a typical market basket of consumer goods and services

consumer sentiment index (CSI) An economic indicator produced by the University of Michigan that measures the degree of optimism that consumers feel about the overall state of the economy and their personal financial situation

continuation pattern The persistence of the underlying bullish or bearish trend

contractionary monetary policy A type of monetary policy that is intended to cut back on the rate of monetary expansion to fight inflation

contrarian An investor who goes against the consensus concerning investment strategy

contrary indicator A measure that assesses what others are doing and suggests you should do the opposite

conversion price The effective price per share paid when converting a share of preferred stock or a bond into common stock

conversion ratio The number of shares of common stock received for converting a preferred share or bond into common stock

convertible A security that can be converted into shares of common stock upon the decision of the holder

convertible bond A bond that may be exchanged for a certain number of shares in the issuing company

convexity Refers to both a measure of and an adjustment for the curvature in the relationship between bond prices and yields

correlated The degree of return co-movement between two assets

correlation A measure of comovement that varies between -1 and $+1$

coupon bond A bond that pays a coupon payment

coupon rate T interest rate paid on a bond, expressed as a percentage of the face value of the bond

covariance An absolute measure of comovement that varies between plus and minus infinity

covenant The terms of agreement between a bond issuer and the bondholder

cover the short To return borrowed shares to the broker

covered option An option written when the seller already owns the underlying asset

covered put Selling a stock short while selling a put on the stock

cross-sectional analysis An analysis of several firms in the same industry at one point in time

cumulative dividend A feature of preferred stock wherein a "skipped" dividend has to be made up before the issuing firm can pay any dividends to common shareholders

cumulative voting A system that permits each stockholder to cast all their votes for one candidate

currency future A contract for the future exchange of currencies

current ratio A measure of liquidity: current assets divided by current liabilities

current yield A bond's annual interest payments divided by the current price of the bond

D

daily limit The maximum amount of allowed daily price change on a futures contract.

data-snooping problem Reliance on chance observations in historical data as a guide to investment decision making

date of record The day on which an investor must own shares to receive the dividend payment

day order An order placed with a broker that is canceled at the end of the day if it is not executed

days sales outstanding The number of days required to collect accounts receivable

dealer A market maker who buys and sells securities for their own accounts

debenture An unsecured bond or note supported by the general creditworthiness of the firm

debt ratio The ratio of debt to total assets, which measures the use of debt financing

debt securities Longer-term debt instruments

debt-to-equity ratio The ratio of debt to equity that evaluates a company's financial leverage

debt-to-total assets ratio The ratio of debt to total assets that measures the proportion of the firm financed with debt

dedicated bond portfolio An investment strategy that matches the receipt of cash flows with the investor's need for funds

default premium An additional amount of interest rate necessary to induce an investor to invest their money in a risky security instead of an otherwise equivalent risk-free security

default risk Lender risk that the borrower will fail to pay the interest payments and repay the principal

deficit spending Government spending, in excess of revenue raised from taxes, of funds raised by borrowing

defined contribution plan An employee-funded retirement program in which the employee makes the funding and investment decisions

deflation A general decline in the price level of goods and services

delta An option's hedge ratio, which is the rate of change of an option's price for changes in the value of the underlying asset

depository institution A financial institution in the United States (such as a savings bank, commercial bank, savings and loan association, or credit union) that is legally allowed to accept monetary deposits from consumers

derivative instrument An instrument whose value is linked to the value of something else

derivative security A financial instrument with value stemming from changes in the value of some other (possibly financial) asset

designated market maker (DMM) The NYSE market maker responsible for maintaining fair and orderly markets for assigned securities

dilution A reduction in earnings per share due to the issuing of new securities

direct listing Existing outstanding shares are sold to the public for the first time on a secondary market with no underwriters involved

director A person who is elected by stockholders to determine the firm's goals and policies

discount The difference between the traded price and the NAV when shares are selling for less than the NAV

discount rate The interest rate charged to commercial banks and other financial institutions for short-term loans they take from the Federal Reserve Bank

discount yield A yield calculated on the basis of the face amount of the bill and using a 360-day year

distribution The mathematical function that gives the probabilities of occurrence of different possible outcomes for an experiment

distribution date The date on which a dividend is paid to stockholders

divergence A disagreement between market direction between indicators

diversifiable risk The portion of risk in an investment asset or portfolio that can be eliminated through diversification

diversification The reduction of risk through owning a variety of different types of assets

diversified portfolio A portfolio of assets that includes various asset categories, such as stocks, bonds, and cash, for the purpose of reducing risk

dividend A payment to stockholders that is usually in cash but may be in stock

dividend discount model A valuation model that discounts future cash flows to the present

dividend received reduction (DRD) A policy of the U.S. Internal Revenue Service (IRS) allowing corporations to only pay taxes on between 35% and 50% of dividends received from other corporations

dividend reinvestment plan (DRIP) A program that permits stockholders to have cash dividends reinvested in stock shares

dividend yield A measure of annual return from the dividend income only

Dogs of the Dow Investment strategy that selects the 10 highest dividend yield stocks of the DJIA

dominating portfolio A portfolio that is superior to others based on better risk and/or return

Dow Jones Industrial Average (DJIA) A stock market index of 30 prominent companies listed on stock exchanges in the United States; its components are weighted by their market prices

Dow theory The idea that market movements can be predicted by studying trends in the Dow Jones Industrial Average (DJIA) and Dow Jones Transportation Average (DJTA)

due diligence The investigation or exercise of care that a reasonable business or person is normally expected to take before entering into an agreement or contract with another party

duration The weighted average time to maturity of a security's cash flows

E

E bond A war bond issued by the U.S. government in 1941 to finance World War II, with face amounts between $18.75 to $10,000 and a maturity of 10 years

EE bond A low-risk savings product that pays interest until it reaches 30 years or you cash it in, whichever comes first

efficient The condition that a stock price that is an unbiased representation of its value

efficient frontier All of the efficient portfolios

efficient market hypothesis Theory stating that security prices fully reflect all available information

efficient portfolios The highest return portfolios for a given level of risk

environmental, social, and governance (ESG) investing An investment strategy in which securities must meet ESG standards

equipment trust certificate A mortgage bond secured by assets with substantial resale value

equity benchmark A performance standard to be evaluated against

equity REIT An REIT with an ownership position in real estate

ESG Risk Ratings A measure of the degree to which a company's economic value may be at risk due to ESG factors

Eurobond A bond issued by a U.S. company that is denominated in U.S. dollars but sold abroad in foreign markets

excess return A security or portfolio return less the risk-free rate

exchange rate risk The risk that exchange rates may go against your favor when you are scheduled to receive one currency in the future and will need to convert it to another

exchange-traded fund (ETF) A tradeable fund share that mimics an index or basket of stocks

ex-dividend Stock that trades exclusive of any dividend payment

ex-dividend date The day on which a stock trades exclusive of any dividends

expectations operator The use of E() to denote that a value is an expectation

expected returns The amount of profit or loss that an investor anticipates receiving on an investment

expense ratio Total fees and trading costs expressed as a percentage of fund assets

extendible security A bond where the term to maturity may be extended at the option of the issuer

extra dividend Cash paid in addition to the firm's regular dividend

F

face value The principal to be repaid on the maturity of a bond

factor betas Stock or portfolio sensitivity to a factor in a multifactor asset pricing model

factor loadings See *factor betas*

fallen angel A formerly investment-grade bond that has become a high-yield security because of lowered credit ratings

Fama–French 3-factor model Common multifactor asset pricing model that incorporates market portfolio, size, and book-to-market based risk factors

Farm Credit Act Legislation passed during the Great Depression in the United States offering short-term loans for agricultural production as well as extended low interest rates for farmers threatened by foreclosure. Small farmers were able to refinance their mortgages with the aid of twelve district banks, called Banks for Cooperatives

FED A name for the Federal Reserve System, which is the central bank of the United States and is charged with maximizing employment, stabilizing prices, moderating long-term interest rates, supervising and regulating banks, maintaining the stability of the financial system, and providing financial services to depository institutions, the U.S. government, and foreign official institutions

federal funds rate The overnight interest rate that banks charge each other to borrow or lend excess reserves

fill or kill An order to be immediately executed or canceled depending on the trading price

financial asset An investment instrument issued by corporations, governments, or other organizations that offer legal rights to debt or equity cash flow

financial future A contract for the future delivery of securities, such as stocks

financial institution A company engaged in the business of dealing with financial and monetary transactions, such as deposits, loans, investments, and currency exchange; types of financial institutions include banks, brokerage firms, insurance companies, trust companies, and investment dealers trading either on their own behalf or on the behalf of clients

financial instrument A contract that generates a financial asset

financial leverage The use of borrowed funds to acquire an asset

financial planner A person who guides customers through the investment process to meet current and long-term financial goals

firm commitment An agreement with an investment banker who guarantees a sale of securities by agreeing to purchase the entire issue at a specified price

firm size A company's market capitalization (shares outstanding × price)

fiscal policy The use of government spending and taxation to influence the economy

fixed-asset turnover Ratio of sales to fixed assets, which tells how many fixed assets are needed to generate sales

fixed-income securities A category that includes bonds, preferred stocks, and other instruments with fixed income cash flows

fixed-income security A security that promises to pay a fixed income stream in the form of fixed dividends or bond interest payments

floater A floating-rate note that pays interest that is set weekly and tied to the most recent 13-week Treasury bill rate

floating A security whose payments to purchasers adjust based on some variable market rate of return

Foolish Four An investment strategy advocated by The Motley Fool that buys four DJIA stocks based on dividend yield and price

forecasting Predicting future values of a variable

foreign exchange instruments Contracts involving the exchange of one currency for another

foreign exchange rate risk The risk that business or investment cash flows will be impacted by changes in the exchange rates between currencies

forward contract A *customized* agreement to buy and sell an underlying asset at a particular date in the future for a locked-in price that is not traded on an organized exchange

forward PE ratio The ratio of stock price to the next 12 months of earnings per share

front-end load A commission paid at the time of a fund purchase

fund family A mutual fund firm that offers many portfolio choices

fund of funds A mutual fund that owns the shares of other mutual funds

fundamental analysis A method of determining a stock's current value.

futures contract An agreement traded on an organized exchange to buy and sell an underlying asset at a particular date in the future for a locked-in price

futures price The price agreed to in a futures contract

G

gamma The change in delta to the changes in the value of the underlying asset; the second derivative with respect to the price of the underlying asset

general obligation bond A municipal bond backed solely by the credit and taxing power of the issuing jurisdiction rather than the revenue from a given project

geometric average The average compounded growth of an investment

good-till-canceled order An order placed with a broker that remains in effect until it is executed by the broker or canceled by the investor

Government National Mortgage Association (GNMA, or "Ginnie Mae") A government agency that guarantees timely payments on mortgage-backed securities, providing liquidity in the market for home loans

Great Depression A severe worldwide economic depression that took place mostly during the 1930s and was prompted by the U.S. stock market crash of October 1929

gross domestic product (GDP) The monetary value of all finished goods and services made within a country; usually calculated for years or quarters

gross national product (GNP) GNP for a country is equal to GDP plus residents' investment income from overseas investments minus foreign residents' investment income earned within that country

gross profit margin Percentage earned on sales after deducting the cost of goods sold.

growth-at-a-reasonable-price (GARP) A stock strategy that seeks growth stocks that are not overvalued

growth-stock investing A stock strategy that seeks firms with high earnings and sales growth

growth stocks Companies expected to have above average rates of growth in sales and earnings

Guaranteed Student Loan Program A provision of the Higher Education Act of 1965, which had taxpayers guaranteeing loans made by private lenders to students

H

head and shoulders A popular price chart pattern that signals a reversal to a bear market trend

hedge To insure a position in financial instruments against risk

hedge fund A limited partnership of investors in a portfolio using high risk methods seeking high returns

hedge ratio The number of shares that must be purchased for each option sold to have a perfectly hedged position

hedging The use of derivative contracts to immunize against risk in an underlying asset that the party already has a stake in

high-water mark The highest end-of-year value of a portfolio

high-yield security Any debt of low quality and high risk

histogram A bar graph used to indicate frequencies of occurrence in various ranges

holding period The amount of time that an investment is held by an investor

holding period return (HPR) The investment return over a specified period

hybrid REIT An REIT that generates income from real estate debt and equity

I

I bond A security that earns interest based on both a fixed rate and a rate that is set twice a year based on inflation. The bond earns interest until it reaches 30 years or you cash it in, whichever comes first

idiosyncratic risk Risk that is unique to a particular asset, also called nonsystematic risk

immunization Matching the duration of a portfolio to the timing of the investor's need for funds

in the money An option having positive intrinsic value

income Cash in-flows from an investment, like dividends, interest payments, or rent

income bond A bond that pays interest during a period only if the company makes a certain amount of money during that period

income distribution Payment of interest and dividends

increasing rate bond A bond whose coupon increases over time

index fund A fund whose portfolio mimics a specific index of the market

indifference curves A line showing all the portfolios for which an investor would be indifferent to owning

individual retirement account (IRA) An account set up at a financial institution that allows an individual to save for retirement using before-tax income

inflation-indexed bond A bond whose interest payments are tied to the costs of consumer goods as measured by an inflation index, such as the consumer price index (CPI)

inflation premium An interest rate adjustment necessary to compensate an investor for expected inflation

initial margin The minimum starting equity for an investment position

initial public offering (IPO) The first sale of common stock to the general public

insider ownership Shares owned by the company's management, directors, and anyone with access to the firm's key information

institutional ownership Shares owned by financial firms, like pension funds, mutual funds, insurance companies, and hedge funds

interest Money paid by a borrower in compensation for the use of the lender's funds.

interest rate option An option to buy and sell debt securities

interest rate risk The potential that a rise in overall interest rates will reduce the value of a bond or other fixed-rate investment

intrinsic value The value of an option at the current market price of the underlying asset if the option were to expire now

inventory turnover The speed with which inventory is sold

investment The purchase of an asset for the purpose of storing and (possibly) increasing value over time

investment banker A finance professional who helps companies and governments acquire capital through the issuance of financial securities

investment horizon The length of time until an investor needs to cash out their investment

investment style A fund's investment philosophy or strategy

investment type The kind of securities held by the fund, such as stocks or bonds

irrational bubbles Extreme change in financial asset values that can't be tied to changes in economic fundamentals

irregular dividend Dividend payments that either don't occur in the regular intervals or vary in amount

J

January effect Phenomenon of unusually large positive rates of return for stocks during the first few trading days of the year

Jensen's alpha Abnormal return measured from the capital asset pricing model (CAPM)

K

kurtosis A measure of how "fat" the tails of a distribution are

L

laddered bond strategy A strategy involving investing in bonds with different maturities

law of large numbers (LLN) From probability and statistics, a concept that states that as a sample size grows, its sample mean gets closer to the population average

leverage The ability to pay a relatively small premium for market exposure in relation to the contract value

leveraged ETF An ETF that uses debt and derivative securities to magnify an index's return

LIBOR The London InterBank Offer Rate, the interest rate at which large international banks lend to each other

lifecycle fund A blended fund that starts with higher equity allocation and slowly changes to higher debt securities allocation as the retirement date nears

limit order An order placed with a broker to buy or sell at a specified price

limited liability A legal status where an investor's financial liability is limited to their investment in a firm

liquidated A company sells all its assets, pays creditors, and ceases operations

liquidity The ease with which assets can be converted into cash with no or minimal loss or cost

liquidity/marketability premium An interest rate adjustment necessary to get an investor to invest their money in a security that might take time or require a discount to sell

load fee A sales commission

lockup The amount of time an investor is prevented from redeeming shares

London InterBank Offer Rate (LIBOR) The benchmark interest rate at which major global banks lend to each other

long-term equity anticipation securities (LEAPS) Options that are typically longer than nine months in duration

low-load fund A fund that charges sales fees ranging from 1 to 3%

M

M1 The portion of the money supply that is composed of currency, demand deposits, and other liquid deposits

M2 Includes M1 plus savings and time deposits, certificates of deposits, and money market funds, all of which are less liquid than the components of M1

maintenance margin The minimum amount that a party to a futures contract must keep on account to cover shifts in the underlying asset that cause them to owe money to the other party

managed future A futures contract managed by a professional management company

management fee A fee charged against the portfolio to fund the operation of fund

margin When purchasing assets on margin, the money borrowed from a broker to purchase an investment and the difference between the total value of the investment and the loan amount; when entering into a futures contract, the amount each party is required to keep on account against future movements of the underlying asset's price against them

margin account An account that holds securities purchased with a combination of cash and borrowed funds

margin call A broker's demand for additional collateral when the equity has declined below the maintenance margin level

margin debt The amount borrowed to buy or maintain a security investment

marked to the market Refers to the action of calculating the gain in value to a futures contract due to changes in the underlying spot price; is usually performed once a day at the close of trading

market breadth A measure of the number of issues that are rising relative to the number that are declining

market bubble A significant overvaluation of economic fundamentals in the stock market

market index bias Distortion of beta estimates caused by imperfect proxies for the market portfolio

market order An order placed with a broker to buy or sell at the current price

market portfolio The portfolio with all risky securities in proportion to their value

market risk premium Risk-reward for taking market risk, defined as the return on the market less the risk-free rate

market timing Investment style that attempts to buy into the stock market before a bull market move and sell before a bear market move

maturity date the date that the final repayment of principal is made on a bond issue

minimum variance portfolio The portfolio of risky assets with the lowest risk possible as measured by variance (standard deviation) of return

modified duration Duration divided by one plus the YTM that measures the price sensitivity of the bond to interest rate changes

moments Attributes of a statistical distribution used to describe its shape

momentum Stocks with higher (lower) prior returns will continue to achieve high (low) returns in the future

momentum indicator A popular indicator that includes rate of change, MACD, and Relative Strength Index

momentum strategy The strategy of buying and holding securities that have been rising

money market fund Mutual fund that invest solely in money market instruments

money market instrument Short-term debt security that trades in liquid markets

money market mutual fund A fund that invests in cash reserves, or short-term IOUs

Money Market Mutual Fund Liquidity Facility (MMLF) A mechanism set up by the Federal Reserve to allow prime money market funds to take out secured loans against their assets rather than having to redeem them during runs on money market funds

monopoly power A firm's ability to price its product or service substantially above the competitive level and persist in doing so

Morningstar Analyst Rating An analyst grade on expected fund performance

mortgage bond A bond issued to purchase specific assets and that is secured by that asset

mortgage REIT An REIT that invests in real estate–oriented debt

moving average convergence–divergence (MACD) A trend-following momentum indicator that shows the relationship between two moving averages

multi-growth firm A firm that experiences periods of different growth rates

municipal bond (muni) Debt securities issued by states, cities, counties, and other governmental entities whose interest is generally exempt from federal income tax

municipal/Treasury (M/T) ratio The yield on a municipal bond index divided by the yield on an equivalent-maturity Treasury note or bond. In general, this ratio should be less than 1.0 due to the tax exemption on munis

mutual fund An open-end investment company

mutual fund flow indicator A mutual fund inflow, outflow, and credit balance information

N

naked option An option written when the writer does not own the underlying asset

negative screen A way to select securities by filtering out companies that fail certain criteria

neglected-firm effect The tendency for lesser-known companies to outperform better-known companies

net asset value (NAV) A per-share value of a mutual fund's stock, bond, and cash reserve holdings

net profit margin The ratio of earnings after interest and taxes to sales

no-load fund A mutual fund that does not charge a commission for buying or selling shares

nominal interest rate The quoted rate on an investment

nominal rates Annualized interest rates based on simple interest only

noncumulative dividend A feature of preferred stock allowing for a dividend on the stock to be skipped by the issuer with no penalty or repayment necessary

nonstationary beta problem Implementation difficulty due to betas' inherent instability over time

nonsystematic risk Risk that is unique to a particular asset, also called idiosyncratic risk

O

odd lot A trade that is not a multiple of 100 shares

odd-lot indicator The number of trades using odd-lots to gauge individual investor buying and selling

open-end fund A mutual fund that continuously offers to sell and buy shares

open interest The number of a particular derivative contracts in existence

open market operations An instance of a central bank buying or selling short-term Treasuries and other securities in the open market in order to influence the money supply, thus influencing short-term interest rates

operating profit margin Percentage earned on sales before adjusting for nonrecurring items, interest, and taxes

optimal portfolio The best portfolio for an investor based on risk, return, and utility

option A derivative contract giving the right to buy or sell an underlying asset for a pre-specified price at the owner's discretion over a predetermined time period

out of the money An option having zero intrinsic value

overbought An insufficient future demand at the market top

oversold An insufficient future supply at the market bottom

over-the-counter The informal market for shares not listed on an exchange

P

P/E effect The tendency for companies with a low stock price to earnings per share ratio (value stocks) outperform high P/E ratio companies (growth companies)

participating A feature of a preferred share or bond where a promised amount is paid each period, but also can possibly receive "extra" payments from the firm if some financial benchmark is met

participating bond A bond that pays both interest and a form of dividends

passive investment strategy Investors hold a diversified mix of assets over long periods to match their benchmark return

passively managed An investment style in which securities are not chosen by a manager but instead identified in an index

payment for order flow The compensation a brokerage firm receives for steering client orders to a market maker for trade execution

payoff diagram A graphical depiction of the value of a derivative at expiration as a function of the value of the underlying asset

payout ratio The ratio of dividends to earnings

PE model A model to estimate a future price using the future PE ratio, earnings, and growth

PE multiple The PE ratio used for valuing a company

PE ratio The ratio of stock price to the earnings per share

PEG ratio The PE ratio divided by the growth rate of earnings

penny stocks Equities priced below $1

perpetual A feature of a security where it never matures

perpetuity model A dividend discount model in which all future dividends are the same

personal consumption expenditure (PCE) A measure of imputed household expenditures defined for a period of time

poison pill A defense mechanism used mainly in hostile takeover situations

portfolio A combination of investment assets

portfolio manager A finance professional in charge of making buy, sell, and hold decisions for a portfolio

positive screen A way to select securities by identifying companies that excel in certain criteria

preemptive right The right of current stockholders to maintain their proportionate ownership in the firm

preliminary prospectus Initial document detailing the financial condition of a firm that must be filed with the SEC to register a new issue of securities

premium The difference between the traded price and the NAV when shares are selling for more than the NAV; used to refer to a bond selling for more than face value

prerefunded municipal bond A debt security that is issued in order to fund a municipal bond

price disclosure The practice of using futures prices as an indicator concerning expectations of future spot prices

price overreaction The tendency for a price to change too much in response to an announcement

price sensitivity The variance in bond price caused by changes in yield

price target An analysts' estimate of the future stock price

price-to-book ratio A measure of relative value that divides the price by the book value per share

price-to-cash flow ratio A measure of relative value that divides the price by the cash flow per share

price-to-sales ratio A measure of relative value that divides the price by the sales per share

price underreaction The tendency for a price to change too slowly in response to an announcement

price-weighted index A stock index computed by components' prices being summed and then divided by a divisor

primary market Sale or purchase of securities by the firm that issued them

primary trend A bull and bear market that lasts anywhere from less than one year up to several years

principal The amount borrowed in a bond issue

private equity firm A private investment firm that purchases, operates, and resells companies

private information Information that has not been formally released to the public

private placement An issue of securities that are sold to pre-selected investors and institutions rather than on the open market

probability density function A function measuring the relative likelihood at various points that a given number will fall in a certain range

producer price index (PPI) A measure of the average selling prices received by domestic producers for their output

profit Financial gain earned from the difference between the revenue and the expenses from an investment asset or business

programmed trading Automated trading of portfolios of securities initiated by computer when certain circumstances occur

protective call Combining a short in a stock with a long call

protective put The simultaneous purchase of the underlying asset and a put on that asset

proxy battle A group of shareholders trying to gather enough shareholder proxy votes to win a company vote

public information Information available to the public

public offering An issue of securities that are sold on the open market

purchasing power risk The chance that future cash flows won't be worth as much because of inflation

put–call ratio A ratio of the trading volume of put options to call options

put option An option contract that gives you the right, but not the obligation, to sell an underlying asset at a certain price

Q

quick ratio (acid test) A measure of liquidity: current assets excluding inventory divided by current liabilities

R

random walk A concept that stock price changes do not follow any patterns or trends

random walk with drift Slight upward bias to inherently unpredictable daily stock prices

rate of change (ROC) A comparison of the current price with a previous price, usually 10 or 12 days ago

rate of return The annual percentage return realized on an investment

ratio analysis A method of gaining insight into a company's operation through examining its financial statements

rational bubbles Extreme change in financial asset values that tied to changes in economic fundamentals

real asset Physical asset that has a value due to its substance and properties, like precious metals, commodities, real estate, land, equipment, and natural resources

real estate investment trust (REIT) A publicly traded company that manages property and/or mortgage loans

real risk-free rate The theoretical interest rate of an investment that carries zero risk; because even Treasury securities carry the risk of unexpected inflation, the risk-free rate is unobtainable in reality

realized return The amount or percentage of money gained or lost over a holding period

recapitalization A modification in a firm's sources of financing, such as the substitution of long-term debt for equity

receivables turnover The speed with which a firm collects its accounts receivable

recession A period of temporary economic decline during which trade and industrial activity both go down; by common consensus, recessions are generally agreed to occur if GDP falls in two successive quarters

registered representative A person who works for a financial firm trading investment products and securities for clients

registration Process of filing information with the SEC concerning a proposed sale of securities to the general public

regular dividend Steady dividend payments that are distributed at regular intervals

repurchase A company purchasing its own shares of stock

repurchase agreement A sale of a security in which the seller agrees to buy back (repurchase) the security at a specified price at a specified date

required return The minimum amount of expected return to compensate for the risk of holding an asset

reserve requirement The amount of cash that banks must have on hand, in their vaults or in their account at the closest Federal Reserve bank, to return deposits when customers demand them

reset bond A bond with a coupon that is readjusted at set intervals

resistance line A graphical depiction of price points at which selling pressure (supply) has emerged in the recent past

retention ratio The ratio of earnings not distributed to total earnings

return The sum of income plus capital gains earned on an investment in an asset

return on assets The ratio of earnings to total assets

return on equity The ratio of earnings to equity

revenue bond a category of municipal bond supported by the revenue from a specific project, such as a toll bridge, highway, or local stadium

reversal pattern A change in trend signal

reward-to-variability measure Excess return earned for each unit of total risk taken

reward-to-volatility measure Excess return earned for each unit of systematic risk taken

rho A change in the value of an option with respect to changes in the interest rate

rights offering Sale of new securities to existing stockholders

risk The possibility of loss; the uncertainty of future returns

risk averse The degree to which a person desires to avoid risk

risk aversion The magnitude of preferring lower uncertainty (risk)

risk-free asset A security with a certain future return

risk-free rate The certain future return from the risk-free asset

road show A series of sales presentations to potential investors by the underwriting firm

round lot The general unit of trading in a security, normally 100 shares

S

secondary market A market where securities trade after issuance by the firm

secondary trend A short-term move in the market that runs contrary to the primary trend and usually last from three weeks to three months

sector rotation A form of market timing in which investors rotate between sectors over time

sector rotation strategy Rotating over time which sectors are over- or underweighted in a portfolio

securities analyst A financial professional who analyzes and makes recommendations regarding stocks and other financial assets

securitization The process of turning illiquid assets such as accounts receivable into liquid assets which can be sold

security market line Linear risk-return trade-off for individual stocks

security selection The process of selecting the assets for a portfolio

sell-side analyst A person who communicates to the public about their stock recommendations and forecasts

semistrong form Premise that stock prices reflect all public information

sentiment An investor mood of optimism or pessimism regarding the financial markets or economy

Separate Trading of Registered Interest and Principal Securities (STRIPS) Treasury securities that let investors hold and trade separately the individual interest and principal components of eligible Treasury notes and bonds

serial bond A bond issue where a portion of the issue is scheduled to be retired each year until maturity.

Series 7 exam The General Securities Representative Qualification Examination, which assesses the competency of an entry-level registered representative

Sharpe ratio Risk premium earned relative to total risk

Shiller PE ratio A version of the PE ratio that uses ten years of earnings adjusted for inflation

short ETF An ETF that tries to replicate the opposite direction of an index's daily change

short interest The number of shares sold short in a firm

short interest ratio Short interest expressed in terms of an average day's trading volume

short sale The sale of borrowed stock used to profit from a falling stock price

short-sale interest The number of shares sold short in a firm

short squeeze The pressure on short sellers through margin calls caused by rapidly appreciating stock prices

simple interest Interest earned on principal alone

sinking fund A fund into which periodic payments on a bond issue's principal is made in order to ensure orderly retirement of the debt issue; A pool of money required by an issuing firm to be accumulated over time in preparation of the buyback or settlement of a security issue

skewness A measure of distribution symmetry

small-firm effect The tendency for small capitalization companies to outperform large capitalization companies

socially responsible investing (SRI) An investment strategy in which companies are selected that have positive social impacts

SPAC Investment vehicle that raises capital in its IPO and then goes looking for a private company to purchase, which causes that firm to become a publicly traded firm

speculation An investment that offers a potentially large return but is also very risky; a high probability that the investment will produce a loss

split coupon bond A bond that initially pays not coupon, but which starts paying a fixed coupon after a set number of years

spot price The current market price of a commodity for immediate delivery

spread The difference between rates on high-yield and investment-grade bonds

staple goods Specific consumer goods consumed by people on a regular basis

star rating Morningstar's backward-looking rating for a fund's past performance

statement of cash flows An accounting statement that specifies a firm's cash inflows and cash outflows

stock The shares into which ownership of a corporation is divided

stock dividend A dividend paid as stock instead of cash

stock fund A fund that makes equity investments

stock index futures A futures contract based on an index of the market

stock index option Option on an aggregate measure of the market, such as the S&P 500

stock split The number of shares issued to shareholders increases simultaneously with a price decline so that the value of each holding remains the same

stop loss A stop order placed to limit a loss in a position

stop-loss order A standing order to sell an asset owned when the price goes down to a specified level

stop order A sell order at a specific price designed to limit an investor's loss or to assure a profit

straddle The purchase of a put and call with the same exercise price and expiration date

straight ladder A bond investment strategy where an equal amount of face value of bonds is purchased with different, but equally spaced over time, maturities

strike price The price specified in an options contract at which the underlying asset can be bought or sold at

strong form Premise that stock prices reflect all public information and nonpublic information

Student Loan Marketing Association (Sallie Mae) A publicly traded U.S. corporation that provides private student loans.

style box Morningstar's depiction of a fund's portfolio expressed in market capitalization and value/growth orientation

subprime lending The practice of lending to borrowers with low credit ratings

sunk cost A cost that has already been paid and cannot be recovered

support line A graphical depiction of price points at which additional demand for the stock has emerged in the past

surplus An amount of an item in an economy that is more than people demand

sustainable investing An investment strategy that considers environmental, social, and corporate governance (ESG) criteria to generate financial returns and positive societal impact

swap A contract to exchange the cash flows from one underlying security with those from another

syndicate A selling group assembled to market an issue of securities

systematic risk The risk inherent to the overall investment market

systemic risk Return volatility associated with the overall market

T

tax anticipation note Debt issued by states or municipalities to be repaid from future tax revenues

T-bill A short-term U.S. government security

technical analysis The study of historical price and volume information to forecast future prices

term premium An interest rate adjustment necessary to get an investor to invest their money in a security that will take longer to earn a return

tertiary trend A very short-term stock market trend that reflects minor price moves

theta Change in the value of an option with respect to changes in time to expiration.

ticker symbol The unique stock identifier assigned for trading in a particular market

ticker tape A paper or electronic representation of stock prices appearing in a linear manner

tier 1 capital The core capital held in a bank's reserves

time interval bias Beta estimation problem derived from dependence on the return interval used

time value of money The concept that the money you have now is worth more than the same amount received in the future due to its potential ability to grow

times interest earned Ratio of EBIT divided by interest expense, which measures the safety of debt

time-series analysis An analysis of a firm over a period of time

total asset turnover Ratio of sales to total assets, which tells the amount of sales generated by total assets

total risk Diversifiable plus non-diversifiable risk of an asset

tracking error The standard deviation of the difference between the returns of the portfolio and the returns of the benchmark

trading index (TRIN) ratio A common indicator of advancing and declining stock, and up and down volume, to measure market imbalance

tranche An issue of bonds that is a portion of a pooling of like obligations (such as securitized mortgage debt), where the parts of that portion have the same maturity or rate of return

Treasury bill (T-bill) A short-term U.S. government debt obligation backed by the Treasury Department with a maturity of one year or less

Treasury bills A short-term U.S. government debt obligation backed by the Treasury Department with a maturity of one year or less

Treasury Inflation Protected Services (TIPS) A Treasury bond whose principal value is indexed to an inflationary gauge to protect investors from the decline in the purchasing power of their money

Treasury Investment Growth Receipt (TIGR, or Tigers) The first zero coupon bonds derived from regular Treasury bonds

Treasury receipts (TRs) A type of bond that is purchased at a discount by the investor in return for a payment of its full face value at its date of maturity. Treasury receipts are created by brokerage firms but are collateralized by underlying U.S. government securities

Treynor Index Risk premium earned relative to systematic risk

TRuPS Hybrid securities that are included in regulatory tier 1 capital for Bank Holding Companies and whose dividend payments are tax deductible for the issuer

trustee An agent appointed to act in the interest of bondholders

U

underwriter A large financial institution that guarantees the performance of a public security issue

undiversifiable risk The risk inherent to the overall investment market

unit trust Privately held type of closed-end fund

unrealized capital gains An increase in fund value caused by a rise in the value of fund investments

unsystematic risk The portion of risk in an investment asset or portfolio that can be eliminated through diversification

utility A measure of satisfaction or welfare obtained by a portfolio

V

valuation The process of determining the current worth of an asset—the present value of future benefits

value investing A stock strategy that seeks firms that are undervalued

value stocks Securities considered to be temporarily undervalued or unpopular

value-weighted index A stock index computed by components' market capitalization being summed and then divided initial index capitalization, then multiplied by a base value

variable interest rate bond A bond that pays a coupon rate that varies based on market rates

vega Change in the value of an option with respect to a change in volatility in the underlying asset

venture capitalist A firm specializing in investing in the securities of small, emerging companies

voting rights The rights of stockholders to vote their shares

W

warrant A call option issued by firms on their own shares

weak form Premise that current prices reflect all stock market trading information

Y

yield The return offered by a bond

yield curve A plot of bond yield against bond maturity

yield spread The long-term Treasury bond yield less the government short-term Treasury Bill yield

yield to call (YTC) The yield that an investor will earn if the bond is held until it is called before maturity.

yield to maturity (YTM) The yield that an investor will earn if the bond is held until it is redeemed at face value at maturity.

Z

zero coupon bond A bond that pays no periodic interest coupons; all interest is paid at maturity

Index